CLOAK & GOWN
Scholars in the Secret War, 1939–1961

As *Cloak & Gown* shows, the paternity of the CIA by the OSS is clear. Of the thirteen thousand men and women who worked for the OSS, a great number helped establish the CIA. Of these, Yale men, and a few women, were numerous. Overall, the OSS recruited from the Ivy League universities—because those universities continued to require the ability to speak a foreign language for graduation—and from the largest of the state universities as well. Initially the American spy game was peopled largely by scholars.

Why? Before Pearl Harbor, for example, the U.S. Navy had few maps, no visual information on any of the Pacific islands over which war with the Japanese might be fought. Only scholars could provide the information that was missing. The same was true in preparing to fight in North Africa, in the Middle East, and even in Europe. By the end of the war, the OSS had achieved the finest index of strategic information in the world and, by doing so, changed the face of university education in America. From starting behind all major nations, at the end of the war only the British and Soviet forces could compete with the OSS.

Here are intimate portraits of the men and women of the OSS. They include safecrackers, experts in Ajerbaijani, the blue blood of society (Paul Mellon, David Bruce, John P. Marquand, Jr., William Vanderbilt), and the bartender from the Yale Club. Its critics called it "Oh So Social." Its admirers called it "Oh So Secret." Its story has never been told so well—until now.

Critical Acclaim for CLOAK & GOWN

"Winks also trots out a rich array of characters [and] probably the best profile of James Angleton we are likely to have. . . . Engrossing and illuminating."
—*The Baltimore Sun*

"Superbly researched . . . fascinating stories"
—*Dallas Morning News*

"An exemplary scholarly examination of a staggering host of primary and secondary sources"
—*San Francisco Examiner*

"A very special book—one that affords insights as well as intelligence"
—*Kirkus Reviews*

"It is a delight."
—*The New York Times*

1939 CLOAK & GOWN 1961

SCHOLARS IN THE SECRET WAR

ROBIN W. WINKS

QUILL
WILLIAM MORROW
NEW YORK

From "Gerontion" in COLLECTED POEMS 1909–1962 by T. S. Eliot, copyright 1935, 1936 by Harcourt Brace Jovanovich, Inc.; copyright © 1964 by T. S. Eliot. Reprinted by permission of the publisher.

Winks, Robin W.
Cloak & gown.
Bibliography: p.
Includes index.
1. Intelligence service—United States.   2. Scholars—
United States.   3. Universities and colleges—United
States.   I. Title.   II. Title: Cloak and gown.
[JK468.I6W48   1988]   327.1′2′0973   88-30560
ISBN 0-688-08665-9 (pbk.)

Printed in the United States of America

First Quill Edition

1 2 3 4 5 6 7 8 9 10

BOOK DESIGNED BY BARBARA MARKS

To friends and colleagues who helped:

W.E.W., R.T.A., E.M.W.,
R.V.D., J.G.A., T.C.M.,
T.J.N., G.W.P., A.B.G.,
W.L.P., S.K., G.C.,
D.R., AND C.K., JR.

ACKNOWLEDGMENTS

Were I to print here the customary list of acknowledgments to those who helped me, I would require several pages. Except for those individuals—and relative to the total, there were not many—who asked not to be identified, I provide full acknowledgments in the notes to each of the chapters, so that rather than handing the reader an indiscriminate list of names, I try to show in general terms how each person helped. There were, of course, some whose help was so basic that their names should appear in every chapter—and indeed, a few do, though related to specific information concerning specific individuals. However, I must acknowledge here those individuals who are indicated by the dedication. I use initials only, in tribute to the manner of the dedication in Sherman Kent's classic work, *Strategic Intelligence for American World Policy* (Princeton: Princeton University Press, 1949). There Kent acknowledges seventeen colleagues, "Africans Honorary," who worked with him in the early African section of Research and Analysis at OSS. Several who helped me throughout suggested that they would prefer to take on no more flesh than their initials would suggest.

Nonetheless, I wish explicitly to identify and thank Chester Kerr, Jr., former director of the Yale University Press, who had faith in the project throughout; Daniel Rose, who provided ready and warm encouragement when it mattered most; Susan Steinberg, of the Sterling Memorial Library at Yale, who went to extraordinary lengths to see to it that I received books as they were needed; Julie Lavorgna, who conquered my ill-typed drafts to produce letter-perfect copy; my editor, Bruce Lee, a masterful editor; and my dog, Bishop Berkeley of Cloyne, who insisted that I arise from the typewriter twice daily and face reality.

CONTENTS

CHAPTER ONE

THE UNIVERSITY

RECRUITING GROUND

A university at war is a peculiar place—that is, considerably more peculiar than usual. At all times a university thinks of itself as a community, being of the world but distinctly not in it, with all the symbols and trappings normally associated with the emotions of nationalism. A university will have a national anthem, offhandedly though with deep emotion referred to as the school song; it will have a flag, a mascot, a set of well-sung heroic leaders—largely athletic though at times academic—and a sense of its natural boundaries, which define "the campus precincts," sometimes as sharply as any rising nation state in nineteenth-century Europe. A university is, of course, a place of learning, but confident universities, even in America—where there is a tendency to believe that all one learns must be taught—recognize that a good bit, perhaps most, of the learning goes on outside the classroom. Within a university there is a sense of hierarchy, of constituencies ranked within themselves, that recognizes the legitimate claims of faculty, students, alumni, and (sometimes) of staff and of donors, if donors and alumni are not, as they generally are in private universities, the same. To be a freshman is very important, for it sets one's feet on the lowest rung of a ladder, which is rewarding, demanding, and very desirable; to be an instructor or assistant professor provides the scholarly minded with a continuation into professional life of the same sense of expectation, anticipated achievement, and mentorship. The creative faculty member will often be the child who has survived.

Those outside the university think of it as an ivory tower, removed from "the real world," while most of those inside the university believe that it is a very real world of its own, and they look out upon those not fortunate enough to lead "the life of the mind"—a phrase elastic enough to cover both the study of Goethe and the instruction of seventeen-year-olds on their comma faults, not to speak of squash games and attendance at interminable committee meetings—with a certain detachment, a sense of irony, and a definite feeling that the turning of a well-wrought sentence is of far greater significance, as well as of greater visceral pleasure, than the selling of one of Detroit's new automobiles. While the public, "out there," thinks of assistant secretaries of state as reasonably important figures, it is a rare full professor at a major university who would think of himself as merely the equal of a subcabinet officer. Universities are suffused with a sense of caste, and older universities especially so. True, universities justify and reward the digging out, writing up, and possessing of arcane knowledge as an end in itself. Why, one might ask, as Bach is once said to have been asked, does one compose? For the greater glory of God—and because I enjoy it, was his apocryphal reply, and academicians respond with the same happy self-indulgence about their work. A university floats on paper and rewards the creation of more words on paper. A private university self-validates its sense of community: whoever is professor of subject X at Harvard or Princeton is, by definition, "one of the most distinguished scholars in the country" (if not the world), even though, by objective criteria, one may find a dozen or more scholars at other universities (usually referred to as "smaller," seldom as "lesser," though these "smaller" universities are frequently far larger in student enrollment) who have had a greater impact on their field.

A university is not, however, a place of snobbery, though it will strike those outside the charmed circle of passwords as, at the least, remote. A university, if it is any good, is open-ended: the person of the most humble beginnings may rise to the highest office. To be sure, he is most likely to do so if he takes on something of the coloration of the university—at Yale, for example, YWAT, otherwise known as the Yale Way of Thought (the y pronounced as a long e). He must judge delicately how much of that coloration is natural to him, or he will be thought a parvenu, a climber, merely ambitious rather than incidentally ambitious. To truly enjoy such an environment, the individual—student or faculty—must harbor a well-calibrated sense of annoyance at the institution, entering into a muted adversarial relationship with YWAT, both in order to move the institution just that little bit away from what it was to what it could become, and also to assure at least the sense if not the reality of independence. The student who never misses a football game, a class, a prom, or a chance to drink a Green Cup at Mory's is not always well regarded, for a university both demands acculturation and scorns it: this is its esprit de corps. The student is told to be an individual, is then reminded of school spirit, and must, with the Greeks it is hoped he will study, find a happy moderation between independence and conformity. Only those students who assume (and make a point of disclosing their assumptions) that the anthem, code words, or way of thought at their university are inherently superior to all others are snobs, and most students and faculty accept that there are at least a few other places that, in their own peculiar way, may turn out men and women of, well, nearly the same caliber. Full professors at Harvard and Yale used to, and still generally do, receive an invitation to appear in Who's Who in America, simply by virtue of that achievement; they know that this "honor," like so many honors, is an act of theater, and while they may take delight in ceremony, in gowns and hoods, in addressing each other in faculty meetings as Mr. President, or Mr. Dean, they are not so pompous as they sound. They understand the nurturing value of tradition while knowing that some of that tradition has little purpose beyond being fun. In such an environment one might reasonably expect to find a number of people, students, faculty, alumni, and staff, who have a wide-ranging curiosity, a somewhat childlike desire to collect experiences and to see places, to know because knowing in itself is fun: that is, a number of people ideally suited for the rather unconventional life of an intelligence service, and in particular, of the Office of Strategic Services in World War II.

None of these peculiarities of a university changes during a war, though they take on new intensities and certain customs refract the light a bit differently. Patriotism, for example—that emotion some think simple, and for cause of which some will repeat inane mottoes like "My country, right or wrong"—is a singularly complex abstraction, and its meanings are debated as intensely as other abstractions more commonly discussed in the classroom, like justice and honor and integrity. While there are many subjects at a university about which people are passionate though not at all serious—football in the Ivy League is a case in point—in wartime seriousness and passion are wed. Those who want to keep America out of war will use the most excessive language in defense of their goal, and those who wish to see America enter the battle will commit their hearts and minds to steering their country toward that end. In wartime middle-aged professors of Victorian literature will put on hard hats and organize air raid warnings for their buildings, even though thousands of miles away from the scene of conflict, because they know that such objectively silly activities draw the community together, in part by giving it a way to laugh at itself, in part because, as they count off the students who descend the stairs into some makeshift cellar in a reinforced basement, they know that a laying on of hands has occurred: the young men who have left for the battlefront are reaching out to touch the young men who will follow them into battle the next year.

A university like Yale, founded in 1701 and elegantly conscious of its age, will have more traditions—more foolishness, if you will—than most other universities. This foolishness will have been tested by time: it is unlikely to include asking new students to roll peanuts across the campus with their nose, or the systematic harassment of anyone identified as new by the color of a hat, or the need to win at any game so badly that the teacher of that game (called "coach" by his followers) could command a student's absence from the classroom. In wartime the measured pace of instruction and of play, the balance between mind and body, the leisurely weekend in the city or at the shore, will naturally give way to a quickened sense: war is urgent, and it is important that the university harness this sense of urgency. And so, from 1941 to 1945 Yale was quite a different place from what it was in, say, 1937; and it never was the same again.

Nathan Hale stands in front of the headquarters of the Central Intelligence Agency in Langley, Virginia, and he has been standing there since September of 1973. Hale is widely regarded as "the first American spy," though the unspoken addendum must always be, "to lose his life for his country," since there were other spies, who survived, during the American Revolutionary War. Hale was a Yale graduate, and the statue by which employees of the agency pass to and from work each day is a copy of one that stands on the Old Campus at Yale University.

Somehow the idea of Yale as a place, and of intelligence work as an activity, became linked, if not by Hale, then by the events of World War II. Commonly authors assert that CIA people tend to be from the Ivy League (to which the University of Virginia and West Point are sometimes admitted); or more specifically from Harvard, Yale, and Princeton. Others suggest that the rise of specific individuals within the intelligence hierarchy may be attributed to their being from one of these institutions.[1]

More than once a non-Yale, indeed non–Ivy League member of the Office of Strategic Services in World War II would find, at some remote outpost in south or southeast Asia, or in Africa, that both American and British intelligence officers, whether desk bound or spooks back from the field, would conclude a festive occasion by linking arms and singing the "Whiffenpoof Song." Somehow this song, with words distinctively appropriate to the art of spying, had become associated in the minds of the Allied intelligence groups with the sometimes romanticized derring-do those officers liked to feel was being demanded of them. Never mind that the song derived from Rudyard Kipling's "Barrack Room Ballads"; even when the British joined in singing it, it was the words of Yale's "Whiffenpoof Song" they most often used.

Yale University, or at least Yale College, is older than the Republic and mindful of that fact. It is often said to have produced more graduates who have served in the government, or in the military, than any other university of comparable size and age.[2]

Until recently it had seen more of its graduates go into intelligence work (to the extent that one can quantify an inherently inexact figure) than any other university. Yale College had always imbued its students with a sense that they must serve their country even as they might serve themselves. This was no less so of those students who protested against the war in Vietnam, or against the injustices of racism in the 1960s and '70s, than it was true of the hundreds of graduates whose names are inscribed in marble in Yale's Memorial Hall, the dead of all of America's wars, for while it is true that some protesters simply wanted to escape the draft and not be killed, as it was true that there were those who wanted to see the United States get out of Vietnam because they thought American lives ought not to be lost on those they identified as "gooks," it was also true that many who fought in that war, and many who fought against the continuation of that war, were unconsciously united in a conviction that their actions were rooted in a desire to serve their country. Many of those students who went to the barricades in 1970, determined, as they thought, to return their country to the idealism they felt it had once championed, would have joined the OSS in 1942. In both wars students saw the humanities and the social sciences as being in the service of civic virtue.

And so the figure of Nathan Hale, noose hanging loosely upon his neck, hands trussed behind him, collar open, as he looks unfaltering out across the Virginia countryside or over Yale's Old Campus from Connecticut Hall, in which he had lived as a student, is an appropriate if ambiguous tie between the generations. Inscribed on the statues are the words Hale is traditionally believed to have said when he faced death: "I only regret, that I have but one life to lose for my country." (For years introductory students in Yale's American history survey course were led through a short exegesis of texts to examine the few, and suspect, sources by which this statement entered popular mythology. The conclusion from the sources had to be that no one really knew what Hale had said, though he probably said something rather like these words. Some teachers first queried their students on what they had always believed Hale had said, and usually received the answer, "I only regret that I have but one life to give for my country," offering an opportunity to discuss the difference between the enthusiastic and the more passive verbs.)

Nathan Hale was ill-prepared for his mission, accomplished no intelligence objective, and though he clearly conducted himself with courage, was—in the words of a later director of the CIA, Allen Dulles—"quite possibly the wrong sort of man" to be in the business. Hale was celebrated for his courage, for his intentions, and in time for his mythic qualities, which have led, as his accomplishments could not, to his being regarded as "the father of American espionage."[3] For this honor he had to wait, however.

Born June 6, 1755, Hale received his B.A. from Yale College, as did three members of the so-called Culper spy ring, in the class of 1773. Three years later George Washington sent Hale, then a captain in the Continental army, on his spying mission. Washington believed strongly in military intelligence, having taken the lesson, to which he was an eye witness, of British General Edward Braddock's defeat at Fort Duquesne by the French in 1755, a defeat attributable to Braddock's failure to learn the strength of the French. Now, in 1776, with the British in New York, Washington wished to know the number of enemy troops there and of their movements. It is not known why Washington accepted Hale, who had volunteered, and little has been learned of the details of his mission or capture. Apparently he landed on Long Island from a boat that carried him across the Sound from Connecticut. He pretended to be a schoolteacher—some say a Dutch schoolteacher—and armed himself with his Yale Diploma, perhaps to authenticate his scholarly cover. The cover was, as cover should be, close to the truth, for Hale had taught school in East Haddam and in New London, both in Connecticut, and he was fond of quoting from the classics. Most accounts say that Hale was able to pass through the British lines as an unarmed civilian, but that when he sought to pass back through the lines he was stopped for questioning, and that he either betrayed his real purpose in his anxiety or that he answered straightforwardly that he was seeking military information. Some accounts say that he lied, trying to convince the British that he had come into their lines to receive their protection from enemies of the Crown. Yet others say that his notes were found in his shoe, proving that he was a spy. One account says that he was betrayed by his Tory first cousin, a Harvard graduate. There is no firm evidence for any of these suggestions, which appear to have entered into the Hale story as means of logically accounting for his capture. Whatever happened, Hale was found out, and on September 22, 1776, he was hanged as a spy.

The words attributed to Hale were reported by an English officer who, though present at or near the hanging, is believed to have had them passed on to him secondhand and to have re-

corded them years later from memory. Another source says that
Hale's last words, in keeping with arguments made by spies before and since, were "It is the duty of every good officer to obey
any orders given him by his commander in chief." If, in fact, Hale
spoke of his regret over having but one life, he was paraphrasing
a line from Joseph Addison's play *Cato,* which was popular in
1776 and which he could assume would be recognized by his captors. That Hale showed composure and resolution, facing death
with a request for a Bible, is not disputed; apparently he was denied the Bible, which made it possible for subsequent accounts to
declare that the British provost marshal who was presiding had
torn up Hale's notes of farewell and perhaps suppressed the final
words, on the ground that "The rebels ought not to know that
they had a man in their army who could die with that much
firmness."[4]

Though Hale failed in his mission, Hale is remembered. Successful espionage was carried on throughout most of the Revolutionary War by the Culper ring, probably the first organized spy
network in American history. Established by Washington, the
network was assisted by Major Benjamin Tallmadge, also of Yale's
class of 1773, with Enoch Hale, Nathan's brother, and Robert
Townsend (who took the cover name of Samuel Culper, Jr.), both
members of that Yale class, and two others. Townsend proved to
be the most effective agent and passed information from New York
to Washington with some regularity and to good effect. Yet, while
it may be said that "every schoolboy" (a person who no longer
exists, one suspects) knows of Nathan Hale, virtually none knows
of the Culper ring.

Hale, too, remained unknown until he appeared in a book published in 1779, and thereafter his story unfolded with modest additions over the decades. He returned to life in 1914, when his
statue was placed in front of Connecticut Hall as a gift from George
Dudley Seymour, a George Washington University graduate of
1880 who had a lifelong interest in Yale memorabilia and who
had, the year before, received an honorary M.A. from Yale. Based
on contemporary descriptions, as no portrait existed, the statue—
slightly larger than life—was the work of Bela Lyon Pratt. Copies
of the statue came, in time, to be placed in front of Nathan Hale
House, a dormitory at Phillips Academy in Andover, Massachusetts; the First Congregational Church in Bristol, Connecticut; and
the Nathan Hale Court at the Chicago *Tribune.* Nine smaller versions were made for placement elsewhere, and when a half-sized

copy that was originally in the garden of Hale's childhood home in Coventry, Connecticut (also the gift of George Dudley Seymour), was moved to Washington, D.C., where it was placed at the side of the Department of Justice, Coventry eventually received one of the smaller figures. The last copy went, in 1974, to adorn the lobby of the Yale Club in New York City.[5]

And thus, by peregrination and duplication, Nathan Hale arrived at Langley. His case officer in his new role, reported in the press as "faceless and unidentified," was a scholarly Yale graduate of the class of 1935, Walter L. Pforzheimer, who had served as legislative counsel and assistant general counsel to the Central Intelligence Agency. Late in 1972 Pforzheimer asked the university for permission to have Yale's statue duplicated; as a longtime benefactor of Yale and a member of the university's powerful Library Trustees, Pforzheimer knew who and how to ask, and within six weeks he was informed that he could have the statue cast for the new CIA building, that the cost would be $6,000, and that the original plaster cast had been destroyed in a fire at the foundry. However, in 1969 Yale had loaned its statue to the foundry so that a new cast might be made, while the Yale statue was being cleaned, and this cast, at Mitchell College in New London, Connecticut, was made available. While the CIA hoped to dedicate the statue on Hale's birthday, June 6, in 1973, this operation went little better than Hale's initial effort, for the plinth was delayed, and the statue was finally erected on September 11.[6] Though some alumni had protested the temporary disappearance of the Hale statue from the Yale campus in 1969, erroneously thinking it had been removed as a symbol of militarism in that most agitated year of campus turbulence, no student organization at Yale appears to have remarked Hale's reincarnation near the entrance to the CIA headquarters. In August George D. Vaill, assistant secretary of the university and the person who had been the cut-out between spy and case officer, wrote a short piece for *American Heritage,* a popular and widely circulated publication, on the cleaning and dedication of Yale's statue in 1969. Vaill's article was reprinted, with some alteration, in the CIA's in-house magazine, *Studies in Intelligence,* and when Vaill wrote the CIA requesting a copy of the reprint and a photograph of the statue, he was told that this material was classified.[7]

Perhaps more closely linked to Yale in the public mind, which probably gave little thought to where Nathan Hale may have gone to college, was that greatest of drinking songs, which told of some

Whiffenpoofs out on a spree. By World War II the song was ir-
retrievably identified with Yale; and when it was used in an inspi-
rational wartime movie, *Winged Victory,* in 1944, it was also
identified with the risks of war. When Charley Yost was on his
way to Bangkok to be chargé d'affaires at the American embassy
in September of 1945 (and on his way to be an ambassador and
confidant of presidents in the after-war years), it seemed perfectly
natural to this Princeton graduate that, when he called on Lord
Louis Mountbatten in Delhi and again in Kandy, Mountbatten, his
beautiful witty Lady, and a departing OSS detachment would all
nostalgically sing the "Whiffenpoof Song" together.[8]

Just as the symbol of Nathan Hale had changed, the amateur
taken as the symbol for the professionals, so had the song changed.
When Kipling wrote his "Barrack Room Ballads," he had in mind
the despised private soldiers of the British army, those without
rank, the fallen sons of the nobility who had once been gentlemen
and now served in the uttermost corners of the empire. Kipling
was especially taken by the fact that they led a double life: often
appearing in police courts as drunken, beer-soaked reprobates,
lost to venereal disease and almost mindless battles, those former
gentlemen who had "gone for a soldier" were, as well, the "smart
neat young officers" who formed the thin red line that defended
the empire from the untold conspiracies of the Russians, the Germans, the French, the Pathan—the list was endless. Kipling was
fascinated with the thought of the double life, as Robert Louis
Stevenson had been when he wrote *Dr. Jekyll and Mr. Hyde,* and,
drawing upon the popular rhythms of the British music hall of his
day, sitting night after night at Gatti's, in London, Kipling created
his ballads, meant to be read and yet capable of being sung.[9]
"Gentlemen-Rankers" was in particular about gentlemen who had
fallen into the amorphous mass known as "all other ranks," sons
of the aristocracy, often disinherited, in disgrace, who had entered Her Majesty's service in India:[10]

> *We have done with Hope and Honour, we are lost to Love and*
>   *Truth,*
> *We are dropping down the ladder rung by rung,*
> *And the measure of our torment is the measure of our youth.*
>   *God help us, for we knew the worst too young!*
> *Our shame is clean repentance for the crime that brought the*
>   *sentence,*

Our pride it is to know no spur of pride,
And the Curse of Reuben holds us till an alien turf enfolds us
And we die, and none can tell Them where we died.

The chorus followed:

We're poor little lambs who've lost our way,
Baa! Baa! Baa!
We're little black sheep who've gone astray,
Baa-aa-aa!
Gentlemen-rankers out on the spree,
Damned from here to Eternity,
God ha' mercy on such as we,
Baa! Yah! Bah!

First written in 1893, these words were well known by the turn of the century when, in the early 1900s, a group of young Yale men formed the Whiffenpoofs. Members of both the Yale Glee Club and the Varsity Quartet, five men in particular soon were looking for more opportunities to sing, and in a different style: James Howard and Denton Fowler of the class of 1909 and Carl Lohmann, Meade Minnigerode, and George Pomeroy of the class of 1910. Joined by others, this group wanted to do as the University Quartet did, to sing at alumni dinners and smokers (which, being stag, required verses that would, in the jargon of more recent times, emphasize male bonding). They met weekly to sing together purely for their own pleasure, and the proprietor of a bar on New Haven's Temple Street, Louis Linder, was happy to have them choose his place, Mory's, soon to be known as "the dear old Temple Bar," since the Whiffenpoofs brought in customers to hear them try out unrehearsed songs.

The group was so successful they decided that they needed a name and that they should arrange for their perpetuation, when Lohmann's gorgeous bass, Minnigerode's effortless tenor, and Pomeroy's inventive genius would be gone. They chose, after much debate, a name drawn from a fish story then being told in a popular musical called "Little Nemo": the Whiffenpoof, a "water-dwelling creature who rose to the surface to accept cheese offered as bait and squawked his gratitude" before returning into hiding. The name was appropriately silly, carefree, memorable, and perhaps just a little sad.

With name chosen, the Whiffenpoofs wanted a theme song. In

Columbus, Ohio, one winter night in 1907, a member of the Yale
Glee Club had heard someone singing an unpublished form of
"Gentleman-Rankers." As the words were taken up by those
present, the chorus repeated several times, the melody being picked
out on a piano, the Whiffs who were present knew that they had
their song. Minnigerode and Pomeroy collaborated on a new version, which quickly became the most popular, and in time the
most famous, of Yale's drinking songs:

> To the tables down at Mory's, to the place where Louis dwells,
>   To the dear old Temple Bar we love so well,
> Sing the Whiffenpoofs assembled with their glasses raised on
>   high,
>   And the magic of their singing casts its spell.
> Yes, the magic of their singing of the songs we love so well,
>   "Shall I wasting," and "Mavourneen," and the rest;
> We will serenade our Louis while life and voice shall last,
>   Then we'll pass and be forgotten with the rest. . . .

Bitterness had turned to bittersweet, altering the chorus. The first
night the Whiffenpoofs sang their theme song at Mory's, all knew
that this would be their, and Yale's, "national anthem," to be
sung, they decided at the moment, "at every meeting, all rever-
ently standing!" "Gentlemen," Lohmann pronounced, "this is
immense!" And so it was, the signal song, the password, the code
word of those young men of Yale.[11]

The "Whiffenpoof Song" moved a little closer to being a national anthem in 1936 when Rudy Vallee, a 1927 Yale graduate
famous for his nationwide radio broadcasts, used the song. Vallee
had not been a Whiffenpoof, but he liked the song, and when he
appeared on an NBC radio show in 1936 called, somewhat grandly,
"Yale Around the World," he heard one of his classmates, Ben
Cutler, sing the now familiar version. Vallee used the song on the
next week's show and recorded it for Victor's "Bluebird" label
and, soon after, promoted the publication of sheet music—declining to have his picture appear with the music, knowing this would
not be acceptable to the Whiffenpoofs. Thereafter, despite considerable resistance on the part of Yale officials who found the use
of the song for commercial purposes "reprehensible," and a good
bit of acrimony on all sides, Vallee sang the words often, and both
recording and sheet music sold in the hundreds of thousands.[12]
Helped along later by *Winged Victory,* by Fred Waring and his

Pennsylvanians, and by Bing Crosby, the "Whiffenpoof Song"
became, if not a national anthem, the anthem for those who thought
of themselves as "the legion of the lost ones . . . the cohort of
the damned," "Gentlemen-Rankers out on the spree," ". . . till
an alien turf enfolds us / And we die, and none can tell Them
where we died": "Gentlemen songsters off on a spree . . . God
have mercy on such as we." When, in March of 1945, Professor
Norman Holmes Pearson of Yale's Department of English, on leave
of absence as chief of the London branch of X-2, the counterintelligence operation of the OSS, rose to address fifty Yale alumni
assembled at the Allies Club, he recognized almost no one, so
quickly had the war changed the university, but he and all present
(even two soldiers whom Pearson had flunked in his course) rose
at the end of his talk.[13] Out across Pall Mall floated the words,
first of Yale's nearly official anthem, "Bright College Years," sung
a bit incongruously to the air of the German anthem of World War
I, "Die Wacht am Rhein," with its closing lines, "Oh, let these
words our watch-cry be, / Where'er upon life's sea we sail—'For
God, for Country, and for Yale!' "[14] And then, of course, all linked
arms and serenaded Pearson with the "Whiffenpoof Song."[15]

The early OSS depended heavily on just such a sense of elitism.
It, too, was anarchic: it favored the idiosyncratic individual, the
person of odd curiosity and distinctive knowledge, the freewheel-
ing thinker who went past tested systems and conventional wisdom to the untried. In any academic community there are scholars
of whom it is said that they have twenty fresh ideas a day, ten of
them quite mad, five naive or stupid, three without point, and two
exciting and potentially of great value. Most bureaucracies, seeking to homogenize their members, would not tolerate so low-level
a return; any sound university will bear with eighteen expressions
of madness, stupidity, and nonproductivity in exchange for two
of great value. The U.S. Department of State was like the conventional bureaucracy: two acts of madness would more than offset eighteen acts of conventionally performed bureaucratic
procedure and would end a career. The OSS was like the university: put itching powder into safes, soon to be delivered to the
Germans, so that file clerks would be discomfited? parachute drop
thousands of pornographic pamphlets onto the grounds at
Berchtesgaden, so that Hitler might be driven mad with sexual
desire? develop a science of "crateology"—of knowing what kinds

of machine parts are in a crate from its dimensions—or invent exploding donkey turds that could be mixed with the real thing on the roads of Morocco? Why not give it a try? The OSS was an elite which also individualized, which rewarded unusual, even frankly peculiar thought, and on occasion, action. OSS recruiters turned naturally to universities, for many of them thought like dons; that they would turn in particular to the great private universities and colleges, whose leaders did not have to justify their acts of madness to state legislatures and taxpayers, or who did not sink the creativity of their students in programs of vocational training and rote memory, was equally natural. A training is not an education, though it forms a part of the larger, and the OSS knew that while it wanted skilled safecrackers, it also needed men and women able to recognize the value of the content of the safes once cracked.

There were, of course, less attractive similarities, other compatibilities, between the private universities and the OSS. In academe the person—tenured faculty or administrator—who has sunk to incompetence is generally maintained by the institution in a job that needs, at least marginally, to be performed, one in which an individual's failings do little harm to the institution. The OSS fired almost no one, and while it contained an extraordinary assortment of very able people, it also harbored a goodly number of mild incompetents, often transferred from the military, amongst its end-of-war 13,000 employees. Elites feel able to rise above their own rules, since they create them: no one can attend faculty meetings for long without discovering that rules are normative, not binding. No one can read the files of the OSS without realizing how often rules were cast aside. Both environments were pathological: academics and intelligence officers generally think it inappropriate to show emotion; if they do show anger, it is usually as a tactic. University teachers devote many hours to telling their students to express dissent; they also appoint the best students to their faculty, in a conscious laying on of hands, and expect them to abide by orders, or at the least, by the local form of YWAT. Those who succeed in a university are not good bureaucrats, they are individuals with a feel for the politics of the bureaucracy. Even after June of 1942, when the OSS took on military coloration, the organization shared the sense of tension, the schizophrenia of purpose, the explosive and complex political nature of a university campus.

A good bit of self-directed rhetoric goes on in any university. The graduate student is induced not to question the value of the goal, the Ph.D. or other degree, that one has set for oneself, lest one inhibit achievement of that goal. In a self-reinforcing elite environment, one does not question the achieved goal even afterward, since it is by virtue of that achievement that one is identified with the elite. This leads to a cozy sense of self-satisfaction, to the conviction that although the outside world (or the department chairman) may not recognize the value of what one is doing, one is right to do it, for it is by virtue of one's work that one remains individualized. Academics do not often suffer from identity crises, because their identity is within their work: they are, in that sense, at work all of the time (some literally so, in part from fear of inquiring too closely into the actual value of the work being done, which would challenge the elite status and the basis for individualization, and in part because work—doing that which one does well—is a buffer against one's incompetence in other areas of human endeavor). These are precisely the kinds of individuals valuable to the OSS or the CIA, and especially to the work of researching and analyzing intelligence data. (Such characteristics are also precisely wrong for clandestine activities, and thus units within an organization like the OSS or CIA are psychologically at war against each other, and movement from one branch to another is not easy.)

For the academic the rhetorical sense of superiority through the possession of knowledge is essential for facing the daily grind, turning again to the otherwise boring article, braving the students who, fresh as each class may be, will still ask the same questions year after year. Psychological survival is not achieved without effort, and the environment must be managed, knocked about with one's elbows until it takes a shape comfortable to one's sense of self. This is not selfishness, for in reshaping the environment the academic is also reinvigorating the educational process. Again, the parallels with the OSS are obvious: there is a need for far-ranging individualists who truly believe that solutions to problems can be found, who believe that environmental constraints help make problem solving interesting, being part of the puzzle, not simply incumbrances to be cursed. A university community is a political environment; so is an intelligence community. Neither is based on equity. No wonder that there would be, in the early years of the OSS, such an affinity with the university community, or that even today the grounds of the CIA headquarters at Langley, Virginia, are called not the base, precincts, post, or station, but "the campus."

Students at a university like Yale thought well of themselves, and with some reason. In a nation driven by commerce, in a university that also heralded other forms of success, men admitted to Yale knew that they would, unless unlucky or intolerably lazy, take their places in society. They might, on their examinations, show a tremendous familiarity with wrong dates, and there would be those from conventional backgrounds who might always show an exceptional lack of talent when it came to artistic judgment, but the first could be dismissed as something that could be looked up and therefore needn't be remembered, and the second was a mere matter of opinion. What really mattered was taking the game seriously, at least while playing it. Charles Seymour, Yale's wartime president and a leading authority on World War I, once confessed to a colleague that he had survived at Yale when others who were initially thought to be the better scholars had not because of such a judgment. In the second term of 1910 the Olympians of Yale's history department, which then included Wilbur Cortez Abbott, George Burton Adams, Charles McLean Andrews, and Max Farrand, giants all, held their annual meeting to decide upon the one graduating Ph.D. who would be appointed to an instructorship. All assumed that Frank Klingberg (later of the University of California in Los Angeles) would receive the nod, for he had pursued the most difficult course and had achieved the best record; further, he and another likely candidate were in Adams's seminar, and Adams was thought to be the most powerful member of the Olympians. On the afternoon of one of the last meetings of that seminar, as the students gathered to await Adams's appearance—always dramatically at precisely four minutes after the appointed hour—fire alarms sounded from the City Hall, followed by a second and a third call. The nearby county jail was on fire, clearly visible from the library where the students met. "I've got to go," said Klingberg, "I can't miss a fire like this," and off he ran, soon to be followed by the second-ranked candidate, and a third. Seymour made to go with them, then stopped, mindful that Adams's seminar would be a shambles. "And where are the others?" Adams asked as he entered, "with a touch of pepper"; gone to a fire, he was told. "Fire," exploded Adams. "*Well*." And then with an effort, "We'll start today with that fifth cartulary of Charles the Bald." Three days later the Olympians announced that Seymour had the appointment.[16]

This hard, gemlike flame with which historians were meant to burn is basic to the rich particularity of a place like Yale. No one, for example, should govern Yale who did not have a Yale degree. This proposition, arising from early eighteenth-century needs in an institution founded by clerics who had broken away from Harvard College because it was becoming too liberal, produces a peculiar syllogism. The faculty takes pride in the fact that they, not some elected body of regents, state trustees, or panoply of vice presidents, govern. The governance of the Yale faculty, specifically, stems from a Board of Permanent Officers. Every member of the faculty of Yale College who has attained a full professorship is a member of the board. But one may not be a member of the board without a Yale degree. Thus follows the logic, that upon promotion to a professorship, the faculty member will simultaneously be awarded, by the corporation of the University, an honorary M.A. degree. And the secretary of the university would personally call round to the professor's house, there to present him with his statement of elevation. Probity, integrity, the sense that the life of scholarship is serious business, and yet the ever-present awareness that all of this is, if not silly, just a little odd, and endearing for all that, was central to the institution.

This delicate sense of irony was best expressed by Wesley Sturges, who was dean of the Yale Law School. Sturges understood Yale very well, perhaps because he had taken most of his degrees elsewhere, and he would greet new law students on their first day at the school with the observation, "I do not know why you have come to law school. If you want to make lots of money, you are in the wrong place. There is a law school about a hundred miles from here on the Charles River that would prepare you for that. The function of the Yale Law School is to train presidents of the United States." The point was, at the time no Yale Law School graduate had ever been president of the United States.[17]

During World War II the voice of Yale, in truth the voice of liberal education in a time of war, was the dean of Yale College, William Clyde DeVane. No person was more responsible for preserving, and acting on, the conviction that it would be disastrously wrong to abandon the liberal arts in favor of the killing arts, however grim the news from the battlefront might be, and no one did more to see to it that amidst the clamor for courses in demolitions and airplane maintenance, room must be left for the humanizing subjects that strengthened a capacity for abstract and objective thought. DeVane, some thought long after the war was over, had saved the university.[18]

DeVane had come to Yale from South Carolina, the descendant of French Huguenots and a transfer from Furman University in the midst of World War I. He passed an unhappy war, teaching draftees to ask for ham and eggs in French, but this tedium led him to understand the value of leisure and of privacy, two qualities he associated with university life which, in 1942, he saw swept utterly away from the Yale campus. Widely read, DeVane believed that the apt quotation from literature was most likely to make a point universally understood; he also cherished the cool head that did not choke under pressure: in high school he had once won a basketball game for his team by sinking twenty-one consecutive foul shots, and he loved the intricacy and controlled tension basic to football, that brawny chess game that required, as he well knew from his own undergraduate days, far more brains than most spectators ever imagined. In the first year after World War I, DeVane shared a writing course with Philip Barry, Stephen Vincent Benet, Archibald MacLeish, Thornton Wilder, Henry Luce, Briton Hadden, Walter Millis, and Wilmarth Lewis, as distinguished a group as was ever assembled in such a seminar, and he cherished both the connections that Yale brought him and the good that he could do for Yale students through those connections. Leisure and privacy, he knew, required a sense of tight control over oneself and one's time, to do all that must be done, to never appear hurried, ruffled, or angry. He knew the typical undergraduate complaint, then as now, that professors give out assignments as though theirs was the only course a student was taking, and he knew that it was right they should do so, both because a professional sense of passion ought to lead the scholar to feel that nothing other than his own demands mattered and because it was good for the student to learn how to deal with conflicting demands and pressures.

Of DeVane it was later said that "everything he was asked to do he looked on as an opportunity." He seldom said no to an assignment or an invitation, in part because he liked the pace of challenges added to challenges, and in part because he had a vision for the institution that was all-embracing. He had, by the war years, enormous influence, but he never seemed to wish to have power. He, with Seymour, helped the university adjust to war.

Seymour had become president of Yale in 1937, an obvious choice, with his Cambridge and Yale degrees, his experience at Versailles as chief of the Austro-Hungarian division of the American Commission to Negotiate Peace, his distinguished years as a Sterling Professor of History (a Sterling chair being Yale's highest academic achievement), and since 1927 his careful and wise use of the provostship, which he had made into the second-ranking office in a university that earlier had seemed to harbor, below the presidency, a bevy of competing deans. Seymour was the interior Yale man: a member of the most prestigious of Yale's secret societies, Skull and Bones, a close follower of the two most beloved sports, football and crew, a staunch conservative who championed compulsory chapel because of the Burkean social values it taught, a superb, somewhat aloof diplomat who seemed down to earth only in the rare moments when, reaching across his desk for one of his six corncob pipes, he paused to rethink a phrase that had displeased him. Seymour was "dyed in the Blue," as a friend remarked, a man who thought one should take everything in life seriously except himself, though he usually hid his reservation from the faculty.

Even before the United States was in the war, the war's tensions were brought to the Yale campus. In 1936 a student-organized Peace Week had crystallized isolationist sentiment, and each year the Yale Political Union, an undergraduate body founded in 1935, would devote major attention to the growing crisis in Europe. As the Germans struck across Poland on September 1, 1939, college students traveling in Europe found themselves scrambling to get out of the war zone and back to America, while young Britons in universities in the United States hurried to find passage home. A group of Law School students, fearful that the United States would be drawn into a war that, they were convinced, it must avoid at all costs, organized for the purpose of "building an impregnable hemispheric defense and staying out of war in Europe and Asia." Eighteen men met to form College Men for Defense First, which soon linked fifty-nine institutions (including several that were coeducational, despite the organization's title), with Yale providing by far the largest number of members. In 1940 this group, led by R. Douglas Stuart, Jr., became the Committee to Defend America First. A College Committee for Defense First, based on the Murray Hill Hotel in New York City, took Senator Robert A. Taft, a Yale graduate of 1910 and a trustee of the university, as its primary spokesman. Taft was joined by Hanson W. Baldwin, Herbert Hoover, and Robert Maynard Hutchins (of the Yale class of 1921), the president of the University of Chicago.

By the autumn of 1940 the campus was in ferment. A very active committee for conscientious objectors, with advice from the chaplain of the university, Sidney Lovett, who had been a CO in World War I (though not, as it developed, in World War II), opposed the draft, and late in 1940 it rallied around David Dellinger, Yale '36, who had gone to federal penitentiary in Danbury for refusing to register. An America First unit was formed at Yale, with Richard Bissell, '32, a young assistant professor of economics (and future employee of the CIA), and an undergraduate, Kingman Brewster, Jr., '41 (a future president of Yale), as spokesmen. Brewster was summoned to testify before the Senate Committee on Foreign Affairs when it held hearings on Lend-Lease in February of 1941, and he was able to report that 1,486 Yale students had declared themselves isolationists. Against the America Firsters there was an equally vocal group of undergraduates led by McGeorge Bundy, '40, and many faculty who, as Norman Holmes Pearson, then a new instructor in English, would remark, were 150 percent interventionist.[19]

In the meantime a group of Yale faculty decided that they must do something for the British. They could unite, interventionist and isolationist alike, on helping British children escape the war. It was, perhaps, typical of Yale that, having decided to help wives and children who were under threat of bombing in England to find homes in America, the faculty would settle on Oxford and Cambridge universities as the source of those most likely to "fit in." The master of Berkeley College, Samuel B. Hemingway, together with Dr. John F. Fulton, Sterling Professor of Physiology, contacted the national Committee for the Care of European Children and, finding it ill-organized, decided to act for Yale alone. In July of 1940 ninety-seven children between the ages of five and sixteen (and twenty-three mothers) arrived in New Haven via Montreal, to which the Yale committee had gone in greeting. (Seven children and one mother arrived later, having been held up in Canada with visa problems.) The Yale faculty raised $227,850 to meet school tuitions for the children and to pay rent on apartments for accompanying mothers, and ties were struck that remained firm long after the war.[20]

When the Japanese struck at Pearl Harbor on December 7, 1941, debate over intervention ended. Students streamed out of their rooms, rushing aimlessly about the city, some in tears and most, with bravado, vying to pronounce the most hideous of deaths on the Japanese. From Vanderbilt Hall, on the Old Campus, freshmen moved in more purposeful ways, down the nearby streets, invading the lounge of the Taft Hotel, trashing the lobby, smashing windows, battling against the New Haven police, who suddenly found themselves with a full-fledged riot on their hands. Later no one seemed able to explain this violent reaction, though most acknowledged the need to strike out at something, at someone, to vent the energy that had been building all through the term.[21]

Yale immediately shifted to a full court press so that undergraduates might complete their degrees in three years. Students who left for active service at once were assured of readmission after the war. By the summer of 1942, with army, navy, marine and air force reserve units in place, and special war courses on civilian pilot training, explosives, mapmaking, naval cryptography, and aeronautics introduced, Yale was on a full war footing.

By the summer of 1943 Yale had become a military camp. Rooms intended for two men now held six, single beds replaced by government-issue double bunks. Persian and Oriental carpets which had adorned common room floors were gone, the hardwood shone to a military polish. Seated and served meals in the dining halls, with silver and crisp napery, gave way to standardized trays and cafeteria service. The Old Campus and the Cross Campus, the principal greenswards, were beaten into dust, the carefully manicured lawns surrendered for parade grounds. Popular lecturers, accustomed to having students hang on their every word as they built to resounding conclusions, normally to halt dramatically at precisely the fiftieth minute, found their perorations rudely interrupted by military marching bands. The ultimate inelegance of army butt receptacles—for which read, standing ashtrays, or what many at Yale had decorously called "gentlemen's friends" from an earlier time—appeared in the corridors. Only three of the residential halls—Timothy Dwight, Jonathan Edwards, and Trumbull—remained open to civilian undergraduates, down to 700 in number, while the army took over Berkeley and Calhoun, and the navy and marines gave the rest a barrackslike atmosphere. Yale was, the unreconstructed on the Yale faculty complained, simply a military camp for seven thousand men, only a tenth of whom were pursuing traditional programs and then in untraditional ways.[22]

There were blessings, too. Yale's budget was enhanced by having over two thousand more students than usual, nearly all of whom met their bills, or had them met by the government. In 1944 Yale fielded its first undefeated football team in two decades, since the navy and marines allowed their men to play (the army refused), and though there was no victory over Harvard, which had abandoned football in 1942, Yale claimed, perhaps a bit unfairly, at least a regional championship. There was a new source for bawdy jokes (Yale men, it was said, liked barnyard but not boudoir humor, a most unlikely story), as when a course in logic used a report allegedly sent back by a soldier/anthropologist in the Marianas of an islander who established the ultimate syllogism: "Today I was 86 years old. Had an erection. Couldn't bend it with two hands. Ditto, at 88. Ditto at 90: Could bend it with two hands. Am growing stronger." And there was always the romantic sound of air force songs, more resonant of the sadness of war than any others. There was a new burst of Cole Porter tunes—widely regarded as Yale's special property from his years on the campus—replete with the special Porter brand of double entendre. Best of all, at the end of the war a flood of more mature and committed servicemen would be returning, to further move undergraduate life away from the air of elegance that, some faculty thought, had not been appropriate even before the war.[23]

There were sad and harassing moments too, especially when the university was compelled to provide information on all "enemy aliens" on the faculty and to require them to turn in their cameras to the campus police and to certify that they had changed their radio sets so that they could not receive short wave. Thirteen faculty were thus singled out in this silly season, including such scholars as Paul Hindemith in the School of Music, Theodore Ernst Mommsen in history, and the philosopher Ernst Alfred Cassirer. Though Carl Lohmann, the university secretary, to whom this bit of idiocy fell, tried to make light of it publicly, he was unhappy, and with good reason.

The registration of aliens, their radios, and their cameras, though technically handled through the office of the university secretary, actually fell to a virtually unknown employee of, apparently, the FBI and Yale jointly. This was Harry B. Fisher, the tip of whose iceberg was not fished to the surface until 1984, to reveal a distinctly unappetizing side to the university's cooperation with government authorities.

Fisher had been installed at Yale in 1927 as a liaison officer between the FBI and Yale, to help protect Yale students against the vices of prostitution, narcotics, and alcohol, the purchase of which was then illegal. Fisher had worked with the then-dean of Yale College, Clarence Mendell, and had put undercover agents along the College Highway—the route up the Connecticut Valley from New Haven to Dartmouth College that encompassed Smith and Mount Holyoke colleges for women—to stage raids on roadhouses and centers of prostitution. Fisher reported to a euphemistically named Social Research Committee at Yale, which was concerned, as he wrote, with "attempted black-mail, indecent pictures, homosexuals, liquor drops and girl drops within the campus buildings, etc., etc.," with the conceivably legitimate parietal purpose of protecting innocent young men against being "saturated with . . . a loathsome disease"—and not incidentally to save the university much embarrassment. Fisher, the brother of a Methodist Episcopal bishop, and himself a minister, was worried about a wider range of problems, including "the white slave traffic; the drug traffic; immoral conditions in traveling carnivals, circuses, theatres and agricultural fairs; gambling, illegal liquor selling, obscene books and magazines; Sabbath desecration and political corruption."

Originally Fisher had made private reports on the consumption of alcohol at fraternity parties, on law students who imported women for immoral purposes, and on "Faculty-Student Booz Parties" at the homes of medical students. With the aid of informers and the cooperation of the campus police (the first university police force in the United States, dating back to 1894) he was able to launch a program designed more for protection than punishment. By the mid-1930s, with access to alcohol legal once again, he recognized that his budget might be reduced, but by then he had made himself generally valuable to the university, investigating drinking at football games, checking on immorality at Yale-owned off-campus dormitories, and advising on how best to use the new college system to protect the morals of minors. At the outbreak of the war, however, Fisher was either thrust into, or grasped at, widely expanded and quite new responsibilities: the clearance of Yale faculty and students for sensitive wartime employment and the vetting of aliens, both as to their activities at Yale and the suitability of their being employed or even enrolled as students.

In this way the university allowed matters of educational policy to be blurred into questions of administrative procedure, putting at risk important precepts of academic freedom. With Mendell no longer dean of Yale College—there is no evidence that DeVane cooperated with Fisher at all—the program fell under the surveillance of Charles H. Warren, director of the Sheffield Scientific School and, more important in terms of undergraduate matters, master of Trumbull College. Warren gave Fisher high marks for tact and thoroughness. The latter was certainly the case: with his assistance the FBI conducted over four hundred investigations of individuals at Yale (and at Wesleyan University) in 1942 alone, including fifty inquiries into Yale men who had applied to the Department of Justice (which included the FBI) for jobs, hundreds of others who applied to the War and Navy departments, the OSS, the Department of State, or the Office of Economic Mobilization, and "76 girl cases." In for a penny was in for a pound apparently, for since Fisher already had obtrusive capacities in the Yale community, he was made "Special Custodian" of enemy aliens at Yale.

Fisher's actual position is unclear, though it appears that he was paid mainly by Yale, probably with some additional funds, perhaps on a case basis, from the FBI. It was probably better, if professional snooping had to be done—and few were likely to gainsay it in wartime—that it be done by someone subject to Yale administrative authority, though it is difficult to know just where authority lay, especially when Fisher wrote as late as 1951 that he had "instructed" Yale's registrars on matters of confidentiality. He was, in one sense, on the side of the angels—or of one angel— for Fisher insisted that only FBI agents had the right to ask for confidential information (a view overruled by Lohmann, who included the intelligence services, the State Department, and the Immigration Service in a memorandum to masters and deans in 1951), though this appears to have been an argument made less in defense of the privacy of individuals and more to protect FBI turf. Fisher concentrated during the war on students of Japanese background, interfered at least once to try to persuade the Yale economics department not to renew the contract of a Japanese scholar who had taught in the Army program, and poked about into the affairs of the Institute of Human Relations, presumably because it was viewed as somewhat left-wing. Tact, however, would hardly apply to his remarks about the conscientious objectors, "a strange group, particularly since Pearl Harbor," whom he thought far too active. He hoped Yale would "remove" these people from the student body. To its credit Yale refused to do so and, later, told Fisher that the FBI was not to tell him, or he to tell Yale, about the investigatory bodies with which the university would or would not cooperate. When Fisher retired in 1952 he seems not to have been replaced.[24]

For Yale, and for American higher education generally, the effects of the war would never be forgotten. The university had been transformed; with the arrival of postwar veterans, its student body matured; with the development of its wartime institutes, especially in the social sciences, its links to the government had been forged, for good or ill, so that pure research would be harnessed to the service of the state. As thousands had gone forth from Yale, and thousands upon thousands more from every campus in the land, to serve openly in the military forces of the nation, so had hundreds entered the covert service of the nation. From Yale's class of 1943 alone, at least forty-two young men entered intelligence work, largely in the OSS, many to remain on after the war to form the core of the new CIA. Rightly or wrongly, a historian could, in assessing the link between the university and the agency, declare in 1984 that Yale had influenced the CIA more than any other university did. This generalization was extended by a student journalist into the judgment that for four decades "Yale had influenced the Central Intelligence Agency more than any other institution, giving the CIA the atmosphere of a class reunion."[25] The laying on of hands, quietly and effectively, in the college and in the classroom, at the master's tea and in the seminar, over a cup at Mory's and during a break in crew practice, had by the 1950s become so accepted, as John Downey, a graduate of 1951 remarked, that it was taken for granted that one would serve the nation in some way; for him the choice lay between the CIA or fighting in Korea.[26] At the end of World War II, as the campus talked of returning to normalcy while knowing that it would not, the idea of service in "the intelligence community" was only one, and by no means the largest, expression of the Yale notion that, for students having "paced out a cloistered life," service to nation marked an appropriate next phase of growth.[27]

In June of 1946 the university closed its books on the war, with a major service of commemoration for those from Yale who had given their lives in that conflict. President Seymour and the university chaplain presided over the solemn ceremony, the reading out of 397 names. The list was inclusive—it embraced Franklin Roosevelt, deemed to be a Yale man by virtue of an honorary LL.D. granted in 1934—and it ended with the names of five faculty. There were forty-three names from the class of 1943, thirty-five from the class of 1944, and a devastating seventy-two from the class of 1945. Yale did not know, at least officially, how many of these men had lost their lives while serving for the OSS or one of the other intelligence organizations, though a careful reading of the private memoranda from the university secretary's office, where circumstances of deaths were recorded for the Roll of Honor, would suggest that the number in intelligence was at least sixty (with one suicide).[28] President Seymour had, a few weeks earlier, declared that the university should now return to a peacetime schedule; still, no one thought it likely that this would be so. Uniforms would disappear from the campus, rooms would, it was hoped, be a bit less crowded—a hope not realized—and acceleration could be forgotten as a bad dream. But nearly everyone thought there was going to be trouble with the Russians, and many on the faculty simply redirected the focus of their research. The tone of urgency that had pervaded the campus for half a decade was in no way stilled. Four years later, when in 1950 the memorial tablets bearing the names of those 397 dead (to which a few other names had, in the meantime, been added) were dedicated in Memorial Hall, the nation was at war again, in Korea.

How did forty-two, or more, members of the class of 1943 wind up in the OSS and many more in other branches of intelligence? How did Yale's faculty adjust their research to assist in the work of intelligence? In what ways did the "bad eyes brigade" help the war effort? And what kind of continuity was there between the wartime years and the postwar years when, in the atmosphere of the cold war, the new Central Intelligence Agency was formed? The answers lay in part in dozens of individual biographies, a few of which are told in the following chapters. But the answers also lay in the institutional history of Yale and, in particular, in its various research institutes, in the work of certain members of the faculty, and in the Residential Colleges.

Yale's undergraduate life is organized around its Residential

Colleges, of which there were ten in 1941. These colleges, designed to make living and learning one, were the gift of Edward S. Harkness of Yale's class of 1897, who in 1930 provided just under $16 million so that Yale might create a college plan modeled, so far as possible and appropriate, on the college system at Oxford and Cambridge universities. Although Harkness had secretly offered the benefaction some time before, the Yale faculty declined to accept it until it was learned that Harvard, which had accepted a like offer from Harkness, was moving to such a system (though there residences would be called houses rather than colleges). It was typical of the loyalty of Yale's alumni that the donor, rather than turning away from the university in anger, had openly renewed his offer. The first seven Yale colleges took in students in the autumn of 1933, the tenth in 1940; two postwar colleges would be added in 1962.

These colleges were far more than glorified dormitories, though they served the dormitory function as well. Each had its own dining hall, each a common room and often two, parallel to the senior and junior common rooms of Oxbridge. Each had its own kitchen, game room, squash courts, and a variety of activity rooms, typically including printing presses, woodworking shops, perhaps a little theater, and as tastes and needs changed, music rooms or photography studios. Each had a substantial library, both to take pressure off the main library and further to assure that study was associated with the residence as well. As one college master was wont to tell entering freshmen to the point of tedium, a dormitory was, as its root implied, a place in which to sleep, while a college was meant to form a binding sense of community, of collegiality. Sometimes the colleges did this, equally often they did not, and if they did the chemistry was usually (and often wrongly) credited to the master and his wife—for all masters were, until 1971, men.

The masters were respected, but they also were the object of much jealousy, for at a time when a full professor might be paid as little as $6,000 a year, each master, without respect to his normal rank (and not all were full professors) received $10,000, a splendid house ranging up to thirty rooms in size, and two or three resident servants (until the war came to take them away). Faculty jockeyed constantly if decorously for masterships. Though such enticements did not invariably attract the best people, most masters were conscientious in the pursuit of what they took to be a civilizing mission. Young people are, as one master would remark

later, "hungry, noisy and nocturnal," and the master would try
to temper this energy, make certain that young men left Yale feeling secure about how to take tea and converse with ease in the
company of adults who were neither parents nor professors sitting
in judgment on their course work, and that they would understand
what it meant to "play the game." Truth was, no doubt, that the
real civilizing influence came most often from the master's spouse,
and in some colleges—Berkeley and Pierson were instances—returning war veterans invariably remarked with affection on how
much they had missed Mary Hemingway or Doris Wolfers. Taken
as a group the masters were, in the 1940s, powerful and influential
figures on the campus, in close touch with undergraduates, and in
an especially good position to steer bright young men toward particular employment—the OSS, say, or in the 1950s the CIA.

In World War II and after there were masters who were known
as contact points—seldom recruiters, usually simply conduits—
with the intelligence community, though these masters did not
displace interested faculty, the odd administrator (usually a lesser
dean), or the occasional coach. Six masters were particularly influential in this regard. Arnold Whitridge, '13, historian and the
first master of Calhoun College, had roots in England, and until
he left in 1942 he saw to it that students in his college shared his
concern for Britain. Robert Dudley French, '10, professor of English and first master of Jonathan Edwards College—indeed, the
first master of any Yale college—ran the only High Table at Yale
that could hold a candle to Oxbridge. He was an outspoken supporter of the English cause throughout, differing sharply and publicly whenever he could with his classmate and frequent visitor,
Senator Robert A. Taft. Elliott Dunlap Smith, a Harvard man,
professor of economics and first master of Saybrook College, volunteered to help find appropriate young men for economic analysis in the OSS at the graduate as well as undergraduate level.
Samuel B. Hemingway, professor of English, who had succeeded
President Seymour as master of Berkeley College, was quite persistent in his efforts to place members of the specialized army
language programs in one of the OSS units. Most important, however, were the masters of Davenport and Pierson colleges, together with the fellows—that is, university faculty (and a few
administrators) assigned to take their meals in the college and,
often, to use offices there.[29]

The fellowship of Davenport College, both during and shortly after the war, may be taken as representative of all the Yale colleges. There were, at the war's height, twelve fellows—the number prescribed when the colleges were first opened—and sixteen associate fellows, a category generally reserved for distinguished figures from outside the university who lived or worked close enough to New Haven (usually in New York City) that they might reasonably be expected to attend the fellows' meetings, which took place either weekly or twice monthly, depending upon the custom of the college. By 1950 there were twenty-seven fellows and twenty-three associates, for a total of fifty individuals. All were male. Taking the year 1948 as a median between the larger and smaller fellowships, we find that of forty-eight individuals, thirty held their B.A. from Yale, while six more had first come to Yale for a graduate degree: that is, thirty-six were Yale men by some form of education. Of the remainder, four were from Harvard, three from elsewhere in the incipient Ivy League (Brown, Columbia, and Princeton), and five were from Oxbridge. This left little room for anyone from so exotic a place as, say, the University of Washington, which made it all the more interesting that the first postwar master, Daniel Merriman, was from just that institution.

The network also held for the preparatory schools. While sixteen of the total group had attended public schools, and five had been educated outside the country, the remainder were from the prep schools. Phillips (Andover), Phillips Exeter, Groton, St. Paul's, Hotchkiss, and Taft dominated, with twenty between them. The first four of these would also dominate in the list of young men who, having graduated from Yale during or immediately after the war, entered the OSS, the CIA, or one of the other intelligence groups. (Merriman, the master, had attended Groton and Harvard before taking time out to pursue Alaskan fisheries, thus to wind up at university in Seattle.) These schools had already laid the groundwork of education for civic virtue, and they shared a general approach to education and to prayer. At all, the students could have shared in the prayer "For Courage" (though it is taken from the St. Paul's School prayer book): "For all who have labored for freedom, sound government, and just laws; and for those who have laid down their lives that truth and justice might live, We praise thee, O Lord." [30]

During and after the war this fellowship scarcely fulfilled the cliché of the ivory tower. Thirteen of the fellows had close government connections, eight of them serving with one of the intel-

ligence groups, usually navy or OSS. The associate fellows were
an older body, but even there six were active at high levels of
government: these included Dean Acheson, Groton and Yale '15,
assistant secretary of state throughout the war and, from 1949,
secretary of state, and Archibald MacLeish, Hotchkiss and Yale
'15 as well, Librarian of Congress from 1939 to 1944. Ties reached
even further: the brother of one fellow was a top OSS operative
in North Africa, the daughter of another worked for the OSS
abroad, and several had in-laws that were extremely well placed.
A sociologist might have had a field day studying the kinship patterns of Davenport College, which were at least as complex as
those of one of the South Sea islands then in vogue. Within this
matrix Daniel Merriman, who had joined the faculty in 1938 as an
oceanographer, and who in 1946 became the master, to serve until
1966, steered a number of young men toward the CIA.

   Above all there was Arnold Wolfers, a distinguished professor
of international relations with superb connections in Washington,
who presided over Pierson College* from 1935 until his elevation
to a Sterling professorship in 1949. Both as master and through
the Institute of International Studies, he was active, knowing exactly whom to call and when on behalf of a likely candidate for
any agency of government. Born in 1892 in Saint Gall, Switzerland, a self-styled "Tory-Liberal" with two doctorates, Wolfers
was a natural mediator. Tall, aristocratic, well-dressed, he glit-
tered when he walked, and his crisp, light voice turned quickly
from person to person, "rather like a searchlight." An émigré
scholar who was almost, if not quite, at home amongst New England Yankees, Wolfers made the Master's House in Pierson Col-

---

*Many Yale alumni also identify Alan Valentine as a conduit to the intelligence
world, but this is quite incorrect. Valentine was a brilliant young former Rhodes
Scholar who at thirty came to Yale from Swarthmore to serve briefly as the first
master of Pierson College until he left for the presidency of the University of
Rochester in 1935. He had placed his stamp on the college, especially with his
concern for public service, but despite the mythology he was never in a position
to help with intelligence recruiting at Yale.[31]

   Another master one might assume helped as a conduit was James Grafton
Rogers, '05, professor of law and master of Timothy Dwight College from 1935
to 1942, since Rogers became chief of the Planning Group of the OSS in July of
1942. Rogers had been dean of the Law School at the University of Colorado
and an assistant secretary of state in the Hoover administration. He left a diary
covering his work for the OSS, which has been edited for publication by Thomas
F. Troy. Almost certainly Rogers did contact former Law School colleagues,
but very little evidence of this survives in the record.

lege a center for campus entertainment second only to the president's residence. His wife, Doris Forrer, daughter of a member of the Swiss parliament, was an enthusiastic hostess, and the Wolferses graced the house with eighteenth-century Swiss furnishings of conventional but charming taste. Wolfers's sister-in-law, Anita, who lived in New Haven for a time, would become an OSS agent, work for Allen Dulles in Switzerland, and receive a commendation for most secret and dangerous work—so secret, indeed, that no record of her work survives, and the commendation was ordered removed from the OSS files. When statesmen were to be entertained at Yale, it would be the Wolferses who would do it, formally and well, yet to the light touch of Dixieland jazz, which Wolfers loved to play. Wolfers also stood at the center of a group of faculty, not at all derisively referred to by those outside their charmed circle as "the State Department," who met for lunch regularly at Davenport College, exuding an air of dignity as they trooped into the hall in well-tailored gray flannel suits.[32]

These members of the Institute for International Studies were one of the two best sources for intelligence information and contacts on the Yale campus. In addition to Wolfers, the luncheon table usually included Percy Corbett, professor of government and jurisprudence, whose contacts throughout the British Commonwealth were already formidable; Frederick S. Dunn, also professor of international relations and director of the institute; Jacob Viner for the year he was at Yale as a visiting professor of economics; Grayson Kirk, a visiting fellow at the institute (and postwar president of Columbia University); and Nicholas John Spykman, the nation's leading geopolitician, Sterling Professor of International Relations and, until his health began to fail in 1940, director of the institute. Richard Bissell from the economics department, who was a fellow of Davenport, was also often present.

This was a formidable group who, realizing that faculty at other tables were interested in their conversations, launched a Wednesday seminar, "Where Is the World Going?" at which various State Department issues were discussed. From this seminar Wolfers, who preferred small-team operations, developed study groups to tackle problems sent up from the State Department, to which he went every second week, or to which he communicated through his good friend and Yale Corporation member Dean Acheson. Dunn was known for his quick trips abroad, frequently off on some State Department assignment, traveling light by throwing his dirty un-

derclothing out the window of his hotel and buying more as needed.
A bit deaf, Dunn had mastered the art of agreeing with one before
a sentence was finished, replying with a touch of Celtic crispness,
by which those who didn't know him thought him always on the
verge of taking offense. Viner, who returned often after his year
at Yale, loved dispute, and within five minutes in any gathering
he would provide the substance for a fight. Offsetting this bristling
body there was, until his death in 1943, the very Dutch Spykman,
who sought to forestall arguments by beginning his sentences with
the declaration, "Of course this is so." Here was a group with a
capacity for controlled tension, hard work (and grace) under pressure, and a worldly knowledge of languages.

Under Dunn's direction the institute, organized in 1935 with a
grant from the Rockefeller Foundation, worked closely with the
Department of State on a variety of research projects. The foundation refunded the institute in 1940 on the condition that it become self-supporting in three years, and this meant that Dunn must
seek out contract money. Fortunately, the institute had an established track record. Wolfers had published an influential study of
British and French policy between the first and second world wars.
A. Whitney Griswold, '29, an exceedingly able young scholar who
would be all over the lot without anyone thinking him superficial—instructor of English; assistant professor of government and
international relations; associate professor of political science;
professor of history; professor of history, the arts and letters; and
after 1950, president of the university—had completed a survey
of the Far Eastern policy of the United States under institute auspices. Samuel Flagg Bemis, Farnum Professor of Diplomatic History and, with his Pulitzer Prize, an adornment to the university,
was hard at work on a companion study of United States diplomacy in Latin America, while Wolfers had begun an analysis of
the control of the foreign communications of the United States,
one part of which—on telecommunications—led him to an interest
in codes and ciphers.

The proposed work of the institute for the years after 1940 suggested a strong interest in how the world might be reorganized to
fit American needs. Members of the institute were studying the
question of a United States of Europe, whether resulting from a
German victory or from successful British resistance; others were
looking into inter-American trade relations, and especially the
question of a customs union; another group was working on the

idea of hemispheric self-sufficiency, which would briefly support those who felt Fortress America was an option; and on the premise that "whatever the outcome of the present war, the United States will be forced for many years to come to maintain a high war potential," the staff were launching, with the Law School, several studies of the role of American-style democracy in modern war. Spykman, in the meantime, was continuing his work on the geographic bases of foreign policy. Though they would not have said so, these scholars were working on a history of imperial America, and all of their efforts were of interest to the State Department. Most received assistance from it.[33]

The other major source of intelligence information at Yale, the Institute of Human Relations, was rather more controversial, at least on the campus, some faculty declaring that its rapid move to war-related work smacked of opportunism. The charge is reasonable, though the institute also abundantly demonstrated the value of anthropology, and to a lesser extent of sociology, to intelligence work. The institute's director, Mark A. May, an educational psychologist, seems never to have won full acceptance on the campus, perhaps because his advanced degree was in a subject of which many on the faculty were skeptical, perhaps because he held no degrees at all from Yale other than the obligatory honorary one, and most likely because he did lay himself open to a certain degree of satire.

Less than a week after Pearl Harbor, May announced that the institute would accept contract work from any government agency, and he launched an immediate crash program to study the "cultural and racial characteristics" of the Japanese. George P. Murdock, one of the leading cultural anthropologists at Yale, shifted the emphasis of his Cross-Cultural Survey to the collecting and classification of materials on the people of the Pacific, and he began a fresh study of Micronesia, and especially of the Japanese Mandated Islands. The institute drew up a list of anthropologists throughout the nation who had firsthand knowledge of the islands and sent it to the Army and Navy departments. Another group of scholars signed a contract with Nelson Rockefeller, coordinator of Inter-American Affairs, for a Strategic Index of Latin America. Studies already launched—one on the reaction of adolescent boys to success and failure, another on the point of view of industrial managers, a third on the machine tool industry in Connecticut— were redirected toward the war effort, while the institute an-

nounced yet another major project, "the study of man and war."
In short, the institute responded as academicians often do, with
an eye to grant and contract money and a desire to justify their
actions by creating attractive new projects, reorienting old projects, and announcing large new plans under titles calculated to
have good effect on public relations. The institute confessed, rather
grandly, that its major goal during the war would be "the discovery of the basic principles and laws of learning which apply not
only to human but to all living things." The humanists on campus,
who had been wondering for some years what the institute was
up to, thought this rather silly.

Even so, the institute obviously harbored a number of scholars
who would be helpful to the work of James Phinney Baxter, the
historian who was the first head of the office of research for the
Coordinator of Information, the precursor to the OSS. On leave
from the presidency of Williams College, Baxter urged May to
press forward with the study of the Japanese Mandated Islands,
while May wrote to the COI, even as the shells were cooling at
Pearl Harbor, to ask how Yale could relate the work of the institute to intelligence gathering and evaluation. Professor Leonard
Doob, Yale's leading authority on the psychology of propaganda,
a field obviously related to the production of wartime materials,
was dispatched to see the OSS, Nelson Rockefeller—who he knew
from Dartmouth College years—at Inter-American Affairs, and
Colonel Percy Black of Military Intelligence. May wrote that
Murdock's Cross-Cultural Survey already had files on 145 "mainly
backward peoples"—twenty in Africa, fifty-six in South America,
twenty-three each in North America, Eurasia, and Oceania—and
he offered these files to the COI. On December 27, 1941, May
concluded in a letter to Gordon Allport, with whom he hoped to
coordinate work between Harvard and Yale, that "the Institute
of Human Relations has gone to war."[34]

At the institute, if somewhat on its fringes, was Heber Blankenhorn, the originator of aerial propaganda in World War I. While
at Yale Blankenhorn prepared most of a study on combat propaganda, working on leaflet dropping by pilots. Called "confetti" by
Americans and "nickels" by the British, the leafletting (as the
verb had it) of enemy civilian populations as well as of troops was
of particular interest to the Psychological Warfare Section of the
War Department. Blankenhorn soon left, however, to become a
lieutenant colonel in the OSS, where he designed a black proj-

ect—that is, a secret project for MO, or Morale Operations—and convinced Donovan to organize a special labor unit to contact European trade unions, which he felt could become the center of anti-Nazi resistance groups. The first head of the OSS Labor Desk would be a young lawyer, Arthur Goldberg, later justice of the Supreme Court and ambassador to the United Nations.[35]

A prime target for satire was the Strategic Index of the Americas; another was the Cross-Cultural Survey; a third was a series of *Strategic Bulletins. Time* magazine, from which Henry Luce kept a close eye on his *alma mater* (never to allow an issue to pass without getting Yale's name into it once, it was said), was quite critical of all this scholarly effort and poked fun at the institute, leading May to declare that he had "a very strong negative goal-gradient toward *Time.*" Reading the *Strategic Bulletins* today (on "Food and Water Supply in the Marshall Islands," for example, with its lengthy instructions on how to open a coconut) induces a mildly negative goal-gradient even yet, though not in the way May meant.

The Cross-Cultural Survey shows both the best and the worst that might be drawn from the institute to the OSS. After the war the Cross-Cultural Survey, whose records existed only at Yale, was again expanded and the material duplicated as the Human Relations Area Files, or HRAF, so that full files could be consulted at twenty American universities, the Smithsonian Institution, and universities in France and Japan. Though the categories for indexing differed widely in their applicability to intelligence needs ("304 Mutilation . . . Self-torture; Eunuchs," as against "508 Airport Facilities . . . loading, unloading, and fueling . . ." etc.), HRAF was drawn upon by the CIA at least through 1967, and it was widely believed that a full file had been deposited at the agency's new headquarters in Langley, Virginia, where in a trice agents might call up all that the scholarly community knew about ethnoanatomy (the conception of ideal bodily proportions) in order to adorn oneself to achieve the ideal of erotic beauty in any one of hundreds of cultures.

Yet another Yale group that contributed to the war effort was the Yale-in-China Association. Since 1903 the Yale Divinity School had been active in missionary work in China, setting up hospitals and schools. To the latter bright young Yale graduates, known as Yali Bachelors, were sent out to teach English and to gain a sense of the culture, and the alumni of this body comprised good pick-ings for intelligence work. Yale-in-China was, in a sense, at war well before December of 1941, for it had suffered from severe Japanese air raids on Changsha, where the hospital's four operating rooms were in constant use, the staff sometimes subsisting on a bag of cookies someone brought in. The Yali Middle School in Yuanling and the Medical School in Hunan Province had remained open, as had the Yale School of Science in Yunnan, though by 1944, when Changsha at last fell, the hospital staff had to be evacuated to Chungking, the Chinese wartime capital.

One of the Yali Bachelors, Preston Schoyer, of the Yale class of 1933, made a dramatic escape from China in 1940. Fritz, as he was called, had taught at Changsha for two years after graduation, returned to Yale for graduate work in Oriental history and Chinese languages, and had gone back to teach in Changsha in 1938. After eight bombing raids on the city, Schoyer had taken a party of twenty doctors, nurses, and wounded on board a junk and led them down the Hsiang River under cover of darkness. At daybreak a Japanese plane had, despite the fact that the junk was showing an American flag, made continual attacks on it. Schoyer succeeded in getting the entire group away safely, however, in six weeks of irregular travel to French Indo-China. When America entered the war, he became a major in Air Intelligence, initiating development of the Air Ground Aid Section, attached to Theater Headquarters, China, to instruct airmen in ways to evade or escape from the Japanese if forced down behind enemy lines, and worked with Chinese guerrillas on a number of rescue missions. At the end of the war he commanded a mission to Shanghai to rescue seven thousand Allied prisoners and internees in Japanese camps. His remarkable work, as well as that of several other Yali Bachelors, in particular John Hadley Cox, '35, who went to Burma as an OSS member of Detachment 101 and later operated behind the lines in China, and Reuben Holden, '40, later secretary of the university, encouraged a postwar conviction that Yale-in-China had been an intelligence operation from the outset. It was not, but certainly its staff were in a superb position to gather intelligence information, and it was natural that they would be drawn on heavily once hostilities had begun.[36]

The work of Charles R. Walker, Yale's unofficial "Secretary of War," also intrigued the OSS. Walker, a research fellow in the social sciences, was interested in the military uses of anthropology, and he and Murdock elaborated on a data base that became

part of the Human Relations Area Files. Walker fed pieces of research to Leland T. Chapin in the Office of the Chief of Naval
Operations; he and Chapin then reworked the pieces to make certain "for security reasons" that they could not be traced to either
source. Walker was especially interested in preparing "survival
pieces," and he wrote many that gave practical advice for seamen
afloat on a hot and empty sea and specific instructions, with map
coordinates, on how to move about unnoticed (one hoped) when
ashore on specific islands. He and Murdock also combined knowledge to produce short case studies on how best to get Polynesians
to cooperate with the military in, for example, building an airfield
on an atoll, to help Americans grasp the practical implications of
the communal ownership of property, or to remind them that when
treating with a native chief they must never stand up, since this
was an insult while to remain seated showed the proper form of
respect.

Walker was quick to recognize the potential threat to scholarship that lay in the success of such work, however. It was won-
derful, he thought, that Yale could demonstrate how the research
of scholars "with a purely scientific motive and as wholly remote
from any practical application, [could] turn out in the end to be a
strong weapon for the Navy," but he also feared that "men con-
ditioned by the war to education by contract, will want to come
in and buy so much knowledge for so many dollars" after the war
was over. Walker, who had a broad view of the Yale scene, was
the only person connected with the institute who repeatedly made
pleas for the preservation of the liberal arts.[37]

Walker was a bridge from the social scientists to the humanists;
the reverse lane was built, to the extent that one was built at all,
by Ralph H. Gabriel, a historian. Gabriel, '13, who during the war
taught with Walker at the School of Military Government in Charlottesville, was interested in interdisciplinary studies. One of the
earliest advocates of the creation of a separate program in American Studies, to break down the barriers between history, literature, and the social sciences, Gabriel would carry the message of
American Studies to prestigious postwar visiting professorships in
Australia, England, and Japan; during the war he gave the same
message to the future army overseas administrators, insisting that
officers charged with governance in Germany or Japan must understand the whole culture. He developed lectures for the North
African campaign, for Sicily and Italy, for the reoccupied islands

in the Pacific, for occupied Japan, for Korea and the Philippines, studying each country intensely, shaping talks that were clear, often amusing, and above all, for the overburdened military men and women who attended his classes, memorable. Recognizing that historical knowledge was not valid without a comparative perspective, Gabriel also worked on governments of military oc- cupation elsewhere, examining with particular care Japanese ad- ministration in Malaya, and for historical background, the American record in Veracruz, Samoa, and even New Mexico and Califor- nia. These lectures were then turned into briefing papers which received restricted government circulation, or into reports for the OSS. Gabriel was determined that army officers must see conflict through the eyes of their opponents, and not simply attribute evil motives to them—that is, he did precisely what the historian is supposed to do—and so, perhaps to their bewilderment, he also lectured on Aquinaldo's revolt in the Philippines and on the Pueblo Indian revolt of 1680. Nearly everyone who heard Gabriel lecture, whether in his Yale courses or in Virginia, remembered how well this World War I lieutenant of infantry appeared to understand their own fears of inadequacy.[38]

Gabriel's work was off campus and little known to the univer- sity community at large; this was also true of the Yale contribu- tion to the American Commission for the Protection and Salvage of Artistic and Historic Monuments in War Areas, known as the Roberts Commission. This effort, conducted jointly with Great Britain, worked quietly and effectively to save from destruction, and ultimately to recover from theft by high-ranking Nazi leaders, many of the art treasures of Europe. Part of the work would be done through the OSS, since art historians had to be moved up to the front lines quickly in order to follow a conquering army as closely as possible; much of the work consisted of compiling the kinds of inventories that Research and Analysis was good at, so that invaders might be alerted in advance to artistic treasures in target areas, at least to increase somewhat the chances that those treasures might be spared; other significant art retrieval was done through SHAEF (Supreme Headquarters Allied Expeditionary Forces). Because of the intervention of Norman Holmes Pearson, who in 1942 joined the OSS, some of the work in the field rather oddly fell to X-2, the counterintelligence service of the OSS,*

*See Chapter Five.

though the greater portion of the research was done in the States or from London, and later from Rome, Florence, Paris, and Vienna. In the end over a fifth of all the scholars engaged in this rescue operation were drawn from the Yale galleries or history of art department.

Much of Yale's contribution fell under the guidance of Sumner McKnight Crosby, Yale '32, a debonair scholar bilingual in French, who with the aid of a considerable private income from the Crosby flour business in Minneapolis would devote his life to the study and partial restoration of the Chapel St. Denis in France. An assistant professor during the war, Crosby worked steadily under the American commission's chairman, Dr. William Bell Dinsmoor, president of the Archaeological Institute of America, to supply detailed information on the locations of treasures from both artistic and historical points of view, preparing—with nine other scholars and museum directors—maps that would show fighter pilots what not to bomb, recovering and identifying looted works of art. By 1944 Crosby, Francis H. Taylor, and Georges Philippa, with others, had produced a report on what Hitler, Himmler, and Goering had hidden away, and Crosby hurried off to war areas through the intervention of the American ambassador to Britain, John Winant. Crosby resigned in September of 1945, when he learned that the United States government was bringing from Germany art objects for storage and display on the alleged grounds that expert personnel were not available in the American Zone of Germany, this despite the presence in the Fine Arts and Archives Section of the Military Government of a number of art historians and curators. Crosby and many others viewed this decision as a slap in the face to the various Monuments, Fine Arts, and Archives officers in Germany, and they also suspected it was an effort to appropriate for American art galleries the very objets d'art that had just been rescued from Nazi hands.[39]

Of course, the kinds of contributions to the war effort made by a Crosby, a Gabriel, a Walker, or even by the institutes of Human Relations and of International Studies, were not widely known and, except for Yale-in-China, were unlikely to be made known in any detail on the campus. Nor were there many personal risks involved, though by the end of the war one of the scholars working on the art recovery project had been killed when too close to the lines. Perhaps only the name of Professor Raymond Kennedy, '28, might appropriately have been added to the list of the war dead being carefully compiled in the university secretary's office, for eventual inscription on the walls of the Memorial Hall in Woolsey, and then only because, for Kennedy, the war extended into the 1950s.

Kennedy was a sociologist who had developed a close and sympathetic knowledge of the native cultures of Southeast Asia. After graduation he had taught at the Brent School in Baguio in the Philippines and then was field representative for the General Motors Corporation in Java and Sumatra. During the war he worked with military intelligence, reporting on a variety of ethnographic matters, and was a regular consultant to Morale Operations in the OSS. Some thought him too left-leaning—certainly he was opposed to any reassertion of Dutch colonial rule in the East Indies at the end of the war—and too outspoken, though with hindsight one can only judge the memoranda he wrote for the State Department on the future of Indonesia and Malaya as balanced and prescient. Early in 1945 Kennedy broke with the State Department when an article he was commissioned to write for the department's *Bulletin* was rejected as "likely to offend the Netherlands," but he continued to deliver photographs of Malaya and the Straits Settlements to the OSS and its successors, who in turn gave Kennedy access to secret memoranda prepared for the secretary of state on the increasingly chaotic situation in Indochina. Kennedy was strongly anti-French, and while less anti-British, he felt that the British general who entered Saigon to accept the Japanese surrender was both brutal and inept—Kennedy blamed him for the death of Lieutenant Colonel A. Peter Dewey, a young Yale graduate, the first American officer to die in Vietnam. While Kennedy did not oppose the reestablishment of French authority in the area, he felt that the United States ought not to provide any support if the French chose to use force.

After the war the intelligence community called on Kennedy again, for his field notes, his photographs, and his political point of view, which had so cogently put the anticolonial position, were valued as they had not been during the war. Kennedy was hard at work on a four-volume manuscript on Indonesia and was presumed to have good contacts amongst the independence movement in the East Indies. In June 1949, determined to finish his work and, he told his wife, a sociologist, eager to test the views he had espoused at the OSS school during the war, Kennedy set out to prepare a report on the impact of the West on native cultures. In central Java he and a companion were held up by "freedom fighters" and, given no chance to express the sympathies they held, were accused of being agents for the CIA. They were summarily taken to a cleared field and shot to death. A shocked Yale faculty arranged for a bronze plaque to be placed on his grave in the Christian Cemetery at Bandung.[40]

On balance, the university's playing fields were as important as seminar rooms or the college dining halls as socializing environments, and coaches were at least the equal of masters in being the leaders of men. In 1969 it would be revealed that the chief recruiter for the CIA in its early years was none other than the crew coach, "Skip" Walz; probably only Wolfers, and a professor of history, Wallace Notestein, of whom we will hear more later, had equal influence when students sidled up to ask how they might get into intelligence work. Allen Walz's story is instructive and worth recounting at some length.[41]

Walz was not a Yale man. Having attended the Hun School in Princeton, he had been destined for an Ivy League institution (though the league did not in fact formally exist then), when on impulse he went off with his friend Elliot Roosevelt to play football for the University of Wisconsin. When Roosevelt got married instead, and did not show up in Madison, Walz transferred to New York University, where he was ultimately captain of the football team. In 1934 Walz introduced and coached crew at Manhattan College and was an instructor in speech until 1940, when he accepted the job of crew coach at the University of Wisconsin. Meanwhile, upon graduating from NYU in 1935, Walz was asked by Dale Carnegie to work for his institute; he also became television's first sports commentator before television was commercially feasible. At Wisconsin he quickly became an identifiable figure on the campus, for crew was a "big-time" sport, and being a radio sports announcer, as he also was, was even bigger time.

When war broke out Walz contacted Elliot Roosevelt, who helped him become a lieutenant in the navy. With a natural affinity for boats and the sea, Walz moved rapidly to the captaincy of a destroyer escort. He enjoyed the camaraderie, the moments of extreme tension, and the opportunity to be of service. During the Normandy invasion he brought his ship alongside an LST sinking from enemy fire and a submerged mine, and his ship was credited with saving the lives of at least a hundred soldiers. To the last few he called from his bridge to pass a motorcycle over the rail from the sinking vessel to his own. For the rescue he received the Bronze Star.

Later, having been transferred to Dartmouth, England, to a desk job handling all escort vessels in the European Theater of Operations, Walz used the motorcycle to tour the English countryside. One day, riding in the wrong direction on a one-way street, he had a head-on collision with an English officer who was driving an American jeep. From hospital Walz was ordered to a builder's yard on the Harlem River in New York City to take command of a new gunboat for duty in the South Pacific. Walz left his batman to pack his gear and ship it to Wisconsin; overzealous, the batman included the motorcycle, which when inspected at U.S. dockside was found to contain a copy of the Overlord planning book for the invasion of Normandy, still stamped Top Secret, in its pillion. Walz was relieved of his command and ordered to report for trial by General Court Martial.

Though the military court reprimanded Walz and returned him to active duty, he had made new contacts while preparing his defense and was on the path to a new career. Having no duties to perform, Walz had run the naval district's war bond drive to record heights and had become especially interested in Naval Intelligence, the particular turf of the commanding officer. With the end of hostilities Walz returned to his job as crew coach at the University of Wisconsin, to learn that he had been commended as a liaison between the navy and the CIA. He thus became a lieutenant commander, with the appropriate allowance, a full recruiter for the CIA (with pay), and a full-time coach at the university. (Walz liked to work hard: he also had a job with the Dale Carnegie Institute.)

Shortly after, Walz was invited by Robert Kiphuth, Yale's director of athletics, to come to New Haven as crew coach, and Walz found himself at a university where crew vied with football and swimming for prestige, as it did not at Wisconsin; he was the highest paid crew coach in the country, with an unprecedented salary of $10,000—a fact not made known to the Yale faculty. The CIA asked Walz to continue as a recruiter at Yale, even though the agency had other contacts there, and paid him an additional $10,000 a year for his work.

And so, Skip Walz, Yale crew coach from 1946 to 1950, working simultaneously for the university and for the Central Intelligence Agency on a salary of $10,000 from each, laid his arms on the shoulders of athletic young men, introducing them to official recruiters who would apply the appropriate persuasion. The job was not hard—he found Yale undergraduates far more aware of the CIA, and far more interested in international affairs, than students at Wisconsin had been, and he needed only to put people in touch with each other—and it gave him a sense of doing something patriotic when he was no longer in uniform. He looked for bright undergraduates, in other sports than crew as well, who were going into business careers after graduation, so that they might use their business connections as a cover behind the iron curtain. He checked status, grades, clubs, and he had somewhat vague conversations with those he thought most suitable. Once every three weeks he would meet with a CIA agent at the Reflecting Pool in Washington, passing on names and evaluations. He generally did not know, and did not wish to know, who received or accepted an offer, and on the one occasion some years later when Walz found himself seated in a theater next to someone he had tapped, he left immediately, for he had learned that the first two men he had pointed toward the CIA had been lost in the field, and he did not wish to think past the point of being the contact man. (He did, however, run into two of his recruits in London while there in 1950 as the Olympic crew coach.)

Walz would happily have continued, for he enjoyed his work, he liked the people he met at the CIA, and he hoped that he might be operational himself one day. From New Haven he extended his net to the National Football League, seeking out professional players who had just been cut from the teams in September, who would be hurt, wanting something physical to do, and who would soon have to look for jobs. In this way he delivered twenty-five men to the CIA, to be trained for *parachutage* behind the iron curtain, or so he was told. Then in 1950 a company that manufactured precision gunsight controls, Arma, recruited Walz away from Yale, and he shifted his activities from the locker room and Mory's to the club car between Greenwich and New York City. Walz continued to recruit for the CIA until 1955, when he accepted a vice-presidency at the Canada Dry Corporation, parting company a bit sadly with the agency. These had been good years, and Walz thought they were typical on college campuses, for the CIA was seeking young men, and on occasion women, of sophistication and confidence who believed in the power of knowledge. Walz knew that others at Yale had their own contacts—one might have been a history professor who took an intense interest in crew, showing up at the boat house nearly every day—but he never inquired. The year he left Yale his cox, George Carver, '50, a bright young man who was off to Oxford to study philosophy, chatted with him briefly, though Walz did not think he was interested. Three years later Carver, too, would join the agency.

Yale was not, of course, alone in being a target of intelligence recruitment, especially after the war. In 1948 Frank Wisner, who during the war served the OSS well in Istanbul and the Balkans, became director of the Office of Special Projects, which soon became the Office of Policy Coordination.* A graduate of the University of Virginia and its law school, a naval commander, deputy assistant secretary of state for occupied countries—another position not unlike that of a senior official in the Colonial Office in Britain—Wisner was convinced that the emergent cold war would be both long and central to the shape of the future world order. He wanted people with what he called "that added dimension" for the OPC: young men with high grades, a sense of grace, with previous knowledge of Europe, with a language that went beyond the bookish—Americans study languages, other people learn them, and he thought those who studied under the new techniques at Yale just might actually be able to converse in the language they had studied—young men with an ease with themselves that athletic success can often bring, with a wise awareness of the nuance of patriotism, and with an unfettered sense of curiosity.

Wisner wanted students of history, economics, political science, anthropology; linguistics and applied mathematics were also important; and he got what he wanted. Since foreign languages were valuable, this need further strengthened the tendency to look to Harvard, Yale, Brown, or Princeton, which generally still required competency in a foreign language for graduation—even of football players. Many academic members of the wartime OSS who had returned to their groves were contacted, either to return to intelligence work or to nominate good younger colleagues or

---

*The title Office of Policy Coordination was a euphemism for Covert Action. OPC's approach to intelligence work was rather like a "secret society"—serving the country in ways it did not know. Yale's most prestigious social life turned on secret societies, of which perhaps Skull and Bones was the most exclusive, and the members of those societies deeply believed in the wisdom of their own selection (and perhaps at times in the wonder of it) and were convinced they served Yale in ways that the beneficiaries of their *noblesse oblige* might never fully understand. Of course, it was widely rumored that the secret societies were recruiting grounds as well.

graduate students. Since the OSS, and in particular the Research and Analysis Branch, had been heavy with the Ivy League, Virginia, Wisconsin, and Chicago, the new flow was further reinforced at these institutions. But Williams, Swarthmore, Bowdoin, Reed, Berea—the smaller private colleges—were not overlooked. Recruiting through professors—known as "the P source" (the intelligence community never seeming able to abandon its slightly silly fascination with its own jargon, though here surely there was a healthy hint of self-mockery)—proved highly effective, and by 1948–49 CIA personnel came from seventy-seven different colleges and universities. There was, as yet, no public talk about "invisible government," no thought that a professor who acted as a contact point might be engaged in conflict of interest. The urgencies of the wartime campus simply extended, with hardly the hiatus of 1946, into the cold war and, at most universities, through the war in Korea, not to be questioned until the early 1960s.[42]

Certainly not questioned at Yale. The university faculty had in the main voted for FDR and wanted at the end of the war to see the United States play a leading role in the new United Nations; a good many also shared the growing belief that the Soviet Union would have to be dealt with before the war was truly over. It was natural, therefore, for those who had directed Yale students toward intelligence work to continue to do so. Charles Seymour had virtually validated such contacts while president; his daughter Elizabeth had worked for the OSS in Switzerland and Germany until she became ill at the end of the summer of 1945; and since 1919 Seymour had been on close terms with Allen Dulles, wartime director of the OSS in Switzerland and later in Germany, and after 1953 head of the CIA. In the 1930s Seymour and Dulles had exchanged unhappy notes about American isolationism, and Seymour pointedly congratulated Dulles when he became director and encouraged him to accept a Lamont Lectureship at Yale in 1956. When Dulles visited Yale with his wife, Clover, who was close to Mrs. Seymour, the retired president drew together a group they knew to be compatible with the goals of the CIA for a gala lunch at Mory's. Through his successor, A. Whitney Griswold, Seymour had Dulles meet with a large group of students interested in a career with the CIA, using the Corporation Room in Woodbridge Hall, from whose walls looked down portraits of past Yale presidents. Dulles, Seymour said, had "a rainbow in the soul," and he hoped that there would be others like him to preside over so delicate and so important a matter as intelligence.[43]

   In the 1950s a new generation of college masters found themselves being approached by students who were attracted to intelligence work. Usually the students who made such an approach
were precisely the kind the faculty thought least suitable, but on
occasion one would strike a spark. William Huse Dunham, master
of Jonathan Edwards College from 1956, stayed in close touch
with old friends in the CIA and became a consultant to the critical
Office of National Estimates, or ONE, which his former colleague
in history, Sherman Kent, ran for the CIA. Basil Duke Henning,
who reigned over Saybrook College from 1946 until his retirement
in 1975, took on an assignment or two for Kent in the fifties; Archibald Foord, after service in Naval Intelligence during the war,
assumed the mastership of Calhoun in 1955 and was said to be
more hospitable to an approach than other masters; and Thomas
C. Mendenhall, master in Berkeley from 1950 to 1959, who had
been bagman for a wartime OSS operation,* also may have helped.
All four of these masters were professors of history and all were
students and colleagues of Wallace Notestein.
   To these might be added the name of Georges May, who joined
the French department in 1946 and, with elegance and Gallic wit,
would serve as dean of Yale College, provost of the university,
and a Sterling professor. The sophisticated May understood better
than most that, to borrow another phrase from the poetic Bellinger, "silence itself will come to be the perfect language." When,
in 1969, a student publication declared that May had been a recruiter for the CIA, he simply ignored the charge (for such it was
in the climate of that year). In fact May had worked for the OSS
from the winter of 1943 until the end of 1945, having been a graduate student at the University of Illinois, from which he had joined
the army and been assigned, after basic training, to the OSS. He
had not been invited to stay on after the war, much to his pleasure, though he did credit the OSS, and especially Cora Dubois,
an astringent anthropologist on leave from Harvard, with whom
he worked before she was posted to New Delhi, with teaching
him how to write the crisp prose for which he became noted on
the Yale campus.†[44] He had never recruited for the CIA.

---

*See Chapter Three.
†Amusingly, when Julius Mader, an East German antipublicist of the CIA, produced a handbook on *Who's Who in CIA* (Berlin: Mader) in 1968, in which he
  purported to identify three thousand CIA officers—a book which was immediately branded by the CIA as a work of disinformation—he swept former OSS

* * *

The scholar who teaches must teach with the whole personality. This requires considerable self-awareness. One may hide from others but not from oneself. Instead, one must quite deliberately seek not to hide from oneself. The counterpoint to this need is that one also observes others with care. One must know not only, as teacher or researcher, how to ask the right question, one must know when to ask no question at all. Answers bring closure, often too soon, so that shape is given to knowledge before it should be given, conditioning the questions that follow. One must know how to wait. A quality of quiet watching is essential.

History, philosophy, anthropology, ethnography, all are essential to the cool calculation of meaning of isolated facts. Travel is broadening, and history or anthropology are forms of mental travel. Those who think history but a collection of facts, "one damn thing after another," to be memorized and arranged on the page, are in no sense historians, as any student at a liberal arts university will, or at least should, learn. Often those who think they "like history" (a frequently condescending phrase which makes those who "do history" shiver) merely mean that they like to approach life, or a place, as though it were a text, interpreting it in terms of past reading, which is a form of past experience. This will not do, for disciplines like history and anthropology, philosophy or law, are also about what did not happen, or does not happen, and by extension might well happen differently or have happened differently on a given set of facts. The scholar knows that one ought to feel uncomfortable when in the field, or at research, and certainly in the classroom, for one ought to be aware of the elements of one's own confusion. One is not "let down" by other people, by other cultures, one simply does not understand them, and the interpretation and prediction of behavior, which flows from research and analysis, must rely upon an acute awareness that people will do what they do, not what we think they ought to do—here even Sherman Kent later admitted to at least one, and perhaps two, major intelligence failures on the part of the Americans, who thought that the Russians would "behave sensibly" concerning Cuba, for example, without a full understanding of what sensible behavior in another culture might mean—just as the people of a

---

employees up into his census, and though he listed some 174 Yale graduates or faculty, he managed to miss nearly every figure of significance with the exception of Sherman Kent. Even then Mader said, quite wrongly, that Kent had been a professor of geography at Yale (p. 280).

remote tribe will eat what they eat even though the anthropologist in their midst might wish they would eat what he (and theory) want them to eat.

Scholarship, like marriage, is often based on a working misunderstanding, and one must know this and not expect more. If one understands the elements of a misunderstanding, one need not invariably correct the misunderstanding; rather, work proceeds on the basis of the misunderstood (and thus mutually comprehensible) points. Machines cannot grasp anything so simple; human beings, or HUMINT, just might. Intelligence is, after all, concerned with problem solving, though those who gather the information must never be those who assess it or recommend policy on the basis of it, just as philosophy is, in part, the study of the language by which problems may be solved, history the study of how problems were (sometimes) not solved, anthropology the study of how human beings organize their societies in order to solve problems.

This is not to say that there was an OSS or a CIA "type." While those who were suspicious of the OSS, perhaps thinking that it was a refuge for the socially well-to-do (since it contained more than its share of names from the social register), said that OSS stood for "Oh, So Social," "Oh, So Swish," or (since some also thought it was full of limousine liberals) "Oh, So Socialist," one cannot but be impressed by the diversity of people, just as one is impressed by the pluralism of a university campus. To be sure, a good many had money, having been drawn disproportionately from the private schools and universities, and probably a disproportionate number, certainly in R&A, wore glasses. After that, however, what was needed was the ability to learn at speed, a good mind with, preferably but not indispensably, a broad education, a sense of personal balance, an awareness of nuance that would lead to discretion, some specialized knowledge and, ideally, one or two foreign languages at a level of competence above the textbook. The conviction that what one was doing was essential to the war effort would be useful. One ought, as an operative said, to be so thorough that one would leave nothing to chance but chance itself,[45] and yet be sufficiently modest to believe that chance itself always remained a risk. In the short run one ought to see the world in adversarial terms, though for the long haul one would need to be consciously for rather than against something.

Years after World War II a longtime employee of the Central

Intelligence Agency would suggest that all of this, Yale-in-war and Yale-in-peace, the OSS and the CIA, was an example of "sentimental imperialism." He was not condemning, though he did mean to criticize the inherent naiveté: he spoke of a time when Americans generally, upper middle-class American men broadly, and the Yale community specifically, thought of themselves as having a mission to the world, enjoying "the blessings of liberty," able to reshape the world to its benefit and, not incidentally, to America's. They had health, knowledge, power. One enemy would be replaced with another, but the continuity of purpose, the conviction that to apply one's education in the service of the state was an appropriate thing to do, the certainty that civic virtue grew from the broadly liberalizing study of the humanities, of cultures other than one's own, and of the languages that framed those cultures, these convictions remained, from World War II, across the arch of the cold war, in Korea, into the 1960s.[46]

In time these convictions weakened, just as in time words like *sentimental* and *imperialism* took on heavily pejorative freight, a new generation of students speaking in texts that not all understood. But the sentimental imperialism of the decades of the 1940s and '50s was not, then or now, to be utterly scorned. One could not utterly condemn, nor wholly praise, the desire to "make the world safe for democracy," even while realizing, as Woodrow Wilson had meant, that the form of democracy for which the world must be made safe would be the form best exemplified by and most comfortable to the United States. Pride in one's culture, one's history, like pride in one's work, or in one's university, was the glue that gave coherence, and force, and both the sense and at times the reality of accomplishment, to a society that, perhaps, had lacked the good grace to be confused, as it would be by the 1960s. Yale had, as President Seymour remarked upon his retirement in 1950, the university by then swollen by returned veterans, been made more serious by them and by the best motivated and most intelligent classes ever, held "on the three-yard line."[47] That would not, of course, be good enough in the new, tense, disorienting postwar world.[48]

CHAPTER TWO

THE CAMPUS

LANGER, LEWIS, KENT & CO.

The wartime Office of Strategic Services, though not a central intelligence agency, came far closer to combining all the purposes of intelligence than any democratic society had previously allowed itself in peacetime. Originally established as the Office of the Coordinator of Information on July 11, 1941, when the United States was not at war, the COI (which reported directly to the president) was transmuted into the OSS on June 13, 1942, and placed under the Joint Chiefs of Staff. This organization, COI and OSS, would combine the functions of at least four British intelligence organizations: MI6, the Secret Intelligence Service; SOE, the Special Operations Executive; PWE, the Political Warfare Executive; and the Foreign Office Research Department. The last corresponded somewhat to one of the first COI branches to be set up, Research and Analysis, or R&A. Nearly everyone *outside* OSS agreed that R&A was the most important unit *in* the OSS.

Inside the OSS R&A could not compete for prestige against SI (Secret Intelligence), or SO (Special Operations, a title behind which all kinds of derring-do might be assumed to hide), or even MO (Morale Operations, or "black" propaganda). Above all there was X-2, breaking from the acronymic labeling, covering counterintelligence; these were the tough, silent jobs that made strong men quake.* In an atmosphere of male bonding, SI and X-2 were the coaches, the clever men, the quarterbacks, while SO housed the rest of the jocks. R&A gave refuge to the weenies and wimps, the glassy-eyed students on the campus who came out to cheer the team on and who burrowed in the libraries, moles of a kind that neither Marx nor John le Carré meant when they used Francis Bacon's term. Or so many SI, SO, and X-2 members felt.

With stunning obviousness the Research and Analysis Branch soon came to be known as "the campus." The name stuck, not only to R&A: when R&A was carried over into the CIA, the rubric was applied to the entire operation, to the CIA headquarters in the District and later as well, when the CIA moved out to Virginia. In an information industry, which is what OSS and CIA most fundamentally were, or ought to be, the entire operation came to be known as "the Company," the place as "the campus," a wedding of business and academe often thought to be hostile to the goals of "the University."

When the Japanese attacked Pearl Harbor, there was no one who did not agree that it was a disgrace the United States had no centralized intelligence research capacity. While the fastidious might share Henry L. Stimson's alleged view—"alleged" because there is no hard evidence that the secretary of state ever really said the words attributed to him in dozens of books, that "Gentlemen do not read each other's mail"—when he closed down Herbert Yardley's Black Chamber in 1929 by denying it State Department funds,

*OSS BRANCHES
R&A—Research and Analysis, SI—Secret Intelligence, SO—Special Operations, X-2—Counterintelligence, MO—Morale Operations, OG—Operational Groups, MU—Maritime Unit, S&T—Schools and Training, FN—Foreign Nationalities. On the last, see page 498, note 27.

there could be none after 1941 who did not understand the need
for as much information on a potential enemy's strengths, weak-
nesses, and intentions as the intelligence community could get.

"Intelligence community" has always been an unduly cozy
phrase. Not only does it imply a degree of happy cooperation among
the various bodies charged with obtaining and analyzing intelligence when cooperation has not been the invariable norm, but it
also suggests a concert of purpose and interest that simply does
not exist. Even British and American intelligence agencies did not
invariably share information in the midst of World War II, and
the spies of most war-time allies continued throughout the war to
ferret out information on each other: certainly the intelligence
community is in no sense international, even when information is
exchanged with one's allies, since the purpose is to serve the national interest. Those who work most comfortably with the moral
ambiguities that arise from reading each other's mail must be nationalists—not necessarily "patriots" in the narrow and much
abused sense of the word, but men and women who subscribe to
the notion that if each nation put its own interests first, there would
probably be greater rather than less stability in the world, and
certainly more predictive capacity over how a nation's leaders
would respond to any given situation. The "intelligence community" is restrictive to itself, to a single nation. It is also often
divisive within: just like a real community, a suburban one with
solidly middle-class values, worried that the next neighborhood
may have the better schools and lure the yuppies away while condemning the way undesirables are moving in on the fringes of the
town, setting up shady flea-market operations and lowering the
tone of the whole community.

Research and analysis are at the core of intelligence. While daring, courage, good luck, and tenacity are needed to obtain closely
held information, unless one is dealing with a society that is both
physically isolated and totalitarian, the great mass of information
can be obtained from open sources. Nazi Germany was, in fact,
the second but not the first; the Soviet Union was both. However,
since most "facts" are without meaning, someone must analyze
even the most easily obtained data. And then there is the 5 to 10
percent that the opposition tenaciously tries to withhold. R&A
could, with a good library at its back and scholars skilled in drawing secrets from a library, get at most of the material the operational branches of OSS, and equally important, of the Army and

Navy, State or Treasury, needed. R&A could, with a well-organized and infinitely expansible retrieval system (which in the 1940s generally meant a card catalog not unlike the kind still encountered in most sensible libraries), reassemble the data it had collected to answer specific questions put to it by Army, Navy, State, and others. R&A could, with microfilm and new techniques for photocopying and filing, hope to retain inert data across years, rather than playing the fool's game of "relevance," until such time as the data could prove their own relevance. R&A controlled the most powerful weapon in the OSS arsenal: the three-by-five index card.[1]

R&A's initial successes (which, until the operational units of the OSS were fully ready to go, generally not until 1943, were the OSS's initial successes as well) lay in the study of intelligence rather than in the origination of it. This meant that R&A section heads had to learn how to convince many skeptics of the value of their product. In government this is most often done, at least officially, by providing "proof of effectiveness," proof frequently supplied by manufacturing paper rationales keyed to the current buzz words most likely to loosen funds from the Bureau of Budget. But academics are not very good at providing quantifiable "proof of effectiveness," and they tend to be slow in learning the buzz words of another subculture, though they have plenty of their own. Academics generally work in an environment that respects knowledge for its own sake, or says that it does, and merely knowing, rather than acting upon what one knows, is sufficient reward for many academics, though by no means all. The producer of knowledge is likely to ask himself only whether the knowledge is "interesting, significant, and true." The first two judgments are clearly subjective to the individual or to a group one may win over to one's definitions of interest and significance. The third goal, proof of truth (or "accuracy"), also an academic end in itself, may well not lead to any action whatsoever. What, then, is "effectiveness"? Someone must always be set the task of asking the academic the question, "So what?" So, what difference does it make that mica has these properties, that Hitler had one testicle, that Sicilians still use sixteenth-century vulgarisms, that narrow-gauge track is not the same in New South Wales as in the Sudan? Even more important, someone must ask "So what?" to the grander theories, the broader interpretations, the conclusions reached by scholars who have no responsibility to the action others may think it appropriate to take on the basis of those conclusions.

Selling therefore becomes important, and selling requires confidence. Of this there was an abundance amongst the scholars assembled by R&A; one might even say there was a sufficience of arrogance. Most of the scholars were drawn from Ivy League institutions, most heavily from Harvard and Yale, backgrounds conducive to a certain healthy self-respect at the least; many were, as was the case at such universities in those distant days, men of independent means. As DeForest van Slyck, Yale '20, who worked as a member of the CIA's National Estimates staff after the war, and who was former chairman of Freshman History on the Yale faculty, often observed, one must not be dependent on salary or one could be bought. It is difficult to tell one's supervisor to go to hell for misreading the evidence if one has wife, children, and no other source of income. The reverse of the coin was a certain rebelliousness, impatience with the military demand that information be rendered in forms that were "useful"; if the scholars of R&A were to be arrogantly productive analysts as well as arrogant bastards, they needed someone who could relate to the rough-and-ready language of the locker room. For this they had Sherman Kent, scion of a politically powerful California family, a scholar with a margin of independent income though not the wealth that might lead to boredom, and the saltiest vocabulary ever heard in a Yale common room. To set against Kent's earthy approach there was the austere second director of R&A, William L. Langer, down from the Olympian heights of his Coolidge Professorship at Harvard, and the sleek elegance of Wilmarth S. Lewis, Yale man and dilettante extraordinaire, who directed the Central Information Division. Above all, there stood William J. Donovan, "Wild Bill," the man behind COI and OSS, who seldom wavered in his support for R&A.[2]

Donovan was charismatic, intellectually unconventional, a bit chubby, and certainly not elegant, intensely loyal to those loyal to him, and apparently without fear. Born in Buffalo, New York, on New Year's Day, 1883, Donovan had graduated from Columbia University, taken a law degree there, and begun practice in Buffalo. Though much in social demand, for he was handsome, with bright blue eyes that looked like the pinpoint of a torch (someone in X-2 once remarked, not in a friendly fashion, that when e e cummings asked, "And how do you like your blue-eyed

boy, Mister Death,'' he could have been thinking of Donovan),
he did not marry until he was thirty-one, and then he married
wealth.

Long before the United States had entered World War I, Donovan was preparing for it. As a captain in the New York State
National Guard, he served in the American Expeditionary Force,
became a major in the 69th New York Infantry Regiment, around
which much tradition had grown, and was promoted to colonel in
France. At the second battle of the Marne, in July 1918, Donovan
led his troops in a remarkable advance across the River Ourcq,
and in October, in the Meuse-Argonne offensive, he again was in
the thick of the fighting. There, despite an order to withdraw (an
order Donovan later claimed he never received), he advanced on
the double. At the end of the war he was one of the most decorated men in American history, with the Distinguished Service
Cross, the Congressional Medal of Honor, the Légion d'Honneur,
the Order of the British Empire, the Croce di Guerra, the Order
of Leopold, the Cross Polonia Restituta, and a Croix de Guerre
with palm and silver star.

Riding the crest of a wave, Donovan was elected to Buffalo's
most exclusive clubs, became U.S. attorney for Western New York,
and in 1925 assistant attorney general of the United States. In
1929 he opened a private practice in New York City with a range
of powerful clients, and in 1932 ran for governor of New York, as
a Republican, and lost. Immediately he plunged into developing
overseas clients and both Hambro's Bank in London and Winston
Churchill used him as an agent on legal matters. He also developed good contacts in Italy, especially with General Pietro Badoglio. Franklin Roosevelt, who became president in 1933, had
been a friend for years. Donovan entertained widely, traveled
broadly, and accepted every invitation he received to address either
a large or an influential group. By the time war broke out in Europe again, he knew, or had a friend who knew, nearly everyone
who counted.

Many accounts tell us that Donovan's special influence with
Roosevelt stemmed from the fact that he alone amongst the president's advisers predicted that the British would successfully
withstand the German assault. After Dunkirk, the American ambassador, Joseph Kennedy, was deeply pessimistic, and U.S. Army
Intelligence was giving the British little hope of survival. Donovan, on the other hand, visited Churchill and returned to tell Roo-

sevelt that the British would win in the air; when they did, Donovan stood high in the president's eyes.

Donovan's standing with FDR came from far more than being right on a single issue, however. He was politically shrewd, and being of the opposition party, also provided Roosevelt with excellent contacts—of which he had many of his own, of course—with liberal Republicans. Were Donovan to head up a secret intelligence agency, Roosevelt would be less open to the charge of trying to create a private spy network than if it were to be in the hands of a New Deal Democrat. Further, Donovan was deeply impressed by British Secret Intelligence and, to a lesser extent, by SOE, and since it was assumed that the inexperienced American group would have to learn a good bit from the British, the fact that he obviously stood well with Churchill would help. More than this, Donovan was exceptionally bright, innovative, both physically and politically courageous, and was thought to be an able administrator. As FDR would soon learn, the last was manifestly not so—Donovan proved to be a disorderly administrator who required able assistants around him to get almost any paperbound task done—but happily all the other qualities Donovan was believed to possess proved true. In July 1941 FDR appointed Donovan director of COI.[3]

COI's (and OSS's) relationship to the British would move on a crooked path. Certainly the COI did lean on the British for expertise, including training facilities at Camp X, outside Oshawa, in Ontario, and the British were initially helpful to Donovan personally and to all those who came with his blessing. Early in 1941 Donovan had visited the Middle East and the Balkan capitals under British auspices, and he worked hard at building close ties to SOE. Such ties helped him in his struggles with competing groups in Washington, and especially with the FBI, which opposed the operation of any nation's intelligence services—including the British—on American soil, and also claimed exclusive American intelligence jurisdiction over the whole of Latin America. In time gaps would show between OSS and British aspirations, both in short-term expectations and long-term policies, for as the OSS grew in confidence it found the British insisting that they ought to have exclusive, or at least primary, responsibility for large chunks of the world in which Donovan felt the United States had legitimate interests of its own. By 1943 there would be sharp differences between the intelligence services of the two Allies, as in

Yugoslavia the British began to shift their support from Mihajlovic, the nationalist (some said fascist) leader, to Tito, the Communist. Donovan sent an independent mission to Turkey without
informing the British, set in motion a complex and rather rickety
plan to draw Bulgaria out of the war, and went personally to Mol-
otov in Moscow to discuss this effort with him. By 1944 Donovan's desire to use the OSS to help establish non-Communist
Balkan governments, coupled with British suspicions that OSS
operatives in India and elsewhere were lending moral support to
projected postwar independence movements, brought him into
disfavor with some of the British.

But this clash generally did not extend to, and in the early months
did not affect, a nonoperational, or nonfield branch of the COI
like Research and Analysis. Because R&A was one of the first
branches to be established, because it relied on research techniques generally shared with the British, and because raw intelligence data are, in a sense, without ideological context, capable—
if shared—of being used to the purpose of more than one nation,
cooperation between R&A and British counterparts remained always at a few degrees greater warmth, even as it too cooled, than
general intelligence cooperation in the field after 1943. While Donovan's conduct, capable of being interpreted as erratic, would prove
damaging to his efforts in 1945 to assure the continuation of the
OSS into peacetime, R&A would survive the general demise of
the OSS and be carried over into a new postwar intelligence apparatus, in part because the scholars recruited to do the work of
research and analysis had generally been able to stay on the sidelines during the inter-Allied squabbling and (though less successfully) at the height of the internecine battles within the Washington
bureaucracy.

R&A also benefited from Donovan's administrative idiosyncrasies. Donovan was strongly attracted to R&A: he had a high regard for professors, placing them above diplomats, scientists, and
"even lawyers and bankers"; he valued their "card index" men-
tality; he knew that they could become productive quickly, and
that if he controlled their output and delivered it personally to the
president, he would have frequent reason to visit the Oval Office;
and he was intrigued with the wide range of information R&A
would have to command. Still, this meant that R&A was buffeted
about, its priorities and assignments undergoing constant and confusing change, both by Donovan and, given Donovan's access to

the president, by FDR's own enthusiasms. While some observers
thought this was harmful to R&A, it may well have been benefi-
cial over the middle run. Though no sustained, serious research
could be done if projects had to be put aside to turn to something
Donovan fancied, or said that the president fancied, this draw-
and-shoot atmosphere did induce in the customarily methodical
academics an ability at which most professors are generally not
very good: to meet deadlines under pressure, taking the deadline
as a premise of the work. Normally universities are quite tolerant
of missed deadlines: a better work late is thought to be more desirable than a less good work on time. Yet historians, in particular, must work with the concept of time itself, with time as a limiting
factor: if they are to understand why a given person made the
decision he did, they must know both the information he had when
making the decision, and the time he thought was available to him
in which to make the decision. History is about time. Soon the
scholars in R&A, though ritualistically complaining about the
pressure, had come to accept the need to produce at top speed,
not simply because the nation was at war after December of 1941,
but also because of a desire to get a task done while it still was of
interest to Donovan or the president or before another enthusiasm
forced it to be set aside.

The function of R&A was to provide strategic intelligence to
the departments and agencies of government that required it.
"Strategic" was defined to mean all that information by which the
national welfare was protected. Strategy could include arbitration
and negotiation through the normal channels of diplomacy, the
composition of international law, the offer of political or economic inducements to other sovereign states, the imposition of
political, economic, and moral pressure and sanctions, the threat
of the use of armed force, and as last result, the use of that force.
Obviously for those government bodies charged with acting in such
matters the range of information needed was enormous; equally
obviously, other departments—the State Department for example—thought themselves already capable of getting the information and, even if not, generally were reluctant to share the kinds
of information on which "proffers of inducements" might be based.
Still, everyone accepted that a successful national strategy had to
be based on knowledge of other countries' strategic capabilities,
their probable intentions, and their vulnerabilities.[4]

One must not romanticize the scholars in R&A. The method of

research used in the branch was not, in fact, that of the scholar in the university. The best use of the "scientific method" (a term then popular with historians, though now not much used, even if the actual method employed has changed less than current sensitivity over the word *scientific* would suggest) was to have a single person go through all the stages of a methodology on a single problem. Only a single individual could collect data always with an eye to its place in the problem—"he would tend to collect a larger proportion of relevant data and a smaller amount of irrelevant than someone less familiar with the problem"—and in the collecting operation could sharpen his ability to judge the validity of data, thus testing the quality of sources. Further, only the same person who did the collecting and appraising could be expected to produce the highest proportion of plausible hypotheses; someone coming in cold at the hypothesis stage would have little feel for the data and could not go back for more data, the existence of which the original collector could more readily sense, in order to test the hypothesis. Scholarship is seldom at its best when done by a committee, or even in collaboration, and historians above all are suspicious of coauthorship or of research assistants.

But they would have to set these suspicions aside, finding some way to compensate for the errors they believed any outside assistance would inject into the data. Any ideal employment of the "scientific method" had to be suspended, collective research being necessary to the immediacy of deadlines. This required a division of labor that produced a procedure that was "the exact opposite of the ideal": in the end R&A would consist of "a race of collectors . . . , a race of evaluators, a race of idea men, a race of memo and report producers." The historians liked to point out that in the very selection of data lay perhaps the most profound moment of interpretation, since one could not include all things in any report, especially when scholars who were accustomed to a cursive flow were, at times, required to reduce all matters to numbered paragraphs. Consumers of the reports, anxious to have them yesterday, were not at all interested in the historians' *angst* over methodology, though it led some of the scholars, who recognized the legitimate causes of bureaucratic impatience, to ponder long and hard the connections between scholarship and intelligence, and after the war one of those scholars, Sherman Kent, would produce the most important general analysis of the nature of strategic intelligence yet written.

Those charged with the mobilization of American scholarship were well aware of the methodological problems posed by R&A, and they sought to overcome them by creating a Board of Analysts that would receive the various reports generated by R&A staff and then advise Donovan on how he should best advise the president. Policy-oriented analysis would thus be removed from the hands of those who had a stake in the report. Further, it was quickly recognized that R&A could not undertake simultaneously all tasks put before it, and there would have to be a Projects Committee that determined priorities between conflicting demands. The person who chaired this committee would also sit on the Board of Analysts, assuring that the gurus on high would understand what significance the researchers attached to their product. The head of R&A would chair the board.

The board never worked effectively. Under its initial chairman, the first chief of R&A, Dr. James Phinney Baxter III, the board simply reflected the contending urgencies of the disciplines represented on it, and the strong-willed Baxter, who proved to be an erratic administrator with an unpredictable temper, never was able to draw the diverse personalities on the board into a productive working relationship. An able historian with an established reputation in diplomatic history, Baxter had been lured away from the presidency of Williams College by Donovan in August 1941, and he and Donovan chose the initial members of the board. There were to be a naval officer, a military man, and eight academic specialists. Early members included William L. Langer, who when recruited was not told that he was to serve under Baxter but had thought he would be parallel to him; representatives from Army, Navy, and Treasury; Edward Meade Earle, from the Institute for Advanced Studies at Princeton; Edward S. Mason, a dynamic economist from Harvard; Joseph Hayden, a former vice governor of the Philippines who was now a professor of political science at the University of Michigan; Calvin Hoover, a tough and opinionated economist from Duke University; and as a junior member *cum* secretary, Donald McKay, a political historian from Harvard. To these were soon added Wilmarth Lewis as head of CID, James Grafton Rogers, the former assistant secretary of state who was now professor of law at Yale, and Richard Hartshorne, a geographer from the University of Michigan who chaired the Projects Committee and later became director of research. The board was dubbed the College of Cardinals.

The Board of Analysts was undermined from the start. Donovan replaced members on it at will, Baxter resigned, pleading ill health, before the conflicting methodologies represented on it could be smoothed into a single operation, and the academic tendency to talk at a subject until consensus was reached clogged the calendar. Ambitious heads of sections, convinced of the importance of a report produced in their unit, saw to it that copies went to consumers while the board was still discussing what the report meant. On one occasion the board spent most of a meeting trying to determine, unsuccessfully, whether reports ought to be typed in single or double space. Individually the board members were well placed and very able, and they were frustrated with their inability to function as a group, so that the best and most committed, such as Hoover and Mason, moved on to more challenging and productive work. In the end the Board of Analysts became a totem to which the section heads made occasional gestures, while the real work of R&A, and virtually all of the branch's triumphs, came out of the individual units. This, when realized, encouraged the sections in their entrepreneurship as Langer, after he replaced Baxter as head of R&A, resorted to reorganizations that never quite achieved their purpose. When the board received from the radio news analyst Edgar A. Mowrer, who had undertaken a six-week tour of Asia on behalf of COI, a report that Japan "would do nothing to provoke a major war"—a report dated November 21, 1941—and gave this report credence, it was destined to be ignored.[5]

Donovan, FDR, the Joint Chiefs of Staff, R&A's potential clients, all agreed that R&A ought not to have to be created: everything it would do should have been done before war began in Europe. Nearly everyone agreed that R&A should be organized to endure, for common sense surely suggested the need for something very much like R&A in perpetuity. The war was a new war, in the sense that it involved radically new weapons and, eventually, methods, while the tools of R&A were old tools—logic, imagination, and patient industry—which would not be outdated by wartime developments. Donovan told Baxter, Langer, and Lewis to organize for the long haul.[6]

The R&A men began with a survey of what already existed; they were appalled. They found the materials collected by military and naval attachés at the American embassies and legations "haphazard and indiscriminate." The attachés "saw what was not there, did not see what was there, and in general saw without appreciation of significance." Foreign service officers were little better. Specialists, in the Bureau of Foreign and Domestic Commerce and the Office of Foreign Agricultural Relations, had done very well, however, pointing up the need for specialized knowledge and collections. Since little existed outside university libraries, R&A would create its own collection. This would be Wilmarth Lewis's job. Since such analysis as had already been done on other collections seemed deficient, R&A would establish its own organization by which analysts would best be served. This would be Baxter's job. Since intelligence required its own methodology, R&A would derive this methodology from that of several disciplines. This would be Langer's job.

William L. Langer was among the many scholars who, after the fall of France, were certain that all possible aid short of direct military intervention should be given to the British. Historians, in particular, tended to be Anglophiles: in Britain lay the source of Magna Carta, the source of the language that had bound the diverse American nation together, the source (though together with Germany) of the canons of the historical discipline. When Baxter accepted Donovan's call to direct the Board of Analysts (and thus R&A), Langer, an old friend of Baxter's, was a key member of the small luncheon group that Baxter assembled at the Tavern Club in Boston in July of 1941, and he accepted on the spot the invitation to be director of research for the new organization.[7]

Langer had worked his way up at Harvard, from South Boston and a public school education—though at the highly regarded and very rigorous Boston Latin School—to the Coolidge chair in diplomatic history. He had always believed that history could be useful to society, and he designed a number of projects—texts, encyclopedias, atlases, series of quasi-popular volumes—to demonstrate this. In the months prior to the war he had experienced a sudden failure of confidence, at least as a lecturer, and found that his usual declamatory style, which had been much in demand by Harvard students, had deserted him: in February 1938, "in the middle of a discussion on the Italian peasantry," he was so overcome by a wave of emotion he became dizzy and could not speak, and thereafter, though he resumed lecturing, it was always "a chronic ordeal" that left him feeling panicky. Further, he had recently divorced his introspective, intensely intellectual wife, Suzanne Langer, who was developing her complex and undoubtedly brilliant theories on art, and he had remarried. A break from Cambridge and from teaching was precisely what he needed.

An austere man whose greatest intellectual pleasure was in proving that one could "get at" an answer, Langer was able to command a substantial number of younger scholars. He had gone to Leon Trotsky in Mexico and drawn away from him his papers for the Harvard library, though not to use them for himself. He would readily share his research materials, especially if he thought he would not get to them soon, with his graduate students, not so that they might become junior authors to a book of his—a common academic form of slave trading—but so they might get a leg up on their own work. He was demanding and precise: Langer never tolerated a typing error, once castigating a research scholar for a single typo in a paper, on the ground that if an author could not take sufficient pride in his own work to proofread it with care, he ought not to expect someone less intimately involved with the subject to give it the respect the author had not. If Langer wished a paper to be of a precise length, that length it must be. He was probably truly close to none of his students, with the possible exception of the young Germanist Carl Schorske, though he was, outside the seminar room, warm to all. They stood in wonder of him, and when he moved to Washington, his beck was their call.

At first Langer thought he would turn to the British, whom he presumed to be more sophisticated than his fellow Americans on intelligence matters, to see how they mobilized academics to their war effort. He hurried off to England, packed with military personnel into a lumbering seaplane two to a bunk, taking with him Wilmarth Lewis, who wished to examine collections of printed materials, and Conyers Read, who was appointed head of the British Empire unit in R&A. Not knowing of the considerable academic input at Bletchley, where the Ultra secret was being guarded ferociously against even Britain's ally, Langer was disappointed, and when he discovered such distinguished scholars as Charles K. Webster, in many ways Langer's British counterpart in diplomatic history, or the great authority on Islam, H. A. R. Gibb, working in Oxford on a press-reading assignment, to cull intelligence from foreign newspapers and broadcasts, or when he compared the work of the Interservice Topographical Division to the maps already being produced by his own geographers, he considered he had hold of the more effective handle.

Administratively Langer saw himself as a liaison to the world of scholarship. While he superintended from afar R&A operations in London, Caserta, Cairo, or Kunming, he did not feel any need to visit the units personally, an absence often commented on by those in the field. He hunted up his Harvard colleagues in Washington, drawing on them for information: Alexander Gerschenkron, an economic historian with an intimidating reputation, who was over at the Federal Reserve Bank and who read many languages, could be counted on to help, as could colleagues in the State Department. But once the contact was established, he felt no need to nurse it further along, confident that academicians would wish to help each other whenever called upon. Indeed, the chief complaint his staff had against him, especially when he took over from Baxter in October of 1942, was that while he seemed concerned about their problems, he did not provide the day-to-day moral support they needed. He felt personally put upon by the frequent changes of office quarters—six in all—inflicted on R&A, as when some of the staff was moved briefly into an abandoned skating rink over the protests of the section heads. Most irritating to his colleagues was Langer's tendency to administer by nuance, assuming that everyone would read his hints and nudges as he intended them, so that no one need bear the brunt of direct orders. This was the academic way, and not until mid-1944 did Langer learn that it simply would not work, since academics were quite adept at misreading nuance when they wished to.[8]

Unconscionable time, or so it seemed to Langer, was taken up with petty issues of rank, title, and salary. Many of the recruits to R&A, especially after it began to grow rapidly in 1943, were fresh out of graduate school, and they had no private incomes. Life in Washington was expensive when compared to the cities in which the great graduate schools were situated, often cities with depressed labor markets even further depressed by young wives who were prepared to work for very little in an office or library to help their husbands through graduate school. Even getting enough clerical support for R&A proved difficult, for the Civil Service wallahs who appeared to control such matters remained unconvinced of the significance of those three-by-five cards, and Langer often had to put Ph.D.'s onto running the ditto machines. A former associate professor might, as deputy head of a unit at R&A, be expected to sit down at an interservice committee with a representative from one of the armed forces who bore exalted rank. The associate professor thought himself rather more important than a major while the major had no doubts about the reverse hierarchy. Since rank did prove to have its privileges, a number of recruits to OSS—in the operational units more than in R&A—were taken into the services and given temporary wartime ranks in order to speak on more nearly equal terms with the top brass. Too many academics found they quite liked all this and began to demand from Langer the perquisites of their rank. In universities alone, these scholars proclaimed, were people honored for what they knew, not for the insignia they wore, forgetful that some of them came from universities where full professors still had keys to separate washrooms. Even the Civil Service vocabulary was as impenetrable as the military, and a certain guile was needed to deal with matters of title. As Wilmarth Lewis later remarked, one could get little honor, rank, or salary for "librarians" or "researchers"; so he simply said he was hiring "iconographers," which had the ring of science to it, and he was granted higher grades for his staff.

Though generally above the fray, Langer experienced his own embarrassments. He was told, for example, never to use the word *strategy* in his communications, for this would antagonize the armed services, or to refer to *policy,* for this would disturb the State Department. He ignored this injunction, though not without reflecting on the arrogance of those "haphazard and indiscriminate" reports from the attachés. In order to make the rapidly expanding work of R&A known, Langer began a pamphlet, *The War This Week,* which was a review of the intelligence situation for a variety of potential consumers, and he asked Donald McKay, his Harvard colleague, to edit it.[9] This soon attracted opposition from the Joint Chiefs of Staff, who feared that classified information would leak out (though the pamphlet was issued in numbered, and accounted for, copies, they were correct), and Donovan told the scholars to desist, remarking that academics were "like chorus girls, who have beautiful legs and like to show them"—the nicest compliment ever paid to a footnote. Langer then turned to other types of "publication," usually in mimeographed form, in order to reach out to consumers, though he remained vulnerable to the complaint that he preferred this form of salesmanship, on paper, to the method on which Washington ran, the two-martini "high-level" luncheon.

Langer was more concerned with getting information to poten-

tial users than he was with the notion that an important report
would fall into the wrong hands. He shared with Sherman Kent,
in particular, a general disdain for the way in which the various
intelligence groups overclassified materials. Above all, SI was reluctant to give its information to R&A, even though both were
units of the OSS, which meant that the data SI collected could
not be pumped into the larger picture. Kent said that SI had six
categories by which a document might be denied to someone: restricted, confidential, secret, more than secret, more secret than
the more than secret (here Kent was engaging in a bit of parody
on his own behalf, since these items went to Langer's office, where
he might choose to share them on an "eyes only" basis), and
most extreme and super-secret, which no one in R&A was permitted to see. If one was to get a look at such hot items (which,
when seen, often proved not to be very hot after all), one had to
have equally hot items to trade.

By the fall of 1943 the divisional heads in R&A were in open
revolt against SI, directing a manifesto to Langer demanding that
he do something about the situation. They had learned indirectly
that SI was receiving material from the army based on interrogations of prisoners of war, passing none of it on, and they suspected that SI was accepting fraudulent reports without adequate
testing. Langer therefore put onto a study of SI documents two
of his best analysts from the Economic Section, Chandler Morse,
a man of superbly calm if somewhat elevated self-confidence, and
Herman Liebert, an editor who, being from Yale, was a good liaison with two of the most disenchanted R&A men, Lewis and
Kent.

Morse and Liebert were soon able to produce the requisite horror stories for Langer to take to Donovan. Liebert judged SI order
of battle material, which normally was exempt from R&A evaluation, totally unsatisfactory, pointing out that analysis had to include an evaluation of the source of information—that is, the
historian's concept of provenance—and that paraphrased material, which was the only form in which SI would pass its intelligence along, was as destructive to this sense of provenance as
was the destruction of the precise layering at an archaeological
dig. Analyzing a document "purporting to give information 'concerning the comparative inefficient production of prisoners of war,
working in Germany,' " R&A was able to demonstrate that the
report—which argued that Russian and English prisoners of war

worked for Germany with considerable zeal—came directly from an analysis in a nearly year-old issue of *National Zeitung,* on prisoner-of-war labor in cost terms, which was intended to place a value on prisoner labor in order to estimate the costs of building construction, though with the statistics precisely reversed. Then there was "the case of Super-Secret Document No. 33876," in which Robert Lee Wolff of R&A's Balkan section was asked to come to Langer's office to examine a six-page SI document on an eyes only basis. The document was said to give the German order of battle in Russia and to have been received from "Fighting French sources." Thirty seconds of inspection revealed the document to consist exclusively of verbatim excerpts from official Soviet communiqués published months before in *The New York Times.*[10]

In such an environment academics often found that the one thing they had to sell, and which gave them entitlement to respect, did not, as it would on a true campus, earn them very much, and as a consequence a goodly number became greedy for the merit badges of the military society. "Oh, So Social," "Oh, So Secret," even, "Oh, Such Snobs," might win points back home, where the very idea of secrecy was attractive—and no doubt a fair number embroidered, by implication, what they were up to—but in Washington there were frequent clashes between the administrative types (who in a university were supposed to understand that they were part of a support mechanism only, and who in government often appeared to believe that they ran the show) and the research types. Robert Hayden Alcorn, a Dartmouth man and former teacher, was an administrative-executive officer, and a Special Funds (that is, unvouchered funds) officer, for the OSS, and from his memoirs one could conclude that the professors were petty in the extreme, fighting with him for bigger and better desks, jealous of those who had window views, even demanding that they, like their military counterparts, should have official cars while overseas. Vanity ruled, Alcorn concluded, though he exempted Langer from this charge.[11]

Alcorn most likely was right; yet he and administrative officers like him were part of the problem. He appeared to assume that he was in charge, at least of something, and his approach was one of obdurate misunderstanding, stonewalling temper tantrums rather than remembering that he was to facilitate a harmonious office and that the tantrum was a symptom of a larger problem that he must do his best to cure. R&A earned some of the ridicule, or more often simply gentle jibes, directed to it, as when some of the professors insisted on being called "Doctor" to the point that other units of the OSS called R&A not "the campus" but "the medical school." This academic snobbery arose from the simple fact that on most campuses, Dr. was the most prestigious title, since many had attained professorships without attaining the doctorate, the great Ph.D. mill not having begun to grind fine until after the war. Still, Alcorn had got his sums wrong, for virtually all professors at the Ivy League schools did have their doctorates, so that on those campuses a kind of Harley Street inverted snobbery applied, and one was less often called either Doctor or Professor than plain Mister.

Generally Langer dealt with such expressions of tension by ignoring them for the acts of theater they were. No one, he remarked, had ever said that even the most brilliant academic was necessarily large minded—indeed, often the reverse—and he agreed with Donovan that, however pompous a particular ass might be, if he was effective in his job he simply ought to be asked to sit facing in the other direction. Battles with men in the field over who should be assigned to them and who must remain in Washington, arguments about how best to divide up research—by discipline, by country, or by language—were dealt with calmly (one finds only two angry memoranda over Langer's signature), at arm's length, through correspondence and notes. Langer seldom discussed matters with his colleagues, and those who were most adaptable, or toughest, forged ahead, setting their own courses to a considerable extent. This *laissez-faire* mode of administration awarded the more competitive and able of the scholars, a combination essential to success in R&A, and as a result some of the heads of units moved steadily upward in power and prestige, especially if they opted to remain in Washington rather than seeking out the greater glamour of an overseas assignment. The person most favored by this situation was Sherman Kent.

In any case, Langer was at work on another project from the fall of 1943, and that project both kept him rooted in Washington and limited the time he had to cultivate closer personal relations with his staff. Secretary of State Cordell Hull had invited him to examine all of the official records on American policy toward Vichy France, a policy then hotly debated, and to write an account based on his own conclusions. This was a tricky task: Langer did not wish to write an apologia, and Hull said he wanted nothing more than a dispassionate analysis, convinced as he was that the facts would support American policy. Langer must have known that he was selected in part because his hard-nosed realpolitik, as shown in his diplomatic history, would likely lead him to an approving conclusion. Still, he was given a free hand, the official records being placed at his disposal without any apparent limitation. Thus Langer began a double existence, reporting each evening after he left the OSS to the State Department, to toil over the records that had been set aside for him. He arrived at the conclusion that America's Vichy policy had given the country "an invaluable listening post on the continent, an opportunity both to maintain contact with a traditional ally and to use our influence to restrain the forces making for collaboration with the Nazis, and a certain hold on the French navy and colonial empire." The book, *Our Vichy Gamble,* when published in 1947 created a storm of protest from those who had been anti-Vichy, and Langer was accused of a whitewash, though anyone who had read all of Langer's work would have noted his tendency to be captured by the point of view of his current primary sources. In time he also faced libel actions from Frenchmen named in the account, and some scholars, notably Harry Elmer Barnes, who was a leader of the school that charged FDR with tricking the United States into war, accused Langer of being a hired gun. Langer turned to Allen Dulles and Henry Hyde, old friends from the OSS, for help on the French flank, and after agreeing to make minor changes in future editions, and the forthcoming French edition, Langer was relieved to see the libel actions withdrawn.[12]

As the war in Europe drew to a close, Langer turned his attention back to a hope he had entertained when he first succeeded Baxter as head of R&A: that the branch would become a clearinghouse for contacts between all intelligence agencies and all universities.[13] In the fall of 1942 R&A began to contract out research projects to specialized institutes, first at Stanford and the University of California at Berkeley, and soon after to the University of Denver, Columbia, Princeton, and Yale. No one at the universities appears to have protested these ties, and university presidents and professors courted contracts and consultantships, at times going well beyond the supplying or analysis of information, as when Cal Tech manufactured rockets for the army. Langer now appointed a Committee on Relations between Government Intelligence and Research Work and the American Universities, with a geographer, Preston James, as chairman. While this committee originally included seven academics, Sherman Kent proved to be the continuity figure on it, remaining longer than other members. The question, James said, was how to use "specially qualified faculty men" in future; Kent quietly inserted "and women" into his various draft projections and, conscious that academe was organized through other means than universities, reminded the committee that both the Social Science Research Council and the American Council of Learned Societies had done a good bit to help the OSS find members. Langer and Kent were fascinated with the intellectual and ethical problems involved in the relationship between the academic and intelligence communities, and Kent in particular drafted dozens of general statements on the problem.

One member of the committee also prepared a general argument which, if read in the 1970s, would have appeared remarkably naive. Noting that many members of university faculties travel abroad to "out of the way parts of the world," he believed that anthropologists, archaeologists, geographers, geologists, and art historians could quickly turn their area and language knowledge to intelligence purposes; the academics must, the committee's statement admitted, "exercise great tact in their intelligence activities" since they would be "under more or less constant surveillance"; they could not do truly clandestine work. Their research could, however, be subsidized by American intelligence, and a project might be redirected to include intelligence reporting. Any future American intelligence agency should know of projected trips in advance in order to take advantage of them. The statement concluded,

> it may be pointed out that there is nothing at all discreditable or dishonorable in the projected activities outlined above. American academic personnel who collect intelligence in the course of their legitimate research in a foreign country are in no sense engaged in activities detrimental to that country. . . . Their activities are not in any way designed to "influence" developments in the country in question. Such intelligence work can be done by American academic persons with a completely clear conscience.

When Langer appointed James chairman of the committee, he sent this document to Kent and others as an *avant propos*.[14]

At the end of the war Harvard conferred an honorary LL.D. on

Langer, and President Truman presented him with the Medal for Merit, the highest civilian award. Langer soldiered on with R&A even as OSS was disbanded around him, and when the branch was assigned to the State Department at the time of liquidation, he agreed to serve with Alfred McCormack, who was to be special assistant to the secretary of state on intelligence operations. McCormack had expected to turn this position into the first directorship of central intelligence; when it became apparent that the State Department had no intention of cooperating, and that the R&A staff would be broken up, to be subordinated to the regional desks at State, McCormack resigned. Langer stayed on as special assistant until the summer of 1946, in effect succeeding McCormack as head of the remnant OSS, and then he too resigned.

Though the customary maximum leave of absence from one's institution was two consecutive years (and then normally only for public service), Langer had been on leave from Harvard for four years. He now asked for and received an additional four years, to write a scholarly history of American policy during the war for the Council on Foreign Relations. Langer also continued to propagandize for a standing intelligence body that would draw directly on the universities, for never again ought the universities to be drained as they had been during the war. Langer argued that the government should establish a program for training and research in the social sciences, directly supporting area studies programs in the universities. In November 1950, just after Langer had at last resumed teaching, the fourth director of the Central Intelligence Agency, General Walter Bedell Smith, persuaded Harvard to grant Langer a ninth year of leave so that he might organize the Office of National Estimates for the CIA. Harvard gave Langer more than that—to February 1952, with the strict injunction to return then or resign his professorship.[15]

Thus "Bull" Langer, Harvard historian, became an assistant director of the CIA, with a staff of sixty, and with the explicit expectation that Sherman Kent would succeed him in 1952. For twenty years thereafter Kent remained in the saddle, the Office of National Estimates standing at the center of the CIA as R&A had for the OSS. It was Langer who had done the most to convince the military during the war, and especially "Beetle" Smith, then General Eisenhower's chief of staff, of the importance of R&A's work. Though Langer had not ridden the bounds, had not supped nightly with his section chiefs, perhaps had not kept the morale of his scholars as high when they went overseas as they desired, he had done "the one big thing," as a British intelligence scholar, the philosopher Sir Isaiah Berlin, might have noted: he had seen to it that Eisenhower and Smith publicly acknowledged the importance of R&A's work, assuring that there would be a laying on of hands come the day, which Langer thought inevitable, when a new intelligence agency was created.

Langer remained in the spy business after he returned to Harvard, however, for when President John F. Kennedy revived the President's Foreign Intelligence Advisory Board in 1961, in the face of the disaster at the Bay of Pigs, Langer was asked to be one of the eight members, and "the only strictly intelligence official among them." He remained on the advisory board for eight years, resigning on the election of Richard Nixon to the presidency. By then, Langer argued, intelligence had become too technical, and Langer thought of himself as a rather conventional historian. His missions to review CIA operations in Paris, Madrid, Rome, Athens, Ankara, and Teheran had convinced him that historians no longer could make the kinds of contributions to society they had made in the past, in part because the computer crowd ignored them, in part because the quality of historical scholarship itself had sunk steadily into the morass of "relevance." He looked back with affection to the days of Wild Bill Donovan, who had once said that good intelligence was "no more mysterious than McGuffey's *Second Reader* and just about as sinister." Langer still felt that he could prove that. But now no one had heard of McGuffey.[16]

When R&A was first established, it was rich in scholars of many hues, whether from the perspective of ideology or of discipline. Soon, however, two disciplines began to dominate: history and economics. More slowly, political persuasions, though broadly liberal in keeping with academia in general and the New Deal more specifically, moved toward the center and then the right as a potential threat from the Soviet Union was increasingly perceived. By the end of the war, and certainly by 1946, two scholars in particular had, by virtue of their continuity of service, and even more by virtue of their views, their intelligence, and their skills, set the general tone for research and analysis within any future intelligence agency. One had been Langer; the second was the historian Sherman Kent.[17]

Kent did not set out consciously to create a permanent niche for himself in the world of intelligence, and when he first left Yale to work with Langer, he fully expected to return. But he found his time with R&A at least as rewarding as it had been in the university, and because he liked to solve problems, and saw intelligence as one great problem, he worked harder than most at consciously relating his interest in the methodology of history—on which, in 1941, shortly before going to the OSS, he had written a small book, *Writing History*,[18] that was destined to become a classic—and to justifying the need for true scholarship (not merely "looking things up," as those nifty researchers for the weekly news magazines did) in the OSS and later the CIA. Certainly Kent positioned himself well to be chosen to direct the Office of National Estimates, an office that prepared all estimates on another nation's capacities and intentions, for he wrote the first systematic analysis by an American scholar on the nature of strategic intelligence, timing the book to appear at precisely the right moment in 1949, and he maintained his contacts with the Washington bureaucracy even when he returned to Yale. In a sense he made himself the natural choice to direct ONE. And, in part with intent, in larger part through circumstance, he set out on his path by virtue of the strengths and defects he found in R&A during the war.[19]

Not yet a full professor, Kent was young enough seriously to consider another career; still, with two published books, tenure, and an established reputation in a field that was related to the war effort (France and leftist movements), and the presumption of full control over a key language (though in fact his French, while idiomatic, always came forth with the flattest of intonations), with good political connections, a personal base on the West Coast, and the prestige of the Ivy League behind him, Kent was more likely to rise to the top than other scholars who may have been more distinguished within the profession. This was especially true after Baxter left and Langer began his series of reorganizations.

The reorganization of January 1943 proved effective. Ed Mason became the deputy director, and while the Board of Analysts still existed, it was muted. Later in the year Richard Hartshorne was made assistant director in charge of all research. The Projects Committee, usually chaired by Hartshorne, judged the relative importance of proposed research and adjudicated between the urgent demands coming in from the outside.[20] The research divi-

sions were reduced to those on Europe-Africa (and the
Mediterranean, though this was usually omitted from the title),
with Kent in charge; a USSR Division, a Far East Division, a
Latin America Division, a Map Division, and the major portions
of Lewis's CID.[21] Ranging everywhere was William Applebaum,
an efficiency expert, who submitted branch offices to periodic surprise visits known as Applebombings. Mason serviced the Joint
Chiefs of Staff directly, and thus preoccupied let the research divisions set their own agendas for the constant reevaluation of the
capabilities of the European enemy. Langer set up a mass of con-
sultative committees, much in the manner of a university, by which
decisions were reached very slowly and, when accepted by all
parties to the process, were acted upon very quickly. Several strong
personalities served on the many new committees, though Kent
served on the greatest number, for nearly every subject, whether
an analysis of strategic bombing or estimates of enemy oil production, involved the European section.

Further, it was Kent's unit that was put to the test first, and
when it passed that test triumphantly, his group was taken as representative of all of R&A. Donovan informed the entire staff of
R&A that the invasion of North Africa was at hand, ordered them
to drop everything in favor of producing reports useful to Torch,
and told Baxter, Langer, and Kent to organize the project as they
must. Through the sweltering August and early September nights
of 1942, while Baxter was still nominally in charge, the Europe-
Africa group labored to produce the first sustained intelligence
reports. The researchers worked round the clock, taking only short
breaks every few hours; they brought in friends, smuggled in wives,
called out all the branch's secretaries, to type, run mimeograph
machines, and make corrections. In fifty hours of uninterrupted
work these academics relived their youth, the all-night papers of
their undergraduate years, the massive assault on theses, the perhaps pathetic desire to please others as well as themselves, quoting Napoleon to each other on four-o'clock-in-the-morning courage.
"Fritz" Liebert, as editor, dressed in a natty white suit, grew
grimier as the hours passed, spilling drinks down his coat, but
each morning he retired to the men's room to fit a clean collar
over his otherwise dirty shirt, above which rose an ever heavier
stubble of beard. He was, Kent remarked to him, the symbol of
R&A: elegant and dishevelled. At the end of the fifty hours R&A
had ready an encyclopedic report on Morocco and then, after a
break for a night's sleep, other marathons produced, over the next

two and a half weeks, reports on Algeria and Tunisia. When the military received the reports, they professed to be amazed at the speed at which their request was met, even more at the extent of the content. Donovan told the unit that they had produced "the first victory" for R&A's methodology.

After the reorganization of 1943 some units were favored by events over others, and some unit directors were able to fly before the winds of war more effectively. The Europe-Africa Division under Kent continued to earn a reputation for flamboyant hard work, and its deputy, Rudolph Winnacker, who had come to OSS from a post at the University of Nebraska, proved to be an ideal foil to the ebullient Kent. The section was rewarded for its work in Torch by growth—to 117 people by the end of 1942. The report on Morocco, ritualistically trotted out whenever R&A was asked to demonstrate its effectiveness, was rightly remembered, but it was not the fault of the authors of a similar report on New Caledonia that the U.S. Navy chose to bypass that colony. When sub-Saharan Africa was sheared off from Kent's operation under Ralph Bunche, with only four men and almost no military action, it fell into a backwater. The Balkan section, cut off from the Eastern European unit, may have had more opportunities, but its first chief was unpleasant and the second, Robert Lee Wolff, though exceptionally vigorous, was so intent on getting into the field and experiencing the Balkans for himself, he was found, in the language of the bureaucracy, "too energetic and at times unduly unilateral."[22]

The Central European section, on the other hand, while often effective, tended to be on a boom-and-bust cycle, producing fine reports followed by obviously flawed ones. Franz Neumann, a superb intellectual historian and political analyst, worked to hold the section together, though he was not in charge, being a naturalized citizen, the leadership role falling to Eugene Anderson, a competent if low-key historian. Members of the section clashed repeatedly when it came time to talk about the future of Germany, however. The Italian section, when detached from Central Europe, proved even more difficult in the hands of Gaudens Megaro, a highly unpredictable man who suffered, it was reported, from Megaromania. When Megaro left, Richard P. Stebbins, who had been a co-worker of Kent's, stepped into the post and produced enormous quantities of work, largely by ignoring his six staff members and simply doing it all himself.

The Near East section suffered from too many changes of hands, as the Near East rose and fell and then rose again in priorities and as its members sought to get into the field. In time the section consisted of older prewar specialists who, having the complex language abilities necessary to the area, were viewed as a bit snobbish about their earlier academic achievements, which out-ranked the fresh-faced postgraduate scholars of the other sections. The Scandinavia-Baltic section likewise suffered from a lack of continuity, for when John Wuorinen departed it, the section seemed no more able to work together as a unit than the Nordic-Latvian-Finnish nationalities it studied had been able to do.

This left any competition that might be offered up to Kent's smooth operation strictly to the Western European section. Here the problem was simple lack of energy. Critics rather snidely concluded that scholars whose primary interest was Britain were likely to treasure tea breaks above dirty work in the stacks, and though this was a canard, somehow the section did lack force. Where it performed best was in the outposts, especially in London and Paris, to which the more energetic scholars had sought to be transferred. In May 1944, when the Scandinavia-Baltic section was broken up and reassigned to Western Europe, a third energetic outpost, Stockholm, also became a magnet to draw the most able staff away from Washington.

Kent came in for renewed praise when he proved able to re-solve an apparently intractable problem with the economists, who resolutely refused to serve under historians or political scientists, who (the economists said) worked in "the less exact fields." In short supply and in great demand by other government agencies, the economists generally could force their wishes on Langer. Again, it was the reorganization of January 1943 that altered the balance and gave Kent an opportunity to demonstrate his skills as academic diplomatist.

Though they were viewed as arrogant and irritating, the economists were greatly respected inside R&A. They worked incredibly hard, their morale was extraordinarily high, and they considered no self-appointed task too difficult to tackle. To Langer's pleasure the economists brushed aside questions of overtime or promotion; they also ignored channels, for many of the economists were well placed and had their own contacts. Mason, Langer's deputy, was also head of the Economic Division until he resigned to go to the Department of State in 1944; Emile Despres, an exceedingly able and exceedingly ambitious economist (and the real leader of the

Economic section), came from the Federal Reserve Board to be chief of the division, while Calvin Hoover, whose important work on the Level of Industry Study called for by Potsdam, which gave him guru status, was proving prescient time and again.[23] These men, joined by an outstanding authority on oil production, Walter Levy, and by a corps of fine agricultural economists, attracted to themselves a number of brainy younger men, including two Rhodes Scholars, Walt Rostow, who acquired his own clout by highly effective liaison work with the British Air Ministry, and Wilfred Malenbaum, perhaps the one diplomatist in the group. But as the economists pressed forward, taking all economic matters as their province, setting their own agenda, they came into conflict with the remaining regional sections.

Still, Langer was of mixed emotions. When he discovered the economists trying to engineer a merger with the Bureau of Economic Warfare without his knowledge, he was deeply hurt and briefly, sharply, angry—the economists had perpetrated "the most discreditable item in the history of the branch," he later wrote—to discover that they were disloyal. On the other hand, they had prepared a number of studies that won high praise for R&A: one on German oil supplies on the Eastern front, another on European rations that involved complex tabulations clearly beyond the capacity of the other disciplines, and a fine sleuthing job on the members of the Banque Worms with special attention to their assets in the Western Hemisphere. Further, the economists proved, as the other disciplines had not, that joint research was possible, and R&A was predicated on that belief.

Indeed, even those hostile to the economists had to agree that except for the marathon production of documentation for Torch (to which the economists had contributed too), the most striking intelligence achievements both came from their shop and often were initiated by them. Using material captured from the Nazis, the economists worked out the key to serial numbers of captured truck tires and engines, and from this were able to tell which factory was producing what, and in what quantity. They could spot production bottlenecks—ball bearings, for example—and then target the plants that must be destroyed most urgently. The economists and historians, unexpectedly working together under Donald Wheeler, whose specialty was manpower estimates, found that by careful use of the local German press, which was collected in Stockholm and Istanbul, they could collate obituary notices—customarily inserted by families, especially for officers—and both tell where various German units were and extrapolate figures for their losses. The economists, with help from Eugene Kingman (see illustrations, after page 230), were also able to develop maps that showed the flow of various types of traffic on the German lines, especially when one researcher, Walter Levy, discovered that petroleum received preferential rates before the war and that rate tables were not proportionately altered after the war began, even though the flow of actual goods and commodities was kept secret, so that one could calculate which lines carried oil and target the synthetic plants for heavy bombing.

Then there was the even more sophisticated revision of statistics on armored tank production. In 1942 American and British intelligence were estimating that German production was running as high as 2,000 per month. This figure was based on ground intelligence reports and measurements, from the air and on the ground, of factory area. Problem was, the Germans often built tanks at factories also constructing other heavy engineering items, especially locomotives. R&A guessed the tank estimates were too high. The Germans sought to frustrate estimates, and to inflate them, by not using all the numbers in a given serial number band, for they knew the tanks might be under observation by spies in the factories, and after the war was carried to North Africa, they were aware that OSS agents were scurrying about taking serial numbers off abandoned or damaged tanks left on the battlefield. Then a document showing the register of all tanks held by the 7th Panzer Regiment of the 10th Panzer Division fell into British hands, and it was shared with the Americans. This division had fought throughout the Russian campaign, and access to its numbers confirmed that different serial number bands were not used for different fronts. Combining the materials collected in North Africa and in Sicily, and then with British serial number collections from the Middle East, an OSS analyst, Sidney S. Alexander, was able to produce an estimate of German tank production that substantially lowered the conventional figure. This in turn helped to confirm new order of battle figures. Conversely, once the new method of estimate was tracked across several months, R&A was able to state that, contrary to other reports, tank production in Germany was increasing through 1944, notwithstanding the effects of area raids. This study of serial numbers also bore on the continuing debate about the relative effects of saturation and spot bombing.[24]

Thus, when the reorganization of January 1943 occurred, Sherman Kent had a tiger by the tail, for the economists were riding high and strongly resisted being placed, in an Economic section, under his overall direction as chief of the Europe-Africa Division. Three months later Kent discovered "unreconstructed economists" busily burrowing away on steel requirements in Southeast Asia, even though they had been told to confine their work to Europe, Africa, and the Mediterranean. Kent and Despres fell into contention, with Fritz Liebert as a go-between, and only with strong backing from Hartshorne and McKay from their respective positions was Kent, who showed both patience and tact, able to win the economists over. Thereafter the phrase "the patience of Kent" took on biblical overtones, though Kent never openly compared himself to Job; he did, however, once refer to the economists as his "boils."

In such an atmosphere tensions ran high. Kent's standard means of communication with Chandler Morse, a worldly man-of-affairs who, under Despres, ran the economists, was a kind of controlled quarrel—while Morse made it clear that he was above quarrels, but Right. Kent relieved tensions with his asides (he informed young Andrew Lossky, another historian, that diplomatically a *pis aller* did not, as he alleged Lossky thought, mean elimination in a back alley), just as Preston James, who ran the geographers, and who was, Wilmarth Lewis wrote, "rude & un-housebroken," though a superb scholar, was said to have restored the tensions repeatedly.[25] In the Agricultural section a charge of attempted seduction was hurled at a harried economist who had talked too freely of rape (thereafter always referred to in the division as rape seed, oil-yielding), while an analyst assaulted a guard with a garbage-pail cover before collapsing of a nervous breakdown.

Even before reorganization the geographers were far less troublesome than the economists. Whether as a separate division, or when shifted into other alignments, they seemed eager to have an opportunity to prove the worth of their discipline. There were few prewar geographers who had focused on Europe, and topographic intelligence began at a lower level than political or economic work. Preston James, who initially joined COI as chief of the Latin America Division, proved to be an abrasive yet highly efficient administrator, and Hartshorne, from his position on the Projects Committee, was able to assure the geographers a voice. There was a risk of substantial duplication of work with other agencies,

especially the Division of Maps at the Library of Congress and
the Office of the Geographer at the State Department, and realizing this Baxter and Langer tended to set the geographers service
tasks, developing maps to illustrate R&A reports rather than initiating their own inquiries. With the cooperation of the Weather
Bureau, the geographers did establish a niche for themselves in
the preparation of climate reports, demonstrating their talents with
an early report on weather dates for a possible Japanese attack
on Manchuria. Nonetheless, the geographers were not successful
in establishing the autonomy of their discipline, and they had to
be content with producing monographs on the Pacific Islands for
Naval Intelligence, writing portions of the *Soldiers Handbooks*
which, when they fell into unfriendly hands, such as the economists', were thought a wee bit unsophisticated ("If you come from
Portland, Oregon, you will not find the climate of England
strange"), and doing portions of the studies for Torch, especially
on roads and terrain. With reorganization many of the geographers disappeared into the Europe-Africa Division.

Sherman Kent loved maps, and he did not need to be convinced
that his unit's reports ought to have plenty of them. A new Topographic Intelligence Subdivision was set up under Edward Ackerman, and it in turn was divided into five sections: Transport
Routes, Urban Features and Telecommunications, Industrial Locations and Local Resources, Climate and Vegetation, and Terrain and Hydrography. Later a sixth section, Ports, was added.
From these sections flowed thousands of elegant, meticulous maps,
some of them works of art, giving dramatic point to the intelligence data imbedded in the prose. At the end of the war the geographers concluded that their discipline had been forced into retreat
by other government agencies (they blamed the War Department
most), but they had no complaints of substance with the OSS.[26]

Given reorganization, Kent was also free to inquire into other
areas, and he became something of a generalist at R&A. Arthur
M. Schlesinger, Jr., who was on the Current Intelligence Staff and
writing for the *Daily Summary,* prepared an excellent position paper on the problem of "intellectual guidance" in psychological
warfare research, in effect asserting a need for intellectual unity
within R&A, and in the absence of Schorske, it was Kent's annotated copy that first reached, and impressed, Langer. As a historian, Schlesinger pointed out that the notion held in some quarters
in OSS, that researchers ought to hold no beliefs and make no

judgments, was sheer nonsense, since all research involved both. Spurred by Schlesinger, Kent turned his hand to an early statement about the problem of objectivity in the treatment of postwar Germany, noting how certain words and assumptions that were customary to reports colored the conclusions. Any discussion of postwar food supply being, for example, "seriously deficient," or an assertion that people must be given "enough" food, obviously precluded a hearing from those who felt that the Germans ought not, in defeat, be given enough food at all. When dealing with a nation that had deliberately starved unknown millions to death, "assumptions hitherto valid in scientific writing" might well not be valid. He concluded by calling for comparative analyses, noting that a postwar Germany that had no more food than a prewar Poland would be seriously deprived by Germany's previous standards, and yet were it not to be at least so deprived, so-called objective analyses would have no answer to the question that would be on everyone's lips, "Who got us into this mess, anyway?"

Throughout the period of reorganization, Kent had sought to be on good terms with all. This was not his nature, for he enjoyed a good fight; still, he kept his eye on the goal of reorganization: an integrated, more productive R&A. Langer came to think of him as dependable, as Kent remained ever supportive of Langer. When other units in R&A were broadcasting their frustration with SI, it was Kent alone who wrote a mollifying report, asserting that he had always received cooperative responses when he requested information. This may well have been true, for Kent had learned how to use the soft word. As he wrote, there were times when it was best that the written record be kept obscure; if the man in the next office was stealing government property—he had a real instance in mind—one should, if forced to remonstrate in writing, not refer to a contemptible thief but only to "certain irregularities." If a colleague built a snow mountain outside Kent's room and proclaimed from it that he was a little Napoleon, Kent would reply that, rather than being "a little Napoleon, you're a little drunk," and laughingly cart the offender away. Somehow this boyish approach seemed to work for Kent where a Langer or James could not conceivably have attempted so flippant a response to a personnel crisis.[27]

By 1945 Kent had one other fact going for him, when it came time to assess which section head had performed most professionally: his loyalty was never questioned. There were more danger-

ous threats to R&A's effectiveness than maladministration and
academic tempers after all. There were, without question, members of the OSS, and certainly of R&A, who did not wish to see
the branch perform effectively when attention was shifted more
heavily toward the Soviet Union in 1944 and 1945; there was direct dishonesty, in the illegal use of unvouchered funds and in
using R&A materials to engage in private business; and there were
persistent leaks. Certainly there were leftists in the branch, and
while Langer and Kent were, as academics, quite tolerant of a
socialist leaning in a colleague, they sought to root out any card-
carrying members of the Communist party (Kent strongly suspected two on whom he could not produce the proof, and under
wartime conditions, since the Soviet Union was an ally, he was
unwilling to take action without it). Whether any reports were
deliberately distorted to favor the Soviet Union one cannot say;
certainly some, read with hindsight, did unduly favor the Russian
world view. Still, the USSR Division was highly thought of and
rendered many well-received reports; rather, Communist influence, if it existed, was suspected more in the Latin American and
Italian operations and in the Visual Presentation Branch.

The leaks were another matter, seemingly beyond the control
of R&A. There were neurotics in the branch, certainly, and supreme egotists, who liked for their own reasons to play "I know
a secret" at parties. There was the usual leaking of information
to break through bureaucratic barriers. Most serious, leaks appeared to originate from the Joint Chiefs of Staff. On one occasion General Curtis LeMay, on his way to the Far East, asked for
a list of the most important bomb targets in Japan. LeMay imposed very tight security on the project, sending his own typists
to OSS, supervising the destruction of notes and carbon papers,
and ordering R&A to retain no copy of its own report. Shortly
afterward LeMay, in public commentary, threatened the Japanese
with wholesale destruction from the air. His speech made headlines in *The New York Times,* which appended R&A's list of recommended targets to its article. (R&A clipped the *Times* story,
stamped it top secret, and filed it.) Though the leak probably was
from JCS, it could as well have been from R&A, for it was admitted later that a copy of the report had, despite LeMay's instructions, been retained in house, and by virtue of a peculiar
oversight in security—a portion of R&A took over quarters from
the Office of Education, which mailed out enormous quantities of

printed matter from a branch post office inside the cordon of armed guards at the building doors, and could still post material without going through the security check—the list of targets may have escaped.[28]

Kent was meticulous on matters of security, for despite his parodies of the classification system, he understood that he was dealing with someone else's totems. He recognized the legitimacy of often unapparent reasons for classification, not charging all instances to the human desire to think of one's own work as important. At times arcane reports that touched upon the Russians, or on British colonial interests, were classified lest those allies become aware of potential postwar American policies. At other times reports that were felt to be weak were classified so that OSS would not appear naive in the eyes of the British in particular. There were, of course, genuine security matters at stake too, including human lives, as Kent noted when, learning that a particularly sensitive document concerning partisans and political alliances in Italy had fallen into enemy hands, he not only alerted Major H. Stuart Hughes, the Harvard historian who was in Europe working on Italian matters, so that he would take care not to fall into enemy hands himself, but also wrote two former R&A employees who were identifiable from the report even though they had left the OSS for other work.

Finally, Kent benefited from a role thrust upon him during the intensely divisive discussion of how best to deal with a defeated Germany. On the question of war crimes trials he kept silent, though he thought that showcase trials such as those held in Nuremberg were a mistake, and he was unhappy to see the London staff of R&A shifted almost entirely to doing war crimes research. Were he in charge, Kent noted in his journal, he would simply single out the several hundred Nazis about whom there could be no doubt as to guilt, beginning with Hitler, and summarily execute them. Otherwise, what might happen were America to lose a war one day? On the question of the pastoralization of Germany, however, Kent had opinions that he expressed.

The Central European section, with much input from the economists and geographers, ground out over 2,000 pages on the likely civil administration of Germany and, working with the Western European and Balkan sections, at least as much on military government. These were Civil Affairs Planning Guides, destined for use by the Civil Affairs Division of the Army. Hajo Holborn, the distinguished émigré historian from Germany, acted as liaison on these studies, which also involved the Foreign Economic Administration, Navy, State, and Agriculture, as well as the Army. To produce guides that were consistent with each other within R&A— for there were at least fifty-seven guides, addressed to different questions—was the job of Rudolph Winnacker, Kent's former number two.

An inter-agency committee attempted to direct traffic. If a given planning guide was to deal with de-Nazification, the committee would assign the first draft to OSS; if the subject were the agricultural future of Germany, the Department of Agriculture would take responsibility for a first drafting. The Army would draft the planning guides on the demobilization of the German forces, the Air Force on what was to be done about civil aviation in the postwar era. The drafts would then be reconciled to some extent and sent on to the military government, which was at Shrivenham, in England, where a large staff would try to make up its mind about what to do with Germany, ultimately to produce what was popularly called the SHAEF Civil Affairs Bible.

But the system didn't work, at least between OSS and the other participants. Ultimately there was an agreed R&A position on Germany, which argued that military government was a limited instrument of reform, that all phases of Nazism should be uprooted and anti-Nazi personnel should be put into office, and that the Allied military governments should be of short duration. The Foreign Economic Administration, on the other hand, argued for extensive powers in the hands of the military, to remold Germany into a fair replica of the New Deal. R&A wished to allow German textile production, especially of synthetic fibers, for example, while FEA opposed this both because it would divert much-needed coal and would hinder efforts to break up the cartel formed around I.G. Farben. Eventually the R&A line, which was moderate, was incorporated into the SHAEF Bible, which when read by Secretary of the Treasury Henry Morgenthau and his assistant, Harry Dexter White, led to a major struggle between those who, like White, wanted to pastoralize Germany so that it might never again be capable of significant industrial production and those who wanted to restore its industrial economy as quickly as possible along democratic lines. Ultimately the latter view prevailed, Secretary of War Stimson slowly restoring the earlier line, "step by step," Kent told his journal, "making the Harry White policy shrink into the background."

Kent found himself in the middle of the struggle, from which he emerged with high honors. Holborn did not enjoy the endless meetings needed to arrive at an agreed R&A position on the dozens of issues to which they were to contribute; he was, Kent felt, on the right side of the argument—he was against pastoralization—but he seemed unable to come to terms, in particular, with the members of the Board of Economic Warfare who were advocating a scorched-earth policy. Kent suspected that some on the BEW were doing so less because of their assessment of Germany than because they were Communists and wished to assure that Germany could never again pose a threat to the Soviet Union, a guess on which opinion supported him when White was later accused of being a Communist party-liner. As a result of a crucial Saturday morning meeting between Holborn and his BEW counterpart, Alan Rosenberg, on neutral ground at the Department of State, Rosenberg told Langer that the BEW would resign from the guide project unless Holborn were replaced. Sadly, Holborn, who had more knowledge of Germany than anyone else at R&A, was asked to step down, and Langer named Kent to take his place.

Though Kent felt that, "in a substantive sense, I was in no way up to this job," for he lacked the knowledge of Germany that seemed so essential, he nonetheless got on with it. He recruited old friends, including a dozen or so "chaps" from his African group, to run ditto machines, assemble and staple documents, and filling the air with his colorful French oaths, he got each document ready by midnight the day before it was due. Kent had never accepted the notion that a better paper late was to be preferred to meeting a deadline, and the officers at Shrivenham received their full quota of policy planning guides on time. In effect Kent nailed down by force of will and sheer performance the OSS line on postwar Germany, which coincided with the winning positions.

The major failing of Kent's section, from the scholar's own perspective, lay in its inability to make a convincing case for the recognition of de Gaulle. The rank and file in Kent's shop decided on the basis of their research that de Gaulle's movement was "more representative, more democratic, and more able to contribute to the Allied war effort than any alternative group." The Algiers outpost agreed. Yet, Langer and others at the top in R&A remained unconvinced, and those, whose job it was to promote the view of the analysts did not want to do battle over a matter they felt was so unclear. In the end Kent, too, though he shared the pro–de Gaulle view, backed away. When Langer's book on Vichy France, justifying the anti–de Gaulle policy, was published in 1947, Kent—who faithfully wrote to this former boss to congratulate him on each postwar publication—remained uncharacteristically silent.

At the end of the war the section head who was felt to have done the most professional job was Sherman Kent, and it was Kent who, after a brief return to the groves of academe, would come back to help set up a key unit for the CIA. Kent had benefited from having many friends working for him, and from being on the ground at COI early; he had, for an academic, the unusual ability to be able to get along with nearly everyone and to speak their language. Most of all, he saw how to take advantage of the frequent reorganizations and shifts in responsibility in R&A, and he benefited from having been director of the unit that had first proven the branch's effectiveness with its North African reporting, and then, with reorganization, continued to have the most challenging work to do. He had been one of the first to recognize that policy was bound to shift, with respect not just to the Soviet Union but Britain as well. He proved far-sighted in his prediction that the United States would have to contend with de Gaulle even yet. He remained loyal to his former colleagues, dedicating his book on strategic intelligence to the "old Africans," who had proved the methodology which he championed so effectively. Even his enemies respected him. His skirts were clean. And he found that he rather enjoyed tension.

Wilmarth Sheldon Lewis became chief of the Central Information Division at the R&A campus because he knew Archibald MacLeish and because he was having lunch with the Librarian of Congress one August day in 1941 at the MacLeish home in Conway, Massachusetts. As Librarian, MacLeish had been working with Donovan to get the Office of the Coordinator of Information off the ground. The COI was to be a governmental *omnium gatherum*, a concept that had always intrigued Lewis; it was to receive government reports, prepare its own, and be in direct touch with the president. Scholars would have to be mobilized to this purpose, and Lewis had always liked mobilizing others. And though the COI was already off if not yet running, there was no one from Yale in it yet, or so MacLeish told Lewis over their French Colombard, a point on which MacLeish was mistaken.[29]

Lewis was the personification of the well-heeled, genuinely cultured, independent scholar. By 1941 he had long established, and moved into, the most elegantly maintained private repository of eighteenth-century English literature in the world. This library, and his home, were in Farmington, Connecticut, their contents ultimately destined for the cultural enrichment of Yale. Lewis fulfilled all that Cole Porter could have wanted for such a role: his bespoke English clothes, his witty and authoritative air, his command of the English language, his chiseled features, worldly charm, even his nickname, "Lefty," bestowed on him by freshman classmates at Yale as an allusion to a noted gangster, Lefty Louie Rosenberg, who had been involved in the murder of a gambler, Herman Rosenthal—all this made him attractive to those who enjoyed the company of the debonair. That he had more money than he needed no doubt attracted some: his father had been president of an oil company in California, his mother was an heiress to a great cattle corporation, his wife was a granddaughter of the founder of the Standard Oil Company.[30]

There was far more to Lewis than an American Noël Coward. He was not a scholar in the formal sense of the word, for he was content with the B.A. degree that Yale awarded him in 1920,[31] after he had taken time out to serve in the California National Guard; yet he was a formidable bibliophile, with a collector's passion, the scholar's obsession with discovering the relatedness of things, the researcher's delight in the well-wrought footnote, and the raconteur's ability to give a story real bite. He was shrewd, he seldom missed a nuance in speech or on paper, and he had an eye for detail. He also loved, truly loved, Yale.

Lewis had come to Yale from the Thacher School in Ojai, California, then regarded as the best private school in the West, one of the benefactions of the Kent family. His father was fifty-three and retired when Lewis was born; he died while Lewis was still at Thacher. Yale became the focus for the warmth and respect Lewis might have bestowed elsewhere. As he remarked, "It was an extraordinary experience, coming on from the West," for Yale was filled with "the greatest excitement and rush." Lewis plunged in utterly, winning election to the smart clubs, admiring the exciting figures (like MacLeish) who adorned the senior class, enjoying the sense of security that youthful conceit supports. After graduation Lewis took an editorial job with the Yale University Press, whose director he had met through their common membership in one of Yale's most prestigious senior societies, Scroll and Key. There Lewis would meet across the years, his affection for other

Keys men always bright, with Dean Acheson, Cole Porter, John
Hay Whitney, the Auchinclosses. Keys men acknowledged only
the competition of Skull and Bones, and amongst Bones men were
Henry L. Stimson, Averell Harriman, Henry R. Luce, and Archibald MacLeish. Lewis liked this environment very much, and he
would have stayed in it; in 1922, however, when his mother's death
left him with a fortune, he retired from the press and set about
re-creating the eighteenth century.

Only a fellow scholar or collector might understand Lewis's apparent obsession. Concluding that Horace Walpole, an English man
of letters who, born in 1717 and dying in 1797, embraced the
eighteenth century, was the best access into that culture and that
century, Lewis set out to collect every letter that Walpole wrote
or received, to edit them, and to publish them in a handsome edition through the Yale University Press. "The Yale Edition of
Horace Walpole's Correspondence" would become the largest
publishing project ever carried out through private auspices; the
editorial standards established by Lewis and his assistants, of whom
there were as many as twelve, would be hailed as "the greatest
achievement of editorial scholarship" known, and Lewis would
become "the steward of Strawberry Hill," the name of Walpole's
estate. In 1941 the publication project was well under way—Lewis
knew that he could as easily read proof on the two volumes just
off to press from Washington as from Connecticut—and was expected to be wrapped up in about a quarter century, in perhaps
forty-odd volumes and around about 1965. (As it happened, there
would be forty-eight volumes of correspondence, with ten volumes of memoirs projected, and the Yale Edition would not celebrate its completion until 1983. A full set sells for $2,700. By
then Lewis had been dead for four years.)[32]

To be sure, Lewis had no intention of carrying out drudge work,
neither on Walpole nor for R&A. His fascination was with the
tidy plan by which the apparatus of scholarship—the footnote, the
end note, the bibliography, the index—might be used to give unity
and consistency to disparate information. As he wrote, "Nothing
. . . is more irritating than the practice of hiding the notes at the
back of the book so as not to distract the attention of readers of
delicate concentration. Nothing is better reading (except a good
index) than footnotes."[33] The fun was in the research, the joy in
the journey, so scholarship ought to be on display, up front, where
those of like disposition might learn how to play the game for

themselves. Indeed, life itself was a footnote to a larger story, and the pleasure brought by a well-made footnote was, like the well-wrought urn, palpable as the globèd fruit of which MacLeish wrote. Getting the footnote right was serious business, far more important than a football game (as a successor trustee of Yale Lewis once suggested that the fun and games ought to be reduced to one contest with Harvard "and maybe Princeton"), for a footnote displayed a diagnosis with the precision of a surgeon. Those who didn't understand this were fools.

Of course the worldly Lewis knew that fools needed to be helped, and he left very little to chance. He memorized his impromptu speeches, and then threw the texts away. Fearing there might be some present who did not share his excitement over the footnote, the bon mot, even Walpole, he would slip into a lecture hall and turn off the radiators and throw open the windows to lessen the odds that anyone would fall asleep. The style sheet he wrote for OSS begins with the observation that it did not matter what style R&A adopted so long as it was followed: "It may be true that 'with consistency a great soul has simply nothing to do,' but the less soul in government reports the better." No one who has not felt a tiny flush of pleasure over getting a complex sentence just right, replete with clauses, with double hyphen inserted to represent the dash which typewriters lacked, can understand a man like Wilmarth Lewis. Knowing when to *ibid.* and when to *op. cit.*, when to double *p* and when not to *p* at all, there is very heaven!

And so Wilmarth Lewis moved to Washington at the end of the summer of 1941 and on October 16 reported to his office as the chief of the Central Information Division of the Research and Analysis Branch of the Coordinator of Information. He was paid $6,500 a year, the only salaried job he ever had after leaving the Yale University Press. The division consisted of only Lewis. Mrs. Lewis followed, with chauffeur, butler, and two poodles, one of whom soon had to be sent home, and the family settled into a small Federal period house on P Street in Georgetown. Lewis had arrived to empty offices at the Apex Building, where R&A was to be housed, sitting at night in the Willard Hotel with Bill Langer, trying to figure out what they were to do. Langer told him to do whatever seemed best, and so within weeks Lewis had brought in George Young, the son of a Yale professor, and Kenneth Mac-Leish, who brought in Hubert Howe Bancroft, and the four of them had produced a new system of filing.

   As Lewis liked to point out, the CID files were filled with secret
information that almost anyone could dig out if they knew how; it
was in not knowing that the information became secret. He for-
mulated the plans for filing two hundred thousand documents, for
indexing, cross-indexing, and counter-indexing, so that R&A could,
for example, on a day's notice compile a list of important targets
in Germany in order of their importance. The card catalog became
the talk of Washington, or at least of that part of official Washington that worried about how to find information thought to be arcane, though in truth commonplace enough. Did one want to know
if any Waffen SS men were buried at Bitburg? Why, just get on
the phone to a specialist in German history. Who was this Aya-
tollah Khomeini anyway? Here, there are three hundred card entries, including twenty-six on his indigestion. The spirit of Lefty
Lewis must have hovered, grimacing over the arrogance of the
seventies and eighties, over what Van Slyck would call "the California crowd with no sense of history," over the new, slick younger
men who simply didn't know how to look anything up. The catalog that Lewis built was so good it would make you cry; the State
Department wound up coming to R&A to find out what State itself had by way of consular reports. In the end there were over a
million of those little filing cards, though none counted so weight-
ily with Lewis as the card that enabled CID to win its good name
with the first inquiry put to it: what electrical current is used in
Surinam? Lefty and his three recruits knew, and they never looked
back. When the War College, having surveyed all filing and indexing systems in Washington, chose the CID as its model, no one
was surprised. Lewis's system was, as an admirer remarked,
overpowering in "its detail and complexity."
   Analyzing foreign publications was boring work, requiring a
growing staff able to read across the range of requisite languages,
to retain in memory the vast array of subject headings of interest
to an intelligence agency, and to have both a sense for order, so
that extremely diverse data might be brought into a coherent pattern, and an instinct for research, so that one did not think a task
done before all the peripheral questions had been asked. To put
findings into intelligible language required a reasonably good prose
style and, even more, a judgment as to the appropriate density of
data in relation to the intended audience: too many facts, or too
few, would turn certain readers off. Simple curiosity, nosiness,
and the acquisitive instinct were also valuable. Not many people

were likely to combine these qualities, though one or two did, and for the most part analysis would have to be the work of a team.

Before analyzing materials, the materials had to be obtained. Here COI needed historians with a bibliographical bent, or librarians, or simple pack rats and grubbers. They also needed technicians, since cumbersome materials would need to be reduced to microfilm, no overburdened supply officer being likely to let a hundred pounds of out-of-date newsprint displace military cargo. Microfilming would have to be done overseas, as would most acquiring. There were other intelligence agencies, at State, and Navy, and Army, and in the various wartime mobilization and economic boards, which wanted materials quickly, so that sources could not simply be retained at R&A until someone had made his way down through the twelfth volume of the annual report of the electrical engineers' association of Italy. There would always be people who thought all such work nonsense anyway, especially when people were killing each other overseas: would a piece of intelligence information, even if demonstrably valuable, be fitted into place in time to be of help, or would the simple might of American industry roll over the enemy while the thick-glasses boys in Washington were still turning pages in the engineering annuals? Even if the reports were gotten out quickly, would anyone pay attention to them? Frequently the men and women in intelligence feared that their work was being ignored, which it was, or being dismissed when read, which it was, and they turned on occasion to risible intelligence to relieve their anxieties, poking fun at their own efforts, writing handbooks on foreign countries such as the one on Rio de Oro, a tiny Spanish colonial enclave on the coast of northwest Africa, the frontispiece of which was a picture of an elephant with the caption, "Figure 1. The elephant. The elephant is extinct in Rio de Oro."

The best solution to anxiety, as most academics know, is more work; there was ever increasing emphasis on obtaining and indexing more materials. From this need, and even more from the need to provide publications for all branches of government that declared a desire for them, there emerged an important committee, originally chaired by William Langer and subsequently by Frederick G. Kilgour, before the war a librarian at Harvard and after the war a librarian at Yale, known as IDC, or the Interdepartmental Committee for the Acquisition of Foreign Publications.[34] IDC's chief of analysis and abstracting was John Ottemiller, shrewd, tough, and crusty, to whom Lewis took a liking, proposing him as the associate librarian at Yale long after the war was over. It was IDC that was to obtain those German newspapers from provincial garrison towns that might reveal the location of a certain regiment, or the telephone directories that, when analyzed, would reveal the organizational structure of a war agency.

By the spring of 1941 only a trickle of printed material was reaching the United States from the Axis nations. When COI was established, Langer was one of the first to search for a solution to the problem, helping to set up a committee for inter-agency discussions. Discussion was continuing when the Japanese attacked Pearl Harbor; on December 22, 1941, Bill Donovan wrote to President Roosevelt to tell him of the acute problem of securing printed matter from continental Europe. Donovan recommended the creation of the Interdepartmental Committee, with representatives from COI, State, Commerce, Treasury, Labor, and Agriculture, and from the Library of Congress. Roosevelt approved at once, and IDC was established. To Donovan's list of agencies were added War, Navy, the Office of Facts and Figures, the Board of Economic Warfare, and subsequently the Office of Scientific Research and Development and the Office of the Coordinator of Inter-American Affairs. When the Office of War Information was created in the summer of 1942, it took over the Office of Facts and Figures and its place on the committee.

The Interdepartmental Committee confined its work to obtaining publications requested by government agencies, so that other branches in OSS were left to take the initiative with respect to publications unknown to the government. Thus about 350 publications were obtained and abstracted regularly by IDC in 1942, a number that grew geometrically as the war progressed. Material not thought to contain intelligence value was rejected, and Kilgour had the ultimate authority on this point.

The committee quickly decided that Switzerland, Sweden, and Portugal were the best places for acquiring Axis materials. Switzerland enjoyed an uninterrupted flow of German-language publications, but it posed a major problem in terms of transport of the materials; Stockholm and Lisbon had air communications to London, from which regular air transport might be used. Further, the British shared the desire for publications and would cooperate.

Though the committee had sought to stand at least a bit apart from the OSS, it soon found itself drawn directly into the operations, usually of R&A, when it sent representatives overseas. The Bureau of Budget demanded signed receipts for all purchases, even of a newspaper, and the committee quickly learned that news dealers would not sign a government document, their own much less a foreign country's. When Kilgour realized that nothing was coming through from the Balkans, he turned to the only solution possible: the use of unvouchered funds from the OSS. Thus IDC became, however much it may have wished to remain independent, yet another OSS operation.

Three problems were never fully surmounted. As the Germans began to note the number of times the Berlin *Börsen Zeitung* was being quoted on Allied propaganda radio, they sensed that just such an operation as IDC existed, and they refused to send their publications to news agents thereafter. However, individual subscribers would still receive their copies, and the agents could be paid to retrieve copies from the subscribers. Then the Portuguese military censor closed down on publications going into Portugal, which forced new arrangements in Stockholm, where news agents were "less amenable to extra pay." Finally, the Soviet Union placed a complete embargo on publications. The sale of all Russian publications for export was rigidly controlled, and even the American embassy could obtain only those publications that the Russian authorities approved. No solution to this problem was found.

Even so, the flow built up rapidly. The U.S. Army Air Transport Command, convinced by Donovan that the publications were important, was as cooperative as it could be in the face of constant shortage of space. By mid-1942 IDC was receiving weekly 8,000 pages of European newspapers and 3,000 pages of economic, political, and scientific periodicals via London alone. From Geneva, where the League of Nations Library placed its microfilming services at the disposal of the committee, there came thousands more pages, until Germany and Italy moved into unoccupied France, after which work in Switzerland ceased. (Allen Dulles, already setting up his spy network in Berne, wanted IDC to leave, for he feared it would draw attention to the OSS in ways harmful to his own enterprise. Since he had bigger fish to fry, the American legation declined to use its pouch for the sending of publications, and this effectively cut the committee off.)

In the end the most important work of the committee originated in Stockholm. The IDC representative there was Dr. Adele J. Kibre, who originally was to have been sent to Lisbon. When the Portuguese refused to admit her, she left for Sweden, where she set up a model operation in cooperation with the British. Here she worked with all the OSS units, assuring the flow of German materials to London and on to Washington. To prevent the Germans from detecting the massive flow of specialist journals to Stockholm, many were obtained through British SIS, the Ministry of Economic Warfare, or by way of Portugal, just as Japanese newspapers later were brought through Argentina. Some 345 German journals, from *Butter und Fettwarenverkehr* to the *Siemens-Zeitschrift,* were acquired in this manner. Since German news would also appear in the Swedish press, the outpost took sixty-four Swedish periodicals and eighteen newspapers, and German-language papers from Estonia, Latvia, and Lithuania—in fact, the post was able to obtain all but two of the publications that were on the IDC's "want list."[35] By 1943 20,000 pages of material a week were going from Miss Kibre's office to Washington.

There were also representatives in Lisbon, Chungking (where David Nelson Rowe, a sinologist from Yale, took on the chore directly for CID until the committee could send John K. Fairbank from Harvard as its first representative), Cairo (which for a time was a key office, for its representative was writing a dissertation on the Wahabi movement and was assiduous about gathering up materials and learning the language), Istanbul, and New Delhi. "Special arrangements" were made in Moscow and in Australia. These came to little, for the Russians searched out any publications that even the military tried to take away with them, and there was little interest in Australian materials. Chungking proved to be the toughest outpost to service, with freight taking months, and equipment being shunted onto rail sidings for weeks, until IDC discovered that if a man in army uniform went along on the train and protested whenever the car was shunted off that he was starving and getting no food, the Chinese would put the car back on the track rather than arrange to get food for him. In this way one very hungry man could get the shipment through in about two weeks.

IDC found, by early 1944, that it was drowning under the flow of information: in six months in 1943 the Publications section processed over 30,000 issues of original newspapers and periodicals and over 66,000 issues on microfilm, and in a single memorable week from four European posts 45,000 pages of foreign publications had arrived. In the end not all could be indexed, much less abstracted, and the material often had to remain inert, available only to the steady flow of researchers who came in from R&A and the several government agencies.

What, one must ask, came of this massive accumulation? At the end of the war the committee compiled a secret history for Donovan and, at his request, listed hundreds of items of intelligence that came from its material. These included:

> The complete details of the total reorganization of the German armaments and munitions industries at the end of November and beginning of December 1942.
>
> The first confirmation of German submarine oil tankers, and the first picture of such a tanker refueling a submarine at sea.
>
> Facts on the conversion by the Germans of captured Russian locomotives from wide gauge to standard gauge.
>
> The discovery of the construction of drydocks in Varna, Bulgaria, an item of interest to bomb target people.
>
> The report of the discovery of 350 million tons of new coal deposits in Jehol, China.
>
> The first description of the new two-man Italian assault boats designed to operate either on or below the surface to attach mines to ships at anchor.
>
> Number and structure of the Waffen SS divisions in Hungary, Slovakia, and Rumania.
>
> Details of the recruitment, uniforms, and insignia of the Russian volunteer units in the German army.
>
> Detailed Japanese laws and regulations for conscription of Formosans.
>
> Probably the first copy of Generalissimo Chiang's *China's Destiny* to reach America. Chiang Kai-shek had forbidden the publication of his book abroad, but this copy made possible a detailed abstract and analysis. The Chinese official abstract in English was completely deceptive.

To be sure, some, perhaps even most, of these items may already have been known to the British and, if shared, to the Americans; others may have been learned through SI or the Russians. Some of the information taken from newspapers may have been deliberately misleading, or too lacking in detail to be of help. Yet, confirmation from IDC material could lead to a serious reevaluation of an agent's report from the field, to the first full picture of Japanese reconstruction of roads in the Netherlands East Indies, to a detailed knowledge of which publishers in neutral Spain parroted the Nazi message. Donovan, Langer, and Lewis thought the work of the IDC important; even had it done no more—and it did do far more—than supply R&A with raw data, its contribution would have been a significant one.

Lewis also presided over the transfer of Pictorial Records, a well-financed COI section that was set up in New York, to Washington. With $1 million, Pictorial Records had nearly two hundred employees who worked, not too hard, at collecting "strategic photographs." Lewis discovered that the army colonel in charge, "who never missed a matinee," had concentrated on military targets in Latin America and the British Isles, to be ready should the Germans occupy those areas. Thinking it might be wiser to focus on Italy, France, the Low Countries, and even Germany, Lewis proposed to take in the transferred section.

Most of the staff's time appeared to be spent sending out questionnaires about photographs held by the news agencies, commercial companies, and Hollywood, after which one of the unit's "procurers" would take a look at the pictures. Only about 3 percent of the material examined was ever copied, yet it often took six to eight weeks for Washington to get a picture out of the New York office. The upper-level staff were intent upon visions of the future, in particular a national photographic archive, so that they spent too much time tidying up pictures for posterity instead of arriving at definitions of strategic photography. Lewis thought the whole operation a scandal, and when Sherman Kent, who was asked to look into the situation, confirmed that the unit had not the slightest notion of what a strategic photograph was, frequently mis-captioned the photos they did supply, and had confused pictures of Hawaiian beaches with the Solomon Islands, Lewis sent an Applebomb, which resulted in Black Saturday, March 6, when the unit was informed that it was to move to Washington.[36] Eighty percent of the employees resigned rather than do so, to Lewis's delight. He retained thirty staff and something under $200,000 and put two young Yale curators, Tony Garvan and Alexander Vietor, to work rooting through Italian engineering publications in the Yale library, looking for photographs of hydroelectric plants and docks. By the end of the war the Pictorial Records unit at the Yale library grew to six people, who selected, analyzed, and photographed 17,780 strategic photographs. Garvan's research on docks and railroads was judged the best that had been done, better than anything turned out in Washington, leading Lewis to conclude that future work of this kind might best be contracted out to able scholars who knew their own turf and were not being harassed by a civil service bureaucracy. In April 1944 Lewis's successor established a Pictorial Records unit in Cambridge, Massachusetts, to acquire strategic photographs from Japanese publications in the Boston area.

Less successful was the decision—not Lewis's—to ask American tourists to scour their albums, attics, and cupboards for snapshots they had taken in Europe, and to send these to Pictorial Records, with the thought that some might reveal harbors, railway stations, and the like. As Lewis noted, the plea was much too successful and hundreds of thousands of photos arrived, "showing equestrian monuments and sea gulls," to the point that no one would open the mailbags any longer. Sherman Kent later estimated that perhaps 1 percent of this flow proved to be of value, and that 1 percent came from professional photographers and writers like Louis Adamic who were approached directly by the OSS for permission to go through their files. On top of the photos there flowed, to Lewis's dismay, thousands of picture postcards, sent back by travelers in Europe in the 1920s and '30s, and now exhumed so that R&A might have a hundred badly colored pictures of this or that bourse, chateau, stadthalle, or schloss.

The problem of what to do with so many pictures was solved by John F. Langan, who had been looking into the question of microfilm for Lewis, helped by $5,000 of Lewis's own money. Langan, who had worked before the war in the still picture morgue of *Life,* had developed a tabulating card index system that was used for motion picture and still photography. Now he experimented with putting microfilm pictures of the photographs onto IBM cards, and by 1944 he had transferred 300,000 pictures to cards he modified to fit his needs. The first card that Langan considered right he had made up with a microfilm square which showed a mobile kitchen at Stalingrad, and he hawked this around the various agency offices. In the fall of 1944 the commandant of the Naval Academy asked the OSS to help a member of its staff compile a dictionary of Spanish naval terms. The navy had turned to microfilm in order to preserve the hundreds of thousands of passages necessary to examine and reexamine the context of a word or phrase, and the reels of microfilm had gotten out of hand. Langan's method was applied to this project with great success, and after the war the Langan Aperture Card, as it came to be known, was widely adopted in government, the Department of Defense taking 90 million of the aperture cards in its first order. Langan had surrendered his patent rights to the government for one dollar, a dollar he never received.[37]

By this time Lefty Lewis had turned his desire for order, possession, and the systematic organization of the sources of knowledge to other ends. MacLeish had been urging him to have "some connection" with the Library of Congress, and Lewis proposed an advisory council of librarians and collectors of which he would be the chairman. He brought together top librarians from major institutions at the Library of Congress beginning in February of 1942, and from these meetings evolved plans for cooperation among the libraries to acquire books being published in Europe during the war which most likely could not be acquired until the war was over, a kind of IDC mop-up operation. The libraries agreed that there should be, somewhere in the United States, a copy of every book published abroad—the librarians were more than a little parochial, since "abroad" did not include Asia at first—though one copy would be sufficient if the libraries worked together to cover the waterfront. This would save money, and perhaps even more important, space, since libraries were bursting at the seams, doubling every sixteen years or so. The answer lay in the Farmington Plan.

Lewis invited the Executive Committee of his Library of Congress Council to Farmington in October, and there, under the leadership of Keyes Metcalf, the librarian of Harvard, and with funds from the Carnegie Corporation, the librarians worked out a plan for the purchase of publications as soon as the war was over. The plan called for each of the fifty-four major libraries to accept responsibility for one or more countries and for specific subject matters. The Association of Research Libraries sponsored a study of American purchases from eight countries as a test, which showed that many foreign books of research value were not coming to the United States, and that wasteful duplication was also quite common. At the end of the war a Library of Congress mission to Europe came back with 500,000 volumes published during the war in Germany and Axis-occupied areas, though acquisition of books in conquered lands proved to be less of a problem than acquiring books from newly emerging nations in Asia and Africa, which were included in the plan when it was put into effect. By 1961 the Farmington Plan covered 145 nations: Dartmouth would acquire all books from Canada, Stanford those from Australia, Northwestern those from Angola, etc. The University of Florida got Surinam, the site of Lewis's first OSS success. Sugar crops were for Purdue, soap for Wayne, railroads also for Northwestern.[38] Lewis had been able to realize his dream for an orderly, progressive cataloging of the entire world: the Walpole system, which had become the OSS system, would now become the American system.

In August 1943 Lewis went to Peru on a State Department mission to bring encouragement to the cultural community there, which had suffered the loss by fire of the National Library. The State Department hoped that the reception of the three *emisarios*—Keyes Metcalf from Harvard and Lewis Hanke, an able Latin Americanist with the Library of Congress, were the others—would tell how the Peruvian government, thought to be under steady pressure from the Germans, felt about the United States. This proved to be a triumphant outing, if a bit risky, since Lewis was still with the OSS at the time, and Nelson Rockefeller had made it abundantly clear that Latin America was off-limits to anyone connected to the OSS.

It may be that Lewis carried out a mission for the OSS while in Peru. In his memoirs, and in the records of the mission, he draws attention to the key players on the Peruvian scene who would have to approve American plans to assist the National Library. These were the president, Manuel Prado y Ugarteche; the leading Peruvian historian Jose de la Rivera Agüero y Osma, a man so venerable he took only different colored pills instead of courses at the official luncheons; and the grande dame of Peruvian society, Mrs. Gallagher de Parks. Lewis's schedule included a talk with the head of the Geographical Society, a long meeting with Dr. Jorge Basadre Grohmann, a leading Peruvian historian and future director of the library, and a discussion concerning building plans with Basadre, Harth Terré, an art historian, Emilio Delboy, architect, and one Jachomowitz, not otherwise identified. Shortly after his return from Lima, Lewis wrote to Colonel Robert Hall, then R&A outpost chief for China-India, who was in Chungking working on a plan to send Japanese Communist intelligence agents to Manchuria and Korea, to tell him that the trip had gone well and that he had worked with Terré, Basadre, and Arca Parró, whom he did not identify—he was, in fact, a statistician and economist—and reported that they were all "secure." While Basadre might have known Hall through a scholarly connection—Hall was a professor of geography from the University of Michigan—it seems odd that Lewis would have thought it necessary to tell Hall of these "secure" contacts and would tell him nothing of the presumably more important meetings, and quite odd that the otherwise meticulous Lewis would not identify these individuals in his memoirs, where he was at pains to note every other person who entered his story.

The trip to Peru, and tension in the office, plagued with a low-level nit-picking "efficiency expert" who had been foisted onto Lewis, convinced him that the whole thing was growing a bit boring. The system was firmly in place and under the eye of Warren Hunting Smith, '27, who had worked on the Walpole project.[39] Washington was less and less agreeable. Lewis had moved to a larger house, only to find that the house next to his was a brothel, which he promptly bought, and he had licked the air-conditioner problem—for few in Washington were allowed the new machines—but he was losing weight, becoming irritable, indeed, he suspected, ill. In November 1943 he resigned, ostensibly to go off to Ottawa with his friend Ray Atherton, who had been appointed the first American ambassador to Canada, to report on Canadian-American cultural relations.[40]

Still, Lewis had created the system by which biographical and pictorial materials of interest in intelligence work were made accessible, just as Yale's Human Relations Area Files had established the organizing principle for the orderly recording of cultural data for the OSS. Under Lewis's patronage John Langan had created his aperture cards, making control over pictorial materials possible. In 1961 Langan sent his lawyer up to Farmington to discuss the aperture cards with Lewis. The lawyer, then president of the Veterans of OSS, William J. Casey, opined that the invention was a very important one—NATO had adopted the Langan card for the interchange of technical information and was using 500 million cards annually—but he shared Lewis's view that the cards would never replace "the Wet Thumb method plus Homo Cerebrum."

So what?

It is impossible to say. Those who require definitive answers ought not to read history. Yet the historians and other scholars who worked so many late hours at their desks through the Washington heat and autumnal rains had to ask this question of themselves, and they had an answer.

First, there was the incredible range of arrayed data, available to those who could make the data dance. R&A had assembled a staggering collection: 3 million three-by-five cards, 300,000 captioned photographs, 300,000 classified intelligence documents, 1 million maps, 350,000 numbers of foreign serial publications, 50,000 books (excluding the enormous flow from the IDC), thousands of biographical files, thousands upon thousands of uncounted postcards. To be sure, all this might be dismissed as many dismissed the Ph.D. which, they said, merely meant "Piled Higher and Deeper." But such a collection was important in itself, even had it remained mute, for it brought thousands of books to the United States that otherwise would never have been available to postwar researchers. R&A caused, in a sense, the reorganization of knowledge, promoted area studies, and was one of the reasons why American scholarship, which in the humanities and social sciences might have been thought to be behind that of Europe when the war began, emerged in the 1950s (aided enormously by refugee scholars and by the destruction of great Continental collections) as predominant on the world scene.

Of course, the collections were not mute. R&A produced over three thousand studies. Consider the "publications" (most in typescript, though some truly published) of the Mediterranean section of COI alone—that is, the first sixty-six monographs and reports issued by the section between October 1941 and November 1942.[41] There were reports on the potential objectives and costs of the German occupation of northwest Africa, on the railroads of French and Spanish North Africa—indeed, these were the first two monographs, as requested by Donovan, on installations, equipment, climate, and health at forty-two towns on trans-African overland routes; reports on the roads of Libya, the fuel situation in French North Africa, strategic matters in the Cape Verde Islands, on psychological warfare in North Africa, on the military significance of the recognition of de Gaulle, on 'Allal al-Fasi, the former leader of the Young Moroccan party, strategic surveys of the Anglo-Egyptian Sudan, the Belgian Congo, of Eritrea, reports on minorities in Tunisia, and on the attitudes of French-language newspapers in North Africa.*

*Sherman Kent, who had an eye for the ridiculous even when he had to practice it himself, added another "accomplishment": a new vocabulary calculated to produce great pain for future historians. His favorite example, by which initials had become words full of meaning, was:[42]

G2 docs AFHQ disagree with D section PWB on the disposition of materials picked up by CIC of PBS or IBS now being directly transmit-

One simply cannot know what effect these and other reports had on the war. Numerous historians, as well as the responsible military figures at the time, gave high marks to R&A efforts in preparation for the invasion of North Africa. Certainly the invading forces were well informed. Yet one cannot with certainty attribute this to intelligence information much less specifically to R&A. The men and women of R&A felt they had made a difference, and it seems reasonable to assume that they had, especially since so many were asked to remain, or were (like Langer and Kent) called back into intelligence work soon after the war was over. Still, in a chain of cause and effect, proof eludes one. There is no smoking gun to prove effectiveness.[43]

After the war Donovan and others undoubtedly orchestrated a romanticized OSS legend, at first in the hope of saving the organization, then in justifying a successor. There is no doubt that the romance of the OSS legend helped sustain the mood by which the Central Intelligence Agency was established between July and September 1947. But to dismiss the accomplishments of the OSS as legend is to forget the obvious point that most legends rest on some fact and that some legends may be substantially true. That Donovan and others emerged from the war larger than life does not mean that Donovan was not every bit the five-foot ten-inch silver-haired man of real life.

People who do not know how to get at information are usually impressed by those who do: in expertise alone there is a tendency toward legend making. There is a tale of how military information came from a single piece of carbon paper which a Japanese army typist used three times and failed to destroy (*e.g.*, the route used by the Japanese to bring up reinforcements, the exact strength of the Japanese 66th Infantry Regiment, and the fact that 80 percent of Japanese forces in a key area were suffering from malaria, a deduction reached from learning the amounts of quinine being given to Japanese troops in the area).[44] The story may be false, yet indicative of a true method; or true, yet insignificant, if not acted

---

ted to PWD of SHAEF for the use of the SO people. AFHQ insists on preliminary clearance throughout MEDTO and then transmittal to CENSORED for dissemination among ISTD, FORD, MEW, PID, and cognate U.S. outfits like R&A, EWD. . . . We hear that MEDTO's S-Force pattern is being copied in ETO (T-force there) but that targeting and priorities are being set by CIOSC (G2 SHAEF). We have no news of JICA METO's possible attitude.

upon; or true, very significant, though unmeasurable; but the tale attracts those who do not think beyond the single dimension. An offshoot of R&A produced an explosive flour, packaged in flour sacks, which could be safely baked as fresh bread or biscuits, but which was nonetheless an explosive (it was called "Aunt Jemima" pancake flour). R&A was the branch that first calculated how much, of what type, of explosive would be needed to blow a given railway bridge. R&A established and staffed the first Japanese language schools. R&A cartographers made the largest globes ever made to that time, sending one to Winston Churchill.[45] Are these significant matters? Probably though not certainly.*

R&A's statistics are impressive, but one must wonder whether so much data could be assimilated adequately. Perhaps so, given the growing staff—in 1945 there were 1,500 in R&A in Washington and 450 overseas—and relatively high morale that fostered long working hours, and the fact that young scholars with doctorates in hand were often working at the lowest levels, so that one could assume intelligence and careful attention to detail. Yet, even if such a quantity of paper could be used properly, R&A was quite aware that there was even more paper that it did not possess and that what it did possess came to it, however systematic the collection agencies in the field might attempt to be, with a large element of chance attached.

The final, rapid pace of the Allied victory in Europe ultimately brought R&A far too much material to handle: two tons of captured German maps taken at Bad Reichenhall, which were shipped off to Caserta, for example, or the entire Prussian State Library, found in the Ransbach Mine near Hersfeld, 2 million volumes piled

---

*As an undergraduate in 1950, I was told by a professor of Japanese history, Earl Swisher, who had worked with intelligence in the Pacific, that shortly before the invasion of Makin, in the Gilbert Islands, the Japanese garrison was estimated to be 4,000 (this proved to be correct within forty) on the basis of a photo interpreter who counted latrines, visible as dark spots on photographs, and multiplied by the customary Japanese army ratio of latrines to men, counting on the local commandant to follow prescribed routine. This, and the "carbon paper" example cited above, are instances of simple deductions which were comprehensible to a lay public, and they were most likely released—though are also most likely true—to illustrate a point. I did not encounter the latrine-count story in print, however, until it was used by Peter T. White in *The New York Times Magazine* on April 3, 1966. In turn White's story was used by Allen Dulles in his collection, *Great True Spy Stories* (New York: Harper & Row, 1968), pp. 291–92. This material, in turn, probably was ghost-written, at least in part, by Howard Roman. Thus the origin of the story is foggy.

in tunnels in no discernable order, around which smoke from a mine shaft fire had wafted for two months. While there was a momentary thought to bring the Prussian library back to the United States, in the end this kind of material, like the maps, was either simply returned or was held for future analysis in relation to a possible Russian threat, as when a great number of aerial photos of the Ukraine were found in the Gestapo headquarters in Salzburg.[46]

Despite the romance that surrounded SI, SO, and X-2, there is little historical disagreement that R&A was the most important unit in the OSS. Stanley P. Lovell, director of research and development for OSS, and as Donovan's "Professor Moriarty" responsible for thinking up a wide range of strategems, including the unthinkable in germ and gas warfare, called R&A "the heart and soul" of the agency.[47] Though R&A never quite won over the old hands in the foreign service, who liked to think of themselves as equally versed in the gathering and evaluating of intelligence information, and despite persistent hostility between the OSS and the FBI on the one hand, and the OSS and Army's G-2 on the other—hostilities that drew R&A into their wake—there was more respect for R&A outside OSS than there was inside the organization. It produced a visible artifact, after all, a report, which could be judged on its own merits.

Less recognized, perhaps, is the fact that R&A also had a major impact on the shape of scholarship in American universities in the first two decades after World War II. It is no exaggeration to say that the rapid growth of area studies programs at the graduate level, in which several disciplines, together with the necessary languages, focused their methods jointly and in genuine cooperation on a given area, grew out of the structure of the foreign service, the OSS, and the work of ancillary groups such as the Interdepartmental Committee for the Acquisition of Foreign Publications. Many of the young scholars who worked for R&A received a major boost in their profession, and in their access to knowledge, during their service in the OSS. Several published their first, or their second, major books on subjects close to their R&A assignments and without doubt enhanced their reputations and acquired academic clout within the new programs at their universities because of the personal contacts, the travel abroad, and the access to systematically organized materials that their work in the OSS provided them. One finds the alumni of the OSS scattered throughout typical area studies programs: Soviet and East European studies, Latin American studies, Near and Middle Eastern studies, Southeast Asian studies, South Asia studies, African studies, Western European studies.[48]

Area studies programs in American universities came to reflect the relative strengths of the area-related staffs in the OSS. The weakest, most troubled area for R&A was Latin America, and as an area of study Latin America continues to receive less attention in American universities than it deserves. The OSS was slow in moving into Near and Middle Eastern studies, and even slower in South Asian studies, and these two focuses for area studies programs remain less well endowed in money, in numbers of scholars, in students studying the relevant languages, than other area programs. The one "area" to which the OSS devoted almost no attention—Canada—remains numerically the least well served in the United States, for full-fledged Canadian studies programs are very few; indeed, most of the study of Canada tended, until recently, to reflect the conventional attitude of R&A: Canada was simply included under the charge of those like Conyers Read who focused on Britain and the British Empire and Commonwealth. In 1964 McGeorge Bundy, president of the Ford Foundation (the funding source most responsible for the effective initial promotion of area studies programs at the graduate level), observed, "The first great center of area studies in the United States was not located in any university, but in Washington . . . in the Office of Strategic Services. In very large measure the area study programs developed in American universities in the years after the war were manned, directed, or stimulated by graduates of the OSS—a remarkable institution, half cops-and-robbers and half faculty meeting."[49] In whatever cramped quarters, spread over how many temporary buildings, no matter how often moved or reorganized, R&A was always known as "the campus"—for it carried the air and the reality of the campus with it.[50]

CHAPTER THREE

THE LIBRARY

JOSEPH TOY CURTISS

In the summer of 1942 the librarian of Yale University, Bernard Knollenberg, unknowingly agreed to cooperate with the Office of Strategic Services to establish cover for an OSS mission abroad. Initially the mission was to have been carried out in Switzerland, but by June of 1943, when all was ready, it was shifted to Turkey. At Yale only one person was fully aware of the mission, and no hint of it reached the public until 1953, when the person responsible for launching it, Donald Downes, a sometime Yale student and OSS agent, wrote briefly and enigmatically about it in his autobiography. The autobiography, which on many other matters was far more indiscreet, was greeted with anger by members of the intelligence community, and Downes's brief page about the Yale library appears to have been ignored. In 1977, all participants in the episode having left Yale, the principal records were transferred to the university from Washington.[1]

The central figures in the Yale Library Project, as it was called, were Downes, Joseph Toy Curtiss of Yale's class of 1923, who was an assistant professor of English when the war broke out, and Walter Pforzheimer, who ran a highly successful Wall Street brokerage firm. To this group were added Thomas C. Mendenhall, '32, who had become an assistant professor of history that same summer, as bagman, and Pforzheimer's son, Walter L., '35 (and Yale Law '38), who was on his way to Officer Candidate School. At Yale no one else, including the president, Charles Seymour, was informed.

Seldom has a project so clearly been part of an old boy network. As librarian Bernard Knollenberg was not, as most Yale librarians have not been, a professional; rather, he was a man of independent means, a person of parts who was both extremely well connected—he addressed cabinet officers, senators, and presidents by their first names—and exceedingly competent. He knew Wild Bill Donovan, who called him Knollie; he shared with Donovan an interest in Nathan Hale and in the history of the early Republic; his wife, Mary, was also well connected in Washington. Knollenberg was interested in intelligence, having served in Naval Intelligence in the Pacific in World War I, where he was admitted to the Hawaiian bar. A highly esteemed tax lawyer in Indiana, Massachusetts, and then in New York, Knollenberg had reached the point by the mid-1930s that he could devote his attentions to his greatest interests, writing on George Washington and collecting fine books. In 1938 Yale had persuaded him to become the university's librarian, a position he would hold until 1944, helping to attract to Yale many distinguished collections; he would leave the university to become a senior administrator, first with Lend-Lease, and then, having resigned his librarianship, as a divisional deputy with the OSS. A graduate of Earlham College in Indiana, with his law degree from Harvard, Knollenberg was a sojourner at Yale but an accepted one.

Knollenberg presided over one of the largest academic libraries in the world: the Sterling Memorial Library, a great Gothic tower dedicated in 1931, which would grow from 2 to nearly 8 million volumes, counting its several appendages. At the building's dedication Knollenberg's predecessor, Andrew Keogh, had taken as his theme the library as "an instrument of learning and of power."[2] The largest and finest structure at any university should be its library, Keogh had observed, and Yale's library was on its way to being the second largest university library in the country. Included amongst its holdings was that small, somewhat idiosyncratic gathering of materials, the Yale Collection of War Literature, begun with items from the Great War and now rapidly acquiring awkward additions. What, James Babb, '24, who was the assistant librarian and chief when Knollenberg was away, was one to do with all those big posters, with those tiny miscellaneous pieces of cardboard, and those wartime pamphlets, some in languages few at the university could read, and all printed on the worst of papers? The university's historians, however, well aware of how valuable a collection of such primary source materials would be after the war, wanted to see the collection grow in a comprehensive way. Russell Pruden, '06, who was the associate curator of the papers of Edward M. House, Woodrow Wilson's confidant, which were kept at Yale, had added to his duties the curation of the collection of war literature as soon as the war broke out, and now he took on a historian, a fellow-Fellow of Yale's Berkeley College, as a faculty consultant: Tom Mendenhall.

Pruden and Mendenhall knew that they had to give the collection utility if it was to grow, and in the late spring of 1942 they wrote an article for *The Yale University Library Gazette*.[3] It read like an R&A recruiting document: want to know what an English restaurant can offer under food restrictions, or how to use an envelope three times in war, or what airplane leaflets dropped by the Germans over France or by the Soviets over Iran look like? Want a piece of fabric from German parachutes that fell on England? Care to see a German caricature of Goebbels, suppressed in Germany and smuggled out in the lining of a trunk? Come to the Yale Collection of War Literature, they wrote, well aware that they were stretching the meaning of literature to the breaking point. They concluded that material from continental Europe was most badly needed, that German propaganda series were essential to the collection, and that the library must cast its net wide, must not exercise a selective process at the moment of collection, since no one could know until the war was over what would prove most interesting, or significant, or perhaps even true. They appealed for readers, alumni, to send items to the collection. Shortly after they issued their invitation Downes, who received the publication, referred it to Donovan and apparently sketched in the outlines of a possible operation. Donovan then called his friend, and Downes's former teacher, Wallace Notestein.

Joseph Curtiss was teaching in the Yale wartime summer session when he received a call from Notestein, the Sterling Professor of English History. Notestein was the outstanding American historian of England of his generation; he was also a crafty collector of people. A graduate of the College of Wooster in Ohio, Notestein had come to Yale to take his doctorate, which he received in 1908, and had then taught at the universities of Kansas and Minnesota, and at Cornell for some years, before being drawn back to Yale in 1928. He already held two honorary degrees, one from Harvard, for his leadership in developing the school of English studies at Yale, and in time British institutions would extend similar honors to him. Notestein enjoyed the merit badges of life and saw no reason to hide it; he looked after his students, seeing to it that they were well placed in research and teaching jobs; and he liked to be a king maker, putting people in touch with each other, arranging promotions, encouraging aspiring college presidents, standing just a touch behind the scenes. As Curtiss later remarked, it was entirely logical that the call should have come from "Note."

Years later, when interviewed, many former OSS and CIA employees who had gone to Yale would single out Notestein as having most impressed them with the relationship of history to the "real world." Notestein had tasted the "real world" when in 1919 he was attached to the American Committee to Negotiate Peace. He, too, knew Donovan. In 1942 Notestein was sixty-three years old and on the verge of marrying Ada Louise Comstock, the president of Radcliffe College. He was also bogged down in his major book, which had been going badly and was not likely to go better so long as the war was on, and as scholars will do when they find themselves unproductive, he was heavily engaged in campus politics including, he hoped, the ultimate elevation of one of his students to the presidency of Yale. Notestein felt that some government experience, such as President Seymour had acquired with Woodrow Wilson at Versailles, was important to a presidential candidate, and he had his eye on two assistant professors of

history, Tom Mendenhall, who increasingly was becoming a one-
man show in holding the undergraduate curriculum together in that
department, given faculty depletions through the draft and volunteer service; and Sherman Kent, the French historian who was
already making a name for himself in Washington with the OSS.
Absence, Notestein thought, often improved a candidate's chances,
and he was seeking ways to help others among his students and
friends to be away from the campus for a while. Notestein was,
an OSS man who knew him well observed, "a natural conspirator." (The man who did ultimately become Yale's next president,
not a Notestein student, saw this tendency less romantically as a
"usual coating of Notestein blah.") Now, having tried first to reach
another former history student of his, William Huse Dunham, and
Frederick W. Hilles in the English department, Notestein told
Curtiss to wait for him. Curtiss, though in English, had taught for
Notestein in history—crossing over between the two disciplines
was far more common then than now—and Notestein said he had
some more history work for him to do.

Twenty-five minutes later Notestein slipped into Curtiss's suite
(he was a residential fellow in Jonathan Edwards College, whereas
Notestein, then fellow of Pierson College, had no college office),
closed the windows, checked on the doors so that the undergraduates who lived above and below Curtiss would hear nothing, and
said that he had just received a telephone call from Donovan.
Someone was wanted to go abroad, probably to Switzerland.
(Curtiss later recalled that Notestein told him the idea came from
Allen Dulles, but this seems unlikely.) Curtiss was a paid-up
member of the "bad eyes brigade" and could expect to get permission from the Selective Service to leave the country. Notestein told Curtiss to go to the Yale Club, opposite Grand Central
Station in New York City, to its cavernous second-floor lounge;
he was to wear a blue suit and a purple tie—not a combination
Curtiss cared for—and look for a man who would be seated in a
corner near the portrait of President William Howard Taft; the
man would light a cigarette and immediately put it out. Notestein then left for the golf course, where he spent many of his
afternoons.

On the train down from New Haven Curtiss thought over the
potential offer to which he assumed he would have to respond.
He was relatively well traveled, he spoke fluent if not always accurate German, and he was reasonably well informed on Euro-

pean politics. He had been a Sterling Fellow at Yale in 1930–31, and this had enabled him to spend the winter traveling in Italy, the Lebanon, Jerusalem, down to the red rose "lost" city of Petra, and to Turkey, accompanied part of the way by his colleague, Bill Dunham. He had also walked along the Mosel, put in a good bit of time in Munich beer halls, and had renewed his contacts with France and England, where he had spent some earlier time working on his dissertation. He did not much care for the English, remarking on how a visit there made one appreciate America. The English, he had written, were "a decadent race, worn out, and what the country really needs is a visitation by the Black Death followed by earthquake and fire." When the equivalent struck from the English skies in 1940, Curtiss regretted having made a joke of his discomforts in this way; he was sure that his friends would realize that anyone writing that toilets were more important than tea parties and electric lights more important than ancestral oaks had been facetious. Further, while he believed that the responsibility for World War I had to be shared equally by all the Powers, he was clearly pro-British in 1940 and deeply disturbed by the apparent triumph of Fascism in both Germany and Italy. Service in Switzerland would be welcome.

Curtiss may have worried just a little about his earlier remarks when he had traveled in Europe, especially when he went again in 1933 where, suffering from tuberculosis, he spent a good portion of the year in a sanatorium in Salzburg, and the next year in another sanatorium southwest of Vienna (from which he wrote, "Austria is a hot bed of intrigue, and I love it"). He spent a second year recovering in a small villa in Merano, in the South Tyrol. Here his affection had been won over by the Austrians, largely pro-Hapsburg, and he read widely in Austrian history and literature. The South Tyroleans were, except for the industrial city of Bolzano, overwhelmingly German-speaking, and Mussolini's dictatorship was especially harsh in the area. Curtiss had told his friends to say "Heil Hitler" to Notestein for him, twitting his mentor who, like all liberals, had "his feet in the Nineteenth Century and his head in the clouds." By the time Curtiss returned to Yale in the fall of 1935, after further travel in Europe and along the eastern littoral of the Mediterranean, he had come to believe that if the French had been willing to meet German requests for easing the terms of the Versailles Treaty, Hitler might not have come to power. He also believed that Hitler was an unrelieved menace, and Curtiss feared, in particular, for the Jews.

Curtiss was, by the early 1940s, rather disenchanted with Yale. His interest had been in the new interdisciplinary program, History, the Arts and Letters, and though he declared himself happy to be called an assistant professor of English, or an instructor of ceramics for that matter, it was English history that he wanted to teach, had taught, and was not teaching. He was interested in the historical uses of astrology and magic, for he was fascinated with how people could accept nonsense for reality and with the evolution of the scientific mind—an interest he shared on the margin with Notestein, whose Ph.D. assertation had been on witchcraft— and he hoped to pursue "the matter of Britain" (*i.e.,* Arthurian legends) and the emerging field of intellectual history. But Yale's rigidity had forced him into teaching English. Curtiss was also tired of living in a residential college that, for all its physical appearance of an Oxbridge college, seemed one long round of teas with the master and students, a series of repetitive and petty duties, and wounding routine. The thought that he was about to be asked to become assistant air warden for his college, as his colleague in English Dick Purdy had agreed to do in Berkeley, horrified him. Curtiss wanted to serve his country, he wanted to do something directed against the Germans, and he also wanted out.

The recognition signals at the Yale Club proved unnecessary; there was only one person in the lounge, a heavy-set man suffering from what seemed to be a perpetual head cold: Donald Downes.* Downes knew Yale well, having attended it at various times between 1921 and 1935, and he had the persuasiveness of the born teacher, which he had been at schools in Connecticut and Massachusetts. He was also a historian, which Curtiss liked, and he had experience in "the business," having worked for British Security Coordination in New York City before the COI had been created. In time Downes would earn Curtiss's unadulterated enmity, but at the time he simply judged Downes to be a man who had more ideas than stability. Downes proposed that Yale's war collection should be used as a cover under which a Yale scholar would go overseas, probably to Switzerland, ostensibly to purchase Continental war literature for the library but, in fact, to gather the kinds of information so essential for Secret Intelligence

*On Downes, see Chapter Four.

and the office of Research and Analysis. Curtiss immediately agreed
to go.

Since Allen Dulles was soon to be sent to Switzerland, Curtiss
went on to talk with Dulles at his home in New York City. Over
tea together he sensed that Dulles was not deeply interested in
the project—Dulles was always more attracted to the clandestine
side of intelligence than to the more mundane matters of research
and evaluation—and Curtiss was told that he would be thrown
onto his own to get abroad, since all available space in trans-At-
lantic crossings was taken up by essential military personnel. Dulles
stressed that only he and Downes, within the OSS, were to know
the details of the project, and that no one at Yale, including Notestein, should be informed. Though Notestein had behaved as though
he had been told of the plan, in fact he had not been as yet, having simply been asked to pick out a young colleague who knew
German and point him toward Downes. Dulles emphasized the
need for a genuine cover—that is, Curtiss must be seen to be collecting materials abroad for the Yale library, establish an account
to pay for those materials, and send items back to the library,
though it would be well to have the knowledge of even this cover
operation limited to as few people at Yale as reasonably possible.
For the real job someone would be needed to handle funds, a
bagman, who would most likely have to know something of the
operation but as little as Curtiss could get away with. Given the
cover, the OSS would not be able to help with arranging a passport and visas, for he must carry out all the steps essential to
getting overseas precisely as he would were he truly working for
Yale. There should be no further contact with the OSS in Washington or New York. However, Dulles's profile was no lower in
New York than it would be when he set up the OSS operation in
Berne (where he put a brass plaque on his front door), and almost
immediately New York and New Haven papers carried small items
about Curtiss having called on Dulles, speculating on the purpose.

Curtiss invoked Carl Lohmann, the Whiffenpoof of the class of
1910, who in 1927 had become secretary of the university, and
asked his help in obtaining a passport so that he might go abroad
to purchase materials for the World War II collection. Lohmann
called an old Yale friend, Harvey Bundy, then a special assistant
to Secretary of War Henry B. Stimson, to ask for intervention,
and Bundy declined. Curtiss then approached Sherman Kent at
Research and Analysis, for Kent, as a consultant to the war col-

lection, would be a natural person to intervene. Kent, ever shrewd, guessed that something more than collecting bits of parachute was in the wind, and Curtiss backed off, declaring that "he would not soil his hands" by having a friend in the OSS help him get a passport. (Later Kent would be fully in the know and would use Curtiss, through R&A, to supply materials for both SI and later X-2 work.) So the assistant professor of English from Yale presented himself to the passport office at the State Department in Washington and asked that a passport be issued to him. Within a few days his request was refused personally by the formidable director of the office, Mrs. Ruth Shipley.

Curtiss had been hoisted both by his cover and by the petty jealousies often endemic to academic life. Downes told Curtiss that, despite Dulles's warning, he might keep in touch on a private line, and he reported, when Curtiss called, that he had been busy securing the cover by finding a way to launder the necessary funds. Downes was now preoccupied with new schemes, however, and he had passed the project to a close friend and classmate, Robert Ullman. Ullman had invited the young Walter L. Pforzheimer to dinner at his New York house, cautioning Pforzheimer to tell no one, including the senior Pforzheimer. At dinner Ullman introduced Pforzheimer to two other representatives of the OSS and explained that the OSS wanted to send someone to a neutral country in Europe with the Yale library as a cover. Since the cover job would have to be performed, someone able to do both jobs was needed, and that someone would require a good bit of money. No one at Yale was to know the details. Above all, a "certain high officer" of the university must not be told. This was President Seymour, who felt that, if not drafted, his faculty should remain at Yale and attend to civic virtue; faculty members like Curtiss, who were junior and/or untenured, sometimes had their names removed from the faculty directory if they volunteered for military service, and while this policy could not apply to tenured faculty, excision contained more than a hint of official attitude toward volunteering. Nor could the provost, the number-two officer of the university, be allowed to know, for he was thought to share the president's view. Yale's supervisor of contracts with government agencies, Marcus Robbins, was of course cut out completely. Mendenhall, a former Rhodes Scholar and devoted to England (and to Wales, on whose cloth trade he had written), and Notestein—to whom the sometimes garrulous Downes had in fact outlined the mission—would provide liaison at the university as needed.

And so it was arranged. Pforzheimer, as a trustee of the Yale Library Associates and a previous donor to the university, was to make a "gift," on behalf of himself and "other interested Yale alumni who insisted on remaining anonymous," of $25,000 for the project. If all went well, additional money was to be provided each year. The OSS would supply the money to Pforzheimer, who would launder it. Since Pforzheimer was then in the army, having enlisted the previous April, and was to leave for Officer Candidate School in a matter of days, he could not expect to continue to monitor the sum, though it must appear that he was doing so, and therefore it was agreed that his father, Walter Pforzheimer "without the L.," would be the person to whom Mendenhall, ostensibly on behalf of the war collection, should send accounts and requests for transfer of funds. The OSS would then be cut out from any further contact with the money—a technique that the OSS's successor agency, the CIA, would use with a variety of cultural institutions twenty years later.

That same evening Pforzheimer called his good friend, the assistant librarian, Jim Babb, to tell him there was an alumni group interested in making a gift to the war collection.[4] Usually quick to accept money, for Babb was, behind the scenes, even more effective than Knollenberg in building Yale's collections, the assistant librarian responded with a grunt. After a second grunt he abruptly said, "Call me tomorrow," and hung up. The dinner group dispersed disappointed, some worried that Babb's response suggested that cover already had been blown. The next morning Pforzheimer called again, and Babb explained that he could hardly recall the conversation, having taken sleeping pills that night after being ill in bed for several days. Offered the $25,000 again, Babb accepted it on the spot; Pforzheimer told him Mendenhall would fill him in on the details. (The only information Babb was given, of course, was the cover story.) Babb then insisted on knowing who the donors were; Pforzheimer declined on the ground that this group of alumni did not want to be nagged by Yale for further funds. Knollenberg wrote happily that Yale could now have the finest war collection on the Eastern seaboard, perhaps even surpassing the Hoover Library at Stanford: ". . . the possibilities are dazzling." Then followed letters and telegrams from Knollenberg, Lohmann, and finally President Seymour, thanking Pforzheimer for the gift and asking that they be told in confidence the names of the other donors so that the corporation could pass a vote of thanks. Pforzheimer remained silent and, institutional courtesies served, Yale accepted the money, which Pforzheimer formalized on behalf of himself and his alleged associates on October 8, writing from Officer Candidate School in Miami Beach. The OSS had transferred the funds eleven days before.

On Downes's advice Mendenhall had told Babb to announce the gift, which he did on September 15. As soon as notices appeared in the press, the Joint Committee on Importations of Foreign Books protested to the American Library Association. The ALA insisted that Yale should not be allowed to benefit alone from any passport, or facilitative assistance, extended to its faculty member. The directors of the New York Public Library and the Harvard libraries, sensing that Yale's entire effort might go down the tubes if the ALA persisted in its pettiness, met with Mendenhall and Babb and worked out a compromise: one half of the materials Yale obtained should be distributed to a group of other libraries—and any library wishing to join in what became the Associated Libraries Group could do so—which would reimburse Yale for the costs. This would double the number of books that would come to American libraries while still enriching Yale disproportionately but appropriately. Harvard, Princeton, Columbia, Michigan, Minnesota, and Iowa also wanted in on the act. It was, in fact, as Mrs. Shipley explained to Curtiss, the ALA that had brought pressure to bear on the Department of State not to issue him a passport.

Curtiss now took matters into his own hands. Considering Downes insecure, and in no position to know that Downes had departed for a bit of derring-do in North Africa, or that Ullmann had left arrangements in the capable hands of a close friend of Downes's, Sidney Clark—whom Curtiss was not to contact in any case—Curtiss signed his own compromise memorandum with the ALA on November 17. Accepting the terms laid down, he was nonetheless well aware that whatever he did for the libraries would be quite secondary. Indeed, he had no reason to help them: they had cost him four visits to Washington and had wasted three months of his time. Curtiss again presented himself to Mrs. Shipley, and this time she approved, apparently convinced that the Treasury would refuse the transfer of funds in the Pforzheimer "gift." However, Treasury entered no objections (Curtiss believed that

Downes had informed someone there of the real intent of the transfer, though the records suggest that the call was from Donovan through a friend at the Guaranty Trust Company in New York). In the meantime, confident that all would work out, Curtiss had reported in mid-October for three weeks of training in how to be a spy. Most of the conventional instruction, he expected, would be irrelevant: one did not need to know how to garrot a sentry when in neutral Switzerland.

By the time the agreement was signed with the ALA and the passport was in hand, however, Switzerland was no longer in the cards. The landing of American and British forces in Morocco and Algeria on November 8, 1942, cut off all civilian access to Switzerland, particularly after German and Italian troops moved to occupy Vichy France on the early morning of the eleventh. (Allen Dulles, on his way to Berne, slipped across the border by train from France the night before.) Curtiss, trained, with passport in hand, was contacted by the OSS, who asked him where he wanted to go now. Turkey and Sweden had always been possibilities, even as Switzerland had been discussed; now they were the only possibilities.

While Curtiss spoke neither Swedish nor Turkish, he had traveled fairly widely in Turkey, especially in 1937 when he had visited Asia Minor, Greece, Cyprus, and Portugal with William Borst, a student of his who had just graduated and who, in 1942, was again at Yale as an instructor in English. He had never been to Sweden, and Turkey sounded a bit more romantic. The hope of providing cover for Dulles in Switzerland was gone, and when Curtiss was informed that he was being transferred to a new branch of OSS, X-2, from the old SI, to which Dulles had been attached, there seemed not even this thin thread of connection to the original plan. With little hesitation Curtiss opted for Turkey. This might gain the added advantage of dampening the ardor of the Associated Libraries, a desirable goal since the more accountants involved in the project the less secure the cover. After all, the gift had been announced for one year only, though if the project proved useful it was understood that the anonymous donors might well continue to fund it. Pforzheimer would find it increasingly difficult to explain away 25,000 anonymous dollars each year to upwards of a dozen members of a congress of colleges.

The university was by now accustomed to Curtiss's frequent trips to Washington in plea of his passport and visas, and so he

had announced that he would be away again from October 19. On
that day he had traveled to Baltimore by train, was met by a man
wearing a red carnation and, with three other men who alighted
from the same train, was hurried into a waiting car. Curtiss thought
all this a bit obvious, and his feeling that the OSS was not truly
discreet would grow as his assignment developed; in compensation Curtiss became ever more discreet himself. Driven west from
Baltimore—an hour on the local train, as he would learn later—
Curtiss found himself at a large, verandahed house, ca. 1900, set
on seventy acres of well-screened land. There were nine men in
his training group, with a new group brought in each week as one
rotated out. Though Curtiss was not told, the Schools and Training Branch of the OSS was still trying to decide precisely how it
should train its people, and a good bit of the program was exper-
imental. As applied to Curtiss it was also all rather casual, he felt,
because he was to be rushed through and sent off as quickly as
possible. Since he was 4-F, he was excused from the more stren-
uous parts of the course.

What there was proved to be "good fun." He learned a little
telegraphy, Morse; he skipped the rudiments of detonation. Other
recruits crawled through a cellar with .45s in their hands, to have
a figure dressed as Hitler leap out upon them; this too Curtiss
passed by. He took, and enjoyed, map instruction. He and a companion were set down at night, God knew where, with only a
compass, instructed to find their way back in two hours. Everyone had a cover name (Curtiss, who never cared for jargon, always thought of it as a nickname) and was told to reveal nothing
of himself; they were never to say "I," so that they would learn
to think of themselves impersonally, and never to refer to their
childhood. They were sent to Baltimore (or, in some instances,
Philadelphia, Pittsburgh, or Richmond), where many ships crowded
the harbors and trains sat on the lines and much military and government work was being done, and with forged papers were told
to obtain a job in the defense industry and return, within three
days, with "a secret." In the end some were taken aside and told
that they had failed the course, after which a friendly instructor
would chat the disappointed candidate up and, asking what he
intended to do with himself now, would truly fail anyone who
forgot that he was, under no circumstances, to talk about himself.
Curtiss, to whom most of this little game was not applied, thought
much of the activity smacked of the Boy Scouts, but since the

training he did have had been fun, he emerged happy enough.⁵

Now the professor waited again. never having had "a job"—for teaching in a university was not "a job," it was, at best, "filling a position"—Curtiss had no social security number, and so the OSS could not begin to pay him his salary, which was to be $4,250, the same as his Yale salary. There were many in the OSS, he knew, who were there partly for the money, but as he had not known what his salary was to be until he completed the training course, he was not among them. Curtiss returned to his suite in Jonathan Edwards College, to wait for his social security number, to wait for his travel orders—for by now it was not expected that he could get himself abroad without some help—and to be visited by friends who had gone into Air Intelligence. One, Bill Parke, who knew only that Curtiss hoped to go abroad to buy books for the Yale library, visited to cheer him up; weeks later, emerging from a shower stall at the barracks in Newport News, Virginia, Curtiss would come upon Parke, who had undergone the same training course (though in full) unbeknownst to either.

Warned that departure would come soon, Curtiss went to Washington for the weekend. He was out shopping for shirts on April 11 when the word came that he was to leave for Norfolk the next night and to take $1,000 with him since money might be slow in catching up with him. Scuttling a meeting with Walter L. Pforzheimer, who was in town after completing the Army Air Force's Intelligence School in Pennsylvania, and who had offered to introduce Curtiss to a man who knew many prominent people "where you intend to go," Curtiss called his friend Bill Borst, who left New Haven on the Washington train to bring his passport and letter of credit to him. With this Curtiss was able to buy travelers' checks and clothing for the journey while waiting for transport from Newport News. He also called a bookstore in New Haven and had some thirty books, mostly German literature, sent so that he might have something to read on the long trip. After five days of waiting, he was put aboard a ship for New York City, thence past the mouth of the Chesapeake once again to Key West, and then onto the *Elisha Mitchell,* a Liberty Ship carrying 10,000 bombs, two tanks, and three OSS agents. Its captain was instructed to join seven other ships and "run like hell for Port Said."

Running like hell was a relative command, of course, as the ships crossed down the Caribbean, passed through the Panama Canal, crept along the west coast of South America, rounding Cape

Horn on June 21 to a general celebration of all on board, and then made for Durban, on the coast of southern Africa, where Curtiss's vessel dropped out of convoy for two weeks for engine repairs. Across the south Atlantic they picked up signals from a ship in distress but had no trouble themselves. From Durban Curtiss wrote postcards to his friends in New Haven, calculated to reinforce the impression that he was off with a group of academics to buy books. Next was the East African coast, to put in at Aden—where they received warnings of potential Japanese attacks, although none came—and then four days up the Red Sea to the Suez Canal. A tedious train journey to Beirut followed, made more tedious by the refusal on the part of a Vichy French officer at the border to accept his papers. Curtiss rang through to the American legation in Beirut, where an assistant to the chief of mission managed to talk the border control into issuing a twenty-four-hour transit visa for passage across Lebanon. After a night in Beirut Curtiss hurried on to Aleppo, where he boarded the Baghdad train on its way to Ankara and Istanbul. Throughout he used his library cover—the American legation officer in Beirut, in some exasperation, declared that he "wouldn't have gone to all this trouble if I'd known it was only about books"—and with bookbag in tow, Curtiss arrived in Istanbul in July 1943, eleven months after Wallace Notestein had drawn his curtains to tell him of the urgency of his potential assignment.

On the long voyage Curtiss had become well acquainted with the two other OSS men aboard, one of whom he had recognized: Harold Lamb, who stuttered badly when tense, and who was already well known for his popular books about Genghis Khan and the Mongolian hordes. Though Lamb's cover—that he was on the way to Iran to write articles for the *Saturday Evening Post* and the *Ladies' Home Journal*—was transparent, given his presence on the ship, none of the men pressed each other about their work. (The other OSS man, a Viennese psychologist with whom Curtiss could practice his German, he never saw again.) Only one man, Bill Parke, who by coincidence was also aboard, knew Curtiss, and he surely guessed that Curtiss was not simply in search of books for American libraries. There came a night when all saw that the various cover stories made little sense in the context of so long, difficult, and expensive a voyage. This was the night when the ship's captain, disturbed that no liquor had been put on board, asked for a delivery to await him at Colon. No delivery came, but a case of rum and a case of bourbon for each of the OSS men was promised, to be sent out by lighter from Cristobal, if the ship did not lose headway. That night, after the ship had drifted down the canal to make sure that it did not outdistance the lighter, they all gathered in Parke's cabin to drink rum mixed with hot or cold water.

Curtiss had arrived in Istanbul with clear if very broad orders—to collect, sort, and evaluate printed materials of interest in the war effort, and to wait until he was contacted. He drew on his letter of credit, bought clothing appropriate to the climate, and opened a bank account. Mendenhall had been instructed not to send any money until Curtiss arrived and asked for a transfer of funds, for if money were sent in advance of his arrival and Curtiss were to meet with an accident on the way, the cover would be blown. Here a small mystery intrudes.

The financial arrangements necessary to live two, indeed in a sense three, lives would have been complex under the best of circumstances, and circumstances were not very good. As bagman Mendenhall was to keep two sets of records, the first set itself in two parts, and open to inspection by the interesting parties, for these records applied to the cover: accounts that would show how the anonymous gift was being spent and that would also show the division, in terms of actual purchase costs (since Yale was supposed to be, and so far as it knew, was contributing the whole of Curtiss's salary), of expenses between Yale and the Associated Libraries. Another set of books would be needed to account for the actual OSS work. Initially, however, to maintain the cover, Curtiss's salary for the OSS was to come from the anonymous gift, though when he later openly took a position in Turkey, supposedly under the American military attaché as a translator of German materials, Curtiss did not think it right to live off the Pforzheimer fund and asked to be paid directly by the OSS. This salary was quite sufficient to his needs in Turkey, though less than he would have had access to in the States, since he could not touch his private income, a Treasury license to take his money out of the country being both unlikely and unwise.

The account books themselves were turned over to Walter Pforzheimer senior, in part so that Mendenhall need know nothing about actual expenditures and in part because Pforzheimer was very good at figures. He kept Account No. 1, for "the World War II Collection for Yale and Associated Libraries," and Account

No. 2 for the "Yale alumni donors." These arrangements would cause "no end of complications," and the books would not be closed on the project until early in 1948, by which time the younger Pforzheimer was assistant general counsel to the new CIA and in a position to help close the matter out.

Here recollections differ when set against the record. Curtiss recalls having plenty of money and is quite clear that he never asked for any transfer of funds from the Guaranty Trust. Yet the file shows cables requesting a transfer in his name. The confusion can, most likely, be attributed to miscommunication between bagman and accountant, to Donovan's original intercession with the bank, to the complexities of wartime currency controls, and cable traffic to Istanbul, compounded by the interest of the Associated Libraries. In any case, the senior Pforzheimer received a cable asking—as the garbled message read—for "twe housand Yale funds," while Mendenhall received one requesting the release of $5,000. The bagmen conferred and decided that Pforzheimer should respond directly, and to read the request as $2,000. Curtiss did not receive the money until mid-August, however; the ALA, which as a matter of cover had to be asked for its funds, mishandled its end and sent checks that were without endorsement and wrongly made out. Pforzheimer tidied up the matter, and then the ALA sent its new check to the wrong address, so that it was delayed in the mail for another month. To this point it appears that Curtiss did not know that any money was on the way, which strengthens the presumption that the cables requesting that money be sent were from someone acting on his behalf rather than from Curtiss. He had found expenses higher than anticipated because of wartime inflation in Turkey, and the exchange rate was quite unfavorable, as Turkey had been flooded with Lend-Lease dollars. He was, however, at no point in need of money, and even after funds were deposited in Turkey for him, he apparently was not informed of them, for he had to be reminded later to draw on them.

Thereafter Curtiss asked to have the money sent to the Near East College Association in New York City, since he had taken up residence at Robert College, outside Istanbul; this meant that the association could wire fund transfers through its Galata office. He then asked for $10,000, and further confusion arose: was the money to be transferred through Guaranty Trust, which had no office in Istanbul, though the Chase bank did have an affiliation with a Dutch bank there, or through the association? In checking,

Pforzheimer learned that Mendenhall had, in fact, authorized the transfer of $5,000 through Guaranty Trust to the Hollandsche Bank in Galata. While Curtiss would buy less and less, as confusion over the money mounted—he had been dropped, it seemed, into "the muddle east"—he was able to acquire mountains of print simply for the asking: before he was finished, two tons of paper would accumulate in various storage areas.

At Robert College, an American missionary school founded in 1863, which in 1913 had taken up land on the heights of Bebek, outside what was still Constantinople, Curtiss struck up easy friendships. A Yale graduate from the class of 1938, David Garwood, who taught English at the college, roomed with him at first, and Curtiss filled their quarters with books, partially because this would support his cover, more because he had nothing else to do. Soon Curtiss was offered rooms in the president's cottage on the college grounds, and there he lived with the new college dean, John C. Bliss, a professor of engineering, and his wife. Curtiss was a renter, helping to meet the inflated household expenses, and from time to time he taught a lesson in advanced English at the college. U.S. Army reserve officers were among the teachers, for most of the regular American staff had gone back to the United States in the summer of 1941, precisely when the college's enrollment had reached its highest point. Mainly, Curtiss spent his first two months sightseeing, ferreting out bookshops, and peering behind counters for old telephone directories, prewar maps, and the like, and buying daily every newspaper he could get his hands on. Since he soon saw that he would attract attention if he did this himself, he employed a Greek assistant, who entered standing orders and brought the papers along to the maid's room at the American consulate, which—with four Yale men posted there—was referred to by them as the Yale Club of Istanbul.

Curtiss had little difficulty maintaining his cover at Robert College, for while there he did exactly that which an academic would do. He taught the odd class as a favor, discussed curriculum questions with Bliss (who was bringing in a revised engineering program), entertained old Yale students and former colleagues who passed through, had tea on occasion with the new president, Floyd H. Black, who had come from the American College at Sofia in 1942 (and who was a special assistant to the American consul general in Istanbul), and passed on the odd book to the college's Van Millingen Library. Had any suspicion attached to Curtiss, it was drawn off by the new American cultural attaché, Donald E. Webster, who was precisely what he appeared to be, a Near Eastern studies specialist in Turkey to promote the stature of the American schools in the Near East. Webster was the channel for grants to the college to study, among other subjects, the currents of the Bosporus, which all could see would be of interest to the spies of every nation. Although Webster was often on campus, Curtiss avoided him, either by being in the city or by simply taking a walk across the leveled central campus to one of the many viewpoints out across the water, or to the Rumeli Hisar, a magnificent fortress built by Mehmet II before the conquest of Byzantium, whose tower rose next to the president's house.[6]

Because there had been an influx of new American teachers in 1942, the students often gossiped about them, trying to guess which were spies, trading romantic stories about which teacher was most likely to have put another body in the Bosporus. Curtiss may have recruited one student to his work—there is an account of an American professor who, claiming that he was a bibliographer, co-opted one Turhan Celik, and a friend of Curtiss's later remarked that he suspected Curtiss had once let his cover slip, though apparently to no harm[7]—but in general Curtiss was too well aware of the tendency of students to gossip; they were, he thought, as bad as diplomats. In any event, Curtiss felt it was best to avoid the students at the college socially, for he could not be certain of their political leanings without asking questions that might draw attention to himself. Once or twice he had a visitor from Yale who hinted of suspicions that Curtiss was up to something—Arnold Whitridge was one such—and now and then he thought his mail was being held up or read. Turkey was, after all, "the land of mystery," Curtiss sardonically wrote to a friend, and he took in stride the occasional suspicions directed at him. Remarkably, there is no evidence that his cover was ever blown, either in Turkey or at Yale, though after the war a colleague who had been in X-2, Norman Holmes Pearson, professed to knowing all about what Curtiss was up to.

Istanbul was a heady center of intrigue—there were four secret and often competing British organizations alone—and Curtiss found his assignment both broadened and, because of the persistent indiscretions of the local head of OSS, "Packy" MacFarland, a good-natured banker from suburban Chicago, also at risk. Lanning MacFarland, as he was seldom called, was ultimately judged by

his colleagues to be "a bull in a China closet" in the "mare's nest
that was Istanbul," an accurate though mixed metaphor. However, MacFarland was close to Donovan, having come in early
with the Coordinator of Information, and he had been assigned
Turkey under circumstances not conducive to well-maintained secrecy, since he had been refused diplomatic cover, and Donovan
had resorted to persuading a reluctant Harry Hopkins to provide
him with Lend-Lease credentials. Nor had MacFarland much time
on the ground, having been delayed until May of 1943. With him
he initially had only two assistants. One, Archibald Frederick
Coleman, a journalist who had served in Naval Intelligence, was
in Turkey as a correspondent for the *Saturday Evening Post,* and
he would in time run afoul of his principal source, Dogwood, a
Czech not further identified in the available record.[8]

The second, Jerome Sperling, who worked apart from Mac-
Farland and Coleman and consequently was not caught up in their
ultimate fall from grace, was from Yale and known to Curtiss,
since he had been an instructor in classics and a fellow of Berkeley College, where Curtiss had often dined with Mendenhall.
Sperling had worked in the Greek province of Elis in the summer
of 1939, technically for the government of Greece, and he spoke
the language. Though at the end of August he had discontinued
his excavations in order to return to the States before war broke
out and made transportation almost impossible, Sperling still had
good friends in high places, including Dr. Spyridon Marinatos, the
director of the Archaeological Service in the Greek Ministry of
Education, and Professor Gorham P. Stevens, director of the
American School of Classical Studies in Athens. With Greece now
closed to archaeological work, Sperling had, with the help of such
contacts, opened up quite legitimate ties with Turkish counterparts, and technically he was now employed by the Turkish government. He was under deep cover when he arrived, though his
connections became known because of the lax security at the outpost.[9] Generally Curtiss would avoid MacFarland and Coleman,
and in turn Sperling pretended not to know Curtiss, even though
he too was living at Robert College.

There were other Yale men in Istanbul or Ankara toward whom
Curtiss gravitated, though he maintained his cover when with them.
Theodore Babbitt, who was Yale's assistant dean of freshmen,
showed up in Ankara (though Babbitt's languages were French
and Spanish) as assistant military attaché, while Charles Mc-

Vickers, who taught political science at Yale, was also in Ankara, as a vice-consul. Those who did know of Curtiss's work, of necessity, were Stephen Penrose, head of Secret Intelligence (SI) in Cairo, and Charles Bradford Welles, '24, head of X-2 in Cairo, to whom it was decided Curtiss should report directly. This was fine with Curtiss, for he knew Welles; they had graduated from Yale College only a year apart.

Welles and Penrose were easy men to work for. Brad Welles was a low-key, well-liked, avuncular officer. In a time when relations with British counterparts were strained, he was particularly good liaison with the British. On leave from his full professorship of classics and ancient history, Welles had simultaneously been an assistant professor of military science and tactics at Yale, for he was a major in the field artillery. (At the end of the war Welles would systematically purge his papers so that his story, whatever it may have been, would not be told.) Penrose, also a serious, thoughtful man, had taught at Robert College before the war, and he had most recently been secretary to the Near East College Association. He was convinced that the academic had a major role to play in intelligence, and when in the spring of 1945 he was offered the presidency of the American University in Beirut, he turned it down to help prepare a report on the need for a postwar centralized, nonpolitical intelligence apparatus (and then, in 1948, he did accept the presidency at AUB).

Penrose was preoccupied with getting OSS operatives behind the lines in Greece which, as the occupying Germans and Bulgarians withdrew, was thrown deeper into civil war. There were, he felt, only two sources of people with fluent Greek available to Americans: academics and archaeologists, who tended to be pro-ELAS (that is, to the left), and second-generation Greeks (who tended to be to the right). Penrose would establish teams that were evenly divided politically and let them report contradictory information, which he then compared against British assessments and with information received from the OSS station in Italy. He relied on Curtiss for his printed materials and on his assistant, a history instructor from Cal Tech, Kermit Roosevelt, for evaluations. (Ten years later Roosevelt would be back in the Near and Middle East engineering a CIA coup against Mossadegh in Iran.) Penrose talked with Welles and with Jerry Sperling about academicians who could work behind the lines, and through Nelson Glueck, a University of Chicago-educated rabbi and distinguished archaeologist, who in 1947 would become president of the Hebrew Union College in Cincinnati, he was able to draw in the American School for Oriental Research in Jerusalem as a cover.[10]

In the meantime, Curtiss had also been brought into the local picture by MacFarland. MacFarland assigned Curtiss the task of being the buffer between the OSS and a Viennese teacher who was obtaining files from the Turks, and introduced him—unnecessarily and foolishly—to the head of the Turkish secret police, from whom Curtiss then received other dossiers for analysis. To make sense of these Curtiss required access to all reports generated by OSS/Istanbul, and thus he learned of the approach to OSS by Count Helmuth von Moltke, who was assigned to Istanbul by the Abwehr with the cover of legal assistant to the German ambassador, Franz von Papen. Von Moltke, who even then was conspiring with the head of the Abwehr, Admiral Wilhelm Canaris, and with the Kreisau Circle, to overthrow Hitler, proposed Plan Herman—that Britain, the United States, and a German "democratic counter-government" based in Austria, should collaborate to bring peace and shut the Russians out from the empire they meant to establish in eastern Europe. When the idea reached the U.S. ambassador in Turkey, then Alexander Kirk, by way of Cereus, the network Dogwood was running for Coleman, he rejected it. Shortly someone within Cereus betrayed von Moltke, who was arrested and executed when he returned to Germany.

Curtiss should not have been aware of the von Moltke proposal, for Curtiss was, in effect, small fry. That he knew of it arose in part from the understaffed nature of OSS/Istanbul, since his analyses were needed. Curtiss suspected that MacFarland's "high, wide and handsome" image was soon to be tarnished, for the Istanbul operation was leaking like a sieve.

It was clear in Washington by late spring of 1944 that Mac-Farland's cover had been thoroughly blown and that all operations in Istanbul were insecure. The British had, from mid-1943, drawn back from contacts with OSS/Istanbul, and in February of 1944 they cut them off entirely. In January a relatively low-level Abwehr employee in Istanbul, Erich Vermehren, with his wife, the Countess Elizabeth von Plettenburg, had defected to the British. In February three more Abwehr defections occurred, this time to two young employees of the Office of War Information, who having no authority to accept defectors had turned them over to X-2. Curtiss had known the Vermehrens slightly in Germany, indeed had visited them in the company of another Yale colleague, Beekman Cannon, then a graduate student in the history of music, in Hamburg in 1938.[11] The Vermehrens were interrogated in Egypt, then in England, and finally in the United States. The other defections triggered the recall of the Abwehr chief in Turkey and a reorganization of German intelligence there, with the Sicherheitsdienst, or Nazi security police, bidding fair to take over. This angered OSS/Berne, which had penetrated the Abwehr at a very high level. Now Berne would lose its double agents in Turkey, and some of its local assets along the way would dry up. From Washington X-2 issued orders forbidding the acceptance of further Abwehr defectors. The chief of SI, Whitney Shepardson, concluded that Dogwood was thoroughly penetrated and that nothing was coming in except chicken feed—deceptive low-level information, some accurate, some inaccurate, deliberately broadcast so that it would be swept up indiscriminately and circulated by the station. Cairo was given high marks while Istanbul was placed under close scrutiny. Since the defections to OWI had caused the British to cut off all services to the Americans in Istanbul, some reorganization was essential in any case.

Soon after it was discovered that MacFarland's personal chauffeur was reporting to the Russian secret service, that the X-2 driver was in the employ of the Turkish secret police, and that a double agent being run by Coleman was reporting to the Germans. (One report suggested these were all the same person!) By then MacFarland could not enter Istanbul's largest casino, Taksim's, without having the band break into "Boo-boo Baby, I'm a Spy," sometimes accompanied by a roll of drums.[12] (Usually the other large casino, Abdullah's, blessedly had no orchestra.) The chauffeur to the American military attaché was also suspect, while the Turks had their eye on the local head of OWI (who had taken a German lover), whom they suspected of running his own spy ring, an unlikely possibility given some credence by the fact that he was a close friend of Franklin Roosevelt's and, moreover, had been briefed by Sherman Kent at OSS before his departure for Turkey. The whole thing was a mess.

From Cairo Welles put Curtiss onto the task of reexamining all OSS personnel files for Istanbul, and some for Cairo, checking for evidence that any of the SI or X-2 contacts had been doubled. Curtiss was also to collate all information brought by an agent, and between agents, to look for chicken feed. He rated the credibility of each report on a scale of A through E and the credibility of each source 1 through 5. He was still at work on this project, having identified one American working with SO in Yugoslavia of whom he had strong suspicions, when the head of X-2 in Washington, James R. Murphy, freshly back from London where he had studied a series of pessimistic reports on OSS initiatives in Hungary and Bulgaria that appeared to have been compromised from Istanbul, decided that he must treat German control over the Cereus network as total. In late June MacFarland was withdrawn to Yugoslavia. Coleman was abruptly brought home, Dogwood vanished forever, and a new head of OSS Istanbul, Frank Wisner, a Wall Street lawyer from Mississippi, was brought in to put Humpty Dumpty together again. By the time Wisner arrived, Curtiss was down to Z-0 analyses: accounts with no credibility from sources with no credibility.[13]

Under Wisner OSS/Istanbul began to get its act together. Reports were now sent directly to Washington with copies to Cairo. Curtiss was thoroughly integrated into the office, becoming the record keeper for X-2, continuing to sift files to identify who was doubling, who was working for the German, Russian, Bulgarian, Japanese (or British) agencies. On occasion he would board the train for Ankara and Baghdad to talk with German dissidents; on occasion he helped members of OWI with their documentation. Forty years later a colleague, Robert Miner, would recall how Curtiss, whom he thought of as "gentle Joe," had reacted with horror when his tough-talking new boss ordered him, with his equally academic assistant, to "rub out" a Hungarian Curtiss had identified as a double agent. And then Wisner, viewed as a whiz kid, was pulled out of Istanbul in just three months to take over a mission for evacuating airmen from Rumania.

And so, in time, the assistant professor of English who had gone to Turkey to obtain information for SI and X-2 and R&A (and incidentally to buy books for a group of American libraries) would become, first, acting head of X-2 and then chief of OSS/Istanbul. To do these jobs he needed to have an office in the OSS, and for this he needed additional cover. Curtiss created his own cover, looking for something flexible enough to extend should the duly assigned head of X-2 not arrive quickly. He told everyone that he had much spare time on his hands and that the assistant military attaché in Istanbul had asked him to help translate German books and documents. In due course the station chief for X-2 arrived, one with whom Curtiss had immediate rapport, Turner T. Smith, a naval officer from Virginia, and the unit grew rapidly, as people were transferred from areas in North Africa and elsewhere that, with the battle now carried to Germany's borders, were no longer important. By now the volume of X-2 material going out far exceeded that coming in, and Curtiss needed his own secretary to prepare final copy for Washington and Bari, so he arranged to have Helen Bliss, the dean's wife, hired. On the day she reported to work, she was startled to find that Curtiss was her boss, so successful had he been in keeping the Blisses from knowing of his real activities. Curtiss was also given the heady code designation, OOS.

Library materials continued to accumulate, in bookshops where they were set aside in back rooms, at the Bliss cottage at Bebek, and in both the consulate and the OSS palazzo. Curtiss took on more recruits, this time for the cover project. Garwood, who spoke Turkish, and Marjorie Mackillup, a librarian on leave from Connecticut College for Women in New London, worked on translations without knowing that their material was destined for use in Washington rather than for the universities. Curtiss now needed someone to handle the cover job itself, since he was fully busy with his genuine OSS work, so a geologist in X-2, John Maxwell, handled it for him. Dean Woodruff, an interrogator with R&A, was drawing heavily on the maps Curtiss had collected to aid him in his questioning of travelers who were arriving in a steady stream from the Balkans, while Robert Bishop, a Chicago newspaper reporter charged with a close study of the situation in Rumania, also used Curtiss's materials until transferred to Bucharest. When Bishop left, Tolly Smith took over as head of OSS/Istanbul, and Curtiss again became acting head of X-2.

Though Curtiss had remained, until late 1944, on the cover budget established through Pforzheimer, he had been given an academic assistant many months earlier, for the cover project had now been attached to the work of the Interdepartmental Committee for the Acquisition of Foreign Publications. London was instructed to coordinate the work of Stockholm, Lisbon, and Istanbul, so that all three were not in pursuit of the same German publications, and Curtiss was told to concentrate on materials from the Balkan nations, from Turkey and from Iran, and to pick up such Russian items as might come to hand as well. Since IDC said that it wanted a copy of "everything" for its clients, including novels and medieval histories—that is, material with low intelligence content—the task was considerable. This kind of material was to be stored at the outpost and shipped by sea when possible. While this enlarged task presented a problem for Curtiss, since storage was difficult (and Istanbul was not selected to be a microfilming station), it was also convenient, as it provided him with a plausible reason for not shipping materials out on a regular basis to any library, including Yale.

As the war in Europe wound down, the outpost was instructed to turn its attention increasingly to information on Japan and, less obviously, to the Soviet Union. SI sent a man to Istanbul to work through the Turkish merchant marine, since Turkish seamen had personal experience with Japanese ports, and Curtiss in X-2 also helped collate information gathered from the Ship's Observers project with materials obtained from the Turks. Everyone at the post was informed of the new emphasis, which they kept in mind even in seemingly idle conversation. An encounter on a beach might prove helpful: "Oh, you were in Japan before the war? I've never been there. And is the swimming as good there as here?" "Hell, once you're in the water, sure, but where I was there was fucking black sand everywhere and mud just under it, what makes for lousy sun bathing." "Which beach was that?—I had always heard Japanese beaches were very rocky." "Shit, most of them are—the one at X and all those along the shore of Y are damned rough, and it's hell to wade in because of the rocks, but at Z you only have to worry about the mud, which you can't see. It slows you down, being just under all that black sand." "Well, I guess I'd rather be here, then: you can't beat the Med for a good swim." The beach information would, that night, go into the file for transmitting, in code via Cairo, to Washington.[14]

In the final year or so of the European war, Curtiss had worked most on two matters. The first was a study of the flow of Turkish chrome into Germany. In September 1943 British and American economic warfare agencies sensed that Germany might be coming up against a shortage of chrome, which was essential to the special alloys needed for aircraft production, as well as in tanks and warships. OSS was instructed to deepen the shortage. R&A, noting that Turkey was the principal source of chrome once the war had begun, studied how to stop or delay supplies. Turkish agreements with the British and French governments to sell surplus chrome only to them had lapsed in 1943, just as the Germans were depleting their stockpile, and despite representations by the British and American ambassadors, and an attempt by the Americans at preemptive buying—which was proving successful in Spain— the flow to Germany continued. When asked to study whether blowing up bridges along the rail route by which the chrome was taken from Turkey to Germany would help substantially, Langer said that it would not. Only two crossings, the Maritsa and the Arda rivers, involved bridges of such size that they could not be repaired quickly, he reported; these bridges could also be replaced with pontoons or ferries. The project remained in thought only until fresh chrome statistics suggested that Turkey was sending even more than its contract called for, that Britain too was hurting for chrome, and that some gesture seemed essential. To Donovan's surprise, both the British and American ambassadors in Turkey then asked explicitly for an "interruption of the railways between Istanbul and Sofia."

Knowing Langer would not change his mind simply because of ambassadorial desires, Donovan sought another opinion, and from a specialist on Balkan railroads he heard what he wanted to hear: that 60 percent of all Turkish chrome destined for the Axis had, the previous year, passed over the Maritsa River bridges, which were just inside Greece and easily reached from Turkey. Donovan ignored the further observation that sabotage against current production of chrome at the source—that is, in Turkey itself—and destruction of Turkish transport facilities would be more effective. In May of 1944, then, two large teams of Greek Communist guerrillas led by a young OSS officer knocked out the two most important bridges. Langer proved correct, however: within a month the Germans had pontoons in place, and Turkish chrome was on its way again. Curtiss, who had collated the information that prompted the two ambassadors to ask that the Maritsa bridges be knocked out, knew nothing of this, of course, until after the war was over.

Curtiss was also busy analyzing "the Istanbul notebook." This was a document that had fallen into his hands through an assistant to the American military attaché; it appeared to be a compilation of Turkish police reports, rather than piecemeal dossiers on individuals, and when set against detailed lists of individual entries and exits that the Turks had sold to the OSS, it looked like a key to "the ecologists of double agency," the happy phrase of Norman Holmes Pearson.[15] When he heard of it Pearson was especially intrigued by the notebook, and he asked to have it sent to London, unaware that the Germans had a duplicate, supplied to them by the same source. Long after the war Curtiss would say that Pearson had instructed X-2 chiefs elsewhere to "let Curtiss in on things," and that he was told in outline of the Ultra secret, that is, that the British had broken the German air, naval, and army codes and were sharing their information with the Americans. This seems unlikely, for Pearson was quite closemouthed about the British, though it is not impossible. Since Curtiss apparently was not "let in on" the single greatest American intelligence coup in Turkey—the identification of Cicero, the Albanian who, as valet to the first secretary in the British embassy in Ankara and then to Sir Hughe Knatchbull-Hugesson, the British ambassador, had been sending a steady stream of high-grade information to Germany through L. C. Moyzisch, the German military attaché—it seems unlikely that he would have been told of the more remote secrets of Ultra.[16] In any event, victory came to the Allied forces in Europe before "the Istanbul notebook" could reveal all that it held.

There were, as Curtiss would later remark, many dull days in his work, compensated for by the throb and mystery of wartime Istanbul. The OSS headquarters was in the old Japanese embassy in Cihangir, and Curtiss worked from subterranean quarters with a window on the Bosporus. He could look out beyond the Leander lighthouse to Üsküdar, and on a good day to the Ulu Dag, high mountains on the distant horizon. There was also the Hagia Sofia to visit, sometimes to exchange ideas with a fellow OSS member who, in his spare time, was taking notes for an architectural history of the great mosque. Curtiss went often to the gigantic Grand Bazaar, by far the largest souk in the world, where—it was reported—there were 4,399 shops and, to his constant delight, the Sahaflar, a secondhand book market in which travel books were jumbled together with old maps, histories, a bewildering array of hand-tooled Korans, or German texts, all under the protecting minarets of the Beyazit mosque. If all else failed to raise the spirits, there was always the ferry ride from the Galata bridge to Haydarpaşa, or up the Bosporus to the landing for Robert College, where he could revive his spirits with raki or thick red local wine. The beauty of the setting never grew stale for him. There were times when it rained on Bebek in great, blinding sheets, turning the country lanes to mud, and Istanbul, if mysterious, was

not truly glamorous, for it was too crowded, often dirty, in the
dry season very dusty, and claustrophobic in its narrow streets.
Yet, somehow it was always fun.

In the meantime querulous correspondence was coming in from
Yale. Where were the books? Curtiss used the fact that the exchange of money was slow to explain the lack of shipments; further, he wrote, he was having to learn arbitrage at first hand, for
the currency situation in Turkey was confused. A moment of in-
attention to detail almost blew Curtiss's cover, for he asked his
mother to file his income tax return for him, correctly reporting a
salary of $4,250, while Yale incorrectly reported that it was $4,000.
He could not explain the reason behind the tax muddle to his
mother, and he had to let the matter rest, hoping no one at Yale
would try to be helpful on his behalf with the Internal Revenue
Service. Walter Pforzheimer was having increasing difficulty
cooking the books, for Tom Mendenhall, overworked with classroom teaching on the crowded campus, had been inattentive himself. When Pforzheimer asked Mendenhall to come into New York,
in April 1944, to clear up the financial tangle, Mendenhall replied
that discrepancies in the accounts arose from the fact that the
ALA was not sharing in Curtiss's salary, that prices had to be
adjusted owing to delays in shipment of books (though no books
were being shipped), that currencies were in chaos, and that all
would come out right in the end. When Mendenhall left Pforzheimer noted that he would "have some tall explaining of payment
of funds" to do, especially to the ALA, though Mendenhall thought
the ALA ought to get the short end of the stick for "horning in"
on the affair anyway.

After V-E day, however, Curtiss turned his full attention to the
libraries, seeking out in particular suppressed Turkish periodicals
and Greek Communist literature. He rendered a clear, if complex,
accounting for all expenditures, advised on how to run the two
sets of books, and began to pack. He happily agreed to receive
books directly on behalf of Harvard. The day after the Japanese
surrendered, Curtiss cabled for permission to return to the States,
and he arrived in late September with boxes of books trailing behind him. When asked why there were not also files of European
daily newspapers in the collection, he explained that they were
unavailable in Turkey and printed on paper that would not last,
though in fact he had simply found that his genuine duties for the
OSS had overwhelmed any daily attention to his other duties, and

daily collecting had proved impossible. Knollenberg, who had long since learned the true nature of the project, and the senior Pforzheimer complained that Curtiss would have done far better had he gone to Switzerland after all.[17] To liquidate the account and transfer the balance from Turkey, Curtiss drew a check to the order of one W. L. Rehm, and inexplicably Tom Mendenhall blew the whistle, asking Pforzheimer what the check was for. With the war over it seemed safe to tell him: Colonel W. Lane Rehm was the head of Special Funds at the OSS headquarters in Washington.

Rehm wrote to George Bowden. Bowden, one of Donovan's most brilliant assistants, had shifted effortlessly from peacetime tax law to the work of a highly confidential staff officer in Washington and then in London. He had been close to Donald Downes and with Hugh Wilson had signed off in 1942 on the OSS funds for the library project. Bowden had left the OSS in 1944, ill and angry over its growing right-wing tendencies (he described himself in a postwar letter to Norman Holmes Pearson as one of the radicals in the agency).[18] Rehm preferred to put his questions about funds to Bowden alone, since Rehm had participated in a "palace revolt" (quickly quelled) against the direction in which Donovan was taking the agency, and Wilson had been the person who had warned Donovan. Jimmy Murphy, for X-2, had reported that Curtiss had done "excellent work" in Turkey, and Rehm wanted merely to clear the books; he had already asked for clarification, and Murphy had asked Pearson, who had been on brief home leave at Yale, to examine the records held by Mendenhall, but Pearson had returned to London, he said, before he could do so. Rehm had been told that Curtiss also drew on unvouchered funds while in Istanbul, and he and his accountant thought such funds ought not to be used for collecting war documents for Yale. The OSS was wrapping up its affairs, charges that it had spent unvouchered funds in a profligate way were being made in various quarters, and though the sum was small, there should at least have been a paper trail to show proper attention to detail. By September 1945 Downes was no longer with OSS, and he had long before turned his files over to Sidney Clark. Bowden assured Rehm that Curtiss was correct, that half the OSS money was to be spent on the purchase of items truly destined for the libraries, the justification being his cover needs, and that only in this way had the "very secret project" remained secure. Bowden thought the files should be closed financially, the price being viewed as "a consideration for undertaking [the] mission," which had proved "very productive of intelligence." The matter was, in any case, clearly delicate, since it was a university that was involved.

In the meantime, Curtiss had returned to the Near East. Yale's classes had already begun when he had arrived, so that he could not quickly take up his teaching duties again, and there was still the matter of clearing up a variety of office routine. Curtiss found himself taking over all remaining OSS activities in Istanbul, including analysis of information on Russian intentions in the area, which he shared with the British, as they did their reports with him. In January 1946 he began to close up the store, and he rendered one last report—or so he hoped—on the tangled matter of finances. There were $19,000 left in the account, since the other member libraries had deposited money to it, and the sum would have to be prorated back to them by some formula that would not reveal that they had, in effect, been used. By now Pforzheimer was quite annoyed, for when he examined the books Mendenhall had kept he found what he regarded as careless errors. Pforzheimer pored over the books and arrived at the surprised conclusion that the contributing libraries had never paid in their $25,000; rather, they had contributed only $4,425, and they owed money to the project. (The funds were subsequently paid in.) Working together he and Mendenhall reached an approximate sense of order—though even today anyone examining the books will find it virtually impossible to make them balance, and something over $2,000 seems to have boiled away while the books were being cooked—and the two Pforzheimers then put their heads together to see how they might deal with the librarians. They could not give a full accounting and properly protect the original project. The younger Pforzheimer advised his father to send a letter to all parties declaring that he had administered the special fund while his son was in the armed forces, that he was thus not privy to all the details, and that a final accounting would follow shortly.

Shortly turned into five months, but in 1948 the file was closed. Jim Babb, who had officially succeeded Knollenberg, was worried, wanting to settle "the matter of the Joseph Curtiss expedition," and when he examined the accounts he concluded that, "of all the Chinese puzzles I have tried to solve in the past 10 years, the World War II Collection distribution and cost analysis takes first prize." Curtiss had not gotten receipts—he could not have done so under the circumstances—so no one really knew how much to charge each library. Using a pro rata basis, Pforzheimer sent the New York Public Library $1,225; money was returned to Princeton, Michigan, Minnesota, and Iowa, all of which had withdrawn from the project when books had not been arriving (Dartmouth and Illinois had withdrawn even earlier); Columbia received a small sum; and Harvard was "probably underpaid." Keyes Metcalf, the Harvard librarian, being no less well connected than the Yale librarian, apparently sensed that there had been a hidden agenda to the project, most likely from Lefty Lewis, and Harvard lodged no complaint. Walter Pforzheimer, patient and exhausted, received Babb's thanks for his tact and goodwill, and sent to Mendenhall his two sets of books with the opinion that, in reality, Curtiss had $130.13 to account for and that he wanted no more of it.

By now Donovan was failing in his efforts to keep the OSS intact. By the summer of 1945 he had seen that he would not win the battle, and he began to send out formal notes of commendation, informal words of thanks, and appeals to friends to remain available to him should the need arise. One such note went to Bernard Knollenberg, then in Washington, to thank him for all of his services, which included "setting up a secret intelligence source in China, Korea, French Indo-China, Burma (with the British) and Thailand." No mention was made of the Yale Library Project, nor did Curtiss receive such a letter.

The OSS was abolished by executive order on September 20, 1945 (to take effect on October 1). R&A was carried over to the State Department as the Interim Research Intelligence Service. At the end of 1945 IRIS, in turn, became the Office of Research Intelligence within the State Department. Here and there small R&A offices survived overseas as well: Honolulu and Istanbul, for example. Though offered a position in Stockholm, Curtiss wanted to return to teaching, and in May 1946 he formally closed the office down.

There was one final, ludicrous act to this muted story. Throughout the war the British had maintained a large intercept station in Bermuda. Under the Princess Hotel over a thousand British employees examined radio, telegraph, and postal traffic. This operation, run by William (from 1944 Sir William) Stephenson's British Security Coordination, passed on to BSC in New York, thence to the FBI in Washington, correspondence intercepted by the Imperial Postal and Telegraph Censorship stations in Trinidad and Jamaica as well as in Bermuda. Britain also intercepted traffic from the United States to Europe, herding ships into port, delaying the lumbering Pan American flying boats, which refueled at Bermuda en route to and from Lisbon. Crews were entertained at the yacht club, and passengers were wined if not dined in the airport lounge or at the Bermudiana Hotel, while a raft of linguists and "trappers" examined the mail on board. At the height of the operation they were able to go through 200,000 pieces of mail for suspicious addresses or markings and submit 15,000 of these to special examination while ship or plane was in port. Curtiss's first shipment preceding the end of hostilities was, in 1944, aboard a vessel that, having sailed from Lisbon, was ordered to put into Bermuda, and there his untidy bundles of pamphlets, brochures, posters, leaflets, timetables—the equivalent of over a ton of labels from tin canned goods—were pawed over, pried apart, scanned for microdots, and packed back together again. Curtiss had not compiled detailed inventories of what he had shipped; what was clear was that only twenty-five of the English titles he had managed to obtain ever reached the United States, and only twenty-two boxes of books ever reached the ALA offices in Chicago.[19]

What, then, had the Yale Library Project accomplished? Not a great deal, one must say, though perhaps enough. X-2 in Istanbul, and R&A as well, had demonstrated their utility overseas, and Curtiss's performance may have helped create the atmosphere by which R&A survived into the postwar years relatively intact. If one presumes a ready-made Research and Analysis capacity important after 1948, this was a contribution. Curtiss had supplied some valuable data to SI and X-2, and he, together with hundreds of others, had demonstrated that the talents of the academic community were of some value to "the real world." The project had brought 4,078 pounds of books, pamphlets, and printed ephemera into American libraries. If Yale's war collection had not overtaken Stanford's, it did contain a number of interesting new goodies: samples of British propaganda in Arabic, Czech, Greek, Persian, as well as Afrikaans, Dutch, French, German, Italian, and Scandinavian languages. There today is a collection of Persian-style prints based on eleventh-century epic poems showing Hitler substituted for Persian rulers, with Churchill, FDR, and Stalin looking on. There are pro-German pamphlets from Holland, there is literature from the resistance movements, and there are COI and OSS reports, slipped in as they were declassified, on the railroads of West and Central Africa, on the ancient aqueducts of Istanbul, on Levantine merchants at the Golden Horn.

Not all came through Curtiss, of course, for Pearson brought items back with him from London, and Kent sent on copies of some declassified R&A studies from Washington. Too, Pruden had written to dozens of Yale men in the armed services, and many had volunteered to help gather up materials. One, Lieutenant Julius Jacobs, sent packets of clippings regularly, and somewhat imprudently admitted that he was in intelligence when, in September 1945, he was sent to "the Bavarian Forest, near the Czech border." Jacobs's flow had continued, from Paris, from Germany, and from points not remarked upon, until the spring of 1946. In the war collection one could still learn what an English restaurant offered under food restrictions and still examine the fabric of a German parachute, as Pruden and Mendenhall had written in 1942. Now one could also study detailed plans of wagons, coaches, marshaling yards, gauges, types of locomotives, fuel depots, repair shops, signal systems, the gradient and length of embankments, of the railway line from Conakry to Kankan. A researcher could check the location of viaducts, learn which had masonry, which piers, could pinpoint the eighteen gasoline dumps to be found in Spanish Morocco in August of 1942, could examine the details of Casablanca harbor as made known to Operation Torch. One could learn, from a person who had clearly walked as well as ridden the line, the actual as opposed to stated carrying capacity of the Dakar-Niger train line. There, obtained from the offices of the Pullman Palace Car Company in Chicago, one could examine the details of the interior of the sleeping cars on the famed Orient Express, often used by Admiral Canaris of German intelligence, while the OSS was, apparently, giving thought to an assassination attempt. Whether any of this matters today, indeed whether it truly mattered in 1942, or 1945, even if answered in the negative, does not set aside this evidence of how scholarly curiosity might be applied in the "real world."

As for the real world, Joe Curtiss did not think Istanbul, or the OSS, or Washington were any more real than his world. He returned to Yale in the late summer of 1946, four years lost to publication and research (though as he had written to a friend, while he might enjoy reading about the War of 1812, "he couldn't quite imagine himself losing sleep over its outcome"), to receive a presidential appointment to the associate professorship (and tenure) that he almost certainly would have earned had he remained at the university.[20] Other friends and colleagues were back from the intelligence wars too: Archibald Foord, Basil Duke Henning, both historians; Brad Welles; Eugene Waith, Norman Pearson, and Ted Hilles in English; even Sherman Kent for a time. The war collection had provided entree to the OSS even for its bursary assistant—a student on financial aid—and he was now back at work on a doctorate. They didn't compare notes much, and Curtiss stuck to his cover story so that only two or three of his colleagues knew that he had served in the OSS at all. These colleagues were on the rise: in a few years Dunham would be master at Curtiss's own college, Jonathan Edwards, while Foord would take Calhoun, Henning would assume the mastership of Saybrook, and Mendenhall that of Berkeley. Curtiss would teach at Yale until his retirement in 1966, having little use for the knowledge of cipher systems, of radio communication, of how to fake documents, that he had learned in 1942, somewhere west of Baltimore, out there in the "real world." His cover in Istanbul was never blown, despite a generally lax environment around him. Someone hostile to the clandestine world of the intelligence agencies could, and correctly, observe that the library project proved the OSS willing to use anyone, to lie, to compromise the integrity of the academic community in order to achieve its ends. But one suspects that, even had the Yale community known in 1945 of the way in which their library was being used as a cover, few would have objected, for hostility toward the intelligence agencies was neither great, nor as yet had it been earned. God alone knew, Curtiss thought, whether the books he had sent back to the libraries would ever be of use to anyone; he had simply to believe that the material collected for the OSS had proved useful, since he was told often enough that it was valued while he was collecting it. Most important, he could pride himself in having done successfully what he had been told to do, never revealing anything to anyone.

With hindsight one suspects the Yale Library Project did not "matter," in the sense that Curtiss's efforts did not produce any truly vital intelligence. The project was typical of hundreds, truer to the real story of the OSS than all the revelatory, overblown, and falsely dramatized tales that retired OSS officers wrote after the war. One can, with the novelist's skills, make the lighting of a cigarette under the bright moon of a Paris lamp post dramatic—

even interesting and true—but if honest one cannot force significance, the historian's final criterion, upon so banal a cinematic moment. Athleticism, derring-do, the cynical use of people, the knife to the throat, all of these were, however, also part of the true story of the boys in Blue, as we will see in a moment, through the eyes of Donald Downes, Curtiss's contact that day at the Yale Club. Yet Downes's story was not typical. R&A was where the scholars were, and if not there, then in X-2. There was, for those addicted to the cloak and dagger, really very little to the story of Joe Curtiss and his time in Istanbul. That was what made it his part of the real world.

CHAPTER FOUR

THE ATHLETE

DONALD DOWNES

No agent for the Office of Strategic Services appears to have been so nearly "the complete spy" as Donald Downes. Close to Donovan, Downes knew where all the OSS bodies were buried. Energetic, knowledgeable about Mediterranean Europe, Downes was deeply involved in one of the OSS's worst disasters: Operation Banana, in Spain. He served with great courage and determination behind the lines in Italy, was engaged in a variety of operations in the near East, and played a useful role in North Africa. While in Washington, Downes was instrumental to several of the most unusual operations ever mounted on American soil.

Some of these operations were patently illegal, and one, which involved burglarizing the Spanish embassy in Washington, earned Downes the undying enmity of J. Edgar Hoover, an emnity that would pursue him into postwar retirement in Italy.

Downes was and is a controversial figure. His friends swore by him. He was an ideal companion, amusing, literate, a superb cook, loyal and concerned for the welfare of others. He was committed to democracy, convinced as the war began that America was the hope of the world, yet deeply disillusioned by the end of the war over the way American leaders had compromised with the forces of Fascism in North Africa, Spain, and Italy. He was not at all afraid of death, "the place," though he greatly feared dying, "the process," and he often referred to his sense of fear. Outwardly he was a relaxed charmer, with a grin on his face that reminded his friends of a child caught with his hand in the cookie jar, but he was burdened with an ever-heavier sense of guilt, as he saw more and more how the spy game was played, how he and his colleagues used others, how human beings he knew and liked were expended in the pursuit of some higher, more abstract, goal. He became deeply ambivalent about his chosen work, pouring out his doubts after the war in a series of novels and short stories, the latter often transparently autobiographical. When he hated, he hated deeply and without reservation: he thought the chief State Department officer in North Africa, Robert Murphy, despicable and said so at every opportunity; he detested Eisenhower, Hoover, and at the time of Downes's death in 1983, Ronald Reagan; he plotted the elimination of Vichy French go-betweens he suspected of working both sides of the street, and he connived at the death of at least one.

There were those who hated Downes with an equal passion. One operative, who felt abandoned by Downes, called him a "fat, worthless bastard." By some he was thought to be insecure, indiscreet, and probably was. When he published his memoirs in 1953, old-line professionals were outraged at the dirty linen he washed in public. He was viewed by those who were well to the right as left-winged, even pink, and though he hated Communists with the same passion as the Nazis, he tended toward socialism quite openly at the end of the war. Downes was one of those operatives around whom a legend formed, as it did around Paul Blum, or the Frenchman, "Colonel Passy," or later around James Jesus Angleton; people liked to speculate about Downes's true nature, his real intentions, his contacts and friends. Long after he had retired, his friends (and the FBI) suspected him of carrying out operations for Israeli intelligence in Italy and the Near East. Because most spies did not admit to espionage in peacetime, Downes (who spied on behalf of the British well before the United States was in the war) was, to some of his colleagues, a little less than clean, one of "the legion of the lost ones." He liked to play the Game enormously, though he never thought of it as the Great Game, his initial Anglophilia notwithstanding. Nor did Downes have the saving grace of being consistent: once intensely pro-British, he came to hate "that rainy, weakened country"; once outspokenly pro-Arab, he became by the 1960s fully committed to Israel; once well to the left, though always anti-Communist, he moved steadily toward the right in his later years. Irascible, in the last two decades of his life frequently ill, the object of one debilitating operation after another "between his navel and his knee cap," even his best friends had to try consciously to remember his good years, when Donald Downes was felt to be one of the best agents the OSS could put into the field.

Downes was, it seems likely, a homosexual in a business that had no tolerance level whatsoever for gays. He solved this problem, for such it was in wartime and always has been in an intelligence agency, by an exclusive association with a friend, an association that endured until 1961. There was a hint or two of Downes's alleged sexual predeliction in his memoirs, and a virtually open admission in his correspondence with one or two quite close friends, but it was not until after the war that his homosexuality was suspected more broadly, and by then, his sexual energies at a low ebb, Downes appears to have left the gay world entirely. His apparent homosexuality would give those who wished to discredit him, to explain his growing sense of anger and his barely sublimated aggressiveness, some opportunities for cheap psychology. Former colleagues believed that the resignation from the OSS of one of Downes's best friends, George Bowden, who had been an extraordinarily effective number two to General Donovan, was caused by the shock of the discovery (though in fact Bowden resigned because he was both ill and increasingly dismayed at what he took to be the rightward trend of OSS leadership near the end of the war). Both Bowden and Downes were said to be whistle blowers in a business that thought all whistles unclean.

In short, Donald Chase Downes, Yale 1926, a moral athlete

amidst the bad eyes brigade, would prove during the war, and proves even now—as an acquaintance remarked—to be "a most delicate case."[1]

Donald Downes came from a Regicide background, his fore-bears having settled in Maryland in the seventeenth century. Born September 30, 1903, in Catonsville, Maryland, Downes was one of seven children. He grew up in moderately wealthy circumstances in suburban Baltimore; as his father was middle aged when Donald was born, and his mother died when he was sixteen, he spent much time with housekeeper-nurses. Late in life Downes wrote an autobiographical fragment on his childhood. He remembered best tastes and scents and least of all scenes. Two incidents that, he thought, ought to have left a mark on him did not: the first was the murder of his grandfather by the drunken superintendent of his canning plant on the Eastern shore, the news coming in at midnight, his father repeating each fact of the murder on the telephone as Downes listened from his bed. The second was the death of his grandmother, who lived with the family in Catonsville, and who one day "simply ceased to exist." Downes grieved that he could not grieve, but he admitted that he had little affection for her from the day she gave his brother instead of him a small silver pig with a tape measure in its belly. Downes remembered far better an older woman at Pine Orchard, on the Connecticut shore, where the family passed their summers, who would drop chocolate-coated peanut clusters to him from her window, and how, when he asked his parents why she never left her house, they told him that she was addicted to gin, her husband having Done Something Terrible and gone away to die. The child Downes detected the tone of cruelty and pleasure in this adult information, and he hated the adult world for it. As he wrote, he never mentioned this, "my first deep friendship," again, and the same intense desire to suppress unpleasant memories that touched him too deeply can be found in his published memoirs, which are not so much inaccurate as simply selective in an unusually complex way.

Still, life in Baltimore was pleasant. His family moved in a literary circle that included H. L. Mencken and others who poked fun at American values, while his mother left no doubt that in marrying a southerner she had stooped beneath herself, so the cycle of the year was built around the moment when she and the children could escape once again to New England. After his mother's death, Downes could muster up no affection for his step-mother, for she was so undeniably southern. Downes was self-conscious about his snobbery—whatever aristocracy might exist in America lay in New England, he thought—and unashamed.

Downes's parents were close to many German-Americans in Baltimore, and his mother was as deeply anti-British as anti-Southern, the heritage of relatives who had fought in the Revolution and of others who were abolitionists. "The Redcoats were always coming, probably guided by Simon Legree and Jeff Davis." Before American entry into World War I mother Downes worked for the German Red Cross Bazaar while father Downes volunteered his time to the Allied Bazaar, and Downes would recall how, the day before German agents blew up a DuPont powder plant in Delaware, his parents had Franz von Papen and Karl Boy-Ed, the German military and naval attachés in Washington, to dinner. The war was fought out at the Downeses' dinner table: Donald sided with his father, England, and those who thought America ought to get into the war sooner rather than later. Yet he was closer to his mother, with whom he shared a tacit conspiracy against the South, and who took him to the Lexington market shopping, where they chewed on dill pickles and pig's feet, walking about selecting the best in fresh foods, before retiring to a raw bar to down a dozen Chincoteague oysters. Looking back, Downes realized that his closest contact with his mother was through food, and his happiest moments as a child were when he could experiment in the kitchen, reading bits of world history while seeing what kind of dish he could produce to surprise her.

His other memories were of early sexual experiences, which seem to have left him little more than curious. There were several occasions, he noted in his manuscript autobiography, when he at nine and a neighbor girl of ten engaged in "hand work," until the girl's imposing father, six-feet-four and with a pointed red beard, began to suspect that something was up behind the privet hedge. And there was the day when one of his mother's friends took refuge in their house, and Downes overheard a discussion of how the husband had run off with a man: he was, the women concluded, a "pervert." Donald slipped out to the dictionary to discover that the word meant one who had turned to error, especially in religion, and since he knew that the friends, like the Downeses, never went to church, he worried that the Downeses were also perverts. Somewhere along the line he also acquired a morbid fear of dust, flies, yellow paint, and stray dogs, just the right preparation (as he noted in 1942) for an assignment to Morocco. There he grew a red beard of his own.[2]

On his thirteenth birthday Downes was delivered by his mother to the Kent School in Connecticut, two years earlier than intended, with the hope of escaping a polio epidemic that had swept through the cities that summer. He fell ill with one of his frequent migraine headaches on the way and awoke to find that his mother had left him in the school's infirmary to return to Baltimore and that the nurses thought he had polio. He knew better, however, and soon found good friends on both the athletic and the literary sides of the school. His roommate, James Gould Cozzens, would become for a time a highly regarded novelist, and through him Donald also became a close friend of Lucius Beebe, poet, railway enthusiast, and fashion plate, whose later New York *Herald-Tribune* columns on food, wine, and gossip much intrigued Downes. (Through Beebe Downes would gain entry to the most exclusive speakeasies during the long national experiment with prohibition.) At Kent Donald acquired one other fear, for Cozzens kept snakes in a box under his bed—at one time there were eleven, including one that was ten feet long—and each fall Cozzens's mother would bring a cage of pigeons, white mice, and rats to stoke up the snakes for their hibernation. As Donald had kept waltzing Japanese mice as pets, the entire scene horrified him. At Kent, too, he learned about the realities of alcoholism, and how it could destroy teachers, his friends' parents, and all sense of humanity. Though he drank, he was ever after on his guard against the affliction.

Downes moved on from Kent to Roxbury, from Roxbury to Phillips Exeter, and then in the footsteps of members of his family, to Yale. At Yale Downes debated, heeled *The Record* (a humor magazine), and tried his hand at theater. He showed an aptitude for languages and the sciences, and he entered on a premedical course, but his sophomore year proved disastrous—he failed one course, withdrew from another, had a D in a third, and was placed on academic warning—and he fell back a year. At first he tried to catch up by going to a summer session at Columbia, where he studied under the noted historian Carlton J. H. Hayes, who would, years later, become his *bête noire* in Spain. Downes's third year was equally unhappy, with poor marks, jaundice, many missed classes, and a severe suspension for an undisclosed infraction (with the written warning that he would be withdrawn from Yale on the next occasion). Warren Hunting Smith remembered Downes, who was a year ahead of him, very well, and thought him even then "quite a character." Downes collected Yale stories and regaled his classmates with gossip about their professors; he loved to keep late hours, reading, visiting, and then to sleep in the next morning, the janitor daily bringing him breakfast in bed. Even then his friends noticed Downes's quick passion, his ready commitment to what he regarded as the moral side in a controversy, and his general lack of respect for another person's system of knowledge: he stood outside other cultures, peering in, curious, unaffected, yet somehow and paradoxically angry with others for their failure to be curious themselves about how reality was essentially a moral construction.

In his senior year Downes roomed alone, did relatively well academically, especially in history and languages, and left Yale with the class of 1926 with the expectation of taking graduate courses in either history or sociology and then going into teaching, first in Great Barrington, Massachusetts. He was, thereafter, officially listed as of the class of 1926—his classmates included Sherman Kent, William B. Kip, John Ringling North, Avery Rockefeller, David F. Seiferheld, and Robert Ullman, all subsequently of the OSS—though in fact he had not completed all of his courses, and he returned to Yale in 1930 and again in 1934–35, formally receiving the B.A. in June of 1935. Downes later remarked that the best thing that had happened to him at Yale were his classes with two historians: George Woodbine, who was extremely demanding and whose course he nearly flunked, and Wallace Notestein, whom he would not have met had he graduated on time, since Notestein did not join the Yale faculty until 1928.[3]

From 1935 to 1939 Downes taught at the Cheshire Academy, in Cheshire, Connecticut, a few miles from New Haven. Norman Holmes Pearson had helped get him the job. At Cheshire he acquired the interest in athletics that he had not had as a student. Though later he would let stand OSS references to him as "a professor" of history, he seems never to have inflated his own claims, and after he completed his degree he moved to Cape Cod, where he taught and coached for five years in a small preparatory school. He then entered upon the life of "paralegal crime" at Notestein's suggestion and with a gentle push from another of his professors at Yale, Bill Dunham.

Downes often traveled in Europe, and he had spent the summers from 1936 through 1939 in Italy, where he had improved his spoken Italian, French, and Spanish, which were quite good, and battered away at his German, which he never seemed able to master. Downes says in his memoirs that in 1939 he read Edmond Taylor's *The Strategy of Terror: Europe's Inner Front,*[4] which alerted Americans to the dangers of Nazi fifth column activities; actually the book was published early in 1940, and it was across the especially gray late winter of 1939–40, while teaching on Cape Cod, that Downes pondered the likely fate of countries he admired. He was particularly taken by Taylor's chapter on "Ideals as Weapons"—an argument that Taylor would develop soon after for the psychological warfare division of the OSS—and was convinced that he ought to do what he could to be of service to Britain. Downes conceived of an anti–fifth column, or sixth column, an organization throughout the countries he expected to be occupied by the Germans, to form sabotage and partisan resistance groups. When, in April 1940, Downes was told that he would have no job the next year, as the school in which he was teaching was closing down because of lack of funds ("and," Downes added in his cynically indiscreet way, "the headmaster's thirst"), Downes took up a letter of introduction to Military Intelligence (that is, to G-2) given to him by a friend. He wanted, he said, a life of cloak and dagger. Downes did not find G-2 responsive.

Downes was not to be put off, however. He was hungry to strike at Hitler, he was without employment, and he was thirty-six years old; he had no time to waste. He called his brother Willard, who was a commander in the Navy Department, and learned that an old friend of his brother, Captain Samuel N. Moore, was acting chief of Naval Intelligence. Downes called on Moore to propose that he ought to make a list of all his friends who had knowledge and skills valuable to intelligence work, and that Downes would combine these contacts to form "information chains, sabotage units, 'black propaganda' cells, economic warfare, and espionage units"—nothing less than an entire intelligence service. Moore was impressed with the scope of the proposal and met with Downes several times, but he could not interest his colleagues at ONI in taking an amateur seriously, and in any event a far more highly placed person, Colonel Donovan, was known to be working on a similar scheme. Moore then told "a big shot in British Intelligence" (almost certainly William Stephenson) about Downes. The best Moore could do, he said, was to get him a reserve commission, give him a letter of introduction to the American naval attaché in Turkey (who could pass him on to a British intelligence unit there), and put him to work on behalf of British espionage in the Balkans. Downes jumped at the offer; he wanted to join the "venerable scoundrel tradition" of the British secret service, to apply his tart tongue, his taste for calumny and provocation, against the enemies of democracy.[5]

Throughout Downes's life there was this odd mixture of schoolboy enthusiasms and naiveté with a cynicism that led him to suspect the worst of those that conventional wisdom—or wartime propaganda—told him were the best. Downes wanted the United States to create a secret service that would rival the British; he thought that Yankee ingenuity could be applied with at least as keen a lack of scruple as the British showed, and he was determined to prove it. There were, he wrote, really only four reasons why a man would want to be a spy, to face suffering, the risks of torture and death that he was certain lay ahead: these were hate, "or hate's offspring revenge"; love of an ideal, an ideology, a religion, or even of a nation or a locality; pure greed, whether for money or physical security and social position; and fear of blackmail. Only the first two motives were reliable; while he thought they generally were not present in the same person, he was, he thought, an exception. He was tired of minor shin-kicking parties, he wrote; he wanted to help the British shovel shit.

Downes had to establish his own cover for going to Istanbul. He approached oil companies and banks, who turned him down; he also tried tobacco merchants. Reasoning that an out-of-work schoolmaster might do better looking to a school for employment, he then went to the New York office of the Near East College Association, luckily on the day the association received a cable from the president of Robert College asking for several new teachers to instruct Turkish army and navy officers in English, so that they might come to the States for advanced studies. These officers already knew German and some knew French. Downes had taught English as well as history, and he had good French and Spanish and passable German: he was accepted on the spot. Having arranged letter drops—people to whom Downes could send his reports—and agreed with Moore on an innocent text code (one which depends on sender and receiver working from identical copies of a dictionary or other book), Downes was briefed by the geographical desk officers in ONI. He drove west with a friend and sailed from San Francisco on the Dutch freighter *Klipfontein*.

The Dutch freighter was, in fact, central to Downes's first assignment. Though the Dutch assumed that the United States would help defend their East Indian ports in the event of a Japanese attack, they refused to supply information on their harbors, and Moore wanted a detailed report, in particular on Surabaya. The crossing of the Pacific was slow and hot; the ship broke a propeller which could not be fixed when they arrived in the Philippines, and the *Klipfontein* limped on to Surabaya, where it was put up for repairs for three weeks. There were eighty missionaries aboard, on their way to run hospitals and schools in Southeast Asia and India, and Downes found them well educated and open minded, contrary to his expectations. Each night he shared their Dutch gin and during the day taught French and American history to their children. When two of the missionaries hired a car to tour Java while the ship was undergoing repairs, Downes joined them on the condition that they spend some time in Surabaya. Posing as a scientist, he took notes on dockside depths, crane capacities, water supply, and the adjacent landing field. When he repeated the exercise in Batavia, the missionaries divined his purpose, and he brought them, and later many of the other missionaries, into his confidence. (In time, several of the missionaries would, on his recommendation, assist the OSS in the China-India-Burma theater, and one of his contacts, Gordon Seagraves, the famous Burma Surgeon, would covertly help Force 101.)

Downes concluded, on the basis of attitudes he observed in Singapore, Calcutta, and Karachi, that the British Empire was doomed. He thought Asia a study in contradiction, especially when, in Bombay, he saw Gandhi arrive at his British dentist's in a Rolls-Royce on which was mounted the injunction, "buy British goods." At Muscat he puzzled over how it was that Britain could produce a person like H. St. John Philby, the Arabist, who was so estranged from his own country. By 1945, however, Downes would understand how British and American patriots could come to the "verge of treason through . . . bitterness," their honor itself a casualty of war, and he considered that he had "come close to growing up" on the long journey up the Persian Gulf.

The Near East, in which Downes worked from October 1940 to March 1941, taught the schoolmaster how to mask a growing sense of despair with outward anger. He found most military men bound by convention, unwilling to try anything remotely daring, and except for two State Department representatives who were busy with the large cloak-and-dagger industry in Baghdad, he thought diplomats simply stuffed. He admired two Englishmen who had broken into the Italian embassy there to take decoded correspondence, and when he met with SOE conspirators over good food and wine, and learned his tradecraft at first hand, he felt "considerable awe" for the men to whom the American attaché had sent him. He spent a good bit of his time cultivating the Japanese naval attaché, but when he suggested to his American contact that the Japanese officer's "appetite for white girls" would make it possible to get information out of him, Downes sensed the shock his fellow American felt, and he simply decided that he would have to use people in his own way. Though he liked the little Japanese, especially so for the Shinto shrine at which he worshiped, Downes got on with the task as he saw it, hiring a young woman to meet the attaché's needs whenever he wanted at a hotel near Taksim's cabaret. At Robert College, where he met his classes faithfully (and, as he would subsequently learn, angered the administration) he tried to spot good fodder for agentry, and when, throughout February 1941, the Turks lived under the nightly rumor of an impending German preinvasion air raid, he happily fed those rumors in any way he could.

In these days before there was an organized American intelligence presence in Turkey, the British welcomed Downes, and he quickly was put onto the job Moore had foreseen: using his American passport to act as a courier into Rumania, then controlled by a few thousand German military instructors and several Gestapo "tourists," or to Bulgaria and, less often, Greece. Downes took into his confidence a spry old archaeologist, Thomas Whittemore, who in the twenties had supervised the restoration of the Sancta Sophia, and who knew everyone who mattered in Turkish society (and in the secret police). When, in November 1940, the Italians marched into Greece, Downes also plunged into the Byzantine politics of Macedonia. He was perfectly aware of what the British would do—if a presumptively neutral American were picked up in the Balkans, they could deny all knowledge of him, or at the least, disavow anything he might have got up to, since one knew how silly American academics were likely to be. Essentially Downes was a courier, carrying memorized messages to the Balkan capitals, most often Sofia, leaving Istanbul each Friday afternoon on the Orient Express. The old train had none of the romance of legend—it moved so slowly, one could step down, pick flowers, and then walk alongside the train as it pulled up grade—but Downes took care to make sketches of its interior compartments, to measure the width of the gauge while stopping for his flowers, to sketch the uniforms (plum-color abandoned in favor of wartime drab) of the few attendants. Feeling a little foolish, he always put a hair across the lock of his suitcase, to see if it was opened on the train; it always was. Upon his return, Downes would report to a British attaché whom he knew only as Commander Brass, to a civilian employee of British intelligence, or to S. W. "Bill" Bailey, a British mining executive with extensive knowledge of Balkan politics, who after Britain broke off diplomatic relations with Rumania and Bulgaria (in February and March respectively) was organizing a propaganda team in Istanbul. He did not go to the British offices, always reporting over coffee at the Pera Palace, Istanbul's leading hotel.[6]

Downes was especially interested in establishing contacts with the International Macedonian Revolutionary Organization, or IMRO, a terror and assassination cadre that operated in Serbia, Greece, and Bulgaria. In Sofia, where he observed the Orthodox Christmas, Downes cultivated any anti-German movement he could find regardless of its political coloration, moving among Albanian nationalists, both Tosks and Ghegs, talking with members of left-wing peasant movements, reporting to the British while storing up contacts for the day when, he was convinced, the United States would also operate in the region. Again Downes's knowledge of food helped, for as he said, only half facetiously, the IMRO leaders all seemed to be pastry cooks, a good cover for moving about the world, and the leader with whom he worked most closely, Smile Voidonov, was interested in equal measure in Macedonian independence, killing Germans, and making crisp pastry. While Downes made light of these months, and passed them off in his memoirs with little commentary of substance, the Macedonians (particularly in Greece) took him quite seriously and remained in touch with him long after he returned to the United States and America had entered the war.

The Macedonians trusted Downes and hoped that he would throw American policy toward Kimon Georgiev and Nikola Petkov, who had realized that the British found them far too left wing. (Georgiev, a former prime minister of Bulgaria, would wind up living in

Washington, and Petkov, a non-Communist agrarian leader, was executed by the Communists at the end of the war.) The British, in turn, thought that Downes was insecure, especially when he used a student at the American College of Sofia, Christopher Yanev, as his contact man, and they concluded that Downes—who was passing all that he learned to the American naval attaché as well— would most likely create problems for them. At the end of March Downes was ordered home by Moore, on the ostensible ground that he would be needed in the States, since war was near. He had by then sent more than fifty coded reports on to ONI.

At the last moment Downes was asked to take some sealed documents from Istanbul to Jerusalem, and he did so by persuading an acquaintance, a Hungarian countess who was traveling on the same wagon-lit, that she was likely to be robbed or murdered while on the train unless Downes protected her, which he did, hiding the papers under her mattress. He and the countess also shared a hired car from Beirut to Jerusalem, the papers hidden, unknown to her, in her coat. Downes carried off these antics nicely, and when he took an "undisciplined peek" at one of the packets of papers, and realized that they were of little significance, he concluded that the entire episode was simply a test of his discretion and ingenuity. He would, he thought, hear from the British again.

But Downes was unable to follow orders and return to America quickly, for he now learned that he could get no passage to New York for six weeks. He settled into the Hotel Saint Georges in Beirut and began to add to his Brown Book—a listing of likely candidates for the intelligence service, beginning with the missionaries he had met on the *Klipfontein* and carrying through with anti-Vichy French and American missionaries in Palestine. All his life Downes would keep these somewhat indiscreet listings—of those that survive in his papers, one is startled to come across names that, upon second thought, seem far less unlikely than on first—of people he felt he could count on for information. Downes then fixed himself up with credentials as a correspondent for *The Nation* and placed the airport at Aleppo under surveillance, until he could attest to the presence of seventeen Junker transport and a company of German parachutists. Despite efforts by the Deuxième Bureau and the Sécurité Militaire to keep him in Beirut, Downes slipped out to Jerusalem with the help of an American vice-consul and provided the British with the first confirmation that the Germans were using the Aleppo airport.

But then the way opened to start home, by bus to Baghdad.

There Downes was again delayed, and he spent his time working with a group that was helping Norwegian pilots, who had escaped via Sweden, Finland, and Russia, to get to the United States, from which they went to Camp Little Norway in Canada, where the Royal Norwegian air force was being retrained. This work proved a godsend, for one of the Norwegians, Morten Krog, later the Norwegian air attaché in Washington, helped Downes get transport on the same flight to Bombay that was carrying the pilots. From India Downes sailed on the *President Grant*—inevitably dubbed the *President Grunt* by the passengers—across the Pacific and through the Panama Canal to New York. The ship's master was pro-Axis, prominently displaying a signed photograph of General Franco in his cabin; the crew below-decks was Communist; most of the passengers, a motley group who went into the Brown Book, were anti-Axis liberals. As Downes later remarked, the odd voyage prepared him for what he was to find back in the States: isolationists, domestic fascists, socialists, democrats, all with their respective views of the war, all trying to collaborate with one power or another, using people cynically to their own ends.

After a debriefing at ONI Downes found himself again unemployed, and through his brother he made contact with the Association to Defend America by Aiding the Allies, where he worked with Mrs. J. Borden Harriman and with Count Carlo Sforza of Italy, a leader among the exiled statesmen of Europe. Sforza, in turn, put him onto the Free World Association, a gathering of European exiles that included Julio Alvarez del Vayo, a former Socialist minister of foreign affairs for Spain, and Pierre Cot, former minister of air for France, and there Downes worked with Clark Eichelberger. These organizations provided excellent cover, and many of the lesser exiles went into the Brown Book, for Downes intended to approach the British for another assignment. In the meantime he worked on pro-Allied broadcasts for the University of the Air, introduced talks by refugee VIPs, and cultivated German labor leaders. In September 1941 he reestablished contact with British intelligence through the BSC.*

BSC had begun early in 1940, when British MI6 had contacted

---

*A discrepancy here may serve to illustrate the contradictions between Downes's published memoir and his papers. In his book he states that he initiated contact with British intelligence (p. 59). In typed answers to a questionnaire prepared in the 1960s, by which he was seeking a renewal of his American passport, Downes naturally stated that a representative of British intelligence contacted him.

the FBI to suggest cooperative measures directed against espionage. It did far more than open Joe Curtiss's mail. William Stephenson, Canadian electronics millionaire and confidant of Winston Churchill, had come directly to President Roosevelt, first to confirm that British research on the isotope U-235 was proceeding rapidly (as it was in the States), and to warn that measures must be taken to keep English research centers from falling into German hands, and second, to tell the president of the rapid progress the British were making at Bletchley in breaking the German code system. Stephenson warned Roosevelt that the British suspected leaks from the American embassy in London, and while these leaks might be intended only to strengthen American isolationists, sensitive information could well fall into German hands. The FBI had taken the position that no British secret agents were to operate on American soil (which included the embassy in London), and the U.S. State Department had maintained that any formal Anglo-American intelligence collaboration would infringe American neutrality. Stephenson then went to the director of the FBI, J. Edgar Hoover, whom he had met through a mutual friend, Gene Tunney, the world heavyweight boxing champion, and proposed limited cooperation to protect atomic secrets, diplomatic traffic, and other information of concern to both countries, and Hoover agreed, provided FDR were to personally instruct him to cooperate. Acting through an intermediary, Ernest Cuneo, one of his confidential advisers, the president did so. On May 20, 1940, Special Branch detectives in London entered the apartment of Tyler Kent, the American embassy cipher clerk, and found nearly fifteen hundred top secret documents.

That same month Stephenson was appointed head of a small MI6 office in Rockefeller Center, to operate under the usual SIS cover as a British Passport Control Office, for liaison with the FBI. His group had no title, but when the State Department required that it register, it became the BSC. In time it would grow to a thousand employees. Stephenson promised Hoover that he would cooperate with the FBI, not employ Americans, and would have no independent agents of his own. He quickly fudged this promise, and Hoover's wrath, which could not so easily be brought down on the well-placed Stephenson, fell like a summer storm on the American agent BSC had employed: Donald Downes.[7]

Downes was eager to be recruited, and when he met with a "Mr. Howard"—in fact Colonel Charles Howard "Dick" Ellis, a top British secret agent who had served for twenty years in the Near East, Russia, the Balkans, and Germany, and who was now Stephenson's number two—at a chophouse looking out on the skating rink at Rockefeller Plaza, he agreed to spy on his fellow Americans to see whether Nazi money was supporting isolationist groups. As his cover Downes proposed to keep his position with the Free World Association and imposed three conditions: that he be paid only expenses (which he drew on handsomely, to buy a new car and to eat truly well), that he be permitted to inform Sam Moore of what he was doing, and that he be allowed to pass any information he turned up to an appropriate American agency if he saw fit. He was able to reconcile working for two masters, be- cause both had, he reasoned, the same end in view, and while he reported to John Pepper at BSC, he also hoped to have access to FDR through Ernest Cuneo, and by that route could keep the president informed in general terms of what Stephenson, Ellis, or Pepper might ask him to do. Cuneo kept Downes at arm's length, for though he liked him, and thought him a charmer, he also spot- ted Downes as a rogue elephant, a "born loser" living in a giddy euphoria of complex plotting. Downes asked him to see if the State Department would let the OSS forge American passports, earning the lasting enmity of Mrs. Ruth Shipley in the passport office; he also asked Cuneo to ask the FBI if they would permit him a letter drop in Buenos Aires, to which the FBI consented, and then Downes sent two agents to Argentina, where they were soon compromised, and tried to parlay the one permission into letter drops for Caracas and Havana as well. He was, then and later Cuneo felt, "running amok."

Thus, Downes, an American citizen, in contravention of any number of American laws, became a spy for British intelligence, with the goal of undermining anti-interventionist organizations by demonstrating, if he could, that they were unconscious dupes of Nazi Germany. He set up a network, arranging cut-outs and mail drops, and focused on the German consulates and the German embassy in Washington. He soon concluded that one German at- taché above others was a likely conduit of funds, and he placed this man under surveillance. Downes was especially interested in Senator Burton K. Wheeler of Montana, a progressive who broke with Roosevelt and announced the formation of an antiwar wing on June 30, 1940; Senator Gerald Nye, whose isolationism had become increasingly intense, and who had many followers who thought that munitions manufacturers were, once again, behind the war; James D. Mooney, head of overseas operations for General Motors; and the always boyish Charles Lindbergh. Downes also investigated a Republican party county chairman in central Ohio, identified an instructor from Amherst College who made frequent visits to a Yorkville pastry shop, apparently to receive funds from the German embassy, and inquired into a variety of "silver and other colored shirt outfits." He told Norman Holmes Pearson of his inquiries in Ohio, and when he went up to Yale he talked with Professor Sidney K. Mitchell, an English medievalist, about the America First movement and the views of its student leader, Kingman Brewster, Jr. He also pried into the work of the German consulates in Boston, Cleveland, and Chicago. Downes had hoped to demonstrate a clear connection between the Nazi Bunds and America First, but he concluded that most leaders of America First, and perhaps of other isolationist organizations as well, were ignorant of the Axis contacts of some of their members, and though in October he was able to prove the transfer of funds from Nazis to groups in Boston and Cleveland, he felt he had failed. On December 7, 1941, he typed out his report to say so.

Downes enjoyed working for BSC, and he was delighted that Colonel Donovan had been charged with the creation of an American intelligence apparatus, and that he was initially looking to BSC for guidance and to the BSC/SOE training program in Canada for a model before COI schools in Virginia and Maryland might be opened. (At some point, most likely between June and December 1941, when Downes's movements remain unclear, he was given a two-week course in mapping, fieldcraft, weapons, demolitions, communications, and cipher, and was taught the rudiments of unarmed combat, which the British more straightforwardly called silent killing. Later Downes professed to prefer two methods: a rock in a sock, which would crack a man's skull, or the sudden thrusting of the index fingers into the corners of an opponent's mouth, which would "tear like blotting paper," or so he hoped.) Downes approved of Stephenson's systematic harassing of America First, even and in particular of Congressman Hamilton Fish, whom Stephenson made to appear to be in league with Hitler. Ellis apparently kept Downes at some distance, however, since he was not British and might well disapprove of some of the more ungentlemanly tricks which Stephenson and others thought up for discrediting antiinterventionist groups. He did come to know David Ogilvy (who remained after the war to become the man responsible for the Hathaway shirt eye patch), Christopher Wren (son of the author of *Beau Geste,* P. C. Wren), Gilbert Highet, who became professor of Latin at Columbia, and the formidable A. J. Ayer, the Oxford philosopher. He also remained in touch with Dick Ellis, and after the war interested himself in the accusations that Ellis had been working for the Germans and, later, the Russians, accusations Downes thought quite mad. But Downes worked most closely with John Pepper, the Stephenson deputy who was on social terms with Donovan.[8]

In this way Downes's path crossed that of Dusko Popov, a remarkable double agent who, as Tricycle, had operated in Britain and was now in the United States. There is no evidence that Downes was aware of Popov's role, as an agent for the Abwehr and for the British, and then for BSC in New York while on assignment once again from the Germans, and their paths may have converged only in their common hatred of J. Edgar Hoover. Both, however, reported directly to Pepper. When Popov came to the United States in August of 1941, he brought with him a questionnaire provided by his German employers, a questionnaire he was to use in Hawaii to record detailed information on Pearl Harbor. As this information was to be passed to the Japanese, Popov concluded that it pointed toward a Japanese attack on that naval base; he delivered the questionnaire to the FBI and repeatedly tried to draw Hoover's attention to its possible significance. Hoover, learning that Popov was keeping a young Englishwoman in what the puritanical director thought of as sin, denounced Popov as a playboy and refused to pay attention to his argument, and the questionnaire appears to have been shelved or, at best, taken as insignificant. While Popov's memoirs, published in 1974—two years after the publication of Sir John Masterman's official report on the work of the Twenty Committee had made known the basic outlines of Popov's activities as Tricycle and had referred to the Pearl Harbor questionnaire*—no doubt embellish the dapper Yugoslav's part in the affair, they clearly and convincingly attest to the irrational dislike the FBI director had for him, for BSC, and for his offense against Hoover's views of sexual propriety. Popov, who was one of the figures upon whom Ian Fleming drew when

*See Chapter Five.

he modeled his fictional James Bond, concluded (correctly) that Hoover was a bigot who (probably incorrectly) had buried the Pearl Harbor questionnaire rather than see it credited to a competing intelligence operation.[9]

Certainly Hoover was irrationally angry when the BSC came to mind, and not utterly without cause, for Stephenson did not keep to his side of the no-poaching agreement, and Donald Downes, in particular, offended against all that Hoover stood for, or claimed to stand for. Downes had, after all, worked actively in support of American intervention in the war, against Hoover's express agreement with Stephenson, and while Stephenson might make some pretense of having personally kept his promise, his surrogate, Downes, clearly had not done so. Indeed, there is some evidence that Downes's first attempt to burglarize the Spanish embassy in Washington, which he attributes in his memoirs to the initial months of employment by OSS, was in fact carried out while he was still working for BSC. (He may also have gone to Mexico on a BSC mission.) One close friend says that Downes entered the FBI headquarters and stole files from their confidential archives as well.

As soon as Donovan had begun to set up COI, Downes had established contact, but he remained with BSC until the Japanese attacked Pearl Harbor. He then went to see Allen Dulles at his office in Rockefeller Plaza to ask for work; Dulles fought shy at first, for the OSS would inherit all the liabilities Downes would bring with him as a former agent of a foreign power that had violated the Neutrality Act. Donovan, David Bruce (who became a persistent supporter of the hyperactive Downes), and others in the new agency would see him only in their homes, for though they suspected that he was under FBI surveillance, they felt that the added distance implied by not meeting Downes at their offices might placate Hoover somewhat. Donovan was prepared to take the risk of taking the tainted Downes aboard, however, and thereafter Downes remained obstinately loyal to a man he came to admire deeply, though not without reservation.

Given an office elsewhere in New York, so that he need not come to Rockefeller Center, Downes hired his niece as his secretary, drew on his Brown Book to help OSS in its recruiting, and settled into a close working relationship with George K. Bowden, former Wobbly organizer and corporation and tax lawyer who was functioning as Donovan's chief of staff in New York. Soon after,

Bowden persuaded Donovan to accept Downes more fully into the fold, moving him into the OSS headquarters in Washington. From there Downes plotted how to obtain the codes and cyphers of four neutral embassies, Spain, Portugal, Turkey, and Vichy France. In March Bruce approved an effort to penetrate the Spanish embassy in particular, for he was convinced that the Spanish were sending information to the Germans, spying on American aircraft factories, and falsifying their records on gas and oil consumption in order to refuel German submarines at sea.

Downes began with the embassy of Vichy France, since most of the staff there were already reporting to some branch of American or British intelligence. He later claimed that the cost of the codes was "a good deal" of amorous time by two of his assistants and the son of a British intelligence official, since one highly placed Vichyite demanded both money and love, not only for herself but for her daughter, a story that rings false, though certainly Downes was not above encouraging the use of sex to achieve his ends, usually targeting secretaries who had access to records. At least nine informants were discovered in the embassy, however, while Downes added a tenth, and when he put his team in place, they found that the military, naval, and diplomatic codes that they photographed had already been passed to the United States (and, he was certain, to the British) by the various attachés.

He therefore turned to Spain. Downes spoke the language, and he decided to begin by planting Spanish-speaking secretaries, who would report to him, in the embassy. Most of the embassy secretaries lived in one of two boardinghouses near Connecticut Avenue. Using a go-between, Downes contacted the presidents of two of the Seven Sisters women's colleges, asking if each would grant a leave of absence to one Spanish teacher. One was found who was of Spanish ancestry and who could, in fact, pose as a secretary, for she had both typing and shorthand. Moving into one of the boardinghouses, she cultivated the embassy secretaries, reporting on them in detail so that Downes would know how best to lure one away from her job. He then persuaded a friend in the International Telephone and Telegraph Company to advertise for a secretary who precisely fitted the circumstances of the target; Downes's plant drew the secretary's attention to the advertisement, and when she applied for the job she was hired at once; in turn, she recommended her unemployed friend to the embassy position. To Downes's surprise, a second embassy secretary followed the first into IT&T, and he then planted his second secretary. The same technique was duly applied to the Portuguese embassy as well.

Downes had, in the meantime, assembled a team of photographers who could also supervise the safecrackers he intended to hire. Using the story that they wished to make color films of folk dancing in the neutral countries, for use by American museums, Sidney and Sarah Black—actually Sidney and Eleanor Clark—settled into a suite at the Wardman Park hotel where they entertained embassy personnel to the point that they became regular guests at embassy functions. They were to draw off embassy staff for entertainment in their hotel suite on the nights when the burglary team was to open the embassy safe and photograph the files. With the cooperation of Colonel Eugene Prince of Army Counterintelligence, Downes acquired an expert in blowing safes, and through his BSC contacts he recruited an expert on picking locks and repairing safes. When all was ready the secretary would damage the lock to the embassy's safe by striking it with a jeweler's hammer, and when the embassy called the manufacturer to repair the safe, Downes had arranged that it should be his man who was given the job. While repairing the safe, his expert would make himself a key so that it would not be necessary to break into it. In this way Downes's team could hope to return to the safe on a regular basis, and the embassy personnel would not be alerted to change their codes before the time was due.

As backup Downes also recruited several anti-Franco Spanish refugees, about half of them acknowledged Communists, to hang around the cafés where the embassy staff ate and to be on hand for possible rough stuff. One day the Spaniards brought to him "one of the handsomest young Americans I've ever seen," a merchant marine in his mid-twenties who spoke excellent Spanish. Downes fitted him up with a tailor and wads of money and told him to prey on the Spanish secretaries at the embassy. Downes doubted that much would come of this, but he liked to move on all fronts simultaneously, and it was pleasant to think about the use of immoral means to attain moral goals, a notion that would, he thought, irritate Hoover nicely when he inevitably learned of it.

The real opposition, Downes believed, was the FBI, for the OSS had no brief for operating anywhere in the Western Hemisphere. He decided, with a kind of childish guile, that he would argue that an embassy was foreign soil and that the OSS had "technical grounds on which to proceed." The rationale was not tested for four months, for Downes's plan worked, his team safely entering the Spanish embassy without challenge, even though they carried four large suitcases, returning with over 3,000 photographs. Downes kept the worried Donovan informed in the most general terms through Bruce, and Donovan warned him that what he was doing was "very much against the law . . . If you get caught we're in terrible trouble." Downes told him not to worry: were he to be caught he would swear that a foreign power was behind him, and if he were put into prison until the war was over, he would count on Donovan to "spin him out" afterward. But Downes enjoyed his derring-do too much, and he let the game go on too long. Hoover thought that someone in the OSS was penetrating embassies in Washington—indeed, Naval Intelligence was burglarizing the Japanese embassy as well—and since he suspected that Downes had carried out just such an operation against the Japanese consulate in New York when he was with the BSC, he knew whom to watch. Hoping to catch the burglary team red-handed, Hoover waited, and at the appropriate moment put two squad cars of FBI agents around the Spanish embassy while the team was inside. The three burglars escaped across the roof, leaving the safe unopened, however, and reported by telephone to Downes, who immediately called his supervisor, who in turn, with Downes, called on Donovan.

This effectively ended Downes's assaults on the neutral embassies, for though Donovan backed him, protesting Hoover's attempt to arrest the OSS agents, Downes had become a Typhoid Mary. Downes was ordered to turn over his projects to the FBI, which to his disgust treated his team of burglars as common criminals. Thereafter Hoover apparently ordered that a file be maintained on Downes—it is said that it grew to over 2,000 pages—and hounded him wherever he went, with accusations of being a Communist, immoral, perhaps a dealer in drugs, accusations that followed Downes deep into the 1960s when he had long left the United States to become a permanent resident of Italy. Downes, in turn, was obsessed with Hoover, keeping clipping files on him, rejoicing in his death, at last, in May of 1972.

There were, of course, many other operations in Washington in which Downes was involved, and he remained active until the embassies project became too well known within OSS itself to allow Downes, who was viewed by many as a loose cannon on the deck of an increasingly militarized, more sober organization, to continue. Before Downes was transferred overseas, however, he had his hand in a baker's dozen of operations, some amusing or abortive or both, some important. Of these, the activity in which Downes put the most stock, though he was kept to its periphery by those who distrusted his judgment, was the creation of a Labor Desk in OSS.

Afterward Downes thought of the many projects, spun out from Washington while he was hoping for an overseas assignment, as the product of enthusiastic amateurs. The top executives at OSS were willing to try any idea that would either hurt the Axis or provide information of use to the armed forces, and Downes, who was technically a member of the Special Activities unit, as it was then called, was profligate with ideas. Bowden had brought a friend of his, a labor lawyer from Chicago, Arthur Goldberg, into OSS, and Goldberg, Bowden, and others created the Labor Desk, drawing at first on the refugee German labor leaders Downes had been cultivating. Reasoning that suppressed labor organizations in German-occupied countries would welcome support, especially if it came from other labor men, and convinced by the success he had with a French labor leader, Léon Jouhaux, to whom he slipped money via Switzerland while working with the Free World Association, Downes talked the subject up. When Goldberg took on the work Downes found himself being edged aside, however. Soon members of the International Transport Workers Federation were supplying target information on the Continent, while a Belgian, Omar Becu, a former official of the ITF, who had already been working for British intelligence, identified existing cells of the federation still functioning in the occupied countries. When ITF representatives met in London in May 1942, Becu offered to identify radio operators and other personnel for recruitment directly into OSS, and a Labor Desk was established at the London OSS outpost as well. From February to mid-December, the Labor Desk and Special Activities worked as a team, from 7:30 in the morning to a final Scotch at Bowden's Q Street apartment sometime after midnight, and thereafter Goldberg, in particular, nursed the labor contacts to a high level of effectiveness. On the suggestion of Heber Blankenhorn, several officials of the National Labor Relations Board were added to Goldberg's staff, and the general counsel to the NLRB, Gerhard Van Arkel, was sent to North Africa as soon as it was possible for him to go, as Goldberg's representative. To his pleasure Downes would find himself working with the labor group again and more closely when he received his own assignment to North Africa following the Torch landings in November.

In the meantime Bowden and Downes were spinning other webs. Downes worked with Dr. Paul Schwarz, a former German consul-general in New York who had resigned when Hitler took over and, in 1938, become an American citizen, and the Baron von und zu Putlitz, former German chargé at The Hague, to prepare an "encyclopedia" of information and gossip on German diplomatic and military personnel, meeting in happy communion over herrings, boiled beef, and beer at Luchow's restaurant. Through Eugene Prince, Downes linked up with a rather foolish German, a well-known former minister of the Weimar Republic, Gottfried Reinhold Treviranus, to help create Project Skipper, by which Treviranus was to contact old friends who would plan a series of assassinations to exploit the factions within the Nazi party: this project was abandoned soon after Downes left for Africa, because the State Department objected to the use of Treviranus, who was viewed as too far to the right. A third scheme was also aborted by the intervention of the State Department, this one Project Freiheit—which was intended to use Paul Hagen, a German labor leader, to organize a plot against Hitler—because he was felt to be too far to the left.

There were also several more modest efforts in which Downes played some small part. One was the creation of a school to train agents how to pick locks and use gadgets by which letters could be examined without leaving a trace. This was put in the hands of Sid Clark and his wife, who following their Wardman Park adventures set up an apartment on Central Park West in New York City. (They also taught booby trapping, knife throwing, and helped those who needed to improve their English.) Another project was the creation, classifying, and storing of a wide range of covers, to have ready at a moment's notice for sending a man abroad—this was the idea of Downes's good friend Robert Ullman, who developed the concept further, arranging with the presidents or chief personnel officers of several companies to take on an added employee for posting abroad. There was the "I Cash Clothes" project, not original to Downes but pursued vigorously by him, in which immigrants and refugees were offered new clothing in exchange for their European suits, shirts, ties, shoes, underclothes, watches, shoe laces, gloves, glasses, knives, buttons, keys, pens, pencils, suitcases, or handbags (into which a long-distance short-

wave radio, the X10, could be fitted)—anything that would be
needed by someone about to be sent into occupied territory. The
OSS canvassed charitable organizations, wrote friends around the
country, and approached needy Europeans directly, giving it out
that clothes were to be parachuted to Europe's poor, but that
American clothing ought not to be used since it would cause problems for the recipients with the Nazi police.

There were, given the athletic enthusiasm of the amateurs, silly
projects as well. Project Penetrate MacArthur was an effort to
shoehorn an OSS unit into General Douglas MacArthur's theater
despite his expressed desires to the contrary. Project Ignatius was
a proposal to use the Vatican diplomatic bags for the transmission
of materials, an idea vetoed by Donovan, who said that he refused
to use either the church or the Red Cross for intelligence purposes. Yet another was an attempt to counterfeit Japanese money
over the opposition of the State Department. There were plans to
demonstrate that Hitler and Mussolini were consumed with mutual homosexual lust, and discussions of how to drop human feces
from the air into water supplies and swimming pools.

Downes was excited about four projects above others. One was
the conception of the Yale Library Project, which sent Joseph
Toy Curtiss to Istanbul, and though Curtiss's efforts proved disappointing in the end, Downes was pleased to have initiated it
through his good friend Wallace Notestein. There was the Ship's
Observers project, picked up from the English and put by Bowden into the Labor Section, as it had become, by which sailors
would report on traffic in the ports in which they called, or agents
would query sailors about beach and harbor conditions: from these
efforts OSS was able to prove that Spain was refueling Axis submarines with American oil, and that American machine tools,
loaded on Russian ships as part of Lend-Lease, were falling into
Japanese hands. (A separate Basque Ship's Observers scheme was
organized in South America with the help of Don José Antonio de
Aguirre, the president of the Basque Republic, who was a professor at Columbia University, and Manuel de la Sota, a Basque
shipowner who had taken refuge in the United States.) And there
was the use of General Alexander Barmine, a former Red Army
general who had sidestepped one of Stalin's purges and emigrated
to the United States, where he was hired as an OSS translator,
and who in the late summer of 1942 provided the first English
translation of Chairman Mao Tse-tung's manual on guerrilla
warfare.

This was all fun, some of it not precisely good or clean, but it was not what Downes wanted to be doing. He knew that there was a *Boy's Own* sense to the cataloguing of handbags, watches, and clothing, and that there was no way to demonstrate the importance, assuming there was any, of something like Project Brenner Pass, in which a two-volume collection of views of the installations at the famous mountain pass was made up from old blueprints and photographs. He also knew that Donovan preferred him overseas, away from Hoover. Downes knew that he and his colleagues were essentially amateurs, without a hard-won knowledge of the limits of their own capacities, and he wanted to be tested against the more experienced British. There was not only a moral athleticism to Downes's view of the world, there was an ever-growing desire to be quarterback of his own operation, one directly against the enemy, behind the lines, with real risks to himself and to those he controlled. He wanted to "go view the land." Furthermore, his protectors were gone: Bruce to the London office, Dulles to Switzerland, Donovan a general and more and more military in his approach to his work. Most of all, Downes had been preparing his team of Spaniards, never called upon in the embassies project, for their "graduation day"—the time when he would put them ashore in Spain or, at the least, Spanish Morocco.

In November the Allied landings opened up a new theater to the OSS, and Downes asked to have his Spaniards sent to North Africa to form an OSS unit as a basic part of the G-2 of an army that was in the field. It was time, Downes thought, truly to grow up. Shortly before Christmas his orders to fly to North Africa came through, his Spaniards to follow by ship. Seven months later he would put the larger portion of his group, mixed Spanish and American citizens, ashore at Malaga to begin Operation Banana, and eighteen of his men, known as the Banana Boys, would walk straight to their deaths. Downes would blame the British, the American embassy in Madrid, himself; what he knew at the end of the most disastrous OSS episode to date was that he was no longer an amateur and that he had acquired a truly damning sense of the limits of his own capacity. North Africa, Spain, and Italy would destroy the schoolboy Downes who thought of spying as simply a game.[10]

Donald Downes once confessed that he had not stayed on at Yale to complete the graduate courses he began because he knew that he would be expected to write books, and he had nothing he wanted to say. Up until his experiences in North Africa and Italy, this seems to have remained so. He published nothing, apparently wrote nothing, was an infrequent letter writer. But sometime in 1943 he began to think seriously about writing, perhaps because he felt he had, at last, accumulated the kind of experiences one could write about, perhaps because he felt a need to think through the many grotesque experiences of the war, and writing them down helped him. Certainly he began to see the historic landscapes through which he moved with a greater sense of place than he had ever displayed. He had touched upon many romantic, historic scenes before, but only Italy seems to have reminded him that history was a living thing: when he came ashore on the Salerno beachhead, near the ruins of Paestum, on the night of September 9, 1943, he was as interested in the so-called temple of Neptune as in his duties, and thereafter he never lost an opportunity, even a dangerous opportunity, to explore Italian or Greek antiquities.

Downes began to make sketches of characters who would people his prose, and he kept at hand small notebooks in which he recorded ideas for stories or one-liners overheard along the way which could become anecdotes to move a story along. Very shortly after V-E Day Downes resigned from the OSS and spent several months quietly living in Amalfi, the Italian coastal town south of Naples where he had learned some of his bitterest lessons. Seated in outdoor cafés, drinking the "divinely dark" Italian coffee, he would eavesdrop, improving his idiomatic Italian, jotting down his thoughts. At one point he had the notion to be a farmer, but when he was told that the earth was not for him—"the earth has ties and if you work in it it will hold you and you will be a peasant"— he filed the wisdom away to be used later. In the end the historian in Downes allowed him to find a kind of peace through his writing, a therapy in turning his fears into often quasi-autobiographical fiction. His novels became the work of the historian he was.

North Africa and Italy cost Downes deeply. He lost his boyish ideals, which he had masked behind a kind of juvenile cynicism, and became for a time truly a cynic. He had, until then, been a genuinely muscular Christian, though he had professed to no church, a moral athlete who deeply believed that by ethical argument he could lead people to see the truth, face reality, or simply devote themselves to the creed of hard work. Though he disliked J. Edgar Hoover, his experiences with the FBI had not yet soured

him, for he knew that he had been breaking the law, and he felt
he had come away with at least a tie score. He had admired Donovan, Dulles, Bruce, Goldberg, when they were in Washington.
But now he was in the field, and he concluded by the fall of Rome
that the quality of men directing OSS in the field was "appallingly
low," that the OSS had become a "convenient dumping ground
for useless career officers" (known as the "whisky colonels," the
spelling perhaps pointing the origin of the phrase to the Irish in
Donovan). Downes had an independent income of sorts, and yet
he felt his organization was being overrun with "playboy bankers
and stupid sons of wealthy and politically important families." He
felt rage that his life might be at the sacrifice of the incompetent.
He was also sufficiently self-aware that he saved up such phrases
as this and used them, years later, in his writing. He was not
precisely a burnt-out case by the 1960s, for he wrote steadily and
took on a variety of commissions, but he was, well after the end
of the war, drawing on the experiences, the very words—that is,
the history—of those few tense months when he was at, or behind, enemy lines. In the end he wrote that the United States had
made a greater effort than any other country to play the Game
fairly—and it failed.

For Downes that failure began with Robert Murphy, the leader
of the Twelve Apostles. Murphy came from an Irish and German
background; he had grown up in Milwaukee, attended Marquette
University, taken a graduate degree at George Washington University, and after a brief stint with the post office had entered the
consular service, serving in Switzerland, Germany, Spain, and
France. In 1941 he was chargé d'affaires in Vichy, the Auvergne
spa that became Marshal Henri Philippe Pétain's seat of government. The more polished members of the foreign service thought
Murphy occasionally showed his lower-middle-class background
and that he was not up to the more subtle French, but on the
record this was scarcely the case, for he performed extremely well
in Paris as counselor of embassy under Ambassador William Bullitt; Charles de Gaulle, who did not like him, remarked in his
memoirs that Murphy was "skillful and determined, long familiar
with the best society and apparently inclined to believe that France
consisted of the people he dined with in town." William L. Langer thought Murphy was the most competent man in the embassy
after Bullitt, and the Germans had great respect for him: he was,
a German intelligence report said, "a man of the world, cultured,

fond of social life, an excellent conversationalist, easy-mannered, able to deal with any situation . . . a man of ideas far above the average from a European point of view, and certainly an extraordinary type for an American.''

Others thought Murphy entirely too cozy to the Vichyites, suspected that he was sympathetic to the French Cagoulard (a secret organization of extreme right-wing synarchists), believed him to be anti-British (which was not true), and were certain that he intended to help the French retain their North African colonies after the war. His personal life was an unhappy one: one of his daughters committed suicide, his wife was a manic-depressive, he felt he had not achieved the prestige in the diplomatic corps he deserved. When at a crucial moment in the French North African venture he began an affair with the Princess de Ligne, a representative of the pretender to the French throne, the Comte de Paris, his friends wrote it off to loneliness and his enemies to right-wing plotting. Both sides agreed that such an affair was, from the security side, potentially disastrous.

Well before Pearl Harbor, COI was interested in French North Africa. It had obvious strategic and resource values of its own, it was a window on some of the issues of colonialism, and most important, since the Germans had left the colonies to the Vichy government, it was a means of access to that third of metropolitan France not yet occupied by German armies. A then little-known American naval attaché to the French government, Commander Roscoe Hillenkoetter (later the first head of the CIA), was sent to North and West Africa in the summer of 1940, and when he discovered 125,000 combat-trained French troops still on active duty, with an even larger reserve, he informed Washington that if France were ever again going to fight in the war, it would be in North Africa. Roosevelt was fascinated by this thought—he always enjoyed making unconventional suggestions to generals—and he instructed Murphy to make a more detailed survey of the French colonies. In December Murphy visited Algiers and Dakar on secret assignment from the president. The French told him that they could hold the area against the Axis (and perhaps against the Allies as well) if they had enough petroleum and military equipment and sufficient consumer goods to keep the native population relatively content.

In the spring of 1941 Murphy was sent from Vichy to Algiers to negotiate an accord with General Maxime Weygand, the delegate of France—in effect the Vichy governor of North and West Africa—by which the United States would grant Vichy France licenses to import American food and manufactured goods into French North Africa. A condition for granting the licenses was that Pétain would permit twelve American economic control officers to be stationed in the French colonies to monitor the flow of trade in order to assure that nothing passed into Axis hands. These, the Apostles (or Disciples, as some preferred), were known to Weygand and probably to Pétain to be intelligence officers. They reported through Murphy directly to Donovan and were stationed under vice-consular cover at Casablanca, Algiers, and Tunis, and also in Oran, Bizerte, and Safi. They were not Donovan employees, however (though later eight came into the OSS), and Murphy operated independently of the COI/OSS.[11]

The OSS had its own operation, both SI and SO, for North Africa. The chief of the latter, appointed in October 1941, was a Swedish-American, Lieutenant Colonel Robert Solborg, who initially operated undercover from Lisbon. In North Africa, based on the international city of Tangier, in the neutral zone opposite Gibraltar, was a marine lieutenant-colonel, William A. Eddy. Eddy, who spoke excellent French and Arabic, having been born in Sidon, was given the cover of a naval attaché and reported to both Murphy and Solborg. North Africa fell, as a result of the agreement signed with the British in June of 1942, into the American zone of intelligence, and so British operatives were technically subordinate to Eddy. Cooperation with the British proved sporadic, and Eddy's divided responsibilities resulted in confusion and mistakes. When Solborg flew directly to North Africa to take part in efforts to persuade the French to stage a coup, contrary to Donovan's instructions, he was recalled, however. For any member of intelligence operating in the French colonies, Murphy's weight counted for the most.

The Twelve Apostles were a mixed lot, having in common little more than a knowledge of France and of the French language. One, Kenneth Pendar, an archaeologist from Harvard, said that they simply "flew over, to drop like so many Alices into the African wonderland."[12] A Coca-Cola branch manager from Mississippi, a wine merchant from Marseilles, a graduate of Saint-Cyr, a former member of the French Foreign Legion, a California oil man, a librarian, a man simply described as "an ornament of Harry's Bar in Paris"—the group was dismissed by the Germans as representing "a perfect picture of the mixture of races and characters in that savage conglomeration called the United States." They were, the Germans thought, concerned largely with their social, sexual, and culinary interests and showed both "lack of pluck and democratic degeneracy." The group proved quite effective, however, both because they were, on the whole, wisely chosen and because Colonel Eddy was extraordinarily competent.[13]

Eddy set up five secret radio beacons and settled down waiting for developments. For the next several months Murphy negotiated his way through the incredibly complex mine field of French politics, working to persuade an appropriate French leader to stage a coup in North Africa simultaneously with an Allied invasion. Obviously he could give only hints, and preferably misleading ones, about the size or probable date of any Allied action, and the delicate path between French dissidents in the general staff, the colonial administration, and Vichy France required courage, tenacity, and a willingness to compromise, lie, and never forget that "important ends justify minor sins." In the end, however, many in the OSS, including Downes, felt that Murphy went much too far in making concessions to right-wing French leaders. The rank and file in the OSS tended to favor de Gaulle, but because he was thought to be a puppet of the British, and because the French military and naval leaders Murphy chose to court were more anti-British than anti-German, he put his weight behind such ambitious figures as General Henri Honoré Giraud and Admiral Jean-François Darlan.

When the powerful Allied force invaded French North Africa at dawn on November 8, 1942, the French forces teetered in the balance. During the next two days Murphy and the Apostles worked without sleep, each with his own assignment, to forestall Americans killing Frenchmen. At points they were successful, at others not, and heavy casualties were sustained by both sides. At Casablanca the French naval squadron put to sea, and much of it was destroyed; General George S. Patton, Jr., after engaging the French shore batteries, declared that he would flatten the city if resistance continued. Those French officers who revolted were crushed by French forces loyal to Pétain. At Oran, in Algiers, three bloody days of fighting were required before the port was subdued, while at Bougie—important, because it was to be the advance base for the seizure of Tunisia, which had to be completed quickly before German reinforcements could arrive—the Allied schedule was thrown into disarray by French colonial troops from Senegal, and the American assault commander had to surrender. In the city of Algiers itself, however, the coup was successful, though by the narrowest of margins, and the key outposts were in the hands of the French conspirators.

Torch produced a dramatic change in the Mediterranean theater. Though the invasion had not gone as smoothly as hoped, Morocco and Algeria were in Allied and "free French" hands. Rommel was now under threat from the rear, taking pressure off the British at El Alamein. The Russians were relieved moderately on the eastern front, and once the Germans and Italians were cleared from North Africa, Allied shipping would have a shorter supply route to the Middle East and to Russia. The "soft underbelly" of Europe would lie exposed. Though the Germans would not be driven from Tunisia until the following May, the first massive seaborne Allied operation had been successful.

The North African invasion was also the first major test for the OSS. Not only did R&A perform extremely well, to the praise of all who used its research in preparing and executing the invasion, but the OSS agents and vice-consuls proved their worth on the ground. The only sour note for OSS arose from the intense British and liberal American opposition to Darlan. Both the Americans and the British had wanted him removed, and the American support of Darlan had created a storm in Britain, precipitating a secret session of Parliament in which the United States came in for much angry comment. A young SI officer, Lyman B. Kirkpatrick, was given a report of the debate (possibly by Anthony Eden) to send to Donovan. He forwarded it through his chief, William P. Maddox, head of OSS, SI, in London, a former professor of political science from Harvard and Yale. Only by accepting the presence in North Africa of a British minister of state, Harold Macmillan, as an adviser to Eisenhower's staff on questions of colonial policy, was the United States able to silence the storm.

However, on the morning of December 24, 1942, just as he left a meeting with Robert Murphy, Admiral Darlan was assassinated at the Palais d'Eté by Fernand Bonnier de la Chapelle, an intense young Frenchman who was a member of the Corps Franc d'Afrique, a Giraudist military unit being trained at Äin-Taya, west of Algiers. While originally instruction at the Corps Franc camp was provided by the British SOE, they had withdrawn their men and had left the program in the hands of Carleton S. Coon, an

OSS agent sent to Äin-Taya by Colonel Eddy.[14] Coon, then professor of anthropology from Harvard, took a tough view of war: if policy required that someone be assassinated, he favored it, and at the end of the war he wrote to Donovan that "some power, some third class of individuals aside from the leaders and the scholars must exist, and this third class must have the task of thwarting mistakes"—that is, must identify the potential danger of a Hitler and his immediate disciples early and kill them. Unhappily, not only could Bonnier be traced to Coon, but Coon was near the Palais d'Eté when the assassination occurred. It was then discovered that Coon had owned a Colt Woodsman pistol, the type of gun used by Bonnier.[15]

Though certain that Coon was not involved, Eddy ordered him to leave Algiers at once, to hunker down with an SOE outfit near Constantine, on the Tunisian front. However, the French felt justice had been done when Bonnier was court-martialed immediately and executed by firing squad early on December 26. Whatever rumors about OSS involvement may have circulated, they were weakened by Giraud's quick action. Soon afterward Bonnier's sentence was posthumously annulled, his partner in the conspiracy was released from prison and given the Croix de Guerre, and everyone admitted that they were happy to see Darlan removed from the scene. Though there is no real evidence to implicate Coon in the assassination, he was, in any event, also included in the rapid character rehabilitation applied to the now safely dead assassin and his coconspirators.

In the meantime Donald Downes had reached North Africa. Though he had left the States by November 17, he apparently spent some time in Caracas, in Venezuela, and touched on Ascension Island. He was briefly in West Africa, and though it would appear that he had arrived in the French colonies before the end of the year—and certainly by January 26, 1943 [16]—he seems not to have been known to most of his OSS colleagues until the early spring of 1943. In Tangier he was introduced by Colonel Eddy to Carleton Coon and Gordon Browne, who had worked together as a team; Eddy warned them that Downes was "politically undesirable" and told them to avoid him. Downes's leftist views had preceded him, while Murphy was moving even more to the right; Downes was thought to have a personal line to the president, and definitely did have a direct line to Donovan; his tasks, which seemed to combine SI and SO functions, made Eddy uneasy. The American first secretary of Tangier, James Rives Childs, whose approach to COI and the Murphy crowd was "correct," shared, perhaps instigated, Eddy's concern for Downes's political reliability.[17]

Well before the invasion Donovan had begun to worry about what Franco might do when Allied troops poured through the Straits of Gibraltar. Would Franco declare war? Would he permit Hitler to send his armies through Spain and Spanish Morocco? What would the 150,000 Spanish troops in Africa do? What would the Arabs of Spanish Morocco do: go with their fellow Arabs from the French colonies, however they might go, or take an independent path? Donovan had decided that he must get in touch with the anti-Franco Spanish underground in the United States, in order to build a network by which he could learn of Franco's intentions and, if necessary, strike at German communication lines through Spain. Downes was the man for this job.

Before Downes left the States he had assembled his rather special team of Spaniards, most though not all of whom were of the left, and he had contacted General José Asencio, onetime secretary of war in the Spanish Republican government, who was among the exiles living in New York. Asencio had formed an underground organization, Acción Democratica, linked to groups in Spain and Mexico. Asencio claimed there was a list of AD agents in Mexico City, and so, after Allen Dulles cleared his trip with the FBI in New York, Downes had hurried to Mexico. While he was there a rumor broke in Washington that, contrary to his pledge to the FBI, Donovan had ninety secret agents—later called the Ninety Humpty-Dumpties—operating in Mexico alone. Donovan denied this, and Hoover wrote him to complain specifically of Downes who, he said, had no clearances to work in Latin America. Indeed, Hoover warned, "appropriate steps" were already being taken to terminate Downes's misrepresentations of his authority.

Though Donovan was ill at the time, he mustered his energy to tell Hoover that Downes was already on his way back from Mexico City, that he had gone there simply to pick up a name list (though he incidentally met with the American ambassador as well) and that the trip had been fully approved by the New York office of the FBI and reported on to Washington. When Downes returned with the AD list and learned of Hoover's intervention, he was convinced that the director was intent on a personal vendetta against him. Certainly, he thought, he was being used as a pawn

in the ongoing squabble among the FBI, COI, State, and Rockefeller's Office of Inter-American Affairs' own intelligence operations in the Western Hemisphere. Donovan, who had been under
heavy sedation, delayed an explanation to Roosevelt, but when
he was well enough to do so he declared that he had no agents in
Latin America at all and that he had "only contempt for the people who will retail such deliberate falsehoods." FDR pressed the
matter, and it turned out that the rumor had originated with Adolf
Berle, who had a roving commission from Roosevelt on intelligence matters. Berle could not substantiate his charge and produced a list of only four agents who, he had to admit, had been
fingered by the FBI. The four men proved, in any event, to be a
short-time inheritance from the ONI, quite legal and fully known
to Hoover. Donovan thus succeeded in making the point that the
"dirty and contemptible lie" about ninety agents had political motivation behind it. Donovan now realized that Hoover was, implacably, intent on destroying the COI/OSS by attacking Donovan's
credibility with the president. Hoover had also lied to Donovan,
telling him that no dossier on him existed. The FBI had been
keeping a file on Donovan since 1924, and with intensity from
1936 when he had been heard to say that if he ever had the ability
to do so, he would have Hoover fired. Donovan therefore was
strongly inclined to protect Downes, for he believed him to be the
victim of one of Hoover's incredibly persistent obsessions. Because of this episode, and that of the burglarized Spanish embassy, Donovan said that Downes had been sent abroad on a
"secret undertaking of great importance to the national war effort." Donovan also sent to North Africa the head of Downes's
burglary team, José Aranda.[18]

When Downes arrived, Gordon Browne met him and offered to
drive him to Fez, where Downes was to join Fifth Army G-2.
With Downes was Breslove, the photographer he had used in his
raids on the embassies. From Fez Downes teamed up with André
Bourgoin, French liaison to G-2 and a Gaullist. Bourgoin, an Alsatian whose real name was either Hauptman or Hoffman and
whom Downes dubbed Marcel, had lived in Morocco for thirty
years; a former agent for an oil company, he ran a large garage in
Casablanca, and he had contacts in every village. Through Bourgoin Downes also came to know Coon and Browne well, and they
too came to respect him and to discount the advice they had been
given by Eddy and Rives. Downes, in turn, admired the two men

for their competence, the ease with which they moved about amongst the Arabic-speaking people of North Africa, and their tough-mindedness. Coon had worked among the Riffians, in particular, while Browne—who had first come to Africa with Coon in 1924—had established many professional contacts over the years he had lived in Morocco as the resident partner of a Boston importing company. Downes felt comfortable with them, and particularly so with Browne, and he hoped to learn from their ability to work with Arab nationalist leaders.

On January 26 Downes was followed into North Africa by his group of twenty hand-picked Spaniards and American leftists, the latter combat-tested from service in the Abraham Lincoln Brigade during the Spanish Civil War. Working with Bourgoin out of Oujda, the Fifth Army Headquarters, Downes infiltrated the German sabotage centers in the Spanish Zone, as British SOE was doing from Tangier, and tried to intercept German agents who were crossing the border, without results. Downes and Bourgoin also worked together to get information from Driss Riffi, a former general of the great Riff leader Abd el-Krim. Driss knew of all Riffian movements in and out of Oujda, which were considerable since thousands of Riffians came annually to work as seasonal harvesters in May. Since many of the Riffians came from the Spanish Zone, they were an ideal source of information, for the railway between Casablanca and Algiers ran within ten miles of the Spanish frontier, and General Mark W. Clark, who commanded the Fifth Army, feared that German agents might attempt to sever the line by infiltration from the zone. Bourgoin in the meantime had infiltrated the Axis schools in the zone and won over the officers who commanded the Berber troops on the frontier, the notorious Goumiers, or Goums. Colonel Edwin B. Howard, the chief of G-2 in Oujda, to whom Downes reported, was very pleased with the work Downes and Bourgoin were doing and more than offset Eddy's negative comments in his reports.

Downes and Bourgoin became fast friends during these dangerous days, and when years later Downes would visit Bourgoin in his Casablanca home and find him shuffling about, his memory of all that they had done together virtually gone, he would rage at old age. They enjoyed testing the limits together, driving out on moonless nights to talk with Arabs, Riffs, Goums who lived well beyond the ten-kilometer limit, a line drawn below the Spanish frontier beyond which, by an agreement made with Spain, no Allied personnel were to cross. They would visit Goumier outposts, arriving by jeep with no lights, and sit out listening to the Goumier flutes and the delicate, intricately woven songs of the Atlas Mountains. Usually nothing happened on these clear desert nights; now and then they would be given an Arab prisoner to take back to headquarters for interrogation; once—lost in the darkness and unable to find their jeep—they were captured by Goumiers two hundred meters from the Spanish frontier and were then released. Once, too, though alerted that the chief of German espionage in the eastern sector of the Spanish Zone intended to come to Oujda to confer with an old friend, the Pasha of Oujda, they utterly failed to waylay him.

They were nearly successful with Karl Frick, however. Frick was running a German sabotage school in Almeria, Spain, and was helping to supply German submarines in Spanish ports. As Black Tom, Frick had been behind the major German sabotage triumph of World War I, the blowing up of a factory in New Jersey. He was also Carlos Frique, Harry Wood, Emilio Darrio, and the German vice-consul in Cartagena: a big catch. Frick was running a smaller demolitions school in Melilla, the tiny Spanish enclave just east of Cape Tres Forcas, and Bourgoin and Downes wanted him badly. With help from many others, the two were able to blow up the school in Melilla and the house of the German vice-consul there, who was reporting to the Sicherheitsdienst, and they shut down an intelligence chain that ran from the Spanish consul in Oran into the eastern part of the zone. The two were also able to trace a clandestine radio station to Beni-Saf, a small town midway between Oran and Oujda, just inside Algeria, and Downes put his "Ducks"—for his group of Spaniards would be known as the Donald Ducks—on watch, with the unhappy result that the wireless operator was killed rather than taken captive. Coon, Bourgoin, and other top intelligence operatives were then put onto the job of trying to take Frick captive when he came to a rendezvous with the Kaid Mansouri on an island of the Moulouya River, which defined the boundary between the Spanish Zone and Morocco. Since General Clark would not allow them to step on Spanish territory, they were considerably hampered, and Coon and his group were still planning some means to get Frick to venture a few feet across the frontier when the Kaid collapsed in a coma and the rendezvous was called off.

Downes's two chief assistants during this time were José Aranda and Ricardo (or Richard) Sickler (later Sicre?), who was in charge of the Spaniards whenever Downes was absent. Downes sent three of his men, led by one Gomez, to Oujda to work out a plan for crossing into Melilla. While Downes was in London in April, he asked Coon to deal with the three. Before Coon could contact them, the impatient Gomez had presented himself at G-2 headquarters (where the official position was that they knew none of the details of Downes's activities) to demand pistols, bicycles, and money for an operation that he would not explain. The Spaniards were instructed to meet with a member of G-2 at the Hotel Majestic in Oujda that evening, where Coon gave them some money and got Sickler to send them away. Coon was not very good with Spaniards, however—he thought of them as little people, Buzharwans, Fathers of Bullfrogs, and "a separate biological creation," and he disliked them for precisely the reasons Downes admired them—and he wanted to deal with them as little as possible. Nonetheless, when Sickler brought three different men to Coon, asking that they be hidden, he worked with André Bourgoin to find both place and clothes, and provided them with cigarettes, Regulare uniforms, a checkerboard, and Spanish playing cards— which have intestines and kidneys in place of pips and numbers, and on which they were most insistent. The Spaniards were getting out of control, Coon thought, and he was very pleased when Downes returned from London to take his band of desperadoes off his hands.

There was also Pink Eye to be dealt with, a tiny, plump, nearly albino agent who, despite persistent warnings by the vice-consuls, Downes quite liked, and about whom he would write one of his first short stories after the war. Downes suspected Pink Eye was walking both sides of the street, and he made it his special diversion to plant on him a "big lie," that after North Africa the Allies would make a Balkan landing, bypassing Italy. But Pink Eye cleverly converted this into a genuine intelligence coup, tricking one of the OSS officials at the Villa Magnol headquarters into naming Naples as the landing site, and Downes, with the help of Bourgoin, decided that they must kill Pink Eye. They were, however, overruled by Eddy, and Pink Eye lived to meet with Downes in the Cafe Doney in Rome after the war, when he sought help in getting his life story published.

Downes found all this activity precisely what he had longed for. He did not like to think about his country's "triple shame," how-

ever—America having betrayed the Spanish Republic to the Fascists and the Republican movement to its Communist minority in
Spain, his fellow democrats having then supported Giraud and
Darlan in French North Africa (an error only partially atoned for
when de Gaulle was made co-equal with Giraud in the French
Committee of National Liberation in May 1943); and also having
failed to take any decisive action against Franco. Downes suspected that if the opportunity were lost, Franco would remain,
even after a total Allied victory, firmly in control of Spain. He
wanted to talk to Donovan about these mistakes. Donovan came
to Algiers in January, after a nerve-racking flight in which his British
pilot had lost his way, flown over the Channel Islands—which
were in German hands—and had come under antiaircraft fire. For
the first time in his life Donovan had taken out the potassium
cyanide capsule he carried and held it in his hands. He had, nonetheless, arrived safely, and he met immediately with Colonel Eddy
to plan for the expected movement into southern Europe. Instead,
he found his OSS units in newly strained relations with the
British.

Part of the problem appeared to be Eddy. Eddy was antiimperial, a view he had settled on when he had taught English at Cairo
University; he was also a much-published scholar, author of books
on Jonathan Swift and Samuel Butler, a linguist who moved easily
amongst the French and the Arabs, and former president of Hob-
art College in upstate New York: he was used to command. In
World War I he had lost a leg, and the stump and attached wooden
leg gave him pain in the heat. Perhaps because of this he drank
heavily, was deeply moody, and had proved hostile to anyone
who joined his operation after Torch, as Downes had done. He
did not like the expansion going on around him, especially as it
brought many new SO bodies to Algiers. Though he preferred operations, he was briefly to be Donovan's chief of SI, SO, and X-
2 for all of French North and West Africa, Libya, southern and
southwestern Europe, Iberia, southern France, and parts of Italy.
For this he was promised 450 new personnel whom he did not
much want.

Another part of the problem was the British. Relations with SOE,
with whom the OSS shared the Massingham base, an interser-
vices signal unit near Algiers, were reasonably good and mutually
felt to be so, as the memoirs of most SOE agents show. Locally
SOE shared Eddy's dim views of SIS and the Foreign Office, which

did not, Eddy thought, believe in the Atlantic Charter at all. The British, Eddy discovered, really could not conceive of Britain without its empire; even Douglas Dodds-Parker, the SOE man who was Eddy's second in command, to whom Eisenhower made a personal appeal that OSS and SOE must work in tandem ("like this," he said, clasping his hands together), could write after the war of Roosevelt's "anti-British sentiments" in total confusion of an American's legitimate distinctions between the British (*i.e.*, the United Kingdom) and the people of their colonies. As Eddy pointed out to Donovan, though nominally in command, he actually had to bow to British wishes on most matters because Eisenhower, who was intent on Allied unity, believed the British more competent.

Indeed, OSS and SOE did not see eye-to-eye on many things: cooperation was often at a minimum. Donovan suspected that SOE was not playing by the rules agreed to in June of 1942, especially with respect to the presumed establishment of areas of primary activity, and he was basically correct. The British still thought of the Americans as amateurs, as most were, and were disturbed that they would not take stronger direction from the more experienced British, both to avoid making the same mistakes SOE initially had made, and also because, understandably enough, they saw themselves as a senior service working on behalf of a nation with more at stake, including defense of its empire. Donovan had understood that OSS and SOE were to form a common establishment for North Africa, and had been given assurances on this point by SOE representatives in Washington, and then had discovered that SOE in London intended to set up quite a separate operation; he felt double-crossed and angry. In the event, cooperation was seldom achieved, and clearly not in North Africa: the exceptions were in Italy after the armistice of September 1943 (though there too the British at first sought to restrict OSS operations to Rome, Florence, and a few other locations and insisted on being allocated two thirds of all support services—supply drops, ground transport, etc.—an insistence the Americans overrode), in western Europe after D-Day, and in Burma. Downes, whose area of operation was North Africa and Italy, experienced only the more unhappy period of OSS-SOE relations.

Nor was cooperation better, at least in North Africa, between SI and X-2 and their British counterparts. Downes, with SI, suffered from "differences in temperament and policies" with the

British, and when X-2 was hived off from SI, he found himself in
sharp disagreement with Colonel Hill Dillon at AFHQ. At the end
of the war the official in-house history of X-2 concluded that cooperation between OSS and SIS had been at a minimum, that
British intelligence had tried to control "and in some cases to
interfere" in OSS work, in part from a desire to keep a handle on
French operations in North Africa, and that Downes was transferred from the X-2 branch to G-2 in June 1943 as a result of the
"unfriendly atmosphere." [19]

There was, in any case, a third problem: Lieutenant Colonel
W. Arthur Roseborough, head of SI in Algiers, a former Rhodes
Scholar, legal secretary at the World Court, and distinguished
lawyer. It was essential that Roseborough be accepted by Eisenhower and the Giraudists, but he was openly supporting de Gaulle
and had made clear his anger with Eisenhower over the appointment of Darlan. Roseborough also generally supported Donald
Downes, whom Eddy distrusted and Donovan backed, and felt
deeply ambivalent about Murphy. By spring, however, Roseborough was successfully shuffled off to Air Intelligence in London
and his number two, Henry B. Hyde, who had held down the
French desk in Algiers, would take his place. Hyde was prepared
to work with the Giraudists, he understood the French perhaps
better than anyone on the OSS team, and he was extremely well
placed, being the grandson of the founder of the Equitable Life
Company, son of a Francophile father who had lived for forty-
two years in France, and married to the daughter of a French
baron. As a bonus Hyde had been educated in France, Switzerland, Germany, at Harvard—and at Trinity, Cambridge. He could,
therefore, read the nuance of English social attitudes nearly as
well as he read the French, and he was resolutely neutral inside
OSS, neither for nor against such individuals as Downes and,
though himself of SI, quite able to work with SO. The weight of
authority passed to Hyde even before Eddy, who was moved up
into the ambassadorship in Riyadh, had left.

In May 1943 the Axis armies in Tunis at last surrendered. There
were 400,000 men, and the Allies were not prepared to guard so
many prisoners. Many were simply disarmed and left on their own
with perhaps one Allied guard per five hundred prisoners. German
officers would steal American and British uniforms and jeeps, talk
their way through the thinly manned roadblocks, and set out for
the Spanish Zone, a thousand miles away. The Americans on the

roadblocks were unable to tell Frenchmen from Englishmen from Germans, it appeared, and more than once an innocently if tragically ignorant soldier would pay the price of his country's isolation from other languages by being killed at his post. But obviously these German officers could not reach the zone without help. Downes and others therefore decided to lay a trap for the Vichy landowners who were hiding the Germans along the route, dressing several Austrians and Germans who had fought in the French Foreign Legion against Hitler in German uniforms, covering them with American helmets and trenchcoats, as though they were escaping, and following them from Algiers to the Spanish frontier, seeing who helped them. Though this tactic turned up several Vichyites, when it resulted in a pitched gun battle at a farmhouse outside Berkane, the operation was abandoned. In any case, Downes had, some weeks before, received clearance for "graduation day."

Eisenhower and Clark were worried about a possible surprise attack through Spain, which would bring the Axis down on their rear. Further, early in 1943 Rommel, who had returned from the Egyptian front, was threatening to throw the Allied troops out of Tunisia and in February, at the Kasserine Pass, was operating in Algeria as well. The Spanish foreign minister, Ramon Serrano Suñer, was believed to have been pressing Franco to enter the war on the Axis side, and though this threat had seemed temporarily stilled after the November landings, there were ominous fresh signs of a likely change in Franco's policy. He and Serrano Suñer had, on the occasion of Franco's birthday on December 5, responded warmly to congratulatory telegrams from Hitler and Mussolini, who urged Spain to join in the fight to free Europe from Bolshevism, and in January the German ambassador to Madrid, Dr. Eberhard Baron von Stohrer, who had been highly energetic in organizing a German propaganda effort in Spain, was recalled, to be replaced with Adolf von Moltke. If von Stohrer's activities had not been sufficient—and the British felt he had been permitted to go far beyond any acceptable definition of Spanish neutrality— what might von Moltke get up to? Further, that same month the Spanish high commissioner in Spanish Morocco, General Luis Orgaz, declared that the international zone of Tangier had been incorporated into the Spanish Zone. Britain protested, of course, refusing to recognize any unilateral action and reminding Spain that Britain had rights in Tangier, as defined in agreements in 1925 and 1928, which she would continue to exercise.[20]

In the meantime, both British and American intelligence had been working to "create a hostile attitude in Spanish Army circles toward Spain's entry into the war." By early 1943 the Spanish military had been extensively subverted, though no one could know whether successfully so until a crisis threatened. The commandant of the Spanish War College and General Orgaz in Morocco had accepted very substantial sums of money, in theory to create a pool to use when the time came for the overthrow of Franco. By July 1942 $13 million had been placed in the fund. (While there was no coup against Franco, it did become known after the war that a junta of Spanish generals who presumably participated in the pool had consistently blocked Serrano Suñer's efforts to get Spain into the war on the side of Germany, but in the first few months of 1943 the agreement that the intelligence agents had struck with the Spanish generals seemed at risk.)

Downes had his own network, largely but not exclusively based on his Ducks. He had been instructed by G-2 to keep a close watch on the airfields in Spanish Morocco, especially for any lengthening of fields, extraordinary storage of fuel, or building of bunkers. In Spain he was to report on German civilian movements around airfields, ports, and military establishments, and also on any changes in those facilities; to focus in particular on Algeciras, on the European coast just back of Gibraltar, and Melilla, opposite on the African side, for any changes in coastal guns, etc.; to contact Spanish military leaders to encourage desertions of entire units in the event of war; and to open up contact with as wide a range of anti-Franco republican elements as possible, in order to have a sabotage network in readiness should the German army enter Spain. Downes was also told to report the Spanish order of battle for the southern port areas and Spanish Morocco as often as possible. The latter, he knew, now stood at 100,000 native and Spanish troops, plus the Spanish Foreign Legion, or Tercio. They would obviously be influenced by the news coming back from the Tunisian front.

This was a very tall order, but Downes's Ducks seemed cut out for the job. Most were Spanish, or spoke the language perfectly, for those he had recruited in Mexico had been Spanish exiles; some of the veterans of the Lincoln Brigade, Americans, could be detected if they spoke too much, but these could be reserved to the Spanish Moroccan inquiries, where a melange of Spanish accents was to be expected. Downes wanted independent means of suborning Spanish officers, for he was uncertain of how effective the pool would be, and he had persuaded Lane Rehm, the OSS finance officer with whom he often had worked, to provide him with $6 million in untraceable old European gold coins, to be deposited with the OSS finance officer in Gibraltar. Downes arranged that any portion of this horde that was paid out should be given only to someone who brought with him Downes's old Navajo turquoise ring and, when asked "Who sent you?," replied "123"—the number of flutings on one side of the ring.

Downes had understood that his group would be kept together, but now he found that Eddy, either because he had not been told that Downes was to operate inside the Spanish Zone contrary to British and American promises, or because he was worried about what Downes and his group of "leftists" would get up to, diverted the Ducks to other purposes. Downes's demolition officers, both Americans, were detached for service in the Far East, and he was given "a nice, big, jolly college boy in a major's uniform," Jerry Sage, a star of the Washington State College football team, in their place. Two other men were detached without explanation. Sage, acting on Eddy's orders, then took most of the group to the Tunisian front on combat intelligence missions. There, while on reconnaissance, Sage was taken captive by the Germans with one of Downes's most important men, a Lincoln Brigader, Milton Felsen.[21] Downes, outraged and convinced that Eddy simply wanted to "make a showing quickly as a paramilitary operator" in order to win personal praise, declared that Eddy knew no more about infiltration work "than Gracie Fields" did. Downes was pleased that his "Joe-college major" had been taken away from him by the Germans—though Sage would carry out a series of remarkable escapes from the prisoner-of-war camps to which he was sent, well offsetting Downes's low opinion of him—but Downes was now reduced to fourteen men, and it would be necessary to recruit more Spaniards.

Accordingly, in February Downes asked permission to visit Vichy concentration camps in the Sahara, where Giraud was keeping large numbers of Spanish Republicans incarcerated. Four to five hundred miles south of Oran, near Colomb-Bechar, these camps were known to be "torture holes," and Downes was confident that he could find abundant replenishment for his team there. His experiences at the camps turned Downes implacably against Rob-

ert Murphy, who had allowed the Giraud government to keep the
victims of the Franco-German armistice there despite the changed
circumstances, for fear of unleashing Communist agents at the rear
of the Allied advance. Downes was interested not at all in the
political opinions of his men: he wished only to know whether
they would kill Germans, subvert Franco, be utterly loyal to him
for the duration of the operation, and could speak Spanish.

Permission was not easily given for a visit to the camps, and
Downes used a stratagem. In his memoirs he writes that "some
press reporters unknowingly turned the trick for me," as they
threatened to write about the camps, and since no American had
in fact ever investigated conditions there, Allied Forces Headquarters sent Downes and a member of SOE to the edge of the
Sahara to report back. What Downes did not admit in his memoirs
was that the press reporters who threatened to write about the
camps were Charles Collingwood and Peter Tompkins, and that
he had put Tompkins up to the threat.[22]

Downes had met Peter Tompkins for the first time at the OSS
headquarters in Tangier, in the old American Legation building,
buried within the ancient city walls in the Mellah, or Ghetto. Surrounded on all sides by other structures, which shared common
boundary walls, the legation was an ideal OSS site, for by skillful
tunneling one could connect the building to other, apparently separate, structures. Here, in a small landscaped courtyard, Downes
met with Eddy, telling him very little of what he was up to, and
with Browne, Coon, and Roseborough, with whom he was close.
Downes must have spent some time relaxing at the legation as
well, for amongst his papers are sketches easily identifiable as the
south loggia of the Great Courtyard, a patio graced by a Fezzan
fountain, the loggia consisting of three Moorish arches with an
elaborate and distinctive wooden screen behind it. The elegance
of such a sketch contrasted with those he also prepared, though
surreptitiously, near Colomb-Bechar.[23]

At the camps the visitors were told that the inmates were nearly
all criminals and that most could not be interviewed as they were
at work building the Trans-Sahara railway from Oran to Dakar.
When Downes insisted on interviewing those who were in camp,
he was given a handsome dinner at which, if there were atrocities
to be revealed, one or more of those who were responsible for the
camps would attempt to implicate someone else. Downes had taken
six of his Spaniards with him, however, and in the meantime they

were going through the camps in search of likely recruits and incidentally gathering up atrocity stories. They learned that punishment, known as being *frit* (fried), consisted of being placed in a
coffin-sized concrete box with a hole above the nose and left for
a day in the Saharan sun: about half of those so punished died.
Life expectancy in the camp was twenty months. After dinner
Downes joined the interview team, and in four days they talked
with two thousand prisoners.

Downes returned and unsuccessfully tried to persuade the
American authorities to close the camps; only when de Gaulle
arrived were they closed and some of the camp commandants court-
martialed. Roseborough's requests were rebuffed by Murphy who,
Downes reported on Roseborough's word, replied, "Art, old fellow, if you have nothing better to do in Africa than to worry about
those Jews and Communists who helped us, why don't you just
go home?" Downes's requests for the release of some of the
Spaniards also met with silence at Allied headquarters. In the end
he formally withdrew his request, returned to the key camp, and
helped those he wanted to escape. A few others he obtained by
requesting their release to him for questioning and then simply
failing to return them to their camp. Two of the Lincoln Brigaders
were then deputed to teach clandestine communications to the
new recruits, setting up a primitive facility outside Algiers. In the
summer of 1943, when de Gaulle closed the camps, Downes added
more recruits and moved his group to Oujda, where, some fifty
miles out into the mountains amidst a great grove of oaks, he
opened his Spanish Finishing School under the guise of a Fifth
Army meteorological station. Downes now had fifty men and a
dozen instructors.

By now there was little of the schoolboy left in Downes, for he
was working intensely, getting little sleep, at a higher pitch of
anger and expectation than he had ever known. Much later he
would suggest that at some point during his time in Morocco he
slipped up, apparently the only time in all his years in the OSS,
and may have entered into a liaison with a young Arab, perhaps
without sufficient discretion since rumors of this drifted back to
headquarters. No matter, Donald's Ducks were ready for action,
and one night Downes brought to the camp a dozen bottles of
Spanish brandy and a special ration and sat down with his group
under the great oak trees and drank and listened away the night,
each part of Spain singing its songs, the Andalusians lighting the

night sky with their flamencos. Downes felt ineffably sad, but he
comforted himself with a *dicho,* a Spanish proverb: *El que no se
arriesga no cruza la mar* (A person who does not take a risk does
not cross the ocean).

With warm support from Donovan, Fifth Army G-2 had authorized Downes to infiltrate his agents into Spain in July. Since this
was directly contrary to pledges made to Franco by the British
ambassador, Sir Samuel Hoare, and subsequently by the American ambassador, Carlton J. H. Hayes—the professor of history
from Columbia University in whose course Downes had sat—
Donovan made it clear that the operation must not be made known
to anyone in the embassy in Madrid. Hoare and Hayes were suspicious, however; they knew that some viewed them as well to
the right, but they had a single goal, to keep Franco out of the
war, and they deeply and correctly suspected the intentions of
their own intelligence services, both SOE and OSS. Throughout
1943, which Hayes regarded as the most delicate year of his ambassadorship, he repeatedly made clear his view that no one in
OSS could be allowed to give the impression that Americans were
present in Spain to fight Spaniards or to overturn the Caudillo's
legitimate government. In his memoirs Hayes singled out the War
and Navy departments for their cooperation and pointedly neglected to mention the OSS. On May 10 Hayes gave Count Jordana, who had replaced Serrano Suñer as foreign minister, his
assurances that the United States would countenance no violations of Spanish neutrality by its own officials, and on July 29
Hayes held a lengthy meeting with Franco in which he presented
several strongly worded requests, none of which would have been
reasonable had he not been able to act as though the pledge of
May 10 were being strictly followed. For Hayes the period from
July 29 to August 7, when he met with Jordana to learn of Franco's reactions, was especially important, for his proposals already
had been sufficiently compromised by an unwise and politically
motivated revelation by Ambassador Hoare, who apparently hoped
to gain credit for the initiative Hayes had taken. This was the
worst possible moment for him to learn of an American operation
on Spanish soil.[24]

On the day Hayes put his requests to Franco, General Donovan
arrived at Oujda to learn of Operation Banana—Bloody Bananas,
as Downes would later call it—which had left Algiers on the night
of July 15–16. The operation continued to run at least until Au-

gust 26. Banana I, working with the possibly dated list of contacts acquired in Mexico City, was to verify a safe house near Malaga and set up radio contact. Banana II was to follow shortly, with more radio operators, intelligence agents, and saboteurs, to set up a network that was to go into action in the event of a German thrust into Spain. Two other fruits had gone ahead on July 10. Pineapple, in which two operatives had been put across the Moulouya River and had gone on foot to Melilla, thence by boat to Malaga, had checked on the continued reliability of various "safe addresses." Apricot had followed with two radio operators and a set. The full personnel and supply would then be Banana, probably in two or three phases, after which would come Orange (Cartagena), Grapefruit (Cadiz), Apple (Algeciras), Cherry (Barcelona), and Lemon (Madrid). Those in any operation would, of course, know only of their own small part, and only Oujda Base Station would know where any group was.

Downes, possibly on advice from AFHQ, probably quite independently, had an additional end in view: to make a demonstration with arms after the Sicilian landings, which began July 9–10, in order to distract Franco with domestic problems so that he would be less tempted to intervene. On July 15–16 the first Banana Boys, as they were now called, were put ashore from HMS *Prodigal,* a former Portuguese trawler, the British having insisted that they retain control over all beach-landing craft. Downes then flew to London to meet with a former premier of the Spanish Republic, Dr. Juan Negrin, a pro-Moscow Socialist, who represented the Spanish exile government in England.

Downes also hoped to meet with David Bruce, who he thought was in London. Bruce had been a loyal supporter, and Downes knew he might need protection from high places. He had just launched a dangerous operation to which he had attached a potential agenda of his own, the British believed him to be insecure, and his American compatriots were questioning his judgment and would do so even more if Bananas went awry. Eddy was upset with him again, for he was bypassing channels to try to get his brother-in-law, Lloyd Lambert (a personal friend of Eisenhower's, and thus of great value to Downes), who was with X-2 in California, assigned to North Africa, even though Lambert had no languages and his expertise, such as it was, related to the Philippines. Nor does Downes appear to have had any authority for his call on Negrin.

But Bruce was away, for Donovan had cabled from Algeria on July 7 telling him to come at once if he wanted to see the Sicilian campaign, and Bruce—who was always willing to take up "the challenge" of any trip—had left for Italy. Bruce was fascinated by the nature of war, and his OSS desk job in London had become somewhat wearisome, so he followed along behind the troops as a fascinated observer. American troops in Italy fought well, he reported after another such experience, but he found them boastful and querulous. An American company of engineers had built a bridge on which they placed a placard, "This bridge was commenced by the __ Co. of U.S. Engineers at 10 A.M. on May 2, 1944 [for his example was drawn from just south of Rome]. All materials were on hand by 4 P.M. on the same date. Bridge completed by 6 P.M. on May 3 and in service at 6:30 P.M. May 3." A little farther down the river the British Royal Engineers had built a bridge, also with a placard: "Built by the Royal Engineers. There is nothing remarkable about this bridge."[25]

A worried Downes returned to North Africa to find Banana in radio contact. In the crisp prose of his official report, which carried the story through August 26, Downes noted that *Prodigal* put ashore near Malaga four SI-trained Spaniards and one Spanish radio operator, all in civilian clothes, and that seven days later radio communications were picked up from Malaga itself. All incoming messages were translated and forwarded to G-2, with a copy to OSS/Algiers. The advance group of Banana Boys therefore seemed secure when Donovan visited Oujda on July 28–29 and was briefed by Howard, Roseborough, and Downes. A "long list of priceless information" was coming in regularly from Banana—the Spanish order of battle, the identity of vessels moving Spanish artillery by sea, data on German activity at the airports— and so Grapefruit was put into Cadiz. Shortly after some parts broke down on the Malaga radio, and Banana II was readied to send in two new radios with spare parts and the additional members of the team. The report then concludes that H.M. Navy called off the operation by Banana II (which was to be accompanied by Orange, Cartagena being ready to receive them) on Foreign Office orders, and that negotiations were under way with the French navy belatedly to get Banana II ashore when Downes left on August 26.

Having received approval from British intelligence, Roseborough had arranged for *Prodigal* to take the second group of Banana Boys to their landing. Banana I suggested two nights when a reception committee would be ready; if no signal lights were shown on either night, *Prodigal* was to attempt a different beach for a third and fourth night. *Prodigal* was to sail forty-eight hours before the first night, giving Banana II and Orange time to be outfitted. When Roseborough, Downes, and Aranda arrived at the appointed hour, midnight, and called for *Prodigal,* they received no answer. After several attempts a sleepy voice responded that he would come ashore, where Roseborough was told all the officers had taken shore leave. Deeply worried, Roseborough asked to see the one officer left aboard, who when awakened informed him that *Prodigal* had received a cancellation order at 1730 hours and that AFHQ liaison was to have informed him. Downes immediately concluded that either a "full-grown Foreign Office rat" was at work or there had been a triple play, Hoare to Hayes to Murphy, with the American ambassador telling Murphy to put a stop to the entire operation. After an hour of palaver with the ship's captain, Roseborough realized that the ship would not sail, as it had received an order directly from the Admiralty: there was to be no further support of clandestine landings in Spain.

Downes, worried sick about what would happen to the stranded Banana Boys in Malaga, who would wait, exposed, for up to four nights on the beaches, argued that the British ships were no longer commanded by the Admiralty, since the entire theater was under Eisenhower. Though Roseborough promised to see Bedell Smith, Eisenhower's assistant, the next morning, he was not hopeful, for he suspected that SIS had deliberately leaked the operation within the Foreign Office. The next morning Smith declined to carry the matter further, and Downes immediately tried to purchase his own outlaw fleet, buying with the help of André Bourgoin two pathetic rowboats, several inflatable landing rafts, and a fishing smack. He also sent a member of Pineapple back to Malaga by the slow and dangerous Moulouya-Melilla-Malaga route to warn the waiting Banana personnel, hoping he could reach them before the fourth night, whey they would know they had been abandoned. He then told the waiting Banana II and Orange, who realized something had gone wrong, and they were "wild with anti-British anger."

These efforts were, as Downes feared, too late. Pineapple never reached Malaga. The Banana Boys had not given up hope until the sixth night, staying on the beach far beyond their instructions, arousing the suspicions of the police, who followed two of them separately back to Malaga when the dispirited group finally gave up hope. Three days later the Banana Boys called a meeting, against all security rules, since their condition was critical. Nineteen of them met in one house and decided to send one of their number to Oujda; as they talked a Falangist raid in full force stormed the building. A siege followed, and in the end all of Banana save one, who escaped in the confusion, were overwhelmed. Eight Banana Boys were killed and ten were captured; twelve police were dead; an abundance of evidence was found to connect Banana with the American army and navy. Under torture those who had been captured named Donald Downes and Arthur Goldberg as the men who had recruited them. All ten died. Before doing so they gave away the local Republican organization, and the Falangist government arrested 261 members of the anti-Franco group and executed twenty-two.*

Downes hardly cared about the storm that broke over his head. The Spanish foreign minister, Count Jordana, who had been increasingly cooperative with Ambassador Hayes, protested angrily. Hayes felt betrayed and protested to Donovan, who was called on the mat. Donovan replied that Downes had acted with the full knowledge of the Fifth Army and that Banana was intended as a security measure, to protect the army's dangerous open flank, and not as a spy operation. Goldberg was called to Adolf Berle's office, for here seemed proof of OSS perfidy, and on instructions from Donovan denied all knowledge of the operation. An apology was made to Madrid, and in November Hayes required the OSS to sign a formal agreement that they would, under no pretense, conduct espionage against the Spanish. Downes expected to be fired and did not care: eighteen of his men were missing, perhaps dead, and he blamed the British who, he thought, had deliberately scuttled the operation to undermine the OSS. He also wildly denounced Ambassador Hayes, calling him a traitor.

One Britisher who served on HMS *Prodigal* remembers the crucial event quite differently. He had been told that the mission was limited to covering a possible German thrust through Spain, and since this looked increasingly unlikely, the mission seemed less important to the British than, given the several purposes in Downes's mind, it really was. Further, he recalls that the landing

---

*While Ernest Cuneo believes the Banana Boys were killed, Arthur Goldberg came to believe that Lord Halifax, the British ambassador in Washington, intervened through Sir Samuel Hoare to have Franco spare them.

party, with an OSS conducting officer, embarked from Oran on the second night and landed eastward of Malaga. As the date of the operation coincided with one of the longest days of the year, with the moon rising at 0100, *Prodigal* had to stand off several miles from the coast and to make the final run in by her motorboat. The landing was uneventful, but later every member of the party was picked up by the Spanish authorities and was "summarily dealt with." The officers of *Prodigal* had rather expected this, for the timing of the operation was bad and the quality of the agents low: "Communist desperadoes bent on settling old scores with Franco." Further, the Banana Boys were insecure, as all their arms and equipment were stamped as U.S. government issue. This eyewitness finds Downes's recollections in error on many points, including the alleged confrontation in the dead of night on an Algiers dock which, he concludes, "is a pure figment of [Downes's] imagination" since, he reports, *Prodigal* was at Oran, where it had been ordered to be on standby notice. All matters of policy and clearances came, in any event, from HMS *Sidi Ifni,* the headquarters of African Coast Flotilla for Algiers, to which *Prodigal* was a tender, and it was there that the OSS encountered difficulties. ACF treated all clandestine organizations, including the British, as secondary to other competitors for priority clearance.

Gordon Browne remembers the matter differently as well. There was no OSS conducting officer, the mission was to provide a demonstration at the time of the Sicilian landings, and it was in no sense amateur. The Banana Boys were carefully selected, courageous volunteers, anti-Franco from a variety of convictions. While Downes was, he believes, in error on some points in his memoirs, he accepts the essential accuracy of the "Malaga episode" as told by Downes in 1953. As Downes was unable to find an American publisher, and his book was first published by Derek Verschoyle in England, he was exposed to prosecution for libel if he had his facts wrong, and Browne believes that the British did fail the Americans precisely as Downes related.[26]

Whatever happened on the dock at Algiers or Oran and on the beach at Malaga, eighteen OSS operatives were dead. During World War II 2,005 American medals for gallantry and proficiency were awarded to OSS men and women. None went to the Banana Boys. In all, 143 men and women of the OSS were killed in action. The largest single OSS loss occurred at Malaga.

                              *   *   *

Though fearing the worst, Downes had not learned of the outcome of Bananas until October, and by then he was in Italy and
in trouble. Downes first was summoned from Morocco to Algiers
for consultation at AFHQ in order to help plan the projected landings at Salerno on September 9. An Italian-American infiltration
group targeted for Sicily had proved ineffective, and Downes was
instructed to do for Italy what he had done for Spain: recruit sev-
enty-five men to accompany the landing. With the help of two of
his Lincoln Brigaders, Irving Goff and Vincent Lassowski, Downes
returned to the North African prisoner-of-war camps to find Italian anti-Fascists. Later he was accused of selecting Communists,
and he admitted he often did so, because they "love to kill Germans." When the day came, Downes went ashore with Avalanche, taking with him a handful of his tenacious Spaniards as
well. He was still in command of the only OSS outfit that was
actually an integral part of an American army in the field.

The landing had taken place in full sight of the great ruins of
Paestum, pink and gold in the sunrise, and Downes was there
with twenty men, four jeeps, and twenty cumbersome cases of
explosives and false Italian documents, all loaded into two trucks.
He was considered an expert on the landing site, having been there
three times to see the temples, most recently in 1938. The day
before the landing the Italian government had surrendered, and
though the officers knew this meant nothing for the moment, many
of the enlisted men had the notion they might be unopposed as
they came ashore. Downes felt happy once again: he had won
$2,000 at poker the night before, had Spanish brandy in a coffee
cup and an illegal cigarette in his mouth, and the most perfectly
preserved Greek temple in all of Italy, the temple to Neptune (or
Poseidon in Greek), stood before him, thirty-six Doric columns
marching away a thousand meters to the north. (Postwar research
would prove that the temple was not to Poseidon at all, but to
Hera.) He now lay among the sand dunes, which were full of lost
troops and odd observers, American and British mixed together,
and listened to the sounds of battle away to the east, the scene
hidden by scrub growth. A dozen P-38s passed overhead, the fighter
umbrella for the landing, and from somewhere a trigger-happy antiaircraft gunner let loose at them, then another battery joined in,
and the huddled group watched, appalled, as their own men shot
down one of the planes. A British major left running with an

American colonel, .45 drawn, to try to stop the shooting and found the young gunner crying like a baby, suddenly aware of what he had done. The goddam-dumb-bastards were in charge again, Downes thought.

For a time Downes was cut off from his group. Walking in the double tracks of some heavy vehicle that had preceded him, to avoid mines, he went in search of water. He found a bulldozer, with what appeared to be a man sleeping on it, until he saw wisps of steam rising from mouth and nose: in fact, two blackened soldiers, roasted almost to charcoal by their own petrol when a shell had gone through the cab. He vomited, looked for dog tags, found one fused and illegible, and went back to the safety of his sand dune. At noon he set out for the Sele River, four miles away, with two men, to look for a snug spot for the generals where, when they came ashore from the command ship *Ancon,* they could rendezvous. Downes, who disliked General Mark Clark's penchant for grabbing headlines,[27] had already written one in his mind: "General Mark W. Clark is ashore with his troops. Situation under control. Victory assured." He set out, walking past dead Germans baking in the sun, picking tomatoes, bypassing houses lest they prove to be booby-trapped. Nothing got done that mattered. On the way back to the beach he was shelled and dug in, face pressed into the sand, then ran—waddled, more like, for after all he was fat and forty—for the shore. The water was royal blue, the tiny, choppy waves looked inviting, and dressed only in pistol belt and holster, carrying his carbine above his helmet, he went in swimming bare-ass naked with a major he had picked up along the way. That night he joined his unit on the beach, self-consciously employing the password which only a Britisher could have thought up, exchanging it with a Choctaw Indian and an American black: "Mailed Fist!" "Hearts of Oak!" The next morning, as they drank their coffee together, the major was killed at his side.

That second day ashore Downes was summoned by General Alfred Gruenther to the *Ancon,* an Old Panama liner handsomely refitted by the navy, where he advised on the situation ashore and was sent as G-2 to Darby's Rangers, three battalions that were taking hell from the Germans around Amalfi. The next morning Downes was to be put ashore at Darby's headquarters at Maiori; as he watched from the deck of the *Ancon,* he saw the first radio-controlled bomb launched by the Germans strike the cruiser *Savannah* and turn it into a dying Moby Dick. And then he went off among the lemon terraces in search of Colonel William O. Darby.

Darby's Rangers were in the midst of earning their formidable reputation. Trained in Northern Ireland in June 1942 by Darby, they were an American counterpart to the British Commandos. All were volunteers; they had taken part in the raid on Dieppe, had fought through the North African landings, the Tunisian campaign, and then, increased in strength, had spearheaded the Seventh Army landings in Sicily. The men were tough, resourceful, utterly disciplined, and unkempt, while Darby was the image of military spit and polish. He cried when his men were killed, and they were killed in great numbers. For eighteen days they would fight to hold the Chiunzi Pass above Amalfi against eight desperate German attacks, and then in fierce winter weather would clear the narrow corridor to Cassino, and finally, at Anzio and Cisterna, would be pinned down by the Germans and virtually wiped out in savage close-quarters fighting. Nine hundred rangers went into the pocket at Cisterna; 50 percent were killed and wounded, most of the remainder were captured.[28]

Downes found Colonel Darby in Maiori and, pointing out that as a civilian he was not bound by the army's rules and regulations, offered to open banks and take whatever money was needed to pay Italian civilians to help get supplies up to the Chiunzi Pass. Using his special detachment, Downes soon had three to four hundred Italians at work ten hours a day moving shells, water, rations, and medical supplies fifteen miles into the pass. Darby wondered aloud whether this was permitted by the Geneva Convention, but Downes, ends-oriented as always, paid each adult Italian $1.00 a day, each child $.75, and gave them two cans of C-rations daily, which had to be opened and eaten on the spot at noon and sundown to discourage the black market. The Italians, who were starving, rushed to work for him, as Downes drew on his unvouchered funds. Later he was criticized by Allied Military Government Occupied Territory (AMGOT) for inflating Italian civilian wages, upsetting the delicate balance of the economy, to which he replied that he had hoped he had come to Italy "to upset the indelicate disbalance of Italian economy." Darby closed his eyes and told Downes to get on with it.

Darby also asked Downes to find a German clandestine radio that was giving away the location of his supply dumps. With twelve men from his special detachment Downes and a hundred rangers took Maiori apart—more apart than he intended, for one of his men, an anti-Fascist Italian he had taken from one of the French North African concentration camps, proceeded to put his ax to doors, furniture, and possessions indiscriminately. Downes discovered this only halfway through the job. "At best," he wrote later, "it is humiliating and degrading to rout peasants out of their beds; paw over their few miserable possessions; expose their poor hoard of rag-like clothes and wormy dried fruits; pry open a box to find it full of pressed flowers, twenty-years'-old wedding candy, the curl from a dead child's head, and a faded cheap print of the Virgin." He hated his man and nearly shot him, but the aerial to the radio—which had been removed just before their arrival—was found.

As the rangers moved on to the mountains overlooking Venafro, Downes settled in to Amalfi to set up the OSS Fifth Army Headquarters in the Hotel Luna, a converted monastery founded by St. Francis of Assisi. From there he contacted Adolfo Omodeo, rector of the University of Naples, who was still at his summer villa nearby. A historian of the *Risorgimento,* Omodeo was a Radical Democrat, and he agreed to send letters to sanitary engineers in Naples to find out what kind of equipment the Allies would need to get the water system functioning again after the Allied victory, for typhoid was an immediate threat as bodies lay piled in the streets unburied.[29] Downes also served as control officer for a two-man mission west of Venafro, and when both men were lost, one—as Downes admitted later—through his carelessness, he was badly shaken. To be a successful spy, he said, required hatred, and he had sent a man behind enemy lines who did not hate the enemy enough.

Two weeks into the landings Donovan arrived, eager to size up the front, to sleep in a foxhole, and to eat K-rations. He was disappointed to find Downes and his men sleeping on clean sheets and eating fresh mozzarella, and the next day, rather than stay at Amalfi, he took Downes with him to look at the Bay of Naples, which was still held by the Germans, and incidentally to visit Capri, having promised a New York society friend of his, Mrs. Harrison Williams, to see how her villa, La Fortino, was faring. (Her husband, a utilities millionaire, was the second largest contributor to Donovan's 1932 campaign.) On the way to Capri Donovan told Downes he was to remain in Italy, but only with X-2, as Colonel Ellery Huntington, Jr., an All-American Colgate quarterback in 1913 and subsequently a Wall Street attorney, was to head up all

OSS activities in Italy.* Downes thought Huntington was simply "a good-natured incompetent," and he told Donovan he refused to serve under him. Further, Donovan now told him, no more Italians were to be used in any capacity if they did not take an oath of allegiance to the House of Savoy. Downes was antimonarchist, and he saw another sell-out to the right coming; furthermore, he knew his men would take no such oath. He refused Donovan again. "This is wartime and those are orders," Donovan barked; "I am still a civilian," Downes replied in a tone "both insubordinate and nasty." Later Ernest Cuneo would say that from this point Donovan knew he could not use Downes effectively, for Downes's direct refusal of his orders was utterly unacceptable. As they arrived at Capri, Donovan told Downes that he wanted Mona Harrison's home protected from being used by enlisted personnel who would not appreciate its value, and Downes snapped that he would not "fight a war protecting Mrs. Harrison Williams' pleasure dome." As Downes told Joe Curtiss after the war, the situation had reached the point where he had to have two shovels, one to dig a hole for himself and the other to shovel the shit that flowed into it.[30]

That night Donovan told Downes that he could not remain in Italy. He had, as Donovan pointed out, stood behind Downes over the Banana disaster, and he believed him to be an excellent agent, but with no grasp of practical politics and no military standing. Huntington had done good work with the Gaullists, had forged an effective link with the head of SOE in London, and would prove capable and balanced in Italy and Yugoslavia; furthermore, Huntington was frying large fish with Allen Dulles and Gero von Gaevernitz in Switzerland, something Donovan could scarcely tell the impetuous Downes. Donovan said that if Huntington approved Downes could remain until the fall of Naples, and he offered him any post outside Italy he wanted. The Harrison villa would be assigned to Henry Ringling North, Downes's fellow Yale-man, brother of the Ringling Circus heir, and Downes could let Donovan know his decision later.[31]

Downes was, in fact, ill and near a nervous breakdown, and Donovan had spotted it. He also had amoebic dysentery. Donovan ordered Downes to return to the States to a civilian hospital

*Several sources mistakenly say that Huntington was a Yale graduate. A visit to the College Hall of Fame near Cincinnati, Ohio, will confirm Huntington's stature both in football and at Colgate.

and to rest, writing a personal check to cover Downes's hospital bills. (It is rather surprising that Donovan offered and Downes accepted this check, for it could have been construed as black-mail, to get the troublesome Downes out of the way.) Downes never lost his affection and respect for Donovan, and he later ad-mitted that he would, with a tiny nudge, have apologized to Don-ovan and have offered to "requisition Mona's god-damn villa and serve if necessary under Charlie McCarthy." He should, he knew, have made any promise necessary about oaths to the House of Savoy, and then subverted his promise. But he kept silent, and when Naples fell on October 1, he knew he must soon be on his way.

As Downes was entering Naples, Peter Tompkins caught up with him once more. Together they requisitioned a large palazzo at 72 via Crispi, summarily ejecting its owner, Achille Lauro, a Bank of America director, newspaper owner, and leading Fascist, to install the OSS group and to serve as a refuge for such Italians as the aged liberal historian Benedetto Croce, who originally had been rescued by the SOE from behind German lines at Sorrento with the help of Max Salvadori, coordinator of Italian exile activities in the United States (and subsequently a professor of history at Smith). The OSS also installed Raimondo Craveri, a young leftist banker and Croce's son-in-law then known to the OSS as Mr. Mundo, and General Giuseppe Pavoni, Croce's choice to lead an Italian volunteer corps against the Germans, at the villa.

The Neapolitan anti-Fascists had risen in revolt against the Ger-mans as the Allied troops moved toward the city's gates, and the retreating Germans had destroyed Naples's water, light, gas, and telephone service. The "sweet, miserable people" of Naples, a city of nostalgic prewar memories, preyed on Downes's mind. Ragged *scugnizzi* pounced on any crust of bread they could find; mothers offered their preteen daughters for sex in exchange for canned goods; Catholic priests sold holy relics; old men cut down telephone lines simply to have the wire; typhoid swept the city; thousands of people roamed the countryside looking for edible plants. The gas dumps were blazing, buildings exploding as time bombs went off, and all the railway tunnels had been caved in. At the University of Naples the Germans had burned the ancient li-brary, containing 2 million books, and had destroyed the Royal Society's quarters and then stood by to prevent Italian fire fight-ers from putting out the blaze. Downes thought the city was horrifying and that the intelligence scene was in chaos.[32]

By early 1944 the economy of the city would turn on theft and prostitution—an official report concluded that "of a nubile female population of 150,000," 42,000 women were engaged in prostitution, and that 65 percent of the per capita income of Naples came from exchange in stolen army supplies. This was not the promised liberation, and Downes felt sickened by all that he saw. Further, two men he liked very much, Tompkins and Bourgoin, who had come to Italy with him, were at each other's throats, the former recruiting to the left, the latter to the right. Downes was, to his surprise, eager to leave.

Downes's support was virtually gone, though at the time he knew of only the most damaging blow—that he had lost Donovan. However, General Clark also wanted Downes removed, for he thought him too much of a "character." Clark had wanted a military man all along, and Downes held no commission; thus Huntington was an ideal choice, and despite Downes's negative views, he served well though only briefly in the job, resigning over a dispute with the British, whose cooperation he was unable to secure. Clark was willing to see Downes get on with some low-level counterespionage work, apparently, but Vincent Scamporino would have none of this, for though he too had been of the Eddy-Downes-Roseborough "independent" school, Donovan had reprimanded him, and the reprimand had stuck. Downes might have continued to be useful in combat intelligence, but no one could be certain that he would limit himself to the close range. Downes had only himself to blame, since he was in fact offered a lieutenant-colonelcy, which he refused, and he had often been warned about his tendency "to go off half-cocked." His continued presence in Italy was creating confusion: Downes's resentment of Huntington was obvious, and the fact that both sometimes appeared to be doing the same job angered Huntington. Downes was ready to leave, and Clark, Donovan, and Huntington were ready to see him go. They had, in fact, shown remarkable forebearance.[33]

Downes was taking notes for short stories again, for he felt an urge to humanize what he saw by anecdote, seeing events through the eyes of others. He called on old friends from prewar days, sent radio operators behind the lines north of Naples, reminisced with Bourgoin, and walked in the Neapolitan sun. He also concluded that he had done "wrong to be right"—his loyalty should have not been to his ideals but to the man he admired most, to

Donovan. He then left for the States, became ill on the flight, and was hospitalized in California until January.

True to his word, Donovan assigned Downes to his chosen post, and when he was well again he chose Cairo. In Cairo he felt that the OSS was united in thinking all members of the Bulgarian Peasant party were Communists (most, though not all, were), and he got no joy there. The head of OSS/Cairo, Lieutenant Colonel John Toulmin, a Boston banker, had been promoted into the job in September 1943, when Donovan had personally relieved the commanding officer and everyone who stood ahead of Toulmin, then the supply officer. Toulmin was holding firmly to Donovan's instructions that no one in OSS should engage in any political activity of any kind. And if anyone strayed, especially if it appeared that they were favoring a postwar republic rather than the restoration of the Greek monarchy of King George II, who was in exile in Cairo, SOE was quick to complain since official British policy was based on the restoration of the king to his throne. At the time, the situation in Turkey looked secure—Coleman was running Dogwood, MacFarland was not yet exposed—and the major problem was the growing schism with the British SOE. In any case Downes felt lost in so huge an operation—OSS/Cairo now had eleven hundred people working for it—and he wanted to work on his own.

Downes did work on the Cairo end of a key mission which had begun well before he had arrived, Sparrow, an attempt to give support to members of the Hungarian general staff who professed to want to desert the alliance with Germany. This delicate operation, which involved coordination between Cairo, Istanbul, and Bari, and cooperation with the Hungarian chief of intelligence, was aimed at cutting Hungary off from Germany in time to forestall a Soviet invasion. The Sparrow team, which was to parachute into Hungarian territory and allow themselves to be captured, was to be interrogated by Hungarian Military Intelligence, which would then take them to Budapest on the pretext that further interrogation was required, and there they would be held at Budapest headquarters while actually conferring with the general staff officers. On March 13, 1944, the team departed for Hungary. A little over a month later they reported. In the meantime the Germans, alerted to the danger that elements in the Hungarian military were working with the Allies, and aware of the arrival of the OSS team, invaded Hungary and surrounded Budapest. Turned over to the Sicherheitsdienst, the Sparrow team was taken to Berlin, returned to Budapest for further interrogation, and finally imprisoned in Colditz Castle, where they waited out the war.[34]

Downes also flew to Beirut, where a cover somewhat like that of Sparrow was used to get him inside the office of the Chef de la Sécurité Publique. By prior arrangement with the Emir Farid Shahab, he was "arrested" at the airport and taken into custody as a spy. Within two hours he was released, having passed his information to one of the Emir's men, and he was then free to spend a day getting indigestion from alligator pears and red-hearted figs, and drinking arrack at Bassoul's Hotel. The beaches he thought extraordinary, and he decided he would try his hand at writing travel essays about Lebanon when the war was over.

By now civil war had overtaken Greece, and despite instructions, Downes could not remain utterly neutral. Anglo-American policy was showing ever wider cracks over the Greeks—Churchill told FDR that Russian intriguing brought on the civil war while FDR told Churchill that policy ought not to be based on the simple recreation of traditional European spheres of influence—and only when Churchill shifted his support toward George Papandreou, a radical socialist who had been spirited out of Greece by British intelligence to be prime minister of a Greek government in exile, did the rift begin to close. At first the Greek Communists had joined Papandreou, but then they dropped out; shortly after Downes arrived in Cairo, Churchill informed the Communists that they must accept the Papandreou government or he would withdraw all support. The head of SOE, then General Sir Colin Gubbins, asked Donovan through William Stephenson in New York to prepare to pull his teams out of Greece in order to demonstrate a common front.

News of this request reached OSS/Cairo informally before Donovan had firmly decided to comply, and the chief of SI there, Stephen Penrose, rallied the SI and SO officers to unite in telling Donovan that such a move would be extremely damaging to all that had been developed by OSS in Greece. In the meantime some pro-leftist OSS reports originating in Cairo had been leaked in Washington to Drew Pearson, and Donovan was under heavy pressure. Donovan supported the judgment of his men, however, and told them to leave matters as they stood. He then wrote to the secretary of state, Cordell Hull, protesting British interference in OSS operations and asking that his view, that the United States must have a policy independent of that of Britain (which he suspected had veered back toward the monarchy), be supported. Hull agreed, adding however that no American agency should in any way appear to be involved in Greek domestic politics.

Then followed a most disturbing event. Toulmin had sought to return to Washington an amateur, though effective, agent who was clearly promoting the republican cause in Greece, George Skouras, the brother of Spyros Skouras, the chairman of 20th Century-Fox motion pictures. Skouras had invoked Toulmin's superior, General Benjamin Giles, commander of all American forces in the Middle East, and Giles had ordered Toulmin to permit Skouras to remain in Cairo and had threatened him with removal from his position. Downes had, in the meantime, developed contacts of his own with EAM, the National Liberation Front,[35] through the Labor Desk of SI/Cairo. The American ambassador in Greece, Lincoln MacVeagh, was warning the State Department that EAM's growth would mean the imposition of Communist party dictatorship on Greece. From the Pericles Mission in Greece came reports that the Greek people would not accept a restoration of their pro-British monarch, whom they viewed as tainted with fascism. Further, Pericles would provide the first report on the arrival of a Russian mission to EAM and warned most strongly of likely civil war. A man whom Downes trusted, Carl Devoe, was writing up the Pericles reports for Washington, and Downes hoped that they would convince Donovan that he must resist British pressure, which was mounting in Cairo, and support EAM before it turned to the Russians.[36] At this point Toulmin collapsed in near-general paralysis, suffering from a massive attack on his central nervous system. Medical tests suggested that he had been administered nicotine poisoning, almost certainly with the intention that he should die.

Toulmin's colleagues believed that one of the Greek factions in Cairo was responsible, but others pointed at any one of the several people who stood to gain from Toulmin's removal. He was flown home and, on August 23, was replaced by Colonel Harry S. Aldrich. (Toulmin was later shown to have collapsed from overwork combined with excessive chain smoking.) The water was further muddied at just this point when Drew Pearson wrote a column attacking Churchill's Greek policy in personal terms, and Churchill replied in anger, certain that Pearson's remarks were based on a leaked OSS report out of Cairo—in Washington Cuneo suspected Downes. The key report, it was soon learned, had been written by the distinguished professor of Greek from Columbia University, Moses Hadas, who was chief of the Greek desk in R&A. Personally conservative, Hadas was also antiimperial, and presuming that he was writing a secret report, he had remarked on how the Germans were open enemies and the British "treacherous friends." Most of Hadas's analysis strikes one, with hindsight, as accurate if strident, but it failed to take into account the deep British fears that a traditional ally, indeed a part of their informal empire, would fall to the Russians, in part because of American naiveté and meddling. Years later, when interviewed by Anthony Cave Brown, who was writing his biography of Bill Donovan, Colonel Sir Ronald Wingate well represented the sense of British grievance, exasperation, and pure arrogance: "We had been at war with Germany longer than any other power, we had suffered more, we had sacrificed more, and in the end we would lose more than any other power. Yet here were these God-awful American academics rushing about, talking about the Four Freedoms and the Atlantic Charter, and criticizing us for doing successfully what they would try and fail to do themselves later— restrain the Russians. Donovan was very lucky we didn't send a Guards company to OSS Cairo."[37] As Hadas had pointed out, the British had already interned from six to ten thousand men from the Greek armed forces and had arrested many individuals in Cairo and Alexandria for security reasons, with no charges laid. The notion of British Guardsmen marching on OSS/Cairo had none of the ludicrous air of Stephenson's trappers opening all of Joe Curtiss's ton of papers; rather, it was a deeply tragic image, and that a responsible officer could conjure it up even three decades later suggested the depth of Allied disarray.[38]

Downes was marking time in Cairo and knew it. That Donovan hoped to rehabilitate him is shown by the fact that Downes was now told that he would be posted to Istanbul, where he had worked well, it was felt, years before, and where the project he had launched, involving the Yale library, was running along at a low level. But OSS/Istanbul objected, informing Donovan that when the news of Downes's proposed return was made known to the dean at Robert College, the dean declared that he would protest to the American ambassador. Downes was, he said, "a fraud, a liar and an extremely insecure man." As the ambassador already disliked the OSS outpost and virtually all of its personnel, such a protest could do nothing but harm. After reviewing the matter

further, the post concluded that it would be unwise to assign
Downes to the area: he was known and could not hope to maintain a cover, his ex-associates opposed his assignment, matters
were in a delicate state with the embassy because of Packy
MacFarland's indiscretions, and the entire operation would suffer
a serious loss of prestige. London was then queried about Downes
and replied that they had no job for him. Later Downes would
write that he was denied Istanbul because he was known and could
not operate under cover, which was part of the truth, though the
whole truth is that he had been thrown out of the Middle East.

On the way back to Washington Downes stopped off in London
to see a niece who was a secretary with X-2 and, in July, talked
with Norman Holmes Pearson, perhaps about his hope to write,
since thereafter Pearson never failed to receive an inscribed copy
of Downes's books. In 1983 Downes said that at the time Pearson
hinted that H.A.R. "Kim" Philby, a top British intelligence officer with MI6, just might be working for someone else. Allegedly
Pearson told him that he suspected Philby, with whom he worked
closely, because of the way Philby studied the day's reports on
Russian activities—actually part of Philby's duties—and then went
on to read X-2 reports on measures being proposed to counteract
the People's Commissariat for Internal Affairs, the NKVD. Thus
perhaps an early chance to justify surveillance of Philby's activities may have been missed.[39]

At some point in August 1944 Downes returned to Washington,
sick of "unlovely British scheming and American ignorance,"
generally filled with suspicion about British intentions. In mid-
September he reported to Q building, where he found the old
Kremlin, the name for Donovan and his senior staff, "cluttered
with colonels." George Bowden had resigned, Donovan was seldom there, the sniping was intense. Downes went to Maine to see
his family and to eat lobsters. He thought about Italy. He thought
about how an agent ought to know that he was right, "to have a
morale of gold, and faith of steel," to carry on. He thought he
could smell blowing his way the "sweet heliotrope odour of unburied dead" from Naples. He thought about how governments
betray the promises made by their secret agents, how the history
of "broken promises is long, uniform, and disillusioning." He asked
Bowden to help get him out.

Bowden was able to line Downes up with a job in the White
House. Though still on the OSS payroll, he would be loaned to

Lauchlin Currie, one of the president's six administrative assistants, and through Currie he might get his opinions on the situation in Greece onto the president's desk. Downes wrote four Greek reports for FDR, then began a series on Sicily, where he thought Churchill was encouraging a separatist movement, possibly with American connivance, since Sicily was strongly pro-American. Next was a political estimate on Italy, attacking Marshal Badoglio as a Darlan. Finally Downes wrote a report on the condition of labor unions in Italy, concluding that if the United States did not support democracy and reform, if it backed the monarchy, Badoglio, and the Mafia, it would have to contend with a large Communist party. None of the reports was acknowledged by the White House, which was taken up with the question of how to deal with a defeated postwar Germany. Currie told Downes to try his hand at a table of organization for an intelligence operation in a civilian government in Germany and to make recommendations as to who might fill the slots he invented. He named himself to a desk on Communism and Russian affairs. None of this activity was realistic, and shortly Currie confessed that Downes's reports had never ever reached the president; Harry Hopkins had simply filed them away. Currie was becoming something of a weak reed; a Keynesian economist educated at the London School of Economics, he would be attacked by Elizabeth Bentley and Senator Joseph McCarthy after the war, and charges of being left-wing were already being used to discredit him.

For Downes the war, and his career as a spy, ended in Italy, to which he now returned. Bowden helped him retain access to OSS communications, and Currie arranged for a White House letter that might help him in emergencies. After writing a series of articles under an assumed name on predicted postwar conditions in Germany and on the approaching Russo-American split, Downes was hired by a news agency, and in February 1945 he arrived in Naples, more ragged and miserable than it had been the day it fell. The city had become "hard, furtive and sneering." He was ashamed of his fellow countrymen and angry with them; sex was against any wall, discipline was a farce, the name of America no longer magic. On his first night ashore he heard a ten-year-old bargaining with an MP patrol for the use of his thirteen-year-old sister. When he tried to write of this grim side of the American occupation, the censors killed his story.[40] He visited Caserta and Rome, the undamaged city, smug and relatively comfortable. He saw how the Allied Commission helped men he considered old-line Fascists get import and export permits, how the church was capitalizing on anti-Communist sentiment to fasten its superstitions more tenaciously on the people. He was sour, unable to see anything good, by now sufficiently anticlerical, anticapitalist, even anti-American, to seem genuinely left-wing, as he had not truly been before. He decided that he might recover his spirits only by getting to the war zone.

Downes caught up with his old Fifth Army friends in Florence—Howard and Arthur Blom of G-2, the former now a general, and General Gruenther, still making up, Downes felt, for the deficiencies of Mark Clark.[41] He learned of Allen Dulles's great coup, negotiating from Switzerland the surrender of the German army in northern Italy—Operation Sunrise—and he wept with the Italians over Roosevelt's death. On April 26 he learned that half or more of the city of Milan was in the hands of Ferruccio Parri, leader of the Commando Volontario della Libertà (CVL), whose release by the Germans had been negotiated by Allen Dulles. Downes knew and admired Parri—a resistance leader who had been able to draw Communists, royalists, socialists, Christian Democrats, and his own Partito d'Azione, or Action Party, together—and he talked Blom into sending him to Milan on the first plane. Though the press was required to return the same night, Blom suggested that if Downes were to disappear, no one would look for him. That night, with an intoxicated pilot, Downes landed at Milan and commandeered a bicycle to ride into the city.[42]

Downes made for the OSS headquarters at the Hotel Milano, and there he found both Parri, whom he wanted to interview, and the OSS liaison with the Committee of National Liberation in Lugano, Switzerland, Captain Emilio Daddario, an attorney from Connecticut. As Downes rode back to the CVL headquarters with Parri, he was told of the death of Mussolini, shot at Dongo on Lake Como. Mussolini's body was now on display in Piazza Loreto, in Milan. From Parri, others at the CVL offices, and those he interviewed at the Piazza Loreto, Downes was able to get one of the earliest stories on Mussolini's death. At the piazza Downes viewed eight bodies hung like trussed pigs from the parquet of an Esso station; he looked upon the body of Clara Petacci, Mussolini's mistress; he learned of how that same square had been used a month before by the Decima Mas, a political police commanded by Prince Valerio Borghese, to hang the bodies of twelve boys accused of being partisans, the bodies left to swing until they swelled and stank.[43]

There was another story to file. The Gestapo remained in control at the Hotel Regina, in the center of the city. Allied forces had not yet arrived, and the commanding officer, a Colonel Rauf, was holding on until he could surrender to them, for he was certain that the partisans would kill him and his men. On the day Allied forces entered Milan, Downes found himself seated at the bar in the Hotel Milano with the famed cartoonist for *Stars and Stripes,* Bill Mauldin. They had a few torpedoes—vermouth, grappa, and Campari—together, and Mauldin got the notion that Downes had just arrived by parachute. Somewhere along the line they decided to look in on Colonel Rauf at the Regina. There was a story, perhaps a cartoon, and certainly an experience to be had there. Slipping up along the side of a building, Downes held a limp, stained white handkerchief out from the edge, or so he recalled—Mauldin didn't remember this part—and they were beckoned forward. A lieutenant, decked out in his death's-head cap, greeted them in English and invited them in. Inside they found an American colonel (who proved to be OSS) discussing the Germans' surrender—Downes didn't remember this—and an Army Pictorial Service photographer standing around hoping to find a scene to record. The Germans wanted to surrender to someone, anyone who could protect them from the partisans, who waited silently outside. Mauldin wandered off and used a Gestapo major as a model for one of his most famous cartoons, "The Last Roundup," a picture of a German being brought in by bearded GIs. Downes tried to get Rauf to talk for a story, but the colonel only wanted the Americans to remain with him until more forces arrived. A young man approached Mauldin and Downes, declared that he was a Dutch citizen though a German soldier, and asked for help; Downes reported him to an SS lieutenant standing nearby and aggressively told the Dutchman that he need not worry about going to a prison camp with the Germans: "Your pals are going to pull off your legs and beat you to death with them, you fink." An SS captain then approached Downes and Mauldin, with a French blonde on his arm and a white Alsatian bitch on a leash, Yvette and Anna respectively, and asked Downes to take Anna off his hands. Downes demanded the huge swastika flag hanging on the wall in exchange and then gave Anna to Mauldin. American tanks pulled up outside, and three American officers entered;

they had no German, so Downes translated. Then Captain Daddario arrived and Rauf surrendered. Both Downes and Mauldin were drunk, but they moved off with their respective souvenirs, one swastika flag weighing twenty pounds and one Alsatian bitch.[44]

The next day Downes called on Major Max Corvo, whom he had known as the recruiter of a Sicilian-American team for the OSS. Corvo suggested that Downes interview a Russian who had been working with the partisans. Downes did so, and this led to further interviews, with two of Parri's assistants, with American interrogation teams, with Parri again. Downes offered Edda Ciano, wife of the executed Italian foreign minister (and Mussolini's daughter), $10,000 advance for her memoirs and was turned down.[45] He was finding that he could, in fact, do journalism; more important, as he talked with a Russian, a German, a Dutchman who had chosen to leave their countries to work for Parri or another resistance leader, Downes realized that he was like them, destined to be an exile from his own country. Italy was his home. On July 1, abruptly, he resigned his last connection with OSS in Italy, maintained more for reasons of sentiment than because he would need to call on his former colleagues for communications, and deciding that the European war had been his war, that he had no interest in the defeat of the Japanese, he determined that the summer of 1945—the longest, hottest summer for the last fifty years— would be passed among the cool chestnut trees of Amalfi.

Downes renewed his ties with Yale, joining the alumni association, getting into contact with some of the Yale graduates and faculty who had worked in the OSS. He began another Brown Book, this time of potential journalistic contacts. There had been William Morgan, a Yale-educated psychologist who remained on with the CIA; August Heckscher, who had left his teaching position in the political science department to work with the Foreign Nationalities Branch, and who as chief editorial writer for the New York *Herald-Tribune* after the war would be a useful contact; there was James Angleton, whom he had met briefly through Norman Holmes Pearson, and who was now in Italy. In Florence Downes ran into Theodore Ryan, a Connecticut Republican and graduate of the Yale Law School, who was working on the salvage and protection of the city's art treasures. There was John McCulloch, from Yale and Oxford, who had edited a Latin American journal for the Foreign Policy Association and then served in Cairo and

Bari. Richard Weil, Jr., heir to Macy's department store, had operated with Tito in Yugoslavia; Downes had known him at Yale and had admired the way he stood up for Tito even though he was a Communist. Another contact was William Cary, from the Yale Law School, who also worked with Tito. Yet another source on the Balkan story was Robert Joyce, who had gone from Yale to the foreign service and who was now head of the SI Balkan section in Bari. Rolfe Kingsley, actually in the Balkans, might be persuaded to help. There might be a story on Sunrise, to be provided by Allen Dulles or winkled out of C. Tracy Barnes, the Yale graduate who had been Dulles's assistant on the operation. Yet, Downes found no stories, no leaks, through his Yale contacts: the old school tie did not help, and Downes turned again to the notes and sketches he had made for writing short stories and novels.

From 1945 to 1955 Downes traveled often to England, France, and Switzerland. He spent five weeks in Germany in the spring of 1954, gathering material for a series of articles that he never wrote. He renewed ties with the surviving Donald Ducks and spent some time in Spain. He looked up old SOE colleagues. He traveled in the Near and Middle East on a project to promote Trans-World Airlines and a travel service in Beirut. (Since he had also been charged with Beirut-related tasks while assigned to Cairo, this led to the rumor that he was, in fact, working for Israeli intelligence.) He visited his family in the States only once in these ten years, living first in Rome and then in a small villa outside it. In 1953 Downes published, through Derek Verschoyle in London, his wartime memoirs, *The Scarlet Thread,* one of the earliest OSS books of its kind. Rinehart offered to publish it in the United States if Downes withdrew his chapter on J. Edgar Hoover, and Downes refused. A second publisher sent Hoover a copy, and he was reported to be in a fury. Then a North American edition was issued by the British Book Centre in New York. The book fared poorly: those with an ax to grind reviewed it unfavorably, on the whole it was ignored in the States, and it made little money. When asked, Donovan called the book "a minor disaster" and urged that it be forgotten.[46] (Years later Downes himself called it the work of a fifty-year-old "angry young man.") The public simply was not interested in an essentially negative account of a subject on which they had been fed a diet of sensationalist prose and motion pictures. Downes suspected the FBI of harassing booksellers, for even the bookshop of his publisher did not have it in stock when a friend looked in, and the clerks professed not to have heard of it. Several newspapers that announced reviews did not publish them, and Downes wrote that Alfred Friendly at *The Washington Post* told him that the book had caused such a furor, he could not have it reviewed until he found a most authoritative reviewer. Finally Admiral Ellis M. Zacharias, who was wartime intelligence chief of the U.S. Joint Chiefs of Staff, and whose book *Secret Missions,* published in 1946, had been well received, did review it, and favorably. The next year, also through Verschoyle, Downes collaborated with Lord Westbury on a cookbook, *With Gusto and Relish,* which was very English, very much of its time, and yet adventurous (how to cook beaver tail). This too did poorly.

Shortly after he published his memoirs, Downes began to be harassed by the Roman Questura. He was told that his 1947 permit to reside in Italy had expired and had been recalled in 1949, though he had not been informed of this, so he stood in technical violation of Italian law. Downes filed for a new permit and called a dozen times at the Questura, without success; he was then instructed to leave Italy and return to qualify for a new permit. He went to France for five weeks and when he attempted to return, he was met at the frontier and refused entrance. As there was a general strike in France, Downes drove to Geneva and from there contacted various friends in Italy, including the writer Carlo Levi, asking them to find out what was going on. Through Levi he was warned not to use any political pressure, and with the help of a friend in the Italian government he at last learned what the charges against him were: that he was a drug trafficker, a smuggler of arms, an agent of the Cominform, had sold "the favors" of high office when he was close to Prime Minister Parri, and that he was "grossly immoral." Testily Downes asked why the Italian government had not included counterfeiting, murder, and Fascism. Had he not also learned through another source that Interpol was actively investigating the drug allegations, he might have thought the entire matter ludicrous.

Downes wrote a lengthy *promemoria,* reconstructing for himself and a few of his friends all that might be said against him, and from what sources. He had, he knew, offended the head of the Italian police by a series of articles in Italian newspapers on former Fascists still in government. The French had, he thought, a file on him which had lain dormant until now. In 1948 he had intervened with the minister of the interior on behalf of one of his former Ducks, who was studying history at the University of Florence, and since the complaint against the young historian had come from the American embassy, he surmised this had angered "the embassy crowd."

With the help of an influential friend in the Italian government, Downes was given a temporary fifteen-day permit after waiting in France for five months. This enabled him to go to Rome to collect possessions and to do a bit of work on two Italian films for which he was an adviser. While there he consulted with the Questura and learned that no one believed the dope, arms, and Communist agent charges, while the immorality charge was "neither sensible nor substantial." (A porter had told the authorities that Downes was leading an immoral life, but since Downes had complained of the porter before, a friendly Questura could easily dismiss the charge as motivated by the desire for revenge.) Downes returned to Paris, filed a new request, and waited another seven months.

At last Downes brought up such big guns as he could muster. He revealed that David Bruce had read the manuscript of his book and approved it. He contacted Bruce, Arthur Goldberg, Gerhard Van Arkel, and Allen Dulles. A contact inside the Italian police told him that someone "well placed" was working against him, so he contacted well-placed Italians he had helped during their exile years in New York, reminded others of how he had worked against Sicilian separatism while at the White House, and called on Raimondo Craveri and a wartime friend from the Action Party, Ugo LaMalfa, who worked with the Italian novelist Alberto Moravia. Downes made it clear that he not only wanted a new residence permit, he wanted to be cleared of all charges (save that of venal sin, which, he said, was true from the age of fourteen, but not actionable).

In the meantime the Italian journalist Luigi Barzini had added to Downes's complications. Barzini told one of Downes's friends, Charles Moses, that Downes had come to his office after the war to offer Cominform documents for sale. Downes admitted he had known Barzini, Jr., since he broadcast for Radio Rome in 1945; he also knew the senior Barzini, who had been wartime chief of the Fascist news agency Stefani. Downes said he had gone to see the younger Barzini at his office at *Il Globo* in 1946 to interest him in buying articles translated from English, but he had never offered any Cominform documents. Still, he could not plug the dike against the steady flow of rumors, for society loves to believe ill of spies and, even more, to assume that anyone who travels extensively with little visible sign of income, or who knows a wider range of people than he ought, is a spy. When Downes heard it was said by a Panamanian diplomat that Taylor Travel, for which he was working in Beirut, was a front for arms running to the Arabs, he felt he ought to abandon hope. He was, Downes concluded, destined to be a fugitive from injustice, and he decided to sit the long wait out in Beirut, where he could live off his travel consultancy while writing "oleaginous globules of advertising prosody," the closest he came to the travel essays he had once hoped to write.

From Beirut Downes poured out letters to friends, regaling them with tales of members of the European community there. One, whom he thought a likable ass, often took him to lunch, but the man was becoming a bit trying because he was certain that Tripolitanian Arabs wanted to assassinate him, and he had his Daimler repainted each week as a disguise. Downes thought no one ought to want to kill a man, however rich, who was also so vague: ask him the time, and he says, "It's about, um-uh, eleven thirtyish sort of thing, what?" "Rum lot, bad blood, Africans and Asians, made to be slaves sort of thing, hum-hem, what?" Downes helped a lady friend with a little detective work, proving by surveillance that her lover (and business partner) was unfaithful, and he nursed a broken ankle while he waited to see what the big guns could do for him.[47]

Then, in September 1955, well over two years after he had been denied reentry to Italy, Downes received a cable from Bob Ullman in Positano: come home, all is forgiven. The Italians would admit him to permanent residency. His big guns, Bruce, Goldberg, Van Arkel (and perhaps Dulles) had apparently brought a cease and desist suit against Hoover, and Hoover had backed away. Though Downes feared that "the mysterious force" that was against him was only on vacation and would return to undo everything, or that some Communist jokester had sent the cable signed Bopeep—the wartime code name for Downes's inside contact at the Italian ministry—Downes wrapped up his work for Taylor and returned, apprehensively and happily, to his beloved Italy. When he had been deprived of it, he had confessed to his memory book that Italy was the only place in which he felt happy and at home. His best years, he said, were spent in his house at Zagarolo, below the medieval town of Palestrina in the Sabine Mountains, on the fast line to Naples and only fifteen miles from Rome.

At last a measure of success came to Downes the writer. In 1959 he published a spy thriller, *Orders to Kill,* to good reviews. Earlier he sold the plot to Anthony Asquith, who produced the picture before the book had appeared—a reverse timing that did not enhance sales of the book—and in May of 1958 the film premiered at Cannes and in Rome. With James Robertson-Justice, Eddie Albert, Paul Massie, Lillian Gish, and Irene Worth, it drew good crowds, favorable critical comment, and three British Film Academy Awards, including one for Best British Screenplay. Downes received $75,000 for his work on the film script. This enabled him to settle into the life of a full-time writer, and later in 1959 he published *A Red Rose for Maria* to excellent reviews. This too was written with an eye to a film, but the film was never made. In 1960 his American publisher, Rinehart, issued *The Easter Dinner,* a story of the Italian underground set in Rome in 1944. (Downes tried to turn this into a play.) Reviews were less favorable, and Norman Pearson, to whom he regularly sent autographed copies, remarked that the human element was missing. Even so, it went into Pocket Books in 1961 and made a bit of money. Also in 1961 Downes helped his friend Peter Tompkins revise *A Spy in Rome* and wrote an introduction for it.*[48]

In 1965 Donald Downes wrote his best piece of work. Provisionally titled "Caldrons Bubble"—not a good choice—it began as a tough-minded, clear, perceptive exploration of how a homosexual former agent was drawn back into intelligence work precisely because of his homosexuality, to allow himself to appear to be blackmailed by compromising photographs into working with the Egyptian secret service. The writing was effective, without Downes's tendency toward the odd pompous phrase; the tradecraft was correct; the attitude was less sentimental than anything Downes had written. His hero, John Farnil, reflected upon what it had meant to be homosexual in the wartime OSS, on how ab-

---

*Downes's sense of what was prudent had improved as a writer over these years. His papers contain the manuscript of Tompkins's book, with Downes's comments; it shows that he tried to calm down Tompkins's vitriolic remarks on prominent individuals. Time and again Downes wrote "wrong" in the margin with respect to a specific fact, but Tompkins let what he had written stand. Tompkins also provided a valuable and extensive set of photographs which were to illustrate the book. The publisher, Simon and Schuster, apparently decided not to use them, however, and they remain in Downes's papers.

stinence had finally been the only means of survival as the military mind took over that organization, and on how the Arabs, who found nothing shocking in homosexuality, turned American prurience and disgust to their advantage. When he had finished seventy pages, and had them typed by Eleanor Clark, who had become his regular typist from afar, Downes sent them to his agent in New York. In due course the word came back that the material was unpublishable—"quite unappealing," not "tasteful," an audience "simply too difficult [to reach] . . . for this particular subject"—and Downes did not write another line of what surely would have been his best book.

Instead he turned to nonfiction. He tried his hand at a short piece on Charles Bedeaux, a Frenchman who had become an American citizen and who made a fortune as the "speed-up king," advising management on how to put in antiunion efficiency systems at industrial plants. Bedeaux had been stranded in Allied-controlled Algiers just after Torch and was jailed by the French as a Nazi-sympathizer who had worked out a plan to lay a pipeline across the Sahara to bring cheap vegetable oil from Dakar to Hitler. Downes had written a report on Bedeaux for the OSS, linking him to various pro-Axis Giraudists, but he believed Robert Murphy had not forwarded the statement to Washington. However, Edmond Taylor had suggested to Murphy that Bedeaux was suspect, and Bedeaux and his son were temporarily imprisoned. Bedeaux was returned to the States, and was under FBI surveillance when he committed suicide in Miami. Downes had long been interested in the Bedeaux affair, partially because he had known Bedeaux's son, who had been a student at Yale, and he thought this would make a good anti-FBI story.[49]

Downes was far more interested in the question of war criminals, however. He had thought the United States wrong to go through the legal proceedings against the big-name Nazis, sharing Sherman Kent's view that they ought summarily to have been killed. He clipped stories of American atrocities in Vietnam, marking references to My Lai and to war crimes. He began an article on the case of Major William G. Holohan, an OSS officer apparently murdered by one of his own men while on a mission in northern Italy. Above all, he pursued the matter of General Anton Dostler, tried and executed for the summary shooting of fifteen U.S. Army commandos, subject to execution under a special order issued by Hitler, caught behind the lines near Genoa when trying to destroy a railway tunnel after the Anzio landings. The case had been controversial then, and remained so, both because it raised significant questions about the definition of war criminals, and because there were many Americans as well as Germans who felt that Dostler had been made the scapegoat of a very complicated affair.* Downes felt this too, and he corresponded at length with the American military officers who had provided the prosecution and defense. This book occupied much of his time between 1969 and 1975, as he drew on old friends such as Bill Casey, Gerhard Van Arkel, and Philip J. O'Brien, all lawyers, to find material for him in American libraries. This, too, might well have been an important book, for Downes was tenacious in his research and thinking clearly, but it was never written.⁵⁰

After Bob Ullman was killed in a motoring accident while Downes was staying with the Brownes in Tangier, Downes decided to move to London. There, from 1975, he shared a double flat at Albany with a British member of Parliament whom he had met in 1949. Downes no longer had any sexual interests, he was afflicted with a variety of illnesses, and he was no longer writing fiction. He had been seeing a psychiatrist in Rome, and he saw another in London: both thought his ulcers, asthma, and colitis were psychosomatic. He often had double vision. He awoke many mornings feeling a sense of suffocation and with "internal" dizziness, feeling faint. The prescriptions left in his papers show that he was on a wide range of medicines. His migraine headaches had passed with youth, to be replaced with cerebral spasms which, his doctor had told him in 1957, accounted for his overaggressiveness. His broken ankle, compounded by falls in which he broke a foot and his coccyx, continued to bother him. He had had four operations since 1956, suffered persistently from diverticulosis and diabetes, and smoked thirty to forty cigarettes a day. Downes sat in his freezing flat, wrapped in a paisley shawl, reading murder mysteries and sipping sherry; there an interviewer found him, in 1977, consciously growing old, going out only for the occasional visit to the Special Forces Club on Herbert Crescent.⁵¹ Just after Christmas, 1980, Downes realized he must be cared for, and he returned to California, "exile sad, more sad returning!," to live with his widowed sister-in-law. There, on March 26, 1983, he died.

Why, Downes once asked himself, had he been a spy? Because of his aggressiveness, which he knew to be nearly pathological at

*See Chapter Six.

times? From the fact that he could hate and love, the only emotions he thought reliable in a spy?—and the ingredients that made the Israeli intelligence service the best in the world, he thought. Certainly not for money, the least reliable, most common, and safest motivation: safest because, if ideology, which was always explosive, were set aside, there were people who could always be bought. Because he liked to imagine himself the hunter in a world of the hunted? Because of a partially suppressed perpetual adolescence, an adult childishness, that would not allow him to grow up? All of this, he thought, though there was something more. There was the need to influence history and yet fool the historians: men like himself had, or at least could legitimately feel they had, changed the course of history in some small way. Yet the historian would never know what they had done, would never catch them, would never get their history entirely right. Downes the historian, the hunter, liked the irony of also being the hunted.

For Downes, his years with the OSS had been the best. After the war he could not imagine that he was changing history. He was simply "a big, fat man with a red beard," who was welcome in many homes, showing up with a paper bag full of the makings for a curry, recalling the war with old friends. In the 1950s, when he had wanted to be taken back into intelligence work, to prove his anti-Communism, to specialize on the Soviet Union, the nature of intelligence had changed as the nature of the enemy changed. Such changes meant that different kinds of people were attracted to the life, men like James Angleton or Richard Bissell. Rigid anti-Communists had been prominent in the OSS, especially toward the end, but they had been balanced by doctrinaire, and more important, pragmatic liberals who were, at least, reasonably well read and educated to the meaning of the language they used. So too were the conservatives of the time; they had read their Burke (especially if they were Anglophiles, as many were), and they did not think *liberal* a term of disrepute, merely a position on the political spectrum. It is a cliché to speak of World War II as the last "innocent war," a "good war," though it is true enough that during the war most people, unaware as yet of Gulag, uncertain of what might happen to Poland, only becoming aware of the Holocaust, could think that something, their good war, was over in 1945. That it was the "last good war"—in the words of Studs Terkel—was not yet known, of course. That the United States had bought world supremacy (until 1949) very cheaply might be understood statistically but certainly not emotionally. The British as a people were no less naive than the Americans: they had accepted great sacrifice and did not want, under a condition now called peace rather than war, to go on doing so. They could have no idea that victorious, they had lost the war, and that forty years later they would be of such reduced significance on the world scene. Nor, one suspects, had Downes foreseen such a result of the anti-imperialism he espoused so intensely in the spring of 1944. No one can be blamed for not predicting the future, and as it went awry, Downes became more hopeful about the past.

During the war most people had closed their eyes to the dark underside of America, for the underside of the enemy seemed—not seemed, was—so much darker. But the America of Sacco and Vanzetti, of corrupt police who convicted a Richard Hauptmann rather than conclude that they did not know who had stolen a baby, a racist America that systematically permitted one sector of the population to brutalize another, and thus built up a heritage of counter-brutalization in return, this America could be forgotten, suppressed, never even revealed, in the heat of a common purpose. Downes had never understood that at such times one does not blow a whistle. When the House Un-American Activities Committee began to spew forth its venom in a way few outside America could understand—had anyone ever heard of, could anyone imagine the duties of, a Parliamentary Un-Canadian or Un-British Activities Committee?—there were those like Downes who felt that Americans had proved to be no better than the people they fought. That such people—moral athletes, believers in playing by the rules, taking joy in the Great Game—were horrified is understandable, though perhaps they did not see quite far enough, for men like Martin Dies and Joseph McCarthy were in no sense the systematic ideologues, the intellectual butchers of free speech, that German and Russian leadership had offered their societies. Such men, hated by Downes if misread, perhaps because hatred was not really a good foundation for effective analysis, were opportunistic, small-minded, fundamentally unintelligent men with mean-spirited political goals of the most selfish nature. The obscenity of the Dies Committee was not that it represented systematic persecution but rather that it practiced a form of random violence.

Downes thought that he did not take life seriously; actually he took it far too seriously. Many OSS memoirs play the war for amusement, rather like Joseph Heller's Yossarian ("Someone is trying to kill me"), without the deep, black streak that ran through

Catch-22, sitting on Downes's book shelf. Perhaps OSS memoir-ists like Lovett, Alcorn, and Morgan found the whole thing quite horrible and thought as many men do in moments of dread that one had best turn to the comic side to survive. Others, and Downes was one, managed to last through the war despite deep pessimism because they had really believed in the world of G. A. Henty and John Buchan, and in the idea that America might transform the world; when they saw this hope, as they interpreted it, dashed by the many compromises of war—with Darlan, with Badoglio, with Stalin, with Chiang Kai-shek—they could take some refuge in the thought that everyone was, at least, intent on killing Nazis. By the time Downes sent his manuscript off to Derek Verschoyle in 1953 the world had changed, the game was different, not really the same game at all. Yet even then Downes held to the convic-tion that, as compared to other nations, the United States (and Britain) had done reasonably well in matters of justice and hon-esty. He understood, and may even have come to terms with, the necessary illiberality of military values. What truly turned Downes irredeemably bitter, removed the humanity from his writing, was his belief that he was being hounded, in Italy, in Britain, by—he was quite convinced, and the odds are that he was right—that protector of American values, the FBI. He had, he felt, served his country well, he had risked his life, he had done important things. He had fought many battles and yet he was forgotten, mentioned in almost none of the popular histories of the OSS that were appearing with the release of the official records. And so he had to recollect, if not in tranquillity then in nostalgia, the part of the war he had seen plain, as he was convinced he had seen it.

How else to interpret Downes's apparent claim, in 1983, that he had been alerted to the possibility that Philby was working for the Russians? Obviously if this revelation were true, it would set a journalistic covey of mole hunters out on the trail once again, able for the umpteenth time to rewrite their old arguments be-cause they had a new "fact" to add. Downes must have known where such a remark would lead, if taken seriously. At the time, and after more mature reflection later, the interviewer to whom Downes made this startling remark concluded that it was simply untrue, that Downes was maundering, too cloudy of mind in his terminal illness to recall dates correctly and, more important, no longer caring about the consequences (and therefore the accu-racy) of his remarks. This seems a prudent assessment. Downes had a tendency to color his narratives; when one tests *The Scarlet*

Thread against official records and the memory of others, one finds it not so much in error as inclined toward a general exaggeration. This exaggeration, where it can be clearly detected, arises less from a desire for self-aggrandizement—for the subtle shifts in perspective inherent in any exaggeration did not always make Downes seem more important and on occasion made him seem somewhat foolish—than from his romantic nature and his intense sense of morality, and of morality betrayed: that is, from a righteousness that, like many self-righteous perceptions, rests on a romantic view of life. In any case, what former intelligence agent has not been tempted (and in several instances fallen to the temptation) to romanticize, inflate, or confuse after the fact? Many men and a few women who were in the game have turned to writing spy fiction, or acting as consultants to Hollywood or Pinewood, or providing "backgrounding" for investigative journalists, usually for a fee. Fees tend to be better, certainly sales higher, if the material provided is at the least exciting. How many people, living on a fixed and miserly pension (and Downes had none), might make expansive statements to a young researcher (for though quite astute and well beyond his years, the interviewer, Timothy Naftali, was an undergraduate in Yale College at the time), especially to one who had searched him out at a time of deep depression? Further, we know that Downes sometimes spoke loosely, meaning to illustrate a general point with an example plucked from the air, not to be taken literally, as when he told an earlier interviewer, Dilys Winn, when she bearded him at Albany to discuss his knowledge of the spy game, that there had been a safe house in London at 8B Ebury Street, though research makes it clear that there is not now and was not then an 8B. Downes was, in essence, often not exact, and his remark about Philby is to be read as saying that Philby might well have been under casual suspicion—indeed, we know that he was, at least soon afterward—and little more. The interview reveals much about Downes's feelings in 1983 and very little about 1944.

Downes always thought of himself as a cynic. Certainly that was often the tone of his prose. Still, to his death he believed that America ought to be the hope of the world, even if it had not yet proved to be so. Downes was not so much a cynic as a sentimentalist, a man who expected the worst of his fellow man and was always surprised when he was right.

**Charles Seymour, president of Yale University, and the
popular lecturer from the Department of English
William Lyon (Billy) Phelps, in June 1939**

Norman Holmes Pearson
graduates from high
school, 1927.

Norman Holmes Pearson in
his senior year at Yale

Dana Durand, one of the first members of X-2, practicing
use of his gas mask in the back garden at Ayot Saint
Lawrence in the spring of 1943. With Durand is Captain
Ann Wilson, head of the local Women's Army Auxiliary
Corps, or WAACs, which became the U.S. Women's Army
Corps later that year.

Norman Holmes Pearson after his return to Yale. This photograph appears to have been taken in conjunction with the publication of Sir John Masterman's *Double-Cross System* and was not used.

H.D., Norman Pearson, and Bryher seated in front of the Sterling Memorial Library during their 1956 visit to Yale

5/23/44
Washington, D.C.

James R. Murphy, head of X-2, in civilian clothes on a Washington street in May 1944

ROBIN W. WINKS

The Ryder Street headquarters was a somber building that, except for a tidy and rather attractive foyer, was "ugly, cozy, and tight," at least in the eyes of Norman Holmes Pearson. He and his number two, James J. Angleton, with their secretaries, shared small offices (which were separated by a temporary partition) on the right-hand side of the building, two floors above the street sign. The building is now the property of the Charity Commission and is 14, rather than 7, Ryder Street.

ROBIN W. WINKS

Pearson's small flat in Hayes Mewes was above a tiny
garage. He often arrived from work well after dark, and
since blackout regulations did not permit his housekeeper,
the invaluable Alice, to leave a light burning, he had a small
panel of frosted glass installed in the window near the door
so that it would reflect back the streetlamp and enable him
to find his key while protected just inside the doorway.

By 1942 Yale was on a war footing. Air-raid wardens
scanned the night sky from a platform on top of the Sterling
Memorial Library.

The campus of Yale University was turned into a military camp, its colleges into barracks, its greenswards into parade grounds, as the war progressed. The cover of the Yale Alumni University Fund Association's annual report for 1942–1943 attested to the military tempo. Forty-three members of the class would lose their lives in the war.

Joseph Toy Curtiss in 1942, at the time of his appointment to the OSS. Curtiss was an assistant professor of English; he would be the centerpiece of an OSS mission to Turkey, using the Yale library as a cover. The photograph accompanied a release by the university's news bureau telling of Curtiss's impending mission to Switzerland to purchase books, thus justifying his absence from the campus.

THE SCARLET THREAD

Adventures in Wartime Espionage

DONALD DOWNES

OSS agent Donald Downes as he appeared on the dust jacket for his book

**Class photo of
James Jesus Angleton,
Yale '41**

**James Angleton in his room at
Silliman College, at work on
his various literary magazines**

**The Yale Literary Magazine. Back row: Whittemore,
Gardner, Abrahams, Angleton, Johnson. Front row:
Tompkins, Thompson, Pauker, Porter, Dahl.**

Sherman Kent, chief of the Office of National Estimates, CIA. Kent had been a professor of history at Yale.

Chester B. Kerr, Yale '36, director of the Yale University Press, who fought for the publication of Sir John Masterman's *The Double-Cross System* in 1972, thus getting into print for the first time an official record from the British intelligence

Arnold Wolfers, master of Pierson College and professor of international relations at Yale. Wolfers often steered appropriate young men into intelligence work and a disproportionate number came from Pierson. Fellows of the College included Wallace Notestein, a principal contact for recruiting; C. Bradford Welles, who left Yale for intelligence; and the dean of Yale College, William Clyde DeVane. The nattily dressed Wolfers was known for his lectures on worldwide strategic interests.

Sherman Kent in 1964 with J. B. Sinninghe-Damste,
director of the Netherlands Internal Security Service. A
cropped photo, showing only Sinninghe-Damste, was
marked Confidential but the photo amongst the coffee cups
was not.

Sherman Kent was especially pleased to have this photograph, in color, from Reinhard Gehlen, who from 1955 was director of the West German Federal Intelligence Service. Gehlen sent this full-dress portrait, inscribed with best wishes to Kent, at the time of his retirement, apparently mindful of the fact that Kent had begun to build a dossier on him in 1944. Kent annotated the photograph, noting that in 1969 it was one of the very few of Gehlen in existence.

Office of Strategic Services, 79 Champs-Élysées, Paris. Seated: Lt. (jg) Vernon Munroe; Mr. Ross Finney; Lt. Commander Dwight C. Baker; Pvt. Arthur M. Schlesinger, Jr.; Mr. Ralph Carruthers; Ensign Lawrence Stevens; Mr. Harold C. Deutsch; Lt. William Koren; Lt. (jg) Just Lunning. Standing: Cpl. Chat Paterson; Lt. Fred Foster; Cpl. Robert I. Kull.

FROM JAMES FREEMAN JAFFRAY, ET AL., EDS., *A History of the Class of 1941* (NEW HAVEN: YALE UNIVERSITY, 1941), P. 139.

Davenport College

EMERSON TUTTLE, *Master*
Curator of Prints in the University

HONORARY FELLOWS
PRESIDENT CHARLES SEYMOUR
PRESIDENT EMERITUS JAMES ROWLAND ANGELL

FELLOWS

RICHARD MERVIN BISSELL, JR.
Assistant Professor of Economics
PHILIP BISHOP COWLES
Assistant Professor of Immunology
FREDERICK SHERWOOD DUNN
Professor of International Relations
HOWARD THEODORE ENGSTROM
Associate Professor of Mathematics
LEONARD WOODS LABAREE
Associate Professor of History
MAYNARD MACK
Assistant Professor of English
CHAMPION HERBERT MATHEWSON
Professor of Metallurgy and Metallography
DANIEL MERRIMAN
Instructor in Biology

MAX FRANKLIN MILLIKAN
Instructor in Economics
GEORGE MOSELEY MURPHY
Assistant Professor of Chemistry
GEORGE WILSON PIERSON
Associate Professor of History
FREDERICK ALBERT POTTLE
Professor of English
THEODORE SIZER
Professor of the History of Art
WILLIAM LEONARD STEVENS, JR.
Instructor in English
CHAUNCEY BREWSTER TINKER
Sterling Professor of English Literature
LEWIS EDWIN YORK
Associate Professor of Drawing and Painting

ASSOCIATE FELLOWS

DEAN GODDERHAM ACHESON
Fellow of the Yale Corporation
MALCOLM PRATT ALDRICH, B.A. 1922
CHARLES McLEAN ANDREWS
Farnam Professor of American History, Emeritus
JAMES TIMKHAM BABB
Assistant Librarian Yale University
LUDLOW BULL
Research Associate in Egyptology
STARLING WINSTON CHILDS, B.A. 1891
NORMAN VAUX DONALDSON, B.A. 1915
THOMAS WELLS FARNAM
Associate Treasurer and Comptroller of the University
CURTIS PHILIP FIELDS
Executive Secretary of the Yale Alumni University Fund

EDWARD BELDEN GREENE
Fellow of the Yale Corporation
REV. SIDNEY LOVETT
Chaplain of the University
ARCHIBALD MacLEISH
B.A. 1915
ALBERT EIDE PARR
Director of the Peabody Museum, Professor of Oceanography
BRUCE SIMONDS
Professor of Music
MALCOLM RUTHERFORD THORPE
B.A. 1913
FREDERICK HOLME WIGGIN
B.A. 1904
THORNTON NIVEN WILDER
B.A. 1920

The Fellows of Davenport College. Bissell left academia for government work, became the driving force behind the U-2, and in 1958 was named deputy director Plans at the CIA. Millikan and Sizer were in intelligence during the war. Mack called them "the Zane Grey boys." Acheson, Babb, Lovett, MacLeish, and the master, Tuttle, who in time was succeeded by Merriman, all played important roles in our story.

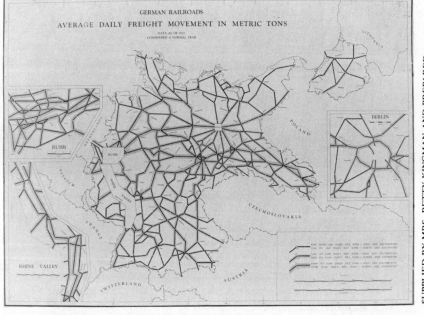

GERMAN RAILROADS
AVERAGE DAILY FREIGHT MOVEMENT IN METRIC TONS
DATA AS OF 1937
CONSIDERED A NORMAL YEAR

SUPPLIED BY MRS. BETTY KINGMAN AND PREPARED FOR PUBLICATION BY MR. EDWARD KLAMM

The chief of Presentation for the OSS was a Yale graduate who had taken an advanced degree in fine arts at the Yale Art School, Eugene Kingman. As chief, Kingman oversaw the production of maps and graphics that were to be used in the visual dramatization of intelligence information. The consumers of the OSS product—Army, Navy, State, Treasury, OWI, and others—were uniform in their praise of Kingman's work. This map, on the average daily freight movement in metric tons along German railroads, was developed from the technique of serial number analysis worked out by the Research and Analysis Branch. Had the Germans known of this map, they would have known of specific areas of penetration (as well as the method of compilation) against which they would have taken action.

Both CIA and other intelligence top brass gather to hear President Lyndon B. Johnson swear in Vice Admiral William F. Raborn, Jr., as director, Central Intelligence, with Richard Helms as DDI, on April 28, 1965. Behind the president and three figures to the right is James Angleton, head of counterintelligence, and next to him, with his hand in his pocket, is Sherman Kent, head of ONE. Next to Kent is Enno (Hank) Knoche, followed by Allen W. Dulles, J. Edgar Hoover, Raborn, Lyman Kirkpatrick, Helms, Cord Meyer, and at the far right Desmond Fitzgerald. From the left are R. Jack Smith, John W. Macy, Jr., two obscured and two unidentified figures, Ray Cline, Thomas Lucid, Colonel L. K. White, another obscured figure, Bronson Tweedy, and the president, followed by James Crichfield and Thomas Parrett.

CHAPTER FIVE

THE PROFESSOR

NORMAN HOLMES PEARSON

I t was Downes who first recommended the youngish Yale
academic Norman Holmes Pearson for a job with the OSS, partly
because he liked Pearson and his critical approach to life, partly
because he thought that, for liaison work in London, the OSS
would require someone who was socially and academically acceptable to the British intelligence services, and he knew that
Pearson's Yale pedigree, which was said to have been further em-
blazoned with a Rhodes Scholarship, would help, and partly because Downes simply liked to feel that he was moving and shaking

others. Downes was an unacademic counterpart to Wallace Notestein, the "natural conspirator," and it is not surprising that after
the war both Downes and Notestein would take credit for getting
Pearson into the game. Since Pearson was actively hoping for just
such an eventuality, neither really needed to have bothered.

Pearson would become the head of X-2, the cryptonym for the
counterintelligence branch, or CI, at OSS/London; he would be
one of the few Yale academics who, after returning to Yale, was
openly if discreetly identified with the intelligence game; and long
after the war he would perform one of his most important intelligence services in helping to get into public print a remarkable
wartime report on counterintelligence, "the greatest work yet
written on double agents"[1]—the judgment was in 1983—Sir John
Masterman's *The Double-Cross System,* the official report on how
Britain had turned all of Germany's agents in Britain during the
war. In a sense Downes destroyed himself by publication, for *The
Scarlet Thread* lost him many of the friends who had remained
loyal, as much for its indiscretions as for its tendency toward self-
aggrandizement, while Pearson preserved his good name in the
annals of espionage by his calculated, cool, and ever-discreet approach to the growing problem of postwar revelations. Some of
his best work, done for the OSS in its final months, were analyses
of the intelligence services of other nations and a sharply critical
report on recruiting methods, but since Pearson was little used by
the successor agency to the OSS, this work remained largely
unknown.

Shortly before Pearson's death one of his colleagues, the poet
John Hollander, who had been on the Yale faculty with Norman,
published a remarkable book-length poem, *Reflections on Espionage.*[2] The long poem had begun with a short one, known as
"transmission 9/17," published separately, which Hollander had
written as a result of reading *The Double-Cross System.* Published
in 1972 by the Yale University Press, this book had been the first
to reveal the work of the Twenty, or XX, or Double-Cross Committee (from which X-2 may have derived its title). Hollander had
been struck by the code names revealed in Masterman's book,
which rang in his head "like bells": thirty-nine of them, from Balloon, Bronx, Brutus, through Mutt, Jeff, The Snark, Sniper, Snow,
to Tricycle and Zigzag. From these he conceived of "a rather
inept, meditative spy named Cupcake . . . communicating with
his control, Lyrebird (a sort of monitory muse)." Then, in the fall

of 1973, Hollander had been brooding over the death of W. H. Auden, whose friendship he had shared with Pearson, and he decided to take a phrase he had granted Cupcake, "daily twilight messages"—the agent's radio transmissions in World World II— and treat them as journal entries, written up at dusk each day. Thus he wrote his poem, ultimately in ninety-eight transmissions, "with spies standing for writers and thinkers, living a kind of hidden life in the actual world." Auden became Steampump, James Merrill—to whom Hollander sent several of the transmissions, at first unsigned and unidentified—became Image, and Cupcake was given the task of brooding "on the epistemology of encoding"— that is, matters of artistic form. Other poets crept into the transmissions—Kilo (Pound),[3] Morosz (Russian for *frost*), Lac (Cal, reversed, for Lowell), and Norman Pearson appeared, not at all in disguise, as Puritan—his cover name with X-2.

Pearson was so delighted with the entire concept, he sent copies of the initial transmissions to Sir John Masterman, who replied with equal pleasure. Hollander had, it seemed, captured precisely the sense of nonce personage, of notional activity (Cupcake appears to be taken up largely with a jigsaw puzzle rather than intelligence gathering) inherent in counterintelligence, a conceit which another literary critic could readily appreciate. For Norman Pearson the spy game—for such he called it—was enormously intriguing intellectually, and while he shared his knowledge of it upon his postwar return to Yale with only a very few who had not played the game themselves, he never lost his fascination with espionage and intelligence as art forms, and with the highly calculated art of forgetting:[4]

> The major work on project Aspasia
> Is now complete and full reports are being
> Prepared. It took time, but as you might conclude,
> The Lady could not be hurried along. I
> Have heard little from the others: the wretched
> Gland will be out of town for a bit, Riddle
> Waits for things to develop, Kidd is silent
> (At least, to me: I'm sure he is off being
> Noisy somewhere). A strange thing, though: yesterday
> I got through ordinary mail a moving letter
> From Puritan (you remember what once in
> Venice the fading Kilo on his pale bed

Said when I told him Puritan, sending his
Regards, "wished to be remembered"?—Kilo half
Looked up: "He is in no danger of being
Forgotten" was the reply—

                        .   .   .

Puritan, no longer
In the service, yet can hardly not be said
To be involved with the work still, and always.

Norman Holmes Pearson would have especially enjoyed the irony of these lines, for at times he felt neglected by his department, his university.[5] He did not speak of his wartime work to his students, and seldom to his colleagues, even to one who, in fact, went into intelligence work in the 1960s. He had, as he wrote to a friend in 1951, lost momentum dreadfully because of his four years of intelligence service, and his major book, on Nathaniel Hawthorne, was slipping away from him while another that he had projected, on Eugene O'Neill, was not even begun. He could not explain to his peers in his department why it was taking so long to recover his momentum, and when student reporters twice asked him directly about his years with the OSS, he replied with vague generalities. He told his immediate family that he had parachuted into Denmark, but he told no one else. Though he believed there was a connection between the academic and the intelligence worlds, not one of his students recalls his drawing such a connection to their attention, though he was the most attentive of dissertation directors, the most careful of seminar supervisors. Most of his colleagues at Yale, especially those who arrived well after the war, disbelieved the few rumors that circulated, and as two of his former colleagues agreed in 1985, most of the postwar generation of new scholars "shamelessly patronized" him, unmindful of his generosity and kindness, "insensitive to his genuine gifts and overly irritated by his fallibilities."[6] As Norman Pearson reviewed his students' essays, wrote his many book reviews, perhaps he reflected, as Lyrebird did, "Today in doing some routine decoding/I thought, as a sad, mild wind brushed with half a/Heart at the papers on my desk, of the days/When no decoding was routine, when ciphers/All gleamed with newness and possibility."

Norman Holmes Pearson was born April 13, 1909, in Gardner, Massachusetts. His parents were well-to-do, and Norman led an intellectually contented, warm life. His father was a merchant and, for a time, the mayor of Gardner, and the Chester Pearson home on Elm Street, while not precisely convivial, was often the scene of serious discussions between the leading bankers, businessmen, and political figures of the town. The Pearsons got down to Worcester from time to time, or to Boston, for social and musical occasions, and they knew well the Berkshires and the White Mountains of New Hampshire as summer retreats. Norman was close to his mother, Fanny Kittredge, and she took an interest in all that he did; he corresponded with her regularly, even when in England working for the OSS.[7]

Until 1938 Norman Pearson suffered from an open, sometimes suppurating, sore on his left hip, the result of a childhood bout of tuberculosis that was mishandled medically, and as an undergraduate he had been in a wheelchair much of the time. One result was the need to retire from time to time to put bandages and plaster on the sore; another was the appearance of being hunchbacked. As he grew older he walked with a more pronounced limp that became in time a heavy, rolling shuffle. He could eat very little, because an extra pound or two put painful pressures on his slight frame. Perhaps to compensate for what he knew would be regarded as a physical weakness—though he did not particularly regard it as such—he tried out for the usual schoolboy athletics, and he took a scholarly interest in the many books for boys that dwelt on athletic prowess. He once said that John R. Tunis was the best of the American lot, but that he much preferred the more rousing tales of G. A. Henty and the colorful escapades of the many more-or-less interchangeable teenage heroes that roamed the pages of *Boy's Own Paper* and its imitators. When, in London, he celebrated V-E Day by climbing well up on one of the stone lions in Trafalgar Square, an OSS partner who understood him well thought that "the professor" had felt it necessary to demonstrate that he could be as physically exuberant as the next. Once when he awoke, flat under a table, dead drunk—for the only time in his life—following a victory celebration in Copenhagen, into which he had entered at personal risk, he was very happy, for it was good to show that he could be one of the fellows. Certainly when he chose to be the first American officer to enter Oslo after the German capitulation in 1945, he could only have made the choice because he simply wanted to be the first, for he could easily have arrived by a safer if slower means. He refused to think of himself as handicapped.

Pearson seemed destined for the life of the mind, however. At

school the young scholar was organized, intense, and well liked.
When only fourteen, he completed architectural sketches—elevations—of the Gardner High School that were used for many years
after as a school display; the elevations still survive in his papers.
(Gardner High School was so proud of him, he was invited back
while still a graduate student at university to give the 1935 alumni
day address.) When he graduated from the public high school in
1927, Norman and his parents opted for a further year of preparation, so that he could be certain to be ready for Yale, and he
went to the Phillips Academy in Andover, Massachusetts. There
he carried away a major prize for oratory, declaiming on "The
Problems of Assimilation." He went down to Yale in the autumn
of 1928, intending to study economics, but when in his third year
he won the Henry H. Strong Prize for American Literature for an
essay on Nathaniel Hawthorne's college years, he was launched
into a new major, toward his life's career, and upon the road of
Hawthorne scholarship, in which he would become one of the
nation's leading figures.[8]

In the summer of 1929 the Pearsons traveled to Europe. Norman kept a journal, as he would do sporadically the rest of his
life, in particular of his impressions of Berlin. Already his most
intense interests were literary and historical. In England he left
his parents to their rainy-day tour of the Shakespeare country while
he had a grand time at the British Museum, where he had the
discipline to look only at the Elgin Marbles; at the Tate Gallery;
a fine lunch on his own at the Shades; and then a rousing run
through the Old Curiosity Shop (as much for what he might buy
as for Dickens), before ordering some clothes on Bond Street.
Not one to abandon a goal already set upon, he carried on to
Kensington Gardens to pay his respects to the statue of Peter Pan
in a pouring rain.

One of Norman's first purchases in his freshman college year
was a copy of Mark van Doren's pioneering *Anthology of World
Poetry,* published in 1928 by the enterprising Albert and Charles
Boni. There for the first time Pearson encountered the world's
range of poetic expression—translations from the Chinese, San-
skrit, Persian, Hebrew, Greek, Russian—and also encountered old
friends from English and American poetry in a new context.
Emerson, Longfellow, Poe, Whitman were there, of course, but
so were poets that had not been taught, even at Andover: Ezra
Pound and "H. D.," at that point the living ideogram she repre-

sented still whiskered with inverted commas. Pearson also liked
the anthology because of the way it brought order into the "Her-
aclitean flow of poetry," and he decided that he would, one day,
capture at least for a moment some part of that flow by doing his
own anthologies. He did not wait long to achieve this goal, for
while a graduate student, in 1937, he published with William Rose
Benét, Yale '07, a two-volume *Oxford Anthology of American
Literature,* which was at once hailed as the best collection of
American prose and poetry available to the general reader. Later,
with W. H. Auden, Pearson would co-edit five volumes on *Poets
of the English Language.* It was generally acknowledged that
Pearson had done most of the work, as is often the case with a
junior partner in a literary enterprise, on both projects, certainly
on the latter.

For Norman Pearson these years at Yale were triumphantly
happy ones. He was an honor student throughout, was an editor
of *The Yale Daily News,* and began his lifelong habit of collecting,
first editions, whole authors, illustrative material, autographed letters. He liked the environment of the university and intended to
stay in it, though he did not precisely lionize his professors: years
later, when living near St Albans, in England, and working for the
OSS, he and a friend played at trying to spot the graying head of
George Bernard Shaw as he strolled about in his garden in Ayot
Saint Lawrence, and when, one day, he saw not only bare head
but beard and then, wondrous to behold, the entire figure emerge
from the garden gate and walk off toward the post office, Pearson
remarked that Yale's famous Billy Phelps, lecturer extraordinary
to young minds first being exposed to English life and letters, could
make an entire lecture out of such a moment and would probably
call it "My Summer with Shaw." (Pearson admitted he might just
do the same.) His was a gentle view of the academic profession:
he thought it so important, he was largely relaxed about it, himself, and those little acts of theater that made everyone in a university so happy.

After graduation in 1932 Pearson set off for Europe, having won
a lesser scholarship at Oxford. He studied also at the Institut für
Ausländer, at the University of Berlin, to improve the German he
would need for graduate school, and then at Magdalen College,
where he earned a second B.A. in 1934 (and, in due course, paid
his fee to pick up the M.A. that Oxford was prepared to award
him in 1941). At Andover Pearson had been vigorous in his at-

tacks on pure race theories and had advocated accepting and as-
similating the talent of the world into the American mainstream,
but during his time in Berlin he was briefly taken in by the prev-
alent rhetoric, and he concluded that national socialism just might
be what the Germans needed. Pearson was deeply impressed by
Hitler's ability to master a crowd. Nevertheless, on the day Germany and Britain went to war, Pearson rejected all things German, even though he confessed to having been "nearly Nazi in
[his] mind" for a short time in 1933.

In 1941 Pearson—seriously delayed by his operation in 1938[9]—
received his doctorate from Yale, working under Stanley T. Williams: his dissertation, an edition of Hawthorne's *Italian Notebooks,* maintained that singularity of purpose begun with his
undergraduate essay. As a graduate student he had joined with
Williams, then the Colgate Professor of English, and with Randall
Stewart, the poet, and Manning Hawthorne, to edit the complete
letters of the great New England writer. (By 1950 Pearson would
be left to carry out this project alone, and the material remained
in manuscript, said to be virtually ready for the publisher, at his
death in 1975, truly the work of a lifetime.) In 1941 Pearson also
joined the Yale faculty as an instructor in English.[10]

Four days after Pearl Harbor Pearson wrote to his friend and
mentor, Ralph H. Gabriel, that because he was a complete interventionist, he was pleased that America was at last in the war.
While he thought being antiwar was a valid literary position—he
sent Gabriel the text of some leftist antiwar ballads—as a practical
matter, England's cause was, and for some time ought to have
been seen to have been, America's cause as well. He didn't know
what he could do in the war himself—he would certainly be rejected by the army—and he feared, as he told his mother, that he
might lose his job at the end of the year, since a rapid decline in
enrollment, as students joined the services, most likely would mean
that instructors would be let go.

Pearson had new responsibilities as well, and they required hard,
practical decisions, for he was newly married, the second husband to Susan Silliman Bennett, the great-great-granddaughter of
Benjamin Silliman, whose ties to Yale were deep. Susan was a
descendant of Jonathan Trumbull, Revolutionary War governor of
Connecticut, after whom one Yale college was named; a second
bore Silliman's name; and Susan's grandfather, Arthur Williams
Wright, had received from Yale the first Ph.D. degree in science

given in the United States. Norman now had two lively and lovely stepdaughters to look after as well, and he doted on them: the story went round the campus that after he had proposed to Susan Bennett, he had formally repeated his proposal to both girls.

A university is a grab bag of opportunities for those who will take them, and Norman Pearson, like Bill DeVane, looked upon whatever he might be asked to do as an opportunity to be improved upon. One such opportunity now came through Donald Downes, who had met Pearson in 1935, and who since 1938 had been a sometime correspondent. Downes asked Pearson to poke into a few matters for him and to find him a Portuguese-speaking academic—this turned out to be C. Malcolm Batchelor, still a graduate student and shortly to be off to the OWI—and both he and Wallace Notestein hinted at work to be done by a new intelligence organization that was just getting into gear. But the year passed, and Pearson was rehired, and these winks and nods came to nought. Instead, Pearson plunged into helping Charles S. Walker in his role as Yale's "Secretary of War," writing a series of letters to thirteen universities—all obvious ones, except for the University of Colorado, where Pearson had passed the summer of 1938 as a visiting faculty member, an exciting experience for one who didn't have his doctorate yet, and where he had become a fast friend of George F. Reynolds's, Colorado's noted Shakespearean scholar[11]—to find out what English departments were doing to assist in the war effort. He received notably useful replies from Reynolds, and also from the three other state institutions to which he wrote (Indiana, Iowa, Rutgers), while some universities—Harvard, notably—gave him a waffly response. (Later Pearson would observe that state universities, having to account to nonscholarly—and sometimes scholarly—taxpayers, knew a lot more about making quick decisions than private institutions would ever know.) Perry Miller at Harvard, the great authority on Puritan thought, was lecturing at Fort Devens, and was finding that newspapermen appealed more to the rank and file, for they had the "right idiom." English departments weren't doing much, Pearson found, for the history, political science, and economics departments had moved out first; Yale was the exception, thanks to Dean DeVane. George Sherburn, from Harvard, did have sound advice for those who taught subjects that the army and navy might not value, however: "I only know my present duty, and my Lord's command—to occupy till he come."[12]

Pearson joined a group eager to persuade President Seymour to be more supportive of senior faculty who entered the services, and he may have fallen afoul of the formidable Lefty Lewis in the matter, for soon after, when Pearson found himself working for Lewis in CID, they proved incompatible. George W. Pierson in history, Richard Sewall, then an assistant professor of English, and others were drawing up a statement to Seymour, and Norman was assigned the task of trying the general idea of some proenlistment manifesto on Lewis without revealing to him the proposed text. At the time Lewis was strongly anti-Seymour, and the party of gentle conspirators feared that he might want to bring up heavy artillery too soon. A copy was slipped to at least two members of the Yale Corporation, the Reverend Henry Knox Sherrill and Reverend Henry Sloane Coffin, the latter a fellow of Pearson's college. This was fairly heady business for untenured and very junior members of the faculty to be playing at. Doubly so for Pearson, for at precisely the crucial moment he was away, in Washington, exploring ways by which he might leave Yale for the duration of the war.

A hint of something in the offing had come to Pearson in the summer of 1942, by way of Downes, when thought was being given to sending someone to Switzerland to purchase materials for R&A, using the Yale University Library as a cover. This assignment went, as we have seen, to Joseph Curtiss and was ultimately diverted to Turkey. Downes had sent Pearson a note from Mexico, where he was picking up his Spanish contact list, to urge him to "give Notey the opportunity to tell you in what connection we discussed your possibly going far afield on a war job." [13] This was a silly thing for Downes to have done, doubly silly given the fact that Pearson wound up in the super-secret X-2 branch of OSS, but it was typical of Downes. Pearson must have thought so too, for he didn't expect much to come of the note. Another wink and nod followed in October, and Pearson went down to Washington to see what he might nose out, especially for overseas work, without success. And then, while staying at the Seigneury Club, near Montebello, midway between Montreal and Ottawa, Pearson received a cable from David F. Seiferheld, asking him to come to Washington.

Seiferheld was a well-placed textile executive with French connections who had graduated from Yale in 1926, in Donald Downes's nominative class. He was working with the Censor unit in Secret Intelligence, and he was developing ties into the German exile community led, in New York, by Dr. Karl Frank, a close friend of Arthur Goldberg's. Downes was working through this same group, and apparently he seized the occasion to press Pearson's name forward once again, with a foreign assignment in mind, since Pearson's English connections were felt to be superb and his German and French at least adequate. But precisely at this juncture CID was in the midst of one of its periodic flaps, and as George Bowden noted, someone was needed to bridge the gap that was opening between CID and SI over the proper treatment of German intercepts. Because Pearson knew Lefty Lewis, someone thought he might be able to tame that tiger. Happy to have a war-related job at last, though disappointed that it would be in Washington, Pearson joined the SI Censor unit in December, reading material coming in from Allied censors in the Western Hemisphere, and providing liaison with Lewis's operation as Seiferheld's number two. The editorial staff of which he was a part had been established only the month before—it included President Seymour's daughter—and because he was in at the beginning, Pearson would be able to help define the job as he did it.*

> *The need for* frissons—*that is most dangerous,*
> *The void in which our people often vanish.*
> Transmission 4/3 (To Image)

Pearson did not last long as a liaison with CID. The work itself was pleasant enough, especially since it called directly on his

---

*One other man may have helped convince the OSS that Pearson was someone they wanted: Charles Beecher Hogan. Hogan had graduated from Yale in 1928; though he did not take a doctorate, he would, in 1943, as the faculty was depleted, become an instructor in English and would, thereafter, help to invent Yale's famous regime of Daily Themes. He was the curator of the Rare Book Room at the university library in 1942, and he and Pearson often conferred over purchases and gifts. Beecher Hogan was one of those Yale figures of the time, not as typical as afterglow would have one believe, who was well educated, sensitive, very intelligent, and quite without financial need, so that he could do what he wanted to do. His name invariably floats to the surface whenever anyone of his generation reflects on who might have been a conduit into the OSS, for he simply—and graciously—knew everyone, at Yale, in Washington, everywhere. As a friend wrote, he was " 'arrayed' like a proverbial lily of the field. . . . The good life rested like a handsome cloak upon his shoulders. But, unlike those lilies, Beecher surely toiled and spun." Bibliophile, Shakespearean scholar, friend of Archibald MacLeish, colleague of Herman Liebert, he was happy to pick up the phone and put people in touch with each other. He had been two years behind Seiferheld. Pearson thought, whatever the case may have been, that Hogan had something to do with his being at OSS.[14]

training, for a censor (a misnomer, as the unit did not in fact censor material, but rather simply read materials—picked out unal-
tered by William Stephenson's operations in Bermuda and
elsewhere—as intently as possible for hidden meanings) had to
know how to read, really *read,* closely, without interruption, how
to interrogate a manuscript to see what an author intended as opposed to what was written, and surely this was what the Yale
Department of English had been best at? There were, to be sure,
also many excerpted letters to be read, and everything had to be
cataloged (happily, by someone else) and sent along, if judged
important, to the appropriate OSS office. But the gems were few,
certainly not like spending an hour in the company of T. S. Eliot,
and the prose seldom seemed worthy of the effort, at least not in
any literary sense. Further, the office was fraught with petty jealousies, and the niggling side that meticulous and repetitive work
may bring out in those who have run to scholarship as a refuge
rather than an adventure surfaced too often, he felt, amongst his
colleagues. There was no doubt, he thought, about the general
importance of CID or R&A, and he enjoyed as much as any man
finding out the annual rainfall in Tibet, the angle of a beach at
Okinawa, or the depth of the harbor at Marseilles; but to his surprise he found he did not much like working with fellow Ph.D.s.
They had, he noted, one consistently valuable ability: they knew
how to apply the seat of their pants to a seat of a chair in a library, and they did not imagine that after four hours of such application nature demanded that they break for coffee—they worked
until they found the answer to the question they were asking—
but while he noted this, it scarcely made for exciting company.
More important, it did not make for decisive company: later he
would remark that X-2 consisted largely of professors and lawyers, and of the two, he preferred lawyers "because they had
been trained to make up their minds on the evidence at hand,
whereas professors prefer to meditate." [15] This was, a little less
precisely, the thought John Foster Dulles, President Eisenhower's
secretary of state and brother to Allen Dulles, director of Central
Intelligence, had in mind when he said that academics argued to
conclusions while diplomats had to argue to decisions.

Pearson also disliked the pettiness of the social life in Washington, of which there seemed a great deal, and above all the preten-
tiousness of the social arbiters for whom the capital has always
been known. He wrote to his wife of one hostess who always

called the Hotel St. Regis in New York the *Sawn Raygee*; he told
the tale of how fashionably dressed women in Chile wore wrin-
kled dresses to show they were packed from Paris (if they bought
their dresses in Chile, they crumpled them), and implied that
Washington grand dames were no better; he disliked the social
closeness to Yale, from which he had wanted a break, as when
he found not only his president's daughter, but Lewis Curtis's
sister-in-law working at the OSS; he discovered he did not think
well of Donovan; as an academic he was suspected of being left-
leaning, and to some proved it when he suggested that the Dies
committee ought to chase down Fascists as well as Communists;
he found the scion of one of the nation's wealthiest families who
was thrust upon him as an assistant "incredibly dumb"; he erupted
often in what he knew was unwise anger.[16]

Most important, Pearson soon found that he could not get along
with Lefty Lewis, and perhaps did not want to. Across a shore
dinner at Harvey's Restaurant Seiferheld had suggested that
something both interesting and important was about to be set up
in England. Seiferheld was caught up in the general feud with J.
Edgar Hoover, which was making life complicated for Downes,
Goldberg, and Bowden, and could not be sent to the London post
himself, as Downes's friend Sid Clark pointed out. Pearson made
it clear that he wanted to go and so, as he put it to his wife,
quoting a jumbled intercept, he had to "sit tight in his pants."
Early in March he was able to reveal to his mother that he was
being sent to England: "The job is not spectacular," he wrote,
"but should be even more interesting than what I have been doing,
and will be one with a great deal more responsibility." This was
a calculated understatement, for he was, in fact, to take the lead
in setting up, under SI's aegis, a counterintelligence division of
OSS in London.

When Donovan first set up undercover operations, he had begun with a Special Activities branch of two divisions: a Special
Intelligence Service, charged with—if the term may be used—
straightforward espionage, and Special Operations (the *special* in
both titles meant simply *secret*), charged with sabotage, guerrilla
warfare, and subversion, roughly the equivalent of British SOE,
Special Operations Executive. SI was referred to as SA/B and SO
was called SA/G, nicely confusing matters, these being designa-
tions originally given by using the last initial of the division chief
at the time: David K. E. Bruce, head of SI, and M. Preston Good-

fellow, head of SO. (The first director of SI, Wallace P. Phillips, a civilian assistant to the director of ONI, served for only six weeks, not long enough for SI to become SA/P.) Counterintelligence work was felt to be a British special talent, and Donovan wanted to tap it. This meant primarily MI6, the organization charged with activities outside the British Empire, and MI5, which operated within the United Kingdom and the empire.[17]

Though COI had been authorized to conduct undercover operations as early as September of 1941, it had initially lacked the capacity to act on the authority, quite apart from the immediate opposition expressed by other American intelligence agencies and the obvious lack of enthusiasm on the part of the British. Indeed, not until October 27, 1943, would the Joint Chiefs issue a directive broadly enough framed to have the effect of lifting all restrictions on the types of information the OSS might collect. Even then, the limitation with respect to operating in Latin America, on which the FBI had been so insistent, continued to apply.[18] Nor did the directive provide SI or X-2 with carte blanche, for the State Department continued to object to certain types of OSS activities in neutral countries. Herschell Johnson, the American minister in Stockholm, insisted that SI and any offshoots could not operate in Sweden, and the OSS professed to accept this limitation, though with crossed fingers, since Norman Pearson's expense accounts clearly show that he was issued Swedish kronor and that he was in Norway on X-2 matters; and as we have seen, Ambassador Hayes in Spain was initially no less adamant about SI, SO, or X-2 activities.[19]

The originators of X-2 were James R. Murphy and George K. Bowden. Murphy was especially close to Donovan; a lawyer who had worked with Donovan in the Department of Justice, he was a slim, quiet-voiced man of utter loyalty who won the admiration and affection of all who worked for him, and who showed a fine eye as a recruiter. As early as December 1941 Donovan had told Murphy to give thought to forming a counterintelligence service within the OSS, to the formation of the kind of register essential to such work, and to organizing a plan for cooperation with the British.

The British were enjoying considerable success, Murphy learned, in detecting German agents operating in the United Kingdom, and while the close correlation of register material was vital to such a task, the greater breakthrough had occurred because they were able to penetrate the German ciphers. This meant, of course, that the British were also "reading" German messages about flight plans and troop movements and were in a strong position on order of battle matters. While the Americans had heard hints of this capacity, naturally enough they were not to be let in on the secret when the United States was a neutral nation, but clearly now there must be liaison with the Americans on the matter of the German intercepts.

So far as we know now, the Ultra secret was the most closely held intelligence coup of the war. Although over ten thousand individuals knew in some small way of this secret, not one word of it escaped to the general public until nearly three decades after the war when, in 1974, the publication of the first book on the subject opened the door to a dozen more. Called, not with exaggeration, "the most comprehensive and effective system for penetrating an enemy's mind that has ever been evolved,"[20] the Ultra secret emanated from a small and rather ugly estate forty miles north of London on a fast line: Bletchley Park. Donovan sent George Bowden, the man who had organized the initial SI branches—insurance, labor, and censorship—off to England to learn all that he could about the operation.

In London Bowden talked with MI6 officials, especially in Section V, which was charged with counterespionage, and he proposed that a small American liaison group be sent to England to prepare summaries based on Ultra traffic. The group would be augmented as the need arose, and if demonstrably valuable, might become the basis for a separate unit. For the time, however, the group would continue within SI, with William Maddox, the Princeton political scientist, in charge until the new men could arrive. Clearly they would be subordinate to the larger, more sophisticated, still-growing Section V, and they would not have their own means of transmitting Ultra information. They would be there to learn.

Bowden's proposal touched several nerves. There were those who resented any suggestion that American intelligence should draw upon, or take instruction from, the British, though Donovan was not among these. (Later, when Sir William Stephenson and others claimed that they had taught the Americans what they knew, or when those charged with creating a postwar central intelligence agency wished to refute the claim that such an agency might become an American equivalent of the KGB, there was a good bit of talk about the paternity of American intelligence. While the issue of paternity, which was in some measure a smoke screen, is not relevant here,[21] the presence of Anglophobia in the FBI and, to a lesser extent, in G-2 at the time of the setting up of the OSS liaison group is relevant.) There were professional rivalries, of course: both G-2 and ONI resisted any arrangement by which OSS would receive future Ultra material, which they felt should be exclusively theirs. There were doubts on the part of some British as to whether the Americans could be trusted with Most Secret information. Despite these reservations, however, Donovan persisted in dispatching an initial team of four men.

Late in February of 1943, Pearson was told of his new assignment. First he and his team members were to take the usual OSS course at the camp outside Washington. He enjoyed it, especially the derring-do bits that satisfied all his "small-boy instincts." The lectures were, he found, first rate, though he liked best a captured German film on the German parachute attack on Crete. At unarmed-combat time the instructor concentrated on showing Pearson what was possible for him, and spotting that he had an unusually strong grip, taught him much "fiendish stuff" about silent killing. To his surprise Pearson also discovered that he was rather good at quick-fire small arms. Those selected as members of his team left something to be desired, he felt, but apparently his companions did not sense his true feelings, for they got along well enough. There was another professor, Dana Durand, a prickly man who was, without doubt, both efficient and brilliant, though Pearson initially pronounced him "a bore" and, three days later, cruelly promoted him to "an incredible bore." (He would, nonetheless, work with Durand in London longer than with anyone else and came to change his opinion.) Then there was John McDonough, Rhodes Scholar and former star quarterback from the University of Chicago who had learned his moves from the famed Amos Alonzo Stagg. McDonough was a "burly sort of hearty who obviously enjoyed a glass of ale" and was a happy balance to Durand. For a moment Pearson thought that Richard Bissell, the former Yale economics instructor, might join the OSS and be assigned to the group, but he was not.

McDonough, who was a captain in the army, got off first, in March, to join with Murphy, who had been sent ahead, in looking for quarters. Pearson and Durand, as civilians, were delayed pending further negotiations with the head of G-2. On April 9 they left for London on an exhausting Pan American flight which stopped at Bermuda, Horta in the Azores, Lisbon, Foynes, Shannon, and Bristol, arriving on April 13, Pearson's thirty-fourth birthday. McDonough, Durand, and Pearson went on almost directly to St Albans, twenty miles north of London, where most of Section V was based, for an intensive training course on Ultra. Two additional men were soon added: Robert I. Blum, from the international relations department at Yale—a rare person in that he had, like his mentor Arnold Wolfers, a professional interest in intelligence work before the war—was reassigned from R&A/London, and in November Hubert Will, a Chicago attorney who had been recruited by Bowden and Donovan specifically for counterintelligence work, was brought in as the first head of the unit. Will was an efficient administrator and a quick study, and though he never warmed to Pearson, whom he characterized as a "Machiavellian, outspoken Anglophile" who, he suspected, formed a personal friendship with the head of MI6, Section V, Felix Cowgill, in part to circumvent the need to go through Will for information. Will did like the group as a whole, however, and when a young Yale graduate, James J. Angleton, '41, arrived, he and Murphy agreed that here was a man they could trust, perhaps because, as Will recalled later, Angleton could remember his lies and never forgot the ends in view.[22]

These men—Murphy, Pearson, Durand, McDonough, Blum, and, a bit later, Will—were the founding core in London of what, on June 15, 1943, had become a separate OSS branch. The folklore of the branch says that Pearson suggested the name, given the several ambiguous ways in which it could be rendered, perhaps because it would mark a break from the alphabet soup of other OSS (and virtually all government) offices, and—though this suggestion came much later—because Pearson considered the liaison work with the British XX Committee to be the most important assignment the new branch was taking on. Yet others suggested that, as Cowgill's unit was designated X-B, Pearson may have promoted X-2 to show the close linkage between the groups. (The British, in turn, referred to the American unit as V-48, for the forty-eight states.) Whatever the origin of the designation, there is little doubt that X-2 hewed closely to the British at first, developing only slowly an independent American line on counterintelligence, while SI continued with secret intelligence. X-2's tasks, as time passed, involved both counterintelligence and counterespionage, whatever the formal duties assigned to it.

Pearson thought X-2 the right ambience for Yale men, and from time to time he would recommend one for assignment, though there is little evidence that these recommendations were accepted in any systematic fashion until he succeeded Will as chief of X-2/London. Later Pearson would suggest that Angleton was assigned to London through his intervention, but this seems not to have been the case. Calvin Tenney, who like Pearson had graduated from Gardner High School and who had just finished his doctorate in French at Yale, did become Pearson's flatmate in London in 1944, until Pearson, exasperated with Tenney's untidy habits, asked him to leave; and Pearson may have played some role in getting Daniel T. Moore, Jr., who had graduated from the Sheffield Science School at Yale a year ahead of him, assigned to X-2.[23] Pearson also succeeded in persuading headquarters to send to him his excellent CID secretary, Susan Tully, who joined X-2 in June. He was not, however, the person who initially determined the shape of X-2 in London: this fell to Jimmy Murphy, the man most widely admired, the man with Donovan's ear.[24]

During this time OSS won the right to a more independent, though still clearly subordinate, position on Ultra, and Donovan and Murphy decided that the new unit ought to work out of London, primarily from the MI6 offices at 14 Ryder Street. There liaison with SI remained easy, for the head of all of OSS/London was David Bruce, by marriage a member of the Mellon family (itself a significant contributor to the ranks of the OSS), a skillful diplomat—after the war Bruce would be U.S. ambassador to Germany, France, and the United Kingdom—and from January 1942 to January 1943 the overall director of Secret Intelligence.[25] Only twenty-five members strong in June of 1943, the new X-2 grew to over 500 personnel worldwide by the fall of 1944.

Between 1943 and 1945 the OSS developed a comprehensive American accumulation of information on enemy espionage agents and cover organizations. While there was some overlap with FBI files, which concentrated on agents operating within the United States, and the British registry was older and larger, the OSS registry was uniquely strong along the Mediterranean. Techniques for filing were unabashedly taken from the British (whose strengths naturally lay in the coverage of enemy agents working within the United Kingdom and France) and were adapted as needed to the areas in which SI and X-2 were to do their greatest work. By the end of the war the collection consisted of cards on 300,000 individuals, "the second-best CE [counterespionage] storehouse in the world." The OSS, in cooperation with the Allies, chiefly the British, contributed to the apprehension of 1,300 enemy agents in military zones alone and was primarily responsible for rendering ineffective German "stay-behind" networks—intelligence groups left to be overrun as the Allied troops advanced, then to work from behind the Allied lines—in Italy and played a significant cooperative role in neutralizing the German stay-behind network in France. X-2 and SI, working together, also identified eighty-five members of German and Italian espionage groups in Mozambique. By the end of 1944, when there were sixteen X-2 field stations, information was pouring in on nearly a million individuals, through liaison with other allied CE organizations. The French, Norwegian, and Italian services made their files completely available to the OSS, while relations with the Danes, Swedes, Dutch, Belgians, Greeks, and Turks "were similarly satisfactory"—meaning that they responded readily to queries, though they did not allow the Americans to search their files.* Information was shared regularly, through the State Department, with American ambassadors in neutral countries, so that representations might be made against individuals spying (particularly in Spain and Turkey) on behalf of enemy nations; with the Visa Division of the State Department, on foreigners applying to enter the United States; and with the FBI, ONI, and MIS (Military Intelligence Section of the War Department.)[26] After the war Pearson would single out the creation of the registry as X-2's greatest accomplishment.

The Ultra materials were essential to the building of the registry, as they were essential to judging the enemy's intentions, and Pearson and his fellow X-2 agents were the key link for OSS directly to Ultra. Accordingly, they were chosen because it was assumed that they could learn quickly and would mesh with the British easily. They were briefed and trained—indoctrinated was Pearson's word—at St Albans, both because it was on the way to Bletchley Park and because Section V had its principal offices there. And then they were set up in London, where they could easily liaise with all relevant intelligence bodies, British and American, and could, as X-2 developed, reach out to the Continent.

---

*Though Pearson later wrote that the Poles opened their files, he did not include them in a paragraph he drafted in 1949 for the official history of the OSS.

This liaison work turned on Pearson, and on who he was or was presumed to be, not on what he knew. Downes had advised Donovan and Seiferheld that whoever set up this early experiment in counterintelligence must be able to learn from the British, since they were the masters at the game; at the same time, the person must not be slavishly Anglophilic, as many academics tended to be, for he would have to bring a critical eye to the British operation so that the Americans would remain independent of, and ultimately improve upon, the British system. Learning, Downes argued, had to be between social equals if OSS were not forever to be the junior partner. A Yale man, an academic, might carry it off, he thought, and certainly ought to if also a Rhodes Scholar (which Downes believed Pearson to be)—though he acknowledged that the British could be quite snobbish about Rhodes Scholars, who were thought of as the best of the colonials and thus eminently teachable, though not necessarily as yet equals (this was before the postwar creation of Fulbright Scholarships, the first holders of which were, when they arrived at Oxbridge, referred to as the Halfbrights, creating a hierarchical situation by which the Rhodes Scholar moved into full acceptance). Pearson was encouraged to use English academic terms and, apparently, to inflate his résumé slightly, for most of his British counterparts called him a don, and though he was in fact an instructor still moderately fearful for his tenure, he converted his brief 1938 summer appointment at the University of Colorado into an associate professorship on the record and was referred to then and in the literature since as "a Yale professor." This established the necessary prestige, since in the English system the title of professor was reserved to the head of a department and carried the same connotation as a chair does in an American university. Because he knew that many professors in Britain did not hold doctorates, a degree not yet either required or even honored, he also saw to it that he was referred to as Professor Pearson, never as Dr. Pearson, and he advised his other doctoral colleagues—Durand, Blum, and Tenney—to do the same. Durand refused and was soon branded by the British as arrogant.[27]

The English were not, and are not, precisely snobbish about American academia. They did think that there were perhaps only four or five American universities of significance, and most likely none of equality to Oxbridge, and they had a frightful problem with the state universities, which they constantly confused, just as they often confused the states. If no one on an admissions committee at Oxford could be found so recently as 1970 who had heard of Emory, Tulane, or George Washington universities, excellent institutions all, one ought not to be surprised that a far more insular, and desparately beleaguered, England of 1943 doubted the very existence of institutions with names like the University of Southern California (did this mean there was a separate state of that name? or that there was also, therefore, a University of Northern Alabama? Well, no, not yet). Nor could the bright lights of Oxbridge be blamed for not understanding the idea of tenure—against what state or church did their appointees need the protection of tenure?—or the intensely *nouveau riche* rank consciousness of even so egalitarian an institution as Yale. Surely they were not entirely wrong to think that the odd pattern of an American undergraduate curriculum (as a college freshman Ezra Pound studied algebra, public speaking, German grammar, American colonial history, English composition, Latin, and American government, four subjects more appropriate to secondary school and two irrelevant for the English gentleman) did not precisely prepare a student to sup with the greats. Pearson, like many an American after, found the English perfectly open, happily biased, inclined to assume that he was there to learn from them, and cheerfully ready to load his desk with bumf until he called halt. That was what new boys were for, to have "heavy desks."*

The work load at St Albans was not, in fact, particularly heavy, though it was instructive, and for the first time Pearson was given a thorough course in security. He, McDonough, and Durand took a cottage, Abbotshay, at Ayot Saint Lawrence, north of St Albans. After being shown around the operation at Bletchley Park, they were briefed on the structure and functions of the various divisions of MI6—there were fifty-three individuals whose assignments they needed to know about to some extent—and were given special instruction on the manipulation of rumor, the monitoring

---

*Among the British scholars at work at Bletchley Park were the well-known historians J. H. Plumb, Geoffrey Barraclough, Asa Briggs, and Edward Crankshaw. Roy Jenkins, later of Common Market fame, and Leonard Palmer, professor of comparative philology at Oxford and decipherer of the Minoan and Mycenean inscriptions, were there. So was the novelist Angus Wilson, who once threw off his clothing to race naked around the swan pool in front of the main house. All were individuals of impeccable logic: when one scholar declared to a lady colleague that he would throw her out a window if she rebuffed him, and was met by the taunt that he was incapable of throwing anyone out a window, he threw himself out to prove her wrong on the logic of it.

of enemy mail and enemy wireless, in analysis, and on countersabotage and the running of double agents. They were also filled
in on the use of double agents in Canada and South Africa, and
on the work of the Balkan, Norwegian, Iberian, and Irish desks
and (rather more generally) on BSC in New York, on India, Gibraltar, and SIME, or Security Intelligence Middle East. Between
times they had lunch at the White Hart, in St Albans, or drank
beer at the Brockett Arms, on the road home. Dinner was often a
can of baked beans at the cottage: they knew they would eat reasonably well once they got to London.

The three were in St Albans until mid-July. They enjoyed the
English countryside, and though they could hear the Flying For-
tresses passing overhead, and listened on the wireless to William
Joyce, or Lord Haw-Haw, broadcast his venom from Germany,
the war seemed remote. Life was made more exciting by Pearson's game of Shaw-spotting. At Easter Sunday, Pearson was
deeply moved, and realized just how long Britain had been at war,
for that day church bells all over England rang for the first time
since Dunkirk, nearly three years earlier, the bells having been
reserved until then as a signal for invasion. Three years, he thought,
had been a long time to live in fear of invasion, and now the tide
had turned, as the bells so clearly said. When, at the end of the
service, the congregation stood to sing the national anthem, Pearson was glad to be fighting a war with them.

In mid-May, when Pearson, Durand, and McDonough saw Jimmy
Murphy off at Euston Station, on his way to North Africa, they
knew they were on their own. This was especially so for Pearson,
who was to be the principal liaison with Section V and on all
Ultra matters. From now on only Blitz, their bomb-scarred Fiat,
and the rail to Euston would provide a lifeline to the "genial un-
reality" of London and the world at war.[28]

The war was, in fact, nearby, at Bletchley. At first Pearson's
primary charge was to learn the system there and then to provide
liaison between X-2, the appropriate intelligence bodies, and the
American contingent that began arriving at BP in April. To do this
Pearson was given a fast, and certainly incomplete, course in the
art and science of the code masters.

Cryptology combines cryptography and cryptanalysis.[29] The first
is the study of how to render messages unintelligible to outsiders,
generally by transforming a plain text; the second involves decoding, deciphering, and decrypting the encrypted messages. The

British were, by 1943, systematically reading most of the high-level encrypted German messages, just as the Americans were breaking Japanese military and diplomatic ciphers. The British had applied the term *Ultra* (accompanied by a classification) to any decryptions of German high-grade codes and ciphers, or to any discussions of the subject, while the American equivalent for the Japanese material was Magic. (Eventually popular usage led to the use of Ultra for the decryptions of all Axis high-grade codes and ciphers, but this was not the case when Pearson was at X-2.)

Technically administrative control over Ultra material was exercised by MI6, and this meant that Pearson had to move about a good bit. The designation MI6 was a reflection of the time when counterintelligence fell to the military, but in fact both the Government Code and Cipher School, which had been under the authority of the Admiralty, and MI6, had been transferred to the Foreign Office. Physically the GC&CS had been located at Bletchley, while MI6 had been at 54 Broadway (hence the customary reference to MI6, and SIS, as simply Broadway), a short, thick thoroughfare that ran off Victoria Street midway between the Houses of Parliament and Victoria Station. (The general OSS headquarters would be at 40 Berkeley Square, close to the American embassy—in which there was also an OSS office—and at 72 Grosvenor Street, not far from any of the crucial addresses, when one could take advantage of the many passageways and cut across the royal parks on foot.) In turn, X-2 established a safe house on Ebury Street, just to the west of Victoria Station, so that an agent need walk only a very short distance, and the general neighborhood, being filled with rooming houses, would not be suspicious of transients. (The safe house was *not* at 8B.)

Most of MI6, and nearly all of Section V, had been forced out of London by heavy bombing, to Station X, the designated evacuation headquarters for MI6. (Station X was, in fact, Bletchley Park.) The MI6 Central Registry had moved only as far as St Albans, however, and Section V, finding a need for constant access to the registry, had left BP for St Albans as well, taking up a Rothschild mansion, Glenalmond. At Bletchley the work of cryptanalysis was carried out on a wide range of traffic, and special huts were set aside for the Ultra materials, which were intercepted in one hut, decrypted into a German plain text in a second, translated, given a priority rating from Z to ZZZZZ, routed to appropriate liaison intelligence officers in a third, and encrypted again into an English text for secure delivery to the ultimate recipients, where they would have to be decrypted once more. The careful division of functions between the huts, the security exercised over the Ultra materials by subsequent reencryption, and the barriers maintained between the various liaison groups, British as well as American, did much to assure tight security.

What made this elaborate and extremely successful operation possible was a machine, which had begun as Enigma. The Germans had worked on electric ciphering and deciphering machines, had made frequent changes of settings to disks and rotors, and had developed Enigma, a machine with combinations of settings so great, they comprised an integer (any one from three to seven) to be expressed with twenty-one zeros behind it. One of the most complex of the Enigma ciphers was used for German submarine traffic; this, Triton, the British broke in December of 1942. (A relatively easy cipher was used by the German Luftwaffe, and the British began to break into it in May of 1940.) Until June 1943 the Germans were also reading the British naval convoy ciphers; when the British realized this, they changed their ciphers, while the Germans refused to believe that Enigma could be broken and made only routine changes in their own ciphers. Hence, by the arrival of the Americans, the flow of Most Secret Ultra traffic of interest to the Allied forces was enormous.

The British owed to the French and the Poles, and to German carelessness, the fact that they were now routinely reading the high-level ciphers. The Cryptanalysis Section of the French Intelligence Service, led by Gustave Bertrand, had obtained instructions and keys to Enigma. In the meantime the Polish Intelligence Service had put several mathematicians onto Enigma, and even before the war the Poles had been able to read three quarters of the traffic originating from the machine. The Germans had made Enigma far more sophisticated, however, and the Poles had not been able to break the subsequent encryptions. Instead, they had obtained one of the machines, which had been kept at a railway station in Warsaw over a weekend, awaiting collection by the German military attaché, and photographed and studied the machine before returning it. The Poles had then built their own copies of Enigma.

The Poles also developed a machine of their own, the Bomba (later rendered at BP as a Bombe), a primitive computer that scanned and calculated encrypted material from Enigma. In July

1939, realizing that Poland was likely to be invaded, they had given to the British and the French their documentation on Enigma and one each of the Polish copies of the machine itself. To make certain that the Germans were unaware of this, the Polish cryptologists escaped to Romania immediately after the German invasion, and SIS spirited them away to France and England. Thus the fact that the British had Enigma, and that having mastered it, they were producing Ultra, remained unknown to the Germans—and to the general public until, in 1967, a Polish author wrote of Enigma, and in 1974 the British Chief of SIS's Air Department during the war, Frederick W. Winterbotham, wrote of Ultra.[30]

It was Winterbotham who created a secure system by which Ultra material could be gotten to the military commanders in the field. He established Special Liaison Units, known as SLUs, at each major military headquarters. Whether the military unit itself was British, American, or both, the SLU radio operators were British, and they received directly from BP, either by one-time pad or Typex cipher—a system based on a RAF machine—all decrypts from Enigma and from other German encryption systems. At each headquarters only a very small number of senior officers would receive decrypts from the SLUs, and once they had read the material, it was returned to the SLU for destruction. Following D-Day, the Americans appointed a single Special Intelligence Officer, or SIO, to receive the decryptions from the SLUs; there were only twenty-eight SIOs, most of whom were drawn from G-2.[31]

Bletchley town was a grimy, dull industrial waste—Aldous Huxley had branded it the drabbest of all, and for this it had much competition—set down midway between Oxford and Cambridge. Bletchley Park, the former estate of Sir Herbert Leon, a wealthy businessman, was undistinguished. A Victorian Tudor-Gothic mansion with all mod. cons., it squatted monstrously behind a circular pond in which swans on occasion dipped themselves. An American with an architect's eye, Landis Gores, described the house lovingly when he first saw it:[32]

> . . . a maudlin and monstrous pile probably unsurpassed, though not for lack of competition, in the architectural gaucherie of the mid-Victorian era . . . built about 1860 in an undiscriminatingly imitative Tudor vocabulary out of an endemic dark red brick with beige coadestone

trim, quoins, voussoirs and keystones . . . further hopelessly vulgarized by extensive porches and solaria as well
as by batteries of tall casements in intermittent profusion, all of painted wood trim . . . mingling with what
could only be termed incoherent abandon two-centre
Gothic, three-centred Tudor, four-centred Perpendicular
and ogival Flamboyant arches with English stick and
French trefoil tracery . . . the profusion of top-story ga-
bles faced with cottage-style half-timbering, not to mention an overpowering copper-roofed, octagonal-walled to
onion-topped pleasure dome with finial immediately
suggestive of the pseudo-Orientalism of the Royal Pavil-
ion at Brighton; oriels, turrets, bay windows and embra-
sures, all capped by myriad multi-potted chimneys in
totally wanton location and configuration: altogether in-
choate, unfocused and incomprehensible, not to say
indigestible.

Pearson simply pronounced the mansion, which he did not need
to view daily, as "unlovely."
Happily this structure was relieved by relatively pleasant gardens, though a series of temporary Nissen huts had been dotted
down within them to house the technical operations. There was
an intriguing ha-ha, that landscaping ruse by which grazing cattle
and sheep might be hidden from the view of the house, and—
more inspiriting—a pub on the grounds, where warm weak ale
might be had in large quantities. The whole was surrounded by
barbed wire and was patrolled intensively. The smell of cedars
and good pipe tobacco helped give the illusion of time gone by
when the lord of the manor might have sat on his terrace and
gazed upon all that he had wrought, but since ten thousand people
worked at Bletchley Park, the ha-ha hid people rather than cattle,
and there was a general sense of being just tolerably cramped.
One flower bed had survived.[33]
At BP two bodies of Ultra decryptions were especially important, and they had been given their own code names. Enigma intercepts that raised special problems went to a section known as
ISK. Named after a famed cryptanalyst, Alfred Dillwyn Knox,
who had cracked the Abwehr ciphers, Intelligence Services Knox
included material from the Russian front. More embracing was
ISOS traffic, or Intelligence Services Oliver Strachey, hand-enci-

phered material named after a legendary figure from the code-breaking days of World War I, who was working now at BP. The OSS also had to compete for this traffic, for Stephenson in New York wanted to be the sole channel for OSS to ISOS; ultimately X-2 won the right to read both ISK and ISOS in London, and since in general only paraphrases were sent directly to Washington, the London office was essential if material was to be acted on at once.

Pearson soon got to know Oliver Strachey, for they shared a friend in common, the composer Benjamin Britten, and once he was settled into his London flat, Pearson would go along to Britten's flat to hear Britten and Strachey, who was a fine amateur musician, play together. Pearson also had a good contact in Humphrey Trevelyan, a Cambridge don who had been at work on Ultra from the beginning, and who had spent some time at Yale before the war. "Humpty" and Mollie Trevelyan (Pearson's sister-in-law) often entertained Pearson in their drafty house in Trumpington, near Cambridge, and Pearson brought them small gifts and, in 1944, was one of the legal witnesses to Trevelyan's transfer of his property in the Lake District to the National Trust. Most likely neither Strachey nor Trevelyan told Pearson anything outside official channels, but his friendship with them may have helped to assure that he got all the ISK and ISOS material that was his, and his country's, due.

Another feature of BP was the Index. After an intercept from the Luftwaffe or the German army had been broken and converted into the original German, it moved on to Hut 3, where future professors and young academics translated the deciphered signal, assessed it—without commentary, as the text must be distributed raw, since Bletchley was not an intelligence center with access to other sources of information—and directed it to an appropriate recipient. In Hut 3, as translation and analysis proceeded, items of interest in the contents of the message were marked for filing in the Index, the largest intelligence index in Britain. Whenever a name or place appeared in a subsequent intercept, it would be checked against previous occurrences. (A copy was kept, in case of bomb destruction at BP, in the Bodleian Library at Oxford.) The Index had begun in a single shoe box; by the end of 1943 it occupied a large room in Block D, with nine women on three shifts, drawing out the indexed material as called for: every unit, every man, every gun, every engine, tank, or ball

bearing number noted in any German cipher. One American reporting for work at Hut 3 early in 1944, the newsman Alfred
Friendly, looked upon the Index room, its worn furniture and
thumb-bent filing cards, and summed up his view of the difference
between British and American intelligence: the British had this
room, with its hundreds of thousands of cards, while the Pentagon, he said, had rows of shining new filing cabinets with nothing
in them.[34]

Friendly was unfair, for he did not know of the vast filing system set up by Langer, Lewis, Kent and company at R&A, but the
sense of his judgment was correct: until well into 1943 the United
States had lacked any coordinated overall plan for the use of the
kind of intelligence contained in the Ultra decrypts. General Eisenhower had certainly recognized the significance of the special
intelligence that Ultra represented, and he had drawn on it for
Operation Torch in November 1942; the OSS had understood the
importance of Ultra, or Donovan would not have been so insistent
on access to the product; certainly the U.S. Navy and Air Force
used Ultra, and the American counterpart Magic, to good advantage—indeed, most historians agree that it was the reading of the
Japanese Fleet Code JN25 by the Navy's Combat Intelligence Unit
that made possible the overwhelming American naval victory at
Midway on June 4, 1942. But there was no equivalent to the operation at Bletchley Park. This could be achieved most simply and
effectively by putting Americans into the picture at BP itself, a
step taken only when Eisenhower and others now realized that
Ultra must not, in the face of an impending advance on Fortress
Europe itself, continue to be used in a haphazard manner. If those
shining new filing cabinets were not filled, then an American group
must go to the dog-eared cards of the English.

The first American to arrive on assignment to BP, in April 1943,
was Colonel Telford Taylor, a Williams College graduate who,
after taking a law degree, had gone to Washington to work in the
New Deal. Taylor, who represented the Special Branch of the
American Military Intelligence Service, which had been created
in 1942, was a man of toughness, clarity, and great energy: at the
end of the war he would be a prosecutor at the Nuremberg War
Crimes Trials and, in time, a professor of law at Columbia. Colonel Alfred McCormack, then deputy director of Special Branch,
had chosen the American Ultra team to work interchangeably with
the British at BP. He also created a second group, the Ultra rep-

resentatives, or "advisers," about twelve in all, who disseminated intelligence to the field, in direct contact as needed with the
twenty-eight SIOs. Both groups were initially trained at BP, together with those members of SI, and later of X-2, who arrived
after Pearson and company. The men from MI5 and the U.S. Army
Signal Corps, about sixty at top strength, worked primarily in Hut
3 and in Hut 6, the cryptanalytical center for army and air force
traffic. A few worked also in Hut 8 and a little later in Hut 5,
which "belonged" to MI5. (There were not in fact eight huts, of
course, just as there are not necessarily nine armies because one
is called the Ninth Army.)[35]

Most of the Americans, like their British counterparts, had academic backgrounds. Princeton was most heavily represented,
though there were, in Taylor's group, eight from Yale. One, William Bundy, '39, who after the war would become an assistant
secretary of state and editor of *Foreign Affairs,* headed up the
cryptanalyst side for the Signal Corps and was head-of-watch in
Hut 6, where by the end of the summer 250 people were at work
in three shifts. Bundy drew in Gaspard d'Andelot Belin, his old
college friend, and they were joined by Langdon van Norden, a
graduate of the Yale Law School, and George Church, '33.[36]

The American unit charged with handling Ultra intelligence in
the European Theater was officially MIS/WD/London, and by an
agreement of May 7, 1943, its members shared in all the Ultra
product. The unit had three chief functions: at BP it examined
incoming messages and chose those that should be sent on to the
field, and it examined all summaries and selected those that should
be transmitted to Washington for G-2. After training at BP, the
liaison officers went out to the field commands to handle the incoming processed Ultra traffic, to integrate it into the total intelligence pattern for the daily field headquarters briefings. One officer,
based in London, with a staff of two, handled Ultra diplomatic
traffic, and another, William Calfee, was liaison on American
counterintelligence to MI5, MI6, and from BP to the OSS. In August 1943, when Taylor's deputy, Samuel McKee, Jr., a professor
of European history from Columbia, arrived to handle the placement of the SIOs, systematic service to Washington began. As
Taylor and McKee were frequently visiting the field commands,
day-to-day supervisory responsibility for American activities in Hut
3 fell to Frederick W. Hilles, known as Ted, a professor of English from Yale, and it was Hilles who provided the continuity so

badly needed as new Americans arrived. In the summer of 1944 McKee returned to Washington to coordinate the handling of Ultra materials in the Pentagon, and the meticulous Hilles, promoted to lieutenant colonel, took over as the number two. Then, just before V-E Day, Hilles met Taylor when he arrived at the airport with the message that he was being assigned to the Nuremberg trials, and Hilles was left in charge of the entire operation, to wrap it up, and to write its official history. In July 1945 he closed MIS/WD/London down.[37]

Reasonably enough the British at BP initially resented the Americans. The British were exhausted, ill-fed, and as of June 1943 most had gone for six months without a day off. All were German-speaking and had lost many friends on both sides. The Americans arrived, bouncing, decked out in new uniforms (jokingly saying that they had seven different types), with an abundance of alcohol and tobacco. By then Bletchley was breaking roughly fifty-six ciphers daily; to train 3US alone was a major task; to indoctrinate them to be truly, reflexively paranoid about security required yet more attention; and when U.S. naval officers arrived as 4US, the whole thing had to be done again. There was, then, very natural resentment, and that it passed so quickly was due in good measure to the diplomatic skills of McCormack's hand-picked group, and to the realization by the British that the Americans, though green, would ripen quickly and that they were needed.

Most of the American group came from New England and had traveled in Britain before the war, and as Taylor observed in handing over to Hilles, these factors alone helped make for a harmonious relationship. BP was heavily Cambridge, while the Americans were far more diverse educationally, but nearly all came from well-to-do social positions, and since law and academe were overwhelmingly in control at BP, the natural "variety of stimuli" easily discovered by such people (as Taylor put it), and the fondness they had for information for its own sake, meant that nearly everyone found the work, however much it did mean applying the seat of one's pants to a chair for long hours, intrinsically interesting. No one doubted that it was important work, and morale remained high throughout the war.

Within weeks, then, the Americans had become part of the scene. There continued to be only one acceptable time for tea, but coffee might be had at any time. Cricket continued in the evening, but baseball took over the lunch breaks. Romances blossomed, and nearby pubs chilled their beer by setting it out on the windowsill in winter. The Americans liked to rag the Wrens—every one of the Americans was a scholar of sorts, but they played up to the British expectation of colonial crudeness, calling out from their desks as the women from the Index walked by, "how about a slug of rye, babe," purporting to raise a glass of Tennessee ambrosia which, in fact, was merely cold unpalatable coffee. By the end of 1943 the British knew an American leg-pull when they felt it.

The British continued to feel that the Americans' greatest liability was an insufficiently alert attitude to security. The War Office and Air Ministry had been extremely reluctant to share Ultra with Washington and did so only after a struggle and then provided they were informed by Taylor of all items passed. There were occasional modest lapses, not about Ultra itself but about BP as the focus of some highly confidential work. These were inevitable: as the need for staff at BP had grown, donnish types had taken up every living space in the village and then in villages for miles around. Woburn Abbey had been taken over by the Wrens and renamed The Wrennery. The Americans, most in uniform, would be observed on their literary pilgrimages and in the pubs, or coming back from London's Euston Station on the train in groups of eight or ten. There were car pools, and cricket matches, and attendance at local church services, so that BP itself was scarcely a secret.

Even so, at least one shrewd and determined academic wife guessed at her husband's location. Taylor, McKee, Hilles, and some of the other Americans lived at The Hunt Hotel at Linslade, near Leighton Buzzard, and drove over daily to Bletchley. None ever told their wives where they lived, much less where they worked, but Hilles, like Pearson, liked to describe his weekend literary encounters and journeys to his wife. In his second year he had managed to get away on a three-day bike ride through the Cotswolds, and as a student of eighteenth-century English literature he had, by reference to Thomas Gray, Oliver Goldsmith, and other poets, given some sense of what he had seen. There were also the more frequent day trips, often on official business, to Cambridge or London. Susan Pearson, by careful calculation of the travel times her husband sometimes mentioned in his letters, was able to trace from a large English atlas he had left in their Connecticut home, a general circle in which he must be located.

Breaches of security take many forms. It is the custom that the head of the British Secret Service (then Major General Sir Stewart Menzies) is referred to only as "C," even in his presence. Landis Gores was visiting Hut 5 one day when one of the analysts, Arthur Cathles, a Scot, told him of how he had briefed a high-ranking visitor, none other than "C" himself, on his work and had addressed him by name. A shock of surprise passed through the room, whereupon Cathles said that if Menzies did not want anyone to be aware of his presence, he ought not to wear the Menzies tartan in public. This custom seems less significant now: nearly anyone interested can learn that Sir Christopher Carwen is the current "C." Menzies, however, felt especially keen about personal secrecy.

Pearson also passed to his wife his code name, though she may not have realized it. Describing how he often worked until midnight, but got little time to himself because people he did not see during the day came in to talk, he said that he had to stop and chat on occasions in order to keep office morale up. If he ever wrote his autobiography, he told Susan, he would call it "My Brother's Keeper": "I really am the Last Puritan."[38] Pearson was, of course, Puritan; Murphy was Saint.

There were far greater security problems than these. Any person briefed on Ultra was under orders to avoid all risk of danger of capture by the enemy, lest they be forced to tell what they knew. This included Pearson, of course, even had he been physically able to engage in combat or operate behind enemy lines. He was nonetheless faced with the problem, though at a distance, three weeks after he became acting head of X-2/London, charged with general responsibility for western Europe. On September 26, 1944, Major Maxwell J. Papurt, X-2 and cleared for ISOS, was captured by the Germans, together with Gertrude Legendre, a Charleston society figure who was to be in charge of the OSS/Paris message center, and two other members of OSS. Though they managed to conceal from their German captors their OSS connection, neither MI6 nor OSS could know this. Fearing that Papurt would be tortured and might speak of Ultra, Donovan and Menzies ordered a special watch on German secret wireless traffic, to see what the Sicherheitsdienst would do. They feared the worst when the ISOS yield went down because the Germans introduced a new cipher system.

The whole thing was very regrettable, and quite unnecessary, as Papurt and the group had basically been on a jaunt to "hear some gunfire." Under the impression that Wallendorf, immediately inside Germany from Luxembourg, had been captured, they had set out with an X-2 driver, only to fall into a German ambush just short of town. Papurt and the driver were seriously wounded so that escape had been impossible, and after being questioned, the captives were sent off to imprisonment in Diez Castle in Limburg. Even if Papurt did not talk soon, he was a ticking time bomb.

Pearson refused to panic and advised Colonel Russell Forgan, the acting chief of OSS/London, that he did not believe Papurt had talked and that he thought the Germans had switched from Enigma to one-time pads in a series of new security measures, probably because of an assassination attempt on Hitler in July. He also felt that Papurt would not break, having "a certain natural capacity" for bluffing his way out of tight spots. Papurt would, he reasoned, talk about his previous work with the Army Counterintelligence Corps in North Africa, if he had to, which would deflect interrogators from the larger target. Indeed, the greater problem was likely to be with Menzies and MI6, for Papurt's capture may have confirmed the British in their belief that the Americans ought not to be trusted with ISOS materials.

Pearson was correct. The changes in German ciphers were routine, and Papurt talked with his interrogators only about matters he could reasonably believe they already knew. In July of 1945 Andrew Berding, chief of X-2 in Germany, obtained a copy of the German interrogation report on Papurt, and it reads precisely as Pearson had predicted. Papurt was killed in an Allied bombing of Limburg, and Ms. Legendre was released by the Germans and crossed into Switzerland.[39]

By now X-2/London had grown to a staff of sixty, and Pearson's main concern was no longer Ultra, since there were several to carry out the many tasks relating to its dissemination and protection. His principal attention was going to a subject on which he was one of the very few members of X-2 to have full clearance.

What problem, if I were to go wrong, would set
Me brooding: not "Am I trusted?"—trust, as we
Know, is only one of many biases;
"Am I useful?"—the question is always
"How?"; but "What has the work, in the end, revealed?"
                                        Transmission 2/5

In July the X-2 contingent had moved from St Albans to Ryder Street, where Pearson, Durand, McDonough, and Blum were given offices, with their own secretaries. In December the burgeoning

X-2 took up part of another building, on St. James's as well, though officially Pearson and Durand kept their desks at Ryder Street and moved back and forth between the two buildings. This was, Pearson found, exhausting, but having offices in two (and at times three) places helped. He usually ended up the day back at Ryder Street, however, because in a pinch he could count on getting a meal there, since a cook was kept on the premises for those who, like Jim Angleton, worked around the clock and slept on cots in their offices. Pearson preferred to slip out, often with a friend, and walk the hundred feet up the road to Quaglino's, where he could entertain one of the liaison officers from the Allied intelligence units. Pearson could see what the special meal of the evening would be by slipping along to a first-floor office, for its window looked directly into Quaglino's kitchen. Because the British could not afford to eat there, Pearson usually felt he had to justify going by taking a guest, though on occasion he would slip alone under cover of darkness across Ryder Yard and enter the restaurant through its kitchen door.

After he was installed at Ryder Street, Pearson was asked to be X-2 liaison to one of the most secret committees in Britain. Pearson's most significant wartime service may have been as the X-2 contact for the Twenty Committee, the official title of the group also known as the Double-Cross Committee, the XX Committee, and the Twenty Club. This committee had grown out of an informal group set up in the summer of 1940 by the directors of intelligence; called the W-Board, it had consisted of the heads of Military, Naval and Air Intelligence, the chief of MI5, and the intelligence officer of the commander in chief, Home Forces. These overburdened men soon realized that a working committee, meeting regularly to discuss how to neutralize German espionage efforts in Britain, would serve their joint needs best, and the W-Board established W-Section, which became the Twenty Committee. This committee was charged with counterespionage, then with the actual acquiring of intelligence, and later—by coordinating planning on how best to handle disinformation via doubled German agents—with deception. MI5 established a special section, B1(A), under Lieutenant-Colonel T.A. ("Tar") Robertson, to identify the German agents as they arrived in the United Kingdom.[40]

When German agents were successfully doubled, B1(A) assigned a case officer to each, to send a judicious mixture of accurate and false data to the Abwehr listening posts. Messages planted on the Germans had to be cautious and clever: believable, enticing, the kind of information an agent might be expected to obtain, just marginally contradictory between agents, since they reasonably would be expected to learn different "facts," and above all, never compromising of the Ultra secret itself. This did not prove too difficult *vis-à-vis* the Abwehr, which wanted to believe its agents and seldom seemed to suspect that they might be under duress; indeed, under its chief, Admiral Wilhelm Franz Canaris, the Abwehr was an abysmal failure, failing to forecast Torch, or Husky, or Overlord, and its uniform record of failure led ultimately to its collapse. What worried the British, and later the Americans, was the counterintelligence division of the Wehrmacht, which in 1943 was in two sections, Fremde Heere West (Foreign Armies West), in the hands of a brilliant intelligence officer, Colonel Freiherr Alexis von Roenne (until he was executed for his participation in the plot against Hitler of July 20, 1944), and Fremde Heere Ost (Foreign Armies East), in the hands of General Reinhard Gehlen, a figure on whom Sherman Kent, at work in R&A in Washington, was building a dossier. Overlord would have to fool FHW, not just the Abwehr.

The Twenty Committee first met on January 2, 1941, at Wormwood Scrubs prison, which was then MI5 headquarters. Responsible to the W-Board but with considerable independence, the committee's work was shrouded in secrecy, for no British secret, not even Ultra, on which the committee drew and of which its activities were, in effect, an ever-growing by-product, was more closely held. Had the Germans at any point suspected that one, much less all, of their agents had been turned, and that the Abwehr was sending its queries directly to the British, the Germans might well have abandoned all their presumed agents, would certainly have changed their codes and sent in new agents who, in turn, would have had to be detected and doubled (or executed), and would quite likely have realized that their Enigma ciphers were being routinely read. Thus by the time Pearson arrived the Twenty Committee was engaged in the most intense work of all intelligence: a deception that, once entered upon, simply had to succeed.

The work of the committee had intensified in the early winter of 1941–42, when the ISK section at Bletchley had broken its way into the Enigma traffic. This meant that all the main lines of the

Abwehr's Berlin communications network (which for Great Britain radiated out from Hamburg) could be tapped. The British had long been planting lies—"whispers," or "sibs"[41]—to deceive the Germans about their plans, and about morale on the home front, but sibs were of use only if one could know how the Germans had responded to them. Ultra, and other intercepted traffic, made this possible. The Chiefs of Staff had become intrigued with the idea of deception, not the original purpose of Ultra or of the Twenty Committee, and in October 1941 somewhat precipitously set up a new system which, after some initial fumbling, not only proved valuable but became the primary occupation of the Twenty Committee. A new group, subordinate to an inter-service body of the Chiefs of Staff Committee, known as the London Controlling Section, or LCS, was instituted. LCS was put in the hands of Colonel John H. Bevan and was charged with the running of strategic deception. Bevan was placed on the Twenty Committee. By this time B1(A) had captured every German spy sent into Britain by the Hamburg *Stelle* of the Abwehr. Those who had not been turned had either been imprisoned or, if they proved utterly intractable, quietly executed. By this combination of stealth and ruthlessness, the British would have some 120 double agents in all; some of these were used for only a day or so, but thirty-nine would, by 1943, be playing a substantial role in Britain's efforts to deceive the Germans from the U.K.

Ewen Montagu, the admiralty's representative on the Twenty Committee, had gone to the United States in November of 1941 to clear the air both with the Americans and with "Little Bill" Stephenson's BSC, and perhaps to establish XX in North America. Caught there, as it were, by Pearl Harbor, Montagu did not return to London until the following February. By then the Americans had been informed of the existence of Ultra, and of what the Most Secret Source was capable, and it was clear that in due course American intelligence in one of its forms ought to be represented on the Twenty Committee in London rather than in New York. Montagu, who served from the very beginning at the committee's weekly meetings, would still be representing the DNI on May 10, 1945, the 226th and last meeting of the committee.

The chairman of the Twenty Committee was Sir John Masterman. He was an Oxford don, a historian with both academic and practical knowledge of Germany—he had been studying German history when World War I caught him in Freiburg, from which he was sent to imprisonment in Rühleben, where he spent four years perfecting his knowledge of the language. An outstanding athlete in cricket, field hockey, and tennis, Masterman seemed a natural for MI5. For himself, he wanted to take part in the war but realized he was too old, and too inexperienced in military matters, to see any front-line activity. He had, as he admits in his autobiography, lived for twenty years "under the weight of an inferiority complex, never frankly admitted and never openly expressed," that he had been inactive in the first war. Put in charge of the Twenty Committee, he found his niche.

Masterman is a controversial figure. Montagu thought him the soul of "tact, equanimity and common sense," while David Mure, the secretary to the A Force, later the Thirty Committee, a deception group operating from Cairo under Brigadier Dudley Clark, thought him humorless, a self-aggrandizer, and quite undisciplined: an intellectual who had never heard gunfire.[42] Masterman also was a rather conventional man, and so described himself, though his smooth, detailed exercise in selective total recall, *On the Chariot Wheel*,[43] is one of the most closely calculated scholar's autobiographies ever written. Throughout his memoirs he depicted himself as limited, unimaginative, climbing with grace and some good fortune (and diligence and care, though not grueling hard work) to academic success—after the war he was provost of Worcester College and vice-chancellor of Oxford—and a modicum of public fame. Born in 1891, Masterman had come from a solid if undistinguished North Riding background, growing up amongst politicians and clergymen, and with two servants. His official portraits, hanging in Christ Church Hall, Oxford, and in Worcester College, show a tall, chiseled, rather handsome man, the first at eighty, the second at sixty-one, though unmistakably the same: well-tailored suit with English loose-collared striped shirt and solid-colored tie, jacket open to show a vest with four buttons done up and one carefully not, a steady gaze looking straight out upon the viewer, a calculated image of frankness. His colleagues must have thought him a good scholar; the distinguished and prolific historian A. J. P. Taylor did not, and in his own autobiography hazards the guess that it was Masterman who blocked his getting the Regius Professorship at Oxford.[44] Masterman was, as a historian, in fact quite unproductive, with little on the written record that would lead one to think highly of him. There is a play, a very intelligent insider's guide to Oxford, two relatively successful murder mysteries, a "straight" novel, his elegantly framed autobiography—and *The Double-Cross System,* hailed by most reviewers as one of the few postwar masterpieces on intelligence.

Pearson admired Masterman. They shared an interest in *Boy's Own Paper* (though Masterman may have cared more because his father, who had been in the navy, had written for it, than because he collected boy's books). They enjoyed making up quasi-fantasy character sketches (B.C., as he was called, once wrote how one could judge a person's character from the way he knocked on a door, while Pearson thought he could judge a man from how he ordered a drink). They both enjoyed the intrigues of the Senior Common Room; both were watchers, and one suspects, rather lonely, not in the sense of having no friends or social activity but in the sense of being drawn in upon themselves, with lives to which no one else could be admitted. As Masterman remarked, at school such people give the impression of being older, mentally a step ahead of the rest. This had been as true of Pearson as it was of the young man who had crammed his way into Oxford on a scholarship. Pearson did not visit Masterman at his bare wartime accommodations in the Reform Club, because those with knowledge of the Twenty Committee were not supposed to mix much socially, but after the war they corresponded warmly.

Masterman had been assigned to Tar Robertson's section. The idea of running the German spies that were turned over to B1(A) was not Masterman's: he credits Dick (Goldsmith) White, once his pupil at Christ Church and a former Commonwealth Fellow in America, who had left the teaching of history in favor of intelligence work. It was Masterman who set out the objects of the system, however. There were seven:

1) to control the enemy's system;
2) to catch spies;
3) to learn as much as possible about the personalities and methods of the Abwehr and other German intelligence bodies;
4) to make the German codes and ciphers reveal their secrets;
5) to study the questions asked by the Germans as evidence of their intentions;
6) to influence their plans by the answers sent back; and
7) to deceive the enemy about Allied plans.

Masterman deprecated his role in this significant work by suggesting that one of his most important decisions, as chairman, was to have tea and a bun always provided for the members of the committee. He credited the near-perfect attendance record of the members solely to the tea and bun.

The members of the committee moved back and forth between their respective offices, usually by bicycle, from MI5, by then at the top of St. James's Street, to MI6, which had offices both by the St. James's Park Underground Station and at Ryder Street, to Norfolk House where (in 1944) Eisenhower had his headquarters, to the War Cabinet offices under Storey's Gate. Because Pearson could not ride a bicycle, he was given a desk in Masterman's office across from Boodle's Club. On the committee there was, in addition to Masterman, Robertson, and Montagu, either John Drew or Sir Findlater Stewart, who represented the Home Defence Executive, John Marriott and later Billy Luke, secretaries to the committee, Martin Lloyd, a schoolmaster down from Rugby who was Section V's secretary to the committee, and someone from COSSAC (Chief of Staff, Supreme Allied Command), a SHAEF representative, and others—fourteen in all. Pearson was privy to the ISK and ISOS traffic that came before the committee—though those code names were banned, and the OSS called them PAIR and ICE respectively—and he listened to the case officers who reported on the running of their double agents. Except for members of the committee who were also case officers, such as Tomas Harris, no one on it actually met any of the double agents.[45] Pearson began sitting in on the meetings as soon as X-2 came into existence, and he continued almost to the last meeting. He did not attend, of course, while in the States—from February to May 1944, when he was replaced by his deputy, Edward J. Lawler, who represented himself at the committee meetings as a New York newspaperman though he was, in fact, a former investigator for the U.S. Internal Revenue Service.*

*It is not clear whether Pearson was a member of the XX Committee, or sat in on its meetings as an observer. No full list of members is available, and as American liaison Pearson might well not appear on such a list or not have been counted in the total. The late Ewen Montagu, in correspondence with Walter L. Pforzheimer, though discussing a different subject, appeared to throw some doubt on whether NHP was a member of the committee (Montagu to Pforzheimer, Dec. 11, 1981, in Pforzheimer's possession). I believe that Pearson functioned as though he were a member, but technically was not a member. This raises the question of how Lawler functioned, of course, and one presumes that he did so in the same way. It has been suggested that Robert Ingersoll, Yale graduate and wartime news correspondent (cleared for top secret material), rather than Law-

The deception plan for Overlord was named Bodyguard, and the plan included a daring invention, an entire army that did not exist, FUSAG, or First U.S. Army Group, notionally under the command of General George S. Patton, Jr., and preparing for an assault on the Pas de Calais. The double agents run through the coordination of the Twenty Committee were focused on building up credibility for Bodyguard, but some had a life of their own. The most successful of these was Garbo, the code name for Juan Pujol Garcia. In February 1942 Pujol had convinced the Germans that a large convoy was sailing from Liverpool to Malta, diverting the U-boat command to empty waters. Now he built up a team of six or so notional subagents, so that he could account for the heavy flow of (false) information sent to the Abwehr, and in 1945 he sent a Wren notionally to Southeast Asia Command in Ceylon, from which came reports to him, actually concocted in London, for the Abwehr to transmit to the Japanese military attaché in Berlin. For such work Garbo would receive the German Iron Cross and the British M.B.E.[46]

Toward the end of the war it was suspected that one of the doubled agents, Treasure, the code name for Lily Sergueiev, was a triple agent, working for the Russians as well. Treasure was used in the Overlord deception and, in December 1944, was closed down, according to Masterman's end-of-war report, because she was of no further use. However, some time after the war Pearson told Donald McCormick, a British historian of intelligence services who writes as Richard Deacon, that he had learned from an X-2 agent who was in liaison with the Russians that Lily Sergueiev had given the Soviet Union detailed plans of Anglo-American military operations in the last weeks of the campaign. Both Pearson, who admired Masterman, and McCormick, who did not, felt that Masterman was so intent on the immediate battle, he had failed to prepare for the battle to come.[47]

After the war Pearson also regretted that he had not followed up on his mild suspicions of H.A.R. Philby more closely. He had

---

ler, sat on the committee in London in Pearson's absence. John B. Oakes, now of *The New York Times,* has been mentioned as a possible liaison, since he was with X-2 in London, and there is agreement that Pearson's replacement was in journalism. Oakes, however, says that he was not with the Twenty Committee, though he believes he attended meetings in France of a subbranch, or outreach group, of the committee. The Ingersoll Papers, at the Yale University Library, provide no clarification.

mistrusted the man, though he liked him, and Masterman had warned him to exercise caution around "Kim." But Philby was entitled to read ISOS materials, which often related to Russia,[48] and to know what was going on with X-2 in Iberia, for these were his designated chunks of turf.

Pearson had been unable to get beneath Philby's smooth veneer, a combination of charm, superciliousness, and (given his stutter, and the bit of spittle one was likely to take flying) aggressive unpleasantness which rather intrigued him. After he defected to the Soviet Union, in 1963, Philby called the X-2 contingent "a notably bewildered group," and in his memoir, *My Silent War,* he lost no opportunity to belittle it. Philby said that Pearson readily admitted he had "come to school" when he first met him at St Albans, and Philby turned this modest and truthful admission into a snide remark. Even so, Pearson tried to ingratiate himself with Philby, deprecating both himself and the OSS. Philby misread Pearson, whom he thought rather "hail-fellow-well-met, and have you heard the latest one about the girl in the train" (indeed, one wonders whether he focused on Pearson, since he calls him Normal rather than Norman in his book).[49] Since he was, unbeknownst to MI6 or OSS, working for the Russians, Philby had good reason to wish to diminish the significance of any Russian-related ISOS material the Americans received, and in retrospect his insistence that the Americans were not to be trusted makes sense.

In February 1944, after SO virtually had amalgamated with SOE to form a Special Forces Headquarters, Special Counter-Intelligence units, or SCIs, were set up. The SCIs, made up of British and American officers, were to deal with stay-behind networks in France once the invasion had been launched. Knowledge of these networks came from ISOS, and the function of the SCIs was to bring ISOS to the field, to eliminate enemy intelligence assets, and to manipulate those who were permitted to survive. This was, in part, an expansion onto the Continent of the Twenty Committee's double-cross system, and Pearson therefore often went along to the SCI War Room on Ryder Street to confer with Bob Blum, who was deputy chief of the War Room, and to see how the Channel crossing affected the system. Since Felix Cowgill's Section V was charged with the protection of ISOS, this brought Cowgill and Pearson even closer together.

From the outset the two men had liked each other. They had

become close at St Albans, and remained so, even when Cowgill
was on one of his frequent campaigns to tighten up security over
ISOS, which might mean trying to cut down on American access.
(Pearson's feeling for Cowgill may have been stronger because he
found the vice-chief of SIS, Colonel Valentine P. T. Vivian, rather
mannered and artificial.) When on the verge of transferring from
St Albans to Ryder Street, Pearson learned that the Cowgills were
attempting to bring back from Canada their two young children,
sent there in 1941 for schooling and to escape the bombings, and
Pearson tried to help speed their return. In the end he was not
able to do so, and the children had to wait until mid-1944, but in
the meantime they spent a good bit of time in the homes of the
Murphys and the Pearsons, and Cowgill was genuinely moved by
Pearson's concern. Soon after moving into Hays Mews Pearson
gave Cowgill his first two-egg breakfast in years.[50]

Understandably then, Pearson was badly upset on two grounds
when Cowgill suddenly resigned, on January 18, 1945, and handed
over charge of Section V to Major T. I. Milne. Pearson liked Tim
Milne well enough—he had been on his frequent drinks list, and
was one of twenty-six Britishers he had to his official Fourth of
July party the previous year (Philby was another)—but he knew
that Cowgill's resignation meant a promotion for Philby. Cowgill
(or Menzies) had denied ISOS materials to the FBI while giving
X-2 the freedom of Section V's files, and Philby professed not to
be able to understand this, unless it was simply Cowgill using the
OSS to bolster his position in MI6 against his detractors in MI5.
This was nonsense: Cowgill was acting faithfully on the October
1943 agreement, on orders from Sir Stewart Menzies, and on the
basis of his understanding with Pearson. To be sure, Cowgill was
in a difficult position, for his section had grown very rapidly, most
of its traffic had to do with German intercepts, and he did not
read German, his direct knowledge of the country being limited
to a five-week tour in 1937. But Cowgill was happy to share with
the Americans, for this left him free to do that which he knew he
did well, administer. Further, as he pointed out, he had been ordered to share ISOS, and as an old Indian Police hand (and in-
spector-general of the Northwest Frontier), he knew that little could
go wrong in obeying orders. He also had the statistics on his side:
his colleagues may have been angry over his internal security
measures, but Section V had, through ISOS, identified 3,575 enemy agents in western Europe.

However, Cowgill was now passed over. He had made too many enemies, and Philby had connived too well. Menzies had decided to combine Section IX, created in the summer of 1944 to deal with Soviet espionage, with Section V, once Germany had been defeated. Cowgill had assumed he would direct the combined unit, though he was, in the eyes of some, a bit slow to turn his attention from Germany to Russia. He had reason, he said: the war with Germany was not yet over. Thought to show poor political judgment, believed unlikely to be able to handle the problem of Soviet subversion (though this had been his specialty in 1938), Cowgill would not do. On Vivian's suggestion the directorship of Section IX went to Philby, who had been maneuvering for it, less by promoting himself than by weakening Cowgill. Cowgill retired, to take up a post with British military government in Germany, and Milne took over Philby's Iberian responsibilities.

Pearson immediately wrote to Cowgill of his distress, drafting and redrafting his letter with care. Durand also wrote, almost as emotional as Pearson, of how Cowgill had brought the Americans up and taught them all that they knew. Cowgill had successfully conducted a "noble experiment in Anglo-American cooperation." Pearson was more personal: "We never had to waste words, and that was the greatest compliment you could pay me." V-48, Pearson told Cowgill, affectionately using the British term, was his creation. They would not, they promised each other, lose touch.[51] Pearson followed the now more remote Philby's career thereafter, to his resignation from the secret service, under suspicion, in 1953, and his sudden disappearance from Beirut, to seek political asylum in Moscow in 1963. Cowgill, in the meantime, nurtured in retirement a special jonquil, the Susan Pearson, which he showed at the Royal Horticultural Show and planted in his daffodil bed at home.[52]

With Cowgill gone, Pearson took less pleasure in his immediate work. He was busier than ever, what with the Art Looting Investigation Unit reporting to him, and the increased traffic coming from Ultra, and the general liaison and some supervisory responsibilities for the whole of western Europe. But his most intense interest in these last months of the war in 1945 was, once again, the Twenty Committee. Sir John Masterman was at work on a report, a history really, of the Twenty Committee, and as soon as the committee wrapped up its last meeting, in May, Masterman set to revising. He asked some members of the old group, apparently including Pearson, to read sections of it.

Sir John had written his report solely for the files. In 1947, however, Clement Attlee, who had become the British prime minister, suggested that the story ought to be told in some form. The Chiefs of Staff said no. There were obvious security risks so soon after the war—unreconstructed Germans might, through some private means, retaliate against the families of the double agents who, though not named in the report, might be identifiable to the knowledgeable in some instances; one could not be certain in 1947 that the same means would not have to be employed in the future; there was, of course, the Russian angle to consider. Against the security risks there was the way in which the reputation of MI5 could be bolstered and the general sense of satisfaction that a battered British public might gain from publication. At some point, as Masterman noted, the two needs would cross, and on balance publication would be to the government's advantage. But when?

Masterman continued to argue for publication, especially as hints about the systematic nature of wartime deception began to appear in the books of others. However, the publication of several intelligence memoirs,[53] none of them particularly revelatory but all containing more information than seemed wise to the more cautious military and intelligence professionals, stiffened official resolve against allowing Masterman to get into print. Not until 1961, therefore, did he begin to press hard, putting the question formally to Roger Hollis, the head of MI5 at the time. Hollis said no, and the prime minister, Alec Douglas-Home, agreed. But as British intelligence fell into disarray in the 1960s, with public revelations concerning Philby's treachery and a clear tilting of the balance away from the war and immediate postwar public assumptions about MI5, MI6, and SOE, Masterman saw his chance, and in 1967 pressed his argument for publication again. He was "depressed by the low state of the reputation of the Security Service"—a condition for which he blamed the service's inclination to keep its good work unknown while its failures inevitably became public—and was convinced that the service could not do its work if it became widely unpopular, since it depended upon being thought well of by the public, lest informers, money, and recruiting dry up. Any technical secrets revealed in a 1945 document were, by the late 1960s, out of date; any names that might be deduced from the document, provided it were very modestly sanitized, were already known or were of individuals who were dead;

the new enemy, the Soviet Union, most likely knew of the activities of the Twenty Committee in any event, since Philby had known a good bit of it. Further, though he realized the argument was not compelling to nonhistorians, Masterman felt most strongly that he had an obligation to tell the truth about work which profoundly influenced the war, work which, if unknown to them, would lead future historians to make serious errors in their evaluations of Torch, Mincemeat, Overlord, and other military campaigns.

Masterman had, clearly, decided to buck authority. Perhaps his cleverest ploy was to list among his publications in *Who's Who* a book, *The Double-Cross System,* which no one could find. (In 1957 he had crept up on his subject by rather audaciously describing a double agent in his mystery novel, *The Case of the Four Friends.*[54]) Masterman had, at one time or another, received approval to publish from the Foreign Office, the Home Office, MI5, MI6, and the Chiefs of Staff, though never at the same time, and more of the work of the Twenty Committee was leaking out. Two books were being prepared for publication in 1971 that were rumored to deal with German agents in Britain. These leaks embodied errors, Masterman knew; would it not be better to set the record straight? He feared that the deciding authorities would say no by diversion, and they did: why not combine his report with a projected history of deception, already in the hands of Peter Fleming (and subsequently of Professor Michael Howard) or hold it until Professor F. H. Hinsley could incorporate it into his projected massive history of intelligence during the war?

In the end Masterman simply went outside channels. In April 1970 the British government again had declined permission for him to publish. No doubt ego was, by now, also involved in Masterman's decision: he wanted to publish quickly, and he surely did not want to see the work of the committee he had chaired disappear into someone else's book, especially if—as in the case of Hinsley's project—that book seemed years away. (On this point he was prescient, for the Hinsley history did not begin to appear until 1979, the volume in which the Twenty Committee might first have been discussed until 1981, and the richest volume until 1984, with one yet to come.) Further, as Masterman wrote, "men of 80 are apt to grow impatient." He would publish in America, where the Official Secrets Act did not apply. This he called his Plan Diablo.[55]

At some point James M. Osborn,[56] a longtime friend of the Yale

library, the Yale Press, and Yale enterprises in general, who had
become a good friend of Masterman through both wartime and
Oxford connections—especially Osborn's many benefactions to the
Bodleian—discussed with him how the Yale University Press might
be an ideal publisher. Masterman was not seeking money—he had
already offered to give "any part or the whole" of royalties to
MI6—and doubted that the book ought to go to a commercial publisher anyway, since they might want him to glamorize the taut,
dry prose of his report. Yale had an excellent reputation on several grounds: it was one of the three or four largest university
publishers in the States; it had published David Dallin and other
authors on intelligence earlier; it had its own operation in London, so that distribution in the United Kingdom was far more likely
than with most American university publishers; Pearson, his wartime colleague, was at Yale and could write an introduction for it;
and the director of the press, Chester Kerr, was noted for his
interest in Britain, his shrewd business judgment, his willingness
to do battle, and his imaginative list. Masterman gave Osborn a
portion of the manuscript to show to Kerr.

Though Masterman created the impression with Osborn and Kerr
that he had held his manuscript very closely, he had in fact allowed a certain number of friends to read it: Norman Collins, who
after the war was Deputy Chairman of Associated TeleVision
Corporation Ltd., his wartime colleagues and fellow historians Lord
Robert Blake and Hugh Trevor-Roper, his English agent A. D.
Peters, and most likely his solicitor, Christopher Harmer, who
had been acting secretary to the Twenty Committee in 1943, when
John Marriott, the permanent secretary, was away. Portions of
the manuscript had been read by Edward Pearce, the director of
the Press Association in England, and by John B. Oakes, by then
head of the editorial page at *The New York Times,* who was brought
into the picture by Harmer. Further, Masterman's American agent,
Harold Matson, presumably read the manuscript before submit-
ting it to American publishers. There were twelve submissions, in
fact, though Masterman later referred to only nine, and the readers for those publishers presumably read the manuscript too (all
recommended rejection, on the grounds that the report was "too
British" and "too technical"). Any one of these readers might
have made a copy.

Masterman's English agent, A. D. Peters, was informed
throughout, though he wrote to Matson that he did not want to

handle the book, even in America, since "Secret Service departments can be vindictive and unscrupulous." At one point Matson
thought Masterman was going to get a $45,000 advance on the
book from Viking, but this did not materialize, and Masterman,
"like a cat on hot bricks" about getting a decision, told him firmly
that money was not the object. Kerr offered Matson an advance
of $5,000, which was unprecedented for the Yale University Press,
and promised both a quick decision and speedy publication. In
the meantime Ladislav Farago, who had learned of the manuscript, was trying to get access to Masterman's report, for when
he had finished the research to his book, *The Game of the Foxes,*
then in press, he had been unaware that the German agents of
whom he wrote had been turned, since the Abwehr records in
Bremen that formed the basis for his study could hardly be expected to reveal this. Farago proposed a mutual sharing of manuscripts, which Masterman turned down, saying that his report
was classified; later Farago suggested that the report could be more
accessible to American readers if provided with an introduction
(it may have been at this time that Pearson was contacted, since
Masterman preferred that the introduction be written by someone
who understood the report from the inside); and finally Farago
offered to "annotate" the book and write explanatory footnotes.
In the meantime the manuscript had also been sent to Donald
McKay—Farago's publisher—for consideration, even though negotiations with the Yale Press were well forward, and McKay held
it longer than other publishers, suggesting an interest and a possible "modest" advance of $5,000. (Learning of this, Kerr reaf-
firmed his offer of the same sum, or that he would match any
other offer, a helpful clarification since, probably unknown to him,
the only telegram Masterman had received from Matson concerning Yale's offer had contained an error and read $500.) Farago
was the go-between at McKay, having urged a friend of his there
to solicit the manuscript, and he may have had a brief opportunity
to examine the material before it was rejected by McKay. Either
this copy, or a copy sent to William Morrow and Company which
went missing after Morrow declined the report, possibly circulated more widely than Masterman intended.

Masterman worried about the American publishers. They had
little to fear from British security; after all, it was he who was
taking the risks. At some point Masterman let Professor Michael
Howard, who, being at work on the official history, had every

right of access to the report, and Donald McLachlan, author of *Room 39,* which had also encountered British security objections before its publication in 1968, read the manuscript, and they were suggesting that the Yale Press was, perhaps, not "big enough" to handle the legal problems likely to arise. Farago said he had now been told that Masterman's manuscript would undermine his own book, and as this assurance came from "a high official" well known to Masterman, Sir John wanted to get the book out very quickly, before one of the several copies that had been circulated escaped to the public. Professor H.L.A. Hart, who had worked with the Twenty Committee, and who was now professor of jurisprudence at Oxford, cautioned that the report was technically the property of H.M. Government, and if one of the copies leaked, and was used by an author less scrupulous than Masterman, he would have no legal recourse, since the report was not in fact his property.

After an uncustomary moment of caution, Kerr vigorously pressed Yale's case. In April 1971, over lunch with Masterman, he had expressed some surprise to discover that the report was not declassified and suggested that perhaps Yale ought not to proceed. He discussed the problems of publishing a classified British report with Marshall Best at Viking and worried that Simon Michael Bessie at Athenaeum, an old OSS hand, had expressed an interest. But after a meeting with the advisory committee to the press, at which its historian member, C. Vann Woodward, recalls saying that the country had fought a war with Britain nearly two hundred years before to establish its right to be independent of British law, and that the press ought to get on with publication, and after getting wind of Farago's interest, Kerr returned to the hunt, talking again with Yale's lawyers in London and suggesting that Kingman Brewster, as a lawyer as well as president of Yale, should come into the picture. There was the possibility of an interesting, and publicity-making, law case, for one Yale professor of law, Ralph Brown, who was on the publications committee, had reported after some research that HMG most definitely could claim the document, while another professor at the Yale Law School, Alexander Bickel, who had recently defended *The New York Times* for publishing the Pentagon Papers leaked to it by Daniel Ellsberg, held differently. In any event Yale could win a case if one were ever brought, he said.

Kerr rather enjoyed battling with the Home Secretary, and he decidedly enjoyed stonewalling Farago, who was now "in a sweat" because the Home Secretary wanted to see the quotations that were, it was said, going to appear in his book as taken from Masterman's report. How had Farago got a copy anyway, Matson wanted to know? Then, late in 1971, Farago's book appeared, with its references to Masterman and the Double Cross Committee.[57] In the meantime Kerr had bearded the Home Secretary.

Masterman's Plan Diablo had worked. He did not publish his report illegally, for in the end the British authorities granted permission. Though action against him was initially contemplated, the British decided to permit publication if certain passages were excised from the report. Masterman, Kerr, and Ronald Mansbridge, the head of the Yale Press in London, with the advice of Christopher Harmer, met with officials of the Home Office. These "admirable negotiators" were almost entirely successful: Kerr recalls that some sixty excisions were asked for by the Home Office and that in the end he agreed to only a dozen.[58] The report was passed for publication in October, and the book was scheduled for publication in February 1972, clearly to a sped-up production schedule. The self-styled man of conventional wisdom had become a successful rebel.[59]

It is not clear, and hardly matters, whether Masterman or Kerr asked Pearson to write the introduction to *The Double-Cross System*. What is clear is that Masterman sent Pearson several pages from the original report, prior to its very slight revision for the press, so that he could prepare a foreword. Comparing these pages with the published book shows that Masterman had, in preparing a final copy, revised enough to loosen up his prose so that an ordinary reader could follow it, while also condensing at times to highlight conclusions of significance.[60] In his foreword Pearson told nothing of his own role on the Twenty Committee, though he did say that he could endorse the authenticity of the report; he made the scholarly case for the report's value, said a little about Masterman, and slipped in a plug for a novel, *The Serpent Sleeping,* by Edward Weismiller, one of the young men who worked for him in X-2, because the book told of the handling of a turned agent (most probably Dragoman, who worked out of Cherbourg, though Pearson did not say so). He also coined his happy phrase for those who planned the deception schemes, "the ecologists of double agency." This was Pearson's last published statement concerning intelligence.

Masterman's book did well both financially and critically. Most reviewers recognized it for the unique document it was: an only slightly censored report, written immediately after the events described, of a most unusual, very important, and extensive intelligence exercise which involved a significant element of inter-service and Allied cooperation. The book was a happy antidote to the superheated prose of spy thrillers and the often irresponsible, and unadmitted, speculations found in more popular nonfiction accounts. One or two academic critics wrote somewhat snidely of the book (including, in an incomprehending statement, a writer for the *Yale Review*) and in England inter-service rivalries, which had resurfaced after the war, led to a few attacks on Masterman, either for publishing at all or for giving the impression that he was the mastermind behind the committee. This he did not do, though some reviews in the popular press did so for him, and some of his critics may not have read what he (and Pearson) actually wrote. Masterman made it clear that he never met a double agent himself, that he ran none, that he was simply the secretary and now the historian of the enterprise, and he stated clearly that the British use of double agents had begun in the Middle East, not with the Twenty Committee. Pearson also stressed that others, notably Ewen Montagu, had already told part of the story of deception. Masterman's cool, restrained prose, speaking of chilling deeds and appalling risks, almost by indirection making it clear that uncooperative agents had been killed, required careful reading, and not all gave the book its due. It was, nonetheless, an instant classic of espionage and intelligence, and it quickly went into paperback and into translations in German, Italian, Portuguese, and Swedish. In English alone, 45,000 copies sold in cloth and 200,000 in paper.[61]

Masterman came to Yale shortly after the publication of his book. He stayed with Chester and Joan Kerr, met with students and faculty as a Chubb Fellow, and banqueted in Chicago with Yale alumni. He went on to address the Council on Foreign Relations, officers of the CIA, and numerous television audiences. Masterman reflected, not sadly, on the decline of the spy, as increased communications and new technologies tipped the balance from HUMINT to SIGINT, and off the record he told a few good tales that spoke ill of the dead, as historians often do. He returned to England, to write his autobiography, to collect his father's short stories, and to compose the preface for the wartime memoirs of the head of Czech military intelligence, Frantisek Moravec.[62] In

1980 Masterman died, already known as the man who had breached the dam, for his book was the first official record of British intelligence to get into print, and it paved the way for all the other revelations to come.

> *Transmitting the truth is always a problem.*
> *Facts we can encipher, and they then become*
> *Sendable messages: why do not the truths*
> *Climb obediently into disguises. . . .*
> Transmission 2/1 (To Image)

Outside work, life had remained rich for Pearson. There were the performances of Shakespeare in Regent's Park, always sold out but, through clever planning and occasional queuing, never to Pearson. There were Dame Myra Hess's piano concerts. There was lunch at Claridge's or Prunier's, even more often at Boulestin's or Quaglino's.[63] There were journeys to Oxford and Cambridge now and then to visit old friends. There were trips to the Peak District, to Cornwall, to Sussex. There were moments that were particularly memorable: lunch at the Reform Club with E. M. Forster—apparently Forster showed Pearson the manuscript of his revelatory novel *Maurice* and asked for his opinion of it— or at the Ritz with Graham Greene, who was with SIS at the time; drinks with Ralph Vaughan Williams, dinner with Compton Mackenzie, tea with Norman Douglas or Elizabeth Bowen, the successful pursuit of a piece of the mineral sillimanite to send to his wife as a reminder of her distinguished scientific forebear. Nothing, or almost nothing, was ever boring. Even fire watch, or the less frequent Sunday as a duty officer at Ryder Street, or being fitted for a suit at G. Keogh's on Sackville Street, or walking along for a haircut at Trumper's, "by appointment to His Majesty," could be made interesting. Pearson was one of those people who understood that no lecture is dull, no task truly tedious, no conversation with a bore boring, for one could always shift one's attention to the conversations overheard in the queue, to a discussion of the use of fallen locks of hair in wartime, to thinking about what it was that a lecturer was doing that made him so dreadfully soporific, to asking why a bore was a bore. These were the natural defensive maneuvers of the scholar against the risks of becoming inattentive, and they served him well as an intelligence officer.

Pearson had found himself working ever harder as Ultra and Twenty Committee responsibilities increased and X-2 grew, first in North Africa and Italy, then in France. He was acting chief of the London branch, from July to October 1943 and chief from September 1944 to January 1945. Throughout all this time, from April 1943 until after the end of the war, he was also head of the Iberian-North African desk in London (thus his frequent contact with Philby), and he was charged with liaison with Scandinavia and the Low Countries as well. He traveled extensively on the Continent, as his expense accounts and some of his letters show, to Lisbon, where he made the obligatory rounds of the bars likely to yield strategic information (and good grilled prawns) and listened to the sad *fados* sung in the bistros. Just after Christmas of 1943 he was in Madrid, helping to establish an X-2 station there by negotiating directly with Ambassador Hayes. He delivered some fine suit cloth from his tailor to Prince Umberto of Italy, he returned from Paris with a potential double agent whom he put up in his house, he called round at the War Room from time to time. The X-2 work was miscellaneous, often unpredictable, always interesting.

Certainly the OSS had been right to put Pearson in London and leave him there, for he got on famously with nearly everyone. He entertained over lunch even more frequently, MI6 officers, MI5 officers, Norwegian and French intelligence officers. He lunched with Professor Gilbert Ryle and Captain Martin Evans of the Radio Security Service, he had drinks with his SIS counterparts, he presented little gifts, sent through Susan, to friends and acquaintances. He recognized the diplomatic value of skillful gift giving. At Christmas 1944 he sent bottles of gin to several MI6 and MI5 friends, and whenever he traveled abroad his expense accounts were dotted with the evidence of his generosity on behalf of the OSS: in Madrid there were flowers to the wives of those who helped him, a toy train for the son of the doorman at his hotel, twenty-one bottles of perfume, and a grand dinner for the British intelligence representatives, while in Lisbon he brought lipsticks, chocolates, dolls, cognac, two alarm clocks, and twelve pairs of stockings. A man who remembers to bring Kleenex and fresh razor blades in wartime is always welcome.

Pearson dined on occasion with David Bruce, got to know the outpost's directors of SI, including Bill Casey, and generally tried to cultivate good relations with the heads of other outpost branches, but he avoided most of the rapidly growing OSS contingent—2,900 strong by the summer of 1944, and spread out in nine different locations—since security dictated that X-2 remain lean and out of sight. Once, when he went into Norway—presumably not by parachute, since it was in late June of 1945—he was accompanied by Captain Lester Armour, last OSS commandant in London, and Morris (or Moe) Berg, former Princeton baseball star and, after the war, lionized spy, who was then special assistant to the director, and on another occasion he slipped quietly over to Paris to visit his counterpart at the OSS headquarters at 79 Champs Elysées, apparently in the company of non–X-2 types, but these appear to be the only instances when he did not travel alone or with fellow X-2 operatives. He was gregarious, with an appearance of social openness, but by both personality and position he was in fact a loner.

Pearson's days were brightened shortly after V-E day when Richard Ellmann, the future literary scholar who, having been spotted by Jim Angleton, had joined the OSS, was posted to London. Ellmann handled two projects for Pearson, one the investigation of two agents, an Englishman who, after being dropped by parachute into a French town, had taken a French mistress and then been captured, and an American, subsequently dropped into France, who took the same mistress. Pearson also put Ellmann, saying that he was the only person in X-2 he could trust to spell, onto writing up citations for Bronze and Silver stars. Since nothing could be revealed in the citations, they had to consist of elaborated boiler plate, which required the skills of a literary critic. Ellmann wrote a hundred such citations, which Pearson signed; NHP then told him to write one up for himself, and Ellmann was awarded a theater command certificate of merit for writing up certificates of merit.

Everyone who worked with Pearson remembered him with affection. This was not always the case at Yale, so one might conclude that Pearson and X-2 found happiness with each other. Ellmann recalls Pearson's kindness: eager to pursue Yeats, Ellmann asked for a week's leave so that he could go to Ireland to see the widow. Pearson said to take two, and during that leave Ellmann was shown an entire room full of Yeats's manuscripts, thus launching his career. There was also the sad problem of an X-2 linguist who worked under Pearson. Word was flashed to the outpost that the translator's wife had killed his two children and that she was defending herself by saying that her husband was a homosexual. The employee frantically cried that his wife was lying;

she was a nymphomaniac. Bruce wanted this very unseemly business kept well away from OSS, as did Pearson, and through Bruce
they were able to hush the matter up, letting it out that the employee had suffered a nervous breakdown and was being sent home.
Pearson seemed more concerned for the employee's state of mind,
however, than for keeping OSS skirts clean.

Pearson was also recalled for his intensity, his almost gnomic
briefings, and for his sense of fun. He began his briefings, without
notes, from behind his desk; soon he would sit upon it, and then
he would progress to the top of a safe, to the windowsill, in constant movement, a huge foulard handkerchief hanging down his
chest, witty and complex material flowing from him. William Hood,
much later a top professional with the CIA, felt that Pearson showed
"a fantastic professional imagination" for tradecraft and conspiracy and credited him with being the first to recognize just how
good at counterintelligence the youthful James Angleton would
be. He could always turn either a briefing or a minor disaster into
a good story, as when the OSS had to withdraw the entire first
edition of a Turkish grammar, prepared by a member of staff who
had been trained in linguistics at Yale, because her Turkish informant had misled her, giving her "I fuck" for "I am." Pearson
thought this one of the happiest events of the war.[64]

Though he often worked until midnight, pushing the paper any
bureaucracy generates, and while he operated behind no enemy
lines and killed no one with the techniques taught him at Camp
C, he was in fact the typical, the representative spy. Fiction, romance, film require the dramatic; X-2 was perhaps the most dramatic of all OSS branches, for by its nature counterintelligence is
vital, tense, meticulous work, and for a few, dangerous work—
James Bond was in counterintelligence after all. Pearson would
have said, rightly, that his life held all the drama he needed. He
knew the war was there, in the skies, for in St. James's he often
had to make his way around piles of rubble, buildings that had
fallen in a bombing raid. There were the V-1 bombs, launched
upon London in June of 1944, the doodlebugs, self-flight rockets
that sounded much like a sewing machine in the distance, followed by a long moment of utter, eerie silence, and then an explosion that sounded exactly like a gas main blowing up, succeeded
by the buzz of V-2s. Pearson was at his post throughout the entirety of the V-bomb attacks, when 6,080 Londoners died and another 40,000 were injured, as Hitler and the wizards of Peenemünde

rained over 1,100 bombs down upon the city. One exploded in
Jermyn Street, just outside Pearson's window, when he was away,
and for days he worked with his office boarded up and the dust
of ceiling plaster on the floor. Could he not at least claim the
bomb fell while he was there? No, good spying required accuracy,
even in letters home, not romance.

Pearson had a romance with the city of London, however. Many
in X-2 did not care for it. Blum wanted a French posting, and in
September 1944 he got it, as X-2 chief in Paris. But to Pearson
the job he had was precisely right. He worked well with his MI5
and MI6 counterparts, sharing with them an unsleeping ear for the
thought unsaid, the nuance altered in mid-sentence, the steady
stare that belied the speaker's words. He loved the English language and thought it not at all unpatriotic to say that the English
used it well. Walks in the London night, down the sea-dark lanes;
almost aimless wanderings about the West End, past low buildings, a few half lit, "soft and warm in chiaroscuro"; trips to
Bletchley, to introduce new men—one of them, William Ladd, the
grandson of a former colleague at Yale—and to savor the landscape; even the long, drilling, ever penetrating rains that ushered
in the almost impossibly damp cold of an English mid-winter were
to him a joy. He *was* a romantic, and as he walked up from Ryder
Street, past the Ritz and Brown's Hotel, down Hay Hill and across
the bottom of Berkeley Square to his comfortable studio house in
Hays Mews, just along from a pleasant pub, I Am the Only Running Footman, settling in just above the tiny kitchen where his
lady-of-all-purpose, Alice, who shopped for his chops and did his
dishes, would leave him notes reminding him to eat this and to
drink that before it spoiled, he knew he had all he wanted. And
then to take a drink to his balcony, look out across the darkened
city (and, incidentally, down into the garden where Queen Wil-
helmina, in exile from the Netherlands, had planted geraniums),
this was his reward. His walks, his flat, even his job cosseted him
against the overseas conflict. He was convinced that what he was
doing was important, and on those Tuesdays perhaps very important. He was sad to be away from Susan and the girls, and yet he
probably had never been happier in his life.[65]

Still, Pearson felt that he was not doing enough, that his physical handicap, to which he never openly admitted, and perhaps his
love for England, were limiting him. As the assault on Fortress
Europe intensified, OSS personnel were shifted from place to place

at bewildering speed, while Pearson remained a rock rooted in
London. He was visited by nearly everyone coming "out of the
dark," telling tales of derring exploits, bringing (as Brad Welles
did, returning from Egypt) bottles of Scotch with Arabic on them,
giving him precious gossip from Yale—Donald Gallup, from the
University Library, and Louis Martz, as assistant professor of
English, were especially hailed for their juicy knowledge—or
showing up to fight the war with him. His biggest surprise was
Eugene Waith, an instructor in English at Yale, whom Pearson
never expected to see, and who proved to be an exceptionally
able controller of enemy agents, and interrogator, for X-2. Drafted
in the summer of 1943, Waith had been slotted to be a clerk in a
message center; instead, because of his excellent French and German, he had been sent to Camp Ritchie for intelligence training.
He was recruited into X-2 in June 1944, in England, trained to the
interpretation of intercepts, and attached to SHAEF. Pearson was
delighted to see him, though within weeks Waith was off again,
going into Paris just behind the advancing armies. Assigned a stay-
behind German agent, he controlled him until the agent was killed;
assigned another, Muleteer, whom he ran as a double agent, he
was able to entice in the paymaster, whom he captured and interrogated, learning much about the German army on the Rhine. He
was, Pearson was proud to learn, one of the best controllers in
France.

One day in August 1944 Pearson wrote to his wife, Susan, of
his sadness that they had lived apart for so long now, exchanging
their carefully numbered letters, Susan spending as much of her
time as possible at their summer home at the Connecticut shore,
on Johnson's Point, in Branford. He tried to share his emotions
with her, to describe so that she might truly see what he saw. He
was fascinated by the air raids, by the beauty of the "candela-
bra," flares attached to parachutes and dropped by German planes.
He liked the way searchlights laced the sky, as flashes beyond
sound lit up the night. At times specks of bright green would flash
across the sky, on and off, in a signal of some message he could
not read, a fighter racing pell-mell through the blackness, the lights
"little more than fragments, occasional vowels hurled through the
air." He crafted his letters in his loneliness, and his concern for
his wife's loneliness, with all the care that might have gone into
his books, had he been at Yale. And as he reflected on those who
seemed to be doing things so much more dramatic, he thought of

the inscription he wanted Susan to put on his tombstone. He had found it, he thought, in Stendhal's *Rouge et Noir,* and he felt that it described him well: carve, he said, *"médiocre avec éclat."*[66]

Pearson was pleased to have played a small, but key, role in the work of the OSS Art Looting project as well. (Or just possibly the reverse. In his diary David Bruce noted a conversation with Pearson and Hubert Will in which they discussed the possible use of the project as a cover for X-2 activities.) This arose in part from a report from R&A prepared for the American Commission for the Protection and Salvage of Artistic and Historic Monuments in War Areas, in October of 1943, on looting and damaging of artworks in Europe. The report proved so useful to the commission, OSS was asked to do further research. Donovan responded by establishing, in November 1944, a special Art Looting Investigation Unit, initially with six members. Looted art was traced, records were compiled on several thousand individuals who had sold art, perhaps improperly, to the enemy, and lists were made of the purchases of German galleries and museums. A "target list" of enemy personnel known to have engaged in art looting, who were to be captured and held for interrogation in Germany, was also circulated, and from June to October 1945 those on the list who were captured were interrogated at a special detention center in Austria. Particular attention was given to the Hitler museum and library in Linz, to the Goering collection, and to the activities of Einsatzstab Reichsleiter Alfred Rosenberg in France. At a nerve center set up in the Neuschwanstein castle, the unit compiled a register of 21,903 objects confiscated from Paris alone.[67]

While methodologically the tiny investigation unit might have fallen to R&A, this would not do, for the investigators had to have access to ISOS, as R&A did not, to be able to go in immediately behind the advancing troops, and the unit, since it was charged with interrogation, had to have mobility and access to immediate information. Further, art historians assigned to SHAEF in Project Orion were having difficulties with their British counterparts under Sir Leonard Woolley and with both the British and American military because of their generally lowly ranks. In the late summer of 1944 Francis Taylor, director of the Metropolitan Museum of Art and the person most directly concerned with the protection and recovery of cultural materials in war areas, made aware by Theodore Sizer of the need for an intelligence connection, called on Whitney Shepardson, head of SI, and Norman

Pearson of X-2, in London. Pearson proposed that the art historians be formally attached to X-2 and that a "Cultural War Room"
be set up in London, as X-2 was able to get higher simulated rank
for its personnel and promotion came more easily overseas. Sumner Crosby, from Yale's history of art department, worked out
the details so that some of the work technically fell under Pearson's command.

This was both convenient and cozy, since many of the members
of the unit were well known to Pearson, having Yale connections.
There was Deane Keller, an associate professor of drawing and
painting, who reported graphically on the moral degradation of
Italy; Glanville Downey, the librarian of the School of Fine Arts,
an extraordinary linguist with nine languages; Frederick Hart, from
the art gallery, an expert photographer; Charles Henry Sawyer,
Yale '29, director of the Worcester Art Museum and master of
Timothy Dwight College after the war; Sizer, a Walpolean, a Har-
vard man, professor of the history of art and director of the Yale
Art Gallery, who recorded the exploits of his fellow Harvard men,
Mason Hammond, James S. Plaut, and Theodore Rousseau—the
last two with X-2—all at least as important as the Yale contingent;
Richard A. Rathbone, an assistant professor of drawing and paint-
ing; L. Bancel LaFarge, '25, an architect; Sumner Crosby; and
John Marshall Phillips, '28, X-2, whom Pearson came to know
well, since he lived in a flat just above Pearson's neighborhood pub.

Pearson especially valued Crosby and Phillips, who joined X-2
early. A connoisseur of international reknown, a Quaker, the most
knowledgeable man in the world on early American silver, an assistant professor of the history of art and after the war director of
the Yale Art Gallery, a devotee of ice hockey and Buck's fizz, the
creative teacher of a popular undergraduate course, "Pots and
Pans" (early American arts and crafts), Phillips had that oft-men-
tioned, truly rare gift, a photographic memory: he did not forget
names, dates, signatures, or marks on a piece of silver. He had
arranged at the close of the New York World's Fair to have the
silver belonging to the Royal Family and the London Guilds kept
in the vaults of the Yale Art Gallery; this, and the later discovery,
while working on the Goering collection, that a Jan Vermeer
painting showed a seventeenth-century pewter tankard with a lid
which had a thumb-piece that was in the nineteenth-century style,
which led to the unmasking of the most notorious art forger of

modern times, Hans Van Meegeren, made him very special. After a short stint in counterintelligence in Boston, then in Lisbon, he had come to London; there, as one of the very few Americans to be a liveryman of an ancient guild, the Worshipful Company of Goldsmiths, he could vote for the Lord Mayor. Such a man, with such an eye, was obviously priceless to an art investigating unit.[68]

In addition to the recovery of vast hordes of Nazi loot, the group, working closely with the British, can be credited with useful liaison on the protection and restoration of much that was monumental and artistic in Italy. General Mark Clark felt he was fighting a war in a "goddam art museum," there were so many directives about what to save and how. Working against time in Algeria, a team of scholars had plotted on sets of detailed maps of Italy, of every town and city, the areas to avoid, and had created a photostatic gridded map for every city in Italy with three or more monuments—churches, ancient ruins, superb examples of Renaissance and Baroque architecture. Eisenhower had then issued an order, probably drafted by Woolley, for the protection of these monuments. If military necessity dictated destruction—Monte Cassino would be an example—then the lives of men must, of course, take precedence over monuments, but all commanders were charged with the most careful examination of what military necessity entailed.[69]

Near the end of the war, invalided back to the States, Lieutenant-Colonel "Tubby" Sizer, former air force intelligence officer, well trained in seven different ways to kill with his bare hands, restorer of Santa Maria della Catena in Palermo, faced the problem so many returnees did. When he arrived in New Haven, *commendatore* of a grateful Italian government, happy to walk once again through the Yale gallery, an art museum without rubble on its floor, he was asked by his eldest grandchild, "Grandfather, did you kill any Italians?" "No, Sandy, I did not kill any." "Grandfather, then did you kill any Germans?" "No, Sandy." "Well, Grandfather, did you sock any?" And even that he had not done. He had merely served art.[70]

Pearson's last year in London, most of it as the chief of the branch, was particularly satisfying. He did miss the companionship of Jim Angleton, now transferred to Italy, their meals and opera together, the impromptu party, the odd literary pilgrimage they shared, but there were dinners and drinks with three other men Pearson found especially congenial, Blum for a time, Cowgill, and Philby. There was the exhilarating turmoil of V-E Day, when Pearson joined the milling crowd at Piccadilly, and climbed the lion in Trafalgar Square, and got drunk with Cal Tenney and Ed Lawler, and had his car stolen. There were trips to Paris, where he walked all over the city with Angleton and Tenney, both temporarily transferred there, and took meals at the vast Allied mess hall, called Willow Run by the men and, since so many women met men there, Bull Run by the women. There was a visit to the Moulin Rouge and le Ciel ("the thrill was equivalent to seeing one's great-grandmother in the bathtub") with Angleton. There was the pleasure of sharing in the interrogation of Kurt Kuntz, commandant of a German concentration camp in Oslo, and seeing him reduced to fearful blubbering. And there were sad moments, when he learned of the death of a friend, and had to write to a child, to explain to him the meaning of his father's death. Even then, Pearson did not forget what his code name meant to him, for he told young Robin Fowler that "We are all Puritans, we Americans, and we know that we are our brothers' and our fathers' and our children's keepers."[71]

But by mid-summer of 1945 Pearson was anxious to get home. He and Susan had exchanged a sad correspondence, in which she revealed she had had an operation and could have no more children. On V-J Day, as he joined the celebration, quieter this time than on V-E Day, Pearson learned that Susan was undergoing a second operation and with a herculean effort got through to her on the phone. Four days later he arranged to go home, and from then until the end of his service, he commuted from the Wardman Park Hotel in Washington to New Haven. On September 28, Murphy, Pearson, McDonough, and Durand reunited in Washington and set out for a farewell reception in honor of Wild Bill Donovan: held in a roller-skating rink, with refreshments of Coca-Cola and hot dogs, for which Donovan picked up the tab, a grateful government apparently unable to find the money to do so. Then it was back to Europe in mid-October, as head of X-2 for the European theater, to help close down the branches in England, Germany, and Austria, and a rough return to the States on the aircraft carrier *Enterprise*, to arrive home to stay, on Christmas Eve, feeling "almost like Santa Claus." After several months of writing up reports, keeping an eye on the post-victory reorganization of SIS, and giving thought to how double agents might be used against the Russians in northern Europe, Pearson packed himself and Susan off on a long holiday journey to Mexico. In May 1946 Pearson resigned from what was, by then, the Central Intelligence Group and prepared to return to Yale.[72]

What kind of people had worked for X-2? A personnel file for 183 individuals provides a reasonably clear picture as of the spring of 1944. As the file contains résumés on such individuals as Pearson, Angleton, Curtiss, Will, and others on whom there is substantial data for cross-checking, one may take the files to be more or less accurate. The file, of ninety-six men and eighty-seven women, suggests the following picture.[73]

The X-2 group was well educated, though democratically educated: any notion that it was overwhelmingly drawn from the Ivy League is incorrect. Of the total of 183 employees, 148 had gone to college while only thirty-five had not (of these, however, at least half had taken courses in secretarial or business schools). Seventeen held law degrees, eleven had taken doctorates, sixteen (including several of the women) had M.A. degrees, two held the Harvard M.B.A., and one had graduated from medical school. Seven were professors. The group had attended eighty-seven United States and eleven foreign universities, or ninety-eight universities in all. The heaviest concentration was from Columbia, with ten; this included M.A.s taken while the employees were at work in New York. Yale had produced eight of the members of the group, Harvard six, and Smith College five. (If the Harvard Law, Business, and Graduate Schools are added, the Harvard figure rises to thirteen.) There were four each from the University of California at Berkeley, George Washington University, Northwestern, Princeton, and Wellesley. The state universities were well represented, with three each from the universities of Michigan and Oregon, two each from the universities of Alabama, Indiana, Kansas, Maryland, North Carolina, Washington, and Wisconsin, and from Ohio State. In addition to Columbia, Yale, Harvard, and Princeton, other so-called elite institutions included Brown and Cornell (one each), Pennsylvania (two), Chicago (three), Stanford (two), and one each from Cal Tech, MIT, and Duke. The small liberal arts colleges—Amherst, Bowdoin, Hamilton, Oberlin, Swarthmore, Williams—were present. So too were the private women's colleges: in addition to Smith and Wellesley, there were two each from Mount Holyoke, Radcliffe, Sarah Lawrence, and Vassar, and one each from Agnes Scott, Bryn Mawr, Goucher, Millsaps, and Sweet Briar. Religious institutions were also present in good number: six individuals had gone to Roman Catholic institutions, and one each to Christian Scientist, Mormon, and Quaker colleges. Educationally the net had been spread widely across the country, from Occidental on the West Coast to Memphis State in the South to Fitchburg State Teachers College in New England.

This education brought with it an astonishing array of language ability. Eighty-four members of the group were fluent in one or more languages, and all but thirty-three were "good to fair" in at least one language. Thirty-seven were fluent in two or more languages—one person was fluent in four, and "less than fluent" in four more, while another was fluent in two and less than fluent in eight more languages—and one was fluent in five. French, Spanish, and Italian were commonplace, with German, Portuguese, and Greek well represented. Three members of the group spoke Chinese, three Hindustani, three "spoke" Latin; also present were Polish, Danish, Norwegian, Swedish, Hungarian, Czech, Slovak, Hebrew, and Azerbaijani. One read Coptic; another was fluent in a variety of Italian dialects, yet another in several Arab dialects. No one was fluent in Russian.

The range of previous experience was also broad. By 1944, X-2 had in its midst a professional singer, a concert pianist, the former head of the English department in a school in Peking, several socialites, young girls just out of high school, two former instructors from Robert College in Istanbul, four young men who had grown up in China as the sons of missionaries (including two who had gone to the Shanghai American School together), the head of a nursing program in China, the former buying agent for the British in Portugal (a specialist in fish oil), a woman flight instructor, the superintendent of a mattress factory, the son of the writer John P. Marquand, a Coca-Cola executive, a football coach, a bartender (from the Yale Club), several interpreters, a beauty parlor operator, a skiing instructor, a member of the California State Legislature, the daughter of a diplomat, at least three men and two women of great wealth and two men and three women who had not finished high school, and the former steward, forty-five years old, to Donovan at his law firm. The average age of the group was thirty-four.

Experience took other shapes, of course. Forty-four of the men had come to X-2 from the army, two each from the navy and air force, one from the marines. Six had been in the State Department, seven had worked for the FBI, two for ONI, one had been a customs agent, and nineteen were transferred from other branches of the OSS. Eighteen had been born outside the United States—one of these, David Zagier, was born in Poland and had subsequently held Russian and South African citizenship; understandably he came in for intense security scrutiny—and sixty-nine had one or both parents born outside the country. Of those born in the United States, no section of the country dominated. The range was as geographically democratic as it appeared to be socially so.*

One also notes the discrimination against women so common in government service at the time. The women were fully as well educated; they spoke the same number of languages; they average to the same age; they had traveled abroad. But all were secretaries, translators, filing clerks, or—in one instance—a decoder. (Two were listed as "secretary and associate desk head," roughly an administrative assistant.) While women rose to be head of station in R&A, as in Stockholm and New Delhi, none achieved executive functions in X-2.

> *We must not forget. We must keep asking for*
> *Ciphers more difficult, each month, to use, lest*
> *Our care and hope vanish into the message,*
> *Coding having become too much a matter*
> *Of sighing, flopping into one's chair, reaching*
> *Wearily for the new grid of the week, and*
> *Starting with the calculations. The noisome*
> *Flutter of papers, like a flick of fear brought*
> *By an unwitting wind, would be too welcome.*
> Transmission 4/3 (To Image)

With the loss of Cowgill to Germany, and the closing up of the Twenty Committee, Pearson had only one truly intense interest left to bring the same sense of pleasure to his week that his happy,

---

*The personnel file also reveals interesting idiosyncrasies. One member, very much a part of OSS, was nonetheless carried in the Dead File. Another, a secretary, had her file annotated that it should show that she was working for X-2 in Ceylon while, in fact, she was working for Duncan Lee, a Yale graduate in Donovan's secretariat who became head of the China section of SI. One, Sylvia Press, later under heavy attack from Senator Joseph McCarthy for alleged left-wing activities, appears in the file in two contradictory résumés and apparently changed her mind about one of her languages. (She was expelled from the CIA after a "reinvestigation" and describes her experience in a novel, *The Care of Devils*.) And then there is the professor of a language who nonetheless lists his ability with it as slight, either a remarkable display of modesty inside X-2 or of chutzpah at his institution.

mixed work load had done. This was his warm friendship with the poet he most admired, H.D., "the imagiste." His relationship to H.D., that is, to Hilda Doolittle, the Anglo-American poet, became steadily closer the longer Pearson remained in London.[74]

He had first read H.D. in 1936 and immediately concluded that one day she would be recognized as a major poet. In 1937 he had met her at Benét's home, and they at once became friends. Benét and Pearson had included H.D. in the *Oxford Anthology of American Literature*—her first appearance in a volume meant, in large measure, to enshrine the American classics—and they had corresponded steadily thereafter. H.D. had, of course, appeared in the anthology compiled by Mark van Doren that, in 1928, so impressed Pearson.

Pearson was a collector of people as some collect experiences, not in any pejorative sense, but because he wanted to understand twentieth-century American prose and particularly poetry, and he rather thought he would understand it better if he knew those who produced it. Throughout his life he played the role of the man of letters, encouraging poets, writers, painters, and scholars, whether émigré Estonian poets such as Aleksis Rannit, who obtained his postwar position at Yale largely through Pearson's intervention, or young translators and poets like Alastair Reid, who would make the Chilean poet Pablo Neruda known to a generation imprisoned in the language of their tongue. He had, by the war, already set off on the long path to persuading other cultures to take America seriously, by showing that Americans also took their cultures seriously.

The day after he arrived in London, April 13, the day before he left for St Albans, Pearson called H.D., who greeted him as an old friend and at once announced that he must come to "the Reading"—he thought she was talking about a move to the English city of that name, until he realized she thought the fact he had arrived in time for the first of the major wartime poetry readings (this one in aid of China Relief) was "an arrangement of God." He went along immediately to H.D.'s cramped flat on Lowndes Square, near the Knightsbridge tube station, where H.D. lived with her constant companion (and cousin), Bryher—the pen name of Winifred Ellerman, taken from one of the Scilly Isles off the Cornwall coast—writing, raising chickens, and enduring the devastation that had blossomed around them. As it was unsafe to go out at night, there being so many collapsed buildings, and later buzz bombs, the two women felt imprisoned in their flat, and they liked to entertain. Pearson was a regular and always welcome guest, and though he frequently brought some rare treat—butter, sugar, biscuits, sweets, a pineapple, a turkey—from the American commissary, he was wanted and waited for because of his charm, wit, obvious affection for H.D. and regard for the writing of both, and his oft-stated intention to see to it that H.D., at least, would have "a shelf of her own" in Yale's rare book collection. Further, Pearson had made life far more pleasant for H.D. by rescuing her daughter Perdita from a job as a typist at Bletchley Park, helping her to find a flat just opposite H.D.'s, and getting her a job with OSS—in fact, as his and then Jim Angleton's secretary—so that Perdita could use her talents as a linguist. Pearson greatly enjoyed the company of these intense, highly literate, sometimes distrait (the word required, when applied to H.D., the French pronunciation to capture Pearson's sense of the atmosphere) women.

There were days of double pleasure, tea and "dull yellow cake" with the Sitwells—Edith, Osbert, Sacheverel—and dinner at Lowndes Square, and at times there were poetry readings, a very little bit of excellent whiskey (Bryher was wealthy, and though she appeared not to know it, H.D. had plenty of money: they simply refused to live as though they had, except for shopping at Harrod's), and good reminiscing. Far too seldom H.D. would speak, obliquely, as Pearson honed his ear for nuance and his tongue for the half-sentence, of how she had been a disciple of Ezra Pound, of her psychoanalysis with Freud, of her husband, Richard Aldington—whom she had divorced in 1938—or of D. H. Lawrence. She was also taken up with spiritualism at the time, with table tipping and the like, an interest Pearson did not share.

Some H.D. scholars were fascinated by the question of whether she had slept with D. H. Lawrence.[75] Respecters of privacy might well ask whether it matters. In many cases, it matters hardly at all for understanding an author's work whether X slept with Y or not, but with someone such as H.D., it appeared to matter greatly, for it would seem, from the way in which she had turned from the promiscuous Aldington, and in her bisexuality, that her womb-vision (of which she wrote in her *Notes on Thought and Vision*[76]) was especially important to her. H.D. scholars were not simply sophisticated voyeurs, as scholars sometimes can be; they wanted rightly enough to discover who shared what shadowed secrets of the body. Pearson shared this view. He was not at all nosy about sexual matters, referring to them in only the most veiled ways even in his private correspondence. Though he would have been intrigued by the current debate over whether *The Scarlet Letter* came forth in anguish from a Hawthorne torn by an incestuous relationship with his sister, NHP would not have been the first, or the tenth, to see that as the primary question of Hawthorne scholarship. Rather, in H.D. and Bryher he sensed a vulnerability, a sexuality in no way threatening, which seems to have drawn him to them. He was the most steadfast and loving of husbands, that perhaps rare creature, not only a devoted but a truly content father, and because of his sensitivities to language, to light, to his own quiet needs as he applied plaster and bandage to his open wound, to his wife's own delicately poised sense of order as both a triumph and a threat, he was able to read others well. As several friends of his remarked, one always felt, when with Norman, that one was being watched, not for any ulterior purpose, but because watching people was for him the most effective way of relating to them. When he had watched enough, and had made up his mind, he usually reached out and did something kind. He was, then, an ideal companion at tea, and it is no wonder that H.D. and Bryher, the Sitwells, Benjamin Britten, and the rambunctious Humphrey Trevelyan found him good company. Indeed, in her memoirs Bryher says Pearson was essential to their survival.[77]

His Sundays with H.D. helped Pearson through the long months of desk work, and he looked forward to them, analyzed them, wrote to his wife of them with a wry amusement and clear-eyed respect, almost consciously shaping these letters to a more literary form. The Sundays were obviously good for H.D., too. She became productive again in 1944, producing *The Walls Do Not Fall,* her first full book of poetry since 1931, dedicating it to Bryher and asking Pearson to write the foreword. This, the first book of her trilogy, broke forth from her as she looked upon the ravagement of London, "a city in ruin, a world ruined . . . almost past redemption." Pearson was determined that when he returned to Yale—for by now he was confident that he would do so, and that he might even enter politics—he would take this major, neglected poet and make her well known.[78]

H.D. and Pearson corresponded when Pearson returned to Washington and renewed their Sunday dinners when he came back to London in May of 1944. He became her literary executor, never failed to visit her when in London after the war, and in 1957 edited the first major anthology of her poetry, *Selected Poems.*[79] He was, one of H.D.'s biographers concluded, the only anthologist to comprehend her entire range. As Louis Martz, Sterling Professor of English at Yale and a good friend of Pearson's, remarked of NHP in 1984, H.D. "trusted him and loved him," and for him she collected her work, had it retyped, and sent everything to Pearson for deposit in the Yale library. In 1956 he persuaded the BBC to give a ninety-minute broadcast of her version of Euripides' *Ion,* her last prewar work, and that same year arranged a seventieth-birthday celebration of her poetry at Yale, where in a carefully orchestrated perambulation she was hailed by faculty, students, and press. In 1960 H.D. came again to the States, this time to receive the Gold Medal of the American Academy of Arts and Letters, and Pearson was there, hosting a champagne party; three thousand people attended, to hear H.D. and St. John Perse, who also received the medal that day, read. Pearson remained a constant in her life, a life that had, she felt, been filled with rejection. When she could not go to Brandeis University to receive an award, Pearson accepted it for her; when she felt confused by a publisher's contract, he reviewed and revised it; when, ill in Zurich, she turned toward Jungian analysis, he followed her intellectual path; and when, also in Zurich, she died in September 1961, he began the systematic organizing of her unpublished manuscripts. Just as Norman Pearson saw to it that H.D. continued to be productive beyond her death, editing, placing with publishers three more books, so did H.D. do the same for NHP: his last publication, released four years after he died, was an edition of her memoir of Ezra Pound.[80]

> *I ask for nothing*
> *More than to do the work, to be able*
> *To work. It is not given us to complete*
> *It; neither are we free to desist from it.*
> *I wish to be assigned a new frequency.*
> Transmission 9/13

After the war Pearson also remained in close touch with General Donovan and took on some assignments for the Central Intelligence Group and, briefly after 1947, for the CIA, but there is no evidence that he ever acted as more than a go-between for the agency. During the period in 1945–46 when Donovan was losing his battle to preserve the OSS, Pearson responded as he could to the charge that academics were likely to be Bolsheviks, or that (as the columnist Dorothy Thompson wrote) something more was needed in the future than "a superman organization of ex-paratroopers and Yale sleuths." He prepared succinct reports, and traveled to Washington to lecture, on the wartime British, French, German, and Russian intelligence organizations. He may have read and reviewed an OSS secret report on the lessons to be learned from the French Resistance—a report that could have been classified secret only because it would have angered the British, since it tended to ignore the SOE role in France (though a section on the capture, and the turning, of enemy agents, even without reference to the Twenty Committee, might also have been damaging). He read and reacted to memoranda on possible future X-2 counterintelligence activities. In 1949 he responded to Donovan's request that he review the history of X-2, which was part of the laborious and lengthy general history of the OSS. Pearson was unhappy with parts of the manuscript, rewriting sections, adding pages on the manipulation of double agents.[81]

Pearson believed strongly in the need for centralized intelligence, for a meticulously maintained peacetime registry, and in the use of double agents. While his primary contribution on the last subject, as we have seen, was his help with Masterman's *Double-Cross System* in 1971–72, Pearson maintained a general interest throughout the cold war. He collected the many articles on the derring-do of the OSS that appeared at the end of the war, though he suspected that Donovan and others had inspired them, during Donovan's efforts to preserve the OSS against its postwar detractors.[82] Pearson knew that these articles exaggerated the work of the OSS, but he did not feel they exaggerated its importance, or what a similar body, more carefully constructed, and with more systematic recruiting, could accomplish. Pearson, Murphy, and another old friend from X-2, Paul Medalie, conferred from time to time. Above all, as he reflected upon the OSS generally, he was inclined to agree with Donald Downes's critical assessment: too many recruits had, in the end, proved unqualified. This was not the fault of the OSS, however: he lay the problem at the door of the service academies and the universities.

Accordingly, when the National Security Council—the body to which the CIA was responsible—authorized a study, conducted in 1948 by William H. Jackson and Matthias F. Correa, on intelligence coordination, Pearson sent along a paper he had prepared on the theory of Controlled Enemy Agents, or CEAs, and after Jackson became the deputy director of Central Intelligence, Pearson provided—presumably at Jackson's request—a pungent memorandum on intelligence training, or more properly the lack of it, in the service schools. Pearson recommended that the case method be used, as in business and law school, so that all West Point and Annapolis graduates might comprehend the uses of intelligence material. This was, as he put it, "an academic question which is not an 'academic' question." Pearson assumed that the CIA would recruit its younger personnel from universities, and he urged that each university have within it informal talent spotters who would forward names of likely candidates to the agency. He also wanted the agency to maintain cross-indexed lists of individuals who knew the more exotic languages, as the British did. "I can recall numerous students, of the highest caliber, who have, for example, passed through Yale equipped with unusual facilities." He could not now recall their names, however, and though students tended to assume that their professors remembered them for years afterward, few did, each new class crowding from memory the previous one, so that some registry of talents ought to be maintained. This meant that each university needed to have at least one faculty member who could also advise students on careers in intelligence, and to do so, that faculty member would have to be reasonably well informed on the agency's hiring policies. He concluded by suggesting five men who had served under him in X-2 who might form the nucleus of such a group of advisers: Eugene Waith, back in the Yale English department (thus suggesting that Pearson did not care to serve in such a capacity); Edward Weismiller, then teaching English at Pomona College; his old flatmate in London, Calvin Tenney, teaching French at Wesleyan University in Connecticut; H. Donaldson Jordan, the chairman of the Department of History at Clark University, a specialist in British history; and Reginald Phelps, a highly regarded associate dean of Harvard College.[83] (Neither Jordan nor Phelps was approached.)

There continued to be visits with old MI6 friends, too, especially with the Cowgills, whenever the Pearsons went to England. They exchanged small presents, Pearson supplied Cowgill with American books on espionage, writing each other notes on the credibility of each new book that took up the Philby case. Bob Blum also kept in touch with Cowgill, as did Jimmy Murphy, and Pearson in turn with them. Not long before his death Pearson attended a gala reunion of the veterans of the OSS in Washington, where he sought out Jim Angleton. These friendships endured all that came after the war, proof that the affection between Cowgill and the Americans was not based, at least solely, on the calculated self-interest imputed by Philby. When Cowgill had left the secret service, Pearson had sent along a silver tea caddy, carefully not inscribed with the names of the forty-eight X-2 employees then in London, as a token of that affection. When asked about those Americans in 1984, Cowgill simply said, "they were a good bunch. A truly good bunch."

The war had seriously delayed work on Hawthorne's letters, perhaps had even made that work seem less important. When Pearson returned to Yale, he joined a group who had served in the war and who, having lost half a decade of academic productiveness, seemed to take too long to get back into stride. For whatever reason, as with Joe Curtiss, Archy Foord, Duke Henning (or, of those historians who remained at Yale throughout the war, Lewis Curtis and Tom Mendenhall), there was a flourishing of brilliant teaching—Pearson's courses were at once, and enormously, popular—and a long silence of the pen. Pearson, who returned to an assistant professorship, had to wait for promotion to the associate professorship, and tenure, until 1951, and then, even more egregiously, another twelve years for the full professorship.[84] A bit of this he attributed to the postwar nature of academia: universities were filled with young scholars of less-than-affluent backgrounds, in a hurry because their income depended upon their promotions, writing furiously (he never denigrated such writing as mere scribbling, as one or two of his friends did) to win those promotions. Prewar Yale had not thought that, in failing to publish, one would perish, and in any event, he had not failed to publish. New editions of Hawthorne came forth regularly, there were four collections of essays, he wrote frequent and invariably well-regarded pieces on Thoreau, Cooper, Gertrude Stein, and twentieth-century American literature (and once, as an apparent departure, since most readers were unaware of his engagement with practical affairs of state, an essay on the German-Soviet Pact of 1939).

Norman Holmes Pearson's most ambitious foray into writing professional history, this essay on "The Nazi-Soviet Pact and the End of a Dream," was his weakest piece of writing. Written in 1952, thirteen years after that day in August 1939 when Stalin

gave Hitler the green light for his invasion of Poland, news of
which demoralized those American writers who had once enthu-
siastically embraced the "glorious rise of the Soviet Union," the
essay quite simply reads badly. Pearson liked, as do many literary
critics, to convey half his meaning by shading, brief phrases that
would resonate in the reader's mind, carrying the eye along the
slippery slopes of literary allusion. The problem with allusive writing
is that for every clever phrase which embraces a reader, letting
him feel an insider to a reference, there is a phrase that excludes
another reader. The essay is not history at all. At moments it
sounds like the intelligence officer at work: "They are the results
of general failures of assessment" is the curt conclusion about
why crises occur; there are mock profundities (". . . for Americans the final examinations come only, if ever, at death"); at moments there are paragraphs so opaque, they might be in code.
When Pearson the critic limited himself to discussing American
literature, remarking upon the dominant strain of self-criticism in
American literary classics, on how even the most hostile writing
showed love for America because it was "goading her toward the
achievement of an idea," or when he reminded his readers of
Pound's remark that irony could not be negative since it always
posits an ideal that had been corrupted, the essay was intelligent
and clear eyed. Old friends run through the essay, most obviously
Archibald MacLeish, and for anyone familiar with Pearson's wartime work, the allusions double upon themselves. He must have
had fun doing the piece, and he was obviously intrigued by his
theme, set by a line from T. S. Eliot, "After such knowledge,
what forgiveness?" But the desire to remind us of Lear's prayer
(though Lear is not quoted), "pray you now; forget and forgive,"
removes the essay from even the portico of the house of history,
since historians are not engaged in the business of forgetting or
forgiving. Asking Eliot's question, they answer differently. The
essay is, in retrospect, simply a curious exercise, though read today it suggests what Pearson's strengths in counterintelligence must
have been.[85]

What Pearson did superlatively well was to promote and give
shape to the growing postwar interest in interdisciplinary studies,
of which American studies were perhaps the first and certainly
the most luxuriant foliage, especially overseas. In 1963 Pearson
became chairman of the American studies program at Yale, a post
he held until his death, and he devoted untold hours to furthering

American studies both in the United States and abroad, lecturing indefatigably in foreign universities. Indeed, his fatal illness—he died on November 6, 1975—arose from a hurried, exhausting lecture tour in Japan and South Korea, for there, as in Scandinavia, he was the American scholar most in demand when the academic community needed someone to make the case for the seriousness of the United States as an object of scholarly pursuits.

Pearson's illness was never publicly explained. He had attended one of five International Bicentennial Conferences on American studies that the cultural division of the Department of State and the United States Information Agency cosponsored abroad, this one in Fujinomiya, Japan, and had then gone on to Korea to consult and lecture, while other stars in the American studies firmament—Pearson's one-time student, for example, William H. Goetzmann, that year president of the American Studies Association and a professor at the University of Texas, who went to Singapore to lecture—fanned out in East and Southeast Asia. Some of those who persisted in their belief that Pearson was working for the CIA laid his death to the North Koreans, alleging that he had been assassinated by poison or germs while in Seoul. As this was the time when rumors were thick that the Russians were using poison-tipped umbrellas to eliminate American agents (they were, or their surrogates, the Bulgarians, were in fact using umbrellas that projected tiny poisoned pellets to kill dissident émigré writers and dropouts from the KGB, but not Americans), some of his former students concluded that his death proved he had been working for "the Company"—or that because he was working for the company one could conclude that he was poisoned—a circular argument that appears to have been accepted, at least for a time, by his widow.*

To some extent Norman Pearson encouraged such speculations. While he never told his doctoral students any of the details of his work for the OSS, and none suggests that he ever sought to steer them toward a career in postwar intelligence, he did drop the rare hint from time to time about what he had done in World War II, especially to those not working directly under him. One of his former graduate students recalls that Pearson said he had

---

*Ms. Addiss has shared with me the death certificate, which makes it clear that death was from viral pneumonia, complicated by emphysema, kidney failure, and in the end a massive heart attack.

thought up "the man who never was" caper (not so),[86] another that when the story of Philby's treachery broke, Pearson mentioned working with him at Ryder Street, a third that Stanley Williams, Pearson's old dissertation adviser, once confided about 1953 that Norman was "working on something" for the CIA. In truth, he worked so hard, traveled so often, spoke in nuanced half sentences so frequently, such notions were bound to appear as mushrooms overnight when he returned from East Asia.

Norman Pearson was a person who saw life as a series of hurdles, of fences to clear, books, articles, reviews to write, doctoral candidates to guide to completion (there were sixteen of these), committees to chair, lectures to give. None of this was viewed precisely as "work," however, for while each posed a challenge and each must be given the seriousness due, spending one's days doing precisely what one liked to do could scarcely be thought of as work. From time to time his wife, Susan, was ill, and there was a diminution in social life, but the marriage remained a source of pride and pleasure. Pearson was not, no more than most scholars, one to take a few drinks with the boys in the evening, though he did treasure his lunch at Mory's, his calendar always filled as it had been in London, with an old friend, a major writer passing through New Haven, a student to be gingered along, sometimes accompanied by one drink and almost always by a cigarette or two. Talk flowed well, and with Norman at the table, often well enough even from those not thought capable of a witticism.

There was always something a trifle conspiratorial in Norman Pearson's manner, and this apparently was so before the war as well as after, so that one cannot accuse him of playing at the game of nuance merely because he honed it over espresso at Quaglino's. He was, as one friend remarked, a person who took pleasure from hinting, very broadly so that the hint could not be missed by any save the utterly obtuse, that he had just had lunch with Winston Churchill; the pleasure, both for Norman and for his companion, came from the fact that unlike others who enjoyed a game of wink and nod behind which there was no substance, if Norman hinted, he was invariably hinting at a truth. For this one could forgive a lot, since a good story was likely to follow, full of anecdote and double entendre. He was, perhaps, a slave to his self-imposed obligations, always searching out another first edition, perusing dealers' catalogs with the intensity of a shrike, aware that great universities maintained great libraries only because of the stern self-discipline of donors who were never dulled by their devotion. His collections on H.D., Pound, William Carlos Williams, John Gould Fletcher; his massive collection of nineteenth-century boy's books; his set of the work of Posada, a Mexican graphic artist; his many paintings by literary figures, all these he gave to Yale; his Eugene O'Neill collection to Yale and Princeton; other gifts to Harvard, Bryn Mawr, the Library of Congress. Three offices full of books, set out neatly on shelves in the tower of the Hall of Graduate Studies, testified to all who visited him to his omnivorous reading. And at home there was more, including a collection of early Eskimo carvings in ivory (which were, he liked to tell visitors, distinctive because carved on whale penises) which he sought out in personal journeys throughout northern Canada and to Greenland.

Pearson's monument was real, though invisible: no American studies program was better known abroad, or more highly regarded, than Yale's in his lifetime. Something went out of the program with his death: foreign students of America reported that no one at Yale seemed to care for them, that the program had turned parochial. There were, within it, better scholars in the sense that there were more productive scholars, but they seemed not to care about those foreign students who wanted to learn about a culture imperfectly understood and, as a culture, quite unappreciated in their lands. One, Orm Øverland, had admired Yale, and Pearson, enormously in the 1960s, and had been grateful for the way Pearson had subtly led him to finish work begun in America in enthusiasm, work difficult if not almost impossible to complete at home—in this case Norway—where library facilities were lacking. Øverland would return to Yale the year after Pearson's death, degree and American studies chair (at the University of Bergen) secured, to discover that the attraction of American studies at Yale for foreign students and scholars had depended on Pearson; now no one cared whether they were there or not. In his entire sabbatical year at Yale, Øverland was entertained in the home of a single scholar, a person not in, indeed little regarded by, American studies.

These foreign students had not realized how much Pearson had influenced the atmosphere at Yale until he was gone; when, in 1980, two French scholars of established reputation arrived for relatively short-term stays, to find themselves not only ignored but viewed as a positive annoyance, since entertaining them properly was a burden, there was at last a realization, outside Yale and to some extent within, that Pearson had mattered far beyond the books he never wrote. As Øverland noted, Pearson had realized "that the international standing of American Studies at Yale to no small degree depended on the attraction of the program for foreign students and on the continued ties between these scholars and the program. . . . Norman was Yale. There were many brilliant scholars and teachers, but he was the one who cared."[87] He cared because he realized that, if his were to be the American Century—as for a brief time in the 1950s and '60s it looked as though it might be—American scholars must care about more than their next book, their American students, their standing in a profession circumscribed by a narrow nationalism.

There were honors, of course. Norman Holmes Pearson was twice a Guggenheim Fellow, a rare distinction; a fellow at the Huntington Library in California; president of his guild, the American Studies Association; a chancellor of the Academy of American Poets; he served on committees for the National Book Awards, received gold medals and framed certificates and presentation items from around the world. One suspects, however, that the awards he cherished most came to him, all, at the end of World War II, poised between the instructorship he had left and the assistant professorship to which he returned. There were four decorations which, now and then—when an invitation gave permission—he would wear, each of them a reflection of a world far outside Yale: the Knight's Cross first class of the Norwegian Order of St. Olaf, the French Médaille de la Reconnaissance, a rosette as a chevalier of the Légion d'Honneur, and the United States Medal of Freedom.[88]

CHAPTER SIX

THE THEORIST

JAMES JESUS ANGLETON

hree branches of the Office of Strategic Services survived the war, the dissolution of the OSS, and the short, intense postwar period when Congress feared that the creation of a centralized intelligence agency might lead to a covert American Gestapo. These were Research and Analysis, the largest of the OSS operations, which was widely viewed as the most effective branch, SI, and X-2, the counterintelligence branch which, in London and elsewhere, had not only proved its worth but could be seen to have peacetime relevance. R&A went, at first, to the Department of

322

State, where a small group of carry-overs hibernated quietly while Donovan and others politicked to get the OSS or something very like it reestablished, and SI and X-2, merged, were taken under the wing of the War Department. Both resurfaced in 1947 in the newly created Central Intelligence Agency.

R&A and X-2 had one interest in common, though in most respects they were highly disparate: they were concerned with the theory of intelligence. Both posed those same questions, though with different emphases and intent, that historians posed: of any given information, was it significant? was it interesting? was it true? They differed, of course, in their definitions of such terms—significant to what? interesting to whom? what is truth?—but, unlike the action-oriented, operational wings of the OSS, they called for men and women who were patient, methodical, curious, able almost as if by instinct to see relationships between the parts and a whole, people who at once understood what E. M. Forster meant by his dictum, "only connect." Those who worked in R&A and in X-2 had a sense of place, for some largely from books, for others from knowing Italy, or England, or Istanbul as James Joyce knew Dublin: because they inhabited it with their mind, and their future, not merely with their body. They understood the function of trivia, of miscellaneous information, and understanding it could both remember an enormous range of data and assimilate that data into a coherent pattern that others might miss. They wanted to understand another society, often in order to understand their own; they tended to think that there truly was something called "national character," despite the possibility that such a belief would lead to stereotyping others, for they believed that Americans, or English, or Italians, or Russians tended—tended as a nation, as a collectivity, not invariably as individuals—to behave in a certain way given certain conditions. They were theoreticians of human nature, with the human condition fragmented into that easy and admittedly at times misleading set of receptacles for collecting and analyzing data, the nation state.

Such American theory of intelligence that developed during World War II, or at least until mid-1944, was derived in good part from the British, and while the Americans built up their practical knowledge, little independent methodology grew from that knowledge. One of the fundamental considerations of a scholarly community—the question of how a discipline's methodology evolves, and how "correct methodology" is to be judged—had received

little attention by Donovan and most of his "thousand professors"
as they frantically sought to keep up with a war that often moved
more rapidly than their own information base. Some of the Americans, men like Sherman Kent at R&A and James Angleton in X-
2 in Italy, realized that the accumulation of facts was moving ahead
of the theoretical ability to handle the facts to any effective purpose, and they soon turned their attention, even as the mud slide
of data threatened to engulf them, to questions of theory. In time
a self-conscious methodology, a scholarly procedure, would
emerge—the publication in 1949 of Kent's *Strategic Intelligence
for American World Policy* provides as convenient a date as any—
and this methodology was a product of the two branches which
had derived the most from their British counterparts.

There are many legitimate claimants for the title of theoretician
of American intelligence. Certainly the major figures associated
with cryptanalysis would stand high in such a competition, especially William F. Friedman, the geneticist from Indiana who headed
the Signal Intelligence Service between the two world wars. Code
breaking is directed to the core methodological problem of intelligence: how to penetrate the enemy without the enemy knowing,
and how then to use that penetration to calculate the value of an
agent's services. Narrowly, cryptanalysis turns upon the theory
of mathematics, upon computer science; broadly it arises from the
widest possible view of human nature and thus of the social sciences most broadly. Thus even the most technical of intelligence
methodologies overlaps with the least technical. Analysis conducted by computer, pattern discovered by machine, must be
grasped within the context of a theoretical body of knowledge and
by a methodology that derives ultimately from traditional disciplines. While enhanced capacity, better tools, add to the density
and complexity of data that can be handled, and thus alter the
questions that may be asked, the intent of the questions does not
change, and it is that intent that is shaped by theorists. The gap
so often thought to exist between theory and practice, between
the person who "thinks" and the person who "does," is not valid
at the level of methodology.

This being so, three other individuals appear to have strong claims
as primary theorists of American intelligence in the first decade
of the cold war. These are Sherman Kent, the scholar who, after
a brief return to academic pursuits at Yale, came back into harness in order to apply his theory of strategic intelligence; Allen

Dulles, who professed to dislike theory but who, by virtue of his practices, effectively defined covert action in terms of operationally acceptable methodology; and James Jesus Angleton, the person who brooded longest, and perhaps with the greatest penetration, over the specialized methodology of counterintelligence. The theoretical concerns of each was an expression of personality.

Angleton was, and is, a student of ambiguity, "the Poet" to many who knew him—a name given him by Charles Murphy of *Time* magazine, who rather admired his style—a man who even today, well over a decade into an enforced retirement, intensely taps upon the table and says that everything begins—and ends—with the proper methodology. Kent was a professor who never lost his interest in seeing whether a properly applied methodology of research would not lead to operable truths, and he encapsulated that methodology in the Office of National Estimates, properly the heart of the CIA, over which he presided for years. Dulles, quintessentially scholarly in manner, dressed in tweeds and puffing upon his pipe as he peered out from behind his spectacles, widely regarded as the "prototypical American spymaster" during his tenure as director of Central Intelligence from 1953 to 1961, would publicize, legitimize, and romanticize, in popular articles and anthologies, the idea of the spy as a valid, necessary, even primary defender of American values. Borrowing a leaf, perhaps half unconsciously, from the Harvard Business School, Dulles championed the case study approach to intelligence; yet, he was also the creator of an aura, even a theory of romance that, to the dismay of many in Congress, in the public, in the universities, in the CIA itself, ultimately was used by very unromantic individuals to justify the unjustifiable: failure (as at the Bay of Pigs) and—along with the FBI—the trampling on the very values romance was accustomed to defending.*

All three would have agreed with James Joyce who, when asked what a writer must do to survive, responded that anyone concerned with language must live by "secrecy, silence, cunning." This is what the intelligence game was about to these men. Angleton, though not the professional historian, may have understood

---

*One well-informed OSS/CIA employee on whom I tried my list of theoreticians told me that I should add Arnold Wolfers (see Chapter Two), who he said had great influence on John McCone, director of Central Intelligence, 1961–65. McCone fundamentally reorganized the administration of the CIA.

the point even better than Kent. If Angleton did not discover Edward Hallett Carr's famous analysis of causation in history, the 1961 Trevelyan Lectures—published as *What Is History?* the following year—until 1985, he always shared its assumptions. Indeed, the words of another eminent theoretician of history, Robin G. Collingwood, the great Oxford metaphysician, historian of Roman Britain, autobiographer, might well have been those of Angleton in a reflective mood, for he knew that intelligence, like philosophy and history, depended on "going to school with the poets in order to learn the use of language": language was "a means of exploring one's own mind, and bringing to light what is obscure and doubtful in it." The intelligence officer was, as Collingwood might have said, less a jeweler than a lens-grinder.

Angleton was, as the possibly admiring, certainly distancing epithet "the Poet" implied, a man whose devotion to theory was virtually poetic. He was never able to abandon a real affection for many with whom he worked, an affection that by his theory required suspension, nor could he be unaware of the ambiguities, and in the end of the inexactitudes, of his chosen poetic form. The literary critic William Empson, in his remarkable if somewhat obscure essays on literature, *Seven Types of Ambiguity* (a book well known to Jim Angleton), explored the effect of ambiguity on understanding. Empson might, as he chose for analysis lines from the Elizabethan poet John Webster, have had in mind a question of patrimony that, unlike the question of the relative influence of the British on the OSS, really matters: from what did the self-destructive CIA of the late 1960s spring, from what, and whose, theory?

> *Oh, my worse sin was in my blood;*
> *Now my blood pays for it.*

In London Hubert Will had concluded that James Angleton was ends-oriented and could remember his own lies: surely a necessary brace of qualities for a successful spy. He also had the professional's necessary interest in ambiguity: an intense commitment to the elimination of ambiguity where sources conflicted (rather than the amateur's tendency to attempt to reconcile conflicting statements, as though both might be true, rather than both being false) combined with the ability to live with the unresolved so that one did not force a premature resolution out of sheer discomfort. Ambiguity related, of course, not merely to factual accuracy; perhaps more important, it related to moral meaning. Angleton's phrase, "a wilderness of mirrors," originally introduced to the public vocabulary in an interview given to Thames Television in Britain and taken by Angleton from T. S. Eliot's "Gerontion," was meant by him to describe the nature of Soviet foreign policy, and yet it was reasonably enough applied by the only person who has attempted a reasonably extended biographical statement, journalist David C. Martin, to the last fifteen years of Angleton's own work.[1]

In 1975, so steeped in the nuanced language of counterintelligence that he hardly realized that others might not pick up on his meaning, Angleton made a serious mistake, saying that "it is inconceivable that a secret intelligence arm of the government has to comply with all the overt orders of the government." The remark is usually reported as having been made to the Senate Select Committee on Intelligence, chaired by Senator Frank Church of Idaho, as though part of formal testimony. This was not the case. During its inquiries the Church committee had rented a suite of offices opposite the Dirksen Building, where CIA employees were interviewed under oath, always with a court reporter present. A question had been put in the open committee hearing about the CIA's failure to act on a presidential order to destroy lethal substances developed by CIA scientists—a dirty business indeed—and the query had given rise to a variety of moral, ethical, and procedural follow-up questions. Subsequently Angleton was being interviewed on other subjects by Loch K. Johnson, an investigator for the Church committee, and when he had concluded his testimony—or so Angleton believed—he stood up and uttered the gratuitous words, which the court reporter took down; they were then entered into the record by Senator Richard S. Schweicker of Pennsylvania, who read the interview material.

The intent of Angleton's observation, which he had not thought of as part of his official testimony, was misunderstood by Schweicker. The senators concluded that Angleton was telling them that the CIA was free to ignore the government and to lie to them, though he was simply encapsulating in one observation all the ambiguities he felt by then as the agency's chief mole-hunter; obviously if a high official of the government were thought to be working on behalf of the Soviets, the agency might resist following an order from that official; more important, Angleton was saying that there might well be overt orders from "the government"

—that is, from the executive branch, to which the CIA was responsible—which would be countermanded by covert ones, since leakage had reached the point that overt orders were likely to be known quickly to the press and thus, he felt, to the nation's enemies. When next called, Angleton withdrew the statement, for it was presumably better not to have any discussion on the witness stand of whether "the government" was, in fact, issuing covert orders or not, and the withdrawal made him look even worse. Angleton had been undone by his own love of ambiguity and his skills with the nuanced sentence, for he had not sensed that a nuance, like a calculated indiscretion, did not communicate well if one's opponent (for such Church surely was) did not recognize it as such.[2]

Angleton spent most of his life inside environments that treasured nuanced language and that used insider vocabularies of their own: the English public school, the Ivy League university, X-2 in the war, the CIA after. Just as spies may not realize how odd they sound at times, so do schoolmasters, professors, and the intensely literary not recognize that their speech is far from normal. By the time Angleton had retired from the CIA, he had given over three decades of unstinting service to what he regarded as the high ideals of his country, and he was truly frightened that those ideals were being destroyed by the Soviet Union, by American youth, by his own government's fecklessness. Some thought that his was the voice of paranoia; Angleton simply felt that the nation was in a state of emergency, that the country faced a grave threat, and that one of its primary guardians, his own agency, might have been compromised, whether by a Soviet mole or by an uncomprehending Congress. (Some few in the agency even suspected that he was that mole himself.) Whether Angleton really believed that there was an active Soviet spy within the agency is not clear, but if there were even a remote possibility that such a mole existed, the methodology of counterintelligence required that he behave as though the possibility were a probability. In the end, faithfulness to his own methodology, in conflict with the CIA's bureaucratic need to clean house, to "get right with the people," terminated his career.

James Jesus Angleton was born on December 9, 1917, in Boise, Idaho.[3] His father, James Hugh Angleton, of Illinois, had ridden with John J. Pershing in pursuit of Pancho Villa after Villa's raid on Columbus, New Mexico, and had married a beautiful, seventeen-year-old Mexican woman from Nogales, Carmen Moreno. (James's middle name, Jesus, was pronounced in the Spanish manner, not as in English.) There were three more children: James's brother, Hugh Rolla, born in 1920, and two sisters, Carmen and Dolores. Until James was ten, the family lived in Boise and then for four years in Dayton, Ohio, the headquarters of the National Cash Register Company, for which the senior Angleton was sales manager and then vice president for overseas operations. In December 1933 Angleton took the family to Italy, having purchased the NCR franchise there, and they prospered, living well on the Via Monte Rosa and at the Palazzo Castiglioni on the Corso Venezia in Milan. As president of the U.S. Chamber of Commerce in Italy, Hugh Angleton grew very close to the American ambassador in Rome, William Phillips, and to Thomas Watson, who had been a sales manager for NCR before founding IBM. By the late 1930s Hugh Angleton was probably the best known American in northern Italy.

To his Via Dante offices Hugh Angleton received visitors from all over Europe, friends he had made while vice president of NCR, or members of the closely knit "NCR family." From these visitors he received information on arms manufacturing, especially in Germany, and statistics on the duration of running time of various models of German engines, on fuel capacities, and on flight distances between factories. Angleton also traveled to NCR factories in France, Germany, Poland, Rumania, and Hungary, setting up what his son later described as "an internal spy trade" which would be of benefit to the United States when war broke out. An extrovert, a fine horseman, a professed admirer of Italy and Germany, Hugh Angleton cultivated the German naval attaché in Rome and used contacts in the Rotary Club, which in Italy involved many highly placed business and government figures, to keep tabs on such matters as the travel plans of the Italian foreign minister, Count Ciano. A Mason, Angleton also drew on the banned Masonic Order to keep informed on the inner machinations in the Fascist party. (He kept his Masonic pin and ring in the false bottom of a jewel box.) On one occasion, while traveling in a private railway compartment to Rome, Angleton was warned by a fellow Mason, who proved to be a high official in the Interior Ministry, that his telephone had been tapped, and thereafter he provided information only to a service attaché at the Rome embassy and limited meetings with his contacts to occasions when he was on an outing with his children. From 1939 to 1941 Angleton was thus an unofficial spy for the United States.

In the autumn of 1941 Ambassador Phillips warned Angleton that war was surely coming. After a quick trip to Paris to make arrangements for his NCR employees there, Angleton returned to Rome, where the ambassador offered to provide a diplomatic passport so that he might remain in Italy. Angleton did not accept the passport, however, for he feared—correctly—that such documents would provide little protection in the event of war; and he, his wife, and two daughters hurried to Switzerland. There they hired a van and drove to Lisbon, catching a ship which arrived in New York City on the day of the Japanese attack on Pearl Harbor.

Angleton promptly enlisted in the army, and after military government school joined the OSS, working for William Vanderbilt, a former Republican governor of Rhode Island, who was the executive officer for Special Operations. For a month Angleton was carried on the rolls of X-2, and in that capacity went to Italy in October 1943, giving rise later to the story that he and his son James "worked side by side" in Italy, though this was not so. Blown out of a jeep in Italy, his leg shattered, Angleton was assigned to General Clark's staff. At the end of the war he gathered up his family and returned to Milan and then to Rome, living at the Villa Angleton on the via Adolfo Carcani, just off the Appian Way, until 1964. the Italian government had confiscated his business, and when Angleton went back to Italy few of his assets could be recovered, so that he worked hard to reconstitute the family finances. Hugh Angleton senior died in Idaho in 1973.[4]

Though the four Angleton children were educated as American expatriates, James later recalled that he felt "quite American" and did not feel at all isolated from his country. Nonetheless, education abroad helped him to view America from a distance, to discover within its culture what he felt to be unique and desirable, and also to be aware of its innocence, isolation, and parochialism. James had spent summers camping in the Haute-Savoie and, as he grew older, in various English preparatory schools, and a year at Chartridge Hill House in Buckinghamshire. In September of 1933, on the advice of Edward VIII's chaplain, an old Malvernian, he was put into Malvern College in the rolling hills of Worcestershire. There James did well in French, German, English, and history, played soccer, was a corporal in the Officers' Training Corps, and became a house prefect. He left Malvern in December of 1936, spending the spring and summer of 1937 traveling on the Continent. That last summer Angleton, a Life Scout, took part in the World Boy Scout Jamboree at Birdsong, a camp in Scotland, just as he had participated in the 1933 jamboree at Göndöllö, in Hungary. His brother, Hugh Rolla, went to the Chartridge Hill School and then to Harrow, finishing a year behind James. The sisters were educated abroad as well, Carmen at the Merrymount School in Rome and the Warren School in Kent and Dolores in Montreaux. The two boys went on to Yale.

James Angleton is invariably described as brilliant; he is, and it is therefore assumed that he was an excellent student. In fact, at Yale he was, at least as conventionally measured, a poor student, excelling in those subjects that interested him, frequently missing class, and on occasion failing examinations in subjects that struck no spark. As a freshman he maintained an average of 72, respectable in the days before grade inflation, and he lifted this to a 73 the following year, with strong performances in Italian and English, which was his major subject. By his junior year, however, he was heavily caught up in the campus's literary life. He failed "English Poets of the Nineteenth Century," taught by Chauncey Brewster Tinker and Richard Purdy; he received a D in beginning Greek; his course on Shakespeare, taught by Sam Hemingway, resulted in a declining C. Only Italian and an intriguing course in which Norman Holmes Pearson was an assistant held his interest enough for him to earn Bs. Everyone who remembers Angleton agrees that he could easily have been an honors student, and most assume that he was Phi Beta Kappa when he graduated, though in fact the situation did not improve. The senior year brought another F, in "English Literature of the First Half of the Eighteenth Century," taught by Ted Hilles, and three Ds, one in the "History of the English Language," a second year of Greek, and a special reading and discussion course on classical civilization, from which Angleton withdrew at mid-year in favor of a new course in his favorite subject, the prose and poetry of the twentieth century. Even here, however, he was interested in only the most contemporary of poets, and his grade of B, as in his remaining course, on literary critics and philosophers, in which he was especially attracted to Croce and I. A. Richards, scarcely reflected what he knew.

He was, in fact, deficient for graduation, for the English major required the mastery of Greek through the third year, and Angle-

ton had not attained that standard. Happily, with war on the horizon, this requirement was waived because of his sound command
of Italian, and when he repeated Hilles's course, in which he now
received a passing mark, he was deemed to have fulfilled the requirements. Nonetheless, he failed his departmental examination,
and only when reexamined, in July of 1941, did he pass and, after
some delay because fees were owed the university and money had
been frozen in Italy, he received his degree, standing in the lowest
quarter of his class. The date of the award was November 8, 1941,
and Angleton was already enrolled in the Harvard Law School.

Hugh Angleton, also an English major, was admitted from Harrow with a record of straight passes. He took much the same
courses as James, and after a strong freshman year and a less
good sophomore year, did consistently well, emerging with a solid
B average which, had it not been for a graduate course in Proven-
çal attempted in his senior year, would have been a B-plus. The
brothers took no courses together, though both lived in Silliman
College in 1940–41. Some writers would confuse Hugh and James
later, and either or both with their father, because of the similarities of name and, with the two boys, of educations. Confusion
was surely compounded when James Jesus Angleton's résumé in
Norman Pearson's X-2 personnel file was headed James Hugh
Angleton.

Despite his grades, those who knew Angleton felt that he
understood literature exceedingly well. His friends thought the
downward slide of his grade in philosophy, for example—a fairly
heady course on philosophical ideas in contemporary literature,
which bathed undergraduates in Tolstoy, Schopenhauer, Nietzsche,
Isben, and Shaw—was because Angleton already knew as much
as the instructor did about the writers and, when he realized this,
was unable to retain an interest in the classroom exercises. (This
was unlikely, however, as the teacher was M. W. Urban, the
chairman of the philosophy department, German-educated, and a
noted authority on both Schopenhauer and Nietzsche.) Reed
Whittemore, a future poet of distinction, had met Angleton in Welch
Hall on the Old Campus, when both were freshmen, and they had
struck up an immediate friendship, rooming together for the next
three years. Whittemore recalls Angleton as wanting to be a doer,
someone who would promote literature, more than a critic, but he
also feels that Angleton had a natural feel for the best in the mod-
erns. It was as a campus literary figure that Angleton made his

mark, then. To those who knew him only from a distance, Angleton seemed a bit odd, certainly different; many assumed that he was English, for he always dressed well, at first in the large-collared English shirts of the time, and he spoke with a strong English accent. His fascination with contemporary poetry simply added to his singularity.

Angleton plunged into literary work as soon as he arrived at Yale, as one of the founders of the *Freshman Weekly* and an editor of *'41*, the class publication. As a sophomore he edited *Vif*, a *revue française inter-universitaire* that strikes one, read nearly five decades later, as a remarkably sophisticated undergraduate effort. As the *rédacteur en chef,* Angleton succinctly stated the primary goal of the magazine—to be critically interesting and clear—and inveigled a piece from Billy Phelps, printed one of Reed Whittemore's earliest prose efforts, and through the intervention of President Seymour and of the Yale Art School, won permission from Ferdinand Léger to reproduce some of his work. *Vif* solicited advertisements from any establishment with a pretense to a French connection, and several French restaurants announced their 50¢ lunches in its pages. Angleton's most striking coup, however, was a handsome announcement from a campus institution, Rosey's, a Wall Street tailor and dry cleaning shop that catered to young men who did not know how to sew on a missing cuff button, and Rosey's became for the time, Rosey le Tailleur. Included on the masthead of *Vif* was the name of James Houghteling, also of the class of 1941, who would join with Angleton in going into intelligence work.

This was the time when Angleton was first known as a poet. (In the CIA he was also known as Mother, Orchid, the Gray Ghost, the Cadaver, the Fisherman, the Fly, and Virginia Slim, a multiplicity of names speaking of the legend that had built up around him.[5]) Many of his intelligence colleagues later found Angleton's intense interest in poetry strange, though since poetry often is a complex form of code, it seemed more than natural to those who shared his Talmudic interest in the elliptic. But at Yale he was, in fact, truly a poet, and he spent a good bit of his time in his room, often very late at night, writing poetry. In *Vif* he published two original efforts in French, "Pianola à 2 francs" and "Caresse primordiale," both immaculate, which would suggest that the 70 he received at the same time in his French course was based on minimal effort.

But the *Freshman Weekly* posed no challenge, and *Vif* lost its
financier after a second issue, so Angleton moved on to what would
be his most striking effort: *Furioso,* a magazine that, though edited by undergraduates—Whittemore and Angleton—would prove
of some significance in the history of modern American literature.
Launched in the summer of 1939 as a magazine of verse, *Furioso*
survived until the spring of 1953. The magazine was clearly intended for an audience outside the university, and despite its
origins, was not a "campus publication." The two poet-editors
led off with a warm introductory endorsement by Archibald
MacLeish, who urged Angleton, in an open letter, to bring back
to poetry "the watchers and waiters" (a happy phrase that might
well describe the later Angleton himself) and shove the critics
back to their appropriate place, as commentators after the creative act rather than, as MacLeish feared they had become in poetry, those who would define what the poet ought to do. *Furioso*
opened with a bang and kept the noise level high: Richard Eber-
hart, William Carlos Williams, Dudley Fitts, John Peale Bishop,
Wallace Stevens, e e cummings, Ezra Pound, Selden Rodman,
Horace Gregory, Marya Zaturenska, Arthur Mizener, William
Empson, Reuel Denny—the list was big with promise and rich in
performance. *Furioso* would, its editors said, "give the public [the]
real poetry that has been kept from them."

Angleton worked simultaneously on the Yale *Lit,* a more traditional student publication, and though he was faithful to it, the
time spent in the Chi Delta Theta room, musty with the tobacco
smoke then essential to all aspiring writers, was of less interest.
The *Lit* tried to shock the university with a mild attack on the
senior societies, but this created hardly a ripple, and Angleton
concentrated on trying to get more original poetry onto the pages
of the journal, helping to attract unpublished work from Mac-
Leish, who had once been an editor of the *Lit* himself.[6]

At the *Lit* Angleton alienated several of his fellow board members by his manner, his intensity, his tastes. One thought he was
"a fanatic in the making," though whether for good or ill he could
not say; another saw him as a "mysterious Satan," somehow dé-
classé, especially when his close and like-minded friend, John
Pauker, also a poet, passed around pictures of the aging, over-
weight Pound in the absolute nude. To some of his *Lit* colleagues
Angleton seemed sly, living to a pattern of "mysterious guile"
which appeared to be an end in itself. Years later, when his career

in intelligence was public knowledge, he was misremembered as having denounced Milton (though in fact Milton was a favorite poet) in favor of Gerard Manley Hopkins, and for his praise of the early *Cantos,* thus confirming his "demonic self" to those who feared "a dark conspiracy against Right, Truth, Reason, Tradition, Gentlemanliness, and the Ineffable Good." Image, *persona,* confusion, complexity—a quiet personality with flamboyant tastes—these were the fragments of memory dredged up forty years later by classmates who were not close to him; one who was close diagnosed a desire to "abandon sense and tradition for intentional difficulty and unintelligibility . . ." for a "a love of conspiracy."

Angleton's principal triumph for *Furioso* was to persuade Ezra Pound to travel to New Haven. Angleton was good at tennis and golf, and he had spent a summer playing in Caen, from which he had gone off to see Pound in Rapallo. A fine photographer, he had taken pictures of Pound at tennis, and Pound was so pleased, he accepted the young editor's invitation (urged on by e e cummings as well) to visit Yale when he came back to the States in 1939. (Angleton's photos appeared for years as accompaniment to articles on Pound, until his work for the CIA required removal of the credit line from them.) Pound stayed with Whittemore's family in New Haven for a night, stuffing all of the guest towels under his bed, wet, before coming into the living room to read from his copy of Li Po. Whittemore and Angleton were counting on an important poem from Pound for *Furioso,* and he disappointed them by giving them his one-page "Introductory Text Book," allegedly in economics, which was in fact four quotations from John Adams, Jefferson, Lincoln, and Washington strung together. They kept after him, however, and eventually he yielded up to Whittemore a bit of poor poetry and a stunning obituary on Ford Madox Ford. Still, the public side of the visit to Yale went reasonably well, at least in contrast to Harvard, to which Angleton and Whittemore drove him, for there Pound spread his anti-Semitism on thickly. Years later, according to David C. Martin, when Angleton was chief of counterintelligence for the CIA, he visited the expatriate and discredited Pound in Genoa, though in fact he never did so. Rather, in 1943, when the Department of Justice was gathering a dossier on Pound, Angleton provided information on the poet's fondness for Mussolini and Fascism. Angleton felt that intellectual honesty required separating the man from his work, as the

so-called New Criticism argued, and if Pound were to be condemned, it ought to be in response to the right question.[7]

If his literary work meant more to him than his classes did,
Angleton did not remain uninfluenced by the Yale faculty. There
was Pearson, who encouraged both Whittemore and Angleton, and
shared, in particular, their interest in Pound and in William Carlos
Williams. Angleton visited Filmer S. C. Northrop, professor of
philosophy and master of Silliman College in Angleton's last year,
two or three times a week, and he was often in Arnold Wolfers's
living room, for the master of Pierson College (in which Angleton
and Whittemore lived as juniors) had funds to bring in poets such
as Robert Frost to read from their work. Both liked the young
man, Wolfers remaining in touch afterward, and Northrop warmly
mentioning Angleton in the preface to his famed work, *The Meeting of East and West,* published in 1946. Angleton also liked Alfred
Bellinger, though primarily for his poetry rather than his profess-
ing of Latin, and he shared an interest with Joseph M. Bernstein,
a graduate student who taught in the French department, in Bau-
delaire, Rimbaud, and Verlaine. His instructor in the introductory
course on Greek civilization, Jerome Sperling, who wound up in
the OSS in Istanbul, invited Angleton to join him pot hunting in
Greece, but the war forestalled a visa. Above all, Angleton enjoyed his course on Dante, and he often went to dinner with An-
gelo Lipari, the professor, who wrung from him graduate-level
work. (The course was shared with William R. Johnson, '42, who
after the war would work for the CIA and with Angleton.[8])

There were two young instructors that the editors met in Pierson College, Arthur Mizener and Andrews Wanning, who taught
in the course Angleton worked most at, on the "Problems of Poetry." Mizener and Wanning and another young teacher, Raymond Short, encouraged Whittemore and Angleton in their efforts
to think big about *Furioso,* warning them to keep their own work
out of it so long as they were students lest it be branded "a student journal." Later Angleton singled out Wanning, Whittemore,
Eugene O'Neill, Jr., and Richard Ellmann, who was already de-
voting himself to the study of Irish literature, as his best friends
on the literary side—there were, of course, other friends, from
Dayton, through soccer, and as entry-mates. One may suppose
that Angleton admired Dean DeVane and Chauncey Brewster
Tinker, since he campaigned vigorously, if unsuccessfully, among
his literary friends to have the college year book dedicated to one
of them.

Wanning was especially encouraging, and Angleton would go around to his suite in Pierson College, which, as a junior fellow, Wanning shared with Charles Seymour, Jr., son of the president of the university and a scholar of European art, the subject that would take Seymour into wartime intelligence work. The gangly Angleton struck Wanning with his sincerity and conviction, the complete loyalty he gave to his literary heroes, and his determination to challenge a Yale establishment that, except in Wanning's course, allowed for little teaching of poets more recent than Tennyson and Browning. Angleton was often on the defensive at *Furioso* meetings, since the group, united in its interest in modern literature, was somewhat to the left, while Angleton, though perfectly aware that "there was something wrong about Fascism," was also uneasily defensive of Mussolini. This had made Pound's appearance on campus difficult and disappointing for him, for though he admired the poetry extravagantly, he found that Pound's right-wing and anti-Semitic rantings made him uncomfortable.

Far more successful, Angleton thought, was his work as an impresario on behalf of William Empson. Empson was returning from China to England in the company of I. A. Richards, the critic Angleton particularly admired, and both were in Cambridge, Massachusetts. After a soccer game there, Angleton sought Empson out and persuaded him to give a lecture at Yale. He then persuaded Dean DeVane, who did not care for Empson's work, to provide the necessary fee. Angleton mailed invitations to dozens of poets and stayed up the night before the scheduled event until 3:00 A.M. slipping notices under student doors. When he returned to Whittemore's room he found the speaker passed out, apparently from alcohol, and feared the worst. The next day, however, Empson stood before his huge audience for long moments in silence, and then, as he finally began, at first haltingly and then with newfound vigor, he captivated the crowd and so won over the dean that DeVane said he might offer Empson a permanent job at Yale—though when Angleton broached the subject with Empson, the critic said that he must return to England. Some years later Angleton would encounter Empson again at one of Bryher and H.D.'s soirées.

Angleton was no bookworm. He played varsity soccer for three years, until sidelined with a broken ankle, and just missed his varsity Y by the margin of a point, when Williams upset the team. He cared about winning and later remembered both his closeness to the Swiss coach, and "the worse bus ride in his life" as the defeated team was driven back from Williamstown. He was a member of the Political Union, was active in the Italian Club, and was said to have spent a great deal of time playing the pinball machines at George and Harry's, a student restaurant just across the street from Silliman. A night owl, Angleton sat up all night, reading and smoking, often with a new Boni and Liveright volume in his hands. As a sophomore Angleton lived off campus at 312 Temple Street with Whittemore, and they often took lunch at Corby Court, a club for aspiring lawyers just behind the pinball machines, where he made additional friends. Angleton frequently borrowed Whittemore's car, which, as a local lad, Whittemore could stash safely nearby, to drive into New York or up to Mount Holyoke. There was also fly-fishing, a lifelong passion of Angleton's, and he would borrow the car to slip away by himself to try his hand in the quiet pools of the Housatonic or the Farmington River. Angleton was incredibly attractive, tall, gangling, but in no sense awkward, with deep, piercing eyes and the hint of a perpetual smile, which suggested an aloof, ironic approach to life. He was, in fact, friendly and generous, though his elegance, the fact that he was a touch older, his English manner, put some of the less sophisticated Yalies off.

Angleton was often short of funds once the war began, for he had to look after his brother and Carmen as well, and money was sometimes slow in reaching him. The elder Angleton had encouraged a number of Italian artisans to develop crafts—handmade shoes, cashmere sweaters, Venetian glass, silk neckties—and many of these found their way to Jim Angleton's college room, often to be stored under his bed, and on occasion to be taken along as a gift to one of the poets he was cultivating (he met Marianne Moore while delivering a sweater to cummings). One day, to Whittemore's dismay, Angleton stuffed the metal master to the recording they had made of Pound's performance in Cambridge in with the ties under his bed in Silliman, and there amongst the Italian goodies it went missing forever.

It was at Yale that Angleton, always inclined to keep his own counsel, "began his undercover work," or so Reed Whittemore recollected much later. When Angleton began his own literary magazine, not to be shared with others, he delivered it secretly to student rooms at night, slipping it down outside their doors. He was writing oracular, Sapphic poems, was reading Dante furiously, was seldom delivering a course paper on time, though he was always ready with a convincing explanation of why he could

not. When *Furioso* was launched, it was Angleton who contacted
Graham Peck, Yale '35, to do for the cover its famous, quite striking, and mysteriously vatic figure out of the *commedia dell'arte*
who steps from the ivory tower as poet-prophet to make a pro-
nouncement. Years later Andrews Wanning received a late-night
phone call from Angleton, asking where Peck might be found,
and whether he thought Peck might serve for the OSS as a spy
on the Russians in Mongolia, since in 1940 he had written and illustrated a charming book, *Through China's Wall,* about his life
among the Mongolians and in China. Wanning told Angleton he
thought not.

Angleton remained in New Haven through the summer of 1941.
He could not return to Italy, there was no transport to England,
there was another issue of *Furioso* to do, and there was that departmental examination to pass. He was writing to his classmates,
asking them to place copies of *Furioso* in local bookstores. The
four years had been interesting ones. Seymour had been inducted
as president, the Political Union had voted no confidence in FDR,
Orson Welles had come to town to do Julius Caesar, and Sonja
Henie had visited New Haven and given an incomprehensible interview. Angleton had lunched with Thomas Mann, had seen
Eleanor Roosevelt and Wendell Willkie parade upon the campus,
had voted (with the majority of students) in favor of aid to Britain
in 1941, and had taken in the prom; he had even sung "Bright
College Years."

But the four years at college had seemed simply another experience, not decisive, enjoyable enough and little more. He did not
reply to Yale alumni questionnaires, appearing in the alumni news
only once, because classmate Robert Van Puersem, who also went
into intelligence work, wrote of running into him in a tea shop in
London, where he reported Angleton was with the OSS and
"making himself very useful in a very non-furious type of work."
The Harvard Law School, from which Angleton did not graduate,
lost touch with him by 1947 and tried to update its records by
asking Yale for help, but there was nothing that even the most
sweeping of intelligence machines, a private university's fund raising
and alumni office, could do to help. Angleton was simply known
to be "working for the government." Yale, Harvard Law, and
literature no longer figured in his plans.

As with many bright young men in the OSS, Angleton's recruitment was more or less by chance; once there, however, his inter-

ests and personality were pulled to intelligence work as iron filings
to a magnet. From Harvard Angleton had intended to go into the
family business, after studying international law and contracts. He
was well into his studies, particularly attracted to Roscoe Pound
and his course on property, immersed in the literary community
in Cambridge, when in the spring he was drafted. (Harvard granted
him one year of credit toward his degree.) Though he could have
gone into the army as an officer, using his father's contacts, he
preferred to begin as a G.I. He was in the infantry at Fort Law-
ton, Washington, when an interviewer singled him out for the
Provost Marshal General's School at Fort Custer, in Michigan.
There he was interviewed by a former FBI agent, Colonel Melvin
Purvis, who had been turned into something of a cult hero as the
man who had shot John Dillinger. Purvis impressed him and offered a choice of three jobs, one to check on lost equipment (for
which, read stolen) that was believed to be in North Africa, another to work with the Army Counterintelligence Corps, a third
with the OSS. Largely because he knew little about it, Angleton
chose the third. He was put through the OSS Schools and Training course pursuing the usual fun and games routine, including
infiltrating the office of the chairman of Western Electric, and was
assigned to the Italian desk in Washington.

Angleton wanted a posting abroad. A corporal in Washington,
he would receive quicker military promotion overseas. He could
use his knowledge of languages in "more applied ways." He had
been fascinated by the S&T lectures on countersabotage and the
security of troops, and this had led to an interest in clandestine
operations. He did not much like Washington (much later he would
call the city "a jungle"), and he knew that he would adjust easily,
as some others in OSS might not, to life abroad. He liked and
admired Jimmy Murphy, the head of the new unit, X-2, that had
been created two months before Angleton arrived in Washington.
And so one day, while at his desk writing reports, Angleton saw
Murphy coming by and bearded him: he was ready to go to the
field, he said, and needed no more training. Murphy liked the direct approach and sent him to England.

At the time James Murphy still hoped he might get State Department cover for X-2 personnel abroad, and he was working
through Robert Murphy, whose standing was high with Roosevelt
though ambiguous at State. James Murphy was beginning to think
that the next task would be to detect Soviet intelligence agents in

the West, including those who worked under the cover of their own embassies. The NKVD had begun as a defensive intelligence organization with the goal of saving the revolution in Russia, but in its Cheka guise it had turned into an offensive operation. In this Murphy was joined by Norman Pearson, privy to the secrets of the British use of double agents against the Germans. At some point between August and December 1943 Murphy mentioned his concern to Angleton, who was fascinated by the notion of penetrating the enemy by exploiting its own agents.

It is not clear when Angleton decided to make intelligence work his life's career, but most who knew him in Britain or Italy agree that they sensed in him a commitment that ran well beyond the needs of the moment, a fascination with the theoretical issues behind each problem as it surfaced that was extraordinary. When he was posted to London, to handle Italian matters for X-2 under Pearson, he was the only man who brought an army cot into his tiny office at Ryder Street, to sleep as well as work there, emerging only now and then to reward himself with an excellent meal at the Connaught Hotel or at Quaglino's. He spared no one, he kept meticulous records, he drove his secretary, H.D.'s daughter Perdita: he was single-minded. Some wondered how he could stand it, for his office, room 23-B, was always a fug of tobacco smoke, since the windows at Ryder Street were kept closed at all times, there being no central heat. When a bomb fell outside his office and shattered all the windows—the second time in two months— Angleton was back the next day, in heavy overcoat and muffler, at work even as glaziers were putting in new glass.

Angleton was, in fact, already thinking about the question of methodology: could there be a science of counterintelligence? He and Pearson, whose office was next door, discussed this from time to time, as Angleton did also with Murphy, who was often in London. Angleton's on-the-job training was with Ultra, which focused his attention immediately on what would become his chosen field. Later, in Italy, Angleton would learn more from men like Paul Paterni, who had been on White House detail with the FBI (and who became deputy chief of the Secret Service), and Charles Siragusa, future deputy chief of the American offensive against narcotics and head of the Illinois crime commission. Success in London and success in Rome, coupled with the fact that Angleton never really knew any other kind of intelligence work, having moved almost immediately into X-2, Ultra, and the mysteries of counterintelligence, combined with his personality, his education, his languages, his sense of Europe, to determine his career after the war.

Angleton brooded upon the practical lessons that Ultra, and double agentry, taught. Penetration, Angleton said over and over, was the key to counterintelligence. This meant that we must penetrate the enemy; equally it meant that we must assume he would attempt to penetrate us. Total integrity of communications was essential, for any leakage could compromise not one, but all penetrations. Sharp compartmentalization of operations, so that the flood waters of failure could be blocked between compartments, was important. No one should know anything he did not need to know to do the job assigned him. Data could speak across the decades, so that strict confidentiality must apply even when, to those who did not know how one compartment related to another, it might seem irrelevant. Above all, so that one did not simply clone one's own insights, recruiting must not be in one's own image. Murphy had said all this, and the British sometimes practiced and often taught it, and to anyone in intelligence such injunctions were commonplace, but Angleton felt that most of his American co-workers assumed that once the war was over, the injunctions would not matter. He thought they would. The line between being obsessed, paranoid, dedicated, prescient, though broad, is also faint, and those who knew Angleton then and since used just this sliding scale to describe him.

What were the specific lessons of Ultra, Angleton wondered? If one is prepared to pay a high enough price to deceive the enemy—if one will permit a city to be bombed, rather than warn its residents and thus reveal that one has broken the enemy's codes (as one entirely false story concerning the alleged sacrifice of Coventry had it)—one can make an unreal world real. Those with access to knowledge of one's movements, and the enemy's movements, must be protected at all cost: in the final analysis mercenaries, and even those simply without access, are expendable. Ultra made it clear that if a superior source was in place, agents could be sent into another system, an orchestration could be built up, to the point that layer upon layer of confirming information would also support the deception. In a descending order of importance, therefore, those interested in penetration must control doubled agents, diplomatic channels (or "back channels"), journalists' reports, cooperating agencies (such as the FBI), and businessmen. Each level would reinforce the next. It followed, however, that if one's own side could orchestrate an unreal world to deceive the enemy, the enemy would hope to do the same. Thus one must be suspicious of all sources and test all levels of information, examine all instructions, for any possible contribution to the unreal world that was pointed against one's own interests. For the object, of course, was to live in a real world while thrusting the enemy into an unreal one.

Such a world view contained many dangers. This year's friend might be next year's enemy, so that one limited even a friend's view of the real world to the short range. The enemy might be induced to act on false information and yet act in a way inimical to one's own interests, or reach a right conclusion from the wrong information. One would need always to be testing one's own colleagues, for one of them might be an unwitting dupe of an enemy deception and thus misevaluate information. The various levels of reinforcement might well not be amenable to sufficient coordination, and the gaps left between each group could reveal that a deception was in progress. One might, indeed, become confused oneself. Further, there were ethical questions, profound ones in a democracy in which deception was considered wrong. And that which might be accepted as necessary in wartime would not be accepted in time of peace. But then, in a time of undeclared war, but war nonetheless, a cold war, a war of subversion, a war against terrorists, what standards were to prevail?

Years later one of Angleton's successors as chief of counterintelligence would conclude that the best policy was common sense: that is, that 80 percent of the information the intelligence community gathered, perhaps even 95 percent, meant exactly what it appeared to mean, and that most operations had as their goal the most obviously identifiable target—the principle of parsimony in intelligence work. Angleton would, in time, therefore be dismissed by many within the intelligence community as paranoid. This response was not precisely to his point, however, for he would have agreed with the judgment that most things in life, even in the life of an intelligence agent, were exactly what they seemed. But what of the 20 percent, or even the 5 percent? If an enemy were prepared to commit vast resources, great patience, perhaps sacrifice the lives of agents, to create that 5 percent, then must the importance of that 5 percent not in fact be greater than all of the rest? And must not one test all facts, examine all motives, in order to judge which might fall into that 5 percent? Angleton's crit-

344 CLOAK & GOWN

ics would complain that because he spoke in nuance and invariably had a hidden agenda, he assumed everyone else did as well—that is, that he was essentially a person of genuine humility who did not realize that his mind scaled the heights of complexity while most minds remained firmly on the ground below, believing himself to be the norm, an average person simply with different interests—while Angleton might have replied that people often had hidden agendas of which even they were not aware. The argument was circular, endless; at base it was about human nature, theory against practice. That which man could conceive of, however evil, man could and most probably would do; that which was theoretically possible would, most likely, prove to be done in practice.

The principal by-product of Ultra was counterintelligence. The Special Liaison Units formed for the purpose of being knowledgeable about and transmitting Ultra, but not for taking interpretative action on it, were at the heart of the proper use of information. Ultra would provide a framework of certitude for communications to the field, making possible *Funkspiel,* the "radio game," or triple-deception messages sent out solely to keep an agent who was under control alive. No one who was tainted by constant contact with hostile personalities should ever be in a position to set policy, for quite apart from emotion, the hostile source may have deliberately misled. If Germany could make this mistake, so might the Allies. Ryder Street could not, must not, make decisions about the meaning of Ultra. Espionage was directed toward compromising the enemy's security of communications; counterintelligence, then, was devoted to protecting one's own, and to protect one's own best, one had to understand the capabilities of the enemy with respect to penetration. (There was a risky problem here: that one would equate capabilities with intentions.) Intercepted communications, if used by safe hands, might well permit the evaluation of the effectiveness of double agents, since such intercepts would represent a superior source unbeknownst to the double agent. Thus one must at all costs conceal the knowledge that one was intercepting communications, and the person for whom this was the primary goal would always counsel against taking action on anything learned from those intercepts. Yet the point of the intercepts for those not in counterintelligence was to be able to take action against the enemy. Therefore some higher authority, neither in counterintelligence nor in operations, must establish and judge the priorities.

In this game London was the place to be in 1943–44. From London prior to D-Day the OSS directed most of its western European operations. Angleton came to know a wide range of OSS operatives, to get a sense of far more than X-2. Here were men like David Bruce, Arthur Goldberg, William Casey. Here he met Paul Blum, Thomas Karamessines. Here were SI and SO operations presided over by his father's old friend, William Phillips, who had established good relations with SIS and SOE. The setting and the people were congenial. One coworker whom he found especially compatible was the young, very promising poet, Edward Weismiller, of whom Norman Pearson later wrote. After the war Weismiller would write several well-received volumes of poetry and an unusually fine intelligence novel, *The Serpent Sleeping,* about a naive young man who, as interrogator, came to doubt the guilt of a young woman who was charged with collaboration with the enemy.[9] Born in Wisconsin, Weismiller had gone first to Swarthmore and then to Cornell College in Iowa. He had published his first book of poetry, *The Deer Come Down,* while still a junior in college; the book had appeared in the prestigious Yale Series of Younger Poets in 1936, and Angleton had noticed it soon after. From a Rhodes Scholarship to Merton College, Weismiller had returned to graduate study at Harvard. His sister had married Westbrook Steele, a driving, dynamic fund raiser for Lawrence College, and Steele had become the young poet's surrogate father, since his own father was fifty-four when he was born. To get Lawrence into the black, Steele had created an Institute of Paper Chemistry in Appleton, and the institute was now involved with the OSS, producing various types of paper, including the paper for counterfeit Japanese and German money. Weismiller had five years of college French, and Steele had used this to get him an offer by the OSS in June 1943.

Weismiller did not stop writing poetry merely because the OSS was training him as an agent who would learn how to kill, and when he reached London he found that Angleton would do for him what the poet John Berryman had done at Harvard: read his work and "squeeze water out of it." Weismiller liked darkly ominous statements (he and Angleton shared a fascination with the levels of meaning in that undergraduate favorite, "What is truth? said jesting Pilate/And would not stay for an answer"), and he said Angleton helped to quiet him down. Both were intrigued by the fact that they had been trained to lie about the extent of their knowledge, the reverse of what a poet does. Weismiller thought that Pearson, who "did tortuous things with gusto," loved the exercise of power and achieved much through "calculated diffidence," while Angleton seemed more abstractly interested in "the levels that lies [deception] could take one to." In due course, under the code name Dwarf, Weismiller operated in and out of Cherbourg, where he played a central role in running Dragoman and subsequently a second double, Skull.[10]

During his time in London Angleton also attracted the attention of David Bruce, who reported on him most favorably, and he became something of a confidant of Norman Pearson. Later Angleton would remark that Pearson was an exceptionally able officer, being both "very energetic and very devious," and he regretted that Pearson had not stayed on to work for the CIA, since he was so skilled a negotiator "in the academic manner." It was from Pearson that Angleton first learned that the art of negotiation was the use of third persons, for a go-between, however he conceived of his own role, could almost always be "run" to some degree by the party with the superior source. Further, he admired Pearson as an articulate lecturer and felt that he gave the best briefings— in effect, that he was the best teacher—he knew.

Certainly Angleton felt he was fortunate in being put by Pearson onto Ultra so quickly. He immediately recognized the value of ISOS, sensed that he must master the flow, the rhythm, the content of the material. Like nearly everyone labeled a genius by coworkers, Angleton put in desperately long hours at his work, poring over the intercepts "as though they were the Dead Sea Scrolls." Much later a journalist would say that Angleton worked with a British team to "master" the German codes, a statement Angleton tried to correct.[11] He did, however, quickly grasp the importance of those broken codes and was soon viewed as an adept at their use, and when in Italy he continued to draw on ISOS to verify material from other sources.

To those in the office, Angleton was always "a strange man, a genius." With his jet black hair, expressive hands, and piercing eyes, as well as emaciated good looks, he was enormously attractive to women, but even so they shied away from him. Andrew Berding, dashing, witty, was the hit of Ryder Street with the English as well as the American secretaries. While others—William Hood, Gerstle Mack, John Marquand, Jr. ("a bit weedy, but nice"), and Kim Philby ("reliable and charming")—seemed to have fun,

Angleton's pleasure took other forms. When free he would visit with T. S. Eliot, write poetry in his office or, wearing a coat and hunched over his fire, produce reports that were, he said, too urgent to wait, so that one of the secretaries would have to remain behind after hours to type them, making her way down through his always complex manuscript, in which there were footnotes, and notes to notes, and marginalia, and sheets decorated with commands, "To X," and "Over," and "Insert B here." No one was surprised when one day a typist came up with one of his poems, stuck in the middle of a report. Yet, however hard he drove the staff, outside the office Angleton was always amiable, inquiring about how the secretaries were faring, if a bit distracted, preoccupied. He seemed always, one said, to be "moving on to the next question."

Angleton had few close friends in London, and while he dined with colleagues, and pursued the odd literary contact, he appeared to have little life outside X-2, and the bachelor flat he had taken at 8 Craven Hill, near Paddington Station. He did not renew his ties at Malvern, perhaps because it had been pressed into war service as a training establishment for Free French cadets. Indeed, Angleton was especially pleased to draw fire watch, for this meant he could do dictation until 1:00 A.M. His secretaries found Angleton interesting to work for, since so much fascinating material crossed his desk, and they respected him for his obvious dedication, but one thought him not so much filled with solitude— a positive quality—as mired in loneliness. With his premature stoop, heavy glasses, long hands and fingers—the Goya look, one said, while another secretary compared him to the film star Gregory Peck—Angleton seemed to be hiding behind his work. He was, one former secretary affectionately said, "like a little wet dog," and though she was younger than Angleton, she thought of him in a motherly way. Grace Dolowitz, on the other hand, perhaps because she was a translator and had finished a doctorate on Proust at Bryn Mawr, was somewhat less moved. French ISOS material arrived from Bletchley untranslated, and Angleton had to depend upon her far more. But he was never close to any of the women in the office, including one, who brought the mail around in a little cart, who was so strikingly beautiful that, somewhat cattily, she was always referred to as "the piece of furniture."

Truth was, Angleton was a bit shy, and by now he was happily married, so that it never occurred to him to express an interest in any social life that extended much beyond X-2. On July 17, 1943, two weeks before he took up his duties with X-2, he had married Cicely d'Autremont, a vivacious, exceedingly bright Vassar junior from Duluth whom he had met when she was at summer school in Boston. On August 18, 1944, their first child, James Charles, was born, and Angleton deeply regretted not being in the States to be with his wife; Pearson wrote Susan that Angleton was "beaming like red coals of a fire, and making very contagious his feeling that all's right with the world." To celebrate Angleton had saved his cigar rations, so that he might distribute them as custom demanded, and he promised Pearson two tins of oysters and a bottle of champagne for a celebration dinner, which (having taken a lesson from his secretary) he threatened to cook himself. On the night, as Angleton was preparing his cordon bleu dish (steak, from Ireland), he discovered, while slicing mushrooms, that he had forgotten the oysters, so off he went "in his usual wild way" to find a taxi, while his guests contented themselves with stuffed tomatoes, until Angleton returned, in high good humor, bearing some fresh sweet corn as well.[12]

Angleton's secretaries may have thought of him as a loner, but he felt he had all the friends he could absorb. There were his British counterparts, in whom he felt especially fortunate: Colin H. Roberts, Dick Brooman-White, Felix Cowgill, and "Kim" Philby. Roberts in particular fascinated him: a classicist, Roberts told him of how, as a youth, wanting to be a paleographer, he had written a museum that had hundreds of papyruses, and when they sent him some, Roberts, by steaming each papyrus in his bathroom, found among them a fragment of text from the New Testament. He wrote a piece on his find and was then supported in his studies by a paleographer from Berlin. Angleton liked all the elements of the story: the persistence, the element of chance, the cooperation among scholars. Roberts was his direct opposite at Ryder Street, being on the Italian desk, and it was to Roberts that Angleton took his cables for approval; from Roberts he learned how truly to understand Ultra, for many of the messages were corruptions with groups missing, and one needed a powerful sense of contextual language to fill in the gaps. Roberts was, Angleton felt, his "tutor," and they happily pooled their meal rations to have the odd festive leg of lamb together.

Brooman-White was more theoretically inclined, the man who best grasped the relationship between MI5 and MI6. He and Angleton often talked of the postwar years, of how allies that had been overrun would have to be helped, of the problem of stay-behind teams that would have been left in those countries by the Germans in anticipation of their liberation. Brooman-White was a specialist on Iberia; it was he who had recruited Philby from SOE. Later Conservative whip, Brooman-White often speculated with Angleton on the future of Britain, and on the possibility that there might be trouble with the Russians when the war was over.

The pro-American Felix Cowgill was another good friend, though Cowgill was closer to Pearson than to Angleton. Warm, open, Cowgill would drop in to go over papers in person. Cowgill personified the spirit of wartime cooperation. He, and Nicholas Elliott, and another Britisher who was responsible for the training handbooks, and who took Angleton to lunch at the Athenaeum from time to time—these were his friends, his teachers, his full and sufficient buttress against loneliness.*

There were, of course, American friends as well. For Norman Pearson he felt affection. Angleton called Pearson "hi ho, silver tongue," in recognition of his superb briefings, and he watched with some amusement the apparent competition between Pearson and Hubert Will. He enjoyed happy, detailed, gossipy sessions with Pearson at Quaglino's, joint literary outings, daily interchanges in the office. Angleton liked Gerstle Mack, the American who sat under Pearson on the Iberian-North African desk (though perhaps more for Mack's knowledge of French art than for his work on Spain). He was delighted when Dick Ellmann came through on his way to France and took him to lunch, where he gave Ellmann a copy of a book on the Gobelin tapestries to "whet his appetite." Above all, Angleton liked the group, the team, the feeling of belonging to an intense and important common effort.

---

*Despite having known Philby, Angleton does not include him among his mentors. There are several reasons why Philby might be left off the list of those who were both friends and instructors. The most obvious is that Angleton may well feel he learned nothing from Philby during his time in London. Another might be the reasonable conclusion that what he learned from Philby was learned only well after, when Philby's treachery made it necessary to rethink several matters, including London. Another could be that Angleton views learning and mentorship in positive terms and that he feels he learned only negatively from Philby's actions. Philby was not, in fact, despite the romantic aura that surrounds his name, particularly adept at analysis or counterintelligence, and there is no good reason to see him as more intelligent than Roberts, Brooman-White, or Cowgill— merely cleverer.

X-2 struck him as being very much like what he believed an academic community to be, supportive, self-confident, hard-working. It was Murphy and Pearson, he concluded forty years later, who had built up that sense of trust, who had inspired the group with a careful, sophisticated, yet almost joyful approach to work. When Angleton was transferred to Italy in late August, as the commanding officer of SCI Unit Z, he kept in close touch with both. Counterintelligence, he felt, would be "the queen on the board," and he knew he had found what he wanted to do.[13]

Pearson also kept in touch with Cicely d'Autremont, for he thought of Jim Angleton as his protégé, and he wanted him to receive only good news from home. From Tucson, where she stayed through much of the war, she asked Pearson to keep an eye on her husband, who she feared would be careless in the face of the V-2 attacks and would work far too hard, sleep in too many dank air raid shelters, and be blown up at the theater. (This last was not likely: theaters, unheated—their audiences dressed in overcoats—were not places to linger, and performances all began, given the double summer time to which the British had resorted, so as to finish by dark, before the rocket attacks started.) She asked Norman to write her a few lines from time to time, telling her what Jim did not, and Norman was only too happy to do so. Just before Angleton left London for Italy, she sensed from one of his letters that he was on the verge of exhaustion, and she appealed to Pearson to compel him to take a short rest; the appeal came too late, for Angleton already was on his way to Bari, thence to Caserta, and on to Rome before Pearson had received the letter.

Putting in the long hours that Cicely feared, Angleton was rising rapidly in X-2. Recruited when he was twenty-six, and a corporal, he would soon have the simulated rank of major (and actual rank of captain). By February 1944, a little over six months after coming into X-2, he was chief of the Italian desk for the European Theater of Operations. Then there was an inspection tour to Italy, a brief posting to Paris, and that return to Italy in November as commander of SCI Unit Z, until March 1945, when he was made chief of X-2 for all Italy, at twenty-seven the youngest X-2 branch chief anywhere. Though he continued to write Pearson friendly, almost avuncular letters, complaining of the appointment of a staff member who, "like a great many young men, knows little or nothing about the business," he was clearly quite unable to see himself as a young man any longer. In truth, Angleton was not a

young man, as his coworkers were quick to realize. He had got
on extremely well with the British, who took his secretiveness for
reserve, and would with the Italians, who took his reserve for
secretiveness, and he was recognized as highly gifted, mature, "a
strange genius." If Angleton knew this was the reputation developing around him, he did not mind a bit.

It was in Italy that the "legendary Jim Angleton" was born.[14]
He felt he did nothing to enhance the stories growing up around
him, and perhaps he did not, but a person as committed as he
was, as concerned about postwar as wartime policies, as hard-
working and different, was bound to generate legends whether he
intended to do so or not.* The story went round that at the OSS
training course he had once told another recruit that it was obvious he was very good at basketball, judging from the way he
jumped. This was to feed the notion that Angleton had remarkable
insight. Angleton then was said to have confessed that he had
seen the recruit playing on the Italian national team before the
war: this assured credibility and fostered a sense of the clever.
The story was an elaboration of a harmless remark—Angleton had,
in fact, seen the Italian national team play in Trieste before the
war—but it stuck. There were those who insisted that Angleton
learned about French wines solely to impress his French counterparts (though his knowledge was real, whatever the motive, and
it predated his work with the French), or that he did not really
play chess, though he was often seen seated in front of a board,
when he did, in fact, play the game well enough. Over the years
Angleton's work, his manner, his personality attracted innumerable stories. As David Atlee Phillips, a CIA chief for the Western
Hemisphere Division, would observe of Angleton, the man had
become a Delphic Oracle with an "awesome reputation nurtured
over the years by word of mouth." When Phillips first joined the
agency, a friend pointed Angleton out to him in the hall one day—
and when Phillips finally sat at table with him, Angleton proved
to be an entirely different person.[15]

Angleton went to Italy at a good moment. SCI units were at the
height of their importance, and Angleton had extensive personal

---

*Allen Dulles daughter, Joan Buresch, has remarked that few people in the CIA
truly became "a legend," however good they were. Her father was one. Paul
Blum—of whom more in a moment—was another. Angleton was a third. She
sensed this even as a child.

knowledge of how they should handle Ultra material. Further, he
was the only American cleared for Top Secret Ultra, as the chief
of other SCIs was a Britisher, and this access coupled with his
unusual grasp of the value that could be gained from Ultra and
his mastery of its techniques put him in a unique position. He was
determined that his unit would produce, and he applied all his
imagination, his enormous nervous energy, and his remarkable
persistence to showing what could be done. The object was to
defeat the enemy, using every resource available, and to bring the
war to a close as quickly as possible. There were, perhaps, secondary agendas, but there was no hidden agenda.

And produce Angleton and his SCI coworkers did. They were
to deal with the incredibly complex problem of the Italian partisans, who were of a bewildering variety of political hues; to keep
those who were clearly Communists applying themselves to the
common war effort rather than diverting supplies and using information for postwar purposes; to help rebuild the Italian intelligence services, hopelessly compromised by their cooperation with
the Germans and almost as hopelessly fragmented in their views
of the future Italian national interest; to liaise with other OSS units
and the British over the no less Byzantine problems of the Balkans, and especially the Yugoslav partisan groups; and to bend
all these secondary agendas to the principal goal, getting information about the intentions of the primary enemy, which was a
still dangerous Germany rumored (and by Dulles in Berne reported) to be preparing to make a last stand in some Bavarian
redoubt. Naturally, as the SCI unit moved on all these fronts, a
variety of functions accreted to it, or were created by it, for Angleton and his colleagues were entrepreneurs of intelligence, eager
to show, just as R&A had been in Washington, the potential of
their product. None of the achievements of SCI/Z, or of X-2, or
later of SSU (see page 371) were completely or even largely of
Angleton's own making, of course, but the initiative and the insight to see how a product might be improved were often his.

Some meritorious achievements were badly needed, for the OSS
in Italy had blotted its copy book in several ways, and there were
to be more blots to fall. Partially because X-2 fell outside the main
operational risks, and in part because Angleton was alert to the
risks, X-2 would incur no debits and a goodly number of credits.
At the end of the war he would receive a well-earned Legion of
Merit for his "clear, concise, and comprehensive" work in Italy.

OSS had rather smeared its copy book with the British a few months before, having employed an Italian, Paolo Poletti, in SI, only to have him turn out to be, or appear to be, a German spy. Knowing how to relate to the British, Angleton quickly smoothed over ruffled feathers on both sides. Murphy had been insisting that no agent be employed anywhere by the OSS without first being vetted by X-2, and the ramifications of the Poletti case, involving an Italian princess, Maria Pignatelli, who had been privy to many OSS secrets and now appeared to be an informer for the Fascists, put SI at a disadvantage and X-2 in the OSS driver's seat in Italy. Aided by information from Allen Dulles in Switzerland, X-2 would furnish the evidence against the princess, when SI, for which she ostensibly worked, could not get it. In the end it was Angleton who would confirm that Princess Pignatelli had, in fact, been passing information to both the Germans and Italians. She had, it appeared, been the one who was most responsible for betraying Peter Tompkins's mission in Rome.[16]

Angleton had an unusual ability to get his sums right, or appear to be right when others were clearly wrong. He seems to have established this reputation most clearly in the embarrassing Vessel affair, already in progress when he reached Italy. After the Allied liberation of Rome in June of 1944, a Vatican contact had begun to let the OSS see reports said to be from the apostolic delegates in Japan. The SI chief for Italy, Vincent Scamporino, had cultivated what seemed a superb contact within the Vatican, known as Source Z, from whom what appeared to be very high-grade information about Japan was flowing in considerable quantity. X-2 was instructed to protect Source Z, henceforth to be known as Dusty, and to prevent hostile penetration into the distribution system. Earlier Donovan had helped the founder of Pro Deo, a Catholic intelligence service, to flee from Lisbon to New York, and had then helped to reestablish him at the Holy See, and it was hoped that Dusty was a *quid pro quo* representing a line directly into the oldest, and perhaps the best, intelligence system in the world. Such was the regard for the Vatican's sources of information that all initially concerned had judged the Vessel material accurate and unusual. Though cautious, SI was sold on it, and SI sold Donovan. By the end of 1944, Dusty was being handled at the highest level, by Brigadier General John Magruder, Donovan's number two for intelligence.

Even so, Angleton had his doubts. He thought it unlikely that penetration at so high a level could continue for so long. Further, Donovan had sent out a general though nonbinding directive stating the OSS was not to employ any spy, or accept any intelligence, until both had been checked by X-2 and, if Ultra were involved, with the MI6 registry in London. Angleton knew the registry and its watchdog, and he knew Ultra: Vessel and his cutout had not been checked. Angleton ordered close surveillance on the cut-out, a Russian émigré who, he soon learned, was in contact with a Jesuit priest who had spied for the Italians in Latin America before the war. Though this looked all right to some, Angleton felt it at least as important to know who the priest was spying for now as who he spied against. Angleton held back, saying that Vessel was not yet clean, and that the sheer mass of the flow made him doubtful. To produce so much intelligence there had to be a ring. Was a ring likely in the security-conscious Vatican? And if so, who was in it?

But Washington could not wait. Good news was needed, especially from Italy, where OSS had not done too well. SI and X-2 were instructed to check on Vessel. Though SI insisted that it alone would handle the material, X-2 continued to investigate, in part because Jimmy Murphy judged SI as possibly open to penetration by the Germans, Italians, Communists, or British. Perhaps Angleton should have moved more rapidly—as he explained later, he had over a thousand cases of espionage to check on, and he could assign only a few of his officers to the Vessel enquiry (at the time he had only thirty men)—and perhaps Donovan was not insistent enough on a thorough vetting of the source (he was, in any case, in the Far East at the crucial moment). Clearly Vessel was a quite exceptional spy, or just possibly a fake, and Angleton opted for the latter judgment. In Washington Earl Brennan, Scamporino's case officer in SI, a man with deep Italian contacts of his own, came down for the former view.

Generally the Vessel material was about Japanese responses to Allied bombings, or about the redeployment of troops in the Far East, and it could not be checked quickly against an independent source. At the end of January 1945, however, Vessel included a reference to Myron Taylor, who had been FDR's personal representative to the Vatican. Angleton checked with Taylor's staff and detected some inconsistencies in the material. Still, these could be explained away, and after four days of checking the questionable report, SI/Washington decided it was accurate, classified it

Top Secret/Control, and released it to the White House. Soon after, however, Vessel sent other reports that contained details that might be checked, and General John E. Hull, chief of the Operations and Plans Division of the U. S. General Staff, with whom the reports were shared, denounced them as Japanese propaganda, perhaps a deception plan. Vessel might well be honest but, if so, he was being duped. Others in Washington also had begun to doubt the Vessel material. Colonel Peter G. Mero, OSS chief of Signals and Communications in Italy, and Robert P. Joyce, the political officer at Allied Supreme Headquarters for the Mediterranean Theater, independently concluded that, at the least, Vessel was not exclusive to the OSS, and was thus not secret, and on February 4 Joyce reported that Angleton, who had evidence that no fewer than ten intelligence services were buying the material, would take appropriate action. On February 16 Washington was able to confirm that Myron Taylor had not had the conversations that were reported in such detail in the Vessel material.

Though Angleton had counseled caution with respect to the material, he could not state, even in messages to Washington, precisely why. There was no Ultra traffic relating directly to the Vatican, so that he had to read such information as he could get out of the Città del Vaticano as a blank counter against the German and Italian information that did resonate off ISOS materials. Using Brennan's earlier contacts Angleton, notwithstanding Donovan's stated decision not to use the Vatican, had been cultivating his source directly within the Vatican—later identified as Giovanni Battista Montini, then a bishop and under-secretary of state at the Vatican and later Pope Paul VI. This contact may have developed further as a by-product of the negotiations then underway between Allen Dulles in Berne and the German high command in northern Italy to arrange for a separate surrender, for Angleton's source appears to have been privy to all that the German ambassador to the Vatican, Ernst von Weizsaecker, was reporting about Pope Pius XII. (A key Berne source, the so-called George Wood information—code name for Fritz Kolbe, a well-placed employee of the German Foreign Ministry—was judged by Angleton to be "one of the best . . . any intelligence service ever had.") Through his cut-out, Filippo Setaccioli, Angleton concluded definitively that Vessel was lying, not duped, though he could not reveal the sources giving rise to his conviction until some fact which he could verify independently of his source—

such as the reference to Myron Taylor—appeared in the Vessel reports. To be doubly certain that he was reading the situation correctly, he ran surveillance on Setaccioli, who worked for Italian intelligence, using one of his best men, Louis Cerutti.

No one individual could take credit for demonstrating that Vessel was false, but Angleton came out of the affair well, since he had expressed caution, and then doubts, from the outset. (Later some colleagues would complain that by delaying a firm response until other information supported his reservations, he would look good either way—if Vessel were verified, he was simply being systematic and careful, and if Vessel were proved false, he had shown the proper caution.) Washington instructed SI to break off with Vessel, while X-2 continued in contact, paying Vessel $500 a month, in hope of finding out who he actually was.[17]

Angleton succeeded, and won general plaudits from all except SI, who may have felt burned. The X-2 team put onto the case identified Vessel as Virgilio Scattolini, a Florentine journalist and author of pornographic books—one, *Amazons of the Bidet,* a staple of the Rome market—who after a religious conversion had begun to work as film critic for the Vatican's daily newspaper, *L'Osservatore Romano,* from which he was, in due course, fired. By then he had learned much about the Vatican, and his fertile pen created many false stories for the newspapers as well as for the several intelligence agencies he serviced. Angleton's surveillance team uncovered evidence that Scattolini was run by an official from the Secret Intelligence Service, who may have hoped by surveillance to pull out the identities of American, British, Russian, and other subagents and contacts. Angleton decided not to blow the whistle on Scattolini for he might even yet prove useful, a decision that would pay dividends three years later.

When Angleton arrived in Italy, one of his first tasks was to review the traffic that had gone between Lieutenant Irving Goff, a left-leaning SI officer responsible for communications with partisan groups in the North, and Communists who had agreed to cooperate with the Americans. Goff had built several all-party agent chains from his base near Brindisi. To keep Communist leaders from using the OSS wireless for party purposes, it was agreed that they would accept certain limitations on their messages. Goff showed any purely Communist signals to his commanding officer, Lieutenant Colonel William D. Suhling, before sending them out. All the traffic had seemed well within the bounds of the agreement until November 10, 1944, just as Angleton arrived, when Suhling read a signal from a Neapolitan Communist recently back from Moscow, to a party chief in northern Italy. The Allies had recently decided to disband guerrilla operations in the north for the winter, and the Communist signal was full of exhortations to greater efforts—"Do not give any rest to the Germans and the Fascists. Attack them with all weapons. Destroy them, kill them"—which Suhling read as a possible Communist challenge to Allied authority. The OSS commander for the Italian theater, Colonel Edward Glavin, decided that the specific signal did not violate the agreement that Communist groups would not send messages along "party lines" but agreed that Goff's back traffic should be reviewed.

Goff's agent-chain was one of seven, but he alone dealt with the Communists. From the moment of the Allied landings at Salerno he had been authorized to be in constant contact with the Communist leaders in Naples, just as André Bourgoin was to deal with professional Italian intelligence personnel. Others, under the direction of Captain André Pacatte, established chains with the Christian Democrats, the Socialists, the Partito d'Azione, and air force, with naval personnel, and with the Garibaldi brigades, who were viewed as ambiguously aligned, though possibly under the control of the Communists. These were assigned to Lieutenant Roger H. Hollingshead of SO. From November 18, 1943, when the first radio contact came from Rome, Goff was thus the only person authorized to deal with partisans who were unequivocally identified as Communists. Pacatte had made a long report, in which he praised R&A and X-2 (and Berding and Angleton specifically) for their work, was somewhat dismissive of SI, and concluded that Goff was "loved by his men, a good careful organizer, and while dealing with Communist [sic] has managed to keep the American and military point of view."[18]

Goff was meeting regularly with Palmiro Togliatti, the Italian Communist leader who had returned from a long exile in Moscow on March 28, 1944, for Togliatti could best affect the immediate agenda: to make certain that arms dropped to Communist groups to fight Fascists were not being stashed away for postwar activities. Anti-Fascist signs were going up all around Bologna and other cities in the north, warning that imperialists were coming up from the south in the guise of liberators. Inventory over drops was next to impossible, but it was obvious that radio sets, arms, sabotage equipment, a good bit of money, and some gold had gone missing, and while simple venality might explain part of the loss, clearly a good bit must be going into Communist hide-holes. Loyalties within the partisan groups appeared to change with bewildering speed and variety, and the Americans generally found themselves ill-prepared to comprehend the realities of wartime Italian politics at a local level.

Inevitably there were complaints that some OSS agents were taking a pro-Communist line. Colonel Clifton C. Carter, who had been head of OSS/Italy prior to Glavin's appointment, had pointed his finger at the group that he said had been recruited by Donald Downes. This was a half-truth: the most intense of the pro-Communists, Milton Wolff and Irving Fajans, though members of the New Model Donald Ducks, had joined after Downes had left Italy. Carter had pressed his view on Glavin, while Major Graham Erdwurm, chief of X-2/Caserta, was trying to sort out charges by the head of Army CIC, Colonel Earle B. Nichols, that some OSS officers ought to be returned to the United States promptly since, whether Communist agents or not, they were supplying improper military information to the Communist party. SI Chief Scamporino felt that Goff was, at the least, exceeding his instructions in his too-ready cooperation with Communist partisans. Thus Glavin ordered Angleton's unit to work through various lists of possible enemy agents and to review SO and SI contacts and support groups as well.

Peter Mero also asked SCI/Z to work closely with the chief of the Army Signals Office, Colonel Robert E. Schukraft, to examine traffic between OSS-sponsored partisan groups. Soon SCI/Z was reviewing Goff back-traffic, inter-partisan exchanges, SO and SI support groups generally, and lists of enemy agents. All Joan-Eleanor traffic in the north of Italy, regardless of purpose, was reviewed. (Named after the wives of two inventors, Stephen Simpson, who had set up a worldwide communications network for COI in 1942, and DeWitt R. Goddard, an RCA engineer, Joan-Eleanor involved a receiver so small it could easily be concealed by an agent on the ground—and as Pacatte found, slipped into a load of manure for transport—while a larger set, aboard an airplane, automatically recorded conversations on a spool of wire.) The review was intense, exhaustive, and lengthy—it took just under five months.

The review revealed no pattern of violations by Goff or the Communist partisans. Colonel Nichols and Major Erdwurm con-

cluded that Goff had done no wrong, though his views might lead
him to do so in the future, and Nichols said that Goff and three
of his men ought to be posted back to the States. Suhling's operations officer, Major Judson B. Smith, and Lieutenant Colonel
William P. Maddox, to whom Glavin showed the opinions, both
declared that Goff had performed extremely well under difficult
circumstances and had done precisely what he was ordered to do,
welding diverse parties and factions into a common front. In the
end the men were promoted, Goff was awarded the Legion of
Merit, and they were sent home.[19]

At the same time X-2 was involved in another inter-American
affair, the Holohan case. On September 27, 1944, Major William
G. Holohan, a Wall Street lawyer and graduate of the Harvard
Law School who had been Colonel Suhling's executive officer and
had been eager to lead an operation behind the lines, was dropped
near the Lake of Orta, north of Milan, with six men. The mission,
code-named Chrysler, was made up of Italian-Americans from SI,
SO, and OG (or Operational Groups) and three Italians. Almost
from the outset Chrysler went badly. The group spent a month in
hiding and on the move; the first drop of supplies and stores was
betrayed; the Communist and non-Communist partisan groups
squabbled over the division of arms; and in December, it was reported, the group had been attacked by Germans and Holohan
was captured.

Soon, however, rumors began to circulate that Holohan had been
killed, perhaps by the Sicherheitsdienst, perhaps by the Communists, perhaps by his own men. Murphy instructed Angleton to
examine all ISOS decryptions of German intelligence at the time
of the alleged German attack on Chrysler: no reference to such
an operation was found, and one ISOS intercept revealed a rumor
from a German intelligence officer that an American senior officer
had been murdered. Peter Mero thereupon took up the pursuit
and, with others, concluded that an on-site investigation was required. In June 1945 Donovan dispatched a team of experienced
OSS officers, led by Captain Bernard M. W. Knox, a Jedburgh
and, after the war, professor of classics at Yale and director of
the Dumbarton Oaks Hellenic Center, to the Lake of Orta. Despite plumbing the lake they did not find Holohan's body. After
the war the U.S. Army's Criminal Investigation Department returned to the chase and in September 1946 produced evidence
that Holohan had been murdered by his OSS intelligence officer.

The evidence was insufficient to bring charges, however. In 1950 another CID agent, Major Henry L. Manfredi, returned to the case. Among those useful to him was Angleton, still in Italy, by then as chief of CIA counterintelligence in Rome. Manfredi found Holohan's body by dragging the Lake of Orta at the spot an informer indicated. The wireless operator from Chrysler now gave a lengthy handwritten confession, stating that he and the SI officer had killed Holohan and taken the considerable quantity of gold and lire he carried with him. Later he withdrew the confession, and in the end, though there was strong circumstantial evidence independent of the confession, no one was brought to trial: the statute of limitations had run out on any charge of embezzlement, and the United States had lost jurisdiction, both civil and military, on any charge of murder committed in Italy. While the Italian government attempted to extradite the two former OSS agents, their lawyers were successful in resisting this. An Italian court convicted both *in absentia*.[20]

Of course Angleton had known what a powerful weapon ISOS was well before he came to Italy, for it had been demonstrated in the affair of Anton Dostler and the Ginny mission. On the night of March 21–22, 1944, fifteen men of OSS—two officers and thirteen OGs—were put ashore from two torpedo boats near Framura on the Ligurian coast to blow up a railway tunnel on the main line from Genoa to the German front. The officers wore no insignia, but everyone was in American uniform. Captured on the twenty-third, the Americans were identified as sabotage troops when their rubber landing boats and explosives were discovered. In the view of General Dostler, commanding officer for the region, they stood convicted of being commandos, and Hitler had issued an unequivocal order that all captured enemy commandos were to be summarily executed. On the twenty-fifth Dostler ordered that the American captives be shot. However, those holding them prisoner delayed. The German interrogator, Georg Sessler, a naval lieutenant, had recognized one of the Americans as a man who had delivered ice to the ships of the Hamburg-Amerika Line that called in New York when Sessler worked for the line. He felt sympathy toward them—perhaps because he had been in Abwehr Maritime Intelligence himself—and may have slipped a pistol to one of the American officers. A German naval commander also asked that the execution be postponed, arguing that it was not clear that Hitler's order applied to this case and, in any event, he

wished to deepen the investigation. Both men sent Dostler their
reasons for a stay of execution, copying their request to Field
Marshal Albert Kesselring, the German supreme commander for
Italy. Dostler was adamant, however, pointing out that officers
who did not execute Hitler's Commando Order were themselves
subject to court-martial. The fifteen Americans were executed on
March 26. Late the same day Kesselring replied with a stay of
execution.

When it was realized that the stay was too late, orders went out
to destroy evidence of the executions and, on March 28, a cover
communiqué was issued declaring that a commando unit of fifteen
men had been annihilated in combat. The Germans intended that
the communiqué should be intercepted, of course, but they did
not know that Bletchley would also intercept a top-secret coded
message from Kesselring to Hitler telling him that American troops
had been liquidated as instructed by the Commando Order. It was
Angleton who was reading the traffic in London. Shortly after an
Italian priest came through the American lines and was picked up
by the CIC net. Under interrogation he described hearing ma-
chine-gun firing and soon after finding a fresh grassy mound where,
he had been told, some Americans had been buried. Donovan ordered that Dostler be captured alive during the American advance—which, with troops still tied down at Anzio and below
Cassino, was much delayed—and tried.[21]

The Dostler trial would set precedent for the war crimes trials
that took place in Nuremberg many months later. In the fall of
1945 Dostler was found guilty. Sessler, who had been sent to the
Combined Services Detailed Interrogation Center (CSDIC) opened
up at Rome's Cinecittà, told how he had come down from Vienna
and had been an interrogator and translator for the American OG
group. Dostler's interpreter throughout the trial, a German who
had come over to the OSS, was a member of Angleton's unit, and
he gained the impression that Dostler hardly understood the nature of the charges. Dostler's defense, that he had simply obeyed
a clear military order, was carefully argued on his behalf by
American counsel (though not, Donald Downes later concluded
as he worked on his never finished book about the Dostler affair,
argued well enough). Kesselring's successor, General Heinrich von
Vietinghof, asked for mercy for Dostler; the Pope asked that the
sentence be commuted; Dostler's wife and daughter addressed a
plea of their own. At the end of November the American author-

ities reviewed the case and petitions and ordered that Dostler be executed on December 1, as he was. Dostler's clear order to execute the Americans, read in the ISOS traffic, had been his death warrant.

Sessler survived, though at the expense of strained Anglo-American intelligence relations. As head of German counterintelligence in Genoa and coastal Italy, Sessler had been an important catch. He had surrendered his network to the Americans, and he had cooperated over the Dostler affair. From the available evidence his role at the time of the executions had been an honorable one. (And he may have also worked for the British, though this is quite unclear.) The Americans had hoped to keep the British from learning that Sessler's network had passed to them, and they feared that the British might put him on a trial or even a possible execution list at precisely the time when American intelligence strategy was to interrogate all former German intelligence officers and then bring those with knowledge of Eastern Europe or Communist parties into the fold. The British learned of Sessler, however, and he was put by them into a PW camp. While Sessler's trial was pending, SSU—some thought Angleton personally—bribed his jailers to let him escape, and Sessler was set up with a new identity as a long-term covert agent for the Americans in the south of France.

Just as the Dostler case illustrated the latent power of ISOS material long after its operational date, so did Sessler's interrogation at CSDIC demonstrate the great value of a close working relationship between CSDIC, CIC, and the OSS. Angleton, who had been in charge of SCI/Z from November 1944 to March 1945, thereafter ran all of Italian X-2 from Rome, and he was charged with effecting as close coordination on interrogation and the information that flowed from it as possible. While he did no interrogating himself, he contributed significantly to the form, the technique, and the content of the interrogations, because he helped determine the line of questioning and often the means by which the results were disseminated. Since among the Americans only Angleton was fully ISOS-cleared, he was carving out a unique activity for X-2 in the field: to do research and analysis on German order of battle intelligence covering both the Sicherheitsdienst and the Abwehr, especially after the complex merger of the two in 1944.

Angleton was determined that his limited manpower would not

be wasted on interrogation. The British Field Security Service and American Army CIC covered the front line and worked back to Allied headquarters. There CSDIC, under a British commander, had become a massive holding area for those awaiting interrogation, with elaborate facilities and a large cadre of trained bilingual interrogators who often produced hundred-page verbatim reports. Special Interrogation Units, or IUs, were targeted onto prisoners most likely to prove productive. Angleton's objective was to convey information to FSS and CIC near the front, and to CSDIC and CIC in Rome, based both on what his men learned and on his reading of the Cinecittà interrogation reports. He had placed men under Paul Paterni in Florence, Henry Nigrelli in Genoa, and G. Raymond Rocca in Rome. Now, through Peter Mero, Angleton was given three vans, with radio operators and drivers, and as the front broke he sent Paterni to Milan and the navy man, Charles Siragusa, to Turin. Their reports back, coupled with continued rereading of ISOS, and X-2 use of the CSDIC product, put Angleton at the center of an ever-expanding network of information.

Angleton therefore turned to a comprehensive study of each German intelligence unit—its functions, headquarters, operating locations, facilities, personnel, channels of command, and known field agents. No one else was doing this. As each study was finished, it was sent to the chief of counterintelligence at Allied Forces Headquarters, Colonel Nichols, for dissemination to all CIC units in loose-leaf form. A corps of ten bilingual secretaries under Rocca's guidance collated the materials. Thus the studies could be updated within a day anywhere on the basis of new information from any source, and the most relevant parts—those that would explain the changing *modus operandi* of the Germans—could be sent to forward units in mimeographed form, saving forward-unit typing and assuring that the problem of paper flow would not, in fact, be a problem. By so simple an innovation Angleton both sped the flow of information and, by making it timely, made it genuinely useful.

Angleton's unit also created a series of notebooks of the same type, from which pages could simply be torn and revised ones inserted, of a more sensitive nature. When the front broke, each CIC officer who went forward had complete and up-to-date notebooks which included pictures of buildings and of the faces of key figures (such as Dostler) wanted for trial or interrogation—sketched by a young artist Angleton drew into the unit—together with maps and floor diagrams of Abwehr and other headquarters so that enemy documents might be more likely to be seized before they could be destroyed. These were presented as appendices and also updated almost daily. If a CIC unit on the front made a startling discovery, it did not go through channels but came to the telephone directly (one such discovery was that German signal plans were being sewed into the lapels of coats, and the word was sent back that all captives should have their lapels examined, since German intelligence operatives would, if captured, almost certainly attempt to hide among prisoners from regular army units). The fast communication vans then targeted the new information to the appropriate CIC people. Since the content grew in good measure from FSS, CIC, and CSDIC information, this both assured a closer working relationship and also fed X-2's accreting influence.

For the pictures Angleton sent men out to visit every photography studio in Rome. During happier days German officers had often sent formal photographs of themselves to loved ones at home, and from the studio files X-2 created mugbooks. A massive collection of picture postal cards of northern Italy was assembled so that villas known to be used by the Germans could be recognized. The resulting compilations were turned over via AFHQ to bomber command, to target Abwehr III centers.* A tight working relationship with AFHQ, in which the once rather independent OSS personality was submerged into the military, was one effect of such close and repetitive cooperation.

A by-product of his close association with CSDIC from which Angleton took particular delight was a mimeographed Chinese newspaper launched by his office. Discovering there were many overseas Chinese, in particular seamen, interned at Cinecittà, Angleton cultivated contacts among them since they might have information on Far Eastern harbors valuable to the Pacific campaign. One of his sources was a young, well-educated North Chinese who complained that the Chinese in the camp were utterly disoriented, cut off from ship's news of events in the East. Angleton

---

*Abwehr Drei was counterintelligence, Abwehr Zwei sabotage, Abwehr Einst positive intelligence. Abwehr I quarters were not to be bombed, for both the Americans and the Russians hoped to capture records which would reveal who had worked for the Germans in the occupied countries. American intelligence assumed that the Russians would use the records to blackmail informants to shift their allegiance to them.

liberated a mimeograph machine (a better liberation, he felt, than the cases of brandy routinely liberated as the Allied forces over-ran the retreating Germans in the north), took material that would be of interest to Chinese readers directly from the American newspaper *Stars and Stripes,* and with the help of a priest in Pro Deo, who extracted relevant material from the Vatican press, pro-duced a news sheet that was soon much in demand. The Chinese youth distributed the paper, discussed the news stories, and drew out further information from the previously uncooperative sea-men. This was, Angleton later recalled, "his first contact with the Orient." When he was invited to the Chinese compound, to be elaborately welcomed beneath a picture of Sun Yat-sen, and was told of the irritation of CSDIC's British commander, he had learned an early lesson in politics. Even more, he said, he now realized how for a few dollars a week one could satisfy the information needs of hundreds of people and get information in return.

During the course of such work X-2 came across many docu-ments, often on signals security, that showed what American codes the Italians had broken over the years. These were routinely sent to Mero, who worked closely with Army Signals on them for use by army cryptanalysts and by Mero's very able assistant, John W. Coffey. Knowledge that a code had been broken would, of course, lead to a reevaluation of the enemy's response to mes-sages it had been presumed they had heard but not understood, so that a local archival function with rapid retrieval methods de-rived largely from R&A also developed.

On occasion X-2 would take part in an interrogation, and though not himself involved, Angleton showed considerable interest in the methods of the interrogators, for he knew that the methods influenced the product, and the interrogators' reports, which came to him without interpretation, were essential to his records. He made it clear that no physical injuries were to be inflicted. While American agents subject to capture carried suicide pills, there is only one recorded instance of an OSS agent taking his own life by use of a suicide capsule[22]—the best protection against betray-ing information to the enemy was in simply not knowing much to betray. The presence of a capsule was thus a giveaway; if one were found, interrogation would be likely to take more urgent forms. One could assume the same would be true of enemy agents, and since Angleton's interest was exclusively in big fish, of X-2 targets in particular. Any resort to torture, however, would result in an adversarial relationship and a loss of objectivity on the part of the interrogator. While abjuring torture is often credited to the presumed greater humanity of a democracy, it also arises from the conviction that persons under great pain will confess to almost anything; will attempt to tell an interrogator what the person under torture believes he wants to hear; if permanently disabled and in unremitting pain, may confess to something for which he can hope to be executed. Such methods would seldom produce accurate information, and the object of interrogation was always information, never the humiliation or disablement of the person under interrogation for its own sake.* Interrogation was, Angleton said in his precise way, "the art of elicitation based on prior analyses and knowledge of the service from which the agent derived." Homework, handbooks, and those loose-leaf fillers were the key to useful interrogation. (This was not to discount pure inspiration, as when he spotted, while examining an address book taken from a priest undergoing interrogation by Siragusa's team in Florence, that some numbers were backwards, yielding the telephone number of the SD in Verona, a discovery that broke an enemy agent.) Clearly, the person who evaluated information must not be the person who extracted it, since bias could so easily arise if one had a stake in the validity of the information itself.

One such interrogator was Curtis Carroll Davis, whom Angleton had known slightly at Yale.[23] An English honors graduate of the class of 1938 (and after the war a Ph.D. from Duke University), Davis had been drafted in April of 1942 and had gone to the Air Force Intelligence School in Harrisburg, Pennsylvania. He ended up "out in the Blue" in Tunisia as a combat-intelligence officer with a fighter squadron. In December 1943 he was assigned to CSDIC and served there through most of the shooting war. In August 1945 he was accepted into X-2 in London under Norman Holmes Pearson and was sent to Rome as Angleton's German speaker. Davis remained with Angleton until mustered out of service in 1946. His French was good, his German excellent, though both had been learned through travel and at Yale and were judged a bit bookish: interrogation was a natural assignment. In Italy

---

*The notion that psychological methods constituted a form of torture was not widely held at this time, and certainly CSDIC used as standard techniques the planting of stool pigeons in holding pens, bugging cells and lavatories, and the double interrogation or "sweet and sour" (now called "good guy-bad guy") approach. Paterni and Siragusa were particularly practiced in this role.

Davis's team picked up a remote radio signal from somewhere in the northern Apennines, and direction finding, or DF, and some on-the-spot checking revealed the origin to be a Wehrmacht corporal who was signaling for rescue, having been caught behind the advancing Allied line. While Davis was for going to the rescue at once, Angleton cautioned that there were at least two levels of meaning to any communication: the corporal might even be working for the British, waiting for an American rescue, so that he could spy on American interrogation methods in the field. Angleton would, Davis felt, always turn every object in his hands to catch the light, would always work harder, be more totally loyal to the concept of intelligence, than anyone else. Many people were waiting for Angleton to break, he thought, since he never appeared to sleep; Curtis guessed that he would never break, for he saw Angleton as a "practitioner of detail," a person who received very real psychological sustenance from yet more data, data that would overburden anyone else. After the war he recalled that Angleton refused free army billeting wherever he was assigned, for the gossip of shared quarters, if not insecure (as it was) was certainly time-consuming, and he generally preferred to sleep at his office, to wait for more materials arriving from CSDIC.

Angleton felt obliged to CSDIC, which produced so much grist for his mill, and he asked General Donovan to visit the interrogation center and have lunch. No one of his prominence had done so, and the prisoners in the camp were delighted when they were told Donovan had accepted. Donovan had first to go to the Quirinale Palace to receive an Italian decoration, and Angleton preceded him to the center. Lunch came and there was no Donovan, though all of the prisoners were lined up in their ill-fitting uniforms waiting for him in the hot Roman sun. Angleton called the palace repeatedly and finally, embarrassed for the prisoners, asked to be put through to Donovan, who responded at once and left for the camp. Donovan conducted a magnificent review, shook hands with all the interrogators, and talked briefly with the German high brass who were kept in a separate holding area. The visit gave great satisfaction, and the CSDIC reports, already extremely good, became even better.

Donovan's visit had also alerted Angleton to the agenda ahead. Murphy had told him it was very important to pay attention to whatever Donovan said just as he got off his plane, literally to listen intently to the first words he volunteered, since replies to his questions usually led him to other concerns quickly, and only afterward would he come back to what was really on his mind. Angleton made a point of being in any welcoming group that came out onto the tarmac when Donovan arrived, and when the general got off his aircraft in Caserta, the first thing he said was that the president was concerned with war crimes. Despite the babble of other matters, Angleton focused on this and had war crimes materials dug out and ready for Donovan when he reached Rome. Donovan told Angleton that scholars had made an industry of writing on the question of responsibility for World War I; he was determined there would be no doubt about where responsibility for the second war lay.

It was an interrogation that first brought Angleton knowledge of German peace feelers in the north. A priest, interrogated at length at CSDIC, confessed that an SD chief had asked him to deliver a message for him to the head of the priest's order. Careful inquiry produced the conclusion that this was an approach to the Vatican, possibly by Heinrich Himmler, to ask the church to propose an armistice. This had to be verified, for it was delicate in the extreme, especially since the Russians feared that the Western powers might make a separate peace. Angleton turned to one of his contacts in Italian naval intelligence, who approached the former chaplain of his ship, a priest of the same order, to ask the chaplain to make an indirect approach to the Vatican, seeking an audience for Angleton. Within a day the audience was granted and Angleton was given the substance of the peace feeler, which was sent at once by safe hand to Washington. Nonetheless, Angleton suspected this was a deliberate German provocation to drive a wedge between the United States and the Soviet Union, and as the priest had been jailed, he instructed that he be interrogated again and again. He learned that though the head of the order wrote periodically to ask that the priest be freed, the order did not actually want him back, and this worried Angleton too, until he found that the priest had embezzled funds from the order. This explained the order's *pro forma* requests for his release, but it also threw into question the veracity of the priest's statements. Whatever Washington might make of the report, Angleton decided to persistently deny there had been any such message from Himmler at all.

Another part of X-2's activity almost from the beginning in Italy was to help the Italians to reconstitute their own services. While there were those who argued that any peace treaty should deny Italy use of an intelligence service, Angleton felt this was unrealistic. He worked with the Italian navy, air force, army, and Ministry of Interior under the Badoglio government, therefore, to prepare for the future, for like R&A, X-2 was under instructions to give increased attention to the Soviets. Italy had an enormous problem as the war wound down: thousands of returned prisoners of war were being sent back by the Russians, and many might well be Communists or Soviet plants; there was a massive influx of agents from Yugoslavia and of others from the breaking Greek civil war; there was a stream of Germans from Austria and Vichyite France; Rome, in particular, had become the crossroads of Europe. Angleton had a high opinion of Italian intelligence work, and he did all that he could to help the Italians reestablish the Servizio Informazione Militare (SIM).

The end of the war brought military attachés to the American embassy in Rome. Though the American ambassador wanted close coordination with the OSS, Angleton tried to keep X-2 at a discreet distance, for his men had military cover. The American military attaché, Colonel John Murphy Willems, made a weekly visit to OSS headquarters, and with him Angleton was cooperative. This proved to be a boon later, for Willems would become G-2 of the army, and their cooperation continued long after the war.

Both the embassy and the Allied High Commission were soon placing heavy demands on Angleton's counterintelligence unit. The high commissioner, Admiral Ellery Stone, instructed Angleton to rescue Prince Valerio Borghese from the risk of arrest and possible death at the hands of vengeful Resistance leaders.[24] There was constant traffic between Angleton and Tom Karamessines, his counterpart in Greece. The Yugoslav secret police, OZ Na (Section for the Defense of the People), was clearly working with Communists in Italy, so that it and its successor U.D. Ba (Administration for State Security) required the full research treatment. And when an American aircraft went down inside Yugoslavia, and the Yugoslavs refused to turn it and its equipment over to the Americans, it was evident that Italian Titoists in general must also be observed. Though the plane was returned when President Truman stated that he would send in the 10th Mountain Division, then in Trieste, to recover it, IFF—Identification: Friend or Foe— instrumentation was never recovered. To meet all these contingencies Angleton was building a systematic network for the post-

war world, recruiting new contacts in Italy, largely from the middle
and upper classes, who were likely to be anti-Communist, but also
from any Italian partisans who, interrogation reports suggested,
had broken with the Communists.

Much time also had to be given to preparation for the forthcoming war crimes trials. SCI/Z obtained secret correspondence that
had passed between Hitler and Mussolini, and also with Franco,
together with minutes of Supreme Council meetings, and this material proved invaluable at the trials. As the developing split between Tito and Stalin widened, Angleton also came up with letters
from two years earlier which hinted at the nature of that split.*
SCI/Z bought many documents relating to the international Communist movement, including instructions to the Italian Communist
party, that outlined Soviet intentions with respect to the civil war
in Greece.

Truly, Angleton's unit had produced. What was asked of them
they did.† Every new assignment was seen not as a task but as a
fresh opportunity: as Raymond Rocca observed later, he had to
take initiatives; Angleton had to make his way on the basis of the
material he produced, for unlike so many in the OSS, he had no
law degree, no doctorate, no operational experience. The effort
to disclose penetrations of American signals was, in essence, archival work, the sifting of documents, many two years or more
old, for the additional meanings the passage of time had given
them. Angleton, like any historian or textual analyst, understood
the value of the original documents. Nothing, in theory, was useless, no document irrevocably mute, no inquiry every truly finished. Layer upon layer of meaning could be found in back file
material if one knew the questions to ask. Just as the X-2 had
grown by accretion, so did the registry, so did his proof of effectiveness, so did the theory of intelligence.[26]

With the German surrender in May 1945 OSS/Italy began to
close down. There were still many interrogations to review, and
much information to gather for the forthcoming war crimes trials,

---

*On one occasion Angleton got a stenographer's notebook containing top-secret
correspondence and had to find someone who knew the unusual form of shorthand. This may have been the occasion.

†The only lapse noted in the documentation was Angleton's failure, in 1946, to
transmit safely a "valuable book" sent by Alfredo Pizzoni, who as Longhi had
been leader of the Comitato di Liberazione Alta Italia, a significant position in
the Italian Resistance, to Allen Dulles in Washington.[25]

and there was the tighter focus on Communist and Soviet intentions, but there were no substantive missions to run. It had been Donovan's intent to stay on to create a peacetime unit, so that the United States would not have again to establish an equivalent of the COI/OSS from scratch, but he had pressed much too hard, his reputation had been damaged by a number of OSS gaffes such as the Vessel affair, and President Truman professed to be deeply suspicious of a peacetime intelligence agency, especially of one that was a carry-over from wartime conditions. Effective October 1, the OSS ceased to exist. R&A (and the Presentation Branch) were transferred to State as the Interim Research and Intelligence Service, 1,362 strong, while the remainder of OSS, down to 9,028 in all, was transferred to the War Department. On that date OSS personnel were reassigned to the newly created Strategic Services Unit (SSU), which reported to the assistant secretary of war. Donovan's former deputy, Brigadier General John Magruder, was appointed director of SSU. Lieutenant-Colonel William W. Quinn, a West Pointer, was directed by President Truman to report for duty to serve as Magruder's executive officer. Donovan had recommended Quinn to Truman, having been well pleased and impressed by Quinn's sagacious use of OSS resources in support of intelligence operations by the U.S. Seventh Army. When Magruder retired in early 1946, Quinn was appointed director of SSU.[27]

Angleton had received a cryptic communication from headquarters that a courier was bringing an important message. Eventually the former chief of X-2 in Vienna, Major E. Phillip Barry, arrived to tell him that they were to meet with the chief of staff, who had a For Your Eyes Only letter for him. Angleton drove to Caserta to read the instructions for his new assignment: that all long-term aspects of counterintelligence in Italy were to be turned over to him. The man to whom he would report was Quinn. Quinn and Angleton shared the view that the rush "to bring the boys home" from the European front was a mistake, and that the United States ought to face down the Russians, who were already living up to the dire predictions made by Churchill in the final months of the war. They traveled together in Italy, Austria, and Switzerland, and Quinn thought the young officer showed a remarkable understanding and knowledge both of intelligence and of the cultures involved. Quinn had been instructed to "preserve the intelligence assets of the OSS and to eliminate its liabilities," and he and Angleton saw eye-to-eye on the definition of both. He soon learned that MO and SI were equally high on Angleton, who was believed to know every bridge and every street—as well as every maître d'—in his field of operation. He was tough, another SSU officer reported, and expected those who worked for him to have "detachable testicles," but he was fair. He also continued to produce. Several times Angleton sent Quinn, who had returned to Washington, back-channel messages to say that he had a "gift" for him, and twice in 1947 Angleton produced the code book and related materials of another country.

Angleton did know his parish extremely well, and not only from the cloister of an office; Quinn had rightly seen that he was more than a bundle of theory studded with geographic place names. From his offices on the Via Archimede Angleton forayed out frequently to rediscover the crippled city of Rome. He knew well his agents and their haunts. He remained in touch with Donovan, whom he admired, and wrote often to Pearson, discussing the jockeying of SSU personnel for position. He shared with Pearson a fascination with the immediate postwar reorganization of European intelligence systems. He kept in personal contact with a code clerk in the Vatican, he visited Togliatti, he poured over the Italian press. His student-day habits unchanged, he could be found in the middle of the Roman night, a single lamp burning, reading reports carefully turned face down on his desk so that visitors might not divine even their form, relaxing over poetry, smoking incessantly. In the day he was out again, memorizing locations, streets, acquiring that intimate knowledge of place so essential to a good counterintelligence operation. Called "the Cadaver" by some of the men in his unit, though behind his back, he coughed constantly and was thought to have tuberculosis. (Years later he would take a leave at a sanatorium.) As the commanding officer of the 2677th Regiment, SSU, and only twenty-eight, he was an obvious rising star. Angleton was, Quinn would recall in 1985, not only "unbelievably understanding of the nature of counterintelligence," he was the "finest counterespionage officer the United States has ever produced."[28]

Apparently at the end of the war Angleton never really considered any other career than counterintelligence. As many old OSS hands returned to civilian life, giving up their clandestine networks for the cozier networking of board room and faculty club, Angleton worried instead about his men, to whom he was intensely loyal, and fretted over whether some unwitting successor would cut the strings to his doubles. Although Angleton was supposed to go into the family business, to help his father build back the crippled Angleton enterprise in Italy, he had little interest in it. Angleton never wanted to do anything he could not do well, and he doubted his capacity for business. He also saw many good people leaving SSU simply because no one tried to keep them, there being no initiative from Washington to do so. Quinn made the difference, for he actively persuaded Angleton to stay at his post. Very little persuasion was needed, and Angleton joined a small group of OSS men and women who were making the transition to what would become, in 1947, the Central Intelligence Agency, with the same close-knit atmosphere that Angleton had liked in X-2 and at Yale—three communities in which people had a strong awareness of their responsibilities to each other and a certain "we-they" view of the world. At least six members of Angleton's Yale class of 1941 made the same transition, as did even more from the subsequent two classes. Angleton would rise steadily to become head of the CIA's clandestine wing, chief of all counterintelligence in December of 1954, for two decades thereafter the man the press loved to call "America's legendary master spy."

This notion of "the legendary" bothered Angleton as much as the idea that there was such a person as a "master spy." He often said that the word *spy* ought seldom to be used, and that "spymaster" and "master spy" were the language of the novelist or of the media. One did one's job, keeping a specific end in view, and if thorough, methodologically correct, and prudent, there would be more successes than failures, though there would be plenty of the latter. In counterintelligence, no success or failure was unqualified, however, and generally neither was known to the public (while the failures of the operational units would sooner or later hit the fan, only the successes remaining—if one were lucky—unknown), feeding the mystique about "legends." Human beings need heroes, and a legend is a kind of hero, or by the 1970s, was perhaps an antihero. Angleton certainly understood this, and on occasion he might capitalize on it, but he was convinced that he ought not do anything that fed it, for it would lessen the sense of working together within a team. Later, at CIA staff meetings, when various high-ranking members would gather around the table with successive directors of central intelligence, Dulles, McCloy, Colby, and would ask each other, waiting for the business of the day to start, how their golf games had gone over the weekend, no one ever imagined that Angleton had a golf game to talk about. He did, of course, get away as often as possible to fly-fish, patiently waiting to see what his line might catch, and he loved to get up to his sixteen acres on the Brule River in Wisconsin or, later, to his property outside Tucson, but somehow his solitary activity, his hobbies—tying his own delicate flies, growing orchids, and making jewelry—scarcely seemed the subject of banter. He had no locker-room chatter, he was not one of the boys, and thus legends would accrete to him as work had done in Rome. After all, Angleton could not change his nature and would not change his mind about those people he most admired, who indeed he came to emulate.

Looking back there were, perhaps, four men who had influenced him most deeply: Jimmy Murphy, Norman Pearson, Paul C. Blum, and Gustav Bertrand. With a little more thought, Angleton would mention others who had deeply impressed him—his British colleagues, Cowgill, Roberts, Brooman-White, coworkers in Italy, Mero, Paterni, Rocca, Siragusa. There were influences that lay in the future, of course, for one was always learning. But it was the company of Murphy, Pearson, Blum, and Bertrand that most stayed with him, for whatever he had become himself.

Murphy he had liked and respected enormously. From him he had learned the power of discretion, the advantage of having immediate access to the top, the value of loyalty, the quiet pleasure of a job well done without fanfare. Pearson had combined all of his youthful interests: in poetry, and its encapsulated ambiguity, to emerge, properly understood,with a shining clarity; in looking for the hidden dimension, the buried emotion, whether expressed through body language or nuanced conversation; in the sophisticated running of people. From Pearson, and from his Ryder Street experiences, the young Angleton had learned about the importance of the multilevel notional story, about why an agent had to transmit his own messages, and thus truly be turned, rather than simply being killed, leaving someone else to send out messages in his code name, because of the distinct signature of touch and rhythm that attached, like a fingerprint, to each hand on the key: a double agent had to be alive to transmit, and this affected enormously what he could be told prior to transmission. From Ryder Street he learned the value of having a superior source, such as

Ultra. He was always disappointed that Pearson did not stay with intelligence work, for he found him an excellent critic, always able to improve the product of others. Angleton was quite happy to learn, after Pearson had returned to university teaching, that Pearson's colleagues generally thought of him as a bit of a romanticizer. This would protect the methodology they shared and would mean that Pearson could, on occasion, be used as a consultant by the new CIA. Pearson and Murphy were, in a sense, father figures.

Paul C. Blum was Robert Blum's cousin. "The last of the aristocrats," at least in the clandestine services, Blum had been born in 1898 in Japan, to a French father and American mother, but his environment was worldwide, for he knew Africa, Latin America, and China well. As a teenager during World War I, he had driven an ambulance in France, for which he received the Croix de Guerre with palms. He had graduated from Yale in the class of 1921, entering finance and, later, the professional collecting and sale of Orientalia outside Paris. He liked to move about the world, seeing all, connecting all, traveling only on tankers, not amidst the glitter and luxury of the great cruise lines. Blum was a patriot, not for America alone but for any society that was, by his own definitions, democratic. In the second war Blum joined the OSS and was sent to Lisbon to set up a unit of what became X-2, then went to London for a time, and finally to work with Allen Dulles in Berne, where he took over from Dulles at the end of the war. It was Blum who, on March 3, 1945, made the first contact with the German army in northern Italy that set in motion the "secret surrender," or Operation Sunrise, orchestrated by Dulles and his assistant, Tracy Barnes, Yale '33. After the war Blum would remain in intelligence work—Angleton accompanied him through southern France to the Spanish frontier when he left for reassignment—to become chief of station in Tokyo, and ultimately to retire there. In Japan before the war he had begun his remarkable private collection of Orientalia, and while later he had intended to give his huge library to Yale, the university felt unable to keep it together as a collection, wishing to disperse books to different subject matter areas of the library stacks, despite Norman Pearson's best efforts to persuade them otherwise, so Blum sold the collection to the city of Yokohama, of which he became an honorary citizen (keeping out a few of his prize volumes for Yale anyway). Angleton admired him, for his professionalism, for his joy in books and good food, for his language skills: he was a person who always "enhanced the moment," and until Blum's death in August 1981 they remained in touch. The memorial service at the Yale Club in New York, on September 11, brought back all the old faces: Angleton and Murphy sat side by side.[29]

It was Gustave E. Bertrand, whom he first met in Italy at the end of the war, who Angleton singled out as one of the people he learned the most from in a substantive way, however. Bertrand had been chief of the French cryptologic section in 1939–40 and had played a central role in passing to the British a Polish Enigma machine.[30] From Vichy France he had supplied information to SIS and had correctly predicted that the Germans would overrun Vichy if North Africa were invaded by the Allies. After the war he was, until 1950, deputy chief of the French secret service.* Angleton had shown a particular interest in the French intelligence services from the time André Dewavrin, known as Colonel Passy, had produced intelligence information, using Gestapo tactics as necessary in the basement of his headquarters on Duke Street. In 1946 Dewavrin was replaced by Henri Ribière, a Socialist, who was injured in an automobile accident shortly after, so that the acting director had to rely more heavily on the deputy, Bertrand. Angleton was impressed by French intelligence, for it had proved enormously effective under the most difficult of circumstances. Angleton knew the top members of French counterintelligence, or DSDOC (Direction des Services de Documentation), including the wartime chief Colonel Jean Chrétien, and he thought highly of the first postwar director, Lieutenant Colonel Lafond (code name Verneuil). The 2éme Sous-Direction Technique, a subdivision of DSDOC headed by Verneuil, handled counterespionage in France and abroad, and with its Travaux/Ruraux (TR) operated double agents. The political crisis in France in January 1946 brought Socialists to power, and they attacked the SDECE as being both

*Several accounts refer to Bertrand as deputy chief of the SDECE, or Service de Documentation Extérieures et Contre-Espionage (Department of Foreign Information and Counterespionage). This is not strictly true, as the SDECE as it is known today was not set up until 1945, and it was greatly reorganized in 1958: its previous name was Direction Générale des Etudes et Recherches. However, the initials SDECE are widely used to apply to the earlier period as well. The SDECE is not to be confused with the Deuxième Bureau, which is French military intelligence, or General de Gaulle's own wartime "second bureau," the Bureau Centrale de Renseignements et d'Action, or BCRA, which was linked to the French Resistance. A 5ème Bureau handled border control and army counterespionage.

Gaullist and pro-British, so that Angleton, anticipating major changes, saw to it that he remained in touch with these figures in French intelligence, believing firmly that de Gaulle would be back. Later he would work closely with Philippe Thyraud de Vosjoli, who was chef de cabinet to Ribière and liaison officer for French intelligence in Washington.[31]

Bertrand, like Blum, remained Angleton's friend until death, even during a time when it was suggested that Bertrand may have been turned by the Russians. Through Bertrand Angleton followed the slow-dawning public story of Ultra, and when Bertrand's little noticed but highly revelatory book, *Enigma ou la plus grande énigme de la guerre, 1939–1945,* was published by Plon in Paris in 1973, and plummeted out of sight, Angleton was convinced that British intelligence bought it up in order to suppress it. He liked Bertrand's fertile imagination, his understanding of how the French might once again be a power on the Continent, and through him, felt he understood far better the ancient Anglo-French antipathy. When, in 1958, Bertrand, theoretically retired from the French intelligence service, became mayor of a small port town near Cannes, and the American Sixth Fleet paid a courtesy call, Angleton created a citation to be delivered to the mayor, and sent along a huge clipping file to show how closely he had kept in touch with Bertrand's career. Angleton felt that with Bertrand's passing in 1978, his great Buddha head silenced, the last of the wartime giants who understood both the Germans and the Russians was gone.* [32]

Of course, many other men, and a few women, were influential in his life. In Switzerland there was Cordelia Dodson, later Cordelia Hood, who he thought was a first-rate agent. In Paris there was Owen Dennis Johnson, son of Owen Day Johnson, author of *Dink Stover at Yale,* who had been dropped by parachute to the French *maquis* and remained in Paris under David Bruce after the war. Because of his personality and his work with the *maquisard* Johnson was in tight with French counterintelligence and helped Angleton to understand pragmatic French ways. Another old X-2 comrade, Bittner Brown, who had operated double agents, and who was close to Senator Robert Taft in Ohio, proved a good friend and tutor when he came to the height of his powers during the Korean War as a consultant on military cover and deception in Japan. There was Phillip Barry, the chief of X-2 in Vienna at

---

*In 1950 Angleton received the Légion d'Honneur for his work with the French.

378   C L O A K   &   G O W N

the end of the war, also an adept at the double-agent game, who thought as Angleton did that the Soviets shortly would absorb Czechoslovakia. Friendships were formed and influences felt as most are, by being thrown together in a common assignment and by the discovery of shared views.

Information on Soviet intentions was flowing in from X-2 in Rumania, from Croatia, from returning Italian prisoners of war and, a little later, from returning German prisoners who, having been kept longer and then being released to two Germanies, obviously required the closest attention. Angleton was convinced that the Soviets were bent on European domination, and as he went again through his archival material, this time with Russian-related questions as the exclusive focus, he became aware of the breadth of Soviet intelligence activities. Moscow, it was clear, was exercising direct influence over the political process throughout eastern Europe and in Italy. As this view was held by the majority of Italian intelligence officers, who had far longer experience in operating against Soviet intelligence services, they shared with Angleton their information on Soviet cases going back well before the war.

Angleton knew that the Italian partisans, most of them Communists, had fought bravely against the Germans, but he firmly believed that they had at once shifted their loyalties to an international order and were now working for Moscow. He supported national loyalties: he was convinced that a patriot should work solely in the interests of his country, and while the partisans had done so when the enemy was Germany, they were now working against those interests. Angleton thought national loyalties were a good thing, and he rather quietly admired de Gaulle when he came to power in France, when the American line was to denigrate him for his "overweening pride" and to poke fun at the French *force frappe,* simply because de Gaulle did that which a national leader always should do: put his country first. Given this respect for the legitimacy of nationalism, Angleton could understand the aspirations of other nations and peoples while nonetheless working solely for what he believed to be the interest of the United States, as later when clashes arose in the CIA over American policy in Vietnam. International Communism ran counter to national sentiment (or was Russian nationalism clothed in the rhetoric of internationalism, a rhetoric Angleton always suspected), subverting the institutions of nations. Later he said he was slow to see how

Communism also undermined the fabric of religion. While Angleton seldom spoke of it, he was still a High Church Anglican who believed, rather in the manner of Graham Greene, in the energizing power of guilt.

It was during this time that Angleton began to develop personal ties with Jewish individuals, some of them later to prove to have been central in organizing the Jewish exodus to Palestine in face of the intense, intransigent British opposition. Jews had been persecuted in Italy as in Germany, and they were natural allies. While many were thought to be Communists, they were less likely to accept domination from Moscow than most Italian partisans were, and they were good contacts for storing up against the future.[33] In any liaison one seeks mutuality of interest, and Angleton suspected that mutuality would grow. He appreciated the stability of command that military leadership was bringing into the immediate postwar intelligence community, but he also suspected that the attitudes of West Point and of "the business" would not mix well in anticipating future variables. An intelligence link could continue to function even when diplomats and the military were genuinely angry with each other. These were all considerations as he contemplated the future, and the nature of the Soviet problem. From this time would grow his web of contacts so that, though he never asked to be given "the Israeli contract" in later years, a liaison function was thrust upon him by directors pleased to have someone with so much personal knowledge. Angleton would not actively resist the added responsibility, for his Italian experience had given him great respect for those men and women intent upon creating and defending the new state of Israel. Further, the subject of Jewish emigration, especially from the Soviet Union, was tied to his main preoccupation. Over the long run Jewish emigration from the Soviet Union would provide a valuable source of information on the Soviet system; it would also give the KGB an opportunity to put its agents into the Middle East and, via subsequent emigration from Israel to North America, into the United States.

While most of his coworkers assumed that Angleton's anti-Communism placed him politically well to the right, he had remained in touch with the Italian Communists, and he was invited to the welcoming party given for Togliatti when he returned from his exile in Moscow. Angleton had discovered that Togliatti despised Stalin, though he hid his feelings in the interest of party unity, and as Angleton knew that Italian politics were infinitely complex, he remained flexible and pragmatic in his assessment of local issues. The land of the Borgias, of Machiavelli and Dante, was not to be lumped with the Balkan states, or the Soviet Union, where cunning translated as complexity without the cultural depth that lent intellectual appeal. He was impressed by Italian professionalism and dedication, and he was quite happy that his assignment had kept him in Italy and would return him there on occasion.

Angleton's first major postwar assignment in Italy was to help make certain that when elections were held the Communists did not come into power. To do this he was to build up and support the Italian intelligence services. SSU, the Central Intelligence Group (CIG)—established in January 1946 and which that August absorbed the SSU—and from 1947 the CIA were consistent in their opposition to Marxist groups broadly and Communist parties specifically, but under the circumstances this often meant throwing support to left-liberal groups. In Italy this initially meant the Committees of National Liberation, or CLN. These onetime clandestine committees, made up during the war of republican democrats, Catholics, liberals, socialists, and Communists, had been especially effective in the industrial north. A coalition of parties derived from the CLN governed until there could be free elections, scheduled for June of 1946. The preceding June Ferruccio Parri, the Resistance leader brought back from Switzerland through Allen Dulles's mediation, had been designated prime minister, but he had been forced to resign by the right wing of the CLN, and Alcide de Gasperi, whom Angleton knew well, had succeeded him.

Angleton and others are said to have fed substantial sums of money into the June referendum; he emphatically denies this. The vote, which assured a republican form of government, demonstrated the strength of de Gasperi's Christian Democrats, while the Marxist vote was split between the Socialists, who also were said to have received American financial assistance, and the Communists. In May 1947 de Gasperi's government collapsed, however, and thereafter Italy was governed by an unstable parliamentary coalition that included de Gasperi and generally excluded the far left. Angleton was rumored to be funding the Rome *Daily American,* a rather scruffy pro-de Gasperi English-language newspaper begun in 1946, and Soviet propaganda held that Angleton had sixty journalists on his payroll, that the newspaper was owned outright by American intelligence, and that the American news reporter Claire Sterling, who was a courageous and enterprising investigative journalist with mysteriously quick access to top stories, was working for him. Certainly the *Daily American* took a line of which Angleton would have approved, and Italians of all political persuasions appeared to see the Americans as intimate participants in Italian politics. From the American perspective the entire Italian scene was fraught with instability.[34]

Shortly before the end of hostilities, it had become apparent to Angleton and to others that the intelligence situation was changing, not just with respect to the Soviet Union. Britain hoped to retain its empire and to reclaim its prewar influence, often through monarchs, in Greece and, perhaps, Yugoslavia, Albania, and Italy. France, which had not been very cooperative with American intelligence operations against Italy, had its own agenda. Italy, which had not been a belligerent since 1943, was in an ambiguous position. Diverging national political policies raised serious questions which no one at SSU appeared to be asking.

Both Britain and the United States wanted world order, stability, the predictive capacity that stability makes possible. Each thought that in making the world safe for its institutions, it would be making the world safe for democracy, would improve the welfare of uncounted millions. But Americans were quite sincere in their anticolonialism, as they understood the term, and it would not have occurred to them that in opposing the British Empire they were putting one of their own in its place. The British saw the danger quickly enough, for they were used to being top dog, were not top dog, and did not really expect again to be top dog, which meant that someone else would climb on top. If they were to lose their position as a world leader, they would prefer to lose it to the United States than to the Soviet Union, but they had no intention of losing it at all if they could prevent an erosion of their power. They thought the Americans naive at the least, guilefully intent on supplanting them in all probability, perhaps still unthinkingly unaware of the power vacuums the collapse of their and other empires would bring. Whether with intent or not, the United States would succeed John Bull, and while the moment of truth—the Suez Canal crisis of 1956—still lay ahead, Americans were quite clear that whatever else might lead to conflict with the Soviet Union, they were not going to allow themselves to be promoted into a war by Britain or support a "British Monroe Doctrine" for the Middle East. In December 1946 the British foreign secre-

tary, Ernest Bevin, realized that the United States was unlikely
to support Britain's Palestine policy, and by announcing that they
could no longer meet their commitments in Greece, to which Truman responded with his "doctrine" of March 1947, the British
assured that the United States would in fact supplant them within
their most significant informal empire.[35]

Angleton was wondering out loud whether British policy was
binding through AFHQ on all American components. This was
obviously a matter for instruction from Washington. He put the
question directly, through Murphy, and he later said that whatever ensued was in strict accordance with policy directives. Though
he was rumored to be close to Crown Prince Umberto, the man
who would be king if the monarchists prevailed, and he greatly
admired the discipline and dedication of the Italian navy, which
was strongly pro-monarchist, he acted on the instructions he received. From his actions these clearly were to be supportive of
centrist, democratic, and, as necessary, non-Communist socialist
groups, and to place distance between popular perceptions of likely
British policy and American policy. He began working more closely
with the Italian intelligence community, which had been regroup-
ing since 1943, and Anglo-American coordination began to dry up.
As Allen Dulles reported Robert Lansing, Woodrow Wilson's second secretary of state in World War I, as saying, "It isn't a lie to
withhold information from a person to whom it is not entitled."
Entitlements had changed. Italy, however, had no entitlements
quite yet, as it would not be dealt with as a sovereign state until
the peace treaty had been signed and ratified. This would not be
until July of 1947.

By 1947 Europe was clearly divided between East and West;
Soviet intentions and strengths were plain; George Kennan, perhaps the country's leading specialist on the Soviet Union, had
concluded in July of 1946 that there was nothing the United States
could do to challenge the Russians in Eastern Europe. "There is
no real action we can take there," he said, "except to state our
case." There were those in Washington who thought otherwise,
however: perhaps one could foment rebellion in the new satellite
states, before the Soviet indoctrination program had its full effect
on another generation; perhaps something could be done through
psychological warfare; certainly the Russians must not be allowed
to extend their dominance to Italy. Something covert was called
for, since few wished to take on the Soviet army, thoroughly in

control and of formidable size, while the Allied armies had been substantially depleted. From Harvard William Langer, whose reputation stood high because of the wartime successes of R&A, strongly argued for covert measures; from Yale several faculty members, including Samuel Flagg Bemis, did the same more cautiously. Perhaps by the end of 1946, certainly by the end of 1947, the necessity for clandestine operations was an accepted premise throughout the intelligence community.[36]

But who would run covert operations? The secretary of state, George C. Marshall, refused, since he believed most such operations ultimately became known and would compromise foreign policy. Still, he thought covert operations, if housed elsewhere, to be necessary, especially as the Italian elections, scheduled for April 1948, looked as though they might yet bring the Communists into power, or at least to a strong bargaining position. In the meantime Allen Dulles, once again a Wall Street lawyer, had been raising funds privately to assist the centrist parties in Italy. Perhaps something might be done covertly on a large scale by the U.S. government? Might not the new Central Intelligence Agency, created by the National Security Act of July 1947, take this on? On December 19 the National Security Council, by its directive NSC 4/A, ordered the director of Central Intelligence, Admiral Roscoe Hillenkoetter, to do what he could, including the use of covert activities, to prevent a Communist victory. Though the CIA's general counsel, Lawrence Houston, advised Hillenkoetter that the CIA did not have authority for covert actions, Hillenkoetter assigned the Italian puzzle to the Office of Special Operations, which had inherited nearly a thousand former OSS types from the defunct SSU and transitional CIG. The OSO promptly established a Special Procedures Group, or SPG, and on December 22 it began to shape its plans. CIA analysts were convinced that the Italian Communists would attempt a general strike, possibly even an armed insurrection, before the election. Obviously this must be forestalled, and the elections would have to be influenced.

In the meantime Angleton had returned to Washington in November of 1947 to be a special assistant to Colonel Donald H. Galloway, who had succeeded Quinn as head of the clandestine service, now a major part of OSO. Galloway and others were creating a Soviet Division in which maximum efforts would be made to pull together and correlate all hard information relating to Soviet intelligence. (Previously work on the Soviet Union had

been divided among several divisions.) Much of Angleton's attention was given over to this activity in 1948–49. He wanted to create handbooks on the Soviet Union as he had done in Italy, in
order to override the compartmentalization of the CIA divisions,
and this required lengthy meetings with division heads. At the end
of the European war X-2 had sent to Washington many valuable
captured documents on the Soviets (together with a great deal of
junk), and these needed sorting and evaluation, a task that William Hood took on in a crash program over several weekends.
The first chief of the division, Harry Rositzke, whose experience
had been largely in Germany, insisted that CIA records contained
little of use, and perhaps Angleton saw this as an opportunity to
demonstrate yet again the value and urgency of an archive. Rositzke also wanted only in-house work, with no outside academics,
while Angleton—and in this he had much support—hoped to reach
out to the academic community. Money was made available to
fund Russian language training in several universities and to build
up a cadre of Soviet specialists. By the time Galloway's successor
would take over, the Soviet Division was a going concern.

Angleton was still involved in Italian affairs, of course, both
because of the depth of his knowledge and experience, and because his initial approach to Soviet matters was through an Italian
window. According to the revelations of the 1970s, when a combination of a series of leaks, exposés in the press, congressional
investigations, and unprecedented candor by the then-director of
Central Intelligence, William Colby, had made public a number of
the agency's "family jewels," the CIA was putting nearly $10 mil-
lion a year into Italy to influence elections at the local level, for
campaign expenses, the financing of splinter groups that might divide the Communists, straightforward bribes, and anti-Communist
propaganda. In 1974 one of the "whistle blowers," Victor Marchetti, set the figure even higher, at $30 million a year, or maybe
more.[37]

The greater American efforts were almost certainly the overt
ones, however. Wheat and food goods were sent into Italy to help
alleviate shortages; Truman made it known that he would withhold aid from any Italian government that included Communists;
Italian-Americans were organized to write anguished (and sometimes subsidized) letters to friends and relatives in Italy, telling
them how they should vote; the American embassy exhorted and
courted the middle class. Some policy makers, including Kennan,
contemplated military intervention if the Communists won, and

new weapons and supplies were hurried to the Italian army with the obvious hint that, should the Communists achieve a government, a military coup was called for.

Angleton's role in the 1948 Italian election is, of course, not clear. Later some commentators would declare that the election was bought by the Americans and would credit, or discredit, this largely to Angleton. Certainly this is a gross exaggeration. The election was in good measure determined by events in Czechoslovakia, where only two months before a minority Communist party had seized power and installed a People's Democracy by coup d'etat. While the more sophisticated in the Italian electorate knew that the Italian Communists could not count on the support of the Red Army, and that any attempt to seize power by violent means would most likely bring on military intervention by the Western powers, this was only one step removed from a worst-case scenario, since no one wanted to be occupied again. The quite open promise of future Marshall Plan aid for Italy, and a well-timed early March Anglo-Franco-American declaration on Trieste, to the effect that because they had been unable to choose a governor for the Free Territory they would favor returning the city to Italian sovereignty, were also more important than any American covert measures.

Angleton's contacts were called upon to provide a close estimate of how the election was likely to run. The American ambassador, James Clement Dunn, who as an assistant secretary of state had been brought in on the efforts to evaluate the Vessel materials, asked for the best possible estimate on comparative party strengths. With Raymond Rocca as his liaison in Italy,* Angleton

---

*Rocca, from San Francisco, had gone to the University of California at Berkeley, where he completed course work for the doctorate, his M.A. having been on Fascist Italy. He went into the analytical section of the Foreign Broadcast Intelligence Service, where he learned content analysis. In 1943 he moved to the OSS, first in SI and then, early in 1944, to X-2 in Rome under Andrew Berding. When Angleton arrived in August to take over, Rocca became his executive officer and remained with him until Angleton returned to the States in 1947. Rocca stayed in Italy under open cover, as though writing his doctoral dissertation, and worked on the 1948 elections. He was Angleton's liaison with the Italian service until his own return to Washington in the summer of 1953. After a year at the War College he took over research and analysis for CI, developing case books and case files to help those in operations. Rocca knew Russian and Italian, and, with Thomas Hall, a historian from the University of Chicago, he developed the Russian side for CI. He became deputy chief of CI under Angleton and resigned when Angleton did. Rocca was the CIA liaison with the Warren Commission during the investigation into the assassination of John F. Kennedy.

put out feelers and reported that the race would be very close. This was scarcely encouraging. Angleton then turned to his friends in the Ministry of Interior. The ministry replied that it was best to say that the election was too close to call. Such inconclusive reports may have redoubled the American overt effort and may have contributed to the remarkable voter turnout, for 92 percent of eligible registered voters went to the polls. On the eve of the election the ministry gave Angleton a figure: those favoring the republic, as opposed to monarchist or Communist voters, would win by a majority of 57 percent. When this turned out to be al-most precisely right—the three centrist republican parties took 58 percent of the vote, and of this the Christian Democrats, with 48 percent, comprised by far the greatest bloc—Angleton's faith in the competency of the Italian Ministry of Interior was renewed, and his contacts and methods were further validated.

Angleton was believed to have done more than simply obtain readings on the forthcoming election which, if carefully orches-trated, may have marginally increased the voter turnout. Cer-tainly there was a moment when he contributed at least one concrete measure that may have influenced the election: at his suggestion Rocca called in the Scattolini card. Both the Ameri-cans and the Russians had undoubtedly financed pamphlets, post-ers, and plants in newspapers to warn the Italians of what it would mean if the Communists, or the capitalist imperialists, won the election. Quite possibly the Americans worked closely with the Vatican, which had an obvious interest in seeing the Communists defeated, and at times provided money for a splinter Communist group that would weaken the central party. But only the dénoue-ment of the Scattolini story seems clearly documented.

Early in 1948 Scattolini was believed to have published a two-volume collection of *Documenti segreti della diplomazia vati-cana,*[38] which purported to reveal how the church had intrigued against world peace during the war. In fact Scattolini appears not to have been responsible for this unwise compilation of his and other fabrications, but the product of his wartime paper mill now came back to haunt him, and whether responsible or not, he may as well have been. (Because this was an opportune time to bring Scattolini out of the closet, there were those who thought the CIA might have published the documents in order to force a timely public revelation.) Communist posters appeared on every wall, declaring that "The Front [that is, the Popular Democratic Front, a union of Communists and far-left Socialists] will win." Two CIA officials flew to Rome with the long-held evidence that Scattolini was a fraud, and he was quickly brought to trial under an obscure Italian law that prohibited hostile acts against foreign countries— in this case the Vatican—confessed, was found guilty, and was sentenced to seven months in jail. Raymond Rocca, still in Italy, had the Popular Front posters plastered over with great six-foot posters of his own broadcasting Scattolini's confession, which was strongly anti-Communist in implication. Whether the posters truly influenced the election or not, they were a superb example of timing and, even more, of the use of an asset buried for three years. When Scattolini emerged from jail, a bit short of his seven-month sentence, he quietly disappeared, the election long over.

The CIA was pleased with the result of the 1948 election. The Communist threat at the polls was turned back, the Christian Democrats won handsomely, gaining a majority of both deputies and senators, and Luigi Einaudi became president of the republic. Covert actions seemed to have proven their worth in France and Greece as well. In June an Office of Policy Coordination was created to run secret operations, and Frank Wisner was put in charge.

Though in the CIA, the Office of Policy Coordination was not precisely of the CIA. Established by the National Security Council, it was to remain as independent of the CIA as possible since it was under the policy direction of the Departments of Defense (as the War Department had become) and State, though the chain of command was through the DCI. Thus two clandestine organizations, OPC and OSO, were at work within the same foreign countries and responding to separate chains of command, a potentially disastrous situation. The OPC under Frank Wisner was activist and, in the view of OSO, now directed by Major General Willard G. Wyman, aggressively competing for the same potential agents. In practice the DCI had little control over OPC, which reported directly through the NSC to the secretary of state—it was, in effect, simply in the CIA for board and room. In the meantime a presidential commission under former President Herbert Hoover had set a task force onto the problem of national security organization; a separate National Intelligence Survey Group, headed by Allen Dulles, made its own report directly to the NSC. By now it was quite evident to Truman that he was receiving conflicting advice, that American intelligence did not have its act together, and that he may even have made a mistake in abolishing the OSS so quickly. As he would write to *The New York Times*'s Arthur Krock a little later—in a letter not sent—the United States was "no longer in the gay nineties"; "no nation," he said, "has had our responsibility."[39] The press and the people could not expect to know all things. An obvious lack of coordination could lead to leaks, blown (and thus public) operations, and low morale.

The NSC directed that OSO and OPC be merged. When General Walter Bedell Smith became DCI in October 1950, he insisted that all orders to OPC henceforth come through him. Complete integration of OSO and OPC was ordered in July 1952, though some overseas stations still reported directly to the DCI rather than up the chain of command until 1954. Wisner became the deputy director for plans, and the joint organization over which Wisner presided was redesignated the Clandestine Services. Angleton was in OSO throughout and somewhat removed from these bureaucratic shifts.

It was during the time over which these organizational changes occurred that the American intelligence community began to fear they were not as fully in control of the situation as they had thought. In September 1949 a patrolling B-29 over the north Pacific detected the Russians' detonation of their first atomic device. The outbreak of war in Korea and confirmation that the Soviet Union had the atomic bomb led to a distinct change in CIA estimates. In July 1950 the agency predicted that the USSR would be capable of a general war by 1952, having recovered from the slaughter of the European war more rapidly than expected. CIA anti-Communist operations were intensified in various quarters, including France and Italy. In the spring of 1952 the Christian Democratic vote in Italy fell in a number of important city elections to just under 36 percent. Many moderate Italians felt that de Gasperi had been hewing too closely to the American line, and when the new American ambassador, Clare Booth Luce, wife of the influential publisher of *Time* magazine, implied publicly that Italians would face unpleasant consequences if they voted too far to either the left or right, both monarchists and Communists were able to document their charges of American interference. In the national election of June 1953 the Christian Democrats polled 40 percent, and even in coalition with other centrist parties fell just short of a majority, while the Communists won 37 percent of the electorate. The period when the CIA had felt comfortably on top had ended.

On November 3, Ambassador Luce asked for vigorous covert action in Italy. Otherwise, she predicted, Italy would have a Communist government within two years. Some overt decision must be made over Trieste, which was still festering, and American markets must be opened to Italian trade—both were done, Trieste passing to the Italians—while an expensive covert operation must be mounted over a sustained period, perhaps for five years.

A rising former OSS member, William E. Colby, who had shown considerable courage when parachuted behind enemy lines in Norway during the war, and sound organizing skills in Stockholm afterward, was sent to Rome to run the CI operation under a shrewd station chief, Gerry Miller. Colby was a Roman Catholic, and he cultivated his own ties to the Vatican. Put in charge of the largest covert political operation to date—over $25 million a year was committed to the Italian show—Colby believed he began with a different assumption than Angleton, whom he did not name in his memoirs, even though many readers felt it was obvious of whom he wrote: he wanted to be *"for* a democratic Italy, not just *against* a Communist one."* He felt his predecessors considered counterintelligence to be methodologically negative: it was to prevent occurrences, not to make others happen; to prevent penetration, to prevent a Communist victory, to assume a defector was false until proven otherwise, to begin with the premise that all told lies and for a reason. He also believed that the anti-Communism of the Christian Democrats simply postponed important reforms that were needed if Communism were not to be a recurrent problem in Italy. Of a more benign disposition than Angleton, Colby was delighted with the pleasures of Rome in the time of the *dolce vita;* Angleton had seen the sweet life as simply another expression of the mud slide of decadence that was enveloping postwar Europe, a decadence from which the tightly organized and highly disciplined Soviets might take many victories. Different personalities, holding different perceptions of the best means to an end, these two men were agreed only on the goal: the reorganized Partito Communista Italiano, or PCI, must not win an election in Italy, which was a NATO member country.

Moscow was pumping up to $50 million a year into the PCI, and given the close relationship between party and government in a Communist state, this was natural and easy. The United States ought not do the same, Colby thought, while Angleton was rather more inclined to fight fire with fire, especially if done early enough.

He believed in supporting any duly elected government, but he did not oppose attempts before the event to assure an electoral outcome favorable to the West. Communist organizations—of women, youth, farmers, labor, veterans, artists, academics—had been set up as fronts. Should not the Italian centrists, with CIA help, follow? Ambassador Luce, to whom Allen Dulles was close, thought so, and CIA money soon was flowing to the parties, to cultural, youth, and civic groups, and to the trade union movement.

Colby and Angleton differed on matters of day-to-day operations as well. Colby considered posters were too expensive and that they were distasteful. He felt that the planted rumor in magazine or newspaper was generally ineffective and made an editor dependent to the point that the paper might as well be purchased: a bottomless pit of expenditure. In any event, anti-American statements blocked by CIA money from one paper would certainly appear in another. As he admitted later, by "bureaucratic foot-dragging" Colby managed to divert the money for this kind of activity to "more productive channels." Then when, in 1955, Pietro Nenni, the leader of the Socialist party, began a slow separation from the Communists, Colby was inclined to be supportive of those among the Christian Democrats who thought it wise to inch toward the "opening to the left," while Angleton thought the whole thing most likely a feint. Even if it were not a feint, the Social Democrats might, if they embraced Nenni's party, lose their own right wing and be no better off. In any case, de Gasperi was the duly elected prime minister, and the United States ought not to fiddle with a very delicate but still democratic system. Angleton felt any support for the opening to the left was bad policy and told the DCI, Allen Dulles, so. The debate over the *apertura a sinistra* was fully aired in the agency. In the event, it was the twentieth congress of the Communist party of the Soviet Union, Krushchev's denunciation of Stalin, and the Hungarian insurrection, and not the opinions of CIA bureaucrats, that determined the nature and pace of any party *rapprochement*.

By now there were beginning to be sharp divisions within the intelligence community; indeed, there were many who thought it was no longer a community at all, but far more simply a business. Certainly it was not the Great Game of the world wars. Allied intelligence forces may have squabbled, and at times even undermined each other, but they were clearly focused on Nazi Germany as a common enemy and generally had a common, if not always shared, approach to that enemy. There was no such agreement on how to deal with the Soviet Union, or even necessarily that the Soviet Union was the principal enemy. Much was permitted in war that was questionable in a period when those wars that were fought were all undeclared. There was also an element of fear in the air: few had doubted that in time Hitler would be destroyed, but except for those very few who believed that the Russian bear was a teddy, there was agreement that victory was by no means certain and if achieved would be long in coming. Angleton believed that a state of affairs that many coworkers preferred to view as abnormal and transient was here to stay, at least for his lifetime.

The British and Italians were particularly unhappy over the spread in Europe and, even more for the British, in Asia of anti-Communist front groups supported with CIA funds. The World Assembly of Youth, the Congress for Cultural Freedom, the International Student Conference, the International Confederation of Free Trade Unions, the Asia Foundation—these seemed unwise ventures to many Europeans and, to the extent that it was known at home that the CIA had a hand in them, unwise to some American policy makers. In time, they feared, it would become known that groups like this were covert operations, and they would poison receptivity for groups that were not. As young members of President John F. Kennedy's Peace Corps were to discover, this was true.[40]

Angleton's view was consistent and simple: he felt that pro-Americans ought to prevail, and that they should be helped to do so. Perhaps with echoes from the old OSS Labor Desk in his ears, he defended, in particular, the International Confederation of Free Trade Unions and the work of David Dubinsky of the International Ladies Garment Workers' Union. The hard-core Communist parties would survive, he knew, but surely there was an obligation to counter the World Federation of Trade Unions, which he viewed as controlled from Moscow, as it proved to be. One might not roll back the Red Army, but the ICFTU could roll back Soviet penetration of the world labor movement. Its strict by-laws, which prohibited sending fraternal delegations to any country which did not grant workers the right to strike and the right of assembly, were overt and set an important example. Angleton did not consider the ICFTU was being manipulated by the CIA; its ideas coincided with the interests of American policy. He reminded critics that one of the founding fathers of the American Federation of Labor, Samuel Gompers, had said that American labor must not be satisfied with workers' rights in the United States until the trade union movement showed equal concern for workers' rights abroad. He did not tire of pointing out to the dubious that well before the CIA existed, the A. F. of L. had broken the back of the Communist trade unions in Mexico in the 1930s. The battle was continuing, he said, and would continue well into the future, in the European trade unions. Such views, if known, would not have endeared him to the labor rank and file in the European parties, if for no other reason than the fact that they appeared to justify American interference in party matters in Scotland, or Lyons, or Venice.

Colby apparently differed on the question of labor as well, and though there was as yet no hostility between the two men, the differences of opinion were so clear, there are those who, in the hindsight of the events of the mid-1970s, claim that they had seen the handwriting on the wall.[41] Surely Colby was annoyed to discover that CI was running a "singleton" in Italy, a man who was operating alone rather than through a chain. As Angleton might have replied, this was an acceptable practice, for there were agents who had special authorization for specific tasks and who reported directly to Allen Dulles, usually orally. Colby complained of more systematic use of a singleton, who was believed to be sending written reports in raw form to top policy officials, and he insisted that these reports be circulated more widely, to CIA officers in the Rome station, and eventually to the analytical staffs in Washington, for possible in-house debate and clarification. CI could not expose what it knew to such a range of possible leaks; Colby clearly had quite different views than Angleton of the role of counterintelligence. Colby, it was clear, did not think CI was the queen of the board.*

The long-awaited elections of May 1958 went favorably for the Christian Democrats, and both Colby and Angleton professed to be pleased, convinced that their respective methods had been helpful to the victory, though a major and simultaneous crisis in

---

*In the 1960s Angleton did have three agents in the Italian government whom he had recruited soon after the war, so it is not unreasonable to assume that he had his own men earlier. One was said to be in the Ministry of Interior, another in the *carabinieri,* the third, and most important, in the Ministry of Foreign Affairs. Many doubt this.[42]

France, which brought General de Gaulle to power, almost certainly had greater influence. The CIA, the American government, perhaps even the American taxpayer were happy, for American policy—of which the public saw only the overt manifestations, of course—appeared to have helped materially with the emergence of a stable Europe. The Communist threat had been turned back in Italy, Greece, France; some of the nations were linked with the United States in an alliance that made them, if not client states, at the least compliant. The CIA did not assume that the United States had saved Western Europe from Communism: if saved at all, the principal credit had to go to the Europeans themselves, even if Marshall Aid and clandestine action had played an important role. Attention was, in any case, turning toward Asia, where the situation in French Indo-China was beginning to look dangerous. No one spoke any longer of rolling back the iron curtain, and relations between East and West appeared to have settled into a predictable pattern once again.*

Not all of the operations in which Angleton was engaged were successful, of course. Yet, even where matters went desperately awry, he managed to come out personally unscathed. A particular disaster was sandwiched between the Italian triumphs of 1947–48 and 1953–58; this was the Albanian operation.

In the last months of the war British and American intelligence units in Italy had begun to pay close attention to Albania, not so much for itself—though there were many in Britain who hoped to see the Albanian king, Zog, who was living in exile there, restored

---

*Angleton has not been forgotten in Italy and recurs over and over in the popular press as an *éminence grise*. In 1962 *La Stampa* "revealed" that he was working with the Sixth Fleet to overthrow the government. This canard was repeated in 1972, while the Fascist journals praised him for not "revealing" the names of his coconspirators. His name cropped up in dozens of frantic, and some serious, Italian books on the CIA and the KGB—Italy and India appear to be the two nations most obsessed with the CIA, at least at the level of popular culture— and he was rumored to be working with the monarchists, the church, big business, the Order of Malta, the military, the neo-right (or, for devious reasons of his own, with the Communists and with academics). In 1983, at the time of the publication in *Der Stern* of the alleged Hitler diaries, he was in Italy on a private visit and was confronted by a reporter from the news magazine who obviously thought he was involved with the diaries. "Why are you in Rome?" the newsman asked. "To get a plate of spaghetti," Angleton replied. The reporter apparently thought he had just heard a new euphemism for the tangled trail all those versed in the wonders of CI must follow. In 1984 a casual browse through a bookshop in Milan produced no fewer than a dozen popular books in which Angleton's name was mentioned.

to the throne—as for its strategic relationship to Yugoslavia and Greece. Bari, which had been the center for Fascist propaganda directed to the Middle East, had become the Allied headquarters for their own propaganda broadcasts. BBC bulletins were rebroadcast through Bari Radio and were aimed, for a time, most specifically at Albania. In London files had been maintained on the Albanian underground movement, as well as on the Society of Friends of Albania—a pro-Zog group—and the more liberal Anglo-Albanian Association. From early 1944 it was evident to anyone with even limited access to these files that something was intended for Albania.

Bari had become an SOE base; it also drew in several OSS agents from Istanbul and Cairo, and was, until early 1945, the focus of OSS activities for southeastern Europe. A grubby town, with a facade of modernity created by some cheaply built new buildings, Bari was not regarded as a good billet. There was opera, to be sure, but there were also cobbled streets that were noisy from sunrise to dark with the passage of country carts, open sewers, and an especially gungy market. (In April 1945 the harbor was devastated by the explosion of the SS *Henderson,* an American Liberty Ship, and eighty-two dockworkers, six children playing near the dock, and several of the crew were killed.) To this posting had come eight members of the Yale class of 1941, with others assigned to cover the Yugoslavian-Albanian front. Informants brought material out of Albania to revise R&A's "Who's Who of Albanian Guerrillas," initially prepared in December 1943.[43]

Though plans were made to send Albanians into the northern part of the country to stir up the partisans, Yugoslavia was of far greater concern. There Tito and Mihajlovic represented two potentially viable forces of the left and right, and the prospect of civil war, as well as the stakes *vis-à-vis* the Soviet Union, were regarded as much higher. The OSS concluded that there were about fifty-five different guerrilla groups operating in Albania, under about a hundred identifiable leaders. These groups were optimistically thought to control perhaps 36,000 partisans; no one really knew for sure. Both the British and the Americans judged that the Balli Kömbetar, an anti-Communist group that had managed to hold together both nationalists and mild Zoggists, was likely to be the best bet for support. The situation was made more complex by Yugoslav ambitions in northern Albania and Greek-Macedonian desires in the south, and by the fact that politics tended to divide on ethnic lines, the Balli Kömbetar being based largely in the Gheg-dominated north and the Livisiya Nacional Clirimtare, or national liberation movement, largely Communist and largely Tosk, in the south. In April 1943 an SOE mission had established contact with the LNC and later with the BK, supporting both, and in April 1944 a third SOE mission—a second had ended in disaster in January—tried to reconcile differences between the two groups. In September the Germans had withdrawn from Albania in the face of the Russian advance across eastern Europe, and the LNC had emerged as the dominant partisan group. Then, early in 1945, a few teams were parachuted into Albania to make contact with splinter groups; most simply disappeared, though some made their way to Yugoslavia to report on the confused situation.

The triumph of Tito, and the growing chill between his independent Communist line and the imperialism of the Soviet Union, meant that Albania might provide the only Soviet access to the Adriatic. Attention turned again to those old lists of guerrilla contacts, and an operation was prepared in the hope of toppling Enver Hoxha, whose provisional—and now clearly Communist—government had been established in Tiranë at the end of November 1944. Hoxha had cleared out the middle class, and anyone he thought likely to oppose him, in a series of show trials of "major war criminals," and in December 1945 he had validated himself in a general election. The monarchy was abolished and a people's republic declared, along Soviet lines, in January 1946.

Albanian relations with the West rapidly deteriorated. Yugoslavia claimed Kosovo-Metohija. Small uprisings against the Hoxha government were blamed on the Western powers. The United States Senate, hardly knowing what the issues were but happy to do something for the Graeco-American vote, passed a resolution favoring the cession of northern Epirus—that is, southern Albania—to Greece. By the end of 1946 both Britain and the United States had withdrawn their diplomatic missions from Tiranë. Albania declared the Corfu Channel closed to international shipping, and in a test, the British sent four destroyers into the strait, where two struck mines with heavy casualties. The Albanians insisted that the mines had been left from the German occupation while the British contended that Albania had mined what His Majesty's Government insisted was an international passage. (In April 1949 the International Court of Justice at The Hague found Albania guilty and ordered that compensation be paid to Britain.) Albania drew into its mountainous valleys and clearly wanted nothing to do with the West. As the split between Tito and Stalin became more evident, and as Yugoslavia put ever greater pressure on Albania, Hoxha began to eliminate the pro-Yugoslav elements in the Albanian Communist party, cutting it even further off from all save Soviet contact.

By now Britain and the United States had again focused on Albania. Hoxha was a thorn in Tito's side, and Yugoslavia might take a benign view of efforts to unseat Hoxha. The Russians were a very present danger, having begun to construct a major submarine base on the island of Saseno, thus to gain access to the Adriatic. Food was scarce, and the Albanian people were thought to be discontented, both with their hardships and with the continued purging of the Albanian Communist party. Skirmishing on the Greek-Albanian border suggested instability on which the West might capitalize, while an effective anti-Communist band of guerrillas was said to be roaming the north. Interests in British and American intelligence converged: now was a moment to attempt to unseat Hoxha.

Sir Stewart Menzies, the venerable "C" of MI6, may have been reluctant to put men at risk for such an operation, but his advisers thought the time was right to give Tito some indirect help. Angleton was not consulted, for this was an OPC operation, but privately he thought any operation into Albania was a bad idea, since he clung to the belief that Tito was not to be trusted and that the desertion of Mihajlovic had been "unforgivable"; further, his few agents-in-place ought not to be put at risk for an operation that, he judged, had small chance of success, as they would be of greater value later. Robert Joyce, liaison at the Department of State, shared Angleton's view. On the other hand Frank Wisner strongly favored quick action. A successful operation could further validate OPC and counterintelligence operations generally, might elevate him in the gentlemanly power struggle that had already begun in the American intelligence community, and should bring down Hoxha. Early in 1949 he concluded that it was not too late for a counterrevolution in Albania, which might in turn strike a spark in other eastern European countries.

Accordingly, a mission was put in train. SIS and OPC set up a joint training camp near Mdina in Malta. Wisner's colleagues in OPC were gung-ho on the operation. Wisner chose first Robert Low, and soon after Michael Burke, ex-baseball star from the

University of Pennsylvania, OSS operative during the war, who had been working as a film executive for Warner Brothers in the interim, to join with David Smiley, an SOE man with considerable Balkan experience—he had been with the SOE team in 1943—to train a group of thirty Albanian dissidents in *parachutage* and small boat handling. Two Americans, Low and Robert Miner, who had continued to hone his Balkan expertise and was soon to be chargé in Athens, went to King Zog, then living in exile in Egypt, to tell him in general terms of intended actions. The target date was the end of November 1949, when a succession of moonless nights would provide cover for sending teams in. The goal was an Albanian national uprising.

Even more, Wisner hoped that the Albanian operation would be "a clinical experiment" in rolling back Communism in Eastern Europe. In the end the momentum of the operation, the eagerness of the Albanian exiles to return to their country, and the enthusiasm of Wisner and SOE overrode those who urged caution. Control of the operation fell to a Special Policy Committee in Washington, comprised of the reluctant Joyce for the Department of State, Frank Lindsay for OPC, Earl Jellicoe of the British embassy for the Foreign Office, and Kim Philby for SIS.

The first operation was almost entirely British, there being only one Albanian-American, assigned in part as an interpreter to the training group, involved. On October 3, nine men were put ashore on the Karaburun Peninsula and broke up into two groups. They accomplished nothing: after a long silence, four survivors made their way out of Albania to report that there was little prospect of a mass rising to judge from the villages they had visited. Three of their number had been killed, one captured, and one had simply disappeared. No one appears to have been suspicious about the fact that Albanian authorities, though apparently not aware of precise timing or landing sites, would seem to have known that some operation was expected, since villages in the general landing area had been alerted to be on the lookout for strangers. SOE and OPC decided to go ahead with the larger mission, to train Italian- and Albanian-speaking Americans as well as more "pixies" (as they called the Albanians), to be dropped into northern Albania.

The next Albanian operation was to become primarily an American venture. A U.S. foreign service officer, James McCargar, had been loaned to OPC in October 1948 and was assigned to the Albanian initiative. Despite Karaburun, joint chief for SIS was Kim

Philby. They agreed that security at the Mdina training center had not been tight enough, and that the voluble Albanian community in Rome, from whom the men dropped on Karaburun had been recruited, was a probable source of leaks. Angleton, who was providing routine counterintelligence backup at the time, also attributed the apparent leaks to the Albanians in Rome, since he took it as an article of faith that the KGB had infiltrated all anti-Communist eastern European émigré groups. Further, Angleton had been told of the actual launching of the mission by one of his own Italian contacts, who had used telescopes from the top of a lighthouse in Otranto harbor to observe the departure of the *Stormie Seas,* on which the Albanians had been taken across the Adriatic. He told McCargar—rather gleefully, McCargar thought—the precise details of the sailing, in part to show him how insecure the operation had been and perhaps also to make the point that what Angleton knew Hoxha could have known. Given two quite possible explanations for the leaks, no one apparently found it plausible to adduce yet another source.

Accordingly, OPC redoubled its plan to destabilize Hoxha's regime. Obviously something larger than the pathetic landing on the Karaburun Peninsula was needed. In due course Company 4000 was created, a unit of two hundred and fifty Albanian refugees, largely royalist or Balli Kömbetar in make-up, with American commanders, to be trained in a special school outside Heidelberg. While the Malta trainees had been told where they were going and had been allowed to mix freely in nearby Maltese towns, this group was kept in the dark and was sequestered. In September 1950 the first unit was put into Albania overland, from Greece, and in November they returned, quite without success, even the propaganda leaflets that were to have been dropped to them having fallen on the wrong town. Another unit put ashore by boat was equally unsuccessful. There were many who thought the mission, all too tiny and so badly handled, ought to be abandoned. In April 1950 Wisner appointed McCargar head of the new OPC mission to be set up in Vienna, and he dropped from the picture. (In the event, McCargar did not go to Vienna and returned to the foreign service.)

Wisner wanted to continue, and he appointed a new commander for the project, Gratian Yatsevich, who had extensive Yugoslavian though no Albanian experience. Philby was still the British cocommander, though by now the operation was almost wholly American. OPC decided to target known Zoggist groups and to drop the Albanians by air, since the best landing sites would be in the Martanesh plain, far from Greece or from the sea. Polish crews flying DC3s were used to carry the men in, flying over the border at fifty feet, at the last moment climbing to eight hundred feet to make the drop. The first attempt failed, as the Polish crew could not find the drop zone. A second attempt a week later went badly, for again the drop zone could not be found, but the nine Albanians went anyway, their supplies landing in a village so that they could not retrieve them. They quickly discovered that they were expected and only two escaped, to be imprisoned in Yugoslavia.

One might have thought OPC would have abandoned so unproductive a mission. However, the situation had changed: the Korean War had broken out, and Wisner apparently felt the need for some dramatic coup in the Soviet Union's backyard. One might also have thought that those responsible for the mission would have concluded that it was being systematically compromised. It is on this point that the journalistic accounts create a fallacy. Most say that the Albanians dropped right into the waiting hands of Enver Hoxha's security police, and that it was clear the police had pinpoint information on drop zones and timings. But frequently the drops did not take place where they were meant to, so any information relayed by someone inside the operation would have been wrong. Further, as with the disastrous drop that required two flights, followed by a supply drop well away from the men and almost square on a village, the drops themselves rather visibly could have alerted authorities. It was easy to conclude that the drops were being detected simply because they were badly performed.

OPC began to throw money at the operation, hoping against hope for some success; and the Albanians continued to be sent from Greek airfields into the cold spring darkness of 1951 and into silence. In all, sixty were air dropped, and not a word was heard back from the drop zones, even though the plane crews sometimes lingered dangerously hoping to pick up a signal. Weeks later one or two men would find their way to Greece, to report that they had quickly run into searching security agents, the odd escape attributable to luck. Seldom has an intelligence operation proceeded so resolutely from one disaster to another. Surely the mission could not have succeeded even had it been well planned, for the situation in Albania was not as those who had promoted the mission believed. But slowly it was becoming apparent that the Hoxha government might well have systematic knowledge of the mission, for too often, when a drop went well, there were security forces nearby. Often the Albanians were tracked down and killed. Under interrogation some provided details on their contacts in Albania, or revealed relatives who might be taken as hostage or killed as a demonstration to Albanian dissidents. Up to two hundred agents had been lost; and counting Albanians killed for the appearance of being implicated, the death toll may have been as high as a thousand.[44]

Any slim chance of success had been destroyed by the systematic betrayal of the mission. Unknown at the time was the fact that Kim Philby—he of the name taken from Kipling's book on the Great Game—was working for the Russians. In the same month that the first infiltration team was landed in Albania, Philby was assigned by SIS to Washington as liaison with the FBI and the CIA. He was on the Special Policy Committee, and he worked directly with the American mission commanders. Even before he left England, Philby had been briefed on plans for Albania and had, he admitted later, passed all that he knew on to the Soviet Union. In his memoirs Philby implied that Wisner's self-importance, the general lack of attention to detail by the OPC, and a misplaced optimism about Albanian readiness for revolt, together with a disregard for the Albanian agents who were being sent in as though they were "just down from the trees," were at least as important in accounting for the disaster as any treachery on his part. As one reads the sorry account one is inclined to agree with him.*[45]

Still, the Albanian fiasco redounded to Angleton's credit. When asked, he had supplied intelligence on it; everything OPC had re-

---

*Rumors about leaks are one matter, a security lapse is another, and no one appears to have thought of the possibility of betrayal. Nor may the Albanian operation have been so systematically betrayed by Philby as suggested by recent commentaries. He may have known little about the original Karaburun landings. As to the drops after Philby became joint chief of SIS, he may have been lying when he later claimed that he had given the entire operation away. The American in charge of operations, Yatsevich, says he never gave Philby details. Philby may have been boasting, or may have been covering up for the person who did, in fact, betray the mission. Anything is possible, since Philby's memoir is a well-calculated document that gives nothing away without purpose. Certainly Lord Bethell seems too ready to accept Philby's unqualified and solitary guilt to leave readers of his book entirely comfortable.

quested it got. He had also opposed the operation from the outset. At the cost of the loss of his assets in Albania, he strengthened substantially his reputation for good judgment. Much later, when a disgruntled colleague concluded that Angleton had been a Soviet mole inside American intelligence, the Albanian operation was built into the list of charges, since so astute a counterintelligence mind apparently had expressed no doubts about Philby's loyalties. Weak reeds, these, for most people who worked with Philby at the time, such as Jellicoe and McCargar, were by their own admission completely taken in by him, and depending on the outcome, which Angleton could not have controlled, the Albanian operation might have been a personal black mark. His methodology of doubt had served him well enough once again, and no more elaborate explanation is needed, though more can always be woven.

If one may not accept simplicity, there is some evidence for the argument that Angleton was playing a deeper game with Philby. Sir John C. Masterman tells us that he had been warned against Philby in the long-ago days of the Twenty Committee, when both his chiefs, Sir David Petrie and Guy Liddell, had suggested that Philby be treated with caution. Masterman had passed this advice on to Pearson, or so he recalled in 1975. There may also have been the warning that Donald Downes said he had been given by Pearson and had passed on to General Donovan, though no one knew of this, and quite possibly it simply never happened. Philby suspected that he and Angleton were mutually using each other, and this was entirely possible, since both rather enjoyed the manipulation of men; what Philby may have sensed, however, was less predatory manipulation than cool suspicion. The story later went round Washington that Angleton was supposed to have frightened Philby on one occasion when, sitting down to lunch with him he said portentously, "I am on to you and your KGB friends," until Philby learned that this was Angleton's idea of a good joke. The two did lunch together weekly, more often than not at Harvey's, which was then something like an English chophouse in the rather dreary manner of the Christ Cella in New York today, but they were very seldom tête-à-tête, since other British or American colleagues came along. Angleton once recalled a day in London when Philby had remarked that England needed a good dose of socialism, and he had told Dulles of this, and of his suspicion that Philby was well to the left. Yet many members of the British secret service, like many of the most effective members of the OSS and CIA, were liberals, some even socialists, and reasonable men did not suspect them of treason.

Of course, there had been the wartime matter of the Rote Kapelle. A British counterintelligence unit in Germany had received a letter from a Mrs. Schmidt demanding compensation for the loss of her son, executed (she said) by the Gestapo as a British spy. The chief of the SCI unit cabled London for advice and received no answer; the original file on the matter appeared to be lost, and nothing was done. At the end of the war, however, when Abwehr records were examined, Allied intelligence discovered that Schmidt had been both a British and a Russian agent. This raised the question of why the original file had gone missing: perhaps to forestall an investigation that would turn up a Russian network, most likely the remnants of the Rote Kapelle, or Red Orchestra, based largely in Switzerland and aimed at Germany? Angleton had reason to suspect someone's efficiency in Philby's section, if not their loyalty.[46]

Then had come the Albanian fiasco. The more he thought about it, Angleton concluded that the Hoxha government was too well informed over too long a time to have obtained information piecemeal through leaks in the Albanian émigré community in Italy. Angleton had noted, over those lunches together, that even when drinking the charming Philby showed a remarkable absence of opinions on political matters. By early 1951 he had the most serious of doubts about the wisdom of continuing to work with Philby. If Philby were not a traitor, he was at the least insecure and incompetent.

Angleton was not, however, "baying for blood,"[47] for this was not his approach to anyone he might turn into a double agent. (Philby is often written of as a double agent. He wasn't: a double agent works for two sides. He was working for only one side and always had. He was a spy and a traitor and perhaps several other nasty things, but not a double agent.) Indeed, long afterward one of Angleton's wartime secretaries said that once the Philby story was out she concluded that Angleton had always known and was playing Philby for higher stakes. This seems unlikely. He would not, however, have simply pounced, for the methodology of CI was more subtle than that.[48]

That he didn't pounce made some who could not understand counterintelligence, but who also attributed to Angleton the kind of omniscience that postretirement legend-mongering fostered, suspect that he had known all along and that he was either in league with Philby or working toward the same end. In 1974, in the atmosphere of the Great Mole Hunt, a member of the CI staff, Clare Petty, presented a report to William Nelson, the deputy director for operations, that set out all the circumstantial evidence to make the case that Angleton was a Soviet agent. That Angleton had not spotted Philby, or having spotted him had not turned him in, was a key element in the conclusion. On February 29, 1979, after journalists for *Newsweek* magazine had reported that a CIA team had been examining Angleton's record for two years, the agency issued a terse public statement to the effect that the allegation that Angleton was a Soviet agent had been investigated and rejected. The spokesman for the agency, Herbert Hetu, said there had been no team, that a single member of the staff had come forward with his own study, and that an in-house examination of the charges was sufficiently satisfying on all points that the agency had not relayed the allegations to the FBI, which is charged with investigating domestic spying. When asked about the report, Colby, the director who had pressured Angleton into retirement, responded that "he never had any doubts about Angleton's loyalty." Stansfield Turner, then the DCI, also said that he had no cause to reopen the matter. Angleton was "gratified." When Petty had submitted his report, virtually no one had believed the case, perhaps because Petty already had a record of denouncing his superiors—he had done so against the head of his office in Germany—and he was believed to be writing other reports on personnel. Petty had, in fact, simply applied the methodology of total doubt to its chief practitioner, but virtually everyone who knew of his massive report—and few did, even Angleton never being shown a copy of it—accepted that principle of parsimony, that the simplest explanation is usually the correct one, and that Angleton had been taken in, at least up to the Albanian operation, like everyone else.[49]

Some writers suggest that Angleton was onto Burgess, Maclean, *and* Philby. In his book *The Fourth Man,* first published in London on November 5, 1979, as *The Climate of Treason,* the English writer Andrew Boyle said that Angleton had his own source of information close to the "Cambridge Apostles"—the group that included Burgess, Maclean, Philby, and Sir Anthony Blunt—one "Basil." Boyle also quoted a colleague of Angleton's who had "inside knowledge" as saying that Angleton's contacts came through the Israelis, though this report is surely suspect when the alleged colleague manages even to misdate the founding year of the CIA for which it is said he worked. In any case, Jewish intelligence is supposed to have handed "Basil" to Angleton, and Angleton and his assistants, Newton Miler and Raymond Rocca (called by the alleged "inside source" Jim Rocca), ran him.[50] Boyle says that Angleton did not tell Dulles or Wisner of his coup, waiting to judge the moment "ripe," and that he did not "demur" when the FBI decided to bug Guy Burgess's Nebraska Avenue home while Burgess was working at the British embassy in Washington—though in fact this was Philby's house in which Burgess was something of an unwanted guest. Some of this seems unlikely, though the unlikely is possible. The only reason not to have blown the whistle on Burgess was to angle for a bigger fish.

On May 23 or 24, 1951, Philby told Burgess that his friend Donald Maclean was to be brought in by MI5 for interrogation. Maclean had been first secretary to the British embassy in 1944 and was British representative on the Combined Policy Committee for Joint Atomic Development, from which he may have passed information on American progress to the Russians. He had been under suspicion since 1949, cryptanalysts having broken into some of the material being sent from the Soviet consulate in New York and, with British help, having produced circumstantial evidence that it was coming from Maclean. This had been turned over to Angleton. Maclean was in London with the American department of the Foreign Office when MI5 decided to investigate him further. Burgess fled from Washington to warn Maclean. The interrogation was to begin on Monday, May 28; Burgess learned of this from "the fourth man," called "Maurice" in Boyle's book, since British libel laws prevented his naming the person, *Maurice* being the name of E. M. Forster's homosexual novel, and the fourth man being, in fact, Sir Anthony Blunt, who was homosexual, as was Burgess and, at times, Maclean.[51] The two fled the country over the weekend, to turn up in Moscow two weeks later. Though there was as yet no hard evidence to link Philby more than socially to Burgess and Maclean, it seemed obvious to the CIA that Philby was also working for the Russians. "Beetle" Smith, the DCI, wrote to Sir Stewart Menzies to say that Philby was henceforth *persona non grata*. Philby was called back to London for an intense interrogation at the hands of Helenus (later Sir Helenus) Milmo, a formidable barrister who had worked for MI5 during the war. Angleton knew Milmo's reputation, as did Philby, and both knew him to be a uniquely skilled interrogator. Philby survived Milmo's questioning but did not convince him of his innocence, and he was obliged to resign quietly from the secret service.

The story did not end there, of course. After marking time in England for some years, and presumably continuing to work for his masters in the Soviet Union, Philby was given a job as correspondent for the London *Observer* and for *The Economist* in Beirut. In 1963, new suspicions were directed against Philby, and with additional though still circumstantial evidence in hand, MI5 decided that Philby ought to be interrogated again. This was expected to fall to MI5, to which the new information had come, and it was presumed that the interrogation would be carried out by Arthur Martin, as he had been involved with the Maclean investigation and had been present at Milmo's interrogation of Philby. Angleton thought this would be the case, and he instructed two of his agents, each unknown to the other, to keep an eye on Philby. Angleton wanted Philby returned in physical custody through the station chief in Beirut, his Yale classmate Ed Applewhite, and interrogated by someone Philby did not know.

However, Angleton was to be frustrated again. Sir Roger Hollis, head of MI5, was able to persuade Sir Dick White, then chief of MI6, that since Philby was a former MI6 man, someone from 6 should be sent. A former friend of Philby's who had recently become convinced of his guilt, Nicholas Elliott, thereupon flew to Beirut to conduct the interrogation. Angleton doubted that a man who had once been a good friend of Philby's would break him, and he instructed his agents in Beirut to keep a close watch. Elliott's mission was secret, and presumably only seven other people knew of it, but there is some evidence that Philby expected him. To Elliott Philby confessed that he was a Soviet agent and had been since 1934, and he confirmed that it was he who had alerted Maclean through Burgess. Elliott offered Philby immunity if he would return to Britain, and Philby asked for time to think it over. Elliott then consulted with his chief, who authorized a call directly to Angleton to tell him of the development. Elliott left Beirut with Philby's typed two-page confession on the understanding that if Philby accepted the offer of immunity, the local MI6 station chief would take care of his return. Angleton instructed his second watcher to get the ribbon from the typewriter on which Philby had typed his confession, but it could not be found. On January 23 Philby failed to show up at a dinner party given by the first secretary of the British embassy: he had fled to Russia.[52]

Angleton and others since have thought that the entire proceeding may have been intended to give Philby time to escape. Nicholas Elliott was not at fault—he acted on orders and did not have the authority to arrest Philby—and suspicion fell on yet some fourth man. Later, when the fourth man was proved to be Sir Anthony Blunt, and it was realized that he was in no position to engineer the handling of the approach to Philby, whatever he may have done for Burgess and Maclean, a fifth man was suspected, and some writers, most notably Chapman Pincher, a British specialist in espionage, pointed the finger at Sir Roger Hollis. Wherever responsibility lay, a man who would have been invaluable to the untangling of the mole hunt that had developed in the meantime had slipped the net or quite possibly demonstrated that there was no net to slip.

Again, it is possible to read the sequence of events in such a way as to implicate Angleton, since he had been informed by Elliott from Beirut prior to Philby's escape. There is no known evidence to suggest such a conclusion—merely the methodology of doubt. The simplest explanation remains the obvious one: that the British, never quick to repair, or admit to, penetration had once again behaved as gentlemen. They had not been willing to interrogate Maclean on a weekend, they could not believe that Philby had been working for the Soviets, they attributed American suspicions in 1951 to the hysteria of McCarthyism—a reasonable enough conclusion in the temper of the times—and now they assumed that Philby would do the gentlemanly thing and return to England. It is also reasonable to assume that there were those in SIS who felt it best if Philby simply slipped away, for to rake over these old coals would be hideously wounding. Dozens of other conjectures have been offered.

After all, the fourth man was definitely known to SIS from 1964, when Blunt confessed, and yet he was guaranteed immunity and until his public exposure in 1979 lost few of the merit badges a presumably grateful nation had given him earlier. Sir Anthony was very highly placed indeed—surveyor of the queen's pictures, research fellow of Trinity College, Cambridge, fellow of the British Academy, director of the Courtauld Institute—though not so highly in terms of access to intelligence. He had been a Soviet talent scout at Cambridge, was clearly a traitor, and had received a slap on the wrist. Only when it became known that the "Maurice" of Boyle's book was Sir Anthony was he stripped of his knighthood. Americans were outraged, but there were many in Britain who thought that Blunt had suffered enough from the indignities of his loss. One might conclude that the nations simply thought about treason somewhat differently.

In his book Boyle listed his informants, including a "confidential" CIA source, and there was much speculation that this may have been Angleton, as he knew the identity of both "Basil" and "Maurice." If so, Angleton most likely was after a bigger catch than Blunt, at least initially. Several commentators have wondered why Blunt was given immunity. One possible answer is that this was an effort to get Philby back from Moscow. Blunt's confession had come on April 23, 1964, not so long after Philby had settled into a city that lacked many of the social amenities to which he was accustomed. If allowed to remain in the Soviet Union for long, he would undoubtedly make the adjustment—as he clearly has—but perhaps his apparent fear that MI6 had not been honest with him in its offer of immunity might be allayed if he saw that it was extended to Blunt and subsequently honored.

An enormous literature has grown around the four men, and the search for the fifth in a presumed ring of five, and it will grow even higher. Angleton inevitably will figure in much of it. Some additional bits and pieces of the story will almost certainly come out from American records, as the Freedom of Information Act makes uncovering more possible over the years. But the main story rests in Britain,* and we are unlikely ever to know it: the birthplace of Magna Carta and of modern democracy has no law by which future generations have right of access to their past so far as classified files are concerned. Guesswork will produce more and more speculative books, damaging to British intelligence. Where psychological warfare is concerned, this sowing of mistrust will be as effective as though there really were a fifth man, a sixth, a seventh. . . .

---

*Or in Australia. In November 1986 the British government went to extraordinary lengths to block the publication in Australia of a book that sought to prove how Sir Roger Hollis had worked as a Soviet mole. This book, by a former MI5 officer, Peter Wright, was based on a document prepared some years earlier that had argued the case against Hollis while he was still alive. As a resident of Tasmania, and with his publisher in Sydney, Wright had believed himself beyond

Writers seem fascinated by Philby and Blunt, in particular, because they are articulate, intelligent people with an eye to style, and perhaps because they are one of the guild, they write books too. The public likes to reach out and touch such people by one means or another, walking about with a guidebook to London's "spy sites,"[54] putting a copy of Blunt's new book on Poussin, published by the Yale University Press—which, just in time, was able to whip the title Sir from the dust jacket—on a coffee table for the cognoscenti to recognize.[55] This bookish lot, fascinated by the sense of world-weary disillusionment, by the notion that "we are as bad as they are" that comes from highly successful and highly literate novelists like John le Carré and Graham Greene, frequently quote E. M. Forster (said to have been one of Burgess's favorite authors) to the effect that "if I had to choose between betraying my country and betraying my friend, I hope I should have the guts to betray my country."[56] One friend of Burgess, the scholar Goronwy Rees, has pointed out the essential

the reaches of the Official Secrets Act, but the Thatcher government, perhaps thinking Australia was still a colony, attempted to take action against Wright in New South Wales. The book, Spy Catcher: The Candid Autobiography of a Senior Intelligence Officer, was published in New York City, by Viking, in the summer of 1987, and it contained much material, some of it incorrect, on Philby, Angleton, and others. For my views on the book, see my remarks in the Boston Globe, August 16, 1987. In Britain two journalists for the Sunday Times of London, Simon Freeman and Barrie Penrose, were determined to publish their own analysis, Conspiracy of Silence, and it was evident that several highly placed former members of SIS had talked with them. Were these former officers, as well as the journalists, also to be prosecuted? At the same time a new book from Phillip Knightley, The Second Oldest Profession, stirred further interest in Chapman Pincher's charges. Australians had every reason to want to see the question of the fifth man resolved, since Hollis, on secondment to Canberra in the 1950s, had set up Australian security services.

In the meantime, it became necessary to reassess the nature of the basic literature on MI5, MI6, and the mole hunts in the United States, for it was evident that several books had been colored, if not shaped, by the determination of former officers of MI5 both to reveal what they suspected about treachery at the top of the British secret service and to break through the pallid anonymity of such official histories as the government had permitted to be published.[53] As these stories broke in 1986–87, the long-retired James Angleton said that British intelligence was in a shambles, as it scurried to protect itself, apparently little worried about damage to public confidence, perhaps already damaged beyond repair. There will now be, Angleton thought, talk again of a fifth man, a sixth, a seventh, consciously echoing the remark of the British literary critic Cyril Connolly, who wrote in 1951 when Burgess and Maclean defected, "After the third man the fourth man, after the fourth man the fifth man; who is the fifth man always beside you?" (On Knightley, see my "Mole Tales," The Nation, CCXLIV [April 4, 1987], 436–438.)

fallacy in the literal rendering of this statement, for to most of us our country is also our friends: to betray one's country is to betray "innumerable other friends and it might also mean betraying one's wife and one's family. . . . One's country was not some abstract conception which it might be relatively easy to sacrifice for the sake of an individual; it was itself made up of a dense network of individual and social relationships in which loyalty to one particular person formed only a single strand."[57]

Through all of this activity, Albania, Burgess, Philby, the CIA's counterintelligence people were judged to have performed well. The *wunderkind* who had most persistently derived the theory, and then applied the theory, of counterintelligence had worked across the board. He understood CI as product, that is, as information about any prospective enemy, and he understood it as an activity, as security and counterespionage. He was the theorist and the poet who seemed to have the deepest grasp of the nature of the threat—a subject on which he gave briefings—but he was also an activist with his own contacts. He had long studied defectors, deception, and the techniques of surveillance. He also understood that while there were friendly foreign powers, there were no friendly foreign services—the words were Raymond Rocca's, the sentiment was shared.[58] He had believed that the threat was here to stay in 1945, and he believed it now. "In a wilderness of mirrors. What will the spider do,/ Suspend its operations, will the weevil/ Delay?"

On December 20, 1954, Frank G. Wisner, deputy director (Plans), released a secret memorandum to the Clandestine Services. Effective that day a separate Counter-Intelligence Staff was established as a senior staff reporting directly to the Chief of Operations. S. Herman Horton was appointed deputy chief. James Angleton was appointed chief. It was just a little over two weeks after Angleton, code-name Mother, had turned thirty-seven. He was at the top of the pole.

The story of James Angleton as chief of Counter-Intelligence cannot be told now, at least not well, and perhaps never. It falls into that 5 percent of information that the intelligence communities of the world are dedicated to protecting successfully. Under the rules by which American government records are made available to researchers, additional Angleton material will be opening up, but this will not soon include classified documents. Most of the Angleton record is classified. To tell the story the historian would need to have unfettered access to the archives of the British, French, Italian, Israeli, and Russian intelligence services, as well as the American and, quite probably, others. No such historian will ever exist. The scholar lacks access, assets, penetration, sources, contacts—the entire array of resources by which a professional intelligence officer may, after much time, great expenditure of money, and with the support of his government, obtain an intelligence story. Angleton both tests and proves Sherman Kent's dictum: while much can be learned that is presumed to be irretrievable, one cannot learn enough to tell in the end precisely how interesting, how significant, how true what one does know may be.

Given this barrier, students of intelligence often have taken the easiest, perhaps the only, path open to them: they have guessed, inferred, and sometimes fabricated. For our needs neither the course of full disclosure, nor the total neglect of the subject, is possible. What follows then is by way of a summary, with some observations, but it makes no attempt to relate in full what might be pieced together from the spate of books and articles that in recent years have tried to tell something of Angleton. There are, after all, both a promise made to all who agreed to help with this book—that, in general, inquiry would stop with the early 1960s— and the simple fact that the only primary source from December 1954, when Angleton arrived at the top of the pole, to the present, is Angleton himself, and he is not likely to go against the custom, tradition, and law that prevent the revealing of classified information, especially when he has condemned two directors of his former agency, William Colby and Stansfield Turner, for doing what he believes is precisely that. What he has been willing to say in the past, and one suspects what he may say in the future, is in my judgment accurate and honest, provided one listens carefully to what the message is, remembers what question he is responding to, and takes the words to mean what they say, not what a listener unversed in the issues may take them to say. He is not a man likely to forget Secretary of State Lansing's advice, though in the slight paraphrase of triple negative: "It is not a lie not to tell a person that which he is not entitled to know."

The post-1954 Angleton story would, were the historian's traditional records available, most likely focus on four subjects: the Israeli connection, the Great Mole Hunt, the Church committee hearings and their aftermath, and subject X—subject X, for one can postulate with fair security that there is at least one major subject buried in those records about which as yet hardly a line has reached the public. What follows is a highly synoptic view of the subjects on which the literature, and to this point public attention, has centered; it may, in passing, tell us something about the theory, the methodology, of counterintelligence and perhaps a bit more about the man himself.

Angleton was a strong-minded man surrounded by like-minded men. The CIA was, by 1954, already a relatively entrenched bureaucracy. Angleton was bureaucratically conservative and somewhat uncomfortable with organizational change. Once he was in a position to do so, he wanted to put as much distance between CI, and its operational offshoot CE, and the rest of the agency as possible, because compartmentalization was essential to effective counterintelligence. This would inevitably mean some duplication of effort—he could scarcely tell another unit which, in theory, might have been penetrated, of all that his own unit was doing, and yet it would on occasion have to go over old ground for new scents and would, by the nature of the work, generally not find any new scents—and overlapping of authority, largely to the benefit of CI, which would get and seldom give. It would mean the appearance of inefficiency and waste, for duplication always appears so, especially to those who believe that one ought to get everything out of a book on the first reading and move on, that one ought to interrogate a defector, deeply and thoroughly, and move on, that one ought to complete an operation, celebrate it quietly if successful or bury it deeply if not, and move on. As someone quite hostile to CI and to Angleton has remarked, counterintelligence was like a dog returning to its own vomit.

Of course, strong-minded people can differ without falling out. A sharp disagreement over procedure, timing, even priorities can be healed, however deeply it cuts at the time, while one over fundamental substance will not be. Friends are lost and forgotten, enemies are remembered. An example of the former kind of dispute was the temporary spat over the Khrushchev speech. From his point of view this could have been, and was not, one of Angleton's real coups, and he was for a time pretty unhappy over the handling of it.

In February 1956 Nikita Khrushchev, the Soviet premier, launched a new phase in his attack on the leadership of Joseph

Stalin, charging him with having created a cult of personality around himself. Contrary to Stalin, Khrushchev declared, war was not inevitable and peaceful coexistence with the capitalist nations was possible. In a remarkable seven-hour delivery to the Twentieth Party Congress he emphasized the need for agricultural and industrial development in the Soviet Union, hinted at possible loosening of control over Communist party apparatus in satellite countries, and even said that people might come to Communism by other than revolutionary paths, including victory at the polls. Though the speech was meant to be secret, its substance was not likely to remain so, for too many had heard it, but the actual text was top secret. CI already had feelers out to get a copy of the speech even before it was delivered on the assumption that it would provide guidance on future Soviet policies.

Allen Dulles soon knew of the speech and its general contents. His brother, John Foster Dulles, the secretary of state, thought it sounded as if it would meet the needs of the platform pledges made by the Republican party in 1952 about liberating the satellites of Eastern Europe. Both wanted a copy of the text of the speech very badly; and when Allen Dulles put out a message to all CIA stations to make getting a copy top priority, one came to hand on April 1, All Fools' Day. Whether in fact the CIA paid for the Khrushchev speech remains a matter of dispute. Ray Cline, the CIA's top analyst at the time, wrote later that "a very handsome price" was paid for it—another writer suggested $750,000— though after his retirement Angleton stated for the record that no payment was made, the speech having been passed along "for ideological reasons." Robert Amory, Jr., former deputy director for intelligence, was reported by Harrison Salisbury in *The New York Times* as saying that a copy was obtained from a member of the Polish Communist party; E. Howard Hunt, later known best for his role in the Watergate break-in, said that it had come to the CIA through Israeli intelligence; and an acquaintance of Angleton's much later said that it came directly from Palmiro Togliatti in Italy, he being delighted to see Stalin exposed at last. Perhaps there were two copies, one with gaps and a little later one of full text. The consensus seems to be that the first text came from Poland by way of the Israelis and that, while no money changed hands, the Israelis were given certain undertakings about services. Angleton is the only person who knows the full answer, and he never registered in the files the actual name of the agent

who passed it along. "There are certain matters," he once remarked, "that you take to the tomb," and this was to be one of
them.[59]

However obtained, and whether paid for or not, the CIA had a
copy of the speech. Dulles passed it for evaluation on the overt
side, since its authenticity had to be tested first. Cline convinced
the key players on the operations side, Frank Wisner, Angleton,
and Richard Helms, who was DDP at the time, that the text was
authentic. Discussion turned to use. Wisner put the question to
George Kennan, a close friend, and Dulles sent a copy to him by
courier. Kennan replied in a long letter, suggesting that since the
Russians did not know that the United States had the speech, it
could be used to great advantage as a guide to diplomatic action.
Angleton agreed, for the speech was a superior source, akin to
Ultra, and he was always for protecting the source. Cline was for
publication, for using the speech could be a major propaganda
move. Dulles conferred with his brother, and they in turn talked
to President Eisenhower: the decision was to make the document
public.

Angleton now had another proposal: to doctor the speech and
release it back to the Eastern European nations, from which it
would leak to the United States. It would not then be known that
the CIA had obtained it, the Russians would believe that the
Americans would act on the doctored version, and the doctoring
itself might, through subtle alterations, sow seeds of distrust in
the satellites. Allen Dulles pondered again and decided to release
the speech in its entirety. He advised his brother to have it delivered to *The New York Times,* where it appeared on June 4, with
explanatory notes.

Angleton may have had a second reason to oppose publication
of the speech: he and Wisner were said to be running an operation, Red Sox/Red Cap, aimed at Eastern Europe. Angleton had
recruited a man to train a resistance group, made up largely of
refugees from Hungary, Rumania, Poland, and Czechoslovakia,
to prepare for paramilitary operations in those countries. When
Cline learned of the secret army, he was convinced that it would
not succeed. Angleton thought it might, but mindful of the Albanian disaster, certainly not yet, so he wanted the speech held until
Red Sox/Red Cap was ready to run.[60]

There is also disagreement on the precise text as finally released. Most sources say that it was printed in *The New York*

Times without alteration. There are hints, however, that one or two slight changes were made in the copy sent to *The Times*. A second version, with thirty-four new paragraphs supplied by the CIA, drawn from other known Khrushchev utterances of a damaging nature, was "sourced" to Italy for release to Eastern Europe. The printing of a speech in which the head of the Soviet Politburo indicted his country's own leadership stirred enormous unrest. Rioting in Poznan and elsewhere in Poland gave the independent-minded Communist leader Wladyslaw Gomulka his entrée back to power. On October 23 the Hungarian uprising began. The CIA and Radio Free Europe actively encouraged the rebels. When the nationalist Hungarian leader Imre Nagy announced on October 31 that Hungary would withdraw from the Warsaw Pact, Khrushchev ordered Soviet troops and tanks onto the streets of Budapest, and the rebellion was crushed. Wisner remained convinced that a golden opportunity had been missed by a president who was unprepared to face the Russians down at an opportune moment, and it is said that he went to the Hungarian border to watch the thousands of refugees stream into Austria. Shortly afterward he had a nervous breakdown, and when presumed recovered was sent to London as station chief. This did not work out, and he committed suicide soon after retiring from the agency.

The lessons of the Hungarian uprising were not learned, for no one could agree what they were. Eisenhower had talked the rhetoric of national liberation, but he had not carried through in the crunch. While the CIA performed well in running an escape line out of Hungary, and counterintelligence gained a great deal from interrogations of Hungarian refugees in the Austrian camps, there is every chance that even with support from the top the projected CIA paramilitary operation would have failed. Here was a rehearsal for the Bay of Pigs, for Vietnam, for every military operation in which the United States would, depending upon one's view, either commit too little too late or embroil itself in a distant affair that was none of its business. Angleton rather thought the lesson was that there is no middle ground when the shooting starts: avoid it entirely or commit to it entirely.

Still, wounds over the Hungarian uprising might not heal quickly, but any inflicted over the question of how and when to use the Khrushchev speech remained of the flesh only. The wound of the heart came when the very validity of counterintelligence—not just of its methodology, not queries about its effectiveness, but a fundamental, deep-seated conviction that counterintelligence was not really of any use at all—was brought into question. Two of the questioners were, in time, at the very top, as directors of Central Intelligence: William Colby, who forced Angleton to abandon the Israeli contract, reduced CI personnel, and pressured Angleton to resign, and Stansfield Turner, who savaged him, and counterintelligence, in a book.[61]

There were two major bones of contention. One was the Great Mole Hunt, the other the passing to the public of the CIA's so-called family jewels, its often unpalatable secrets. The first was an internal matter, the second very public; Angleton was central to the first, and though he was not front-and-center on most of the so-called dirty tricks, one that most enraged Congress, the clandestine opening of the private mail of American citizens, was in good measure his baby. He might have survived one, he could not survive both, without the strongest support from the top, which was not forthcoming.

Dozens of books and articles have been written on the Great Mole Hunt. It relates, of course, to the Philby story, though it has far more important independent strands of its own. One strand was connected with President Kennedy's assassination: was the KGB involved or not? Commentators not interested in the substance of the hunt itself have written at length on the effects of the hunt on morale in the agency and on relations with other intelligence services. The subject goes directly to the heart of counterintelligence—to the problems of penetration, defection, and deception—and cannot be dealt with substantively here. Many of the books and articles are almost entirely imaginative, and even the most carefully researched studies must move so deeply into the great swamp of speculation as to require leaps of faith, from cypress knee to cypress knee, far too great for a historian. If the truth were known hundreds of books now on the shelves would be reclassified from history to fiction. But the truth is not known.

American CI has had some undoubted successes in penetrating Soviet intelligence, especially the Chief Intelligence Directorate of the General Staff (GRU, or Glavnoye Razvedyvatelnoye Upravleniye). In the fifties and sixties the CIA recruited Peter Popov and then Oleg Penkovskiy, both colonels in the GRU; both were ultimately executed by the Russians. In 1959 Captain Nikolai Artamonov, recruited by the Office of Naval Intelligence, became Nicholas Shadrin and began to feed the KGB information doctored by the CIA. Shadrin did not return from a meeting he was to have had in Vienna on December 18, 1975, however, and the CIA, without Angleton, was put to the task of finding out whether the agency had been penetrated and Shadrin betrayed or whether he had redefected. The evaluation of defectors is always difficult, since the agent debriefing a defector has to allow for boasting, exaggeration, and the creation of new stories when the truth is used up. Above all, he has to take into account the possibility of a fake defector intentionally sowing disinformation, such as the allegation that there is a mole high up in the agency.

Thus the story of Anatoly Golitsin and Yuri Nosenko becomes especially important. In 1961 Golitsin defected from Helsinki. He said he was a major in the First Chief Directorate of the KGB, working against North Atlantic Treaty Organization targets. Brought to Washington and given the cover name John Stone, Golitsin appeared to be a source of sensational and accurate information. He declared that the KGB already had an agent in the highest ranks of U.S. intelligence, and that "outside men"—Soviet-controlled agents masked as defectors or double agents—would supply disinformation to build up the inside man's credibility. The inside man would then confirm the authenticity of the outside agent. Angleton was a Golitsin debriefer, and he became convinced that Golitsin was telling the truth, and that a mole did exist inside the CIA. Even if one might not, methodology required working to that premise. Golitsin pointed to a trip made under diplomatic cover to the States in 1957 by V. M. Kovshuk, said to have been head of the American embassy section of the KGB. This mission must have been very important for Kovshuk to leave Moscow: perhaps he came to activate the alleged high-level penetration agent? Since the KGB knew Golitsin knew of Kovshuk's mission, Golitsin warned that an attempt would be made to discredit his information. Angleton, a man who believed most defectors were plants, came to believe in Golitsin and went to the extraordinary length of letting him review the personnel files of CIA officers who spoke Russian or had been posted to Moscow to see if he could spot the mole. The mole was presumed to be in the Soviet Division, and eventually officers from that division, upon whom suspicion had been thrown, found themselves being transferred to other, non-bloc postings.

Six months after Golitsin had said that someone would be sent to discredit him, Yuri Nosenko defected in Switzerland. His information ran counter to Golitsin's on a number of points. No-senko laid Popov's detection to Soviet security work, not to penetration, for example. Angleton doubted Nosenko and held to Golitsin. The Nosenko case was not Angleton's, however: it was handled by the Soviet Bloc Division. Routine interrogation revealed that Nosenko was either lying or was confused on various matters, perhaps none of them critical or extending beyond his desire to appear important so that he would be well looked after, except for some material concerning the KGB's possible relationship to Lee Harvey Oswald, Kennedy's assassin. Nosenko tended to confirm that the KGB had nothing to do with the assassination. Since the CIA knew that Oswald had been in Russia, and probably in touch with the KGB, the Russians clearly were afraid that some connection would be made. The CIA did not believe that the Russians were behind the assassination at all, but the KGB could scarcely simply protest its innocence, hence the sending of Nosenko to drop true information. On the assumption that the information would then prove true on a matter of the highest importance the KGB might well have intended that Nosenko use his advantage to sow disinformation on other subjects, however.

The chief of the division, David Murphy, ordered Nosenko subjected to hostile interrogation—that is, solitary confinement in a small room, deprivation of sleep, little food, intensive and angry questioning. The Office of Security designed and built an interrogation chamber and thought it appropriate that Nosenko's discomforts should be as nearly as possible like the conditions under which Frederick Barghoorn, a Yale professor of political science who had been seized by the KGB from in front of the Metropole Hotel in Moscow in 1963, was held when in the Lubyianka, until Kennedy had intervened with Khrushchev personally to obtain his release. (Apparently it had been Nosenko who chose Barghoorn as the target, having been charged with finding a suitable American to kidnap as a bargaining chip in the KGB's efforts to gain release from the United States of an agent who had been arrested in New York.) Angleton may have thought all this a kind of rude justice—though Nosenko was held for three and a half years, Barghoorn for two weeks—but he was not responsible for Nosenko's incarceration and hostile interrogation, and he learned of it only after it had begun. Both Angleton and Raymond Rocca are said to have protested that hostile techniques should not be used in peacetime in the United States. When Golitsin learned of the interrogation he too protested—but this could, of course, be read as a sign that he feared even more what Nosenko might say under adverse circumstances.

The Soviet Division's final report ran to over 900 typed pages: it concluded that Nosenko was a Soviet intelligence agent sent out to deliver disinformation to the CIA, FBI, and the commission chaired by Chief Justice Earl Warren that was investigating the Kennedy assassination. The report recommended that the FBI undertake its own full investigation of Nosenko. When Angleton read the report he was not entirely happy, however. He felt there were times when the interrogation had been badly handled, allowing Nosenko to anticipate questions and prepare answers. When his analysis staff assessed the report, Rocca concluded that the probability that Nosenko was a fake was 85 percent. Angleton then instructed his chief of operations, Newton Miler, to investigate the case once more, making a systematic comparison of all information that had come from Nosenko with all that had come from any other defector. Two senior researchers with no previous knowledge were put on to the case, so that the record might be viewed with fresh eyes. After this review, Miler also concluded that Nosenko was a disinformation agent. The FBI had its own source, however, Fedora, a Soviet intelligence agent under diplomatic cover at the United Nations in New York. Fedora's first contact had come soon after Golitsin's defection, and Angleton had thought at the time that he might well be a plant to neutralize Golitsin's information. The FBI had concluded that Fedora was telling the truth, and he supported Nosenko's information.

Nosenko was then transferred to the Office of Security, where another officer, Bruce Solie, tried a friendlier approach with the assistance of FBI agents. In the end they concluded that Nosenko was, at least in the main, telling the truth. Miler and others in counterintelligence felt that the interrogation had been conducted poorly so that it was impossible from Solie's report to determine precisely what information Nosenko had volunteered and what had been prematurely revealed to him by the nature of the questions. A final review was conducted by a member of the Board of National Estimates, Gordon Stewart, to the conclusion that the evidence could be read either way but that the hostile interrogation had been conducted in such an atmosphere of tension that it was not fully reliable either. Stewart recommended that, though Nosenko's innocence could not be clearly established, the weight of evidence pointed in that direction. Nosenko was released and resettled in North Carolina.

In 1971 the FBI began to doubt Fedora, however, especially when a key assertion of his concerning Daniel Ellsberg, who had leaked the Pentagon Papers to *The New York Times,* proved wrong. The FBI and CIA decided they would simply have to wait to see what Fedora did when he reached retirement age: in 1981, long after Angleton had been forced into his own retirement and Nosenko had been resettled, Fedora returned to the Soviet Union, possibly confirming that he had been a double agent. If Fedora was a loyal Soviet, and supported Nosenko, then Nosenko presumably was a plant; if Nosenko were a plant, and refuted Golitsin, then Golitsin's information must be true. Thus there must be a mole. Angleton had felt methodology required seeing this chain through, following the labyrinth to its inner recesses, and he personally remains convinced to this day that there was at least one mole in the CIA. DCI Colby, on the other hand, concluded in 1973 that Angleton had tied the Soviet Bloc Division up to the point that morale was seriously damaged and careers had been ruined.

Each side has its defenders. Clare Petty[88] had made the worst-case analysis from the point of view of those who believed Nosenko: that Angleton himself was the mole. It was Angleton who wrote off defectors who proved valuable and who allowed one defector in whom he believed, Golitsin, access to the personnel files, producing a series of disruptive and demoralizing transfers. If a mole, or moles, existed, one must be in a senior position to promote and transfer other moles and to protect himself. By Angleton's methodology, he well could be the mole. While Petty's report was rejected, it had made its methodological point.

Those who sided with Golitsin and Angleton felt that there clearly was a mole, and that whether by intent or pure good fortune, he had attained his end when Angleton was forced into retirement. (Thus some would point the finger at Colby.) Golitsin had insisted that the Sino-Soviet split, the Soviet-Albanian dispute, the gradual movement toward more independence on the part of Rumania, were all Soviet bloc disinformation measures. The Prague Spring, when Czechoslovakia attempted to put distance between itself and the Soviet Union, was a sham, he said. Averell Harriman, former ambassador to the Soviet Union and confidant of presidents, was a Soviet agent, he said. Angleton did not necessarily accept all these notions, for it is possible to divide Golitsin's flow of information into two distinct phases, but Angleton accepted enough of them to be identified with them. With Angleton's retirement, the argument went, each of these disinformation plots had succeeded. The mole would remain until his own retirement, obviously not long off since he must be senior himself.[62]

Setting aside the merits of the arguments, two observations are worth making, both suggesting that there were significant flaws in the approach to the Golitsin-Nosenko problem, though perhaps flaws built into the very nature of counterintelligence. First, the necessary dichotomy between the Office of Security, which reports to the DCI and is responsible for overall security of personnel and installation, and the clandestine side of counterintelligence, was broken down and ought not to have been. (Thus David Murphy, who made the decision to handle Nosenko first through hostile interrogation and then through the Office of Security, fell under suspicion.) Compartmentalization had been abandoned at a crucial time, and information was compromised forever as a result of its flow across boundaries. Investigations of future suspected penetrations would be hampered by the memory of the trauma of this one, even though no investigation had ever been undertaken relative to the problem of penetration which was not based on a lead or an allegation from a third party: that is, CI did not go on fishing expeditions, and investigations were not self-generated. Patience, without doubt necessary to such investigations, had become a victim of failed procedure, the long wait for germination associated with CI under Angleton having been abandoned. This, surely, was a mistake.

But Angleton's own logic could not permit of a genuinely unbiased investigation of Nosenko. If there were a mole, he would have told the KGB about Nosenko, for though Nosenko did not defect until 1964, he had in fact been working for the CIA since June of 1962. Thus might Nosenko not have been sent to be discovered, so that he could further the career of his principal accuser? This, Angleton pointed out, was Peter Bagley, the man who had first debriefed Nosenko in Berne and who had written the massive report after the hostile interrogation. But if Nosenko were in fact caught out and eventually "proven" false, who would benefit most? Angleton and Golitsin. Then might not Golitsin be the plant and Angleton the mole? Back to Clare Petty's report. The permutations were unending.

There were four basic possibilities. One, the mole existed, Golitsin was genuine, Nosenko was a plant, Angleton was prescient. Two, there was no big mole, Nosenko was genuine, Golitsin was also genuine though, later, slightly mad. Three, Nosenko was genuine, there was a big mole, and it was most likely Angleton. Four, that there was a notional mole, Golitsin, having been sent by the KGB (perhaps at the suggestion of Kim Philby) to penetrate CIA files (though this could hardly have been anticipated) and to tie CI up in knots. A notional mole would, of course, only work on someone utterly committed to Angleton's methodology.[63] Each of the four theories, all circumstantial, is abstractly possible. That being so, there is a chilling conclusion one might draw: if such a succession of events is amenable to four interpretations, the methodology of counterintelligence will mean that each will have its champions, and if they are to coexist within an intelligence agency, that coexistence is bound to be destructive to the agency. Yet if they cannot coexist, then the methodology cannot, in fact, be tested at its extremities and is not, when the chips are down, really a methodology at all. This is not the same as saying that counterintelligence leads to paranoia, a facile term used much too loosely; rather, it is to say that counterintelligence contains the seeds of its own contradiction.

Intelligence is, of course, evaluated information, and there are hundreds of ways to assist a foreign evaluator to arrive at the wrong conclusions. While strategic deception was central in time of war, since it had immediate relevance to action, it is also important in time of peace, since it involves controlled, purposeful, and intimate contact with potential enemies. Counterintelligence and counterespionage work is, therefore, always in potential conflict with those in any intelligence organization whose primary concern is security. If security is the most important goal, the next logical step after the discovery of an opposition network is to make certain one has found all members of the network and then obliterate it. CE, on the other hand, would wish to exploit the network, to play it back to the enemy. This is highly dangerous if all members have not been uncovered, or if some only pretend to a willingness to be exploited and then pass information in such a way as to reveal that they have been doubled. Those who are security-minded will avoid foreign agents; CE will move in on them. Angleton knew which response he thought most effective, and he recognized that CE was not likely to be fully understood, could not even be fully explained since it depended upon obscuring intentions as well as operations. Security, operational branches, CI, and CE would often be at cross-purposes, and so there would always be suspicion and competition within any centralized intelligence agency.*

When counterintelligence actually works, it becomes a form of political action. As Lenin observed, every intelligence operation has a political object; CI helps to find what that objective is. Since no intelligence body in any democracy is supposed to engage in political activity, the success of any counterintelligence operation has to be hidden. Only failures generally become known. There can be no expectation of public praise, for anything deserving of praise must be kept secret. Counterintelligence functions are positive intelligence. Operations might be closed down, and yet, if penetration of the enemy has occurred, the operation can still run. CE is like putting a virus into the bloodstream of the enemy. Such an approach involves the longest-range views possible; intelligence can never be static, since the definition of the enemy may change, as postwar shifts had shown. One might never know who one's enemies will be, for revolution and subversion may turn even the staunchest allies into the bitterest of enemies decades down the road; one must hide long-range activities from friends as well. Inevitably this will seem, indeed for all practical purposes will be, paranoia. This is not to be helped. There are a few lines

*Counterintelligence and counterespionage are two terms much abused, and the distinction between the two is discussed in several books. Buffs like to argue about whether hyphens are required or not and enjoy pointing out differences that arise when the words are seen as nouns, verbs, or adjectives. Norman Holmes Pearson's papers contain a document, stamped Secret, which sets out the definitions as used by the OSS. CI is "all efforts to neutralize, repress or eliminate the activity of enemy inimical or other persons or groups or governments or their representatives to secure intelligence the obtaining of which adversely affects the national security." CE is a subdivision of CI and involves human agents. It is "all efforts to neutralize, repress, or eliminate the practice of spying or employment of secret agents by enemy inimical or other persons or groups or governments or their representatives to secure intelligence the obtaining of which adversely affects the interests of the United States." X-2 began as CI but in time was referred to as CE in much of the documentation. These definitions are found in typed documents on the theory of the running of Controlled Enemy Agents, on CI double agents in neutral countries, and similar subjects, in Pearson's wooden files, box 2, as noted in the previous chapter, and they appear to be lectures Pearson prepared for briefing newly arrived agents. One may surmise that Angleton was introduced to the terminology by Pearson.

from Stephen Crane that elliptically sum up the delicate balance: "A man feared that he might find an assassin;/Another that he might find a victim./ One was more wise than the other."[64]

Counterintelligence, then, was not meant to apprehend enemy agents, or to operate against the enemy in a defensive way, despite the misleading implications of "counter." Rather, as an offensive operation, CE was meant to use the opposition's human initiatives against itself. This could scale the heights of the absurd if not in the hands of the most clever of men. In 1963, using the pseudonym Christopher Felix, James McCargar had written what is widely regarded as the best general book on the methods used in "the secret war," *The Spy and His Masters.* There he describes a scene from *Romanoff and Juliet,* as played by the actor Peter Ustinov. Ustinov is prime minister of a tiny, unaligned nation caught between the Russians and the Americans. He meets the American ambassador and learns that the Americans know of a secret operation which will give the Soviet Union dominance over Ustinov's country:[65]

> After a bit of reflection, the Prime Minister . . . calls on the Soviet Ambassador. After some preliminaries, he says to the Soviet Ambassador, "They know." The Soviet Ambassador replies calmly, "We know they know." Back to the American Ambassador goes Ustinov. "They know you know," he says conspiratorially. The American Ambassador smiles confidently. "We know they know we know," he answers. Ustinov returns to the Soviet Ambassador. "They know you know they know," he says. To this the Soviet Ambassador replies, triumphantly, "We know they know we know they know." Once again the Prime Minister calls on the American Ambassador. "They know you know they know you know," he says, weary and curious at the same time. The American Ambassador repeats it after him, counting on his fingers. "*What?*" he suddenly cries in horror.

The point was simply—not so simply— to "raise the tension one step higher": never to allow your ambassador to be the one who must count on his fingers. To some this was of the essence of successful spy craft; to others, it was madness, the essence of an escalating cold war which made no sense. The existentialists would tell us that to know what someone else knows is impossible in any case. Knowing what they know, one still would not know what action they might take on what you know, even with a deep understanding of national character. The whole thing was simply too dangerous, a game with such destructive potential it ought not to be played at all. Or so some felt; to others, CI and CE provided superior intelligence, were the very essence of the game, the ideal. Until Angleton ran into a director of central intelligence who simply could not or would not accept the value and methodology of counterintelligence (or, to be more charitable, took the first view, that the risks outweighed the possible gains of sending a Ustinov back and forth across the floor of the stage), he was able to pursue CE, and its most important technique, penetration, almost without hindrance.

Angleton was an ideal man for this game. He could keep track of the agents, doubled, tripled, turn and turn again. Christopher Felix describes the problem well: "The decisive question is precisely which turns are genuine and which are false. This is but one of the problems which makes C. E. an extraordinarily complex affair; the determination of which turns are genuine and which false is a painstaking exercise in the control of information, of who knows what when, that requires constant alertness and a simultaneous grasp of both large perspective and detail. It is obviously an intellectual exercise of almost mathematical complexity."[66] Angleton saw everything in relation to everything else. He saw questions in the round, immediately ticking off relationships, ramifications, subquestions which others did not think of. If a double agent were suspected, might one not learn about that duplicity by an examination of the precise time sequence and content of information, that is, by developing a "chron"? If there were a change in Israeli intelligence, how would this influence South Africa? If Communist China appeared to be breaking from the Soviet Union, might this not be merely a very long-range strategic deception?

It is a truism of academic life that those who are attracted to a particular discipline—to history, or mathematics, or literary analysis—tend to be of somewhat similar personality types, the discipline already reflecting an individual's view of reality, or of how knowledge is organized. A life spent in the chosen discipline will reinforce the personality characteristics to the point that one cannot separate the individual from the disciplinarian: the "good" historian views all subjects, whether Frederick the Great or the label on Classic Coke, in a historical context. At times those who practice a given discipline may not be able to recall the days when they knew that the discipline was only a way of ordering reality. They are unlikely to be able to see that reality as ordered by another discipline will not only differ but may have equal legitimacy. A liberal arts education is "really about history," says the historian; no, it is "really about science," says the scientist. Humanists are the rememberers says the humanist, they open up horizons; so do we, says the scientist. Unless a disciplinarian gets out into "the real world" (which is not actually more real, merely different, though in purely democratic terms perhaps more "real" in that it is accepted as so by a larger number of people) from time to time, the disciplinarian or methodologist begins to forget that most people do not see reality as he sees it, and that they therefore act on different realities. The historian who knows only the discipline of history is not a historian who can be expected to understand human nature, to know that people sometimes act on pure devilry, or that there are those who consider analyzing a problem in terms of the past purely meretricious, a middle-class means of bolstering the *status quo*. All the more so then might a man who has spent his life in clandestine services, whose personality, education, and interests are constantly self-reinforcing, whose employment is self-validating, and whose commitment to a methodology is total, not understand why others would view him as obsessed—or why "the real world" might feel that he, or his branch, had overstepped the bounds when they extended surveillance to the domestic scene, to opening the mail of suspected subversives, and thus suspected him of not speaking the truth to the elected representatives of the American people. One can also understand why such a person would feel it essential not to reveal all of the truth to those representatives, since some of them might be dupes, a few might be conscious agents, of a foreign power, and the American people, not privy to the secret war—and even when informed by newspaper leaks and disaffected intelligence officers of some dark nooks and crannies of that war—could never be expected to grasp the methodology by which they were being protected.

Those who work for counterintelligence make enemies, of course, inside the service as well as outside. They appear to be all-knowing, and at times may nearly be; in any case, they often feel they cannot afford to appear less than so. They believe they are the

CLOAK & GOWN

protectors of "the queen of all secret operations." They lay claims
to needing to know not only about the operations of other services, but of other branches in their own service as well. This can
hardly endear their directors at staff meetings. A politically ambitious director might well use his knowledge to promote himself
within the organization or outside it: this has been the case in a
number of countries. To CI operatives, their functions seem so
self-evidently essential, they cannot imagine an intelligence service without them; to those outside their circle, their knowledge
may seem far more dangerous than any gain that might be brought
to the larger intelligence community from what they learn and do.

This classic balance, this tension within the intelligence community, would remain in delicate poise through the fifties, even
the extremely difficult sixties, to come undone in the early seventies. Angleton's counterintelligence staff had been growing
steadily; despite recommendations after the Korean War that CIA
staff be cut back, he had marched ahead, from a handful of agents
to 125 by the mid-fifties, to the reputed 200 and upwards of the
sixties. Angleton was, in the jargon of an analyst of organizations
and management, maximizing his payoffs by minimizing access to
his data.[67] A monopoly over any specialized information that is of
value confers power on the holder; if the information is not of
value, it still confers the appearance of power. So large, so secret,
so powerful an operation was bound to invite resentment and suspicion. The mole hunt had fed both; the revelations that came out
through or because of the Church committee hearings would cause
the pot to boil over.

Unhappily Angleton followed the logic of his methodology too
far, for late in 1954 he and his staff began to read all the mail
traffic to and from the Soviet Union that entered and departed or
transited through the Port of New York. The decision had been
made at the cabinet level to permit the FBI limited surveillance
of the mails three years earlier, and the Post Office Department
had permitted the photographing of the outside of envelopes, but
the systematic reading of the mail of American citizens, the overwhelming majority of whom harbored no ill intent toward their
country, was unprecedented. It was also illegal. Angleton estimated that the contents of about 2 percent of all incoming mail
would be photographed. He believed that Soviet agents used the
mails routinely because they knew that opening the mail was against
American law and believed that the CIA could not get permission

to do so. The only solution, Angleton thought, was to break the law, and though he did not invoke the notion of a higher law, he believed the rewards in information were likely to be substantial. Before the operation, known as HT/LINGUAL, was brought to an end in 1973, the CIA opened 215,820 letters and developed a computerized register, a watch list, of 2 million names. Angleton did not presume any large percentage of these names to represent spies or traitors; he did assume that those who were in regular correspondence with the Soviet Union might receive information that was useful to an intelligence agency and that some very few might, by what they wrote in reply, reveal leaks in American security. He wanted, therefore, to "know everything possible regarding contacts of American citizens with Communist countries." [68]

Though Angleton was following his methodology to its conclusions, they were conclusions based upon a wrong premise: that methodology justifies all. Not so, at least to "the real world." Even within the CIA, many who were not engaged in counterintelligence decided that the gain was not worth the risk. The possibility of discrediting the CIA, of bringing down upon it congressional inquiries, the wrath of journalists, the renewed fear of those who had always said that an intelligence agency was one step toward a police state, that the CIA was an incipient Gestapo, these risks were simply not worth the information one might gain. Critics of HT/LINGUAL reasoned that highly placed Russian spies were unlikely to reveal anything through the mails, and in the ascendancy of SIGINT, the letter, the microdot, the coded phrase were not likely to be used at top levels. Checking back on copied letters it was found that the thirty-five that had originated in the Georgian Republic, and had been opened, for example, had revealed not one hint of an uprising that took place there in March 1956. Angleton could reply that, since letters to be opened initially were chosen at random, nothing was proven by the lack of useful information; as the index of names grew, so that letters could be targeted, more information could be expected. He also maintained that he had already obtained information useful to those who understood CI. Nor, of course, could he reveal all that he might know about the value of the opened letters, since the CIA itself might have been penetrated by a KGB agent. One cannot desert a methodology simply because it has not yielded results.

Then there was Chaos. The FBI had been putting thousands of requests to the CIA for information on Americans overseas as

part of an effort to discover whether there was any foreign influence on the growing antiwar and student protest movements in
the United States. Presidents Johnson and Nixon were certain that
the anti-Vietnamese war movement was Communist-inspired and
instructed the FBI and the CIA to get the proof. There was no
proof to be had, and each time the DCI told a president this, the
president in effect said to dig harder, there must be. Informers
were planted in student groups, the FBI sent false and disruptive
letters to the wives of activists to convince them that their husbands were entering into casual sexual liaisons, *agents provoca-
teurs* were used. Richard Helms, the DCI from 1966 to 1973, did
not tell Angleton of this operation at first. When Angleton did
learn of Chaos, he approved the effort to find out whether there
were foreign connections to domestic political agitation.[69] The CIA
was not operating in the States, he insisted: individuals had been
put into dissident organizations under cover in order to build
credibility to operate abroad, and if one of them discovered vital
information and wished to pass it to the FBI in California, should
he have gone to Canada to make the telephone call? Angleton no
doubt thought the question ridiculous, but the answer was yes;
even more, the CIA ought not to have allowed itself to be placed
in the position that the question need be posed. Yet it was the
prerogative of the DCI to put anyone into a unit of the CIA and
have him report directly to him, and the DCI believed himself to
be acting on direct presidential orders. To Angleton in 1975–76 it
seemed that the Church committee had left the rails, did not grasp
the issues. Only one or two staff members to the committee appeared to understand that, whatever abuses may have occurred,
there was also a genuine espionage threat to the country. And, in
the end, so too did one member, Senator Howard H. Baker of
Tennessee, who in a long "separate view" to the committee's
final report, issued in April of 1976, having pursued certain aspects of the committee's investigation independently, concluded
that after "some initial difficulties" the cooperation the CIA gave
the Church committee "was exemplary." He singled out former
DCIs Helms and Colby, the present DCI George Bush, and James
Angleton for praise.[70]

It was the mail intercept program that hanged Angleton. The
program had been handled by the Office of Security at first, and
was then handed over to CI for budgetary reasons. After the Church
committee hearings concluded, the Department of Justice looked

into the program with a view to possibly bringing criminal charges, but the department concluded that because of the high-level approvals the intercept program had been given, there were no grounds for prosecution. Angleton was pressed several times over the program, and his answers were evasive and stumbling. Some thought this was because he was caught off guard, or had not thought about the illegalities involved, or was even in a state of shock; others believed it was because he was trying not to drag anyone else into the mire, since the attorney general's office had approved the program earlier and read some of the product in raw form. As the CIA program had been given the color of legality, there was no prosecution, but as the FBI lacked approval from the attorney general, some of its agents were prosecuted.

Angleton viewed the Church committee as adversarial, as it was, and felt he had been sandbagged. On September 24, 1975, when his gratuitous remark about it being inconceivable that a secret intelligence arm of the government had to comply with all overt orders of that government was picked up by Senator Schweiker, Angleton waffled badly: had he said that, Schweiker asked? Angleton replied that "it shouldn't have been said." Schweiker pressed him as to whether he believed the statement; Angleton replied that it had been "rather imprudent" to make the remark. Schweiker asked if he wished to withdraw the statement; Angleton did. Did he mean the statement when he first said it, Schweiker asked? Angleton repeated that he had withdrawn the statement. Schweiker asked once more; Angleton replied that "the entire speculation should not have been indulged in." An open committee hearing—Angleton had asked for and not been given the privacy of an executive session—was no place to explain what he had meant. And, in any case, he did mean it.

But the damage had long been done. In Angleton's view President Gerald Ford, who had, incredibly, revealed to the press the fact that the CIA had engaged in planning the assassination of foreign leaders, and who when caught by persistent reporters on the ski slopes at Vail had thrown the entire issue of intelligence to the Hill, forgetting that he was throwing away part of the executive branch, had never understood the issues. Senator Church, from Angleton's hometown of Boise, himself an intelligence officer in World War II, was intent on running for the presidency and was using the hearings to command public attention and generate public outrage. F. A. O. Schwartz, Jr., chief counsel to the committee, failed to give Angleton a full bill of particulars, so that when he testified he was unprepared. Apart from the damage to morale and the destruction of any remnant of public confidence, Angleton felt that the hearings had given away so much detail, "the other side can triangulate and build up a chrono that's very deep."[71] The entire situation was a nightmare, in part of his own making—he should not have "popped off," he is supposed to have said later, about whether one obeys the president's overt orders or not—but in larger part because William Colby, from September 1973 director of the Central Intelligence Agency, had chosen to lift the lid on Pandora's box and stand by as all the secrets flew into the open.

This is a partial and a hostile view, of course, and it is, moreover, a view that does not speak to all of the moral and ethical issues. It was in some measure nonetheless correct. Church did use the committee hearings to advance his potential candidacy, though this does not mean that all of the charges he laid day after day were untrue. Ford was unclear, and perhaps ill-advised. And certainly Colby had, for whatever motive—because he was the mole? because he was a simple honest man? because he judged that the agency would survive only if the air were cleared?—surrendered the family jewels. Some, perhaps cynics, saw the entire theater in terms of a struggle for personal power; others, including Angleton, thought it arose from the most fundamental inability of Colby to understand, and therefore to value, the nature of counterintelligence. Certainly there was a clash between Colby and Angleton over a basic issue, methodology. Angleton held to his belief in HUMINT, especially as it was understood in CI. Colby was described by an Angleton supporter as a man who did not believe in human resources. He is said to have told Angleton, when the CI chief protested being instructed to give up the Israeli connection, that his agents were "negotiable." Colby was a "drop, fight, and get out man." He espoused "cost effective agent handling," while CI insisted that efficiency could not be put first. Colby was said to have no "memory" for operations—not that he could not recall names, but that he did not see the connections between operations perhaps separated by years—while Angleton had a "ferric memory." The difference was, one horrified if partial onlooker concluded, quite unbridgeable.

Counterintelligence had always been vulnerable within the agency, where jealousy, anger over its queen-bee position, suspicion that some of its agents turned their clandestinity to self-serving purposes, and disinclination to wrestle with the stern dictates of so avid a disciplinarian as Angleton—CIA workers at the defector reception center in Germany are said to have been driven "half-crazy" by Angleton's list of unending, meticulous, apparently pointless questions—had all contributed to make Cinderella unpopular. When Colby applied his concept of "management by objectives" directly from the corporate world (Union Carbide was one dedicated exponent of the phrase), he ended the conservative, hermetic world Angleton regarded as essential for CI. In July of 1973 Colby reorganized counterintelligence according to these management principles, stripping it of many of its functions, dispersing its staff. CI was akin to academia; it worked on connections, inspired guesses, long hours, unconventional procedures; management by objectives was business. It was also nonsense, CI felt. Disagreements over procedure and policy grew, as Angleton dug in behind the trenches of his methodology and Colby showed little inclination to understand what that methodology was.

There were less philosophic differences, of course, dating back to Italy. Angleton had opposed the Bay of Pigs operation, and it was believed Colby had favored it (he had not—he hadn't been asked); Angleton had urged a strong CI program in Vietnam, to cut off the steady flow of secrets to the North Vietnamese and the National Liberation Front, and Colby, as head of the "pacification" program in Vietnam, refused to try to penetrate the government in Saigon (Angleton is supposed to have said that Colby had the blood of American boys on his hands); Colby had told James Schlesinger when he came in as DCI in February of 1973 that he ought to fire Angleton, who he hinted was paranoid, believing that the Russians were ten feet tall (Angleton would have replied that they were, that any totalitarian state was, because of central control over its people, ten feet tall), that the split with Communist China was a ruse, that the KGB ran the Palestine Liberation Organization. Colby apparently thought Angleton was biased and felt that Israel could do no wrong.

The first great cuts in the agency had come under Schlesinger in 1973. He was determined to clear out anyone who had been in the agency for twenty years or more. He wanted to clean out the Directorate for Plans, the DDP, Richard Helms's "Praetorian Guard." There went Thomas Karamessines, as William Colby became head of the new Deputy Directorate of Operations. There went Bronson Tweedy, Princeton '37, and Cord Meyer, Yale '43. There went over a thousand CIA officers, a hundred of them from the DDO. There went HT/LINGUAL. And then, abruptly, in just five months of tenure, Schlesinger was moved over to the Department of Defense, and the feared outsider was replaced by William Colby, the insider who had come up through the ranks. Colby reduced CI by half or more, taking away components Angleton regarded as essential. The end—though precisely what end was not yet clear—was in sight.

On December 17, 1974, Colby told Angleton of his intended reorganization of the relationship to Israeli intelligence: Angleton could remain as a consultant on Israel, but in future management was to come under the DCI. The next day Seymour Hersh, a persistent and able reporter from *The New York Times,* who had got wind of Operation Chaos, called Colby for an appointment, and on December 20 met with Colby and asked about it. Colby replied that Chaos was not illegal—thus admitting to it—and said that in any case it had been terminated. Colby is supposed to have told Hersh about the mail intercept program run by CI as well. The same day, realizing that Angleton's resignation, were he to give it, would seem linked to any story Hersh printed, Colby told Angleton it was time for his decision. (Colby had anticipated the press reaction correctly: Angleton eventually was reported as having directed *all* the domestic spying operations.)[72] Two days later *The Times* published Hersh's story on its front page. Colby already had the family jewels in hand—those reports on wrongdoing within the agency—and now he felt compelled to clear the air with them. Angleton thought this was madness. Hersh had already encountered Angleton, having tried to ask him questions about E. Howard Hunt and Watergate, and had concluded that Angleton had stalled him, though in fact Hersh's call had come on a day when Angleton had not read the paper and did not know that Hunt had come into the Watergate story. Angleton was certain he did not know Hunt, but he had an eight-by-ten picture of Hunt made up to study. He was relieved that he still did not know him. Hersh, in the meantime, had sought his answers elsewhere, and now when Colby implicated Angleton in the mail intercept program, he was prepared to believe the worst. The floodwaters were spilling over the dam and could not be turned back.

Once more Colby summoned Angleton, to tell him that he was being removed as head of CI, though he could have a posting overseas if he wished, perhaps as chief of station in his beloved London. Colby was aware there never had been a meeting of minds and was certain that Angleton was not playing the game of the new management policy: HT/LINGUAL and Chaos were the proximate cause of Angleton's removal, though the true causes ran much deeper. Colby had wanted Angleton's resignation for some time—he thought it was best for the agency.

The felling of Angleton was over policy, not because of the *Times* article, but it would be linked in the public's mind to the scandals about to engulf the agency and, later, as Angleton appeared before the Church and Pike committees—at the latter with two ill-prepared counsel—and the Rockefeller commission (which, unlike the others, he thought got the story more or less right), the repetitive revelations sealed his connection to "the rogue elephant."[73] Angleton resigned—delaying to the last day of the year to gain a cost-of-living benefit in his annuity—and his three chief deputies, Rocca for research, Miler in operations, and Hood as executive officer, followed him out of the agency. After his retirement Angleton was awarded the Distinguished Intelligence Medal, the agency's highest award. It was presented to him by the deputy DCI, Lieutenant General Vernon Walters. Colby was out of town.[74]

These last few years had been bad ones for Angleton personally. The old friends, Dulles—whose eulogy he had written—Wisner, many others were gone. A friend of twenty years, Samuel Papich, long-term liaison from the FBI to the CIA, had retired to Albuquerque, severed in part by J. Edgar Hoover's testy if brief decision to end liaison to the CIA over a dispute arising from the disappearance of a professor of history at the University of Colorado, Thomas Riha, apparently under murky inter-agency circumstances.[75] Angleton's father had died in 1973. His son had for a time been estranged over the war in Vietnam, in which he had served, and there was strain with his other children and, for a time, with his wife. Angleton had been ill with emphysema and an ulcer (and in the hospital the day the decision was made to finally, formally accept Nosenko as authentic). There was the Petty report in 1974, concluding that Angleton himself might be the mole. There had been what he regarded as a series of betrayals and blunders: President Ford had thrown the agency to the wolves; Colby had eviscerated CI; the Israeli connection had been seriously damaged, for when Angleton was liaison with Mossad there had been little need for a large station in Tel Aviv, Mossad having produced Middle East intelligence for both services; Angleton was publicly blamed for the mail intercepts, was linked with a variety of dirty tricks of which he had not even known himself, was accused of having incarcerated Nosenko, of saying that the CIA could, even should, lie to the country and to the country's president. There had been a dreadful moment when Angleton had been interviewed on the telephone at home and had been described by the reporter as disjointed, his mind wandering. There had been a public encounter in which it was said Angleton was drunk. Lyndon LaRouche, convert from Communism to the far right, accused him—a man who had once said that Secretary of State Henry Kissinger might as well be a Russian agent, so much was his foreign policy playing into Soviet hands—of being a Communist himself!* A man whose picture as an adult had almost never appeared in any public place, whose name had been quite unknown to the media, who was not mentioned in any of the many books on espionage, or World War II, or the Soviet threat, was now suddenly in the public eye. This was, or appeared to be for a time, devastating.

With hindsight, any number of explanations have been adduced to account for Angleton's fall. He was simply too complex, even paranoid, for Colby to accept any longer; he had tied the CIA up in knots with his mole hunt; he was a mole himself; he was ill, and drinking; he was the target of a character assassination campaign emanating from Henry Kissinger; he was the victim of KGB disinformation; he was destroyed by HT/LINGUAL, and Sey-

---

*There is a persistent attempt by Angleton's critics to typecast him into a conventional political labeling. Those who appear to dislike liberals refer to him as "one of the liberals who came from the OSS." Those who link him with Chaos and HT/LINGUAL, and who focus on his concern with "the nature of the Soviet threat," think him well to the right. In fact he seems to have been rather apolitical, mainly intent on his job and protecting counterintelligence. In the 1950s, he saw Senator Joseph McCarthy as a threat to the independence of the agency and felt that McCarthy's almost mindless approach to Communism actually encouraged its acceptance by Americans who disliked his tactics.[76] (Angleton is supposed to have asked whether McCarthy might not be in the control of the Soviets.) That Angleton, Raymond Rocca, and James McCargar are said to have worked together to throw other bones to McCarthy and his staff so that they would leave the agency alone is entirely in keeping with Angleton's protective approach to counterintelligence, though in no way does it say anything about his own political persuasions, LaRouche and company notwithstanding. If they did throw bones, they threw the right ones, for McCarthy turned his spotlight on the army, and it exploded in his face.

mour Hersh, and this campaign of destruction was engineered by Colby, who had set him up, or by the Soviets. The more likely explanations do not require a conspiracy thesis, however. Angleton had enjoyed unparalleled access to the top in the agency, for nineteen years being the one director who never knocked when he entered Dulles's or Helms's offices, and he may have grown a bit careless in his cultivation of access, have burned a few too many fingers with his insistence that everyone must be suspect, may have simply assumed too much in a changing agency. Certainly Colby disagreed with Angleton's way of viewing the bureaucracy of intelligence: Angleton wanted tightly compartmentalized units divided by functions, with counterintelligence a world, and perhaps a law, unto itself; Colby preferred organization by geography, not by discipline, so that everyone who was working on the Soviet Union was talking to everyone else, at least near the top. This was the old argument about centralized versus decentralized intelligence back to haunt everyone. Perhaps Angleton was identified a little too closely with Europe, and possibly there had come to be something of a division between the Old Europe hands and the Old Asia hands as the war in Vietnam wound down, though Colby does not think this was a factor or that any such division existed in any significant way. Perhaps Angleton was too close to the Israelis at a time when the Young Turks were tilting a bit toward the Arabs, so that he appeared to want to lock the agency into earlier cold war verities, whether in the Middle East or over Sino-Soviet relations, while others were eager for the kinds of new initiatives that new definitions would allow. Perhaps the KGB was getting better at its job. Every observer then, and most observers since, espoused some combination of these ideas. However mixed, they all testify to the passage of time.

After his resignation Angleton was understandably a bit invisible for a while, and then he began to surface once more, to visit the Army and Navy Club, where he had dined often with Philby, or the Blue Ridge fishing club in Virginia, to attend a dinner in memory of Wild Bill Donovan or retirement parties for old friends. He stayed in touch with Rocca, Miler, and Hood, his three principal deputies. He saw Richard Ellmann again, attending a lecture he gave at the Library of Congress. He got up to New Haven to a class reunion, having had to cancel plans to go to a reunion in 1971, and he had a happy meeting with Norman Pearson before the professor died. He successfully traced down his favorite Chianti Classico, Castello di Fonterutoli, to a D.C. liquor store. James and Cecily Angleton went regularly to the Episcopal church, a handsome New England-styled structure nearby in Arlington, where for a time the preacher was Sid Lovett, the son of the Reverend Sidney Lovett, the much missed chaplain at Yale. Angleton helped some friends with their writing,[77] wrote a bit himself, and read a lot, books, poetry, the weekly Jerusalem *Post*. Pretty soon he was in rather sardonic good spirits again. He remained convinced there was a mole, and he was certain that Shadrin had been betrayed. With some pleasure he testified before the Senate Intelligence Committee on the question of the mole, and he urged President Jimmy Carter to meet with Shadrin's widow, for she had been put through a great deal on behalf of the nation (Carter didn't call). He shifted from Virginia Slims to Merits—no new code name there—ate less, drank Coca-Cola, and followed closely the breaking news stories of the 1980s about Americans who had sold secrets to the Russians, the Chinese, and the Israelis. He certainly had not gone into hiding, as one press report said—after all, his name was in the phone book—and quite often a reporter or researcher would call him for his opinion on some story, to which he almost always responded that he could not comment.

Angleton's most public activity in retirement was the chairmanship of a small group, the Security and Intelligence Fund, which issued quarterly statements on a variety of security subjects—terrorism, the Russian threat, the invasion of Grenada.[78] Angleton's old friend Charles J. V. Murphy, retired from *Fortune* magazine, wrote for *Situation Report* and was a director of the fund, while former Ambassador Elbridge Durbrow, chairman of the American Foreign Policy Institute, was its president. Angleton was also briefly an associate editor of *The Journal of International Relations* with a retired general, Robert C. Richardson III, who later became the secretary-treasurer of the Security and Intelligence Fund. By 1985 Angleton was somewhat in demand through the fund to supply advice and information to members of Congress. From time to time articles would appear favorable to his position on defectors—some critics said that one author, Edward Jay Epstein, was Angleton's "man," though Epstein could be critical too, as Angleton was of him[79]—and he clearly remained in touch with a wide range of individuals in the intelligence community.

Angleton had been present, as it were, at many of the major

events of the cold war, beginning with the first test of American responses in Italy. He had, through his Israeli connection, played a role in the Middle East from well before the Suez crisis. He had, through his mail intercept program, unintentionally provided prime ammunition for the Church committee and, many argued, had helped bring down public wrath on an already shaken agency.[80] Some believed him to be the Deep Throat of Watergate.[81] When he resigned, his files were dispersed, the remainder of his staff absorbed into other offices. Some commentators would say that with Angleton gone, the CIA had no capacity to defend itself against penetration, that CI was in effect dead, and they pointed out that so far as was known the CIA had never been penetrated, unlike virtually every other Western intelligence agency, during Angleton's tenure (unless Angleton was right, of course, about the mole).[82] Others said that his leaving of the agency was necessary to the saving of it. One could ask a hundred people about Angleton and receive a hundred lightly shaded different replies that ranged from utter denunciation to unadulterated hero worship. That the positions could occupy these extremes spoke of the significance and the ambiguity of the role he had played. And in 1985–87, as Americans opened their newspapers to read of the greatest number of spy trials they had ever known, and as an agency that had believed under Angleton that it had never been penetrated found that it clearly had been, at least at some point in the early 1980s,[83] there were friends who thought they could hear the Kingfish— yet another of his alleged code names[84]—laugh from some place high up on the Matapedia River in New Brunswick, where in the summer of 1985 he had gone fishing for three weeks of late mornings, late nights, and solitary lures.*

The theoretician of counterintelligence did not exactly drop from sight. He granted interviews, though cautiously. He complained of disinformation aimed at him, and encouraged his friends to cor-

---

*Virtually everyone who has written on Angleton has been attracted to the image of the chief of counterintelligence, alone, patiently and silently angling for some still, deep-rising fish. The image is fine, and accurate enough, but it misses the real point. Angleton was a fly-fisher. The devoted fly-fisher may carry a hundred or more flies with him and can choose from a thousand patterns. Some flies are literal imitations of real flies while some imitate nothing at all. Counterintelligence is, like Leo Tolstoy's notion of the hedgehog—the creature that knows "one big thing"—quite single-minded, but it is also like Tolstoy's fox, the animal that knows many things.

rect errors about him when they appeared in the public press, or
in journals he instinctively distrusted, in *Mother Jones* (a very
odd speculative piece about CIA influence in Australia)[85] or *Rolling Stone,* or *Penthouse,* or the *National Catholic Reporter.* He
read few of the novels in which he appeared, though acquaintances (and sometimes the authors) sent him copies. When the
notional mole argument was aired in *Harper's* magazine in October 1983, he did not reply, though some of his friends did on his
behalf; *Harper's* printed none of their letters. He knew his Eliot
too well not to remember "Gerontion":[86]

> After such knowledge, what forgiveness? Think now
> History has many cunning passages, contrived corridors
> And issues, deceives with whispering ambitions,
> Guides us by vanities. Think now
>
>   . . .
>
> Tenants of the house,
> Thoughts of a dry brain in a dry season.

He didn't expect to return to his former position—it was not there
to return to—but he saw no reason to abandon his methodology
of doubt. One had to assume the worst, and go on from there.[87]

By the spring of 1987, there were many in the intelligence community and some in Congress who felt that Angleton had, in some
measure, been proven right: The United States, its counterintelligence unit reduced from 300 to 80 persons at the end of Angleton's reign, the idea of counterintelligence itself somewhat in
disrepute, lacked the capacity to respond to Soviet penetration.
Clearly such penetration existed. Whether Angleton's methodology would have prevented it, or would have made matters worse,
is open to debate. Certainly Angleton felt to some degree that his
approach had been justified, and he came out of the shadow just
a little, granting an interview or two, speaking for attribution on
the telephone from his home in Virginia to reporters who were
insistent in their assaults on his answering machine. That spring
Angleton's name was linked to new information about Suez, to a
breaking news story in Australia, and perhaps most significantly
to the revelation in London that British Intelligence had spied on
Britain's own prime minister, Harold Wilson. Just how much James
Angleton might have been willing to tell would not be known,
however. On the morning of May 11, 1987, he died of lung cancer,
still silent on most of the interesting and all of the significant questions.

CHAPTER SEVEN

THE ALUMNI

RETURNING TO THE CAMPUS

"T"he tigers of wrath are wiser than the horses of instruction." James Agee and Walker Evans had liked that aphorism.[1] It had a rather definitive ring about it. In the end, what happens is what happens, and all the instruction about what ought to happen, should happen, the predictions about what will happen, are overtaken by events. University scholars do not much like that phrase, "overtaken by events," for it suggests that events have a momentum of their own and that academic analysis is not sufficient to account for what happens. One can suggest dozens of reasons

439

why the CIA shot itself in the foot and can present dozens of arguments as to why academe and the intelligence community had, by the late 1960s in much of the country, by the mid-1970s in nearly all, put so much distance between themselves. Both were responsible, certainly: academics generally wanted nothing to do with what was perceived as an unethical subgovernment, and for the most part intelligence people were angered at having been rejected by the subculture of which they had thought they were a part. The alumni had been rejected; they were not wanted anymore, not by the generations that had replaced them on the campuses, not even by their former teachers.

Alumni are a generally conservative lot when it comes to thinking about their university. For perfectly understandable reasons, they do not want it to change, or change much, from the place they recall so happily (happily, for if their experience was an unhappy one, they generally do not join alumni associations). It is natural that those who went to Yale when it was an all-male undergraduate college should, on the whole, have opposed the decision to go coeducational, or that those whose sense of pride in the institution grew in some measure from team triumphs in football, swimming, or crew should feel disappointed that Yale's athletic fortunes were on the wane.[2] This does not make alumni reactionaries. Being an active alumnus of an institution is to be caught up in nostalgia a good bit of the time, and nostalgia is a helpful sentiment: it fuels historical preservation societies, funds drives for band uniforms in high schools, political parties, and some churches. Alumni are often the last to realize how the inner dynamics of an institution have changed it. But then, if reminded, they also remember how they changed the institution during their short time within its hallowed walls, or how they may have wished to see it changed, and they generally renew their support, nostalgia reinvigorated by a fresh sense of what a university is all about: it is the preserver of the past and the creator of change.

The alumni of Yale who went into, and remained in or returned to, the intelligence services worked in a closed environment, and they were not quick to see how the postwar university was moving on a different track. Nor did the university sense this, knowing little about what track intelligence operations might have taken, until the war in Vietnam began to show that two parallel tracks do not meet at the horizon. The 1961 Bay of Pigs fiasco—in which two ultimately unhappy Yale alumni, Richard M. Bissell and Tracy

Barnes, were deeply involved[3]—had been the first major shock to
the assumption that the two cozy communities coexisted in an
easy if unspoken harmony, and that shock was caused at least as
much by the simple fact that the Zapata Plan, the invasion plan,
failed, as it was by any strong moral revulsion over it. The real
disaffection grew as more and more people became convinced that
the U.S. Army, the U.S. State Department, the U.S. intelligence
community, and the U.S. president were lying to them about what
was happening in Vietnam. There too honest men and women tried
to do their job with integrity—one, George Carver,[4] the coxswain
whom Skip Walz did not recruit back in 1950, was among those
who sought to prevent falsification of enemy strength records—
but the definitions of the role of intelligence seemed, at least to
most academics, to have so changed as to make it difficult for
them to understand precisely where integrity lay. Was a university that thought it educated people to a comprehension of civic
virtue able to comprehend the grindingly obsessive and politicized
nature of intelligence work in a war like that being fought in
Vietnam?

Certainly a great number of the Yale men who were in intelligence in the 1960s thought not. They felt they had observed a
change in the academic relationship, whether it came from the
Bay of Pigs, or as a result of the deeply traumatic shock of John
Kennedy's assassination, or simply that universities were increasingly staffed by people who had no experience of Eisenhower's
Great Crusade. It is not true that universities rejected the intelligence community: that community rejected universities at least as
early. The mutual rejection may be dated from 1961.

In 1984–85, when a historian wrote to just under four hundred
Yale alumni who could be identified as having worked as intelligence service professionals, he received ninety-three more or less
detailed responses. Most remarked upon the schism and most attributed it to the universities. These were not conservative alumni,
unhappy about coeducation or student protest movements. Most,
indeed, were Democrats or self-nominated liberal Republicans. But
they had as a group concluded that the alumni could not come
home again. Those who had served in the CIA ironically felt this
the most strongly, for they had become the most visible.

The class of 1943 had sent forty-two of its members into intelligence work, largely with the OSS. At least nine had remained
through the transition to work for the CIA. They were proud of

their work, though not always proud of their agency. In 1984 one thought it had fallen into "sleazy hands," another that it had been compromised by "nauseating egoism," by "greed and ignorance." Some were like the good Republicans who were more outraged than any Democrat could be over Watergate, because they had been let down—more than let down, betrayed—by a leadership they had not only trusted but in which they had vested their own faith and their own ego. Yet, they did not all abandon Yale, even if Yale seemed for a time to have abandoned them, and they continued to send their sons and daughters to Yale (though admission was now more of a problem), to show up in New Haven in late May and early June to gather under blue and white awnings to reminisce with their class, even on occasion to teach a seminar or two in one of the colleges, when, in the 1980s, student hostility to the CIA had softened. It was not these men who had put distance between the intelligence community and the academy. These were men who still had the sense of curiosity, and the concern for the academic laying on of hands, that they had as undergraduates. Conservative as alumni, and entitled to be, they wanted to be in touch with the students: impatient, often thoughtless in the sense of not really seeing connections to the past, mindful only of connections to the future, as they too were entitled to be.[5]

One alumnus of the class of 1943, Cord Meyer, Jr., might be taken to speak for all, for the sense of his response was repeated time and again in conversations and letters.[6] He had come to Yale from St. Paul's, in New Hampshire, where he had been "a strong student, a strong person." There had been prizes in all of his six years at St. Paul's, and except for one year he had been awarded a 1st Testimonial. He had graduated Magna Cum Laude, had been a goalie for the hockey team, editor of the school magazine, a supervisor in a dormitory. At Yale he had continued his superlative record, in four years having only four marks of less than A, those being Bs. He completed his degree on December 19, 1943, influenced far more by the world of events outside the university than by his teachers, though he later remembered three with affection: Wallace Fowlie, who made him excel in sixteenth-century French literature; Ted Sperling, the young classicist destined for the OSS; and the historian Erwin Goodenough, a "very strange fellow indeed," who made Plato come alive. Most valuable, he thought, was his course in metaphysics (in which he received a nearly impossible A-plus), George Heard Hamilton's introduction to the history of art, and Nicholas Spykman's two semesters (in which he received two of his Bs) on world politics. He also received an A-plus in military history, and it was the military that claimed him.

He very nearly died of it. As he came ashore with a marine assault team on Guam, he was pinned down under Japanese fire and badly wounded by a hand grenade. A glass eye and wrenching memories of seeing his friends die all around him were his legacy. Invalided home, he published a fine short story, "Waves of Darkness," in The Atlantic,[7] and it attracted considerable attention. In May 1945 he married Mary Pinchot (Reinhold Niebuhr performed the ceremony) and joined the American delegation to the San Francisco conference from which the structure of the new United Nations Organization was to be built. There Meyer was an assistant to Harold Stassen, one of the delegates. His concern for international order and world peace brought him back to Yale to lecture and then into the United World Federalists and the American Veterans Committee as a peace activist. He was shocked by the in-fighting on the AVC, however, and disturbed to see how the Communist group tried to take over the organization through intimidation. In 1950 he joined the CIA, working under Thomas Braden in OPC. This happy home was soon caught up in Senator McCarthy's charges that it, like the State Department, was filled with Red-lining liberals and card-carrying Communists, and in 1953 Meyer was told that he could no longer have his security clearance.

Meyer fought the accusations, and at last he was able to hear the charges against him from the FBI. He was believed to be a friend of Harlow Shapley, a Harvard professor of astronomy and a leftist (he had shared a speaker's platform with him). He was known to have lived off-campus—not entirely true: he was in Davenport College for a time—and to have stayed up all night with a light on in his room. He had written letters supporting groups on the attorney general's subversive list. It took Meyer six weeks to clear this insanity out of the way—it would take William Bundy, Yale '39, and an analyst with ONE, much longer—and when he was able to return to work, it seemed to his friends that his outspoken liberalism had been stilled. He would rise in the CIA, though not to the top, becoming head of the International Organizations Division. His form of facing reality—the title of his memoirs, published in 1980—was to provide covert financing for a number of such organizations, until in 1967 the word got out that the National Student Association had been compromised by CIA support. A complex edifice of dummy foundations, hidden businesses, and publishing houses came tumbling down, and Meyer moved on, to be station chief in London and eventually deputy to William Colby as DDO.[8]

The Meyer story is instructive, for it illustrates one of the important differences between academe and the intelligence community. In most universities one has the right to be wrong. Universities are built upon making mistakes; there could be no valid research were there not hundreds of feints, aborted projects, invalid conclusions. And one must not be punished, or intimidated, for mistakes honestly made. No government bureaucracy could hold to such a principle. To be sure, during the height of the McCarthy craze, academics were dismissed, tenure agreements violated, and many no doubt shrank into the library stacks, effectively silenced. But Meyer's experience goes to the heart of a fundamental difference between an independent university and government: the faculty *are* the university, while any government employee is beholden to the people (as one should be) and thus exposed to any person who may claim to be speaking for the people of the United States.

Perhaps there is no "typical" career path in intelligence, though there surely might be happier ones. One member of the Yale class of 1944 whose career was full of satisfaction, and who liked his assignments to the end, was Edward O. Welles. Welles was a member of the class that sustained the heaviest losses of any during the war. As a schoolboy in Scranton he had read with absorption of the developing European scene, in particular of the Spanish Civil War and the Italian conquest of Ethiopia, and though unlike many of his Yale classmates he had not traveled in Europe, he found he was very well informed by the standards of his peers. He was fascinated with "the course of events" in the truest sense, in the way events moved across the map, in visualizing the landscapes against which the events were to be set. At Yale he was unclear on his career plans, and when Pearl Harbor hit, he was a sophomore and ready "to leap to service." The marines turned him down—his eyesight was not good enough—and he signed on with the American Field Service, intrigued by an interviewer who appealed to young Welles's sense of idealism. He soon sailed for the Middle East with a group of a hundred young men, off to Egypt on a Danish freighter.

The very young and rather amateur ambulance driver served on
the Western Desert, was blooded at El Alamein in the company
of a New Zealand division he came to admire, and until the fall
of Tunis was attached variously through the Eighth Army to the
New Zealanders, the 4th Indian Division, and the Highland Division. As the AFS made plans to move on to Italy in June of 1943,
Welles enlisted in Cairo with the British army, having obtained
State Department clearance to do so, after failing to get into the
U.S. Air Force in Algeria. He soon found himself in a small, tightly
knit British commando unit, the Special Boat Squadron, a subsec-
tion of the Special Air Service, or SAS.[9]

The SAS prepared him for a life in the clandestine service. After
his first genuine training, Welles and his unit were sent to the
Dodecanese Islands, hoping to take them over from the demoralized Italians before the Germans could get to them, but too late.
Welles was reported missing in action for nearly a month, while
he and some of his comrades dodged searchers on Rhodes, in one
of the classic escape stories of the war, taking refuge amidst a
Greek wedding party. After R&R in Palestine, the Boat Squadron
was returned to the Aegean and, from a sanctuary on the Turkish
coast, harassed the Germans. Welles was struck by "the leadership, bravery, and purposefulness" of the very young officers,
and would remain in touch with some of them for years afterward.

Early in 1944 Welles walked into the American embassy in Cairo
to learn that, having become a corporal in a British unit, and with
some very practical experience behind him, he was now qualified
for American service, and shortly he was a member of an OSS
team being dropped from Brindisi by parachute into Croatia, from
which he and his team worked overland to Slovenia. Welles played
the Yugoslav circuit for six months, dodging the local quislings
and the Germans, brought in supplies to the partisans north of the
Drava River, and helped man the rat line (or escape line) that got
perhaps forty American air force men, shot down in Austria or
northern Yugoslavia, back behind Allied lines in Italy. On V-E
Day he found himself in Trieste, still with the Yugoslavs, maintaining a radio link to Caserta, and he reported on the tense confrontation in that disputed city between the Titoists, the Italians,
and the arriving Allied troops.

This had been a heady, productive, satisfying life: a "good war."
Welles returned to Yale in the fall of 1945, graduated in February
of 1947 (though as a member of his '44 class), and thought about
his future. He recalled the war quite vividly as generally "a happy

time.'' Married, not happy in a business venture in Texas, not
really prepared to live his life as a son-in-law in a middle western
family firm, he joined the Central Intelligence Agency when the
Korean War broke out. Having had Balkan experience, he was
soon in operations, and until his retirement in 1972 he put in long,
happy hours at his work, largely in Third World countries. His
career, he thought later, was the result of "luck, determination,
education, relationships with others and most certainly a belief in
what *I* was doing being in our best interests."[10]

Not all the alumni of the CIA could say the same. During the
last three years I have talked, or corresponded with, just under
two hundred people who were or are in intelligence work. They
do not represent a scientific sampling of opinion, of course, for
the group is skewed in at least three ways: they had a Yale connection, they tended to be financially comfortable, and they were
retired or near retirement.* I found it interesting that overwhelmingly they condemned the agency for projects like Chaos and
HT/LINGUAL and for the abortive and foolish plans to assassinate Castro. Generally they argued—and it seems fairly clear that
they are correct[12]—that the CIA played no significant role in the
overthrow of President Salvador Allende in Chile in 1973. Most
condemned the Bay of Pigs operation, though generally because
it was ill-planned and disastrously executed, and a number insisted that the fault for the latter rested squarely on President
Kennedy. I was struck by the number who were angry about these
operations on strategic rather than moral grounds, however: that

---

*For the period dealt with in this book, the Yale connection skews less than it
does for a later period. The Ivy League institutions were havens of the well
connected, and it is not surprising therefore that Ivy League graduates would
populate the upper echelons of intelligence agencies, and for the most part it has
been from the upper ranks that I have drawn my information, since senior officials are both more likely to be retired now and have a more comprehensive
view of any operation. There were major figures from outside the Ivy League,
of course, but as late as the Nixon administration, 26 percent of CIA employees
with college degrees had those degrees from Ivy League institutions and of those,
86 percent were from Harvard, Princeton, and Yale. When advanced study is
taken into consideration, and with Columbia added to the list of four, the dominance is even greater.[11] By the mid-1960s the balance was clearly tipping away
from the Ivy League, and to the extent that one can tell from purely fragmentary
information West Point (always high), the University of Southern California, and
a number of Roman Catholic institutions were rising. This was true in other
elitist government bureaucracies like the foreign service. In any case, graduates
of the Ivy League were not necessarily "the well connected" any longer, for
those universities had extensively democratized themselves by the mid-1970s.

they failed, that they drew the attention of the legislative branch, that they brought on an increased period of media exposure, that they brought the agency into disrepute. Many defended Richard Helms and other senior agency officials on the ground that the executive had ordered certain actions (or appeared to have ordered them), and that the agency is the creature of the executive branch.

But one may wonder how this necessarily changes things. The defense that one was merely following orders did not help the defendants at Nuremberg or those charged with wholesale slaughter of civilians in Vietnam, and in any event a body of well-educated and well-connected individuals might be expected to use a different argument.* Even looking back and in the relative security of retirement, a goodly number of these individuals did not see agency excesses in moral terms. Of course it may be that they simply thought there was little point in discussing so obvious an issue, especially since so many people view ethical matters as purely situational these days. Or perhaps they simply assumed that the definitions of morality held in the "real world" of an insulated university and in the "real world" of the front line in the cold war so obviously would differ that this could be taken as a given. A common education—that we had both read Plato and perhaps Rawls on ethics—did not mean that we would agree. Nor does it in the classroom.

One returns to McGeorge Bundy's enthusiastic statement about the OSS and academe: that the area studies programs in American universities "were manned, directed, or stimulated by graduates of the OSS—a remarkable institution, half cops and robbers, half faculty meeting."† There was, Bundy told his Johns Hopkins audience, and he hoped there always would be, "a big measure of interpenetration between universities with area programs and the information-gathering agencies of the United States." He was certainly correct in his factual statement—R&A in particular, through its methods and through its alumni, exercised a fundamental influence on the shaping of American graduate education in the growth period after World War II. He may have been correct that the

---

*The CIA leadership group still appears to be liberal in its political persuasions. Nixon thought that the CIA was controlled by "Ivy League intellectuals" who were opposed to him.[13]
†See Chapter Two.

OSS (and perhaps the universities) were "half cops and robbers, half faculty meeting," as academics competed for federal and foundation funding to launch and sustain their area studies programs. But his hope for the future was dashed, at least for a time, and it is surely not entirely coincidental that as academe and intelligence communities became estranged, area studies programs in the most socially concerned universities withered. That Southeast Asian studies programs are dead in the United States today may be attributed in part to a national desire to forget its experience in Southeast Asia, but that death arises in some measure from the fact that the dog bit the hand that fed it: most authorities on Southeast Asia in American universities joined the antiwar movement.

Though correct in the substance of his statement, Bundy was wrong in a deeper sense. The goals of government and the goals of the university are different. One is not the handmaiden of the other, nor ought to be. The intelligence community was angry with the universities for not being more supportive, as the flow of good young new recruits dried up. But in the free market of ideas, it was not the function of a university to be supportive.

Quite apart from moral issues, there were many other ways in which the still "well connected," or the "bad eyes brigade," might employ their talents. Intelligence work had simply ceased, on many grounds, to be an attractive option. That it might make itself an attractive option once again was possible, but not likely. In the heady years of the OSS academics were just learning the game: it was secret, it was romantic, it was a way to be genuinely useful and to apply one's knowledge, and it was much better than being a filing clerk or storming a beach in the South Pacific. Further, it was the academics who did much of the basic defining of intelligence, who laid out much of the theory, who through their social connections provided the essential lubrication with counterpart British and other intelligence agencies.

By the 1960s all this had changed. Academe had become relatively powerful in its own right. Its social base had been enormously broadened, dramatically so in the Ivy League. There was no sustained alternative disincentive, a shooting war and draft that would take the young professor away from his study and put him onto a beachhead, for even if drafted the young Ph.D. would, as a result of the hunger for the trained, generally be put behind a desk. In the larger universities academic salaries were now competing with government pay. Most important, academics had discovered that they were not quite as close in thought to the process of intelligence as they had once believed. Apart from all those covert operations, possibly exaggerated because so little could be known about them, and without the same apparent justification that covert operations had in wartime, there was the observable fact that the CIA, and the executive branch, tended to blame failures on the lack of sufficient intelligence. Academics tended to think that it was not faulty intelligence but bad political judgment that was producing disaster, and many believed that simply throwing more research at the problem would not solve it.

Whenever an alumnus of the Yale Graduate School returns to New Haven, he is likely to pass under the great tower of the Hall of Graduate Studies, and there he will read again the words inscribed over the entrance in 1934. They are not the usual aphorism about wisdom, grace, and learning, nor do they declare the virtue of books or that the past is prologue. Rather, HGS, as it is known, speaks out in the words of Rafael Sabatini, a former employee of British intelligence, whose best-selling and pot-boiling romance and adventure yarn of 1921, *Scaramouche,* provides the line. An alumnus making the transition from university to intelligence agency and then, after the Great Diminution of the mid-1970s, perhaps back to the university, would surely have agreed: "He was born with a gift of laughter and a sense that the world was mad." That gift was desperately needed in the days when the public fell out of its romantic enchantment with the James Bond image.

"People who know about spy systems do not write about them. People who do not know about them, or fancy that they know about them, do do some writing." In this way Sherman Kent replied to a young woman from Wellesley College who, early in 1951, had written to him a somewhat naive letter to ask if he would help her with a term paper. In 1951 Kent was correct, though by the 1970s he could scarcely have responded so firmly. He was known for his forthright approach to problems—there was the student who wrote to him in December 1950 at the CIA headquarters, reminding him that he had been in Kent's class in 1935–36 and asking for advice on a "big project" on the historical process, "physico-chemical, psychic, and historical." Kent had replied that he remembered the student well as one of the worst in the class—

but then, he said, it was one of the worst he had ever taught. Kent suggested that the student write to his old colleague from R&A, Hajo Holborn, back at Yale as professor of German history.[14]

Then there was the vulgar and profane side of Kent, the man who could swear like a trooper, who "could throw a knife better than a Sicilian," the man who in 1942 had cast his title in Arabic as "Chief of those who know things about the Great Green water or the Middle of the Lands." He never lost his sense of vulgarity—how was one to explain semantics to the ignorant, he asked? why, with a story: "Husband—'Darling, I've got my semi-annual hard-on.' Wife—'George, you always get mixed up in your English. You mean that you've got your annual semi-hard-on.' " He never lost his feeling that intelligence, though serious, was good fun and a bit romantic, recalling late in life how, on November 4, 1942, he had been picked up in front of the white guardhouse at the Constitution Avenue entrance to Q building in a plain black Chevy (Maryland plates 208-566) and was taken to The Farm for training in how to throw that knife better than the Sicilians.[15] Nor did he ever forget his scholarship, publishing eight years after his retirement from the CIA his book, slowly plugged away at over the years, on the election of 1827 in France.[16] "A damn fine thing to have got out after a quarter century or so of idle pursuits," his friend Abbott Smith, for years Kent's deputy and then successor at the National Estimates board, wrote.[17]

That quarter century of idle pursuits had included nearly sixteen years as chief of ONE, the Office of National Estimates, arguably the most important job in the Central Intelligence Agency,[18] since ONE was charged not with the getting of intelligence, not with the defining of what intelligence is, but with explaining what intelligence means. When Kent wrote his influential study on *Strategic Intelligence for American World Policy,*[19] he provided the text by which succeeding generations of fledgling analysts were schooled, a book that studs the footnotes of those that followed.[20] The Germans, the French, the Russians cited him as one of the prime theoreticians, and even his critics recognized that he had presented best one side of the "intelligence debate."

The "intelligence debate" was framed in 1949 when Kent's book appeared. Kent argued that intelligence should be independent of policy making in order to avoid bias. This was a historian's natural view. A colleague from the Department of Political Science at Yale, Willmoore Kendall, in an essay reviewing the book for *World*

Politics, disagreed:[21] intelligence should set forth alternative courses of action, should be intimately involved in making policy, and should give greater weight to theory. This was a political scientist's natural view. Kent's approach, Kendall said, reflected a wartime state of mind, "a compulsive preoccupation with *prediction,* with the elimination of 'surprises' from foreign affairs." When Kent retired, recipient of the President's Award for Distinguished Federal Civilian Service,[22] he still thought that intelligence professionals should provide the data and the interpretations—that is, the analysis—by which decisions could be made, and that policy had to come from elsewhere.

Kent was pretty appalled at the revelations about the agency for which he had worked so long, as the circus of 1974–76 put one more act after another into the center ring. He was well out of it, of course, having retired at the end of 1967, when a man he thought both thoroughly honest and thoroughly professional, Richard Helms, was at the wheel. Kent had never changed his mind about what was and what was not honest, either. In 1945, still in the OSS, he had sent off a letter, occasioned by his discovery that there were plans afoot to continue "certain black 'morale operations' after the end of the war." He spelled out "the classical formula" on which the liberal state was founded, at least as he understood it, and he declared: "For any U.S. agency to send unregistered clandestine operatives into a foreign country against which the United States is not at war and instruct these agents to carry out 'black' operations either pro-U.S. or anti- any indigenous secret or masked operations hostile to the interests of the U.S. not only runs directly counter to the principles upon which our country was founded but also those for which we recently fought a war." He believed, Kent wrote, in the power of the human mind to solve any problem, he held to the conviction of the essential goodness of mankind, and to a belief in the sanctity of the individual. To destabilize a nonenemy country—he did not use the now fashionable word, though it is what he clearly meant—was wrong. "Should such an operation be contemplated by an agency of the United States government I could not believe that responsible officers of the government would condone it, and if an agency of which I was an employee should embark upon such a venture without the full knowledge of responsible officers of government the course of action I would take should be obvious."[23]

What had happened by the 1960s, then, to make such a ringing charge seem untenable to so many who worked in the intelligence community? Yes, everyone, including Kent, was older and perhaps wiser. Yes, one could hedge about "peacetime" and "non-enemy nations," for the cold war provided an elasticity of terminology that seemed infinite. Perhaps not everyone believed in the essential goodness of mankind any longer. Perhaps there were those who no longer or never did espouse the sanctity of the individual. Perhaps it seemed clear that the power of the human mind could not solve every problem. And perhaps the "intelligence community" was no longer a community, no longer had its roots in the university, or in a profession, or in a commonly held set of beliefs about the "liberal education." As an astute observer of the Washington scene, Stewart Alsop, concluded in 1968, the CIA had been taken over by the "prudent professionals." An earlier generation, of which Kent was a member, had come to intelligence and stayed in, or left and returned, out of another competing, complementary "real world." They had been lawyers, economists, historians, who had taught, who had to learn how to justify themselves and their activities, how to defend their beliefs to others, and especially to skeptical young minds convinced that the past generation had made a mess of things, that the present was just holding on, and that only the next would do better. In no unkindly way Alsop chose Thomas Karamessines, old OSS man, X-2, CE, DDP—the initials trail out like arcane degrees—to make his point: here was a man who was "a genuine professional," a man who was "essentially an espionage professional, and nothing else."[24]

Well, why should one not expect the Great Game to become the Firm, the Company, a business like any other? Other games, the sports and contests by which young men and women had been taught "character," and "how to lose," and "fair play," were also becoming businesses as any alumnus of most universities could see. Another generation removed, into the 1970s, and even the young would be too far out of touch with the convictions of those who thought intelligence was, like the university, an exercise in civic responsibility to fully find their way back. Kent had once been a guide for his fellow OSS officers in the streets of Palermo, which were "absolutely Dantesque": one could not even be certain that anyone read Dante anymore. There were new sensitivities, new debates, to occupy the attention of the young.

It is always instructive to study the hand-written marginal notations that students make in university library books, for they often reveal a running debate. In one of the Yale University Library's copies of Kent's *Strategic Intelligence* such a debate took place in 1986, to the side of his sentence, "After all, it [an intelligence staff] is made up of men whose patterns of thought are likely to color their hypotheses and whose colored hypotheses are likely to make one conclusion more attractive than the evidence warrants."[25] This was the point Kent had made in *Writing History* in slightly more formal prose: "The historian must have a mulish obstinacy, a refusal to be gulled; he must be incredulous of his evidence or he will trip over the deliberately falsified."[26] Rather than focus on the point made, about "patterns of thought," the running debaters proved that point: wrote the first, circling the word *men* in the quotation, "What is this asshole's problem?" In bold hand came the second message, "What's yours?" A third hand elaborated: "Seriously fucking pseudo-feminist. I'm a woman and I understand that this book was written in 1949! Cool out Bitch!" The last, fourth, voice added, "Exactly. Context, ever heard of that?"

Kent would have loved the obviousness of the exchange, the underlying messages, the overt lack of response to his argument, the covert presence of responses, the gender conflict. After all, a man who could seriously formulate Kent's Law of Coups was not likely to miss the humor (the Law of Coups is that those coups that are known about in advance don't take place).[27] He had, however, died, on March 11, 1986,[28] his monument—the National Estimates—dismantled, his scholarly books still on the shelf to serve generations interested in French history (or in Buffalo Blocks, "for the puzzled high powered executive," on how to use sixty-four precision-cut hardwood blocks to produce hundreds of combinations, permutations, and variable designs for the illustration of geometry).[29]

Kent had seldom been in the public eye—a hundred footnotes in scholarly publications scarcely warrants notice in *People* magazine—and his contributions to intelligence are little known outside close students of the field. Certainly he will be remembered, and in time studied, for his work on theory, and for the way in which he developed and presided over ONE and supervised the production of the National Intelligence Estimates. He was not exclusively of the ivory tower, however. Kent was, for example, one of the four key figures who comprised an advisory council

charged with settling problems that might arise with Reinhard
Gehlen in Germany, and it was Kent who represented the Central
Intelligence Agency and accompanied Dean Acheson and Charles
"Chip" Bohlen on a hurried flight to Paris to brief the French
president, Charles de Gaulle, on the nature of the Cuban missile
crisis.

The Gehlen connection always intrigued and bothered Kent.
Gehlen had been head of military intelligence with Fremde Heere
Ost, German forces in the Soviet Union. He had built a strong
organization, and when Germany collapsed he had moved quickly
to make himself indispensable to the United States. Gehlen micro-
filmed his extensive files, hid the films in the Bavarian mountains,
and destroyed his original materials. He then offered the Americans access to his microfilms, and use of the agents in place left
behind as the Russian armies had overrun eastern Europe. Gehlen
was put in charge of an intelligence system targeted solely on the
Communist bloc nations, entering into a written contract with the
U.S. War Department in May 1949, as augmented by a gentleman's agreement with General Edwin Sibert, the former chief of
intelligence to 12 U.S. Army Group, and the go-between for Gehlen to American Military Intelligence. Those who wish to depict
the American military as clasping Germans with knowledge of the
Soviet Union to the nation's breast are unduly enthusiastic: Sibert
arranged to send Gehlen to Washington, and there he hung around
for nearly a year, trying to persuade SSU and G-2 of his potential
value. American intelligence wanted his files, certainly, and possibly his men, but they were quite reluctant to take Gehlen on.
Thus it would not be until the Soviet occupation of northern Iran
that Gehlen was invited to settle down to serious discussions, and
not until the cold war had heightened that agreement was reached.
Gehlen insisted that his organization would be purely German,
and under his control, contact with the American intelligence services being through a liaison staff. He stipulated that once a sovereign German government was established, all agreements were
to be cancelled, and his organization would be solely responsible
to that government. The advisory committee set up through the
American War Department was to keep Gehlen honest, and apparently all was carried out to mutual satisfaction, for in 1955
Gehlen became director of the West German Federal Intelligence
Service. The advisory committee consisted of two senior officials
from the War Department, Sherman Kent and Loftus E. Becker,
later deputy DCI, and a Wall Street banker charged with monitor-

ing the financial side of the agreement. Kent remained in touch with Gehlen until their respective retirements, only a year apart, and he met with Gehlen whenever he visited Germany.[30]

Kent's hurried trip to Paris in 1962 arose in some measure from his most serious intelligence lapse, one he later compared to the wartime disaster at Arnhem: he failed to foresee the Russian missile build-up in Cuba.[31] As he later remarked, he had made that most fundamental error: because all evaluations of the evidence argued that, though Russia certainly had the missile capability, it would be contrary to all logic to deploy missiles in Cuba, and because ONE had concluded that the Russians were rational when it came to the deployment of missiles, he predicted that they would do the sensible thing—not arm Cuba. That they did so showed either they were capable of being irrational (not surprising, he thought afterward; all people are, and the irrational should be built into predictions as a policy option) or that they thought quite differently than Americans did, which he concluded was also true. As President Kennedy readied his response to Khrushchev's initiative, small teams were sent out to show to the heads of state of America's allies the photographic evidence on which the United States was determined to act. Kent had marked areas under missile coverage on an ordinary 1960 Cuban tourist map by cross-hatchings, pinpointing the locations of the missile sites, and had his staff prepare hurried graphics. He and Acheson met with de Gaulle at 5:00 P.M. on October 22, and he returned with Ambassador Bohlen on the afternoon of the twenty-sixth, having also briefed the French press. On the first occasion Kent used U-2 photographs and on the second a low-level color picture of a SAM site "which almost made the old gentleman shout." The Russians began to dismantle the missile pads on the twenty-seventh, and Kent returned home, his demotic French having been put to very good use.*[32]

---

*Kent already knew the Elysée Palace. In May 1960, on the occasion of the Big Four Summit Meeting, Kent had been present and had taken notes, augmented by information from President Eisenhower's interpreter. Two hours after the discussions between the four had ended for the day, Kent was able to send off a cable to the DCI about the results. Bohlen moved more slowly and did not clear the interpreter's version of the State Department cable for three days, and then added his own material to the text. Kent asked to see the text, put it through the pants presser (Thermofax then, Xerox now), and sent the text to the CIA before it reached State. This was known as "taking a few rough notes," and though it showed enterprise, it was probably not a good idea.[33]

Above all, Sherman Kent was a scholar interested in seeing how
far he could carry the methods of history into the world of strategic intelligence. He agreed with that rather offhand judgment of
the British historian A. J. P. Taylor about how trained historians
or journalists could dig out most of the information which interested a foreign government, and in 1951 Kent had put statistics to
this observation: "of the things our state must know about other
states some 90 percent may be discovered through overt means."
(He later raised this to 95 percent.) The first stock of all basic
intelligence rested in the great libraries, museums, and laborato-
ries of the United States—that is, at least 60 percent of the information labeled "intelligence" was accessible to any hardworking
and well-trained undergraduate. Another 30 percent could be found
by overt means, though money and organization were needed for
this portion of intelligence: to subscribe to foreign publications,
to obtain telephone books, timetables, and "above all, newspapers." An intelligence agency would also monitor and transcribe
foreign commercial and state-sponsored radio programs, would
interview Americans who had recently visited foreign countries,
and would send out trained, fully overt observers in any number
of fields, many of them (politics, economics, cultural affairs, military, agriculture) as attachés to the embassies. This left not more
than 10 percent of needed information to be gathered clandes-
tinely. It was this information that was properly labeled "secrets
of state," even where a totalitarian regime might seek to restrict
as secret much that a democratic society left to open-gathering
techniques. To the safeguarding of this 10 percent many nations
would dedicate all of their security procedures. To explain why a
democracy needed a secret intelligence agency, Kent framed his
conclusion in terms of a primer: "To crack into this 10 percent
one's own offensive procedures, techniques and arts must be superior to the other man's defense. The essential ingredient and
the ingredient of overriding importance in one's offensive must
inevitably be the complete secrecy of the operation."[34]
During his time with the OSS Kent had become increasingly
fascinated with the theory of intelligence. One facet of this fascination lay in the questions of definition, another in a desire to
create a special vocabulary of "estimative probability," a third in
showing politicians, rather as though they were students in the
classroom, just how easily foreign intelligence services could obtain information on the United States without penetration of se-

curity agencies, without paying huge sums to greedy men and women to sell them secrets, and without anyone charged with the protection of secrets being lax in that protection. Kent believed strongly in democracy—he too was what might have been called an "old line liberal"—and he suspected that many of the country's politicians did not understand that a democratic society could not expect to keep from another country's intelligence agencies all of that theoretical 10 percent that were "state secrets" by its own definitions. (As we have seen, Kent later suggested that the most a society like the United States could hope to protect "for any period of time" was 5 percent.) This was why a democratic society had to be better at penetrating the "other man's defense," had to be stronger, technologically and methodologically ahead of the "other man," simply better at the game if it were to expect to survive as a democracy. Not for a moment was Kent ready to entertain the alternative: that the United States should abandon the fruits and methods of democracy in order to protect itself.

To make his point, Kent was the father of one of the most revealing, perhaps even bizarre, exercises in the history of the relationship between universities and intelligence. This was the production of the so-called Yale Report, the work of five historians. In the end Kent regretted ever having had the idea.

The notion was simple enough: Kent would demonstrate that his statistical estimate was roughly correct by having a squad of research scholars, none using any security access, prepare a report on the U.S. gross order of battle down at least to the division level, to show what the Russians could know, and probably did know, about American strength. In the spring of 1951 Kent sold his boss, once again William L. Langer, on the idea, and then contacted William Huse Dunham, his old friend at Yale, and asked "Huse" to put together the appropriate team. Given ten to twelve weeks of uninterrupted work across the summer, and given some small help with access to unpublished but public material not yet available in the Yale libraries, these scholars were to examine all possible sources as though they were "an informed and studious Russian team," and to present Langer and Kent with a document which could be compared against the most closely guarded official order of battle information. They also were to prepare an "encyclopedia" on naval strength in major combat vessels, air strength in major components, and types of military aircraft that were in the order of battle.

At the end of the summer the Yale scholars—Kent had been prepared to fund as many as eight through the government's Division of External Research, but five proved sufficient—having "worked like beavers" delivered several hundred pages of material to Kent, with a thirty-page summary. Kent then put a Sovietologist onto the game, to turn the "volume of capabilities" into what would look like a Russian report on probable U.S. intentions. "It was then," he wrote somewhat less creatively than usual, "that the shit hit the fan."

Kent had not informed the director of Central Intelligence, General Walter Bedell Smith, about the project. When he now told Smith that some Yale amateurs had produced a report that was 90 percent correct in its inventory of the gross order of battle, the shocked Smith took the tale to President Truman, who since July had been working on an executive order intended to place curbs on press freedoms when dealing with classified information. On September 23 word of Truman's intentions leaked to the press. The following day he signed the order directing all government offices to put into effect the classification system used by the State and Defense departments, by which the words *restricted, confidential, secret, top secret* would become universal. At the same time Truman insisted that there was "no element of censorship" in the order, which he was issuing, he said, as a result of a study made by a subcommittee of the National Security Council. At once there were concerted protests from the radio and newspaper press.

The order was not, in fact, unduly restrictive, though it was not clearly thought out, and it came at a time when Truman's popularity had taken another of its roller-coaster dips. The Republicans in the Senate immediately attacked him for trying to muzzle the press, all but two signing a statement against any form of restraint on the press. One, Senator John W. Bricker of Ohio, who was intent on an amendment that would take the United States out of the United Nations, offered a bill to revoke the order. General Douglas MacArthur, who in April had been fired by Truman for insubordination, joined in the general attack. Arthur Krock, perhaps the most powerful pundit writing in *The New York Times,* judiciously examined the order and pronounced it flawed, while the Office of Price Stabilization immediately played into the hands of the order's opponents by trying to use it to hide matters merely embarrassing to OPS, not security related.

The beleaguered Truman wanted proof of the need for some

restraint upon the press, and on October 4 he seized upon the Yale Report to justify his case. He delivered a stern lecture about the media's patriotic duty not to divulge information of value "to potential enemies," and gave it as his opinion that the press ought not to have published information on a new secret weapon, the Matador—a pilotless jet-propelled bomber—even though the press had received photographs from the Department of Defense. Truman also attacked *Fortune* by name for publishing the locations and maps of atomic energy plants. He then declared that he had not signed the executive order until a study by "a team of Yale scholars" had proven that 95 percent of classified information held by the government already was in print.

The press conference, described as unusually lively, was in fact a rather earnest seminar in which all parties seem, in retrospect, a bit naive. Certainly Truman was never clear on what classified information was, and he appeared to believe that if he could recognize disloyalty, all should be able to see it plain. He did not acknowledge that the intelligence community's methodological insistence that any nation, including present allies, was to be viewed as a "potential enemy," meant that virtually all information relating to military capacity was classified, and though *Fortune* had received the maps it printed from a government agency, and printed them to provide information on civil defense, he believed the editors should have made a judgment against the government and not used them. To illustrate his point he revealed that there had been two atomic explosions in the USSR, one "a fizzle" and one successful. When Stalin confirmed this the following day, Truman's case seemed substantially strengthened. One reporter asked why printing the fact that the Russians had detonated an atomic device should be classified, since presumably the Russians knew what they had done, and Truman replied that printing such news in advance of obtaining it openly from the Russians would reveal something of American monitoring capability. One reporter, Merriman Smith in *The Times,* asked the shrewdest question of all and received no answer: how did the Yale scholars get at the information so quickly?

While neither *The Times* nor the New Haven *Register* could get at the story, it seemed, an enterprising student reporter for the *Yale Daily News,* Gary S. Thoenen, was more successful. After the Yale News Bureau denied knowledge of the project, he went snooping, taking the history department as a likely place to start.

Thoenen soon learned that five members of the department had
prepared the report that Truman had waved above his head. No
one is more assiduous in defense of a free press than an undergraduate newspaper, and Thoenen kept digging, to report that the
scholars had worked on the "ultra secret" project on the fifth and
sixth floors of the library for six weeks. Within the day he was
able to identify four of the five historians: Dunham, Thomas C.
Mendenhall, the master of Berkeley College; David M. Potter,
editor of the *Yale Review* and the newly appointed Coe Professor
of History; and Morrell Heald, an instructor in history with an
interest in immigration. Thus pinned down, Dunham confirmed his
part in the project. Thoenen then queried Chester B. Hansen, an
assistant to the director of the CIA, who declined to comment.
Hansen went immediately to Kent to ask for his official confirmation of the estimates contained in the Yale Report.

The *Yale Daily News* soon lost interest in the story, in the wake
of the upset in the next two weekends of the Yale football team,
first by Brown and then by Cornell, and the fifth member of the
Yale team remained unnamed. He was Basil Duke Henning, the
master of Saybrook College, and it was Henning who had quietly
taken the 600 pages of typescript locked in a briefcase on the train
to Washington. (Two other scholars, Archibald Foord in history
and Alfred Bellinger in classics, had assisted at the edges.) As
soon as DCI Smith saw how accurate the report was, he ordered
the few duplicates that had been made in Kent's office locked up;
no one at Yale had kept a copy, though the next day a CIA official
showed up in a car bearing medical plates, told the scholars to
gather up every bit of paper they had used, and took everything
away with him. (Dunham told him that he was really asking for
the whole of the Yale library, but the official was satisfied with
the sheets of carbon and scratch notes, remarking as he left that
he hoped the historians had emptied their own wastebaskets during the summer, which in fact they had.)

Dunham had been in class when Kent reached Henning on the
phone and, not identifying himself, told him that the project had
"gone bad," that Dunham should be warned, and hung up. Henning had gone at once to find three reporters waiting outside Dunham's classroom, and since they did not know that Henning was
involved, he decided to intercept Dunham at the end of his lecture
as though the next class were his, and under the cover of exchanging pleasantries as they erased the blackboard together, was

able to warn Dunham. Thus Dunham revealed nothing except to
confirm that he had been in charge of the project. Henning, Foord,
and Bellinger were never named. (This left Henning free later to
work with Arnold Wolfers on a quite different project, on what
the Russians would estimate American foreign policy options to
be if they based their conclusions on the European press, without
his colleagues knowing.)[35]

Kent regretted having launched the project. Truman had not
used the report to make the most obvious point—that it revealed
that the larger part of sensitive information had come from oral
testimony given by high government officials to various congressional committees as published for all to read in the *Congressional Record*—and it was so accurate, the five copies that existed
were now very hot potatoes. Further, some crazies on the political right interpreted the report to show that Yale faculty were
"subversively" digging out information, showing the way as it
were to others who would steal the nation's secrets, and neither
the five faculty nor Kent could explain. The far right cited the
fact that the previous spring Yale had acquired a considerable collection of Chinese Communist books as proof that the university
was under the control of "influences" (the term, much used later,
was Robert Welch's, the founder of the John Birch Society),[36]
and that it was in league, through its graduate Dean Acheson,
with the "Communist-dominated Truman administration." Though
Kent did use Dunham later as a consultant on operational projects, he no longer sought so dramatically to prove the obvious:
that "the Soviet press or the Soviet intelligence organization could
have had as full an account of an American order of battle as they
wanted to."

As he approached retirement, Kent wanted to revise his now
classic work on *Strategic Intelligence*. In the end he decided that
intelligence had changed too much, and that his 1949 book was
too closely argued, and too much like a piece of strong carpentry,
to permit tinkering. The book was reissued in 1966, therefore,
without alterations, though with a new and significant preface.[37]
In a letter to a close friend and longtime colleague who had retired
to Florida, William B. Kip, Kent acknowledged that he faced
"about fifty" hazards in trying to say in the preface what needed
saying. He had inserted a long footnote to mar the first page, discussing how Soviet and American definitions of intelligence dif-

fered, "in the vain hope of short-circuiting the antics of some Soviet propaganda clown." He implanted in the text verbal accident insurance against his colleagues "in the scientific organization, the computer boys, and the counter-intelligence people." Some of the "positive spooks" would, he suspected, be sore enough to blackball him at Mory's for his final paragraphs. He was happy, however, for retirement lay just over the horizon, and "the prospect of never having to worry about another God damn ICBM, or megaton, or grain of fissionable material, [was] positively bracing, *Bracing*, BRACING!"[38]

And what did this new preface say that might disturb the intelligence establishment of the 1960s? His book was now primarily about the "classical analytical aspects of the intelligence task," Kent admitted, for there were other tasks, and the world had changed a good bit since 1949. He spoke of the "weaponization" of nuclear power, of the worldwide population explosion, and of the destabilizing (though not necessarily ultimately harmful) effects of the end to the great European empires. He praised the computer boys, and SIGINT, observing that the collection of data had changed, the day of the filing card was gone; but analysis had not changed in any fundamental way, he thought. There was still "no substitute for the intellectually competent human." He did not define this human, though he worked his way toward doing so in two sustained arguments.

A former high-ranking officer in Soviet intelligence, General Alexander Orlov, had published a book which was issued in 1963 by the University of Michigan Press: *Handbook of Intelligence and Guerrilla Warfare*. Orlov had taken Kent on, arguing that intelligence is hard data and that espionage is the only sure means of gathering it in: one must find the other side's "secret documents." Kent, who argued at length a quite different case, was "but one step from mysticism and metaphysics," Orlov concluded. Kent worried that the Russians would, if they followed Orlov's dictims, make serious mistakes of the kind that might plunge the world into nuclear war. He returned to the argument he had presented to R&A staffers over two decades before: there are no "secret documents" in the romantic sense of the words. On any important subject, there is no single document or even group of documents that contains "the secret." No spy could know enough to spot such a document even if it existed, and no vacuum cleaner approach to espionage, even should it gather up two or three doc-

uments of the highest importance, would lead without all the analytical skills of the humanist to any valid conclusions. Documents
do not speak: they do not declare that they are not "the off-beat
thoughts and recommendations of a highly-placed but erratic advisor," not a draft intended only for discussion, not a record of a
decision rescinded orally the next day. No document says that it
is an approved intention that is in effect. Stealing the wrong documents could lead to trouble; misreading even the right documents would lead to disaster.

On the surface this argument, supported with anecdote, was a
refutation of a position taken by the Russians that Kent was caricaturing very slightly. Chillingly, his letters to Bill Kip made it
clear that his audience was fully as much inside the CIA as in the
Russian government, however. His last sentence, he thought, would
really bother the computer boys, would anger the CI types, for
this was now 1966 not 1949: the basis for action had to be something other than proven authenticity of source. That "something
other" was, "in last analysis, a judgment as to the plausibility of
content—a judgment which a disciplined mind will construct on
the basis of knowledge, wisdom, and plain horse-sense." [39]

Any number of historians will tell you that they do not know
what they think until they write it. History is, in that sense, rather
like research and analysis in the intelligence community. One
evaluates evidence at the time it is first at hand for its authenticity
but not for its significance and certainly not for its meaning. The
customary tests for authenticity should be made when the evidence is found, so that its integrity is as little changed as possible.
In this sense the historian is rather like the archaeologist, concerned at first for the stratigraphy of evidence. A letter to John
Quincy Adams is best read and evaluated within the body of the
Adams papers, before someone else has sorted the papers (generally the historian will not be so fortunate—an archivist will have
been there ahead of him, but an archivist is, usually, a historian
as well), or edited them, to attach tentative dates to them, if the
date is not present in the original. Certainly the historian will wish
to use the original source, not a collection of printed sources which
have passed through the hand, and the mind, of an intermediary.

Assuming the source is accepted as authentic, one must ask,
authentic to what end? Did President Adams, being the important
man he was, expect one day that an inquisitive historian would

read his letter, and thus shade it lightly for posterity? This is somewhat akin to the intelligence analyst's test for a plant. It does not mean, of course, that the information in the Adams letter is false—it almost certainly isn't—but rather that any value judgment that accompanies the information may be—almost certainly is—skewed a bit by Adams's concerns. Knowing the context of the value judgments implicit in the letter requires even wider context, of course—that is, the letter needs to be read while it is still embedded in dozens more of its kind, over a like time period, perhaps to the same recipient, and, as a control, to other recipients. One must also know whether the intent of the letter was to explain, to apologize, to persuade, or simply to be a courtesy, to get a few words on paper in reply to other words on paper.

Fine, says the reader, and so what? The so what is that the historian will read the Adams letter, and hundreds of others like it, without a customer in view: he wants to find out what the letter means. An intelligence analyst will or should do precisely the same, but there is nonetheless a difference at the end of the line: the cost of the apparatus that makes it possible to read the letter (especially if Adams had gone to some lengths to see to it that no unintended reader might ever see it) implies that there is a customer, waiting with more or less impatience for "the product." It is not that this necessarily hurries the process, the evaluation, but it does contaminate it. For the questions, what was the intent of the writer?—what is the intent of the artist?—and who are the intended and unintended readers in the mind of the writer? change subtly the relationship to the customer. To the professional historian writing his biography of Adams, he is himself the customer; to the intelligence analyst, there is a chain of potential customers up the line.

Again, so what? All of this is portentous language for the obvious. But not quite. After the evaluation of the evidence, the historian moves on to its use, as does someone along that intelligence chain. The historian's "use" does not involve any specific action, however, and certainly predicates none of any kind, other than for himself: the act of writing a book or article, or perhaps delivering a lecture. The intelligence analyst's "use" is predicated upon an assumption of some action, or denial of action, that reaches well beyond the self. This makes the analyst's task more difficult and it demands of him the greatest integrity. His integrity is compromised if the probable future use is not also determined by individuals of integrity.

Too bad. The historian writes for himself, and if someone else likes what he writes, that is simply icing on his cake. The intelligence analyst is a big boy, and he knows that his product is out of his hands, and open to abuse, as soon as he passes it along. After all, doesn't the public, don't political parties, take the historian's product, his written findings, and abuse them by turning them to activist purposes: to legislation, or the formulation of foreign policy, or the decision to give money to a particular charity? Grow up.

The reader will, even before now, no doubt have sensed that this is a summary of an actual discussion between a historian and an intelligence officer, a former analyst who also worked in operations. That there are affinities between education as a historian and analytical work in intelligence hardly needs arguing, and it requires no further demonstration here. That there are, or were, or could be affinities between the university's commitment to education for civic responsibility and an intelligence organization's application of the fruits of a liberal education is a substantially more difficult argument, especially on the face of the record, though it was at the least a belief widely held to during the period covered by most of this book. But there is still a point to be made about the historian's way of thinking, one that speaks to the function of this book.

"The historian does not know what he has decided until he writes it." The act of writing is an essential part, then, of the process of research, of evaluation, of deciding about the significance and truth of any inquiry. It is writing—finding the words to express the assessed as well as the felt meanings—that brings research to its point. This writing cannot be solely for oneself, or private, for the search for language to express meaning and conclusion must be deep enough to convey that meaning to a diverse audience, not simply to those who share a jargon, since only if those who do not understand what is being said can be reached, through language, to finally understand what is said, has one achieved any understanding of the meaning of one's conclusions. If one writes only for those who understand through a code language, the search for meaning is forestalled, for the language itself will force meaning upon the conclusions. As a former director of Research and Analysis for counterintelligence remarked, ". . . avoid the small-minded linguistic expert. But language must go to the insights." To write is to know.

This is not a difficult point, though the language to express it is difficult. So the historian experiments, shifts tone and voice, moves from the formal to the familiar, in order to reach out, for he is not limited to channels, to a specific form, to a type of reporting. He is not, in fact, reporting at all; he is talking to a reader. The intelligence analyst narrows his audience, may not assume so diversified a readership as to play much with his own awareness of what his language means. To be sure, the intelligence product is packaged—during the Johnson administration, gossipy items, sometimes of a sexual nature, were added to the daily intelligence paper, since it was understood that the president was more likely to read the paper then—but the packaging is with a specific, targeted consumer in mind.

If one does not know what one believes until one has written it—not "until it is written down," for this would permit of someone else doing the writing, and one must find the language for oneself—it follows that writing is integral to research, not a separate act that temporally follows after research. (This is not a defense of the academic doctrine, much deplored by students who fear that it costs them good teachers, of "public or perish," though it no doubt could be used to that end.) The historian must write to know. The historian knows nothing of significance until he has written. This is intellectually quite different from many disciplines and leads to quite a different approach to research and to the evidence. The lawyer generally begins with a case to prove: he seeks the evidence to make that case and marshals his writing to present that evidence convincingly. The social scientist begins with a hypothesis, finds evidence to support or refute the hypothesis, and tests the hypothesis against the evidence. Both must know what they believe is the case, or hope will be the case, or (with the lawyer) may be paid to demonstrate is the case, before they can finish their "product." The historian must just keep rowing for the shore, which he cannot see, and which he may even be permitted to doubt is there, his only life preserver being the undoubted fact that there is something called "the past."

Intelligence work often faces toward the past, but the far shore is the future. It inevitably suffers from the historical fallacy of presentism. It shares with the historian all kinds of stigmata: the intense stare that gives away the methodological necessity for doubt, the body slump of the patient sifters for the twentieth time of records already known by heart, the happy smile at the discovery that there is another source to examine, that there is more work to be done. But it is fundamentally different. Historians write more books than scholars in most other disciplines, not because they work harder (there is no evidence that they do) or are rewarded more handsomely for their hard work (there is an abundance of evidence that they are not) but because the books are themselves the work.

Thinking about Sherman Kent, and thinking with Sherman Kent, brings one to a conclusion. There are those rare individuals—he was one of them—who could hermetically seal off a compartment of inquiry and return to it, apparently untainted by another kind of inquiry, much later. He remained the professional historian throughout, and valued for that by those for whom he worked. Still, he did work for them, he did not work for himself.* He was an independent, plainspoken, and direct as they come, but when he sat down to write—a capability assessment, a devastating review of a book that had attacked the agency and got a goodly number of its facts wrong—he had a discrete, private, basically homogeneous audience in mind. The intellectual process, valid in its own right, was not that of which he had written in his student's primer on the writing of history: "The last, the most serious, reason why it is worth the student's while to write his own history is that by doing so he will come into intimate contact with the chief philosophical assumptions behind his existence."

The truth is, the affinity that I thought I saw between the work of the historian and that of the intelligence officer remains largely on the surface.† Certainly the skills are transferable, indeed essential to intelligence, and very clearly individuals trained as historians are vital to the intelligence enterprise, and not on research and analysis alone. But training is not an education, just as a university is not a school, however much our culture is prone to

---

*It might be said that neither does the university-bound historian work for himself. In my sense of the word he does, however. A true university (yes, this sets aside trade schools, some sectarian institutions, and universities where presidents, trustees, and state politicians behave like mental swizzle sticks in order to create winning football teams) demands, on the surface, very little of its faculty—only that they show up a few times a week and teach their students and, perhaps, act as an exemplar of their discipline, and show signs of mental life from time to time by venturing into print. (If one is adamant, one can even avoid committee work.) What it does demand—total commitment to the discipline—is very hard, and in no way compares to the nine-to-five job that may be left behind. Of course, there are plenty of faculty members who abuse this privilege of hard work.

†See the essay that precedes the Notes.

confuse these words. While a senior colleague who launched this book by a remark to me on a Yale pathway, that it had never been proper for a historian to work for an intelligence agency, was wrong on the facts—as shown, hundreds of historians have worked for the COI, the OSS, SSU, CIG, and CIA—in the most fundamental sense he may have been correct. Sherman Kent's point is surely correct: much interesting (generally), significant (sometimes), and true material can be learned by the historian's methods of research about subjects that were, one presumes, meant to be kept closed. There is an undoubted connection between the world of the university—the campus, its library, its professors and athletes, its theorists and critics, its alumni—and the intelligence community. To the extent that both university and intelligence communities hold to a mutually understood concept of civic virtue, there are clear affinities within a liberal and democratic society. History is a superb preparation for intelligence work. Intelligence officers, and above all analysts, employ the methods of the historian in their work. Assuming an intelligence agency that is committed to civic virtue, that is led responsibly from within and commanded responsibly from without, university and intelligence community could work together.

But these assumptions, the perception of shared views, seem to many who follow the university ethic today to be false. Too often intelligence leadership has given ground to political imperatives, has forgotten that for intelligence work to be effective it must stand outside the political fray. Universities that permit outside interference, faculties that forget that it is they who govern their universities and who surrender either to politicians or to paid professional managers, abandon the civic responsibility they are meant to embody. Intelligence agencies that permit analysts to reach conclusions that politicians want to hear as opposed to those they must hear, governments that endanger the necessary political and ideological neutrality on which intelligence best thrives by placing those agencies under political appointees, betray civic responsibility. Neither a university nor an intelligence agency is, at root, a propaganda body, even though each may at times find itself trying to sell its message to the public. Historians cannot, by definition, be propagandists.

A historian ought not to set out to prove a point. As an intelligence analyst must, the historian too must go where the evidence leads. But the act of writing that is the essential extension of research—that *is,* in fact, research—and that the university historian owes to the environment and the larger society that supports one often is not permitted to the intelligence officer, so that the final, and essential, stage of analysis is omitted. Perhaps one cannot really be an alumnus, even an intellectual alumnus, of two such institutions, of one that projects ever outward and onward, of another that projects inward and foreshortens the most essential stages of intellectual battle. The two institutions have become very different, however much they share common roots. Indeed, the alumni of any institution may, in truth, return to the campus, walk upon its ever slightly more tatty greenswards, only as outsiders. The institution will have moved on, will have become something else, not what one remembers.

In the moment of writing, the historian decides what one has concluded. Historians do not fail, since there must be no predetermined end to achieve. The achieving of some end, any end, is success to the historian. It is no conclusion of despair to realize, as one completes this inquiry, that the relationship between intelligence work, the university as a liberating institution, and history as a discipline, is interesting. It is also significant. But it may no longer be true.

NOTES

This book began with a casual conversation on the campus of Yale University. I had recently returned from two years' leave of absence, during which I had been the cultural attaché to the American embassy in London, in a program (since virtually abandoned) in which the Department of State and the U.S. Information Agency appointed academics as cultural affairs officers in a few embassies—as I recall, Paris, Rome, Tokyo, and on occasion Athens and Beirut, in addition to London. Richard Nixon was the president, and there were many in the academic community opposed to him, to his policies, and to his party. Remarkably, I thought, no one in government, either at the time I was invited to serve in London or during the time I was there, ever asked me about my politics. I am politically an independent, and it had seemed natural to me to serve when asked regardless of the party in office. I was pleased with the foreign service, and for my country, that there seemed to be little concern with whether I subscribed to a party line, and I had thought that the old academic notion of education for civic responsibility might be given a practical test by accepting the offer to spend two years abroad interpreting American culture to the British and British culture to my fellow Americans, especially among the embassy staff. As it turned out, I was partially correct; at the end of the two years I felt I had received an education very nearly equal to a doctorate in a discipline that I could not quite identify: political science? administration? public speaking? communications?

I was surprised, then, when I returned from the embassy to the Yale campus, to discover that many of my colleagues immediately made the assumption that presumptively more rigid government bureaucrats had not made (or at least not voiced), that I now stood revealed as a Republican. I was even more surprised to find that many colleagues (though somewhat fewer) also assumed that I was a defender of all aspects of the foreign policy of our country, including the Christmas Vietnam bombings, as those aspects were revealed during my time in London. Remembering several lively and open arguments in the embassy over the legitimacy of our policy, I was also surprised by my friends' tendency, contrary to all that academics teach in the classroom, to jump to general conclusions about my own views.

The conversation on the campus had arisen from these circumstances. I had remarked that until recently—that is, until the early 1960s—it had always been regarded as legitimate for a member of the academy to work temporarily in government. I also said that I thought history, in particular, as a discipline that quite literally taught a disciplined way of thought, that should teach people how to recognize the right question when they asked it and how to read for nuance both the spoken and written word, was an ideal education for diplomacy. Indeed, I ventured, history was also the best discipline for the gathering and evaluation of intelligence information, in part because it enabled individuals to assimilate and reorder into meaningful patterns an enormous variety of data.

Perhaps so, my companion remarked, but it was utterly inappropriate, he said, for any scholar of whatever discipline to cooperate in any form with the Central Intelligence Agency. I said that I thought this might well be so, given the revelations of the late 1960s and early 1970s, though I added as my opinion that among the many matters that had gone wrong for the CIA was its growing inability to attract liberally educated men and women who knew that civic responsibility arose in good measure from a shared sense of morality. Too much trust was being put in machines, I thought, and however sophisticated our technology might become, evaluation still relied upon the educated individual. In the jargon of the intelligence trade, I still thought HUMINT more important than SIGINT. (But, then, I still prefer a typewriter to a word processor.) It was scarcely original of me to suggest that an effective intelligence community required effective human beings, and that if those with the most broadly based and appropriate educations did not go into intelligence work, the situation could only grow worse.

At that point this book was born. For my companion, now angry with me, remarked that there had never been a time when academics, and above all when historians, had cooperated with the government over matters of intelligence. I knew this was clearly false; it did not require a specialist in military, diplomatic, or intelligence history to know that in both world wars, and at least until the time of the 1961 disaster at the Bay of Pigs, the academic community had routinely shared information, and more important, conclusions with the intelligence community. (Of course, perhaps by the late 1960s no such "communities" existed any longer, but this did not alter the historical fact.) What intrigued me, however, was that so well-versed a scholar, one I otherwise knew to be worldly and direct, could have argued himself, under the trauma of the sixties, into such a historically false corner. I thought then, one day I will write an article about academics and intelligence.

What evolved was neither an article nor a history of academics in intelligence. Having been drawn into the modest story that has become Chapter Three while doing research on a quite different subject, I first thought to relate how the Yale University Library was used as a cover for an intelligence operation run by the Office of Strategic Services, thus to discharge my mild itch to say something on the subject of academics and intelligence. But research takes its own paths, and as I poked about into my library story, I began to realize that there were several other stories to be told that were illustrative of my general theme. The article thus slowly—slowly, because research and writing were bootlegged off other projects and interests which also had to go forward—turned into a book. At the same time I realized that a great number of the figures who moved in and out of my stories, carrying pieces of it with them, were Yale graduates. Once I had compiled a very full (though I am sure not definitive) list of scholars who served in the OSS, I knew that I could not write of them all. Partially as a matter of prudence, therefore, though also because I reasoned that I might come to understand one academic milieu—the one of which I was a part—where I could not hope truly to understand dozens, I decided to write largely about Yale men (men it would be, since Yale College did not admit women until 1969, and I was determined to end my inquiries in the 1960s) in the OSS and the early CIA.

My decision to end roughly at the time of the Bay of Pigs was purely practical. No sooner had I begun my somewhat spasmodic research than two key figures died, and I realized that I must hurry, especially with respect to the earlier years; the post-1961 period would have to wait for someone else to write of it. Further, while I might reasonably expect to make use of records from the war years, more recent documents would be closed to me, and I had the historian's natural desire to be able to read with my own eyes the evidence I sought. Moreover, interviews would be very important, and since I did not mean to write a book that would be revelatory, except perhaps incidentally and on matters of detail, there was little reason to scare potential informants off by appearing to probe into recent operations, especially when I had no prospect of getting at the full truth of those operations. There was also another reason to stop sooner rather than later: time. A book ought to take a certain length, and preoccupy one's life for a certain season, and then if one wants to try a hand at other types of writing—a biography, say—one must move on. Of course, I could not hope to be definitive within the years I settled upon, nor could I prevent some parts of my stories from hemorrhaging closer to the present than I generally intended, but a series of essays on how Yale men, and especially how Yale scholars, served in intelligence work from 1941 (when the COI, which preceded the OSS, was created) to about 1961 seemed to me to have the right dimension to it: the subject was, as the poet Archibald MacLeish (who himself had played a role in the story) wrote, as "palpable as a globéd fruit." I liked the way it felt in my hand.

Now all research has a central theme, for which a central question must be framed, and a series of ancillary themes, or secondary questions. If these secondary questions are not held consciously, they quickly become hidden agendas. To hide an agenda from oneself is a mistake; to hide it from a reader is folly. There were, of course, additional interests in the subject for me. My academic specialty is the history of imperialism—British imperialism generally, and particularly so on my written record, but comparative imperialisms as well—and the larger question on which I was working was, Is there an American (that is, a distinctly American) imperialism? This question involves many issues: comparative race relations, the impact of American culture abroad, the nature of pre- and postwar competition with the British to shape "an orderly world" as defined by a dominant society, and, not least, the definitions of imperialism and empire. Since the OSS had—or so conventional wisdom holds—been modeled on British intelligence agencies, and since intelligence is obviously one way of controlling and manipulating information and knowledge, and since knowledge is power—all trite truisms—an inquiry into almost any aspect of American intelligence history would be grist for my larger mill.

Then, too, there were questions about the nature of history as a discipline, and whether it had social utility or not, and whether any effort to give it social utility meant the compromising of the discipline—the list will be recognized by any professional historian, for these are the questions historians often ask, as graduate students and as professors emeriti—questions that most historians pose, implicitly if not explicitly, by the subjects they choose for their monographs and by the way they organize the classes they teach. I had long enjoyed the theme of "The Historian as Detective"—the title of a bit of scissors and paste I had put together one Cape Cod summer to show the kind of inquiries from which historians took their fun—and surely here was another slice off the same loaf.

I had been trained as a diplomatic historian, though I was far more interested in the history of race relations, and in how one group used power *vis-à-vis* another. Progression to the study of the British Empire had come logically. I believed that diplomatic history, like military history, often suffered from an unwillingness to look at the truly hidden side of things, that "bodyguard of lies" to which Winston Churchill referred which was invariably brought out to protect an operation (Churchill was speaking of the several deceptions used to keep the Germans confused as to where the D-Day landings in 1944 would occur) or a treaty negotiation. The English historian, A.J.P. Taylor, had remarked that 90 percent of all information gathered by intelligence services is drawn directly from publicly available sources, another way of saying that good research methods are essential to good intelligence, while the American historian of France, Sherman Kent, perhaps reflecting the more open nature of American society, raised this figure to 95 percent, as we have seen, and added that it is the truly hidden 5 percent that justifies much professional spying.* Since I frequently quoted Taylor (and less frequently Kent) to my students in research methods, I felt I ought to put up or shut up: let us see whether, in the stories I decided to tell, I could not get at some of the material, probably insignificant in the main, that lay within that 5 to 10 percent margin. And so another task was added to my agenda: while I was not seeking sensational revelations, I would see whether I could not find the answers to at least a few of the questions that, once the research had begun, I was told I could never answer.

And so, what is this curate's egg, this book the reader holds in his hand? It is a history of a peculiar kind. Most likely librarians, charged with order and symmetry, will classify it as intelligence history, though I would as soon see it on the shelves with Langlois and Seignebois, authors of a classic (though fundamentally boring) treatise on historical methods. Or, perhaps, were such a

---

*Dozens of books tell us that Willie Fischer (or Fisher), alias Rudolph Ivanovich Abel (who entered the United States as Andrew Kayotis and operated, generally, as Emil Robert Goldfus), was "the most important Soviet spy ever captured in America." Perhaps so, though if this is true it merely proves Taylor's point, since Abel most likely never transmitted a real secret to the Soviet Union. Virtually all of his information came from a close reading of *The New York Times* and *Scientific American*. The journalistic judgment on his importance probably turns more on the fact that he was traded for Francis Gary Powers, the pilot of the American U-2 spy plane brought down near Sverdlovsk.

Another apparent version of the Taylor-Kent statement is attributed to the British historian Sir Lewis Namier, who remarked (somewhat muddily) that there are very few profound secrets to which one cannot find a reference somewhere in a printed book if one knows what to look for (Basil Collier, *Hidden Weapons: Allied Secret or Undercover Services in World War II* [London: Hamish Hamilton, 1982], pp. xvii–xviii). This is actually quite a different formulation of the point, and I disagree when the point is made this way.

classification to exist, applied moral philosophy?: for I am interested in "the small platoon," a phrase from Edmund Burke used to denote those persons who, in any society, understand that education is meant to create a sense of civic virtue (by which he meant duty), and I believed that the great private universities of Britain and the United States did, at least at one time, foster that sense.

There is, in fact, very little careful, solid research on the American intelligence community—there is marginally more on the British—even though intelligence history is an essential component of our times. Diplomatic history is, in an important measure, the outward public manifestation of the inward and private acts of intelligence gathering and evaluation. But there are obvious reasons why the field, if such it is becoming, is poorly served. Historians traditionally rely upon documentation, and the intelligence field is based on the denial, the falsifying, and the destruction of documentation. Intelligence subjects can seldom be researched within the life span of participants, so that scholars who must publish so that they will not perish cannot afford to wait about for records to be organized for them; only in the summer of 1984, forty-two years after the events described, were many of the OSS documents opened to researchers. Even when documentation ultimately becomes available, it is suspect, filled with deliberate red herrings, and requires enormous work to understand. When opened, a collection often is so badly organized (from a researcher's point of view) as to appear—the Donovan Papers are an example—to have been filed virtually at random. The rewards are small for a disproportionate expenditure of time, except to those for whom snooping is an end in itself.

As many academicians prefer to denounce the existence of intelligence agencies from a distance rather than come to terms with them, the public, except for the sector that seeks sensations, is likely to discount even accurate accounts, or to think that an author has himself been part of that community, or has compromised normal scholarly canons, in order to gain access to materials; or to think of the field as akin to writing of crime from the inside: unclean. That a portion of the public does thrive on revelations and sensation, a taste fed by spy fiction, means that professional writers dependent for their income on their writing are tempted to overemphasize the sensational or colorful aspects of their findings. The literature is riddled with sloppy, hasty, ill-informed conclusions, with amateur research that ignores the scholar's rudimentary methodologies, with modes of inquiry that overlook virtually all peripheral or ancillary research channels (ironically, in a field in which the ancillary may prove to be the key), and by simple—and complex—falsehood and evasion.

Most obvious of all, within the literature, is the fact that very little of the published material is dispassionate: it tends either to partake of the special pleading generally associated with the memoir, which is natural to a person who has come to the field through participation in it; or to be defensive—one not very hidden agenda being a plea for an understanding that spying is essential to the protection of an open and democratic society from its closed enemies—or wildly, arrogantly angry, as with the work of Philip Agee and the "disclosers."[1]

To these problems one must add the judgment that most books in the field are badly written: either egregiously overwritten for effect, drama, suspense; or given to hypothesized dialogue in order to lend the air of a story to the proceedings (a good hint, there, as to the anticipated readership);[2] or ghost-written, plain tales from the ranks turned into gussied-up fabrications at the hands of professional ghost writers. Many books show signs of haste, being repetitive,* badly organized, simply careless. I have never read in a field so replete with printer's errors nor encountered so many memoirists, including those for whom the English language is their Majesty's, who seem unable to get the language right. These matters, in turn, reveal yet another reality of the literature: often it is competitive, written to deadlines because, once a collection of papers has been made available for research, there will be many rushing through the documentation hoping to be the first to discover one more Big Secret.[3]

No wonder, then, that as a field the literature is not taken seriously by serious readers. This is too bad. It is a very serious field. There are, of course, excellent and honest writers at work,[4] but they are far outnumbered by the careless, the sensation mongers, or the merely beclouded.

Having made so many criticisms of the field, an author stands

---

*Some readers may complain that this book is repetitive at points. This is true, and deliberately so, since there will be readers who are interested in one chapter or another and do not approach the book consecutively: hence re-identification of the players on occasion. I have also given a full citation to each source in the notes on the first time of mention in each chapter, rather than send the reader searching through the entire book under the scholar's usual arcane method of declension of notes.

exposed lest he commit the same offenses. No doubt I have done so to some degree, for this book also suffers from sometimes diffuse sources—the ill-organized Donovan Papers did not leap into an order of battle at my command—and from sources which cannot be tested, much less verified. There is the natural desire, already alluded to, to feel that a book should be of a specific length, and take a certain time from one's allotted span, and not a great deal more (not the same thing as deadline journalism, or even haste, but nonetheless producing a certain sense of personal urgency, since other curiosities beckon, asking to have the fun of research applied to them). Further, it is a truism of historical writing that an author, unless exceptionally strong minded, begins to take on the intonations in his own prose of the manner and rhythm of his principal sources (diplomatic historians tend to write like diplomats), and a steady diet of revelatory and super-heated prose is likely to become infective.

Those who are best at espionage work, it has been said, require boldness, daring, risk, and audacity, all in combination with prudence. This is a hard combination to find. When found, it produces mute documentation. Were the documentation merely mute, however, the researcher could often coax it into speech. The risk is that the speech will be deliberately misleading. More than once while interviewing a former agent, I realized that I was being run— that is, I was being led to a conclusion rather than being allowed to reach a conclusion for myself. Perhaps this is natural to the beast, for persuasion is but a mild word for manipulation, and most agents—and certainly retired ones—hope to see the record justify their actions. While some of the spy books that have grown from trickle to flood in the last five years or so might conceivably be part of a KGB disinformation plot, it is far more likely that current revelations have been leaked by one of the several factions within the British and American retirement communities of former agents. One wing, certain that some major figures in intelligence are double agents or, at the least, insufficiently alert to the skills of the KGB, will shape arguments to discredit those of whom they disapprove: "liberals," "socialites," "fuzzy-headed academics," "one-worlders," etc. Paranoia does not stop with retirement; those low on a totem pole do not stop resenting those higher on the totem pole; suspicion is essential to good work in security services. The result is that both the printed word[5] and the interview, whether formally conducted or simply a friendly chat over a cup of coffee, must be scrutinized for secondary intentions. It is all enough to make the historian very cautious: perhaps too cautious. In the end, then, the leap of faith historians must make between their evidence and their conclusions may be across more troubled and angry waters than is usually the case.[6]

It is easy to fall into these waters. If intelligence officers dislike a book, for its tone, revelations, or simply because they find that one or two facts in it may prove compromising (for which, also read embarrassing), they may let it be known that the book is "riddled by errors," customarily pointing out a few. Any book on intelligence work will contain errors, given the nature and origin of the documentation, and these errors may then be used to discredit quite valid judgments and conclusions which do not turn on the facts in question. The OSS had some notable successes in World War II, and some equally notable failures, but those who wish to romanticize the OSS, or who continue to feel a strong emotional loyalty to its charismatic founder, William J. Donovan, dismiss books that are critical of him and support that dismissal by sometimes quite pedantic criticisms (or silly ones; one review of a book on Donovan declared that the author could have little credibility since everyone knew that Donovan was not, stuffily, William J. but "Wild Bill"). This kind of carping leads readers who want criticisms to be leveled at large targets to discount the seriousness of the field.[7]

How serious is the field? Intelligence history is important, but one can never know how important. Intelligence triumphs and failures are seldom open to quantification, the triumphs often not even to public review. Before World War I Colonel Alfred Redl, Austrian general staff officer and member of Austrian intelligence, betrayed military secrets in a wholesale manner to the Russians. One account says that Redl was responsible for the deaths of a quarter million Austrians on the field of battle; another puts the figure at half a million; a third, noting that total casualties were half a million, prudently declines to attribute the total casualty list to Redl's action, arbitrarily crediting 20 to 30 percent to his treachery. No one can know, for estimates of this kind are unhistorical since they are derived from the "what if" premise: what if Redl had not betrayed his country to the Russians? What if John F. Kennedy had not been assassinated? We do not know, and guessing is not useful, though it may be entertaining. Still, the need to assess the significance of some event or development

is deeply ingrained in professional scholars. The cult of the significant, consisting of those who feel that it is not enough to be merely
interesting and true, has led some writers to declare, for example,
that Britain's possession of Ultra shortened the war in Europe by
two and a half years. How can one know, and why need one feel
compelled to guess?

I have sought to provide citations to printed records wherever
possible and whenever important. I have not thought it necessary
to lead the reader to the precise document that proves figure X in
my narrative had salmon mousse for lunch. A good bit of material
came only from interviews. As a matter of integrity, I told anyone
I was interviewing the intent of my research, and where a potential interviewee was uncertain whether to talk to me or not, I
promised either anonymity—which surprisingly few insisted upon,
removing one of the persistent curses of this type of documentation—or the opportunity to review those portions of the manuscript that were based exclusively on what they had told me (as
distinct from material I could document from another source). I
did not allow anyone to censor what I had written, or to lead me
to altered judgments unless I found a countervailing argument,
with documentation, convincing, but I did agree to remove one or
two names—not to alter them—which an informant felt, on seeing
them in print, had been harmfully indiscreet. Of course, calculated indiscretions are a matter of interpretation, but in this wilderness of mirrors one must trust one's judgment for the final
analysis.[8]

Recounting events forty years more or less after they occur
means that many participants are not alive and that the memory
of others has dimmed. However, when I began this book all but
one of the subjects of my chapters was still alive, and that one
was a person I knew well and had lunched with often. The greater
problem comes from the 1968 decision by the British to move
from a fifty-year rule—that is, permitting researchers access to
records only after they were fifty years old (usually plus-fifty, since
increasingly there is a delay for accessioning and organizing materials at the archive to which they have been sent)—to a thirty-
year rule,* combined with the happy fact that progressively, and

---

*British records on the Suez crisis are now beginning to be available. This will
surely change intelligence and, quite possibly, what I have written about James
Angleton.

especially in 1984–86 (and, one trusts, in each year to come) the U.S. government has released large quantities of OSS papers. This means that one must face the problem that the documentary evidence at times directly contradicts surviving participants.

Normally the historian will accept a document over memory, though in this instance some of the documents may have been intended to deceive and participants may now be striving to recollect accurately (one need not cynically suspect all of trying to run the researcher) in order to set the record straight. Conversely, they may now still be clinging to a cover story created for events forty or more years past. Where direct contradiction occurs, and where reconciliation of the contradictions is important, the historian must simply arrive at one's own conclusions, with apologies to anyone whose memory has been impugned. On the whole, though not always, I am inclined toward the historian's customary judgment that documents, and especially documents that were once classified, are likely to be more reliable than memory so far as they go. What one must keep in mind is that such documents were not intended to go very far and certainly were not written with future reconstruction in mind, even when many of them were written by historians. (This is not as contradictory as it sounds. I have often observed that professional historians, those most angry with people who do not keep their records, are particularly bad about keeping their own.)

One partial solution to this problem—seeking official permission to consult the as yet unreleased documentation, as an official historian would do—I never considered. I did inform one well-placed official of the CIA, a Yale graduate, of what I was writing, since I knew that inevitably the agency would learn of it, and it was best for people to know what I was doing. I never asked for permission to consult any CIA records nor offered to have my manuscript read by anyone in the agency, for I was unwilling to surrender any part of it to the potential censorship of others. No doubt I missed some material this way, but I suspect I kept my hands on more of it.

I am quite aware of two other self-imposed limitations on this study. First, this book looks hardly at all into OSS operations, not to speak of the CIA, in Asia. This arises from the fact that the individuals whose stories I decided to tell did not, or did not often, operate in Asia. The OSS was quite active, and also quite effective, in Asia, and especially in Siam. It ran eleven radio stations, had its own schools for training agents, and controlled thousands of guerrillas who, it is claimed, killed up to 15,000 Japanese. There were 122 OSS operations, including ten to the Andaman Islands, and one to Indo-China to rescue prisoners of war. Eighty-seven Americans, and far more locals, were parachuted into occupied territory. All of this story ought to be told in full by someone with the requisite Asian languages. It will not be told by me. I have barely adequate Malay, but far more important will be Japanese and Thai. True, a journalistic account can be written by someone who knows only English; it would be too bad if this were to happen. When it happens it will illustrate yet another problem with intelligence history.

The individuals chosen for looking at closely were meant to represent a variety of intelligence work, especially in the OSS. Thus I focus in turn on administration, research and analysis (R&A), secret intelligence (SI), secret operations (SO), counterintelligence (X-2), and evaluation (ONE). I try to relate the subject's personality to his academic background generally, to Yale specifically, and to show the texture of thought and the flow of work, even of daily life, in an intelligence job. This means that I verge upon a massive invasion of the privacy of several people who had no reason to believe they would be the focus of some historian's attention. I have, therefore, sought to remember the motto of the great French *Biographie Universelle:* "To the living we owe some consideration, but to the dead we owe nothing but the truth."

A second limitation was the decision to restrict research to the OSS and the CIA. There were, of course, many other types of intelligence bodies, and there still are. Some (the Office of Naval Intelligence, for example) have benefited from sound, professional history written to answer important questions. The story I would most like to see told is that of W. Stull Holt, the American scholar who was in charge of liaison with Britain's MI9, the escape and evasion operation that helped get downed Allied pilots (and others) out from behind enemy lines. Holt sought to achieve the same magic for the American Eighth Air Force, and though his work is attested to in M.R.D. Foot and J. M. Langley's *MI9: Escape and Evasion, 1939–1945,*[9] there is an important record to be set straight. Holt had been a professor of history at Johns Hopkins, and subsequently at the University of Washington, and I had known him and admired his work. A brief foray into his personal papers made it clear to me that he warranted, and could receive, more than the chapter-length treatment I had settled on as my approach. Holt's conclusion on professional history, that it is "a damn dim candle over a damn dark abyss," haunted me throughout the preparation of this book. Nonetheless, I prefer to accept the optimism inherent in Sherman Kent's estimates.

—ROBIN W. WINKS
Berkeley College
Yale University

NOTES

1. Almost random examples include such well-received books as Jules Archer's *Superspies: The Secret Side of Government* (New York: Delacorte Press, 1977), which is riddled with fundamental errors easily corrected from a reference tool (that Allen Dulles was the first director of Central Intelligence, when he was the third, or placing Fidel Castro's revolution chronologically ahead of Nasser's overthrow of Farouk, and without reference to Naguib). Is it not possible that otherwise reputable publishing houses simply fail to edit manuscripts in the field, perhaps on the assumption that no in-house editor could expect to command, and thus challenge, covert information, without any sense of what is covert? Consider, too, the mixtures of truth, half-truth, and plain error (to be charitable) in *Covert Action Information Bulletin* and similar publications. Examine, for example, the hodgepodge of sometimes accurate, sometimes accusatory, sometimes quite simply tendentious material in Konrad Ege's "Introducing George Bush" in *Counter Spy*, V (Apr., 1981), 3–7, a subject about which I know very little and yet can readily spot the moments when the author moves from fact to conjecture, despite a uniformly all-knowing tone; or Ege's "Buying Oman" in the same issue (pp. 22–27), a subject about which I do know a little, and which is relatively accurate, despite opaque phrases that could mean just about anything.

2. Consider Greville Wynne, *Contact on Gorky Street* (New York: Athenaeum, 1968)—also published as *The Man from Moscow*—written cinematically, with flashbacks and forwards further to dramatize an already sufficiently dramatic story.

3. Sometimes the writing is so odd as to be impenetrable—sample Colonel Noël Wild's foreword to David Mure's *Master of Deception: Tangled Webs in London and the Middle East* (London: William Kimber, 1980), in which Wild does a disservice to himself and Mure, both figures well worthy of honor—or the organization so choppy as to lead a reader to suspect the manuscript was produced from ill-sorted filing cards (see Lauran Paine's *Britain's Intelligence Service* [London: Robert Hale, 1979], which repeats identical information on three occasions, mindless of what the reader already has been told).

4. Virtually everyone would agree on Christopher Andrew, David Kahn (especially *Codebreakers*) and F. H. Hinsley; most would add Thomas Troy, Joseph Persico, and Sir John Masterman; and though professionals in the field have at times been a bit hard on Bradley F. Smith, R. Harris Smith, Andrew

Boyle, and Nigel West (Rupert Allason), considering the magnitude of the tasks they set themselves, I would rate them more highly.

5. J. L. Granatstein makes this point well in "Spies," *Queen's Quarterly,* LXXXIC (Autumn, 1982), 529–37. An excellent example of this kind of writing appeared after Granatstein wrote: Chapman Pincher, *Too Secret Too Long* (New York: St. Martin's, 1984), the third book by Pincher intended to show, so far as it might be shown, that Sir Roger Hollis, for nine years head of Britain's MI5, was a Soviet agent or dupe.

6. There are books that strike one as fundamentally sound, yet at times too knowledgeable, too tidy. John Barron's *KGB: The Secret Work of Soviet Secret Agents* (New York: Reader's Digest Press, 1974) is a case in point. The origin of Barron's book is moderately suspect, since the *Reader's Digest*'s desire to alert Americans to the presence of Soviet spies—a desire in itself perfectly responsible—has led many who read for nuance and context to feel that *Digest* publications press the case too far. Still, the basic material usually stands up. One would like the facts without the moralizing, statements of only that which is known or may be properly inferred, as opposed to pressing all arguments to a common breaking point. However, despite these reservations Barron's book strikes me as remarkable, down to its lengthy list (pp. 379–415) of Soviet Citizens Engaged in Clandestine Operations Abroad, with dates of service and information on expulsions.

7. Having learned, for example, that good bits of Charles Whiting's *The Spymasters: The True Story of Anglo-American Intelligence Operations within Nazi Germany, 1939–1945* (New York: Saturday Review Press, 1976) is embroidery and guesswork, one is led to distrust other elements in the book which research might well prove true. A reader might ask, does it matter that Whiting (p. 116) reports that Dr. Hans Bernd Gisevius's visit to Allen Dulles in Berne was made known to the British SIS by Dulles's German-speaking Swiss cook, who noted the initials HBG in a nocturnal visitor's hat; or that, as Nigel West reports in *MI6: British Secret Intelligence Service Operations, 1909–45* (New York: Random House, 1983), p. 223, the SIS agent who recognized Gisevius was Dulles's doorman-cum-butler. Whiting is regarded as full of fabrications, West is generally thought accurate. Yet Mary Bancroft, one of the very few eye witnesses on this point, supports Whiting's account (*Autobiography of a Spy* [New York: William Morrow, 1983], pp. 188–89). And does it matter? Perhaps not, though given the ramifications of most intelligence operations, there is another sense in which it may be quite important to know who the SIS informant in Dulles's household was.

8. There are also official OSS and CIA historians, professionally trained, with unparalleled access to documentation. (As this is written the official in-house historian for the CIA is a Yale-trained scholar.) But almost none of the commissioned histories of OSS units were ever released for publication, and of today's official CIA histories one might quote the aphorism that perhaps the most important task for the official historian is less to remember things than to forget things.

9. (Boston: Little, Brown, 1980). A colleague of Stull Holt's at the University of Washington, Donald Emerson, is at work on this subject. I wish to thank Holt's daughter, Jocelyn Marchisio, for allowing me to examine her father's papers. The aphorism is from Holt. *Treaties Defeated by the Senate* (Baltimore: The Johns Hopkins Press, 1933), p. vi.

CHAPTER ONE   **The University: Recruiting Ground**

1. For examples, consider three highly disparate accounts in three different languages: Alain Guérin, in *Qu'est-ce que la C.I.A.?* (Paris: Editions sociales, 1968), p. 20, asserts that Harvard, Yale, and Princeton supplied the majority of those holding top positions; Camera Press, *Mengungkap Kegiatan Subversip: CIA*, I [Djarkata, 1965], p. 14, asserts that the Ivy League supplies nearly all of the CIA's agents; and Tomori Endre, *Rejtett Szolgalat: Fejezetek a CIA törté-netéböl* (Budapest, 1979), pp. 53–56, 113–14, takes the view that Richard Bissell and James Angleton rose rapidly in the CIA solely because of Harvard and Yale (though both were, in fact, Yale undergraduates).

2. Despite this widely held belief, the statistics suggest otherwise. See George Wilson Pierson, *A Yale Book of Numbers: Historical Statistics of the College and University, 1701–1976* (New Haven: Yale University, 1983), pp. 474–502.

3. Allen Dulles, ed., *Great True Spy Stories* (New York: Harper & Row, 1968), p. xi. Dulles was a Princeton graduate. The claim of paternity occurs in Ronald Seth, *Encyclopedia of Espionage* (Garden City, N.Y.: Doubleday, 1972), pp. 116, 285–86.

4. For various slightly different versions of Hale's life and death, see John Bakeless, *Turncoats, Traitors and Heroes* (Philadelphia: J. B. Lippincott, 1959); Morton Pennypacker, *The Two Spies* (Boston: Houghton-Mifflin, 1930); George Dudley Seymour, *Documentary Life of Nathan Hale* (New Haven: privately printed, 1941); and Thomas J. Farnham, *A Child I Set Much By: A Life of Nathan Hale* (New Haven: New Haven Colony Historical Society, 1978). In "A Possible Source for Nathan Hale's Dying Words," *The William and Mary Quarterly*, 3rd ser., XLII (July, 1985), 394–95, F. K. Donnelly makes a case for John Lilburne, Leveller leader, as a source equally possible to Addison's *Cato* for Hale's "last words."

5. Yale University, Secretary's Office: correspondence between George D. Vaill and DeWayne C. Cuthbertson, Dec. 5, 12, 1973, Feb. 9, 12, 1974. I wish to thank the late George Vaill for reading this chapter in draft and for clarifying several points for me.

6. Yale University, Secretary's Office: Walter L. Pforzheimer to George D. Vaill, Dec. 13, 1972, Mar. 28, 1973, and replies, Jan. 29, May 1, 1973; Renaissance Art Foundry to George Vale *(sic)*, Jan. 23, 1973. The CIA refused to divulge the cost of the statue. To confuse even simple matters may seem natural to the agency: when enquiries are made about the statue, it is stated that it was erected on September 11; however, the typescript of the speech of dedication is dated September 6. On Pforzheimer, see his "Amassing Intelligence: In Search of Truth in Fine Condition," in Dilys Winn, ed., *Murder Ink.* (2nd ed., New York: Workman, 1984), pp. 36–40; *New York Times*, Feb. 7, 1984; and his Yale College Scholarship Record, 1931–35, in Registrar's Office. He too has read and corrected this chapter as well as Chapters Two and Three, offered warm encouragement and astringent criticism, and allowed me access to his remarkable private collection on intelligence.

7. Vaill, "Only One Life, But Three Hangings," *American Heritage,* XXIV (Aug., 1973), 100–101; *Studies in Intelligence* (Winter, 1973), pp. 13, 15; Vaill to Cuthbertson, Feb. 12, 1974 (see note 5).

8. Dozens of instances occur in the literature and in the records. This typical example is cited by Charles W. Yost, in *History and Memory* (New York: Norton, 1980), p. 231. Mountbatten was an admirer of the OSS and its relatively centralized administration as opposed to the lack of coordination he detected between the twelve "clandestine, semi-clandestine, and quasi-military organizations" which he encountered in India (Charles Cruickshank, *SOE in the Far East* [Oxford: Oxford University Press, 1983], p. 253).

9. See Rudyard Kipling, *Something of Myself* (New York: Doubleday Doran, 1937), p. 89, and Charles E. Carrington, *The Life of Rudyard Kipling* (Garden City, N.Y.: Doubleday, 1956), pp. 275–76.

10. Rudyard Kipling's Verse, 1896 edition.

11. James M. Howard, "The Whiffenpoofs: Gentlemen Songsters off on a Spree," *Yale Alumni Magazine,* XXII (Mar., 1959), 9–11.

12. Rudy Vallee and Gil McKean, *My Time Is Your Time: The Story of Rudy Vallee* (New York: Ivan Obolensky, 1962), p. 128.

13. Norman Holmes Pearson Papers, originally in possession of Ms. Susan Addiss (his stepdaughter): Pearson to Susan, his wife, Mar. 4, 1945. See Chapter Five for full information.

14. George D. Vaill, *Yale: A Contesseration of Human Beings* (Bethany, Conn.: Bethany Press, 1979), pp. 65–67. I also wish to thank Mr. Vaill for his help in unscrambling the history of the "Whiffenpoof Song," on which he was an authority.

15. The "Whiffenpoof Song" and Nathan Hale are linked at the Yale Club on Vanderbilt Avenue near Forty-Fourth Street in New York City, where the "Whiffs" perform with regularity (as they do at Mory's), and where there is a plaque to Hale, who was taken as a captive and hanged in Artillery Park, "near this site." America's first spy thus was introduced to the romanticizing process, since Artillery Park was, in fact, not so near at all: at Third Avenue and Sixty-sixth Street. There is another, rather different, representation of Hale at his execution, its inscription agreeing, except for the comma, on his last words. This, an exemplary beaux-arts monument, stands in City Hall Park and is by Frederick MacMonnies, who completed it in 1893 (see "The Nathan Hale Statue," *The Art Interchange,* XXXII [Jan., 1894], 16–17, and the Art Commission of the City of New York file on the statue, kindly supplied by Michele Cohen at City Hall).

16. Charles Seymour Papers, Yale University, Manuscript Group 441, box 11, folder 660: Seymour to George Wilson Pierson, Mar. 16, 1962. Hereafter, unless otherwise noted Yale Manuscript Collections (MG) and Record Groups (RG) cited in this and subsequent chapters are in the Historical Manuscripts Room, which also embraces the Yale University Archives, in the Sterling Memorial Library at Yale.

17. See Charles Alan Wright, "The Fictional Lawyer," in *The Practical Lawyer,* XXXI (Jan. 15, 1985), 88. Yale's presidential record is, in fact, not very good, and the idea of anticipating a Yale man running for president could, in 1946, be supported only by the successful William Howard Taft, and the unsuccessful John C. Calhoun, Samuel B. Tilden, and William "Liberty Bell" Lemke, of the Yale Law School class of 1905, who in 1936 won a million votes for the Union party ticket—the ticket of Father Charles E. Coughlin, the Reverend Gerald L. K. Smith, and Dr. Francis E. Townsend. Of course, postwar Yale would more nearly fulfill the dean's jibe, with Gerald Ford attaining the presidency, George Bush the vice presidency, and Gary Hart, William W. Scranton, Pat Robertson, and others making one or more stabs at it.

18. On Dean DeVane, see the William C. DeVane Papers, MG 1114, *seriatim,* from which I have quoted liberally here; the obituary prepared by his wife, Mable DeVane, *William Clyde DeVane, 1898–1965* (New Haven: The University, 1965); Charles W. Hendel, *In Remembrance of William Clyde DeVane as Dean of Yale College* (New Haven: Pierson College, 1968); and *Yale Daily News,* Special Memorial Edition, October 9, 1965. I wish to thank the late Associate Dean Richard C. Carroll for discussing Dean DeVane's work with me and for sharing his file of the dean's correspondence, and Dean DeVane's son, Milton DeVane, for giving me a selection of his father's addresses and family letters.

19. The source here and elsewhere in this chapter for general information on Yale is the file of the *Yale Daily News* kept in the Historical Manuscripts Room. Pearson's statement is in the Ralph Henry Gabriel Papers, MG 228, box 6: Pearson to Gabriel, Dec. 11, 1941. Also useful is RG 48-B-1, microfilm reels on "Yale Old and New," especially reels 6 and 19. On Lovett, see William A. Wiedersheim, ed., *Uncle Sid of Yale* (New Haven: Yale Alumni Fund, 1981).

20. The Yale story is told in the records of the Faculty Committee for the Reception of Oxford and Cambridge University Children, RG 1212, series I, boxes 2 and 27; in the World War II records of the Office of the Secretary, RG 4-A, series III, boxes 255–59; and in the *New York Herald-Tribune,* July 25, 1940. The larger story is nicely summarized in Merle Witkin, "The Overseas Evacuation of British Children during World War II," unpubl. senior essay (Yale University, 1981), which draws upon manuscripts in the Public Archives of Canada and the Public Record Office of Great Britain. For tone, see Anthony Bailey, *America, Lost & Found: An English Boy's Wartime Adventure in the New World* (New York: Random House, 1980).

21. *Yale Daily News,* Special Edition, Dec. 7, and issues through Dec. 10. I wish to thank Mr. William Dougherty, Yale '45, for describing the rioting of his fellow freshmen.

22. Clarence Mendell, *Mr. Dooley Redivivus: On Acceleration* (New Haven: Branford College Press, 1942), [pp. 5–7]; Mendell Papers, MG 799, box 1; Annual Reports of Yale College, 1942–1945, *seriatim;* Charles W. Hendel, "Dean DeVane and Yale College in War Time," unpubl. paper delivered at the "Old Men's Club," Feb. 14, 1968; and DeVane, "The Scholar Cornered: The Dilemma of National Greatness," *The American Scholar,* XXXIII (Autumn, 1964), 502–511.

23. For an excellent summary of Yale's wartime programs, see Brooks Mather Kelley, *Yale: A History* (New Haven: Yale University Press, 1974), pp. 393–421. Polly Stone Buck offers an informal and anecdotal account in *We Minded the Store: Yale Life & Letters during World War II* (New Haven: privately printed, 1975). See also Loomis Havemeyer, *Undergraduate Yale in the Second World War* (New Haven: The University, 1960). The letters on which Polly Buck drew, with much additional detail, are in RG 41-A-1. The anecdotes here come from the Lewis Perry Curtis Family Correspondence, MG 587, boxes 2 and 6; Sidney

Lovett Papers, MG 1089, series 1, boxes 46, 47; Alexander Witherspoon Papers, MG 528, box 1; Berkeley College memorabilia files, kept in the college office; and Archibald Foord Papers, MG 136, box 1. The air force songs, including an indication that the OSS drew on them for recognition signals, are in RG 1212, series 1, boxes 2 and 3, and series II, box 7. See also Eugene Kone Papers, MS 1221, Yale in World War II, boxes 1-12, which duplicate but also supplement other collections.

24. *The Harvard Crimson* began an investigation of Fisher's work in 1949, but the story was quashed, not to be fully told until 1984, in Sigmund Diamond, "Surveillance in the Academy: Harry B. Fisher and Yale University, 1927–1952," *American Quarterly*, XXXVI (Spring, 1984), 7–43. The account here is taken from Diamond's article, which provides full citations to Yale's records and available FBI files. See also Diamond, "God and the F.B.I. at Yale," *The Nation*, CCXXX (Apr. 12, 1980), 423–28.

25. The first comment is attributed to Gaddis Smith, Larned Professor of History at Yale, in Rich Blow, "The Secret Link," *The New Journal*, XVI (Apr. 20, 1984), 13; the second comment is on p. 3. At least thirteen faculty joined OSS in its first year.

26. *Ibid.*, p. 14. Downey entered the CIA and in November 1952 was captured by Chinese Communist troops in Manchuria, the victim of an overly ambitious fellow CIA agent. Downey was held in a Chinese prison for over twenty years, returning home in 1972. He had, he said, "planned to take some time off after college, but it turned out to be a lot longer than I had planned." I had hoped to include a chapter on John Downey in this book, but I am unable to do so. Mr. Downey is entitled to his reticence and may, one day, tell his own story.

27. The words are those of Alfred Bellinger, of Yale's classics department, in his book of poems, *Day's End* (New Haven: Yale University Press, 1924), p. 8.

28. Lovett Papers, MG 1089, series 1, box 47, folder 422: roll of honor forms. The original forms are kept in the papers of the Secretary of the University and are restricted; Lovett's copies are organized somewhat differently and, when read against the correspondence, suggest this figure. When the Korean War began, the university simply threw out its World War II files and waited to see what the military might ask of it. Basil Duke Henning, master of Saybrook College, was asked to survey the faculty to find out who held reserve commissions, just as Lohmann had done in 1940; he would then maintain the list of faculty members who went to war (Henning Papers, MG 834, boxes 1 and 3). By 1951 the list of *Yale Men Who Died in the Second World War* (the title of Eugene Kone's book [New Haven: Yale University Press, 1951]) had grown to 514. There had been 18,678 Yale alumni in the armed services, and 21,881 men served who were trained at Yale (p. 439).

29. The wartime papers of the masters of Davenport, Pierson, Saybrook, and Silliman colleges are in storage in those colleges. (Only those of Silliman, whose master at the time was Filmer S.C. Northrop, professor of philosophy, failed to prove valuable.) The wartime papers of the masters of Berkeley, Calhoun, and Jonathan Edwards colleges are in the Yale University Archives. The papers of Robert Dudley French, MG 1264, also were useful (on French, see the New York *Herald-Tribune*, Apr. 20, 1953, and *The Times* of London, Sept. 14, 1954). The records of Davenport College are especially full, and thus I draw disproportionately on Davenport in this chapter. I am grateful to the present master, Henry A. Turner, Jr., for giving me access to them. For a list of fellows in 1948 see *Record of the Fellows of Davenport College*, II (New Haven: The College, 1948), with *curriculum vitae* on most. On all the colleges, consult Thomas C. Bergin, *Yale's Residential Colleges: The First Fifty Years* (New Haven: The University, 1983). Also useful as a composite on the class of 1941 was a special file kept by the late Richard Carroll, who kindly shared it with me. Correspondence between some of these individuals and the OSS appears in R.G 226 OSS, entry 37, *seriatim*. I wish above all to thank the late Daniel Merriman, who although ill talked with me at length about Davenport College,

30. St. Paul's School, *Chapel Services and Prayers* (4th ed.; Concord, N.H.: The School, 1977), p. 16. Just as Davenport College is used statistically to represent all of Yale's ten wartime colleges, so too are generalizations about preparatory schools drawn from what I must believe to be a representative example, St. Paul's. The reason for these choices is, simply, that records were more accessible to me. (My own college, Berkeley, suffered a loss of some of its records and memorabilia, while Davenport's materials are quite full. And the rector of St. Paul's, the Reverend Charles H. Clark, gave me access to the school library and to the course records of certain individuals, provided they first granted permission themselves in writing.)

In World War II at least 2,170 alumni of St. Paul's were on active duty in the military services. Of these, 104 died during the war. John B. Edmonds, ed., *St. Paul's School in the Second World War* (Concord, N.H.: The Alumni Association, 1950), which is rich in anecdote and account, reveals that 126 alumni overtly refer to intelligence work, usually the OSS or Naval Intelligence, while anyone familiar with intelligence during the war can readily find thirty-two more (two quite obvious examples, whose service in the OSS and later CIA is known, simply are listed as "Record incomplete"), this still being the day when assistant naval and military attachés were reticent about what they did. Of these 158 men who were with one or another intelligence body, at least forty-two were in the OSS, not including the large if undetermined number who were in the OSS as civilians. Given the small size of St. Paul's— during the war its graduating classes were a hundred or so—these figures are astonishing. For an excellent history of the school, see August Heckscher (who served in the OSS after graduation from Yale), *St. Paul's: The Life of a New England School* (New York: Scribner's, 1980).

31. I wish to thank Mrs. Alan Valentine, of North Haven, Maine, and Karl Kabelac of the University of Rochester Library, who unsuccessfully searched for relevant papers for me.

32. Here and elsewhere in this chapter descriptions of faculty members I did not know personally have been strengthened by conversations with Richard Carroll, long an assistant to Dean DeVane; Professor George Wilson Pierson, Yale's official historian; and the late George Vaill, former associate secretary of the university and compiler of anecdota on Yale personalities and places. On Wolfers, see Kenneth Maclean, *Pierson's Masters and Fellows, 1933–1938* (Stamford, Conn.: Overbrook Press, 1938), pp. 13–22.

33. The annual reports and records of the Institute of International Studies in the Yale University Archives provide information on contracts, research projects, and staff. Wolfers destroyed most of his papers when he left Yale in 1957, though there is a small collection, MG 634, and boxes 1 and 4 proved useful. See also the Nicholas J. Spykman Papers, MG 37-V, box 9; A. Whitney Griswold Letters, MG 255, 1914–1962, box 27 (seen with permission of Mrs. Mary Griswold and the secretary of the university, John Wilkinson); and the Samuel Flagg Bemis Papers, MG 74 (these are unsorted and quite difficult to use).

34. On the institute, see its annual reports, records, and correspondence, RG 37V, boxes 1, 3, 7, 10, 31, 42, and 63. The files of the Cross-Cultural Survey, and the Human Relations Area Files' original slips and related manuscripts, are not organized. They are kept in filing cabinets in a locked room in the Sterling Memorial Library. The *Outline of Cultural Materials* from which I quote subsequently is the 4th revised edition, third printing with modifications, by George P. Murdock *et al., Behavior Science Outlines,* I (New Haven: HRAF, 1967). Copies of the *Strategic Bulletins* are in RG 1212, Yale in World War II, box 2. I wish to thank Professor Leonard Doob for confirming his role in OWI, the late Professor C. Malcolm Batchelor for describing his work to me, and Mrs. Joan Dollard for offering me access to the papers of her late husband, John Dollard. See also Leonard W. Doob's amusing article, "The Utilization of Social Scientists in the Overseas Branch of the Office of War Information," *American Political Science Review,* XLI (Aug., 1947), 649–67. On the initial clash between the OSS and the OWI, see Allan M. Winkler, *The Politics of Propaganda: The Office of War Information, 1942–1945* (New Haven: Yale University Press, 1978), pp. 122–28.

35. Blankenhorn's report on "Soldiers Committees: History of MO Project (Black), 1944–45," stamped Secret, is in MG 688, World War II Collection, box 43B, folder 108, as is the draft of his much longer study on combat propaganda.

36. *Yale Daily News,* Nov. 11, 1940; RG 37A, Yale-China Association (a name assumed in 1975), boxes 94, 113; Schoyer's several novels, especially *The Indefinite River* (New York: Dodd, Mead, 1947); and Reuben Holden, *Yale-in-China: The Mainland, 1901–1951* (New Haven: Yale-in-China Association, 1964). John Hadley Cox owned a fine private collection of Chinese antiquities, largely of tomb finds from Changsha, which in 1939 he loaned to the Yale Gallery of Fine Arts for exhibit. His ties to the Chinese intellectual community were exquisitely tuned, and they became more so during and after the war. Cox had an unusual career in intelligence work, working on both the substantive and the operational sides, and his is among the several stories that ought to be told in detail. Sidney Lovett was another person who recognized the value of Yale-in-China as a listening post, and he once made a study of railroads in China, which he told me of before his death.

37. Yale University, Sterling Memorial Library: personal files of Charles R. Walker. These manuscripts are not organized; they are kept with the HRAF materials in the library. The quotations cited here are from folders 029 and 068. I wish to thank Matthew Seccombe for drawing my attention to this material, and the late Professor Walker for giving me carbons of several of his reports some years ago, in relation to a different interest of mine.

38. See Gabriel Papers, MG 228, boxes 26, 27, 30–33, 35–38, 40. I wish to thank the late Professor Gabriel for discussing his work with me.

39. See Sumner McKnight Crosby Papers, RG 1144, box 1; Theodore Sizer Papers, RG 453, box 5; Henry La Farge, ed., *Lost Treasures of Europe* (New York: Pantheon Books, 1946); and Sir Leonard Woolley, *A Record of the Work Done by the Military Authorities for the Protection of the Treasures of Art & History in War Areas* (London: HMSO, 1947). The late Professor Crosby provided me with a number of contacts which I hope to draw upon one day for a book on the rescue of looted art.

40. Elizabeth P. MacDonald, *Undercover Girl* (New York: Macmillan, 1947), p. 8; Raymond Kennedy Papers, MG 1046, box 1; Yale University Obituary Record, 1949–50, pp. 115–16; teaching materials, in the records of the Institute of International Studies; conversations with the late Ruby Jo Reeves Kennedy. The secret memo on Indo-China is in box 1, folder 00009, of the Kennedy Papers.

The story of A. Peter Dewey, Yale '39, is another that needs to be told. Dewey commanded an OSS unit sent by Detachment 404 to accompany British forces into Saigon. He soon found himself so sharply at odds with British policy, General Douglas Gracey issued an expulsion order against him. On September 26, 1945, Dewey was killed by Vietnamese who apparently took him for a Frenchman, when Gracey refused him permission to fly an American flag from his jeep. In 1981 a Vietnamese refugee identified the attackers as a Viet Minh front group (*Periscope* [the journal of the Association of Former Intelligence Officers, or AFIO], X [Winter, 1985], 10). Dewey, Chevalier de la Légion d'Honneur, his body never recovered, was memorialized at the Cathedral of Bayeux. His story is told briefly, in differing versions, in most books on this period of French colonial, or Vietnamese, history, and in Edmonds, ed., *St. Paul's School in the Second World War,* pp. 134–35, with minor inaccuracies. See Geoffrey T. Hellman's brief appreciation of Dewey in Dewey's posthumous book, *As They Were* (New York: Beechhurst Press, 1946). That the circumstances of Dewey's death remain controversial is attested to by the sharp attack on him by British writer Dennis Duncanson (*Times Literary Supplement,* Aug. 21, 1982) and the equally spirited defense by Harrison E. Salisbury. The official story appears in the National Archives RG 226, OSS, entry 110, box 25, folders 277 and 284, including a report by Captain Herbert J. Bluechel.

41. The following paragraphs are based on an interview with Allen Walz at his home in Rancho Mirage, California.

42. See William R. Corson, *The Armies of Ignorance: The Rise of the American Intelligence Empire* (New York: Dial Press, 1977), pp. 306–310, though there are errors.

43. Dulles lectured at Yale again in 1958. Charles Seymour papers, MG 441, folder 254; Allen W. Dulles Papers, Princeton University, box 86: Seymour to Dulles, Feb. 19, 1919, Dulles to Seymour, Dec. 26, 1959.

44. Interview with Professor Georges May, 1984; *The New Journal,* II (Feb. 9, 1969), 6. I wish to thank William Kahrl, author of this article, for clarifying several points for me, and William F. Buckley, Jr., for helping me to establish contact with key individuals.

45. The remark is from Michael Burke, *Outrageous Good Fortune* (Boston: Little, Brown, 1984), p. 161.

46. I wish to thank E. J. Applewhite, '41, of Washington, D.C., for a discussion of "sentimental imperialists" in the postwar years, and Richard T. Arndt and Osborne Day, '43, for making it possible for me to gather with several former employees of the CIA.

47. Kelley, *Yale,* p. 393.

48. A reader might justly complain that no hard figures have been provided on how many Yale graduates went into intelligence work. The answer cannot be known, by the nature of the subject. I have suggested various figures that may be taken as indicative: forty-two members of the class of 1943 went into intelligence work, largely the OSS. Julius Mader's very faulty compilation provides 174 names, most of them not the same as the forty-two. I have said that at least sixty of the 397 individuals memorialized in 1946 were in intelligence work for at least part of the war. Personnel rosters of the nine OSS branches provide some other names; X-2, the most secretive of the branches, had at least twenty-two Yale men working in it, including three I would not have identified otherwise. Philip Agee and Louis Wolf, eds., *Dirty Work: The CIA in Western Europe* (Secaucus, N.J.: Lyle Stuart, 1978), generally concerned with a much more recent period, provides résumés on 307 individuals, ninety-seven of whom came from the Ivy League, twenty-two from Yale. (Higher numbers come from Harvard [35], Georgetown [31], and George Washington University [27].) But figures like these are of little use as hard data, and conclusions must remain subjective. Most fundamental is the fact that no list could be anything like thorough: after all, subjects of the next three chapters, Wilmarth Lewis, Joseph Toy Curtiss and Donald Downes, appear in none of the lists referred to above.

CHAPTER TWO   **The Campus: Langer, Lewis, Kent & Co.**

1. See Bradley F. Smith, *The Shadow Warriors: O.S.S. and the Origins of the C.I.A.* (New York: Basic Books, 1983), p. 361. Smith devotes one chapter to R&A, and while his conclusion—that R&A was a fundamental "building block" for the CIA—has been challenged by several writers (a debate not relevant to my own interests), this chapter is the fullest short history of R&A yet written.

2. I wish to thank the late Mr. DeForest van Slyck for describing his work for the OSS and the CIA, and the late Sherman Kent for telling me in detail of his work with R&A.

3. The best book on Donovan's pre-COI career is Richard Dunlop, *Donovan, America's Master Spy* (Chicago: Rand McNally, 1982). It is not sound on COI/OSS.

4. Kent's draft paper on this subject is in the Sherman Kent Papers, Yale University, Manuscript Group 854, box 25. Now consisting of 39 boxes, the Kent Papers are unusually valuable. Boxes 16–38 are closed to research at this time. I wish to thank Mr. Kent for the unusual confidence extended to me in temporarily lifting this embargo.

5. See Smith, *The Shadow Warriors,* on these and other problems with the Board of Analysts. Unhappily, the papers of James Phinney Baxter have not been processed by Williams College and are unavailable to researchers. I wish to thank the Colorado Historical Society in Denver for sending me copies of its file of James Grafton Rogers manuscripts, collection 536, almost all of which are on the OSS. See in particular his testimony to the value of R&A in box 8.

6. The following account of the history of R&A is drawn in part from the draft

"History of the Research and Analysis Branch in the Office of Strategic Services, June 1941–September 1944," in Record Group 226, OSS, entry 99, box 76, folder 45. This draft is not without its biases, and I have attempted to correct for them through conversations with a number of scholars who worked for R&A—of the historians listed in note 19, I have talked or corresponded with twenty-three—and through the Langer and Kent papers. The draft was apparently begun by Conyers Read, extended by Herman Liebert (see Harvard University, Pusey Library, William L. Langer Papers, Box 8: Liebert to Langer, July 9, 1946), and completed by an unknown hand. Marked Secret, in part because of the sharp personal remarks contained in it, the report was terminated incomplete (RG 226, entry 1, box 13). Langer was unhappy with it, and when Kermit Roosevelt began his in-house general history of OSS—*War Report of the OSS,* finished in 1947 and published in 1976 (New York: Walker and Co.)—he sent his caveats to Roosevelt with a copy to Donovan (Langer Papers: Langer to Donovan, Apr. 14, 1947). Langer's twenty-nine-page apologia was highly defensive in tone, and he criticizes the division historians as being "in no position to judge" on the matters on which the individual histories reported. Since the branch history frequently criticized Donovan for not paying enough attention to R&A activities, Langer wrote, "I am eager to go on record as saying that General Donovan and his chief assistants at all times showed a genuine and lively interest in all the problems and activities of the branch." Langer's response provides a useful history of R&A from his perspective (U.S. Army Military History Institute, Archives, Carlisle Barracks, Penn., William J. Donovan Papers: box 67B, no. 350, Mar. 1, 1947). Other draft versions of OSS histories may be found in RG 226, entry 1, box 11; the history of the project itself is in entry 99, box 15.

7. See *In and Out of the Ivory Tower: The Autobiography of William L. Langer* (New York: Neale Watson Academic Publications, 1977), pp. 128–29, 180–208. Except for minor changes this is Langer's 1975 manuscript, "Up from the Ranks," in the Langer Papers, HUG (FP) 19.46, 19.19, 19.3. I wish to thank the Harvard University Archives for allowing me access to these papers, and Mrs. William L. Langer of Cambridge for giving me the necessary written permission. I also examined the papers of Crane Brinton in the Harvard Archives, which contained no relevant material. I should like to thank Carl Schorske of Princeton University, Richard Frye of Harvard University, and Marshall Dill of the University of Michigan for discussing their work in OSS with me. On Langer's techniques as historian see Carl E. Schorske and Elizabeth Schorske, eds., *Explorations in Crisis: Papers in International History, William L. Langer* (Cambridge, Mass.: Harvard University Press, 1969), a collection of Langer's essays presented to him on his retirement.

8. See, for example, RG 226, OSS, entry 1, box 15, folder 18: Crane Brinton to Conyers Read, Dec. 19, 1944. Brinton's belief that the chief of R&A, "like Charlemagne, has got to travel through his own empire," was simply not shared by Langer, who was a far closer student of Bismarck. On Read see *Conyers Read, 1881–1959: Scholar, Teacher, Public Servant* ([Fairfax, Calif.: 1963]), especially Langer's essay, pp. 9–17. For a long list of complaints about rank, the reproduction of reports, space, etc., see RG 226, OSS, entry 1: "group manifesto," Division Chiefs and Assistant Division Chiefs to the Director, Sept. 17, 1943. For complaints on another subject—the draft—see Kent Papers, box 34: Kent to Baxter, July 13, 1942. Also, Wilmarth Sheldon Lewis amusingly de-

scribes his COI/OSS period in *One Man's Education* (New York: Knopf, 1967),
pp. 334–58. See also his collection of essays, *Read As You Please* (Cleveland:
The Rowfant Club, 1975).

9. I wish to thank Ruth C. McKay for sharing with me her husband's file
copies.

10. See RG 226, OSS, entry 1, Evaluation Committee: David Cass to Donald
Wheeler, Jan. 27; Wheeler to Chandler Morse, May 19 (two memoranda of this
date); Isaiah Frank to Morse, May 20; Frank J. Manheim to J. R. Forgan and
J. A. Montgomery, May 21; S. J. Van Hyning to Wheeler, May 26; Harold C.
Deutsch to Langer, Sept. 16; [Kent] to Deutsch, Oct. 2; Charles Burton Fahs to
Langer, Nov. 3 with enclosure of Nov. 2; and Liebert to Langer, Nov. 17, all
1943. Mrs. Jamie Ross Fahs is writing a biography of C. B. Fahs.

11. See Robert Hayden Alcorn, *No Bugles for Spies: Tales of the OSS* (New
York: David McKay, 1962), Chapter 5 throughout.

12. Langer set out his approach in the preface to *Our Vichy Gamble* (New
York: Knopf, 1947), pp. vii–ix. The conclusion is a well-reasoned defense of
American policy, explaining why it seemed wise to hold to Vichy and not to
espouse the cause of Charles de Gaulle. With hindsight one surely would wish,
at least, to question Langer's judgment that "de Gaulle was a hireling of the
British" (p. 394), and given Langer's access to OSS reports, one may wonder at
the observation that the Department of State "seems to have underestimated the
extent of de Gaulle's following" (p. 394). His conclusion, however, is appropriately tough minded: "Sentiment played no role in the decision. We were not
partial to the fascism of Vichy and we were not unsympathetic to French aspirations. Our objective was to safeguard our own interests" (p. 395).

13. See Langer, "Scholarship and the Intelligence Problem," *American Philosophical Society Proceedings,* XCII (Mar., 1948), 43–45.

14. See Smith, p. 372 and 472 n. 22; RG 226, OSS, entry 1, box 1, Intelligence
Collection Activities: Jesse H. Shera to William Applebaum, Aug. 10, 1945; *ibid.,*
box 2: Robert T. Crane to Donovan, Feb. 14, 1944, and Langer, *aide memoir,*
Aug. 31, 1945; *ibid.,* box 3: Langer to Carl J. Kulsrud, June 30, 1944; *ibid.,* box
23: Jay S. Seeley, Activities Report, Nov. 13, 1944; entry 37, "American Universities and Field Intelligence" folder: Charles F. Edson to James, Aug. 29,
1945.

15. There are minor discrepancies in the record, of no importance to the discussion here. In his memoirs Langer says that Truman personally called President Conant at Harvard; in a letter to a former member of ONE, Ludwell
Montague, who was writing an in-house CIA history of ONE, Langer says that
it was Smith who called Harvard (Langer Papers: Montague to Langer, Aug. 11,
25, and Langer to Montague, Aug. 19, 1969).

16. Langer was unfair to himself. In his presidential address to the American
Historical Association, "The Next Assignment," Langer took up the cause for
the role of psychology in history and, by implication, in intelligence. In part this
may have arisen from work his brother, Walter C. Langer, had done for the
OSS, for—with unnamed collaborators and researchers—Walter prepared a secret report on "the mind of Adolf Hitler" (OSS, MO Branch, "A Psychological
Analysis of Adolf Hitler: His Life and Legend," 4 vols. typescript, declassified
1968, copy in Cross Campus Library, Yale University). In 1972 this report was
published in a somewhat altered form, with a foreword by William and an intro-

duction by Walter, as *The Mind of Adolf Hitler: The Secret Wartime Report* (New York: Basic Books). The last quotation is from Marian Wilhelm, *The Man Who Watched the Rising Sun: The Story of Admiral Ellis M. Zacharias* (New York: Franklin Watts, 1967), pp. 87–88.

17. The following history of R&A is based primarily on the Kent Papers, the OSS files cited throughout the chapter, and a massive manuscript history of the OSS, with lengthy sections on R&A, in the Donovan Papers, Carlisle, Penn., box 102A, especially IV. See also box 67B, files 350, 351, box 72A, and Liebert to Langer, May 22, 1945, in box 66A, file 60. Serial number analysis is discussed in RG 226, 1/10, Sidney S. Alexander to Preston E. James, May 26, 1945.

18. (New York: Appleton-Century-Crofts, 1941).

19. Why Kent, if ONE required the talents of a historian, and not someone else? After all, the list of historians who worked for the OSS reads like a *Who's Who* of the profession. A short list, with indicative postwar positions, includes the following:

James Phinney Baxter III, president of Williams College;

Carl Blegen, professor of history, University of Cincinnati, and a leading authority on American immigration and ethnic history;

Crane Brinton, professor of history, Harvard University, perhaps the leading historian of ideas on the European front;

Dr. Frederick Burkhardt, director of the American Council of Learned Societies;

John Christopher, professor of history, University of Rochester, who with Brinton and Robert Lee Wolff wrote an extremely influential (and extremely successful) textbook, *History of Civilization,* immediately after the war, a text which became one of two that dominated the market for the immediate postwar generation of undergraduate students. Brinton, Christopher and Wolff, as the text was known, reflected the synoptic view the authors developed while in the OSS, and it would not be totally revised until 1983;

Dr. Ray Cline, who wrote a first-rate volume in the official history of World War II and then returned to the intelligence profession. He became the CIA's deputy director for intelligence from 1962 to 1966;

John Clive, professor of history, Harvard University, a major figure in nineteenth-century British studies;

Gordon Craig, professor of history, Princeton and later Stanford universities, author of the leading books on the role of the military in German history;

John Curtiss, professor of history, Duke University, an authority on France;

Harold C. Deutsch, professor of history, University of Minnesota, also an important figure in the development of modern German history in the United States;

Donald M. Dozer, professor of history, University of California, Santa Barbara, a Latin Americanist;

Dr. Allan Evans, a Harvard medievalist from Yale who remained with the Department of State after R&A, transferred to State at the end of the war;

John K. Fairbank, professor of Chinese history at Harvard University, the leading sinologist of his generation;

Franklin L. Ford, professor of history, Harvard University, and dean of the Harvard Faculty of Arts and Sciences during late 1960s student disorders;

Felix Gilbert, historian at the Institute for Advanced Study in Princeton, New
Jersey, an elegant diplomatist:

S. Everett Gleason, who worked with William Langer in the OSS and after,
and returned to become the State Department's historian;

Moses Hadas, professor of classics, Columbia University, who wrote on the
expansion of the Roman Empire;

Samuel W. Halperin, professor of history, University of Chicago, and after
the war editor of the *Journal of Modern History*;

Henry B. Hill, professor of history, University of Kansas, who developed
French history there and later at Wisconsin;

Hajo Holborn, Sterling Professor of History, Yale University, who worked on
occupation policy for Germany at the end of the war and wrote on the history of military occupation, becoming a dominant figure in the training of
postwar Germanists;

H. Stuart Hughes, professor of history, Harvard University, who moved on
from where Crane Brinton had left off in European intellectual (and especially Italian) history, and unsuccessfully ran for the House of Representatives in Massachusetts;

Sherman Kent, who left Yale to preside over ONE, the Office of National
Estimates, at the CIA;

Clinton Knox, who also left the historical profession, becoming ambassador
to Guinea;

Leonard Krieger, who returned from the OSS to become a professor at Yale
and then of German intellectual history at the University of Chicago;

William L. Langer, the outstanding European diplomatic historian of his generation;

Val Lorwin, professor of history, University of Oregon, and the nation's leading authority on the Low Countries;

Herbert Marcuse, who moved from history to philosophy at Brandeis and the
University of California, and from the contemplative life to that of guru to
the student revolt during the war in Vietnam;

Henry Cord Meyer, professor of history, Pomona College, another leading
Germanist who left Yale for the West Coast;

Saul K. Padover, professor at the New School for Social Research, authority
on Jefferson and democratic thought, and a pioneer lecturer on American
history at a wide range of universities overseas;

Michael B. Petrovich, professor of history, University of Wisconsin, who developed Russian studies there;

David H. Pinckney, professor of history, first at the University of Missouri
and then the University of Washington, a major force in French history and,
like Brinton, Craig, Fairbank, Holborn, Langer, and others, a president of
the American Historical Association, perhaps the highest honor the discipline can bestow on one of its own;

David M. Potter, professor of history, Yale University (and later at Stanford),
who with Ralph Gabriel and Norman Holmes Pearson firmly established
American studies at Yale;

Conyers Read, professor of history, University of Pennsylvania, an authority
on Elizabethan England and the prime mover behind the Council on Foreign
Relations in Philadelphia;

Henry L. Roberts, professor of history, Columbia University, who followed Geroid Robinson, also of R&A, in developing a front-rank Russian studies program at that institution;

Elspeth D. Rostow, University of Texas, who with her husband, Walt Whitman Rostow, worked out major interpretations on American foreign policy;

John E. Sawyer, economic historian who left Yale to become president of Williams College and then of the Mellon Foundation;

Arthur M. Schlesinger, Jr., professor of history, Harvard University, polymath, adviser to and historian for the Kennedys before his translation to a Schweitzer chair at the City University of New York;

Bernadotte E. Schmitt, who after the war lived in retirement, lauded as the leading revisionist historian of the causes of World War I;

Carl E. Schorske, professor of history at Wesleyan and then Princeton University, an authority on European intellectual history;

Raymond Sontag, professor of history, University of California at Berkeley, the first of the old OSS team to publicly remind the student generation of the 1960s of his service and of why academics had felt it appropriate to engage in intelligence work, which he had continued to do as a consultant to ONE;

L. S. Stavrianos, professor of history, Northwestern University, who carried the idea of global history further than any other scholar, in a series of notable texts;

Richard P. Stebbins, a man Sherman Kent felt could turn out more work of high quality than anyone else in his shop, who became director of the Council on Foreign Relations;

Paul R. Sweet, who also remained with the State Department, in charge of its official histories and archives;

Alexander Vucinich, professor of history, San Jose State University, a leading authority on Eastern Europe;

Wayne S. Vucinich, professor of history, Stanford University, who covered the same waterfront;

Paul L. Ward, who became the executive director of the American Historical Association;

Albert Weinberg, technically a political scientist, although the author of a fine historical analysis of American imperial expansion, who remained in government work after the war;

Robert Lee Wolff, professor of history, Harvard University, that institution's outstanding authority on Eastern Europe;

John H. Wuorinen, professor of history, Columbia University, who covered Scandinavia and in particular Finland;

T. Cuyler Young, professor of archaeology, Princeton University, who with Richard Frye at Harvard, who also was in the OSS, pioneered Iranian studies in the United States.

These and dozens more, scholars like George McCune, Amry Vandenbosch, Oscar Falnes, Emmet J. Hughes, Charles Burton Fahs, Thomas L. Blakemore, and W. Norman Brown, who gave shape to intelligence, and through their time in intelligence gave shape to their careers, attested in 1965, when Langer sought to draw up an OSS historians' veterans list, to the connection (as Ray Cline somewhat melodramatically put it) between "secrets, spies, and scholars."

20. The Projects Committee generally met every two days. A typical meeting might discuss five projects submitted for consideration, with four given the green light, and would receive from the chief editor up to fifteen completed reports to be reviewed for sending on to the Joint Chiefs. These would be a mixture of long-range projects ("Present tensions in Canadian-American relations," to be prepared by Elizabeth Armstrong), background pieces (the current status of Jews in Europe, by Robert Lee Wolff), and immediate needs (biographical notes on Japan's Shidehara cabinet). The Joint Intelligence Committee might also request that a project be classified top secret, with no details presented to the group, except for information on where the work load would fall. For examples see RG 226, OSS, entry 1, box 6. On the shift of priorities from Europe to the Far East and to Eastern Europe and the Soviet Union, see *ibid.*, box 2.

21. A small Arctic Section was proposed, but it was left as already consti- tuted, under the air force and G-2. Its personnel, comprised of fifteen scholars, most with degrees in geology, under Laurence M. Gould, who had been second in command of the Byrd Antarctic expedition of 1928–30, included Richard F. Flint, a professor at Yale. OSS asked to have Gould and Flint transferred to its work (RG 226, OSS, entry 1, box 9).

22. See Kent Papers: Kent to Mrs. William Kent [his mother], Dec. 29, 1942, on the size of the section. For a fine example of Wolff's style see his interview of Dr. E.F.S. Hanfstaengl, said to be a lapsed Nazi, in RG 226, OSS, entry 1, box 4: Nov. 18, 1943.

23. Hoover's Papers, in ninety boxes, are in the Duke University Archives, Durham, North Carolina. On Hoover's work for OSS see his *Memoirs of Capi- talism, Communism and Nazism* (Durham: Duke University Press, 1965), pp. 199–220.

24. RG 226, OSS, entry 1, citations: Alexander to Preston E. James, May 26, 1945. On the general question of strategic bombing see the excellent introductory essay in Gordon Daniels, ed., *A Guide to the Reports of the United States Stra- tegic Bombing Survey,* Royal Historical Society *Guides & Handbooks,* Supple- mentary Series, no. 2 (London: Royal Historical Society, 1981), pp. xvi–xxvi.

25. Wilmarth Lewis Papers, Walpole Library, Farmington, Connecticut, Sey- mour file: Lewis to Charles Seymour, Oct. 28, 1943.

26. One of the geographers, Harold Wiens, who returned to the University of Michigan to complete his doctorate, was able after the war to demonstrate the importance of the work he had done for OSS with a series of important publi- cations written while serving on several faculties, including Yale and the Uni- versity of Hawaii. These included the influential *China's March into the Tropics,* published by the Office of Naval Research in 1952, and *Atoll Environment and Ecology,* published by the Yale University Press in 1962.

27. The Foreign Nationalities Branch also read and processed information, going through the American ethnic press in twenty-three languages, largely Eu- ropean or Middle Eastern. The FNB kept tabs on contacts between foreigners in the United States and peace and labor groups in Europe, studied whether émigrés were influencing the content of *The New Republic* or *Nation,* and ana- lyzed attitudes taken toward new political leaders in Germany in 1945. See RG

226, OSS, file 1, box 3 in particular. On occasion the FNB used its contacts to alert Langer to possible turncoats inside R&A. When the remnants of OSS moved into the State Department, the FNB became the Foreign Nationalities Interim Intelligence Service.

28. Herman W. Liebert, "Comments on 'Donovan and the C.I.A.,' by T. F. Troy," MS. list of suggested corrections sent to Walter L. Pforzheimer, July 9, 1981. I wish to thank "Fritz" Liebert, librarian emeritus of the Beinecke Rare Book Library at Yale, for sharing this material with me, and for discussing his work in R&A at some length.

29. Material on Wilmarth Lewis, unless cited otherwise, is taken from the Lewis Papers kept at Lewis's Walpole Library in Farmington, Connecticut. There are both general correspondence files and files on specific individuals. The latter include Anthony Garvan, John F. Langan, Charles Seymour, and Jesse H. Shera. There are also relevant files on Lewis's trip to Peru in 1943, on Military Training, and broadly on "Washington," where COI papers are to be found. Included are the COI Index Guide and Lewis's style sheet. I wish to thank Mr. Donald Engley for giving me permission to consult the Lewis Papers and Ms. Catherine Jestin for guiding me through them and the house. See also Lewis, *One Man's Education* (New York: Knopf, 1967), pp. 334–66. Some details in the memoirs, especially on Lewis's mission to Peru, have been corrected by Professor Lewis Hanke, of the University of Massachusetts, to whom I am most grateful. Jesse Shera was Lewis's librarian in COI/OSS, and there is a considerable anecdotal correspondence with Lewis in the Shera Papers in the Case Western Reserve University Archives. I am grateful to Jeffrey Rollison, Case's assistant university archivist, for searching these papers for me.

30. See Geoffrey T. Hellman's "Profiles: The Steward of Strawberry Hill," *The New Yorker,* XXV (Aug. 6, 1949), 26–37, and (Aug. 13, 1949), 31–41, from which part of the following description is drawn. Also useful is *"Life* Explores World's Finest Walpole Library," *Life,* XVII (Oct. 23, 1944), 116–18. While generally admiring, Hellman does quote from a diatribe on the Walpole project by Cyril Connolly that appeared in the London *Observer* in 1943. Later an even sharper attack was launched by the distinguished English historian J. H. Plumb, in "Horace Walpole at Yale," *New York Review of Books,* V (Sept. 30, 1965), 9–10, which is a review of volumes 32 through 34 of the Walpole Correspondence. Plumb thinks Walpole, "the dilettante son of Sir Robert," not worth the effort; feels that the lavish editorial techniques are spreading "like measles among the Aztecs," and that use of Walpole as representative of the eighteenth century is "a mischievous and distorting cultural attitude." The correspondence is, however, "a monument to the finest standards of American editing which is now the best in the world." Lewis and the Walpole editors did not reply, though Brendan Gill of *The New Yorker* and Vera Liebert did so on his behalf (*ibid.,* Oct. 28, p. 40, and Dec. 9, 1965, p. 41). Hellman devoted only a few paragraphs to Lewis's work with COI, but he was quite familiar with it, and personally friendly to Lewis—though he does not confess his interest in his article—since Hellman had worked with the OSS, beginning in Lewis's shop. Later he apparently thought to write a history of early COI (see Thomas F. Troy, *Donovan and the CIA: A History of the Establishment of the Central Intelligence Agency* [Frederick, Md.: University Publications of America, 1981], p. 558). Hellman did write humorously of "how to be a secret agent" in *How to Disappear for an Hour* (New York: Dodd, Mead, 1947), pp. 46–51. He also helped prepare a memorial book, *Yale '28 War Record* (New York: A. Giraldi, 1946).

31. In keeping with Yale's custom, Lewis was always listed as an alumnus with his entering class, 1918.

32. Warren Hunting Smith, "Horace Walpole's Correspondence," *The Yale University Library Gazette*, LVIII (Oct., 1983), 17–28.

33. With apologies to Mr. Lewis, publisher and author have agreed that our notes belong at the back of the book.

34. The following material on the committee comes from the secret manuscript history of the committee's work, possibly written by Wallace Deuel, in RG 226, OSS, entry 99, branch histories, box 76, folder 46. This excellent history, eighty-five pages in typescript, is without date. While not in final form, it is clearly an advanced draft. The committee was occasionally known as ICAFP and at times in the records "Periodicals" was erroneously substituted in the committee's title for "Publications."

35. *Ibid.*, entry 1, boxes 61, 63.

36. On office organization see in particular *ibid.*, Functional Directory of Personnel, Oct., 1942: Office of the Director, Branch of Research and Analysis, box 4.

37. There are three folders of Langan correspondence in the Lewis Papers at Farmington. See also the short statement on the Navy's Aperture Card System in *United States Naval Institute Proceedings*, XC (July, 1964), 137–38.

38. On the history of the Farmington Plan, see Keyes D. Metcalf and Edwin E. Williams, "Notes on the Farmington Plan," *Libri*, I (i/1950), 13–19.

39. I wish to thank Dr. Smith for his help and for providing me with the names of several other contacts in CID. On his work see *The New York Times*, Nov. 25, 1983.

40. While writing a book on Canadian-American relations, I once asked Wilmarth Lewis if I might see the report he wrote. He replied that he believed he never wrote one, and if he did he had no recollection of what it was about. On his resignation see Langer Papers, box 7: Lewis to Langer, Nov. 9, 1943.

41. "Index to Publications: Mediterranean Section Coordinator of Information," Kent Papers, box 27. Classification was not yet utterly out of hand: only twenty-three of these documents were classified as secret.

42. MS. without title on the problems future historians would face in using intelligence records, 1946, pp. 40–41, in *ibid.*

43. For a typical "accomplishments" list see "Accomplishments of the Research and Analysis Branch, OSS from 1 January 1943 to 28 March 1944," in RG 226, OSS, entry 1, Office of the Chief, R&A.

44. See Arthur Widder, *Adventures in Black* (New York: Harper & Row, 1962), pp. 22–23.

45. These examples are from one of the books by which the OSS was romanticized, though at a later date: Alcorn, *No Bugles for Spies*, p. 71.

46. RG 226, OSS, entry 1, box 1: Kent to Solon J. Buck, archivist of the United States, Aug. 10, 1945, and box 19, "Salzburg, Austria Mission," file.

47. See Stanley P. Lovell, *Of Spies & Strategems* (Englewood Cliffs, N.J.: Prentice-Hall, 1963), p. 184.

48. Friendships formed or strengthened in the OSS continued after the war, the scholars criticizing and reinforcing each other's research. Of the fifty historians listed in note 19, all but two wrote postwar books in which they thanked at least one wartime colleague for reading a manuscript. See H. Stuart Hughes, *An Essay for Our Times* (New York: Knopf, 1950), for a typical example: he commends Felix Gilbert and John Sawyer for criticizing, among other chapters, his very good analysis of "The Transmutation of Marxism." A significant work by an OSS historian who explicitly acknowledged the importance of his OSS experience and colleagues to his subsequent career is Robert Lee Wolff, *The Balkans in Our Time* (Cambridge, Mass.: Harvard University Press, 1956). The exceptions were Herbert Marcuse and David M. Potter. The latter's name never appears on OSS lists, though he did serve briefly (see Yale University, Eugene Kone Papers, MG 1221, Yale in World War II, box 1: "Faculty in the War"). At the time only thirteen Yale faculty were acknowledged to be with the OSS.

49. Bundy, "The Battlefields of Power and the Searchlights of the Academy," in Edgar A. G. Johnson, ed., *Dimensions of Diplomacy* (Baltimore: The Johns Hopkins University Press, 1964), pp. 2–3. See also Ray S. Cline, *The CIA under Reagan, Bush & Casey* (Washington: Acropolis Books, 1981), pp. 61–63. This is a revision and expansion of Cline's *Secrets, Spies and Scholars: Blueprint of the Essential CIA* (Washington: Acropolis Books, 1976), in which see pp. 41–43.

50. In addition to Smith and Lovell, others who rate R&A very highly in relation to other OSS branches include John Magruder, the deputy director of OSS, as early as September 11, 1943 (he felt only R&A and CE had fully proven themselves (RG 226, OSS, entry 110, box 52, folder 517: Magruder to Donovan, Sept. 11, 1943); Barry Katz, in *Herbert Marcuse and the Art of Liberation: An Intellectual Biography* (London: NLB, 1982), p. 115—Katz is now at work on a closer study of the role of philosophy and the social sciences in the OSS, and he has called R&A "the social science equivalent of the Manhattan project"; and by context and inference, Stewart Alsop and Thomas Braden, *Sub Rosa: The OSS and American Espionage* (New York: Harvest reprint ed., 1964). I am grateful to Joseph Alsop for giving me permission to consult the Joseph and Stewart Alsop Papers at the Library of Congress, and to John Alsop for meeting with me. The Alsop Papers contain useful OSS material, though none proved relevant to the present study.

In an interesting assessment Donovan's first biographer, Corey Ford, says that R&A was clearly superior to anything the British or Russians could do, or that the Germans chose to do, and that R&A maps were "unparalleled" (see Ford, *Donovan of OSS* [Boston: Little, Brown, 1970], p. 152). I wish to thank the Dartmouth College Library for giving me access to the Corey Ford Papers.

CHAPTER THREE   The Library: Joseph Toy Curtiss

1. Unless otherwise indicated, this account of the Yale Library Project is drawn from the following sources, to which further specific reference will not be made. The genesis of the project, and the financial problems arising from it, have been pieced together from the accounting and letter file held by Walter L. Pforzheimer, transferred to the Yale University Library's Historical Manuscripts Room in 1977, together with supplementary OSS documents obtained by the library through the Freedom of Information Act in 1981. Joseph Curtiss's reports on expenditures, and the account books, are in the Yale University Library, Yale in World War II Collection, Record Group 1212, series I, boxes 2, 2A, 10 and 11. The World War II Collection at Yale (Manuscript Group 688) also contains much relevant material. The collections of papers of Lewis Perry Curtis, William Huse Dunham, Archibald Foord, A. Whitney Griswold, Basil Duke Henning, Sherman Kent, Bernard Knollenberg, Thomas C. Mendenhall, and Wallace Notestein, all in the Yale University Library, fill in many details and contain the Curtiss letters referred to. Also useful are the clipping files of Russell Pruden, held in the Master's Office of Berkeley College, and the wartime records of the masters of Jonathan Edwards and Pierson colleges. The Records of the Secretary of the University (RG 4-A, boxes 255–57 and 259), the papers of the university librarian, and the official papers of President Charles Seymour provided small items of corroborative detail, as did the accession records of the Sterling Memorial Library. Of these collections, those of the secretary, and the Dunham, Griswold, and Kent papers, are restricted.

The files of the Near East Foundation, held at the foundation's office in New York City, unfold the history of Robert College during World War II. The minutes of the board of directors' meetings, the dockets of the board of directors, and general files on the college were examined there. Other records of Robert College, held at the college offices in New York City, are not open to researchers while being reorganized. They were searched for me by Michael A. Lutzker, archival consultant to the college, to whom I am most grateful. The official records of the American Library Association, housed at the University of Illinois Library, where the records of the Joint Committee on Foreign Importations may be consulted, were searched for me, and several relevant letters and reports were found. A few Curtiss items may be found in RG 226, OSS, entry 134, boxes 297, folder 1, and 298, folders 3–6.

Three other collections of manuscripts, which are closed to researchers at this time, were of substantial use. These are the private letters of Norman Holmes Pearson, owned by his daughter, Ms. Susan Addiss; letters of Sidney Clark; and the papers of Donald Downes, which are in my possession. The Downes papers are destined for the World War II Collection at Yale.

More rewarding than the manuscript sources, as valuable as they proved to be, were interviews with the participants. I wish to thank Joseph Toy Curtiss, Thomas C. Mendenhall, and Walter L. Pforzheimer, in particular, for meeting with me on several occasions; Beekman Cannon, Mrs. Sidney Clark, Basil Duke Henning, and the late Sherman Kent for providing much useful information across coffee, tea, and bourbon respectively; and John Waller, Turner Taliaferro Smith, Lawrence Houston, and Carolyn Bland, formerly of the CIA, for sharing their knowledge of the Istanbul, Cairo, and Bari operations with me. Mrs. John I. B. McCulloch was also most gracious in telling me of her husband's work in Cairo, Caserta, and Bari. Conversations prior to their deaths with James T. Babb, William H. Dunham, John McCulloch, and Norman Holmes Pearson, while not concerned specifically with the Yale Library Project, also add flesh to the story, as did a visit to Robert College in Istanbul in 1984. I wish to thank Steven Rosenthal for making further inquiries on my behalf at Bebek and for supplying me with useful photographs, Helen D. Bliss, Brevoort Cannon, Bozkurt Guvenc for responding to my queries, and Robert Miner for corresponding with me about Curtiss. Above all, this chapter could not have been finished without the ready cooperation of Messrs. Curtiss, Mendenhall, and Pforzheimer, who reacted to it in draft. I also thank Richard Frye and Douglas W. Bryant, executive director of the American Trust for the British Library, who read its penultimate version.

The only substantial printed reference to the Yale Library Project is in Donald Downes, *The Scarlet Thread: Adventures in Wartime Espionage* (New York: The British Book Centre, 1953), pp. 75–76. Downes is uncharacteristically discreet about the project and does not mention Professor Curtiss by name. There is a reference to "young historians" in a context that could imply that there may have been a second Yale scholar sent overseas. There is no evidence for this, and I believe Downes's statement to be an imprecise reference to Notestein, Mendenhall, and Pearson, who are named by Downes.

2. Keogh, *Dedication of the Sterling Memorial Library, 11 April 1931* (New Haven: The University, 1931), p. 135.

3. Pruden and Mendenhall, "The Yale Collection of War Literature," *The Yale University Library Gazette,* XVII (July, 1942), 14–20. Kent's article, "War Collection," is in the *Yale Alumni Magazine* (Mar. 22, 1940).

4. Some years before his death I talked with James Babb about how surprised I was to find in the Yale library full sets of German and other scholarly publications running right through World War II. Our conversation was about the oddity of scholars continuing to publish even as the ceiling fell in on them, and while at the time Babb showed me some of the accession slips on these publications to prove that many of them had arrived during the war and not been bought up afterward, he made no mention of the Yale Library Project, and I lacked the wit to see the oddity the accession slips posed. Sometime later, while I was working in the Yale Archives, Ruth Gay, who was preparing a catalog to the World War II Collection, drew my attention once again to the few papers then in the archives relating to the library purchases, and I determined then to make this a case study in the use of cover for an intelligence operation.

5. This description of Curtiss's training is taken from conversations with him, as supplemented by the manuscript "History of the Schools and Training Branch OSS," in the National Archives, Record Group 226, OSS, entry 99, box 78, folder 60 (printed in 1983 by the Kingfisher Press of San Francisco as edited by William L. Cassidy). This history adds the tale of a student who posed as a Yale professor, wrote a letter of introduction on Yale stationery from the dean of men to the president of a large company in Pittsburgh, claimed that he was interested in the postwar training of returned veterans, and was given an extensive tour of the plant. Fortunately (for the trainee), the president to whom he had addressed the letter was away from the factory on the crucial day, and a vice president authorized the tour, for when he returned the president called the dean of men at Yale, who was a close friend, to learn that no such professor existed. The FBI then traced the trainee to the OSS facility. The bogus professor may well have been quite pleased with himself, however, for he was in fact a Yale graduate, and most Yale students assume that they can satisfactorily imitate their professors.

Several memoirs and biographical accounts of OSS members describe the presumed training, or assessment of that training, which individuals experienced. More often than not, these descriptions are not precisely accurate to the specific person. For example, several accounts tell how candidates were told to climb, in the dark, up a long shaft, hang by their fingers, and on command drop. One account adds the detail that while one or two refused to do so, and one climbed back down in the dark rather than drop, yet another spat out his chewing gum and, upon hearing it strike the bottom, knew how far the fall was. (The distance was from ten to eighteen inches.) The problem with incorporating such a detail into a memoir is that it generally does not apply. Apart from the obvious fact that any one person might not experience the norm, the norm itself was constantly undergoing change in the Schools and Training Branch. Curtiss did participate in the "schemes," however—the infiltration of industrial centers—and got himself a job with a forged document. The "schemes" were discontinued entirely in July 1944.

The same problem of generalization applies to the Assessment Program. No program was established until December 15, 1943, when a Candidate Appraisal Board was set up. The program was intended initially only for personnel scheduled for overseas assignment. There were three different places where assessment took place—station "S," a country estate in Virginia; "W" in Washington; and "WS" in California. Further, as recruitment to the OSS and posting abroad increased, programs of various lengths were devised: three-day assessments, one-day screenings (known as "quickies"), six-hour assessments ("specials"), one-day schools, etc. Any effort to describe a "typical" training assessment or program will almost certainly fail if its purpose is to describe the actual experience of a particular person. Individuals were not, in any case, privy to their own assessments (see *ibid.*, folder 61: manuscript history of the OSS Assessment Program, draft, confidential; and the OSS Assessment Staff [John W. Gardner, Henry A. Murray, *et al.*], *Assessment of Men: Selection of Personnel for the Office of Strategic Services* [New York: Rinehart, 1948]).

6. For background on Robert College at this time, see Robert L. Daniel, *American Philanthropy in the Near East, 1820–1960* (Athens, Ohio: Ohio University Press, 1970). Bliss was said to be a COI contact (see RG 226, OSS, entry 106, box 21, folder 166: Bertha Carp).

7. The story of Turhan Celik is told in Edward Hymoff, *The OSS in World War II* (New York: Ballantine Books, 1972). On the basis of internal evidence I feel that Hymoff's book cannot be accepted in detail on this matter.

8. Langer accused MacFarland of running a "loose ship" (RG 226, OSS, entry 1, box 15: "Cairo 1944," and box 19: "Middle East Expeditions"). Statements here concerning other OSS personnel in Istanbul are drawn largely from the interviews listed in note 1. Further detail can be found on most of the individuals I mention in the standard books: R. Harris Smith, *OSS: The Secret History of America's First Central Intelligence Agency* (Berkeley, Calif.: University of California Press, 1972 [subsequent citations are to the Delta reprint edition, 1973]); Anthony Cave Brown, *The Last Hero: Wild Bill Donovan* (New York: Random House, 1982 [subsequent citations are to the Vintage reprint edition, 1984]), Bradley F. Smith, *The Shadow Warriors: O.S.S. and the Origins of the C.I.A.* (New York: Basic Books, 1983); and Anthony Cave Brown, ed., *The Secret War Report of the OSS* (New York: Berkley, 1976). This last book represents a condensed reorganization of two earlier volumes, to which Cave Brown has added very useful commentary, but on Istanbul, Cairo, and the Balkans, one must also consult the two original volumes and their introductions by Kermit Roosevelt: *War Report of the OSS* and *The Overseas Targets: War Report of* *the OSS* (New York: Walker, 1976). Roosevelt and a small team originally wrote these in 1946–47 as official histories. See also Coleman's article, "Snapdragon: Story of a Spy," *Metro Magazine: The Magazine of Southeastern Virginia,* May 1977, pp. 24–31, 64–69.

9. See Sperling, "Explorations in Elis," *American Journal of Archaeology,* XLVI (1/1942), 77–89. Sperling was one of two Yale faculty who were serving in the war effort under circumstances by which Yale was initially unaware of even a cover operation. Sperling's name was omitted from the Yale lists of faculty on leave for the war effort, until it was added some time later in pencil to the file copy (see RG 1212, series I, box 2, folder 21).

10. The situation in Greece was exceptionally complex. As the Germans withdrew, the British had moved so cautiously it was widely believed that they were waiting for the monarchist groups in Greece to stifle the pro-Communist organizations. Britain and the Soviet Union apparently had reached an understanding: no Soviet troops were to enter Greece, which would remain in the British sphere of influence, while much of the rest of the Balkans might be presumed to fall to the Soviets. Winston Churchill who, as Harold Macmillan remarked, seemed unable to give up his fondness for kings, was doing all that he could to restore the monarchy in both Italy and Greece. While there was sharp division between the British Foreign Office and the Special Operations Executive (SOE) with respect to postwar policy, that disagreement was especially sharp over Greece, where the majority of SOE operatives were to the right. The British had, in any event, tried to keep the fledgling OSS out of those areas they regarded as properly theirs, for the British feared, with some reason, that the OSS would prove hostile to attempts to reimpose colonial rule after the war. Thus the SOE had refused to cooperate with the OSS at crucial times in Spain, in Greece—where they felt there should be no American operatives at all, allegedly on the grounds of American naiveté—and, of course, in such traditionally British-oriented areas as the Middle East and South and Southeast Asia.

Under these circumstances the Americans often distrusted the British, tried end runs around them, putting missions into Greece without making them known to SOE, and generally believed that SOE's huffy disinclination to communicate was due to jealousy, or fear that the Americans would be more liberal than the British liaison officers would be, rather than to a concern for security. Though there was clear fault on both sides, one cannot help but conclude, on the basis of the extensive published literature, that American intelligence was, on the whole, fully as good as the British, that the American government was quite well informed on Greek and Balkan matters broadly as a result of OSS and other agents in Istanbul, Cairo, and London, and that those Americans who favored a more liberal approach to postwar Greece were the more farsighted. American dislike focused on the British commanding officer in Athens, General Ronald Scobie, and the record strongly supports their view that he was an extreme reactionary. Most OSS officers concluded that ELAS (Ethnikos Laikos Apeleftherotikos Stratos: National Popular Liberation Army), in particular, was not getting a fair hearing from the British.

Especially useful accounts, in addition to those in the general histories cited in note 8, include John O. Iatrides, *Revolt in Athens: The Greek Communist "Second Round," 1944–1945* (Princeton: Princeton University Press, 1972), and

Iatrides, ed., *Greece in the 1940s: A Nation in Crisis* (Hanover, N.H.: University Press of New England, 1981). Iatrides forcefully makes the point about the quality of American information. Richard Clogg, "The Special Operations Executive in Greece" (*ibid.*, p. 109), concludes that the OSS operatives had an advantage over those from SOE because the majority were Greek-Americans who spoke the language. He disagrees with the assessment of their political leanings, however, finding them generally to the left and contrasting them with Yugoslav-Americans, who tended toward the Chetnik side. See also Bickham Sweet-Escott, *Baker Street Irregular* (London: Methuen, 1965), and J. G. Beevor, *SOE: Recollections and Reflections, 1940–1945* (London: Bodley Head, 1981). The literature is, of course, both vast and contentious.

11. Interview with Beekman Cannon, former master of Jonathan Edwards College and professor of the history of music at Yale. The Vermehren matter needs further exploration. Almost all of the published accounts contain discrepancies or direct contradictions. The most straightforward is in Lauran Paine, *German Military Intelligence in World War II: The Abwehr* (New York: Stein and Day, 1984).

12. It is interesting that five of the individuals I interviewed told this story. Either it is quite true, or it spread by word of mouth among OSS operatives in Istanbul to the point that it was fully believed to be true, which in this business is the same thing.

13. Several individuals, mentioned briefly in this chapter, of whom "Jimmy" Murphy is an example, consented to interviews, and I draw more heavily on them elsewhere in this book. I did not raise the library project with Murphy, however, since I was most interested in his relationship to Norman Holmes Pearson, and because a colleague, Timothy Naftali, was also interviewing Murphy for a general history of X-2, so that I thought it pointless to tax a person with questions not central to my own needs. On German penetration of Cereus see Cave Brown, *Last Hero,* pp. 394–410.

14. With thanks to Dr. Richard T. Arndt. See also Downes, *The Scarlet Thread,* pp. 76–77.

15. From Pearson's introduction to Sir John C. Masterman, *The Double-Cross System in the War of 1939 to 1945* (New Haven: Yale University Press, 1972), p. xiv. On another occasion Professor Pearson used a different form in a conversation with me: "the ecology of double agentry."

16. On Ultra, see Chapter Five. The standard books on Cicero are Moyzisch's own account, *Operation Cicero* (New York: Coward-McCann, 1950), and Elyesa Bazna, in collaboration with Hans Nogly, *I Was Cicero* (London: Andre Deutsch, 1962). They must be supplemented with many other books and clearly do not tell the entire story.

17. R&A did send an agent to Switzerland to acquire books. His name, confusingly enough, was Donald Downs, which naturally led to confusion with Donald Downes. See RG 226, OSS, entry 1, box 24. Reports to Donovan in conformity with General Order No. 63: Downs to Donovan, n.d., and box 19, Ramon Guthrie to Kent, final report.

18. Yale University, Beinecke Library, Norman Holmes Pearson Papers: Bowden to Pearson, Mar. 4, 1946.

19. The BSC intercept operation was described in H. Montgomery Hyde, *The*

Quiet Canadian: The Secret Service Story of Sir William Stephenson (London: Hamish Hamilton, 1962), and less anecdotally in Stanley E. Hilton, *Hitler's Secret War in South America, 1939–1945: German Military Espionage and Allied Counterespionage in Brazil* (Baton Rouge: Louisiana State University Press, 1981), pp. 199–201. In the meantime, something funny had happened on the way to the publishers, and a variety of highly romanticized versions of Sir William's accomplishments—which were considerable, and needed only to be retold in a calm tone of voice to be seen as considerable—appeared, of which the most questionable was William Stevenson (no relation), *A Man Called Intrepid: The Secret War* (New York: Harcourt Brace Jovanovich, 1976). For example, Stevenson reproduced forty-four photographs which even an untutored eye—mine—could detect presented problems. Some were scarcely relevant and were present simply to drag in buzz names, such as Kim Philby or Ian Fleming; two maps, which had appeared elsewhere, were incorrectly described as to provenance; three photographs purporting to be of Eric Bailey, a King's Messenger, might have been of just about anybody, and three pictures identified as of Madeleine, an SOE agent who was dropped into occupied France, were (for those who remembered the picture) fairly obviously stills from a wartime movie, *School for Danger*. Thus one does not know quite what to make of Stevenson's descriptions of the intercept operation, though they continue to be accepted by the more synoptic writers (see, for example, Robert Goldston, *Sinister Touches: The Secret War Against Hitler* [New York: Dial Press, 1982], pp. 79–101). Though Stevenson wrote that he had included BSC papers in materials he presented to the archives of the University of Regina, the archivist there says that the gift includes no such papers.

The first warning bell on the Intrepid inflation was sounded by Phil Johns, in *Within Two Cloaks: Missions with SIS and SOE* (London: Kimber, 1979). In 1985 Nigel West, in *A Thread of Deceit: Espionage Myths of World War II* (New York: Random House, 1985), blasted the credibility of other photographs in *A Man Called Intrepid* and demolished further claims made there and in a subsequent book by Stevenson, *Intrepid's Last Case* (New York: Villard Books, 1983). The questions of whether Stevenson confused evidence, or enlarged on the identification between Intrepid and Sir William Stephenson, are not important here, except that the debate forces one to discount many BSC stories until such time as BSC papers truly are open to researchers. This, in turn, makes it difficult to be accurate about what may have happened to the materials Curtiss sent when, indeed if, they were intercepted in Bermuda. A search of the papers on the Postal Censorship Unit in Bermuda, in files 3/2, 11/14, 19, 21–25, 30, and 31 of the Harford Montgomery Hyde Papers, Roskill Library, Churchill College, Cambridge, does not answer the question. Mr. Hyde, who kindly gave me permission to examine the closed collection, finds the story apocryphal.

20. Curtiss suffered, as would Norman Holmes Pearson a little later, from not being able to make his war service known to the faculty, and his promotion to an associate professorship was awkward and unpopular, leaving Curtiss angry with his department and his college. Sometime in 1945 President Seymour had learned of the general nature of Curtiss's true work in Istanbul, and he had told Robert French to tell Curtiss that he would receive a presidential promotion if the department was unwilling to act. French did not deliver the message, and when Curtiss returned in 1946, he said that he was going to accept a position in the Department of State. Notestein talked with Seymour while Lewis Perry Curtis, one of Curtiss's best friends, worked on French. The department declared that it could not judge a scholar without publications and that it was trying to absorb the largest number of non-Yale-educated teachers (surely a task) in the history of the university, having been given thirty-two new instructors to meet the swollen enrollment caused by returning veterans. Curtiss was badly needed, since he had experience with undergraduates, and the department let it be known that while it would not act on its own it would not oppose presidential intervention. Frederick Hilles, a rising star in the English department (who understood the problem, having just returned from secret service at Bletchley Park in England), also argued on Curtiss's behalf. Though French remained complacent if apologetic about his handling of Curtiss's return to the campus, on instructions from Seymour he destroyed Curtiss's letter of resignation. Alfred Bellinger, who was chairman of the promotions committee, confidentially advised that a presidential appointment would be necessary, and Seymour acted accordingly.

Though hurt, and especially upset over the "baleful influences" in Jonathan Edwards College, Curtiss—who was taking a vacation on a ranch near Santa Fe, New Mexico, in order to be away while the decision was being made—accepted the associate professorship and, to his credit, never used his work with the OSS as an excuse for not writing. He would retire still an associate professor, his story never told. (See Lewis Perry Curtis Family Correspondence, MG 587, boxes 3 and 5, on what Dunham called the *"affaire* Curtiss.") I wish to thank Dr. Stanley Hordes, historian of New Mexico, for identifying the San Juan Ranch, on which Curtiss spent the summer of 1946, for me.

CHAPTER FOUR   The Athlete: Donald Downes

1. The remark, intended as sympathetic, is from Ernest Cuneo. The principle sources on Donald Downes are his memoirs, *The Scarlet Thread: Adventures in Wartime Espionage* (New York: The British Book Centre, 1953), and his papers. These papers were originally traced by Timothy Naftali, who was then writing his senior essay at Yale and developing his forthcoming book, a history of X-2, and I wish to thank Mr. Naftali for putting me in touch with Downes's sister-in-law, Polly W. Downes, of Northridge, California, who subsequently gave the papers to me. They are to be deposited in the World War II Collection at the Yale University Archives. The papers consist of the manuscripts of Downes's books, a substantial quantity of letters, a fragment of autobiography, research files, medical papers, photographs, and appointment diaries. The papers also included a detailed typescript journal covering the period November 12, 1942, through January 5, 1944. While this journal was originally thought to be by Downes, a close examination argues that it was written by one of Downes's friends, almost certainly the war correspondent Peter Tompkins. (The manuscript for Tompkins's *A Spy in Rome,* published in 1962, is also amongst the papers.) Unless cited otherwise, material in this chapter comes from the published memoir, the papers, or correspondence and interviews with Downes's colleagues and friends. I do not cite the manuscripts separately, as they undoubtedly will bear different designation after processing by the Yale Archives.

I wish to thank Mr. Gordon Browne, who worked with Downes in the OSS, for sending me several letters that he and his wife exchanged with Downes, and Mrs. Sidney Clark, who gave me several letters between her husband and Downes, and who talked with me at length about their work. Tompkins discussed Downes with me and supplied a copy of the Pacotte Report. I also thank those who responded to specific queries: Eric Ambler, Charles Boxer, the late Charles Collingwood, Max Corvo, David C. Crockett, Ernest Cuneo, Fergus Dempster, Arthur Goldberg, William Mauldin, David F. Seiferheld, Martin Stevens, Sir William Stephenson, Dimitri von Mohrenschilt, E. C. Wharton-Tigar, and the Cheshire Academy. Another colleague, Gerhard P. Van Arkel, died shortly after I contacted him and was not able to answer the questions I had put to him. Alfred C. Ulmer also agreed to meet, but we were ultimately unable to do so.

There are three additional sources of significance. The first is an interview of Downes conducted by Dilys Winn, a student of spy fiction and editor of *Murder Ink.*, at his flat at Albany, London, in March of 1977. I have both the tape of the interview and a transcript of it prepared by Dilys Winn, whom I wish to thank for supplying the material. In this interview Downes is impatient and irascible, and there are points of detail which contradict his published memoir, but the material appears basically reliable. He was, by then, not well, and he was apparently eager to be heard since he had responded to a notice in *The Times* Personal Column, in which Ms. Winn had asked anyone willing to talk about the profession of spying to contact her. A second interview, by Timothy Naftali, was conducted by telephone on February 14, 1983. By then Downes was dying of cancer, his memory was faulty, and he could no longer recall with any accuracy names or dates. At times this interview is contradicted by the official record. Also valuable are the untitled secret draft history of SI, with Donovan's annotations, in the William J. Donovan Papers, Carlisle, Pa., box 122A, vol. II; and Carleton Coon's draft history of OSS Fifth Army, in RG 226, OSS, entry 110, folder 15, box 49.

2. These reminiscences are drawn from Downes's handwritten autobiographical fragment, which covers the years 1905 to 1916. His beard is attested to by a photograph which dates from late 1942 or, possibly, 1943. Later he had a goatee. Max Corvo writes (Aug. 12, 1985, to author) that he believes Downes was married at one time.

3. On Downes at Yale, see List of Registered Students, 1925–26, Yale University, p. 57; *History of the Class of 1926 Yale College* (New Haven: Yale University, 1926), pp. 137–38; Records of Yale College, entrance record and grade records; *Yale 1926–1926S Class Directory* (New Haven: Yale University, 1980), p. 11; and *Alumni Directory of Yale University, 1968* (New Haven: Yale University, 1968), p. 79, in which Downes lists his occupation as "writing and editorial work."

4. (Boston: Houghton Mifflin, 1940). Taylor subsequently wrote *Richer by Asia* (Boston: Houghton Mifflin, 1947), which was on "the pathology of imperialism," and was based in part on his wartime experiences as chief of OSS in Southeast Asia. Downes found this book equally admirable. On Taylor's feeling that the United States should have entered the war in support of Britain after Germany attacked Poland, see his autobiography, *Awakening from History* (Boston: Gambit, 1969), Chapter 17.

5. On Moore, ONI, and COI, see Jeffrey M. Dorwart, *Conflict of Duty: The U. S. Navy's Intelligence Dilemma, 1919–1945* (Annapolis: Naval Institute Press, 1983).

6. On this period in the Balkans, see Bickham Sweet-Escott, *Baker Street Irregular* (London: Methuen, 1965), pp. 61–99; J. G. Beevor, *SOE: Recollections and Reflections, 1940–45* (London: Bodley Head, 1981), pp. 94–128; Douglas Dodds-Parker, *Setting Europe Ablaze: Some Account of Ungentlemanly Warfare* (Windlesham, Surrey: Springwood Books, 1983), pp. 47–52; and Hugh Seton-Watson, "Resistance in Eastern Europe," in Patrick Howarth, ed., *Special Operations* (London: Routledge and Kegan Paul, 1955), pp. 88–113.

7. H. Montgomery Hyde, *The Quiet Canadian: The Secret Service Story of Sir William Stephenson* (London: Hamish Hamilton, 1962), is still the best general account of the work of BSC. It was published in the United States as *Room 3603: The Story of the British Intelligence Center in New York during World War II* (New York: Farrar, Straus and Giroux, 1963). William Stevenson, *A Man Called Intrepid* (New York: Harcourt Brace Jovanovich, 1976), contains more detail, though there is much that is open to doubt in the book. Roy Maclaren, *Canadians Behind Enemy Lines, 1939–1945* (Vancouver: University of British Columbia Press, 1981), contains some useful corrections. On the problem of BSC records, see Chapter Three, note 19. I have examined the BSC papers, including the "Report on British Security Coordination in the United States of America," held by the Roskill Library, Churchill College, Cambridge—for which I am indebted to Mr. Hyde—and find no references to Downes. All employees of BSC were identified by a number in the 48000 (48 states = United States) series, and the Hyde Papers do show that at least two BSC employees were placed in the OSS. On Cuneo, see *CBC Times,* Sept. 13, 1968, pp. 4–5; *Foreign Intelligence Literary Scene,* I (Oct., 1982), 4–6; and his introduction to Raymond Beasson, *The James Bond Bedside Companion* (New York: Dodd, Mead, 1984), pp. xi–xiii. I am grateful to Mr. Cuneo for two long critiques of this chapter and wish to note that he disagrees with some of its conclusions. See also Pierre Cot, *Triumph of Treason* (Chicago: Ziff-Davis, 1944) and the confused material in Ivo Omrcanin, *Enigma Tito* (Washington: Samizdat, 1984), pp. 59–63.

8. The accusation that Ellis was a double, even triple, agent was first given wide publicity in Chapman Pincher's *Their Trade Is Treachery* (London: Sidgwick and Jackson, 1981), and was repeated, with added speculation, in Pincher's *Too Secret Too Long* (New York: St. Martin's Press, 1984). Ellis's character and loyalty are defended, though not on the specific points raised by Pincher, in H. Montgomery Hyde's *Secret Intelligence Agent* (London: Constable, 1982), pp. 143–50, and William Stevenson, *Intrepid's Last Case* (New York: Villard, 1983), pp. 238–56. Ellis is dead; any papers, to which I have not had access, are said to be in the possession of his daughter, though she states that she has none. Pepper, in response to my queries, responded by telegram only that he knew "nothing detrimental" about Downes.

9. See *Spy/Counterspy: The Autobiography of Dusko Popov* (New York: Grosset & Dunlap, 1974), pp. 149–204. For confirmation, and a cooler, no less devastating, assessment of Hoover's arrogance in the matter of Tricycle, see Ewen Montagu, *Beyond Top Secret Ultra* (New York: Coward, McCann & Geoghegan, 1978), pp. 75–77. The Hoover hagiographers have yet to respond to the many criticisms made of the FBI director in recent years. For an example of pre-Popov writing on Hoover, see Ralph de Toledano (a former OSS employee), *J. Edgar Hoover: The Man in His Times* (New Rochelle, N.Y.: Arlington House, 1973), which suggests that the FBI worked closely and in harmony with British intelligence (p. 163). The story of the FBI and BSC is not likely to be told, for the FBI has proved even less cooperative than the CIA with respect to the release of documentation under the Freedom of Information Act.

10. The preceding descriptions of these various projects is taken from *The Scarlet Thread,* pp. 63–84, as augmented by information supplied through the individuals mentioned in note 1, by official records, and a variety of books which, usually in passing, refer to one of the activities, generally not by name. Information on the burglary of the Spanish embassy is wildly contradictory. The account given here leans heavily on Downes, including additional description from his papers. The only important discrepancy appears in Anthony Cave Brown, *The Last Hero: Wild Bill Donovan* (New York: Vintage/Random House, 1984), p. 229, where Cave Brown says that the burglars of the Spanish embassy were captured and questioned at FBI headquarters and that Downes was with them. I have found nothing in the record to support this. One informant (Cuneo) believes this to have been the case, another accepts Downes's version. See also *The New York Times,* June 22, 1973.

11. This background situation is described in Cave Brown, *The Last Hero,* pp. 242–73; Peter Tompkins, *The Murder of Admiral Darlan: A Study in Conspiracy* (New York: Simon and Schuster, 1965), pp. 9–67; William L. Langer, *Our Vichy Gamble* (New York: Knopf, 1947), *passim;* and Charles de Gaulle, *Mémoires de guerre: L'Unité, 1942–1944* (Paris; Plon, 1956), chapters 4 and 6.

12. Pendar, *Adventure in Diplomacy: Our French Dilemma* (New York: Dodd, Mead, 1945), p. 11.

13. For a French intelligence view of the American group, see Colonel Passy [André de Wavrin], Souvenirs, II, 10, Duke Street Londres (Monte Carlo: Raoul Solar, 1947). Robert Murphy presents his views in *Diplomat Among Warriors* (New York: Doubleday, 1964).

14. Coon proved to be an adept at the spy game. Though there are minor errors in his memoirs, they are particularly helpful on day-to-day activities: *A North Africa Story: The Anthropologist as OSS Agent 1941–1943* (Ipswich, Mass.: Gambit, 1980). I am grateful to the librarian of the University of Pennsylvania, who gave me permission to examine Professor Coon's papers, which are restricted, and to Mr. Gordon H. Browne, of Tangier, who plays a major role in Coon's book, for helping me on a variety of matters, and for reading and (with Mrs. Browne) commenting on a draft of this chapter.

15. Edmond Taylor, the journalist and psychological warfare expert who had commanded Downes's attention that bleak Cape Cod winter, said later that a week before Darlan was assassinated he "discovered" by intuition, or its equivalent, that the admiral was to be assassinated, but when he told his superiors they did not take him seriously. Had the French known at the time that a member of OSS had predicted the assassination, the circumstantial case against the OSS would have been increased. See Taylor, *Richer by Asia,* p. 11.

16. There is some confusion over dates. In his memoir Downes says that he arrived in North Africa ahead of his team. In his official report on Bananas he says that the team arrived about January 26, 1943. One source says that Eddy first introduced Downes to the vice-consul "in the spring." Another friend recalls Downes still in the States in January, when he gave a farewell party at which he squatted beside a large fishbowl filled with gold, ladling coins into a money belt "sunk in his capacious middle," chortling that they were his "letters of credit." He looked, the friend recalled, like "a monumental canary in moult." His route of travel is shown by stamps in his passport and entries on other documents in his papers.

17. Downes gives an unfavorable picture of Childs, though he was, in fact, an able diplomat doing a difficult job: see William A. Hoisington, Jr., *The Casablanca Connection: French Colonial Policy, 1936–1943* (Chapel Hill: University of North Carolina Press, 1984). A visit to Childs in Richmond, Virginia, proved unhelpful, as he was seriously ill, but Professor Hoisington kindly offered a copy of the Childs manuscript on which he drew. Childs sets out his own position in *Diplomatic and Literary Quests* (Richmond: Whittet & Shepperson, 1963), pp. 33–55.

18. See Cave Brown, *Last Hero,* pp. 219–22; Kermit Roosevelt, *War Report of the OSS* (New York: Walker, 1976), pp. 22–24; and Thomas F. Troy, *Donovan and the CIA: A History of the Establishment of the Central Intelligence Agency* (Frederick, Md.: University Publications of America, 1981), pp. 140–43. Donovan's lengthy response to the charges of interference in Mexico, dated May 9, 1942, is in the Franklin D. Roosevelt Library, Hyde Park, N.Y., PSF OSS: Donovan Reports, box 166, folder 10. Attached is Sumner Welles, under secretary of state, to FDR, Apr. 29, 1942, which quotes Ambassador George S. Messersmith's report of Mar. 31 on Downes's visit. Downes asked to use the diplomatic pouch to return the AD lists to Washington but was refused.

19. Dodds-Parker's remark and observations are in his *Setting Europe Ablaze,* pp. 117–24. The June 1942 arrangement, as OSS understood it, gave OSS the lead in subversive operations in the area of the forthcoming Gymnast-Torch landings, and in China, Korea, the South Pacific, and Finland, while SOE was to undertake subversion in India, West Africa, the Balkans, and the Near and Middle East. Western Europe was to be shared equally. This arrangement, which was ridiculous on the face of it, was violated repeatedly. See David Stafford, *Britain and European Resistance, 1940–45: A Survey of the Special Operations Executive, with Documents* (London: Macmillan, 1980), pp. 89–90, and two particularly balanced and revealing memoirs, Sweet-Escott, *Baker Street Irregular,* especially pp. 136–40, and Beevor, *SOE,* in particular pp. 81–86. It must be remembered that SOE was the larger organization and achieved far more in France than OSS could do. Of over a thousand subversive operations into France, only eighty were American, and most of these, of course, were after D-Day (see M. R. D. Foot, *SOE in France: An Account of the Work of the British Special Operations Executive in France, 1940–1944* [London: HMSO, 1966], p. 30). The X-2 history, apparently written in 1947, is in RG 226, OSS, entry 176, box 2.

20. Cave Brown, *Last Hero,* p. 225. Spanish cooperation with German intelligence is described in secret OSS report, "The German Intelligence Service and the War," in Beinecke Library, Yale University, Norman Holmes Pearson Papers. See also RG 226, OSS, entry 115, box 35, folder 1 [3]. This file also contains a detailed report on the powerful Orgaz, a monarchist who, the OSS concluded, would behave with neutrality and "absolute correctness." On the conjunction of events in Spain, see Arthur F. Loveday, *Spain, 1923–1948: Civil War and World War* (North Bridgewater, Somerset: Boswell, n.d.), pp. 186–87. This book, by a right-wing former chairman of the British Chamber of Commerce in Spain, is not trustworthy on matters of interpretation, but it does provide an accurate chronicle of events on an almost week-by-week basis. Serrano Suñer presented his views in *Entre les Pyrénées et Gibralte: Notes et réflexions sur la politique espagnole depuis 1936* (Geneva: Éditions du Cheval Ailé, 1947), pp. 235–63.

21. On Sage see two somewhat romanticized articles: Richard M. Kelly, "He Never Stopped Trying," *Blue Book Magazine* (Sept., 1946), pp. 42–51, and Walter Wager, "Slippery Giant of the O.S.S.," *Men* (July, 1961), pp. 32–34, 54, 56, 58, 60, 62.

22. See Peter Tompkins's journal, in the Downes Papers. I wish to thank the late Charles Collingwood—who did not know Downes—for confirming that portion of the story with which he was familiar.

23. See Luella J. Hall, *The United States and Morocco, 1776–1956* (Metuchen, N.J.: Scarecrow Press, 1971), p. 989, and "A Survey of United States Relations with Morocco," manuscript Research Project No. 404, Historical Division, Department of State (Nov., 1957). As it happened, in 1984 I was the chairman of the History Areas Committee of the National Park System Advisory Board when the proposal came before the committee that the Tangier Legation should be designated a National Historic Landmark. Doing so would set a precedent, for no structure on foreign soil had as yet been designated, and therefore a substantial quantity of documentation not generally available was presented to the committee, and I have drawn on this. I wish to thank the late William E. Weld and Ben F. Dixon for discussing the legation with me, and for providing additional materials.

24. The OSS felt Hayes inflicted "Ambassadoritis"—pompous incomprehension—on it. See RG 226, OSS, V.48D Miscellaneous, entry 147, file 36, box 5: talk by Gerstle Mack, Dec. 22, 1944. In October 1944 Hayes agreed to OSS operations in Spain, if they could be "secret in fact as well as in name" (RG 226, OSS, War Diaries, 91/15: Hayes to Donovan, Oct. 5). Hayes makes a good case for American policy toward Franco—certainly better than his historian colleague William L. Langer did for America's Vichy gamble—in his memoirs, *Wartime Mission in Spain, 1942–1945* (New York: Macmillan, 1945). On his apprehensions about the OSS, see pp. 77–78, 126–130, 156–65. The Hayes Papers, in the Butler Library at Columbia University, did not prove helpful except for some correspondence with J. Rives Childs (box 5: May 25, 1943, and Aug. 19, 1944). For the British view, see Sir Samuel Hoare, Viscount Templewood, *Ambassador on Special Mission* (London: Collins, 1946).

25. RG 226, OSS, entry 110, box 46, folder 470: Murphy to Donovan, Sept. 2, 1943, and box 47, folder 477: Eddy to Donovan, Mar. 26, 1943; David Bruce Papers, Virginia Historical Society, Richmond: diary, ms. 1, IV: July 7, 1943, June 3, 1944. I wish to thank Mrs. David Bruce for giving me permission to use her husband's papers.

26. This account is drawn from Downes's report to Donovan, carrying the story as he knew it up to August 26, 1943, but dated March 22, 1944, with a

NOTES

copy in the Downes Papers; and Donovan, memorandum for JCS covering OSS activities in Iberian peninsula, Jan. 1943 to Apr. 1944, Top Secret, dated May 1944, in RG 226, OSS, entry 99, box 15, folder 62; Harris Smith, *OSS*, pp. 74–82; Downes, *Scarlet Thread*, pp. 103–29; Kermit Roosevelt, *War Report of the OSS: The Overseas Targets, II* (New York: Walker, 1976), pp. 25–26; correspondence with Gordon Browne; Winn interview; and correspondence with a British officer, serving with *Prodigal*, who replied in detail but not for attribution, and who reviewed the notes kept by the officer in charge of the final run in for his official report. Information was also supplied by three of the participants named in this chapter, provided it was not sourced to them specifically. The full story on *Prodigal* cannot be known until the British records are made available, and I am inclined to a Scot's verdict.

27. Perhaps the most balanced biography of Clark is by Martin Blumenson, *Mark Clark* (New York: Congdon & Weed, 1984). Clark was described as a "cold, distinguished, conceited, selfish, clever, intellectual, resourceful officer who secures excellent results quickly" (p. v). He thought the British intrigued against him in North Africa and Italy, and he was intensely anti-Communist. Downes thought him obsessed with a need to be noticed and blamed him—as subsequent historians did—for marching on Rome instead of encircling the German army with which he was engaged, for fear that if he did not capture Rome before the Normandy landings began he would not receive sufficient publicity. Still, he was put in command of the 15th Army Group, with British troops in the majority, and they liked him.

28. The Old Fort Museum, Fort Smith, Arkansas, holds a substantial collection of ranger memorabilia, Darby having come from that city. Included is a useful scrapbook of firsthand battle descriptions by which one may reconstruct the engagements at the Chiunzi Pass. Downes is not mentioned in this material. The best published account is James J. Altieri, *Darby's Rangers: An Illustrated Portrayal of the Original Rangers* (Arnold, Mo.: Ranger Book Committee, 1977), pp. 56–67. The larger context is provided by Hugh Pond, *Salerno*, 2nd. ed. (London: William Kimber, 1961).

29. Omodeo describes this period in *Per la riconquista della libertà* (Naples: Macciaroli, 1944), and other books.

30. This remarkable confrontation has two corroborating sources: when Downes returned to the States, he told Ernest Cuneo of it, and Cuneo confirmed it to me. Later Donovan told Browne the same story, who in turn has written of it to me. Donovan's concern about La Fortino was quite legitimate as Mrs. Williams had formally granted its use to the OSS (RG 226, OSS, entry 106, box 15, folder 117: Williams to Donovan, Dec. 2, 1943).

31. See Anthony Cave Brown, ed., *The Secret War Report of the OSS* (New York: Berkley, 1976), pp. 193–95.

32. On the chaos of these days, see Aubrey Menen, *Four Days of Naples* (New York: Seaview, 1979), Peter Tompkins, *Italy Betrayed* (New York: Simon and Schuster, 1966), Norman Lewis, *Naples '44* (New York: Pantheon, 1978); and David W. Ellwood, *Italy 1943–1945* (Leicester: Leicester University Press, 1985). Menen had known Downes in Italy in the 1950s. See also Tompkins, *A Spy in Rome* (New York: Simon and Schuster, 1962), about his OSS experiences in Rome, with Donald Downes's preface, pp. 9–14, and Robert Katz, *Death in*

Rome (New York: Macmillan, 1967), in which Tompkins figures prominently. Croce comments on Tompkins in *Quando l'Italia era Tagliata in due* (Bari: Editori Laterza, 1948), p. 120; on Croce's meeting with Donovan, see Raffaele Colapietra, *Benedetto Croce e la politica italiana* (Bari: Centro Librario, 1970), II, 767. See also Raimondo Craveri, *La compagna d'Italia e i servizi segreti: La Storia dell' ORI (1943–1945)* (Milan: La Pietra, 1980), p. 20.

33. RG 226, OSS, entry 110, box 47: material assembled by Peter Karlow, including selections from the report of Peter Tompkins; report on interviews, Feb. 1947, Karlow to Kermit Roosevelt, Feb. 11, 1947; interview with Major John Roller, Dec., 1944; Final Report, Huntington to Donovan, Dec. 25, 1943, and letter, Huntington to Donovan, Nov. 17, 1943; Downes to Donovan, report on OSS activities in the Neapolitan campaign, Oct. 19, 1943; and file 142, Andre Pacatte to Donovan, report covering the activities of OSS Special Detachment G-2 Fifth Army in Italy, n.d. There are several references to Tompkins, though none to Downes, in Corey Ford's notes on the Salerno operation, in the Ford Papers, Dartmouth College Library.

34. The story of Sparrow is well told in Cave Brown, *Last Hero,* pp. 382–93.

35. Downes's connections with EAM are shown in the context of Pericles, in Kōstas Kouvaras, *OSS—Me tēn kentrikē tou EAM [OSS—with the Central Committee EAM]* (Athens: Eksantas, 1976). I wish to thank Mr. Panos Razis for translating Kouvaras's book for me.

36. See Lawrence S. Wittner, "American Policy toward Greece, 1944–1949," in John O. Iatrides, *Greece in the 1940s: A Nation in Crisis* (Hanover, N.H.: University Press of New England, 1981), pp. 229–31, 396. Devoe's report on the Pericles mission was submitted on August 25; the records remain classified. Most OSS/SI personnel in Greece were infiltrated and maintained by SOE. A search of relevant collections at the Liddell Hart Centre for Military Archives, King's College, University of London—especially the C. M. Woodhouse and Edmund Charles Wolf Myers papers—not unexpectedly yielded nothing on Downes, though the typescript "History of the Allied Military Mission in Greece, September 1942 to December 1944" in 11/1 of the Woodhouse papers, is valuable background.

37. Quoted in Cave Brown, *Last Hero,* p. 609. On the apparent attempt to assassinate Toulmin (on which Downes makes no comment), and the Pearson/Hadas leak—which was not to be laid to Hadas's desk, but to a member of the staff at Donovan's message center in Washington—see pp. 596–609.

38. On British policy at the time see Elizabeth Barker, *British Policy in Southeast Europe* (London: Macmillan, 1975), and Phyllis Auty and Richard Clogg, eds., *British Policy towards Wartime Resistance in Yugoslavia and Greece* (London: Macmillan, 1975).

39. RG 226, OSS, entry 134, box 197, cables: May 12, June 6, 1944; Norman Holmes Pearson Papers, as owned by Susan Addiss: Pearson to his wife, July 11, 1944; Naftali interview. There is no evidence aside from Naftali's interview of this conversation, and Naftali concludes that Downes, who knew that he was dying, was reaching for effect.

40. Downes was especially outraged by the way the Mafia had been used in intelligence work in Sicily, and he feared it was getting a grip on the OSS. For background see Rodney Campbell, *The Luciana Project: The Secret Wartime*

Collaboration of the Mafia and the U.S. Navy (New York: McGraw-Hill, 1977).

41. Downes's favorite Mark Clark story was of an agency dispatch sent out by a war correspondent from the bar of the Excelsior in Florence:

> At Mark W. Clark's dawn today General Mark W. Clark's 15th Army Group troops entered Bologna where a high mass was said in the Cathedral of Mark W. Clark's Holy Trinity to celebrate the liberation of Mark W. Clark's city. General Mark W. Clark attended. The Cardinal Archbishop was also present.

42. Downes's papers include a series of detailed plans of Milan, dated 1942, and copies of the Comitato di Liberazione Nazionale per l'Alta Italia's *Bollettino Settimanale d'Informazioni* for 1945. The latter, in turn, has slipped into it a detailed *Scheme della rete ferroviaria* (a map of all electrified railways) for northern Italy. On it are marked thirty-one points at which a break in the line would disrupt traffic between major cities and industrial points or across the River Po.

43. Downes was quickly scooped, however, by an OSS colleague, Valla Lada-Mocarski, who crossed into Italy from Switzerland the day Mussolini's body was strung up and immediately began a report for OSS which led to his highly acclaimed article, "The Last Three Days of Mussolini," *Atlantic Monthly,* CLXXVI (Dec., 1945), 46–52. The Mussolini Collection of V. Lada-Mocarski (Yale Archives, MG 812, boxes 1 and 2) makes it clear that he had the assistance of Ferruccio Parri, Emilio Daddario, and Cardinal Ildefonso Schuster, archbishop of Milan, help Downes could not have hoped to receive.

The history of the Resistance, like that of the partisans in Greece and Yugoslavia, is complex and controversial, and unraveling either is not essential to understanding Downes. There is, however, a major book to be written on the history of the OSS and the Resistance, especially in Italy. The basic contours of this difficult story may be learned from Charles F. Delzell, *Mussolini's Enemies: The Italian Anti-Fascist Resistance* (Princeton: Princeton University Press, 1961), which has a good bit to say about the OSS, as does Kenneth Macksey, *The Partisans of Europe in the Second World War* (New York: Stein and Day, 1975). Fuller, though less helpful on the OSS, are Henri Michel, *The Shadow War: Resistance in Europe 1939–1945* (London: André Deutsch, 1972), and Jørgen Haestrup, *European Resistance Movements, 1939–1945: A Complete History* (Westport, Conn.: Meckler, 1981). The literature on the Italian Resistance—that is, the period of German occupation of Italy following the Italian surrender—runs to hundreds of books. Most are personal memoirs, or histories of local actions, but a few help provide the background for understanding the situation confronted by Downes and Tompkins and, later (see Chapter Six), by James Angleton. The most useful include Giorgio Bocca, *Storia dell'Italia Partigiana: Settembre 1943–Maggio 1945* (Bari: Editori Laterza, 1966); Edgardo Sogno, *Guerra senza bandiera: Cronache della "Franchi" nella Resistenza* (Milan: Mursia, 1970); Roberto Battaglia and R. Ramat, *Un Popolo in Lotta: Testimonianze di Vita Italiana dall'Unita al 1946* (Florence: La Nova Italia, 1961); and Luciano Bergonzini, *Bologna 1943–1945: Lettere ed osservazioni di Giorgio Amendola* (Bologna: Editrice Clueb, 1980). A valuable bibliography appears in Roberto Battaglia, *Storia della Resistenza Italiana (8 settembre 1943–25 aprile 1945)* (Turin: Einaudi, 1953). See also his *Un uomo, un partigiano* (Turin: Einaudi, 1965), and from the left, Pietro Secchia, *La resistenza accusa, 1945–1973* (Milan: Mazzotta, 1973). The role of the OSS is discussed in Max Salvadori, *Breve storia della Resistenza italiana* (Florence: Vallecchi, 1974), pp. 141–72, which tells of the role of Raimondo Craveri, Edgardo Sogno (who as "Franchi" operated in Lombardy), and Ferruccio Parri.

44. Downes's version of this episode is in *Scarlet Thread,* pp. 189–94, while Mauldin's is in *The Brass Ring* (New York: W. W. Norton, 1971), pp. 266–70. In conversations with me, Mauldin reaffirmed the accuracy of his recollections.

45. On Count and Countess Ciano, see Frederick W. Deakin, *The Brutal Friendship: Mussolini, Hitler and the Fall of Italian Fascism* (New York: Harper & Row, 1962). The diaries of Edda's husband, Count Galeazzo Ciano, had been obtained by Allen Dulles and were published in 1948. On the negotiations see Howard McGaw Smyth, *Secrets of the Fascist Era: How Uncle Sam Obtained Some of the Top-Level Documents of Mussolini's Period* (Carbondale: Southern Illinois University Press, 1975), pp. 57–72.

46. Donovan Papers, box 119A, folder 11: Donovan to Walter L. Pforzheimer, Apr. 13, 1961.

47. Downes's account of his adventure in Kafka-land—his term—together with copies of his correspondence with friends concerning his effort to return to Italy, and his work in Beirut, is in a separate memory book, with *promemoria* (as written in September 1955) attached, in the Downes Papers. These letters also add some details to our knowledge of his wartime operations. Enclosed in the book is correspondence from Robert Ullman at Villa Tre Ville in Positano, from Downes concerning the Barzini allegations, and (in Italian) from Downes to an industrialist, Ivan Matteo Lombardo, an important alumnus of the Partito Socialista Italiana di Unità Proletaria. To Lombardo, Downes identified those he believed were "the mysterious force" behind his harassment: J. Edgar Hoover, General Mark Clark (of whom he had, he realized, made too much fun in *The Scarlet Thread*), and Achille Lauro, the subject of the single most unflattering portrait in his book, and subsequently mayor of Naples. The letters also show that two friends, Charles Moses and Alberto Carocci, did most of the leg work to help Downes during this period.

48. The Downes Papers contain handwritten and typescript drafts of these novels. It is interesting to see how Downes tempered the bitter ending of *Orders to Kill:* the novel most bitter of all, the screenplay sad but with a hint of hope, the treatment for a television series quite upbeat. Downes sent an inscribed copy of the novel (now in the Beinecke Library) to Norman Pearson and admitted that he used in the novel the dialogue that Paul Dehn, one of the scriptwriters for the film, had written. Dehn went on to be coauthor of the film for the 1964 James Bond blockbuster, *Goldfinger.*

Downes seems to have been unlucky in his reviewers. Read today against the novels, the reviews seem often to have missed the point. *Orders to Kill* was in some measure about Downes, for it explored a young American spy, brought up by women, who had qualms about his courage and who twice broke security, once through weakness and once through vanity. Jules Dellman, in *A Red Rose for Maria,* was Downes. *The Easter Dinner* has an element of humor missing in the other novels and yet was seen as dour.

On the film history, see R. J. Minney, *The Films of Anthony Asquith* (South

Brunswick, N.J.: A.S. Barnes, 1976), pp. 165–67, 269; James Robert Parish and Michael R. Pitts, *The Great Spy Pictures* (Metuchen, N.J.: Scarecrow Press, 1974), pp. 355–56; and Lillian Gish, *Dorothy and Lillian Gish* (New York: Scribner's, 1973), pp. 262, 304. I wish to thank the staff of the Yale Audio-Visual Center for obtaining and screening *Orders to Kill* for me.

49. *The New York Times*, Feb. 20, 1944. The story was finally told in 1984 in Jim Christy, *The Price of Power: A Biography of Charles Eugène Bedaux* (Toronto: Doubleday). Christy does not mention Downes.

50. On the Holohan case see Aldo Icardi, *Aldo Icardi: American Master Spy* (New York: Stalwart, 1954).

51. I visited the club and found he is still remembered; his name was carried on the membership list through 1984.

CHAPTER FIVE   The Professor: Norman Holmes Pearson

1. George C. Constantinides, *Intelligence and Espionage: An Analytical Bibliography* (Boulder, Colo.: Westview Press, 1983), p. 322.

2. *Reflections* was originally published as the entire Nov. 1974 issue of *Poetry* magazine and then—with some changes—in book form by Atheneum in New York in 1976. At the time Hollander was teaching at Hunter College; he subsequently returned to the Yale faculty. The quotations in the paragraph are taken from John Hollander's explication of the poem, in letters to the author, both undated, Aug. 1984 and July 1985. I wish to thank Mr. Hollander for giving me permission to use lines from *Reflections on Espionage* as epigraphs in this chapter.

3. Norman Holmes Pearson was among the visitors to Pound at St. Elizabeth's Hospital after the war. Pearson had been on the advisory committee for Pound's Square Dollar Series, intended to be an inexpensive series of literary texts not widely enough read in American schools and colleges. It collapsed when the person charged with carrying it out, T. David Horton, was arrested for interfering with the integration of a school in Clinton, Tennessee. Pearson also helped convince Mary de Rachewiltz, Pound's daughter, that she ought to settle in New Haven, and helped promote a production of his *The Women of Trachis* at Yale. See C. David Heymann, *Ezra Pound: The Last Rower* (New York: Viking, 1976), pp. 214, 229.

4. This transmission from *Reflections on Espionage* is 5/9 (pp. 37–38); the next transmission is 4/3 (pp. 30–31).

5. University of Colorado, Boulder, George Fullmer Reynolds Collection: Pearson to Reynolds, Aug. 10, 1951.

6. Daniel Aaron, Harvard University, to the author, July 11, 1985.

7. A NOTE ON SOURCES, WITH A PROBLEM OR TWO
Pearson kept materials from his school days, and his schooling can be pieced together from copies of the school papers, and from scrapbook items, that are in the Norman Holmes Pearson Papers. These papers are in the Beinecke Rare Book and Manuscript Library at Yale. They consist of twelve boxes in a large wooden file, fourteen boxes in drawers, twelve file boxes of correspondence, and a large cardboard box of ephemera, thirty-nine boxes in all. Additionally, Pearson gave to the university quite substantial collections of books, including

his holdings of juvenilia, in which relevant inscriptions often are written, and papers relating to Hawthorne, Pound, H. D., and Bryher, authors in whom his interest was constant. While his private papers are generally open to researchers, the collection is not organized, having been kept as Pearson left it; future curatorial work on the materials will almost certainly mean that a given document will not be found in the place one would now cite. A general description of the organization of the Pearson Papers therefore seems necessary.

The first ten boxes of those in the wooden file pertain largely to Pearson's work for the OSS, though there is also material on Gertrude Stein, and the last two boxes in this series are on literary matters. Box 9 contains Pearson's journal notes, family letters (including letters from his mother and from his wife), and programs of theatrical and other events Pearson attended in London while on OSS assignment. Folders of OSS materials, directories, personnel files, and reports, are mixed somewhat indiscriminately with notebooks, diaries, newspaper clippings, and photographs in the first six boxes. I have drawn on the letters in box 9 particularly heavily in this chapter.

The four drawers, which contain in all fourteen boxes, are almost wholly personal. Box 5 contains Andover memorabilia, while the first four boxes hold letters from Pearson to his mother. The letters in box 3 overlap with those in 9 of the "wooden file." In general a specific reference to a document will be of little help to a subsequent researcher. This is especially true of the twelve correspondence file boxes, which—despite an obvious attempt to arrange letters alphabetically and chronologically—is sufficiently disorderly to require a general turning over of each item.

These Pearson Papers are further confused by a small intervention on the part of the Central Intelligence Agency. The Pearson Papers contain items not formally declassified, in the sense that they are copies of documents that, most likely, ought not to have been retained. Most of these have, however, been declassified at source, and their originals, or other copies, may be found in the OSS Papers in the National Archives. However, some fifteen of the documents apparently were not declassified at source, and in the spring of 1983 the president of Yale University, A. Bartlett Giamatti, wrote to the director of the CIA, William J. Casey, on behalf of myself and of Timothy Naftali, the Yale undergraduate who was writing a senior thesis on Sherman Kent and Norman Holmes Pearson under the supervision of George Wilson Pierson, to ask that these documents be declassified so that they might be copied. These fifteen documents comprised 292 pages of manuscript.

Rather than declassifying the documents, the CIA sent two agents to the Beinecke Library, and they removed fourteen documents (a fifteenth proving to be a duplicate of one of the fourteen, which at the time were attached to each other). Of these one had been classified as "confidential"—an OSS telephone directory—and was, in fact, perhaps unbeknownst to the agents, readily available in other collections; another is in the Donovan Papers; twelve were classified as "secret" (including the duplicate), and two were "most secret." These removals occurred, unhappily, on a day when the interested parties were in no position to protest: I was in South Africa on research, Mr. Naftali was in Canada, and the curator of the collection was out of town. Since the documents were officially part of the Pearson collection, they were the property of the university, and it is not clear that they could have been so readily removed, though no doubt their classified status meant that they should have been closed to researchers, pending clarification.

In July 1983 the agency agreed to return three of the original documents, and two of the documents (three counting the duplicate) in sanitized form; nine documents were to be withheld in their entirety, with three of the documents that were "secret" now reclassified as "most secret." In November 1983 the university's legal counsel requested the formal return of the documents the CIA had agreed to release. In January 1985 these documents were returned to their original place in the Pearson Papers. One document that was "returned in its entirety" was found to have pages missing.

In addition to the Norman Holmes Pearson Papers in the Beinecke Library (referred to hereafter as NHP/Beinecke), there is a substantial collection of Pearson's letters to his wife, Susan, now held by the New Haven law firm of Tyler, Cooper, & Alcorn, but previously held by Norman Pearson's stepdaughter, Susan Addiss, at her home in New Haven. She courteously gave me permission to examine this material, and I draw on it heavily here. These letters are in two large filing boxes, with letters to and from Norman and Susan Pearson for Jan. 1943 to Aug. 27, 1944, in the first box, and letters from Aug. 30, 1944, to Sept. 9, 1946, in the second box. The Pearsons numbered them as a check against loss. They often wrote each other twice a week, with surprise letters arriving by special delivery mail on Sundays. Susan wrote to her husband somewhat more frequently than he to her: her letter No. 174 crosses with his letter No. 100, for example. (Items from this collection are referred to hereafter as NHP/Addiss.)

Thus, citations to specific documents, files, or boxes in either collection of Pearson Papers would be of only marginal help to subsequent researchers. References to notes taken from documents subsequently removed from the collections would, of course, be of no use at all. I have supplied specific notations when it would prove helpful, or in instances of direct quotation, but in general this explanatory note will stand for citations to the two Pearson manuscript collections.

I am also grateful to Timothy Naftali, who was able to continue his work in the Pearson materials during a time when I was drawn away into administrative activities, for initially making copies of relevant materials, and for his guidance in the use of the two collections. He was the first to use NHP/Addiss. He has shared his senior essay, which won the Porter Prize for the best paper in American history submitted by an upperclassman in 1983, with me, and he is now revising and extending it for publication as a general history of X-2.

I have drawn upon other collections of manuscripts, which are cited in their proper place, and have corresponded and talked with a number of colleagues and students of Professor Pearson. Sixteen of his doctoral students responded to queries I put to them either by letter or in person. Several of Norman's colleagues at Yale have also helped me, in particular Donald Gallup, Alan Trachtenberg, and Eugene Waith. The late James R. Murphy, the head of X-2, and Hubert Will, the deputy head who worked closely with Pearson in London, and two London colleagues from X-2, James Angleton and John Waller, met with me and graciously answered all my queries concerning NHP. Ms. Perdita Schaffner, H. D.'s daughter and secretary in X-2 to Norman Pearson and James

Angleton, was equally helpful. An X-2 personnel roster as of 1944, found in the Pearson Papers, revealed the names of several individuals still living who worked with Norman Pearson, and a few of those have responded to my letters. His London address book provided leads to other individuals; despite a gap of many years, four also responded.

I was most graciously received by Felix Cowgill and his wife at their home in Dorset, and while still bound by the Official Secrets Act, and thus properly cautious, Mr. Cowgill confirmed for me several suppositions about work at Ryder Street. Most of these individuals wished their information to remain without specific attribution, however, and it would be invidious to single out the few who did not from those who did. I provide a list, therefore, of those who met with me, responded to telephone queries, or who corresponded, but do not supply specific citations to their information elsewhere. This avoids use of a citation such as "private information," which seems quite unhelpful.

In addition to those mentioned in other notes, I have received help from Robinson Oligny Bellin, Robert Bone, John R. Brazil, Robert F. Campbell, James L. Colwell, John E. Costello, Robin Denniston, Alan B. Donovan, Richard Lee Francis, Donald Gallup, William H. Goetzmann, Cordelia Hood, Francis Kalnay, A. N. Kaul, Joseph Leach, James Matlock, Dorothee Metlitzki, Reginald H. Phelps, William S. Prince, Alice E. Rockett, Albert E. Stone, Benjamin Welles, Tom Wolfe, and Edward Weismiller.

Finally, there is the fact that I knew Norman Holmes Pearson. He was singularly kind and open when I first joined the Yale faculty in 1957, and we also worked together in the mid-1970s, when he was lecturing extensively abroad in order to promote American studies in foreign universities, and I was chairman of a committee, financed by the U.S. Department of State and the U. S. Information Agency, to mount several international congresses on American studies and the impact of America abroad in the context of the American Bicentennial. Norman Pearson shared my interest in detective fiction, as virtually no one else on the Yale faculty appeared to do in the 1960s, and we both admired and often lunched to discuss the work of popular writers like Joseph Altsheler, creator of a remarkable series of books for boys in the 1920s. As a result, Norman came to speak to me in less guarded terms than I believe he used with most of the faculty, especially about his work for the OSS, and I therefore draw upon my own recollections of our many conversations.

I wish to recognize five individuals in particular without whom this chapter could not have been written: Susan Addiss, for permitting me unfettered time to examine her stepfather's papers; David Schoonover, then curator of the American Literature Collection at the Beinecke Rare Book and Manuscript Library, who made available the Pearson papers; Lindsey Kiang, general counsel for the university, who was persistent and percipient in his pursuit of the materials spirited away by the CIA; and Timothy Naftali, who as I fell further behind in my research and, as I became for a time unable to move about with ease because of an illness, opened up the outer doors to Messrs. Murphy and Will, kept me in good cheer with frequent reports on the progress of his own research, and helped me to establish contact with Perdita Schaffner and Felix Cowgill. We will, inevitably, arrive at somewhat different conclusions from our interviews and examination of the same documentation, because we are asking different questions, and this exercise in what another discipline might take to be competitive rather than cooperative endeavor has been a demonstration of yet another of the subjects of this book: how historians work.

8. "How Did You Choose Your Academic Field?," a series of short replies by various members of the Yale faculty, including Pearson, in the *Yale Alumni Magazine,* XXXVII (Oct., 1973), 13.

9. On Pearson's illness, see Reynolds Collection: Pearson to Reynolds, Nov. 23, 1938.

10. See the tribute to Pearson by Arlin Turner in *The Nathaniel Hawthorne Society Newsletter,* II (Spring, 1976), 1–2. The photograph accompanying the article shows Pearson as he was in the late 1960s, while that in the *Yale Weekly Bulletin and Calendar* on the occasion of his death shows him bearded, as in the 1970s. The photograph accompanying the Pearson obituary in the New Haven *Register* for Nov. 6, 1975, is not of Pearson at all.

11. Pearson taught in the Ninth Writers' Conference, was an editor for the conference organizers, and participated with the Rocky Mountain poet Thomas Hornsby Ferril in a round-table discussion on "The Obligations of the Poet." See Boulder *Daily Camera,* July 16, 1938, and the program of the conference, in the University of Colorado Archives. He was paid an associate professor's salary by Colorado, and Pearson cited that rank in his OSS résumé; he was, in fact, officially designated to the visiting faculty simply as editor (University of Colorado *Catalog,* Summer Quarter, 1938, p. 340).

12. NHP/Beinecke, wooden file, 1: Sherburn to Pearson, Nov. 26, 1942.

13. *Ibid.,* Downes to Pearson, Aug. 25, 1941.

14. On Hogan, see the appreciation from which this quotation is taken, in *The Century Yearbook 1984* (New York: The Century Association, [1984]), pp. 223–25.

15. Both quotations are attributed to Pearson in William L. Kahrl, "Yet Time and change shall naught prevail/ To break the friendships formed at Yale," *The New Journal,* II (Feb. 9, 1969), 3. Kahrl was an undergraduate student of Pearson's at the time, working on a Scholar of the House paper in a program Pearson had originated, and Pearson checked his article for accuracy. Though by 1969 student opinion was generally hostile to the CIA, Kahrl reports that he received only one letter as a result of the article, from Gloria Steinem, who was moved to describe the background of her own brief entanglement with agency funding— the story of CIA funding of the National Students Association had recently broken—and that no one at Yale seemed much interested. I wish to thank William Kahrl for responding to my questions concerning his research. See also the *Yale Daily News,* Mar. 8, 1950.

16. NHP/Addiss: Pearson to his wife, Jan. 8, 12, 15, 21, 26, Feb. 5, 12, 16, 1943.

17. Record Group 226, OSS, entry 99, box 15, folder 68: "X-2 Branch O.S.S." official history.

18. Donovan Papers, Carlisle, Pa., box 122A: draft history of SI, chapter XXX of the history of the OSS, II, Secret, declassified 1978.

19. Johnson was even more adamant than Hayes on the point and no more successful. He was up against a formidable team of academics who knew that Stockholm was teeming with spies. Bruce Hopper, a Harvard professor of gov-

ernment, was the OSS chief, and Taylor Cole, a political scientist and later provost at Duke, was his assistant. The feisty and well-connected Calvin Hoover,
the Duke economist, encouraged the branch to spy on the Russians from his SI
post in Washington. OSS/Stockholm therefore obtained the Russian order of battle and the register of the Soviet navy. See R. Harris Smith, *OSS: The Secret
History of America's First Central Intelligence Agency* (New York: Delta reprint
ed., 1973), pp. 199–200.

20. The judgment is from Ronald Lewin, *Ultra Goes to War: The First Account of World War II's Greatest Secret Based on Official Documents* (New
York: McGraw-Hill, 1978), p. 17. This is the best treatment of Ultra in its total-
ity that we have. The book that broke the story—an earlier leak in the *Observer*
on Jan. 8, 1967, went virtually unnoticed—was F. W. Winterbotham, *The Ultra
Secret* (London: Weidenfeld and Nicolson, 1974). It was written from memory
and has no documentation, though it has the virtue of the freshness of a participant. (One suspects the presence of a second writer, for this book is quite superior to Winterbotham's previous and subsequent books, *Secret and Personal*
[London: William Kimber, 1969] and *The Nazi Connection* [London: Weidenfeld
and Nicolson, 1978].) Accounts by two American participants in the work at
Bletchley are Constantine FitzGibbon, whose *Secret Intelligence in the Twentieth Century* (New York: Stein and Day, 1977) is superficial—but interesting for
its judgment that Ultra was misused at the time of the Ardennes offensive—and
Landis Gores, "Ultra-American: Memories of Service at the Most Secret Source,"
an unpublished memoir. This last is rich in human detail and provides the most
personal record of work at Bletchley yet written. I wish to thank Mr. Gores for
giving me access to the relevant portions of his massive manuscript, which will,
I hope, soon be published. The American side of the story is told in Thomas
Parrish, *The Ultra Americans: The U.S. Role in Breaking the Nazi Codes* (New
York: Stein and Day, 1986). The larger context for Ultra is provided in R. V.
Jones, *The Wizard War: British Scientific Intelligence, 1939–1945* (New York:
Coward, McCann & Geoghegan, 1978). Jones's book was published in London
as *Most Secret War* (Hamish Hamilton, 1978). The significance of Ultra is only
now beginning to make its way into more general accounts. Lord Robert Blake,
in *The Decline of Power, 1915–1964* (London: Oxford University Press, 1985),
who says that every pre-1974 book about the war must now be revised (p. 247),
appears to be the first.

Most books on British intelligence make at best a passing reference to American intelligence, whether OSS, ONI, G-2, or whatever. Books on Bletchley
make even fewer references, since the American contribution was modest. However, six books in particular ought also to be consulted. Gordon Welchman, *The
Hut Six Story: Breaking the Enigma Codes* (New York: McGraw-Hill, 1982), is
another insider's account, and especially valuable. Important on the relationship
between Ultra and the Twenty Committee (see note 40) is Ewen Montagu, *Beyond Top Secret Ultra* (New York: Coward, McCann & Geoghegan, 1978). Peter
Calvocoressi, another participant, has provided the most succinct summary of
the work done at Bletchley Park in *Top Secret Ultra* (New York: Pantheon,
1980); the book makes clear that most documentation relating to Ultra and to
Bletchley broadly is not available as yet in the Public Record Office. (I wish to
thank Mr. Calvocoressi for meeting with me to clarify certain points.) The use

of Ultra by the Royal Navy is discussed in Patrick Beesly, *Very Special Intelligence: The Story of the Admiralty's Operational Intelligence Center, 1939–1945* (London: Hamish Hamilton, 1977). Anthony Cave Brown's *Bodyguard of Lies* (New York: Harper and Row, 1975), which is about Allied deception operations before the Normandy invasion, contains many controversial judgments, but it adds some useful detail to the story of Ultra. Finally, Andrew Hodges, *Alan Turing: The Enigma* (New York: Simon and Schuster, 1983), is an exceptionally compelling look into a man of undoubted brilliance, the mathematician who, more than anyone else, was responsible for the mathematics behind the breaking of the Enigma machine, by which cryptologists were able to decipher Germany's codes.

The operational use made of Ultra is discussed in Beesly, *Very Special Intelligence;* in Aileen Clayton, *The Enemy Is Listening* (London: Hutchinson, 1980), which is on the Royal Air Force's Y Service (which also intercepted and translated the enemy's lower level traffic); and in W. J. Holmes, *Double-Edged Secrets: U.S. Naval Intelligence Operations in the Pacific during World War II* (Annapolis: Naval Institute Press, 1979). Holmes was chief of the naval section that coordinated Ultra with other intelligence. On French use of Ultra see Paul Paillole, *Notre espion chez Hitler* (Paris: Robert Laffont, 1985). Ralph F. Bennett, *Ultra in the West: The Normandy Campaign of 1944–45* (London: Hutchinson, 1979), is very strong in its analysis of how Ultra influenced the war in specific battles. A key question—whether Ultra could have or should have warned of the German counterattack in the Ardennes—is taken up in a review essay by David Syrett, "The Secret War and the Historians," *Armed Forces and Society,* IX (Winter, 1983), 293–328 (but see a response by Adolph G. Rosengarten, Jr., in *Foreign Intelligence Literary Scene,* II [August, 1983] 10–11). Many intriguing questions are raised in Jürgen Rohwer and Eberhard Jäckel, eds., *Die Funkaufklärung und ihre Rolle im Zweiten Weltkrieg* (Stuttgart: Motorbuch, 1979), especially pp. 167–200, 325–403.

The actual military and naval intercepts will soon be available in approximately 500 reels of microfilm as the *Ultra Documents* (New York: Clearwater Publishing). Scholars may then trace the movement of an intercept up the chain of translation, analysis, annotation, and transmission. The cost is $50 per reel.

The extensive literature on Enigma—the German cipher machine, which produced the encrypted messages which became, when deciphered, the major portion (though by no means all) of product Ultra—is not directly relevant here. However, *The Enigma War,* by Jósef Gárlinski (New York: Scribner's, 1980), provides valuable additional background on Bletchley Park, and two studies help document the very significant Polish contribution to the story: Richard A. Woytak, *On the Border of War and Peace: Polish Intelligence Diplomacy in 1938–1939 and the Origins of the Ultra Secret* (Boulder, Colo.: East European Quarterly, 1979), and Wladyslaw Kozaczuk, *Enigma: How the German Machine Cipher Was Broken, and How It Was Read by the Allies in World War II* (Frederick, Md.: University Publications of America, 1984). A sound earlier account came from Gustave Bertrand, *Enigma on la plus grande énigme de la guerre, 1939–1945* (Paris: Plon, 1973).

21. See the forthcoming book by Rhodri Jeffreys-Jones, *A Question of Standing: The CIA and American Democracy since 1947* (forthcoming). I wish to thank

Dr. Jeffreys-Jones for sharing portions of his research with me and for allowing me to read part of his manuscript prior to publication.

22. NHP/Addiss: Pearson to his wife, Feb. 25, 28, Mar. 17, 28, Apr. 15, 1943, and itinerary of flight to Bristol.

23. Other Yale acquaintances of Pearson's whom he encountered in X-2 were John K. Miller, '28, who overlapped with Pearson in Washington and, in October 1943, went on to Algiers and in 1945 became X-2 branch chief in Paris; Richard W. Cutler, '38, a friend of Donovan's, who moved from Air Intelligence to X-2 and worked in London in the fall of 1944; and William M. Wheeler, '35, whom Pearson met when he went to Lisbon as head of the Iberian-North African X-2 desk in London. George Brewer, who was with SO, was in London working directly under David Bruce; a former Yale English teacher and successful playwright, coauthor of *Dark Victory,* Brewer gave many parties in his flat off Grosvenor Square.

24. I found the late James R. Murphy one of the most interesting of the former OSS agents to whom I spoke. We met in his Washington office next to the Army and Navy Club, and though it had taken two rather tentative telephone calls before he agreed to see me, he was charming and gave no sense of being pressed for time when we at last met. I had been told by another former OSS employee who had stayed on with the CIA and only recently retired that Murphy was from Missouri and was an Ivy League graduate, which I knew was not true—though John Read Murphy, OSS, was Yale '42—and I eventually learned that this particular individual liked to feed me slightly wrong information, which he knew to be wrong, to see whether I would have the wit to double-check it. James R. Murphy was, in point of fact, from Missouri and a 1931 graduate of George Washington University. He responded to all that I asked, though at times his memory seemed to fade a bit—always a convenient refuge for those who find they prefer not to answer a question—and he too enjoyed games. At one point he drew my attention to Ernest Hauser's excellent guide to Italian art on his shelf—a book I had reviewed shortly before—remarking that it was a shame it had not sold well, and then waited to see whether I would respond with my knowledge that Hauser was the brother-in-law of the former CIA agent who had helped clear my way to Murphy. These kinds of interchanges were, in fact, standard at any first encounter with many professional intelligence officers, and while at times they struck me as moderately ridiculous—one person would call me only from telephone booths and would take my calls only at other booths—they generally seemed no more irrelevant than the usual jockeying (where did you go to school? and what was your sport?) one encounters in any unclear interview situation in which the interviewee needs to get a fix on the interviewer. Murphy was, however, something of a master at obscuring what he knew and slipping in remarks which, if left unchallenged, would leave the questioner quite without credibility. The bookcase behind his head as we talked was filled with titles on cross examination.

25. I am most grateful to Mrs. David K. E. Bruce for granting me permission to examine Ambassador Bruce's papers, which are partially restricted until 2002. Boxes 4–8 contain five original diaries, and three typescripts, on the OSS years.

26. See Donovan Papers, box 66B, file 206: "Certain Accomplishments of the Office of Strategic Services," and file 207: Murphy to Donovan, Nov. 20, 1944.

27. The English writer, Anthony Cave Brown, in *The Last Hero: Wild Bill Donovan* (New York: Vintage/Random House, 1984), p. 184, refers to Pearson as "one of the country's leading literary dons" (certainly not yet the case), accepts the notion that he was a Rhodes Scholar, and says that he had been crippled by polio and had to wear leg braces to walk. Never having heard of New England's St. Paul's, the prep school in New Hampshire (the source of the sample in Chapter Two), Cave Brown automatically assumes that any OSS officer who had "gone 'to St. Paul's " was from St. Paul's, England. Of course, American writers and academics are just as ill informed on, say, the schools and universities of Australia.

28. NHP/Beinecke, box 9: journal entries, Apr. 19, 20, 24, 25, 26, 28–30, May 1, 12, 18, 19, 23, 28, June 4, 5, 11, 1943.

29. This brief summary closely follows that of Walter L. Pforzheimer, who has written a concise statement on the subject: "Code Breaking—The Ultra Story," *Marine Corps Gazette,* LIV (July 1980), 76–80.

30. The British navy also received Ultra, of course, through its Directorate of Naval Intelligence, which established an Operational Intelligence Centre (OIC). This center dealt with all sources of intelligence, not only Ultra, and X-2 was not involved in liaison with OIC. The Germans used fifty separate ciphers, and on occasion X-2 would receive lower-level (that is, non-Ultra) decryptions, though generally this material, which had to do mainly with day-by-day military matters of a tactical nature, was handled by other intelligence bodies. For this material there was a separate British cryptanalytic center at Cheadle, which broke the specific key being used for the day by the Germans and returned it immediately to the field units. This service, known as Y, operated on a full Allied basis.

31. I especially wish to thank Jean Howard for helping me on matters of detail. As Jean Alington she introduced the Americans to Hut 6 and was one of the three members of 3L, the liaison section in Hut 3, who established priorities for the decoding room.

32. From Gores, "Ultra-American," Chapter 1, sections 1 and 2.

33. In 1970 I had occasion to go to Bletchley often, as the Open University was being organized there, and I visited BP at the time. I returned to Bletchley Park (and to St Albans) again in 1984 while writing this book. Now virtually an outer suburb of London, the area has changed dramatically—even between 1970 and 1984, not to speak of 1945 to 1970—but the major places mentioned in this chapter survive, as even do two of the original huts.

34. Quoted in Lewin, *Ultra,* p. 121. See also Friendly's brief memoir, "Confessions of a Code Breaker," *The Washington Post,* Oct. 27, 1974. On Knox see Penelope Fitzgerald, *The Knox Brothers* (New York: Coward, McCann & Geoghegan, 1977).

35. The literature on Bletchley, intimately part of the literature on Ultra, is summarized in note 20. I wish to thank, additionally, Professor Telford Taylor of the Columbia University Law School, who described the work of the American contingent to me; Colonel Leslie L. Rood, who provided a very full memoir of his time at Bletchley; William P. Bundy, who wrote for me a most valuable account of the Yale members of Bletchley and sent me a draft copy of an article prepared for *Cryptologia;* Professor Louis Martz, of the Department of English at Yale, for searching (in the end, unsuccessfully) for relevant papers of Frederick Hilles; Robert M. Slusser; and Sue Hilles, who talked with me of her husband, helped in a fruitless search for his papers, and showed me his various military honors from the time. Landis Gores and Peter Calvocoressi told me of Hilles's work; Jane Fawcett, who was Jane Hughes when at BP, described the work of her hut to me and gave me several contacts; and Justice Lewis F. Powell, Jr., of the Supreme Court of the United States, helped me with two additional leads.

36. Landis Gores, a Princeton graduate, was able to recall by name fifty-eight of the Americans in the spring of 1985 and account for the background (and often the foreground) of most of them. It is against his list that I have checked Yale names.

37. See National Archives, RG 457, Records of the National Security Agency, SRH-110, "Operations of the Military Intelligence Service War Department London (MIS WD London)," a report prepared by Frederick W. Hilles, stamped Top Secret Ultra, and declassified Jan. 7, 1981. The use of Ultra is nicely shown in *ibid.,* Sh-H-023, "Reports of U.S. Army Ultra representatives with Army Field Commands in the European Theater of Operations."

38. NHP/Addiss, July 7, Sept. 26, 1944. He also suggested titles of books on English rural history that she might read, which provided a clue as to his location. References to Puritan in the Bryher Papers (Beinecke Library: Bryher to Pearson, Aug. 5, Oct. 17, 1944) suggest Bryher also knew Pearson was Puritan.

39. RG 226, OSS, X-2 branch: Berding's memorandum, with German interrogation report attached, July 2, 1945. Cave Brown, *The Last Hero,* pp. 609–11, describes the Papurt affair and quotes from Pearson's report to Forgan, from the Donovan Papers. Ms. Legendre tells of her capture, imprisonment, and flight across the Swiss border in *The Sands Ceased to Run* (New York: William Frederick Press, 1947). I am grateful to Ms. Legendre for responding to questions I put to her.

40. The literature on the double-cross system is substantially less extensive than that on Ultra, in good measure because the book to most fully break silence on it, Sir John Masterman's *The Double-Cross System in the War of 1939 to 1945* (New Haven: Yale University Press, 1972), at first seemed so thorough. One must, however, also read Sefton Delmer, *The Counterfeit Spy* (New York: Harper and Row, 1971), which revealed something of the work of the Twenty Committee before Masterman did, and in particular Delmer's account of the work of Garbo, a double agent he disguises with his own code name of Cato. Montagu's *Beyond Top Secret Ultra* is good on the recruiting of double agents. Two books by David Mure argue that the double-cross system was much less significant than Masterman suggested: *Practice to Deceive* (London: William Kimber, 1977) and *Master of Deception: Tangled Webs in London and the Middle East* (London: William Kimber, 1980). Masterman claimed that all German agents operating in the United Kingdom had been turned, imprisoned, or executed. In a fictionalized account, *The Druid* (New York: Atheneum, 1981), Leonard Mosley builds a case for the possibility that one spy for Germany escaped the British net. (Mr. Mosley did not respond to my queries concerning his book.) Dusko Popov, who was Tricycle in Masterman's account, has written a theatrical autobiography, *Spy Counterspy* (New York: Grosset and Dunlap, 1974). From the German side see Günter Peis, *The Mirror of Deception: How Britain Turned* the *Nazi Spy Machine Against Itself* (London: Weidenfeld and Nicolson, 1977).

41. On "sibs" see David E. Walker, *Lunch with a Stranger* (London: Allan Wingate, 1957), pp. 142–49.

42. Montagu, p. 48, and Mure, *Master of Deception,* p. 11.

43. *On the Chariot Wheel: An Autobiography* (London: Oxford University Press, 1975). The title was taken from Aesop: the fly on the axle wheel cries, "What a dust I raise."

44. Taylor, *A Personal History* (New York: Atheneum, 1983), pp. 206–7.

45. Nigel West (Rupert Allason), *MI6: British Secret Intelligence Service Operations, 1909–45* (London: George Weidenfeld, 1984), p. 214.

46. Masterman lists thirty-nine double agents by code name, from Balloon to Zigzag, with dates when they started and finished work. The real names of many of these individuals are still not known, though the work of Garbo, Mutt and Jeff, Snow, Tate, Tricycle, and Zigzag has been discussed in several accounts. The Pearson Papers in the Beinecke contain a "list of double agents run in England," dated October 1942 (and thus presumably given to Pearson, without updating, about June 1943). This list generally provides the real name set against the aliases—not the code name—but in thirteen instances also relates these to the code names used by the Twenty Committee. Pearson's list shows three double agents—Watchdog, Gwladys, and Cobweb—who do not appear on Masterman's list. Two, Watchdog and Cobweb, are discussed in his text, however, since they operated outside the U.K.—Cobweb in Iceland and Watchdog in Canada. This leaves Gwladys to be accounted for. (Is this Mosley's Druid?) Another list takes up fifteen more CEAs, all operating in France or Belgium, including the notorious Dragoman and Sniper, the latter the only one to appear in Masterman's list. This material is restricted. Garbo is taken up in detail in *Garbo,* by Juan Pujol (Garcia) and Nigel West (Rupert Allason) (London: Weidenfeld and Nicolson, 1985). The American edition, *Operation Garbo: The Personal Story of the Most Successful Double Agent of World War II* (New York: Random House, 1986), contains changes, including greater emphasis on Pearson. The book, in either version, is not entirely satisfactory.

47. McCormick tells of Pearson's remark about Sergueiev in Deacon, *The British Connection: Russia's Manipulation of British Individuals and Institutions* (London: Hamish Hamilton, 1979), p. 179. This book is not generally accessible, having been withdrawn by the publisher shortly after its release. McCormick (to the author, July 7, 14, 1985) reports that after the withdrawal of his book, he did not retain Pearson's note to him. Pearson lists Lily Sergueiev as Natalie Serguiev *[sic]* in his own file. See her memoirs, *Secret Service Rendered* (London: William Kimber, 1968). Constantinides, *Intelligence and Espionage,* p. 405, doubts that she knew the Allied plans. Deacon says that Garbo was Luis Calvo, while West convincingly argues for Pujol.

48. Ronald Lewin's excellent book has very little on the eastern front and only a single reference to ISOS. This was because most of the Russian material had not been declassified when he published in 1978.

49. Kim Philby, *My Silent War* (New York: Grove Press, 1968), pp. 92–93, 261.

50. NHP/Addiss: Pearson to his wife, May 17, June 1, Aug. 6, 1943.

51. NHP/Beinecke: Cowgill to Pearson, Jan. 19, and two undated draft replies, and Durand to Cowgill, from his posting with 12th Army Group, Feb. 20, all 1945.

52. Cowgill and other retired members of the British intelligence community continue to be subject to the Official Secrets Act, and all were careful not to give me still classified information. The British government does not hesitate to punish its former agents for indiscretions, threatening to reduce already small pensions. In the case of my visit to Felix Cowgill, however, there is an additional somewhat amusing, possibly chilling, tale to tell. I had written to Cowgill, who had agreed to see me, though he had replied that he knew very little and his memory was poor. Nonetheless, he gave me his telephone number and directions on how to find him in Dorset. When I arrived in London I called the number given to confirm the visit and was told by an abrupt voice that no one was at that number. I called again the following day, and when I began to speak, the telephone went dead. Nonetheless, I took the designated train at the designated time, wondering what might transpire. Riding first class, I was amused that two men chose to share my compartment, though there were three other nonsmoking compartments in the same coach that were quite empty. I fell asleep on the journey and awoke with a start as the train sat on the platform at Salisbury: beating on the window was an old friend from the American desk at the Foreign Office, calling me by name and telling me to wake up. When I did so he waved me off, smiling. The rest of the journey was utterly without incident, and Mr. Cowgill met the train without comment. It would appear that the British could not resist the temptation to let me know they knew of my visit; whatever intepretation one puts on this bizarre series of incidents, one cannot escape the conclusion that the whole affair was rather childish. It reminded me of my American friend who insisted that he could be interviewed only if I called him from one telephone booth to another. The information he then gave me was readily available in a book that had been published the year before.

53. The first memoir to come out of the double-cross system was Frank Owen's account of Eddie Chapman's work as Zigzag in *The Eddie Chapman Story* (New York: Messner, 1954). However, this book was not widely believed and gave almost nothing away on the systematic nature of British double-agentry.

54. (London: Hodder and Stoughton). On the points in these paragraphs, see pp. 8, 70–74, 79, 137.

55. See Masterman's account of "how Yale brought a happy ending to my 25-year struggle to tell the secret story of British espionage," "The XX Papers," *Yale Alumni Magazine,* XXXV (Feb., 1972), 7–11; and *On the Chariot Wheel,* pp. 348–61. HMG's version appears in John F. Naylor, *A Man and an Institution: Sir Maurice Hankey, the Cabinet Secretariat and the Custody of Cabinet Secrecy* (Cambridge: Cambridge University Press, 1984), pp. 293, 390.

56. The Beinecke Library at Yale holds a presentation copy of *The Double-Cross System,* inscribed "For Jim Osborn/ Without whose interest & help this book would never have been published."

57. Let us worry a bit more over Farago's *The Game of the Foxes: The Untold Story of German Espionage in the United States and Great Britain during World War II* (New York: David McKay, 1971). As seen, Farago's book raises interesting problems. If he used Masterman's report, how did he get it, and *what* did he get? (In print Masterman made no admission of having given anyone access to it, except for King George VI, who could hardly be refused, and who had a copy in his possession at the time of his death in 1952. We know, however, that several people had access to it.) Farago made mistakes in *The Game of the Foxes* that suggested he did not read the report carefully, if at all. Was his time with it limited? Did he see a different version, or perhaps only extracts? Did he see a reader's report, perhaps through McKay? After Masterman's report was published, most historians concluded that Farago's more serious errors were over Lily Sergueiev, to whom he credited undue influence. Given rumors that she had worked for the Russians, could Farago have used a doctored version of the report? One also wonders how, if he did see the full report, Farago missed the fact that what he calls the Abwehr's most successful mission (with double agent Tate) was actually run by the Twenty Committee. Could Masterman have sent slightly different versions to different publishers? There is also the question of why, once Masterman's full report was in print, Farago did not revise his book: the first English edition, published by Hodder and Stoughton in 1972, is the same as the American, and even the sixth edition, published by Bantam Books in New York in 1978, retains the errors. Most authors of books on intelligence become a bit paranoid during the time their manuscripts are circulating to publishers, and problems do, at times, arise. M.R.D. Foot's *SOE in France* (London: HMSO, 1966) was completed in 1962 and then circulated while it was receiving bureaucratic approval. Foot came to believe that a copy fell into the way of Edward Spiro, who as E. H. Cookridge published his *Inside SOE* (London: Arthur Barker) in 1966 as well. See *Intelligence Quarterly,* II (Oct., 1986), 9. My own manuscript suffered from some leakage, for though I sent out only a single copy of the manuscript, that copy was read at three, or perhaps four, publishing houses, and it seems probable that at least one additional copy of it was made during that time, in addition to the one held by my agent. Another laborer in the vineyard called to see me and by his questions revealed that he had seen at least one and probably two chapters of the manuscript. That which one might read, many may read. Being of a suspicious nature I had done that which some other writers in the field do, however, and had planted three false, and quite exciting, "facts" in the typescript. It was the recitation to me of one of these false facts that showed access to the manuscript. I have, of course, removed the "false facts" at page proof.

58. There is no way, of course, to check on what these omissions were. That they were of some significance, and to a pattern, is strongly suggested in a letter from Pearson to Cowgill, NHP/Beinecke: Za Pearson, Feb. 28, 1972.

59. The story of the bringing of Masterman's report to print is drawn from the substantial correspondence file in the Harold Matson Papers, Butler Library, Columbia University: box 68, Sir John Masterman folder. I wish to thank Harold Matson and Mark Wells for giving me permission to use this file, and Chester Kerr for discussing his role in the publication with me, and for searching his own files, though unsuccessfully. Christopher Harmer, C. Vann Woodward, and Kingman Brewster also supplied information. Nigel West says that the arrangement to publish was made through Pearson (West [Rupert Allason], *A Thread of Deceit: Espionage Myths of World War II* [New York: Random House, 1985], p. 70 [published in London by Weidenfeld and Nicolson, 1984, as *Unreliable Witness: Espionage Myths of the Second World War*]). Masterman mentions Osborn specifically in "The XX Papers," p. 9, and *On the Chariot Wheel,* p.

358, as the conduit to the Yale Press, and Osborn confirmed this to me—for I was an obtuse reviewer for the *Yale Review,* and he chided me for what he regarded as an imperceptive statement—so this point seems clear. The James Osborn Papers, in the Yale University Library, contain nothing on the subject, however, and the Yale University Press is unable to find its file on the negotiations, or the original copy of the manuscript. Queries at the offices of the printer yielded nothing. Masterman's papers, at Worcester College, will "not be available to researchers for some time." I thank Mrs. E. Vallis, of Nuffield College Library, Oxford, for searching the Masterman letters in the Cherwell Papers for me.

60. For example, Masterman's summary of the purposes of the double-cross system, which I paraphrased above, originally was expressed as six items; in the book he broke down one of the purposes into two so that he wrote of seven.

61. The book was reprinted, with a correction or two in its index, by Ballantine Books in New York in 1982, to favorable reception. An English reprint edition, which I have not seen, was issued in 1979 (London: Paladin).

62. See Moravec, *Master of Spies: The Memoirs of General Frantisek Moravec* (London: Bodley Head, 1975). Moravec's daughter arranged to have her father's memoirs published after his death. While reviewers judged the book to be authentic, Masterman suggested in his preface that Moravec had exaggerated the importance of at least one agent, Paul Thümmel; he also concluded that the Czech spy service was "the most successful . . . of the war years." F. H. Hinsley, *et al.,* in *British Intelligence in the Second World War: Its Influence on Strategy and Operations* (London: HMSO, 1979) I, 58, published in 1979, show that Thümmel was fully as important as Moravec had argued, without mention of Masterman.

63. One may still, if in search of sights and sounds to invoke the past, take lunch at Claridge's, but Quaglino's is no more. It was a dinner-dance restaurant, very fashionable during the war, before it was wiped out by Annabel's; called "Quagers" by the debutantes of the 1930s (and by Pearson), it featured the only rumba band in London. Its main point was its proximity to Ryder Street, however, and its unremitting Englishness; even in the 1970s one could order Champignons sur Toast, Welsh Rarebit, and Scotch Woodcock. As Pearson wrote Susan (NHP/Addiss: May 14, June 21, 1943), his frequent talk of food in his letters was a reflection of a major concern at the post. At the office they ate "surprizes" for lunch: always two tiny spam sandwiches, a cheese sandwich, and a piece of unpredictable pastry. Meals out were an important break, therefore: "We all talk about food here, like small children, because of the rations. . . . Each dish gets triply caressed with the tongue: once in fact and twice (before and after) in speach."

64. RG 226, OSS, entry 110, box 50: M.O. Benson to Whitney Shepardson, June 18, 1945; *ibid.,* entry 176, box 2: draft history of X-2, p. 48; Bruce Papers: diary, June 20, 1942, July 12, 20, Aug. 1, 4, 1944; interviews with Grace Dollowitz, the late Richard Ellmann, and William Hood. See also Louis Kaufman, Barbara Fitzgerald, and Tom Sewell, *Moe Berg: Athlete, Scholar, Spy* (Boston: Little, Brown, 1974).

65. NHP/Addiss: Pearson to his wife, Dec. 5, 1943, June 6, 8, 1944. I Am the Only Running Footman is the focus of a novel of that title by Martha Grimes (Boston: Little, Brown, 1986).

66. These fragments are from NHP/Beinecke, Susan's letters to her husband, box 9, and NHP/Addiss, his letters to her, various dates in 1943 and 1944. He proposed his epitaph in his letter of Aug. 1, 1944.

67. Bruce Papers: diary, Aug. 21, 1944; "X-2 Art Looting Investigation Unit," official history, in RG 226, OSS, entry 99: Branch Histories, box 15, folder 68. For a general history of the subject, see George Mihan, *Looted Treasure: Germany's Raid on Art* (London: Alliance Press, [1944?]); James J. Rorimer, *Survival: The Salvage and Protection of Art in War* (New York: Abelard Press, 1950); and Thomas Carr Howe, Jr., *Salt Mines and Castles: The Discovery and Restitution of Looted European Art* (Indianapolis: Bobbs-Merrill, 1946). James S. Plaut, a director of the Art Looting Investigation Unit, wrote of how the Germans acquired their collections in "Loot for the Master Race," *Atlantic Monthly,* CLXXVIII (Sept., 1946), 57–63. Lincoln Kirstein told of the discovery and salvage of the Nazi art collection found in a salt mine at Alt Aussee, and especially of the work of four Naval Reserve Lieutenants, Hamilton Coulter of Yale, Craig Smyth of Princeton, Thomas Howe of Harvard, and George L. Stout of the Fogg Museum. See "The Quest of the Golden Lamb," *Town & Country,* C (Sept., 1945), 114–15, 182–86, 189–90, 198–99.

68. See Theodore Sizer, "John Marshall Phillips, 1905–1953," Publications of The Walpole Society, *The Forty-third Annual Meeting* (May 22, 1953), pp. 26–41, corrected proofs, in Yale University Library, MG 453, Theodore Sizer Papers, box 7; and NHP/Addiss: Feb. 11, 1945. See also the report, "Accessions to German Museums and Galleries during the Occupation of France. The Schenker Papers, Part I," Apr. 5, 1945, Secret, in Yale University Library, RG 1144, Sumner McKnight Crosby Papers: box 8, folder 90.

69. See *ibid.,* box 1, folders 3–5, 7; Sizer Papers, box 5 *seriatim* and box 7; MG 1212, box 10, folder 157: Deane Keller to Russell Pruden.

70. Sizer, "A Walpolean at War," an extension of remarks made at a dinner on the occasion of the *Thirty-fifth Annual Meeting of The Walpole Society,* Oct. 27, 1945, pp. 3–27.

71. NHP/Addiss: Feb. 14, Mar. 23, Apr. 1, May 10–13, July 5, 8, 22, 23, Aug. 8, 13, 14, 21, 27, 1945.

72. *Ibid.:* Aug. 20, 24, Sept. 27, 28; NHP/Beinecke, box 10 *seriatim,* and box 1, "Other Systems," and box 3: David D. Zagier to Samuel Klaus, Mar. 4, 1946, and Cowgill file, Pearson to Cowgill, Sept. 6, 1946.

73. This profile is indicative, not definitive. It is based on an analysis of the X-2 personnel book kept by Norman Holmes Pearson, which is now in NHP/Beinecke. Internal evidence dates the book to the spring—perhaps April—of 1944, and it appears to have been taken from Washington to London by Pearson when he returned to Britain in May. There are 216 *vitae,* though a few duplicates, and two different files on two of the same people, reduces the number of individuals to 208. While it is not entirely clear, it appears that twelve of these individuals were not, in fact, hired though their sheets were kept in case of future need, and thirteen of the résumés were set aside in a Dead File. If these names are extracted, there remain 183 individuals for analysis. Not all the files are precisely to the same format, and a few omit information on parents or foreign languages spoken (omissions in this category were recorded as though none were spoken, which no doubt brings the appropriate figure down slightly, since at least one of those who did not supply information on languages is known from other evidence to have been bilingual). In short, the total here is taken conservatively. Nonetheless, at a time when the total X-2 roster was just on 500 individuals, a sample of 183 is sufficient for generalization.

Of the eight Yale men listed in Pearson's file, six were still alive in 1985, and I wish to thank them for helping me both with this chapter and at other points in this book. Joseph Toy Curtiss was essential to the unraveling of the story told in Chapter Three, while Stuyvesant Wainwright II gave me generously of his time as well. I am grateful to Edward J. Burling, Frank B. Nichols, John F. Potter, and one other, for responding by letter to my inquiries, and as mentioned elsewhere to James Murphy, Hubert Will, Turner T. Smith, and John Waller for their help.

74. Pearson mentioned H.D. often in his letters to his wife, and she and Bryher at first appear frequently in his appointments calendar. (He dined so regularly on Sundays with H.D., he ceased noting it in the calendar.) He also comments on the relationship in L. S. Dembo, "Norman Holmes Pearson on H.D.: An Interview," *Contemporary Literature,* X (Autumn, 1969), 435–46.

75. One of my earliest conversations with Norman Holmes Pearson was about H.D. He had seen me carrying a small volume of H. D. poetry on my way to lunch and asked me to join him. I had, in fact, not read the volume at all, was quite ignorant of H.D., and had purchased it only the day before because I was attracted, as I had been as an undergraduate, to the remarkably effective tactile design of New Directions books. I had been wrestling with William Carlos Williams's *In the American Grain,* likewise in a New Directions edition, and had benefited much from the wrestling, so almost on impulse I had decided to take on this, to me, unknown poet. Norman quickly realized I had nothing to contribute to a discussion of H.D., but he liked the fact that I intended to read her, and he gave me some pointers on how to do so. A more senior colleague then happened by—I have forgotten now who it was, for this must have been in 1959—and joined us, noted the volume, and immediately went to the question: was the relationship between H.D. and Lawrence ever physically consummated. I had not known enough to ask the question, and when it was asked realized that the answer was of no interest to me, but in listening to Norman's reply, which I have in effect paraphrased here as I best recall it, I realized that historians tended to overlook the private life of those about whom they wrote in favor of those baked meats set out in the funeral parlor, the volumes of so-called public life and times. Norman's answer, that sometimes it matters and sometimes it does not matter to know the intimate details of a private life, struck me as obvious good sense. To the specific question, which our interloping colleague pressed, Pearson answered no and turned the conversation—this I remember well—to Pablo Neruda, and I, having written a pathetically inadequate undergraduate paper on Neruda a few years before, moved the conversation toward the higher ground of Macchu Picchu.

76. See *Notes on Thought and Vision & The Wise Sappho* (San Francisco: City Lights Books, 1982).

77. Barbara Guest, in an otherwise quite sensitive portrait of H.D. (and a mutedly hostile one of Bryher), suggests that H.D.'s life was marked by "both erotic and intellectual" influences—clearly true—and that as Amy Lowell had

534   N O T E S

supplanted Pound and been supplanted by Richard Aldington, Aldington was supplanted by Pearson. I find no evidence for this, and Ms. Guest seems not to have researched Pearson much—she refers to him as "a former student at Bowdoin College" (Guest, *Herself Defined: The Poet H.D. and Her World* [Garden City, N.Y.: Doubleday, 1984], p. 267)—and concludes that his relations with H.D. are "mystifying." Pearson had a critical mind, and it does not seem especially mystifying that he would have befriended H.D. or become her literary executor. What *is* mystifying is that Bryher, usually so strong a personality, not only consulted Pearson on literary matters but let him alter and edit her work. Pearson wrote the introduction to H.D.'s Trilogy, and she dedicated the last part of *The Flowering of the Rod* to him, but despite the obviously erotic symbolism of the latter, there is no reason to suggest, as Guest does (p. 266), that he "supplanted" Aldington. Certainly nothing in the correspondence supports this—he was effusive in his praise of her work, and always encouraged her to continue, but the first was true of most of his correspondence (Pearson could, as one colleague remarked in none too friendly a way, make buying a fuse a literary event), and the second was, in a sense, his job. For Bryher's view, see *The Days of Mars: A Memoir, 1940–1946* (New York: Harcourt Brace Jovanovich, 1972), pp. v–vi, 90–91, 115–19, 145–46, 155, 161, 170–71, 179.

   78. See Vincent Quinn, *Hilda Doolittle (H.D.)* (New York: Twayne, 1967), p. 30; Susan Stanford Friedman, *Psyche Reborn: The Emergence of H.D.* (Bloomington, Ind.: Indiana University Press, 1981), pp. 7–11; Janice S. Robinson (Stevenson), *H.D.: The Life and Work of an American Poet* (Boston: Houghton Mifflin, 1982), pp. 316–17; and Guest, *Herself Defined*, pp. 253–69, on Pearson's relationship to H.D.

   79. See Katherine Scobey, "The Making of a Poet," *The New Journal*, XVI (Feb. 3, 1984), 26–34. A fuller collection, with an ample and informative introduction, was edited by Louis L. Martz, dedicated to Pearson, and published in 1983: *H.D.: Collected Poems, 1912–1944* (New York: New Directions).

   80. This is *End to Torment* (New York: New Directions, 1979), and further edited by Michael King. See also Pearson's foreword to *Hermetic Definition* (New York: New Directions, 1972).

   81. Typescript copies of pages 512–41 of the official OSS history survive in two slightly different versions in Pearson/Beinecke, together with the changes he proposed and a new section on field operations. In an accompanying letter to Donovan (box 1, wooden file, IV) Pearson suggests that the history ought to recognize more explicitly that it was self-interest which initially moved the British to assist. Rather cozily, he wrote to General Donovan, "One who worked in the game as you and I did" knew that Cowgill's dismissal was probably because X-2 "had gotten them [the British] too much under our control." The official history was declassified in 1976. I wish to thank Felix Cowgill for showing me his postwar correspondence with Pearson, Blum, and others.

   82. Typical examples include Forrest Davis, "The Secret History of a Surrender" (on Operation Sunrise), *Saturday Evening Post* (Sept. 29, 1945); Cabell Phillips, "The Shadow Army That Fought in Silence," *The New York Times Magazine* (Oct. 7, 1945); Corey Ford and Alistair MacBain, "Cloak and Dagger," *Colliers* (Oct. 6, 13, 20, 1945); and Bernt Balchin, "Our Secret War in Scandinavia," *ibid.* (Mar. 9, 16, 1946).

83. NHP/Beinecke: Pearson to Jackson, n.d. This draft of Pearson's memorandum is typed on the back of a copy of an American studies examination for Dec. 15, 1950, which provides an approximate date. On Jackson, see Ray S. Cline, *Secrets, Spies and Scholars: Blueprint of the Essential CIA* (Washington: Acropolis Books, 1976), p. 112. Jackson had inspected X-2/London in 1945. The Clark University archivist searched the Jordan Papers for me and found nothing relevant.

84. Ted Hilles was not among those who had to wait long for his postwar promotion to full professor, which came in 1948, and perhaps because of this he was often at the forefront of senior faculty advocating the promotion of those who had lost momentum on their scholarly work by virtue of military service.

Hilles drew on the many connections he had made at BP to bring the young men, now distinguished scholars holding down prestigious chairs in British academia, to lecture at Yale. He told Tom Mendenhall in 1950 that he ought to visit Bletchley sometime, though not why. He received a British decoration. And he kept in touch with Francis H. Hinsley, the president of St. John's College, Cambridge, and professor of the history of international relations there, for when he heard that Hinsley was to write the official history of British intelligence in World War II, he knew it would reveal one of the keenest minds he had met at Bletchley Park. (See William H. Dunham Papers: Hilles to Dunham, Dec. 21, 1952.)

85. The essay appears in Daniel Aaron, ed., *America in Crisis* (New York: Knopf, 1952), pp. 327–48. (Professor Aaron does not recall why Pearson was asked to write this essay, though he believes the intermediary may have been Franklin Ford, Harvard historian and former member of the OSS.) There is, I believe, an affinity between Pearson's very unhistorical essay in history and his particular interest in H. D. I do not think he recognized that his essay was not history, or that it set out in display all the sins with which "the history of ideas" is usually charged by more empirical scholars. H.D., too, was the most unhistorical of poets. One will find an abundance of historical fragments standing out like commemorative plaques in the lines of Pound, Wallace Stevens, and above all, of Eliot—the last an almost excessively "historical" voice—but one finds virtually none of this in H.D., whose lines arise from word associations, hallucinations, images almost devoid (utterly devoid were it not for the occasional name from Greek antiquity) of any historical resonance.

86. See Ewen Montagu, *The Man Who Never Was* (London: Evans, 1953). This is the account of Operation Mincemeat, which played an important deception role in preparations for the landings in Sicily in 1943. It is most unlikely that Pearson suggested or even knew of the operation (see Charles Cruickshank, *Deception in World War II* [Oxford: Oxford University Press, 1979], pp. 50–84), since "Major Martin's" body went ashore at Huelva on April 30, 1943, though he might well have learned of it through his work with the XX Committee. It is generally agreed that the deception plan was first suggested by an MI5 officer, Charles G. Cholmondeley, or by Ewen Montagu.

87. Øverland, then president of the Nordic Association for American Studies, to the author, July 8, 1985.

88. One suspects that, were one to pursue all of Norman Pearson's literary interests, some small additional information concerning his intelligence work would come to the surface, since a number of writers were, probably unbeknownst to him, engaged during the war in one of the British intelligence agencies. An example would be Arnold Toynbee, distinguished classicist and, after the war, author of *A Study of History*, who during the war prepared the intelligence summaries for the War Cabinet (Richard Deacon [Donald McCormick], *A History of the British Secret Service* [London: Frederick Muller, 1969], p. 354). In 1970, when I paid a visit to Professor Toynbee at his home to discuss an essay I hoped to write about him, he quite suddenly asked me how Norman Holmes Pearson was faring. At the time I was unaware of even the slightest connection between them.

CHAPTER SIX   The Theorist: James Jesus Angleton

1. This is Martin's *Wilderness of Mirrors* (New York: Harper & Row, 1980). In his introduction Martin says that Angleton was at first cooperative with him, then cut off contact. Angleton's friends explain this as resulting from the strategy, as they see it, that Martin followed to get information on Angleton and the second major figure on whom the book focuses, William Harvey: that Martin went to Angleton for information on Harvey at first, without telling him that he would also be writing on Angleton, and not explaining that he intended to dramatize the wilderness he would describe by cutting back and forth between the two men, representing them as utterly different types and intense competitors. Actually, in a letter to Angleton, June 3, 1976, Harvey declared that he agreed "basically" with Angleton's views. Others say that Angleton cooperated when he understood that Martin was writing only an article for *Newsweek* and cut off contact when he learned that a book was in the making. In the meantime a literary agent had approached Angleton to write his own story, and he said no; the agent then went to Martin. Martin says (p. 2) that he intended to write on Angleton, and that it was Angleton who first told him stories about Harvey. Yet others say that Martin's initial interest was in the rumor that it was Harvey who first brought the Mafia into CIA work, largely in order to set up an assassination of Fidel Castro. The actual origins of Martin's project do not matter here, though the conflicting stories are representative of virtually everything that touches on Angleton.

Martin's book is not, I think, as bad as its detractors feel, nor is it as good as most reviewers found it, for Martin finds drama and conflict where little existed, and to the extent that it did exist, sometimes imputes the wrong motives. One does not come away from Martin's book feeling antagonistic toward either figure, however, and there is a clear, if quite curious, sense of sympathy toward Angleton that comes from Martin's pages. Still, it is easy enough to see why the book would irritate Angleton, who may have hoped for a more serious study of counterintelligence.

Jonathan Bloch and Patrick Fitzgerald, *British Intelligence and Covert Action: Africa, Middle East and Europe since 1945* (Dingle, Ireland: Brandon, 1983), p. 243, also credit Angleton with the phrase "a wilderness of mirrors." Since the phrase is now so indelibly linked to Angleton, it is useful to quote what he meant: the wilderness of mirrors "is that . . . myriad of strategems, deceptions, artifices and all the other devices of disinformation which the Soviet bloc and its coordinated intelligence services use to confuse and split the West," producing "an ever-fluid landscape where fact and illusion merge"—thus, not precisely foreign policy, and certainly not (in Angleton's use) intelligence work world-wide. See typescript "Statement by James Angleton in Reference to a Book Entitled 'Wilderness of Mirrors' by David C. Martin."

2. The papers of Frank Church have been deposited in the library of Boise State University in Boise, Idaho; they are not yet organized or open to research-ers. Angleton's remark was made on September 24, 1975. See Senate Select Committee to Study Governmental Operations with Respect to Intelligence [the correct formal name for the committee], *Hearings,* 94th Congress, 1st Session (1975).

3. James Angleton, like H. A. R. Philby, is a staple figure in most books and articles on British, American, and Russian espionage in the 1950s and '60s, and there is little point to a recitation here of titles, especially when many repeat the same information. Sources on Angleton's time before and at Yale are largely official Yale records; the *Yale Daily News* for 1937–41; *The Centennial Yale Banner: The Yearbook of the Colleges of Yale University* ([New Haven: The Class of 1941, 1941]), pp. 94–95; John N. Deming, ed., *Yale 1941 Class Direc-tory* ([New Haven]: The Class, 1976), pp. 3, 141; *Bulletin* of Yale University, *Alumni Directory Number: Living Graduates & Non-Graduates of Yale Univer-sity* ([New Haven]: The Alumni Association, 1948), pp. 266, 275; and James Freeman Jaffray, ed., *A History of the Class of 1941* (New Haven: Yale Univer-sity, 1941). I have benefited from useful discussions and correspondence with men who knew Angleton at Yale: his college roommate Reed Whittemore, po-etry consultant to the Library of Congress and professor of English at the Uni-versity of Maryland; Edgar J. Applewhite, Jr., Robert L. Arnstein, Andrew Berding, Curtis Dahl, Curtis Carroll Davis, Richard M. Ellmann, Roy Finch, Robert A. Gardner, Ambrose Gordon, LaRue R. Lutkins, John B. Madden, John Pauker, Lawrence K. Pickett, William Parsons Porter, Roger Starr, Karl Fred-erick Thompson, Kinsley Twining, Andrews Wanning, and Harold B. White-man, and two who asked not to be named. I wish also to thank Messrs. David Blee, William F. Buckley, Jr., Thomas W. Bullitt, William E. Colby, Max Corvo, William Hood, Bernard Knox, Peter Mero, Newton Miler, Raymond Rocca, and Stuyvesant Wainwright II for meeting or corresponding with me. There are no Angleton papers, of course, though a few of his wartime letters may be found in the Norman Holmes Pearson collection in the Beinecke Library at Yale.

I have also benefited from conversations and correspondence with Angleton himself. He is an intense, organized, quite articulate person who, when recalling such aspects of his work as he chooses to recall, or discussing the methodology of counterintelligence, is indefatigable. His concentration is legendary, as is his recall of names and the precise details of events. Whether over Coca-Cola (his) and beer (mine) in a rathskeller, or at the Army and Navy Club in Washington (where, ludicrously and apparently unnoticed by Angleton, background music played the James Bond theme over and over as we talked), or in a car parked on Chain Bridge Road in Washington, and elsewhere, he was invariably inter-esting, well-read, and quick with an apt quotation. He was not, however, forth-coming on any subject that threatened to range beyond my own research. Rumor has it that Angleton is writing his autobiography, though I doubt it; if he is, it should be an unusually interesting literary document, as much for its construc-tion as for its content.

4. On the senior Angleton see Boise (Idaho) *Statesman,* Mar. 6, 1973. His

arrival in Italy, at Sineti, is documented in RG 226, OSS, entry 110, box 4, folder 487.

5. See Martin, *Wilderness of Mirrors, seriatim;* Fred Rowan, *Technospies: The Secret Network That Spies on You—and You* (New York: G. P. Putnam's, 1978), pp. 184–87; and Burton Hersh, "Dragons Have to Be Killed," *The Washingtonian* (Sept., 1985), pp. 158–61, 192–94, 196–98, 200, 202–203.

6. Full files of these magazines may be found in the Yale University Library. Angleton's last appearance in *Furioso* was in the summer of 1941, remarking on Marianne Moore's discovery of "imaginary gardens with real toads in/them."

7. Martin, p. 21. See also Whittemore, *The Poet as Journalist: Life at The New Republic* (Washington: The New Republic Book Co., 1976), p. 62; C. David Heymann, *Ezra Pound: The Last Rower—A Political Profile* (New York: Viking, 1976), pp. 87, 135; and Boise *Statesman,* July 8, 1976.

8. Johnson emerges as one of the few genuine heroes of the ill-planned CIA evacuation of Saigon, so graphically described by Frank Snepp in *Decent Interval* (New York: Random House, 1977).

9. *The Serpent Sleeping* (New York: G. P. Putnam's, 1962); *Serpent's Progress: The Writing of a Novel, Monday Evening Papers,* No. 15 (Middletown, Conn.: Center for Advanced Studies, Wesleyan University, 1968). Weismiller had also translated *The Young Concubine,* by Makhali-Phal, from the French (New York: Random House, 1942).

10. (Boston: Houghton Mifflin, 1946). On Dragoman see Nigel West (Rupert Allason), *MI6: British Secret Intelligence Service Operations, 1909–45* (New York: Random House, 1983), p. 230. I wish to thank Professor Edward Weismiller, of the Department of English at George Washington University, for discussing his work, and Angleton, with me. I also thank four individuals who were secretaries or translators at Ryder Street for describing work there: in addition to Perdita Schaffner these were Mary Maxwell Ellett Harrison, Grace Dolowitz Levitt, and Margaret Elliott Sherman. Richard Warch, president of Lawrence University, opened the Lawrence archives on Westbrook Steele to me, and John Strange, formerly president of the Institute of Paper Chemistry, and Wendall Smith, described Steele's work and provided access to the Institute's OSS file.

11. Peter Carlson, "Secret Agents," *People* (June 7, 1982), p. 32. Angleton called *People* and dictated a correction, which subsequently appeared with a dismissive editorial aside. See also F. H. Hinsley, E. E. Thomas, C. F. G. Ransom, and R. C. Knight, *British Intelligence in the Second World War: Its Influence on Strategy and Operations* (London: HMSO, 1979), I, 487–89, 491–93.

12. Norman Holmes Pearson Papers, formerly in the personal possession of his stepdaughter, Susan Addiss: Aug. 13, 30, [Sept. 7], 1944.

13. Norman Holmes Pearson Papers, Beinecke Library, Yale University: box 3, folder XX, Angleton to Pearson, n.d.

On Angleton's postings see, among several documents, RG 226, OSS, entry 110, folder 3, box 43: Louis A. Boxleitner to J. O. Brown, Jan. 1, 1943, which refers to Angleton as "now en route to London" to be junior officer for Italy, and V-48 personnel list of seventy-one names, Jan. 21, 1944, with Angleton as V/38/T.1 (chief of the Italian desk); entry 100, box 47, folder 135: Apr. 24, 1944, with request for warrant officer rank for Angleton, who is listed second in order of priority in X-2 to attain that rank; and entry 1, box 14, General Outpost records: Dec. 18, 1945, which lists Angelton *[sic]* as a captain and the commanding officer, 2677th Regiment SSU. Internal reports referred to him as a major. See, for example, RG 226, entry 100, file 142.

Little has been written on SCI units; the best book, in which a picture of Angleton appears, is Akeley P. Quirk, *Recollections of World War II: O.S.S. S.C.I. Unit 6th Army Group* (U.S.) (Fullerton, Calif.: Sultana Press, 1981). I also wish to thank Dr. Charles W. Hostler, X-2 training officer and later chief of station, Rumania, for information on SCI work.

14. What man might not like to be a legend in his own lifetime? Angleton is near that status, surely, if for no other reason than the fact that he is an obvious figure in dozens of spy thrillers. Representative examples include L. Christian Balling, *Mallory's Gambit* (Boston: Atlantic Monthly Press, 1986)—perhaps the best; Arnaud de Borchgrave and Robert Moss, *The Spike* (New York: Crown, 1980); and *Death Beam* (New York: Crown, 1981), by Moss; William S. Cohen and Gary Hart, *The Double Man* (New York: William Morrow, 1985); Alfred Coppel, *Thirty-four East* (New York: Harcourt, Brace Jovanovich, 1974); E. Howard Hunt, *The Hargrave Deception* (New York: Stein and Day, 1980)—Hunt wrote to *Harper's* about using Angleton in his novel: Hunt to the editor, Oct. 27, 1983, unpublished—Marion Layne (Woolf), *The Balloon Affair* (New York: Dodd, Mead); David Lippincott, *Salt Mine* (New York: Viking, 1979); Nicolas Luard, *The Orion Line* (New York: Harcourt, Brace Jovanovich, 1977); Robert Ludlum, *The Aquitaine Progression* (New York: Random House, 1984); Victor Marchetti, *The Rope-Dancer* (New York: Grosset & Dunlap, 1971); Chapman Pincher, *Dirty Tricks* (London: Sidgwick and Jackson, 1980); and Theodore Wilden, *Exchange of Clowns* (Boston: Little, Brown, 1981). The most interesting such novel is *Orchids for Mother,* by Aaron Latham (Boston: Little, Brown, 1977), which is transparently about Angleton, William Colby, and others. Latham also wrote an odd piece, "Orchids for Mother: Behind the C.I.A. Cover Story," *New York,* VIII (Apr. 7, 1975), 27–40, which purports to be the fictional result of research on a straight story about the CIA. He suggests that Secretary of State Henry Kissinger wished Angleton out, and he concludes with the assassination of Orchid who, nonetheless, is able to leak a deception story even after his death. In "Politics and the C.I.A.—Was Angleton Spooked by State?" *ibid.* (Mar. 10), pp. 32–34, Latham wrote of his suspicion that Kissinger had passed the word to phase Angleton out, because of Angleton's belief that the Sino-Soviet split and Russian talk about detente were ruses. This article is chiefly valuable for its quotations from Angleton on Pound, Eliot, Wallace Stevens, and Robert Frost. When asked about such books, Angleton invariably replies that he is not a student of them, though he reads some if they are sent to him, and he is aware that he figures in a recent novel by Saul Bellow. My letters to Latham, hoping to set up a meeting to discuss his pieces, went unanswered.

15. Martin, p. 16; Phillips, *The Night Watch* (New York: Atheneum, 1977), pp. 189–90, 239.

16. An account of the Poletti and Pignatelli affairs may be found in Anthony Cave Brown, *The Last Hero, Wild Bill Donovan* (New York: Vintage/Random House), 1984, pp. 499–507. Angleton's report is in the Donovan Papers, Carlisle, Pa. The OSS commander in Italy, Edward Glavin, had agreed to talk to me about this and other matters, when he died, on July 25, 1984. His widow, Mary

Glavin, has kindly searched her husband's papers for me, without success. Peter Tompkins has discussed his impressions of Donald Downes, James Angleton, and OSS operations in Italy with me. He is at work on his own study of the period.

17. The Vessel affair is recounted in Cave Brown, *ibid.*, pp. 603–705. I could not independently check the ample documentation provided by Cave Brown from the Donovan Papers, for the file numbers have been changed and several of the documents appear to be missing. Box 120, folder 91, labeled X-2 Italy, for example, is missing. Donovan microfilm, originally retained by Cave Brown, is now in the hands of Donovan's son David, though it may be returned to the archives at some point in the future. Cave Brown's references (pp. 861–62) are to telegram files, memoranda, and interviews. See also Donovan Papers, file 206, box 66B, "Certain Accomplishments of the Office of Strategic Services," and file 215, box 66B, "OSS Special Operations in Italy"; *The New York Times*, Sept. 13, 1973; *The Washington Post*, Aug. 3, 1980, which contradictorily says Angleton was taken in and then shows that he was not; and Robert A. Graham, "Has the Vatican Lost Confidence in the Press?" *Columbia*, Aug., 1973, p. 3.

R. Harris Smith, *OSS: The Secret History of America's First Central Intelligence Agency* (New York: Delta reprint ed., 1973), pp. 84–86, 103–106, places greater emphasis on Earl Brennan. Frederic Laurent, *L'Orchestre Noir* (Paris: Stock, 1978), dates the Brennan-Montini collaboration as having begun in 1942 and says that Angleton then developed it (p. 29). I wish to thank Max Corvo, who worked with Brennan and Scamporino, for searching Earl Brennan's papers, which he holds. Mr. Corvo is writing a history of the OSS in the Italian campaign. A Russian report, by V. Semyonov, "Seventeen Moments of Spring," appears in the Moscow *Literary Gazette* of Oct. 19, 1983. It says that Angleton recruited bishops, cardinals, and a future pope, but does not name them. I thank Vasily Rudich, assistant professor of classics at Yale University, for translating this article for me. For Angleton's comment on the George Wood material see West (Allason), *MI6*, p. 225.

18. Pacatte Report, pp. 15, [37, 40].

19. Cave Brown, *Last Hero*, pp. 709–19.

20. *Ibid.*, pp. 721–27, 804–16. Harris Greene is writing a full-scale study of the Holohan affair.

21. *Ibid.*, pp. 479–83.

22. There is a clear suggestion in recently released OSS records that a second agent, Jane Selman, of Operation Ragweed, swallowed an L-tablet a hundred yards from the Swiss border after being wounded by the Germans (see RG 226, entry 110, vol. 48, folder 491: Ernest Brooks, Jr., to War Diary Section, June 11, 1945).

23. I wish to thank Dr. Davis for supplying me with much information by mail, for meeting with me on two occasions, and for other valuable help.

24. Stuart Christie, *Stefano delle Chiaie: Portrait of a Black Terrorist* (London: Anarchy Magazine, 1984), p. 6. In 1986 *Covert Action* magazine said that Angleton and Raymond Rocca received the Croce al Merito seconda classe from the Sovereign Military Order of Malta on December 27, 1946, presumably for this work and their allegedly close ties to the order. See Francoise Hervet, "Knights of Darkness: The Sovereign Military Order of Malta," *Covert Action*, no. 25 (Winter, 1986), p. 31.

25. Princeton University, Allen W. Dulles Papers, XXX: Dulles to Robert P. Joyce, Feb. 13, 1947.

26. On this period see the work of Raimondo Craveri, *La compagna d'Italia e i servizi segreti: La storia dell'ORI (1943–1945)* (Milan: La Pietra, 1980), which is rich in material on the OSS, Scamporino, Corvo, and others.

27. On the transition see Thomas F. Troy, *Donovan and the CIA: A History of the Establishment of the Central Intelligence Agency* (Frederick, Md: University Publications of America, 1981), pp. 296–97, 303, 358.

28. I wish to thank William Quinn for discussing SSU with me. He is at work on a book of his own which should amplify the story significantly. See also Pearson Papers, Beinecke: documents taken and returned as sanitized by the CIA (see Chapter Five, note 7), _____ to Quinn, Apr. 22, and Murphy to Quinn, Apr. 23, 1946.

29. In the introduction to the notes I state that two key figures died at an early stage in the research for this book. Paul Blum was one. Six months after I began serious research, and only a few weeks before I was scheduled to meet with him, Blum passed away. His biography is being written by Robert S. Greene, his cousin, to whom I owe great thanks for his help. On Blum's connection with Sunrise, see Allen Dulles, *The Secret Surrender* (New York: Harper and Row, 1966), and Bradley F. Smith and Elena Agarossi, *Operation Sunrise: The Secret Surrender* (New York: Basic Books, 1979). By selling his books to Yokohama, Blum is said to have "given the city back its history." In 1983 the Yokohama Archives of History honored Blum by publishing, in two volumes, *The Paul C. Blum Collection: A Catalogue of Books,* with an essay by George H. Kerr that touches on his work for the OSS in I, xix–xxv. In 1978 Blum translated Jacques Pezeu-Massabuau's *The Japanese Islands: A Physical and Social Geography* for publication by Charles Tuttle in Rutland, Vermont.

30. Bertrand's account of his work was initially discounted by students of Ultra. More recently it has been taken as largely accurate. On his role in the bringing of an Enigma machine to Britain, and the publication of his book, see Jean Stengers, "Enigma, the French, the Poles and the British, 1931–1940," in Christopher Andrew and David Dilks, eds., *The Missing Dimension: Governments and Intelligence Communities in the Twentieth Century* (London: Macmillan, 1984), pp. 126–38, 267–73. Stengers draws on some Bertrand papers held by his widow. See also Paul Paillole, *Services Spéciaux, 1935–1945* (Paris, Laffont, 1975), p. 64, and Paillole, *Notre espion chez Hitler* (Paris: Laffont, 1985), *seriatim.*

31. On Lafond, Bertrand, *et al.,* see Henri Navarre, *Le Service de renseignements, 1871–1944* (Paris, Plon, 1978); and Nicolas Fournier and Edmond Legrand, *Dossier E: comme espionage* (Paris: Moreau, 1978), which, however, contains several errors. Verneuil and Lafond were first revealed to be the same person in Pierre Nord [André Lèon Brouillard], *Mes camarades sont morts* (Paris: Librairie des Champs Elysées, 1947).

The nature of Angleton's relationship to de Vosjoli should be pursued. When de Vosjoli served as a liaison officer in Washington, he was involved in a variety of matters concerning France, Israel, Cuba, and the United States. In 1970 he claimed to have provided important intelligence to the CIA with respect to the Cuban missile crisis in 1962. Later he contended that the writer Leon Uris used his book *Lamia* (Boston: Little, Brown, 1970) as the basis for the novel *Topaz* and sued; there was an out-of-court settlement.

32. Angleton was well known to many of the top figures in French intelligence. When Christopher Felix visited the director of the Sûrêté Nationale in Paris, the director Pierre Bertaux, replied to Felix's message of greetings from Angleton with a smile, and described him as "un homme macabre." He meant this as a compliment. Felix was struck by the "extraordinary physical resemblance" between the two men: "the same long, thin face, elegantly pointed chin, aquiline nose, sensuous but disciplined mouth, sunken cheeks, deep-set eyes illuminated by a kind of controlled fire, thick black hair surmounting an aristocratic forehead." See Christopher Felix [James McCargar], *The Spy and His Masters: A Short Course in the Secret War* (London: Secker & Warburg, 1963), pp. 129–39. (The American edition, published by Dutton, uses only the subtitle.) Pseudonyms are used throughout. With George Marton, Felix also wrote an excellent novel rich in detail on deception: *Three-Cornered Cover* (New York: Holt, Rinehart and Winston, 1972). See also Roger Faligot and Pascal Krop, *La Piscine: Les services secrets français, 1944–1984* (Paris: Éditions du Seuil, 1985).

33. For obvious reasons only hints here and there tell of the liaison between Angleton and Israeli intelligence. The most useful accounts are Wolfe Blitzer, *Between Washington and Jerusalem: A Reporter's Notebook* (New York: Oxford University Press, 1985); Jacques Derogy and Hesi Carmel, *The Untold Story of Israel* (New York: Grove Press, 1979); Stewart Steven, *The Spymasters of Israel* (New York: Macmillan, 1980); Richard Deacon (Donald McCormick), *The Israeli Secret Service* (London: Hamish Hamilton, 1977); Joshua Tadmor, *The Silent Warriors* (New York: Macmillan, 1969); and Dennis Eisenberg, Uri Dan, and Eli Landau, *The Mossad: Israel's Secret Intelligence Service—Inside Stories* (New York: Paddington Press, 1978). Very little concerning Israeli intelligence can be verified, and these accounts clearly contain errors. A series of articles by Claudia Wright in the *New Statesman* (Nov. 29) pp. 22–23, (Dec. 6) p. 19, (Dec. 13, all 1985) pp. 18–20, sets the Israeli attack on the USS *Liberty,* an American spy ship, in June 1967 (and, prospectively, the discovery in 1986 that an American Naval Intelligence officer was providing classified information to Israel) in historical perspective. One may only speculate as to Angleton's views on the *Liberty* incident, when Israeli aircraft attacked the American naval vessel, allegedly in error, with heavy loss of life. Of the several accounts of the strike on the *Liberty,* only one mentions Angleton: Anthony Pearson, *Conspiracy of Silence* (London: Quartet, 1978), p. 71. Taken together the accounts do attest to the close ties that grew between Angleton and Mossad (the Institute for Intelligence and Special Assignments), especially with Isser Harel and Ephraim Evron, and they suggest that despite Angleton's personal visits to Israel, his failure to anticipate the Israeli invasion of Egypt on October 29, 1956, damaged his credibility with Dulles. See in particular Leonard Mosley, *Dulles: A Biography of Eleanor, Allen, and John Foster Dulles and Their Family Network* (New York: Dial Press, 1978), pp. 374–417. Derogy and Carmel also suggest that the Israelis, perhaps not understanding either Congress or the American press, tended to believe that Angleton was sent packing in 1974 by Colby because of Angleton's insistence on probing links between the KGB and Lee Harvey Oswald, the presumed assassin of President John F. Kennedy. Kermit Roosevelt may have best reflected official CIA attitudes toward Angleton's relationship with the Israelis in his comment in the introduction to the 1976 edition of *The Overseas Targets: War Report of the OSS (Office of Strategic Services)*, II (New York: Walker), xix, that Angleton was simply "too close" to Israel, and this prevented a balanced view of Arab-Israeli conflict. Angleton may have worked with Roosevelt to strengthen SAVAK, the Iranian National Information and Security Organization: see *Covert Action Information Bulletin*, no. 7 (Jan., 1980), pp. 28–31.

34. See Enzo Piscitelli, *et al.*, *Italia 1945–48: Le origini della Repubblica* (Turin: G. Giappichelli, 1974); and especially Roberto Faenza and Marco Fini, *Gli americani in Italia* (Milan: Feltrinelli, 1976), throughout. H. Stuart Hughes, who was with OSS in Italy and France, wrote *The United States and Italy* (Cambridge, Mass.: Harvard University Press, 1953) for his OSS colleague Donald C. McKay, editor of The American Foreign Policy Library. Published well before it was known that the CIA had assisted the Christian Democrats, Hughes's book nonetheless contains intriguing hints of the American involvement: see pages 156–58. In the 1980s Angleton's name was linked again with Claire Sterling, when she (and he) said that the KGB was behind international terrorism and an assassination attempt on the Pope. Among several books, see Roger Faligot and Remi Kauffer, *Au coeur de l'état, l'espionnage* (Paris: Autremont, 1983), pp. 38–40. For a history of Italian politics during this period see Giuseppe Mammarella, *Italy after Fascism: A Political History, 1943–1965* (Notre Dame: revised and enlarged ed., University of Notre Dame Press, 1966).

35. So bald a summary obviously begs any number of controversial questions. On the whole I agree with the general views expressed by the British scholar D. Cameron Watt in *Succeeding John Bull: America in Britain's Place, 1900–1975* (Cambridge: Cambridge University Press, 1984), and by William Roger Louis in his very fine, and full, *Imperialism at Bay: The United States and the Decolonisation of the British Empire, 1941–1945* (Oxford: Oxford University Press, 1977). There are important objections to be made to Watt's treatment of the prewar years, but I believe him sound on the postwar period. The specific perceptions of the relative interests of the two nations in the Balkans and the Middle East are a case study of the larger issue, and that case study, in turn, reflects boldly on the changing views on Italy. Where intelligence policy is concerned, the remark by Richard Bosworth—in his "Italy's Historians and the Myth of Fascism," Richard Langhorne, ed., *Diplomacy and Intelligence during the Second World War: Essays in Honour of F. H. Hinsley* (Cambridge: Cambridge University Press, 1985), p. 86—that modern Greece can be "discussed around the interpretive poles erected by the ex-S.O.E. agent, C. M. Woodhouse, and the ex-O.S.S. agent, W. H. McNeill," strikes me as quite exact. Woodhouse, cited in previous chapters, summed up his view in *Modern Greece: A Short History* (London: Oxford University Press, 1977), while McNeill, a distinguished historian at the University of Chicago, has elegantly restated his position, of which he first wrote in 1947 in *The Greek Dilemma: War and Aftermath* (Philadelphia: J. B. Lippincott, 1947). in *The Metamorphosis of Greece since World War II* (Oxford: The University, 1978).

36. On the question of when the CIA resolved on the need for clandestine activities in Italy see Trevor Barnes, "The Secret Cold War: The C. I. A. and American Foreign Policy in Europe, 1946–1956," *The Historical Journal*, XXIV (ii/1981), 399–415, and XXV (iii/1982), 649–70. Consult also James E. Miller,

"Taking Off the Gloves: The United States and the Italian Elections of 1948," *Diplomatic History,* VII (Winter 1983), 33–55. I have drawn heavily on these valuable articles in the paragraphs that follow. A succinct history is provided in Anne Karalekas, *History of the Central Intelligence Agency* (Laguna Hills, Calif.: Aegean Park Press, 1977), which is a reprint of the unclassified history prepared in April 1976 for the Senate Select Committee to Study Governmental Operations with Respect to Intelligence Activities. Karalekas is reprinted whole in a curious publication, William M. Leary, *The Central Intelligence Agency: History and Documents* (University, Alabama: University of Alabama Press, 1984). See also Tyrus G. Fain, ed., *The Intelligence Community: History, Organization, and Issues* (New York: Bowker, 1977), pp. 215–22.

37. Marchetti, "The CIA in Italy: An Interview with Victor Marchetti," in Philip Agee and Louis Wolf, eds., *Dirty Work: The CIA in Western Europe* (Secaucus, N.J.: Lyle Stuart, 1978), p. 168.

38. Vol. I was *Il Vaticano e la democrazia italiana,* vol. II *Il Vaticano contro la pace mondiale,* both published by the Società Cooperazione Operaia Editrice in Lugano. I wish to thank Raymond Rocca for showing me his set of the volumes.

39. Robert H. Ferrell, ed., *Off the Record: The Private Papers of Harry S Truman* (New York: Harper & Row, 1980), pp. 218–19.

40. Smith, *Cold Warrior,* p. 138.

41. There is no need here to pursue the hostility that developed between Angleton and Colby, or to recount in detail how Angleton ultimately lost in the running battle. The story is covered as fully as possible, and sympathetically to both sides, in Thomas Powers, *The Man Who Kept the Secrets: Richard Helms & the CIA* (New York: Knopf, 1979), and from Colby's point of view in a well-written memoir by William Colby and Peter Forbath, *Honorable Men: My Life in the CIA* (New York: Simon and Schuster, 1978). Angleton has not and will not have his say, as he does not now have access to the classified information necessary to defend himself, and he has said that he will not violate the spirit of his oath of secrecy to defend himself in public. The nub of the conflict appears to have been over the use of Israeli intelligence, however.

42. Martin, p. 182.

43. See Roy Maclaren, *Canadians Behind Enemy Lines, 1939–1945* (Vancouver, B.C.: University of British Columbia Press, 1981), pp. 160–61; C. V. Hearn, *Foreign Assignment* (London: Robert Hale, 1961), pp. 111–22; RG 226, entry 115, box 35: London Field Files and folder 3, Mazzarine Report from London, "Who's Who of Albanian Guerrillas."

44. The fullest account of the Albanian operation is Lord (Nicholas) Bethell's *The Great Betrayal: The Untold Story of Kim Philby's Biggest Coup* (London: Hodder and Stoughton, 1984). Some modest excisions have been made in *Betrayed,* the American edition (New York: Times Books, 1984). Most reviewers have praised Bethell's account as accurate and full, but a few have suggested caution, perhaps because in 1971, in *Sunday,* a New Delhi publication, he was accused of being a KGB agent. He is now said to be trying to create an independent Khalistan through the Committee for a Free Afghanistan: see "How the British Founded Khalistan," *Sunday,* XIII (Feb. 22, 1986), 25–27. The late Michael Burke guardedly told his part of the story in *Outrageous Good Fortune*

(Boston: Little, Brown, 1984), pp. 139–69 (see also *The New York Times,* Nov. 13, 1984), while Philby speaks of it in *My Silent War* (New York: Grove Press, 1968), pp. 194–99. See also David Smiley, *Albanian Assignment* (London: Chatto & Windus, 1984), pp. 159–64. The estimate of a thousand deaths is from Chapman Pincher, *Too Secret Too Long* (New York: St. Martin's Press, 1984), p. 300. The short description of the operation in Anthony Verrier's *Through the Looking Glass: British Foreign Policy in an Age of Illusions* (London: Jonathan Cape, 1983) is useful. See also *The New York Times,* May 9, 1987. I wish in particular to thank James McCargar for his hospitality and help.

Most historians of contemporary Albanian affairs agree that even without Philby's treachery, the operation had little chance of success: see, for example, Anton Logoreci, *The Albanians: Europe's Forgotten Survivors* (London: Gollancz, 1977), pp. 106–109. Christopher Andrew, *Secret Service: The Making of the British Intelligence Community* (London: Heinemann, 1985), p. 493, is of the same opinion. On the other hand, a few writers place the greater blame on Philby, and by implication on those who failed to suspect him; a typical treatment is in Norman Gelb, *Enemy in the Shadows: The World of Spies and Spying* (London: William Luscombe, 1976). Hoxha credits Albanian success to the eternal vigilance he exercised against the imperialist powers: Hoxha, *The Anglo-American Threat to Albania* (Tiranë: n.p., 1982). On the essential Greek background, see C. M. Woodhouse, *The Struggle for Greece, 1941–1949* (London: Hart-Davis, MacGibbon, 1976). On the wartime Albanian foreground see Julian Amery, *Sons of the Eagle: A Study in Guerrilla War* (London: Macmillan, 1948), and Amery's *Approach March: A Venture in Autobiography* (London: Hutchinson, 1973). Albanian writers often insist that the Anglo-American effort had, in addition to active Italian and Greek cooperation, direct Yugoslav support; see, for example, Stefanaq Pollo and Arben Puto, *The History of Albania from Its Origins to the Present Day* (London: Routledge & Kegan Paul, 1981), p. 265.

45. Philby, *My Secret War,* pp. 195–99.

46. On the Rote Kapelle see Gilles Perrault (Jacques Peyroles), *The Red Orchestra* (New York: Simon and Schuster, 1969), and Central Intelligence Agency, *The Rote Kapelle: The CIA's History of Soviet Intelligence and Espionage Networks in Western Europe, 1936–1945* (Washington, D.C.: University Publications of America, 1979).

47. Douglas Sutherland, *The Fourth Man: The Definitive Story of Blunt, Philby, Burgess and Maclean* (London: Secker & Warburg, 1980), p. 136.

48. The literature is substantial. See, in particular, Bruce Page, David Leitch, and Phillip Knightley, *The Philby Conspiracy* (New York: updated ed., Ballantine Books, 1981); Hugh Trevor-Roper (Lord Dacre), *The Philby Affair: Espionage, Treason and Secret Services* (London: William Kimber, 1968); E. H. Cookridge (Edward Spiro), *The Third Man: The Truth about "Kim" Philby, Double Agent* (London: Arthur Barker, 1968); Anthony Purdy and Douglas Sutherland, *Burgess and Maclean* (Garden City, N.Y.: Doubleday, 1963); Andrew Boyle, *The Fourth Man: The Definitive Account of Kim Philby, Guy Burgess, and Donald Maclean and Who Recruited Them to Spy for Russia* (New York: Dial, 1980), published in London in 1979 as *The Climate of Treason: Five Who Spied for Russia* (Hutchinson); Fitzroy Maclean, *Take Nine Spies* (New York: Atheneum, 1978), pp. 222–77; Chapman Pincher, *Their Trade Is Treach-*

ery (Toronto: rev. ed., Bantam Books, 1982), pp. 14–25; and *Too Secret Too Long,* especially pp. 286–302; Patrick Seale and Maureen McConville, *Philby: The Long Road to Moscow* (London: Hamish Hamilton, 1973); Wilfrid Mann, *Was There a Fifth Man?* (London: Pergamon, 1982); Martin Green, *Children of the Sun: A Narrative of "Decadence" in England after 1918* (New York: Basic Books, 1976); John Bullock, *Akin to Treason* (London: Arthur Barker, 1966), pp. 139–50; Verne Newton, "The Spy Who Came to Dinner," *The Washingtonian,* XX (Oct., 1984), 95–96, 100–108; and Robert Cecil, "The Cambridge Comintern," in Christopher Andrew and David Dilks, eds., *The Missing Dimension: Governments and Intelligence Communities in the Twentieth Century* (London: Macmillan, 1984), pp. 169–98, 218–82. The most recent contribution, which says that the CIA warned the British there were moles in MI5, is Andrew Sinclair, *The Red and the Blue: Intelligence, Treason and the Universities* (London: Weidenfeld and Nicolson, 1986). In many ways, however, the most interesting book of the lot is a memoir by a man on the sidelines, Goronwy Rees, *A Chapter of Accidents* (London: Chatto & Windus, 1972). Though two of the titles cited here use the word *definitive,* obviously no such thing exists or can exist.

49. Martin, pp. 209–10.

50. Boyle, *Fourth Man,* pp. 307–11.

51. On the theme of homosexuality that runs through the affair, see in particular a perceptive essay by George Steiner, "The Cleric of Treason," *The New Yorker* (Dec. 8, 1980), pp. 158, 161–62, 164–68, 170–95. Richard Holmes has written a reasoned, angry statement: "Anthony Blunt, Gentleman Traitor," *Harper's,* CCLX (Apr., 1980), 102–109.

52. Pincher, *Too Secret,* pp. 286–304. I wish to thank Cherry Hughes who is writing a biography of Blunt, Nicholas Elliott, and Newton Miler for meeting or corresponding with me. I did, as a matter of methodology, write to Kim Philby in Moscow; I did not expect to get a reply, of course.

53. See London *Sunday Times,* Nov. 9, 16; London *Times,* Nov. 6, 8; and London *Observer,* Nov. 16, 1986.

54. For example, Roy Berkeley, *A Spy's London,* forthcoming.

55. *Poussin* (New Haven: Yale University Press, 1980). Shortly after publication I visited the home of an academic who had placed a Bilston enamel ashtray on top of Blunt's book. It said, "Everything is sweetened by risk."

56. Forster, *Two Cheers for Democracy* (New York: Harcourt, Brace, 1951), p. 67. Forster is often subtly misquoted, and even when quoted correctly, I believe he is being misread here, and it is useful to reread the entire passage. Angleton holds to the conventional intelligence view on homosexuality: that even in a time or a society where it is accepted, so that blackmail is not a major risk, homosexuality creates an instability of relationships that can be damaging to the conduct of an operation or investigation. The same may be said, of course, of a purely heterosexual relationship. He also believes that homosexuals promote their own and that they compare jobs, breaking down compartmentalization.

57. Rees, *Chapter of Accidents,* p. 208.

58. Fain, ed., *Intelligence Community,* p. 338: Rocca deposition, Nov. 25, 1975.

59. Cline's version is in his *Secrets, Spies and Scholars: Blueprint of the Essential CIA* (Washington: Acropolis Books, 1976), pp. 162–64; Angleton's is in

The New York Times, Nov. 30, 1976. The Togliatti report may have arisen from the fact that when he returned from the party congress, Togliatti made some comments about the speech which were printed in the Italian press. E. H. Cookridge (Edward Spiro) says in *Gehlen: Spy of the Century* (London: Hodder and Stoughton, 1971); p. 303, that Reinhard Gehlen, president of the West German Federal Intelligence Service, the BND, got the text for Dulles. If there were gaps in the Polish text (assuming that the consensus is to be accepted), then it may be that Gehlen provided the first full text a bit later (see Dobson and Payne, *Dictionary,* p. 57). Brian Freemantle, *CIA* (New York: Stein and Day, 1983), p. 37, says Angleton knew that the Gehlen service had been penetrated by Russian intelligence, and that the first "indication" of the speech came from James Critchfield, head of the CIA's German division, which led Angleton to turn to his Israeli connections. See also Darrell Garwood, *Under Cover: Thirty-Five Years of CIA Deception* (New York: Grove Press, 1985), pp. 266–69, which argues that getting the Khruschev speech was no big thing; and William R. Corson, *The Armies of Ignorance: The Rise of the American Intelligence Empire* (New York: Dial Press, 1977), pp. 367–68.

60. On Red Sox/Red Cap, see Stephen E. Ambrose and Richard H. Immerman, *Ike's Spies: Eisenhower and the Espionage Establishment* (Garden City, N.Y.: Doubleday, 1981), pp. 237–40. One source says the infiltration and paramilitary teams were an elite corps, another believes they were semiliterate toughs, and yet a third suggests that no such project ever existed. There is also a hint that Angleton tried to invoke his friend Robert B. Anderson, secretary of the treasury, to persuade the Dulles brothers not to release the text. See also Blanche Wiesen Cook, *The Declassified Eisenhower: A Divided Legacy* (Garden City, N.Y.: Doubleday, 1981), on security in the Eisenhower administration generally.

61. Stansfield Turner, a Rhodes Scholar, student at Amherst, and graduate of the U. S. Naval Academy, had served as president of the Naval War College and commander in chief of the North Atlantic Treaty Organization's Southern Flank. Chosen by President Carter to be DCI when Carter's first choice, Theodore Sorensen, ran into opposition, Turner served from March 1977 to January 1981. In his book *Secrecy and Democracy: The CIA in Transition* (Boston: Houghton Mifflin, 1985) he provides an interesting analysis of the CIA's problems and is forthright in his attack on the obvious excesses of the agency prior to Colby's tenure as director. The book is not a balanced assessment, however, for from the moment he introduces Angleton (when James Schlesinger, DCI for five months in 1973, tells Turner he suspects Angleton still has an office at Langley), he is intensely suspicious. Though he must have known the facts, he attributes Nosenko's hostile interrogation entirely to Angleton, and he asserts a variety of positions—such as his contention that the sudden reduction of the espionage staff by 820 positions did no damage to national security—without offering evidence or argument to support his view. He appears to believe that a CE capacity is not needed because SIGINT has replaced HUMINT, incidentally removing the many risks of human error that arise from HUMINT; he then redefines disinformation to suit his own needs and concludes that the only CE requirements the United States has are to deal with domestic spying. Since the FBI handles the home front, CE has no role to play. Though one may commend Turner's ethical stands, the argument is simplistic and a bit slippery. He recommends that the espionage and analytic branches should be merged in order to make CE a team player. This sounds a good idea if one believes that intelligence is still a game, great or otherwise, but it flies in the face of the rudimentary methodology of compartmentalization. The need is less to make CE play for the team than to find a way to see to it that a necessarily somewhat independent operation does not try to steal a base out of a misplaced sense that the coach doesn't know what to do. On Nosenko, see pp. 416–21.

62. On Shadrin see Henry Hurt, *Shadrin: The Spy Who Never Came Back* (New York: McGraw Hill, 1981); Donald R. Morris, "The Spy Who Went Out into the Cold and Never Returned," Houston *Post,* Dec. 27, 1981; and Ernest Volkman, "The Search for Sasha," *Family Weekly,* Oct. 9, 1983, pp. 1–5. Volkman writes of "the Mole Wars" in *Warriors of the Night: Spies, Soldiers, and American Intelligence* (New York: William Morrow, 1985), pp. 167–228. In 1985 a Soviet defector, Vitaly S. Yurchenko, is said to have confirmed that Shadrin was killed by the KGB (*Time,* Nov. 18, 1985, p. 36). Angleton considers Volkman's work very seriously flawed. See also *Accuracy in Media,* XII (Oct. 8, 1983), 20.

The basic developments relating to Golitsin and Nosenko are admirably summarized in Jeffrey Richelson, *The U. S. Intelligence Community* (Cambridge, Mass.: Ballinger, 1985), pp. 221–24. The case against Angleton for the harsh treatment of Nosenko is made most strongly by Turner in *Secrecy and Democracy,* pp. 43–47, but it is also wrong. To set against the indictment of Turner and others, Angleton's defenders often cite William R. Corson and Robert T. Crowley, *The New KGB: Engine of Soviet Power* (New York: William Morrow, 1985), which they have called "the proof of the need for Angleton's methodology." An updated edition appeared in 1986. The best pro-Angleton statement is by Edward Jay Epstein, "Who Killed the CIA? The Confessions of Stansfield Turner," *Commentary* LXXX (Oct., 1985), 53–57. The most interesting books are Anatoliy Golitsin, *New Lies for Old: The Communist Strategy of Deception and Disinformation* (New York: Dodd, Mead, 1984), which does not mention Angleton and is believed by some to have been, at least in part, ghost-written by him (Angleton emphatically denies this and says it is a disservice to Golitsin, though he did prepare a strangely supportive press release on it); John Sawatsky, *For Services Rendered: Leslie James Bennett and the RCMP Security Services* (Toronto: Doubleday, 1982), pp. 204–19; Peter Worthington, *Looking for Trouble: A Journalist's Life, and Then Some* (Toronto: Key Porter, 1984), pp. 278–83, 297, 385–86; Martin, pp. 93–212; and Corson, *Armies of Ignorance.* There are endorsements of Angleton's position in William Stevenson, *Intrepid's Last Case* (New York: Villard, 1983), and Richard Deacon (Donald McCormick), *"C": A Biography of Sir Maurice Oldfield* [the head of MI6] (London: Macdonald, 1985), both taking the view that "no case is ever dead" even when we are. Possible ties to the Kennedy assassination are explored in Edward Jay Epstein, *Legend: The Secret World of Lee Harvey Oswald* (New York: McGraw Hill, 1978), especially pp. 257–74.

63. The idea of the notional mole is put forward best (though not well) by Ron Rosenbaum in "The Shadow of the Mole," *Harper's,* CCLXVII (Oct. 7, 1983), 45–60.

64. *The Collected Poems of Stephen Crane* (New York: Knopf, 1930), p. 61.

65. Felix, *Spy and His Masters,* p. 129.

66. *Ibid.,* p. 132. Felix (McCargar) is still regarded as the best book on coun-terintelligence. Oresto Pinto's *Spy-Catcher* (New York: Harper and Brothers, 1952) was once thought to be a useful, if somewhat romantic, primer on the methodology, and Pinto's list of the ten essential attributes of an agent is inter-esting, but the publication of subsequent books has made Pinto seem less and less reliable.

One of Angleton's deputies, William Hood, who left the Central Intelligence Agency at the time of the "purge"—but who was already planning to retire and was not, in fact, fired with Angleton's other deputies—has provided a model examination of methodology, and of tradecraft, in his book on the activities of Lieutenant Colonel Pyotr Popov, a Soviet military intelligence (or GRU) officer who began in Vienna as a walk-in and worked as a penetration agent-in-place until his arrest by the KGB in 1958. This book, *Mole* (New York: W. W. Nor-ton, 1982), may be the best account we have of field methodology, though it is written in the manner of spy fiction, and thus its contribution to the explanation (and justification) of that methodology has not been fully recognized. Most re-cently Hood has written a novel that follows upon a similar case: *Spy Wednes-day* (New York: W. W. Norton, 1986). Much less good, though useful, is Francis J. McNamara, *U.S. Counterintelligence Today* (Washington: The Nathan Hale Institute, 1985).

67. See Loch K. Johnson, "Decision Costs in the Intelligence Cycle," in Alfred C. Maurer, Marion D. Tunstall, and James M. Keagle, eds., *Intelligence: Policy and Process* (Boulder, Colo.: Westview Press, 1985), pp. 181–98; James D. Aus-tin, "The Psychological Dimension of Intelligence Activities," in *ibid.,* pp. 199–219; and Newton S. Miler, discussant, in Roy Godson, ed., *Intelligence Require-ments for the 1980s: Counterintelligence* (Washington: National Strategy Infor-mation Center, 1980), pp. 40–44.

68. See Frank J. Donner, *The Age of Surveillance: The Aims and Methods of America's Political Intelligence System* (New York: Vintage Books, 1981); David Wise, *The American Police State: The Government Against the People* (New York: Random House, 1976); Athan G. Theoharis, ed., *The Truman Presidency: The Origins of the Imperial Presidency and the National Security State* (Stan-fordville, N.Y.: Coleman, 1979), pp. 238–42; James Bamford, *The Puzzle Pal-ace: A Report on America's Most Secret Agency* (Boston: Houghton Mifflin, 1982); and Richard E. Morgan, *Domestic Intelligence: Monitoring Dissent in America* (Austin: University of Texas Press, 1980).

69. Virtually no one attempts to defend Operation Chaos or HT/LINGUAL, the mail opening operation, for little defense can be made. Here the CIA, or elements within it, were clearly working illegally and unethically, far beyond any bounds of responsibility, even if not precisely as the rogue elephant Senator Church later charged. About the only weak defense that can be made is that there was a consensus in both houses of Congress to perhaps as late as 1968 that the country had to meet an imminent danger from "monolithic Communism lurking globally" so that large defense budgets were hardly scrutinized and intelligence operations were left without congressional oversight.

70. U. S. Senate, Select Committee to Study Governmental Operations with Respect to Intelligence Activities, 94th Congress, 21st Session, Report: *Intelli-*

gence Activities and the Rights of Americans (Washington: GPO, 1976), pp. 99–100, 107–108, 386–87.

71. Quoted in Powers, *Man Who Kept the Secrets,* p. 343, n. 61. This fascinating and well-written volume requires both reading and shopping in: it is the closest book on the subject to demanding its own intelligence analysis that I have seen, for it is full of useful and generally documented information. The CIA clearly does not know quite what to make of it, as shown by three thoughtful reviews by John Bross, Donald Gregg, and Walter L. Pforzheimer in the agency's in-house journal, *Studies in Intelligence,* XXIV (Spring, 1980), 69–88. If someone were to read a single book on the CIA from 1960 to 1975, it should be this book. The Gibbonesque footnotes contain half the pleasure and a good bit of the story.

72. Judith F. Buncher, ed., *The CIA and the Security Debate: 1971–1975* (New York: Facts on File, 1976), pp. 11–12, 85–91; Ray S. Cline, *The CIA under Reagan, Bush and Casey* (Washington: Acropolis Books, 1981), p. 244 [this reference is not in the first edition, *Secrets, Spies, and Scholars*].

73. *The New York Times,* Dec. 22, 24, 31, 1974; Nov. 28, 1985; *Newsweek,* LXXXV (Jan. 6, 1975), 10–13, and LXXXXIII (March 5, 1979), 43; *Time,* CV (Jan. 6), 45, (Feb. 24, both 1975), 18–19 [this last by Charles J. V. Murphy]; Seymour M. Hersh, "The Angleton Story," *The New York Times Biographical Service,* IX (June, 1978), 688–94; *Christian Science Monitor,* Apr. 9, 1975.

74. Freemantle, *CIA,* p. 129.

75. Fain, ed., *Intelligence Community,* p. 388. Papich says that the Riha case was "a very minute element" in the break, despite testimony before the Church committee. Angleton got along rather well with Hoover himself, but there is no doubt about the long-standing hostility between the FBI and the CIA, especially after Dulles's retirement, and there is an important book to be written on the role of the FBI liaison figures, and in particular Deke DeLoach (whose views on the CIA were largely negative) and Papich (who worked with Angleton to achieve both cooperation and a warmer feeling). Though Papich retired in 1970, he was a consultant in the intelligence community until January 1973. For the little that has come into the open, see Robert J. Lamphere and Tom Schachtman, *The FBI-KGB War: A Special Agent's Story* (New York: Random House, 1986).

76. Freemantle, pp. 32–34.

77. Some reviewers profess to see Angleton's hand, as well as his mind, behind various recent publications, mostly notably Golitsin's book. Maybe. He did like to help people tinker with their manuscripts, and after retirement he would recall several such instances, many pre-CIA to be sure, such as the time when he met James Agee in Greenwich Village one night, probably in 1939 when down from Yale, and went over the manuscript of Agee's *Let Us Now Praise Famous Men.* Certainly the book should have had much in it to appeal to the young Angleton: it virtually began with a quotation known to all, "Workers of the world, unite and fight. You have nothing to lose but your chains, and a world to win," which was then glossed, "These words are quoted here to mislead those who will be misled by them. They mean, not what the reader may care to think they mean, but what they say." See Agee and Walker Evans, *Let Us Now Praise Famous Men: Three Tenant Families* (Boston: Houghton Mifflin, 1960), p. xix.

78. *Situation Report,* IV (Jan., 1984), 1–7, compares Grenada and the Bay of

Pigs as "two classic examples of a President in the role of Commander-in-Chief in a Cold War situation," much to President Reagan's favor.

79. Two examples are "The Spy War," *The New York Times Magazine* (Nov. 28, 1980), pp. 34–37, 102–108, and "When the CIA Was Almost Wrecked," *Parade Magazine* (Oct. 14, 1984), pp. 8, 11.

It seems a fair inference that Epstein, who had built a reputation on exploring conspiracy theories, especially on the assassination of John F. Kennedy, did receive information from Angleton for a time and was a conduit for expressing Angleton's views on certain matters (see, for example, Epstein's correction of *Newsweek*'s rather sloppy statement that Angleton had imprisoned Nosenko, an article that appeared on November 18, 1985, and was corrected by Epstein on December 23). But Angleton must have felt Epstein had been a bit unwise in some of his writing, and whatever Angleton may have felt about the bona fides of Arkady N. Shevchenko, he may not have been entirely pleased with Epstein's handling of Shevchenko's book.

Shevchenko was an under-secretary at the United Nations in New York and a Soviet diplomat with the rank of ambassador. In April 1978 he defected, and early in 1985 Knopf published his memoirs, *Breaking with Moscow*, extensive excerpts having appeared in *Time* magazine on February 11 and 18. The book was generally well received as a unique examination of the power that Communist party leadership played in the Soviet Union, and it downgraded the alleged all-powerful role of the KGB. On July 15, Epstein assaulted the book in *The New Republic*, declaring it to be "for all effective purposes a work of fiction." To support this view he cited several errors, some quite minor but others potentially damaging, and by using the intelligence analyst's (or the historian's) creation of a chronology showed that certain events could not have taken place in the sequence described, if at all. When Epstein was in turn attacked by Peter Reddaway in the *Times Literary Supplement* of London (August 30), Epstein responded (September 27) with a rebuttal based on a "chron." It also became known that the manuscript published by Knopf had been submitted to another publisher earlier and that material which Shevchenko claimed to have been reporting to the CIA for two and a half years before his defection had not appeared in that version. Epstein, and no doubt others, concluded that Shevchenko's book was another disinformation plot, perhaps to turn the focus of American intelligence research from the KGB to the party *apparat*.

This series of interchanges was all too typical of what happens whenever a defector (or presumed defector) speaks out (or appears to speak out) in print—discussions of defectors always involve many parentheses. Obviously someone had let the English press know of Epstein's attack even before it reached the pages of *The New Republic*, since reference to it appeared in the *TLS* on July 12. Clearly Shevchenko (or someone) had altered his manuscript. Apparently he had not told the complete truth. The principle of parsimony would suggest that most of Shevchenko's errors arose from faulty memory, from hurrying to get a book into press, and—as perhaps the alterations did as well—from wanting to tell a better story, or from feeling safe enough to confess of the more heinous crime of spying against his country rather than merely defecting from it, or because he was given a good ghost writer. Epstein's attack was shown to be wrong in a number of particulars, and he responded in *The New Republic* on August

26, accepting that Shevchenko "had contacts with American intelligence before his defection" but not backing away from his basic charge that the book was a hoax.

80. For a balanced view on the Church committee, see Loch K. Johnson, *A Season of Inquiry: The Senate Intelligence Investigation* (Lexington, Ky.: University Press of Kentucky, 1985).

81. Perhaps the most interesting analysis of the Deep Throat question appears in Jim Hougan, *Secret Agenda: Watergate, Deep Throat and the CIA* (New York: Random House, 1984), pp. 280–301: interesting because Hougan goes through the evidence supplied by Bob Woodward (who with Carl Bernstein wrote *All the President's Men,* on Watergate, in 1974) as to the identity of Deep Throat. Hougan suggests that Woodward, Yale '65, was pointing to a Yale man, a spook, whom he had come to know during his own time in Naval Intelligence. Maybe. Hougan also discusses at length (pp. 315–20) the career of John Paisley, who worked with the Watergate Plumbers through the Office of Security of the CIA. Paisley was involved in the Shadrin affair and in Nosenko's debriefing according to Hougan, and he says that Paisley was close to Angleton. (Angleton denies knowing him at all. Hougan believes he was probably telling the truth. Richard Deacon [Donald McCormick] says in *Within My Little Eye: The Memoirs of a Spy-Hunter* [London: Frederick Muller, 1982], p. 205, that Paisley was a close confidant of Angleton, but Deacon has been known to be wrong.) In September 1978, Paisley disappeared from his sloop on Chesapeake Bay and was found several days later floating in the bay. His death was ruled a suicide. To have committed suicide he would have had to jump off his boat with his gun in his hand, having first strapped on two sets of diving belts to weight his body, and then shot himself in the water. It is possible, of course. Hougan does not suggest what any of this might have to do with Angleton; presumably nothing.

Though Angleton was mortally ill in early 1987, he cannot have missed the report issued by the House Intelligence Committee on February 4, which, after eighteen months of inquiry, concluded that "Senior managers of U.S. intelligence agencies have downplayed the seriousness of counterintelligence and security failures and have not taken adequate measures to correct deficiencies." See *The New York Times,* Feb. 5, April 8, 10, 1987.

82. See Phillips, *Night Watch,* pp. 307–08, 339–41; Deacon, *My Little Eye,* p. 197; and *New York Post,* Oct. 21, 1985, on the need for "a new James Angleton." A typical response, in the context of the revolving-door defection of Vitaly Yurchenko in 1985, is that of columnist William Safire in *The New York Times,* Nov. 7, except that he is obliquely specific with respect to Angleton: "No wonder so many of us suspect that Mount Alto moles burrow where orchids used to grow."

83. The case is that of Edward L. Howard who fled from Santa Fe, New Mexico, in September 1985.

84. Raymond Palmer, *The Making of a Spy* (London: Aldus Books, 1977), p. 122. Palmer may not know, however: he misdates Angleton's resignation by a year.

85. Philip Frazer, "Dirty Tricks Down Under," *Mother Jones,* IX (Mar., 1984), 13–20, 44–45, 52. The oddness is in the contents, not in the fact of speculation, for Angleton had played a key role in the creation of the Australian Security

Intelligence Organisation (ASIO), as its former director-general, Brigadier C. C. Spry, acknowledged. Angleton was, after Dulles, the number two "honorary Australian" so far as ASIO was concerned, at least in 1969. See Jeffrey T. Richelson and Desmond Ball, *The Ties that Bind* (Boston: Allen & Unwin, 1985), pp. 163–64.

86. In his youth James Angleton had encouraged the poet Marya Zaturenska to publish in *Furioso*. When she released her *Selected Poems* in 1954 (New York: Grove Press), one might have appealed to him above all others, "The Listening Landscape" (pp. 67–68):

Hide no secrets now, for all,
All must be revealed and told
As the bells of judgment call
Melancholy, stern and cold.
Hearing them the Children wake,
At the sound Love's eyes grow dark,
In each flower a sleeping snake
And the Arrows pierce the mark.
All, all shall learn the secret hid
In your secluded rooms, shall know
The name, the hour, and what you did.

87. I wish to thank Richard Bissell, Kingman Brewster, Jr., Carl Burke, George Carver, Osborne Day, Anita Forrer, Charles Gage, Cordelia Hood, Thomas Hughes, William R. Johnson, the late Sherman Kent, Delaney Kiphuth, Mary McCarthy, Samuel J. Papich, John Waldron, and those named elsewhere in notes throughout this chapter for providing me with general information and insights into Angleton and the various operations touched upon here. Five individuals with whom I spoke were most reluctant to be identified here, and I wish to thank them collectively as well.

There are, of course, any number of "Angleton stories" not told here, in part because many are not open to even the most rudimentary verification, in part because some are not relevant.

88. My comments here concerning Clare Petty are taken directly from David C. Martin's book or from James Angleton. Mr. Petty protests these views and states categorically that he did not denounce any superior at any level in Germany or elsewhere prior to his assignment to the CI staff and that he disagrees with other statements here as drawn from these sources.

A Partial List of Yale Graduates in X-2

Personnel in the OSS were reassigned, loaned between branches, or simply not recorded as to educational background, so that any list will fall well short of an accurate count. However, the following list provides a partial count. I have talked or corresponded with the majority of them, and the work of twelve is treated in some measure in this book. Six are deceased. I have found material in the records on all but one.

Angleton, James J. '41
Blum, Paul '21
Buhler, Conrad W. '36

Curtiss, Joseph T. '23
Cutler, Richard W. '38
Davis, Curtis Carroll '38
Ellmann, Richard D. '39
Gray, Gordon '33 Law
Hylan, William H. '37
Johnson, Owen D. '40
Miller, John K. '28
Moore, Dan T. '31
Paige, Jason, Jr. '32
Pearson, Norman Holmes '32
Russell, John S. '41 Law
Russo, Col. Harold J. '24
Sawyer, Charles H. '29
Seiferheld, David F. '26
Tenney, Calvin '32
Wainwright, Stuyvesant, II '47 Law
Waith, Eugene '35
Welles, Charles B. '24
Wheeler, William M., Jr. '35

CHAPTER SEVEN   The Alumni: Returning to the Campus

1. James Agee and Walker Evans, *Let Us Now Praise Famous Men: Three Tenant Families* (Boston: Houghton Mifflin, 1960), p. 458.

2. One football star who went into intelligence work was George S. Seabury. See his picture in Thomas G. Bergin, *The Game: The Harvard-Yale Football Rivalry, 1875–1983* (New Haven: Yale University Press, 1984), p. 178. I wish to thank George Seabury for writing of his work to me, and Frank Ryan, director of athletics at Yale University, for searching the Yale athletic records on Seabury and Skip Walz (see Chapter One).

3. I wish to thank Richard Bissell for talking with me at some length about his work in intelligence, and especially the U-2 project, in which he was intimately involved. I also wish to thank a number of former members of the OSS and the CIA, mentioned elsewhere in earlier chapters, who discussed Bissell and Barnes with me, as did several of their classmates. In the end I decided not to use this material in the present book, since most of that concerning Bissell (and Barnes's participation in the overthrow of Jacobo Arbenz in Guatemala and the preparation for the Bay of Pigs) falls largely outside my time frame. I should have liked to have told the story of Barnes, assistant to Allen Dulles in Switzerland, as a fresh approach to the Sunrise surrender, and through this to have related the remarkable stories of two women, Anita Forrer and Mary Bancroft, as both have been most helpful to me on this and other points; and also because I knew Barnes when, after his resignation from the CIA, he became assistant to the president of Yale University. However, Barnes proves unusually elusive, and to date I have not been able to learn enough to answer the questions I wish to put. Since I think it most helpful to discuss Richard Bissell and Tracy Barnes together, I will hope to write of them at another time. I should, however, none-theless like to thank those who volunteered their time to help me: in addition to those mentioned above, the former Janet Barnes, Cordelia Hood, Paul Mellon, Fritz Molden of Alpbach, Austria, Howard Roman, Mary Jane Taft (Mrs. Ban-croft's daughter and widow of the former dean of Yale College, Horace Taft), G. Harold Welch, and the staff of the Columbia University Oral History Ar-chive.

To tell the story of Richard Bissell, in particular, is to tell the story, at least in part, of both the U-2 project and of the Bay of Pigs. On the former there is a very strong book, which appeared while my own study was in progress: Michael R. Beschloss, *Mayday: Eisenhower, Khrushchev and the U-2 Affair* (New York: Harper & Row, 1986). The fullest account of the Cuban intervention is by Peter Wyden, *Bay of Pigs: The Untold Story* (New York: Simon and Schuster, 1979). The most balanced account, in my view, is by John Ranelagh in *The Agency: The Rise and Decline of the CIA* (New York: Simon and Schuster, 1986), pp. 349–82. The elusive Barnes shows up most fully, though quite insufficiently, in Stephen Schlesinger and Stephen Kinzer, *Bitter Fruit: The Untold Story of the American Coup in Guatemala* (Garden City, N.Y.: Doubleday, 1983) and (very briefly) in Allen Dulles, *The Secret Surrender* (New York: Harper & Row, 1966).

4. Another essay that cannot be written at this time is the story of George Carver. I wish to thank him and his wife, Ruth, however, for providing invalu-able assistance and encouragement throughout this project. Carver has written a good bit himself since his retirement from the CIA, and he appears in several of the standard works on the agency or on Vietnam. A line from his 1952 book (which was his 1950 undergraduate prize essay in philosophy) *Aesthetics and the Problem of Meaning: The Application to Aesthetics of the Logical Positivists' Verifiability Criterion of Cognitive Meaning* (New Haven: Yale University Press), p. 5, n. 10, must not go unheard here, given the conclusion toward which this chapter is moving: "Once we have a satisfactory definition of truth the definition of falsity is simple."

5. I wish to thank three members of the class of 1943 in particular for encour-aging this book at an early stage and for helping to put me into contact with other members of the class. In the end a sufficient number of class members chose not to be quoted for attribution to lead me to postpone writing a separate treatment of the class, but the help of J. Foster Collins, Osborne Day, and Cam-eron LaClair was nonetheless of the greatest value. None of the quotations in this paragraph are to be attributed to any of these men.

6. I thank Cord Meyer, Jr., for meeting with me and providing encouragement and contacts for this study. He gave me permission to consult his school and college records. I wish also to thank Virginia S. Deane of St. Paul's School for her search of the records and Richard Shank of Yale University for making the college record available after receiving Mr. Meyer's approval. The best source on Meyer is his substantial memoir, *Facing Reality: From World Federalism to the CIA* (New York: Harper & Row, 1980). This is a remarkably thoughtful inquiry into the way one man of the liberal persuasion dealt with the cold war. See also Roy Godson, ed., *Intelligence Requirements for the 1980s: Clandestine Collection* (New Brunswick, N.J.: Transaction Books, 1982), pp. 199–219, which reprints a portion of *Facing Reality*.

7. Reprinted in Abraham H. Lass and Norma L. Tasman, eds., *"The Secret*

Sharer" and Other Great Stories (New York: New American Library, 1969), pp. 11–30.

8. Thomas Powers, *The Man Who Kept the Secrets: Richard Helms & the CIA* (New York: Knopf, 1979), pp. 61–63, 256, 285.

9. See William McCormick, *Special Boat Squadron* (London: William Kimber, 1985).

10. I wish to thank Edward O. Welles for sharing his experiences with me.

11. See Rhodri Jeffreys-Jones, "The Socio-Educational Composition of the CIA Elite: A Statistical Note," *Journal of American Studies*, XIX (3/1985), 421–24. I am grateful to Mr. Jeffreys-Jones for showing his article to me prior to publication.

12. We may never know, of course, but I tend to be persuaded by Nathaniel Davis, *The Last Two Years of Salvador Allende* (Ithaca: Cornell University Press, 1985).

13. Henry Kissinger, *White House Years* (Boston: Little, Brown, 1979), p. 306.

14. Sherman Kent Papers, Yale University Library, box 34: Kent to Betty Bredin, Feb. 28, 1951, and to _____, Dec. 12, 1950. Though cited in previous chapters, the Kent Papers require some description here. They are Manuscript Group 854, and they consist of 39 large boxes of materials. Donated to the university in a series of gifts beginning in 1949, the boxes are arranged in order of accession; a preliminary inventory was prepared in June 1983, when the bulk of the papers were opened to research. Kent closed boxes 16 through 38 to research indefinitely, with certain minor exceptions. These boxes contain his manuscript autobiography, which is extensive, readable, and frank—I hope to edit it for publication; papers from his years of work with the OSS and the CIA; some confidential departmental correspondence from Yale; and family financial records. Dr. Kent permitted me access to this restricted material under certain conditions: that no one else was to be given access in his lifetime, and I would not make notes or copies of material available to anyone at any time; that citations to documents would be sufficiently incomplete as to make certain that, after his death, references to his papers by other researchers would, if properly exact, show that they had in fact seen the document in question and not taken their citation from a printed source; and that if, by remote chance, I encountered any document in the files that was not declassified, I would inform him and make no use of it. On this last point Dr. Kent need not have worried: while the material is rich in documents originally stamped with classifications, all except a single photograph had been declassified. This I returned to him. Some sensitive documents given in 1969 have written across them Dr. Kent's personal classification: "not to be quoted until 1980" or some other date, and I have honored these restrictions as well.

15. *Ibid.,* box 31: Henry Roberts to Kent, Dec. 12, 1944; box 34: Egbert Kent to Sherman Kent, Nov. 3, 1953; box 27: Nov. 4, 1942.

16. Kent, *The Election of 1827 in France* (Cambridge, Mass.: Harvard University Press, 1975). The acknowledgments give special thanks to Donald McKay, his wartime OSS colleague. He also wrote "Elector Lists of France's July Monarchy, 1830–1848," *French Historical Studies*, VII (Spring, 1971), 117–27. The research notes to the book are in the Kent Papers.

17. Kent Papers, box 34: Abbott Smith to Kent, Nov. 23, 1975; and Kent to Thomas D. Beck, Feb. 16, 1976.

18. Stewart Alsop and Thomas Braden, *Sub Rosa: The OSS and American Espionage* (New York: Harcourt, Brace and World, 1964), pp. 249–50.

19. Published by the Princeton University Press in 1949. The book almost did not get published, for most academic presses thought the subject of intelligence was not serious enough: as late as 1958 William H. Dunham recommended to the Harvard University Press that it not publish a general study of how intelligence worked because it was not a scholar's subject. Kent had written the book while at the National War College, and he hoped to use it to reenter the field of professional intelligence, so it was important that it be published with dignity and by a highly regarded press. He was still on the faculty at Yale when he submitted the book, however, and he did not think it appropriate that it should go to his own university's press. Nor did he want to run the risk of being scooped, so he could not hawk the manuscript around in multiple copies to a number of publishers. This took delicate negotiations. The manuscript was rejected once, perhaps twice, and then an astute director of the Princeton University Press, Datus Smith, agreed to publish it. The book was handsomely produced, well received, and widely reviewed. (I wish to thank Datus Smith for providing the background on publication.)

20. Examples include Allen Dulles, *The Craft of Intelligence* (New York: Harper & Row, 1963), p. 266, which calls Kent's book one of the three major books on intelligence; Harry Howe Ransom, *Central Intelligence and National Security* (Cambridge, Mass.: Harvard University Press, 1958), and *The Intelligence Establishment* (Cambridge, Mass.: Harvard University Press, 1970); Roger Hilsman, *Strategic Intelligence and National Decisions* (Glencoe, Ill.: The Free Press, 1956); Harold L. Wilensky, *Organizational Intelligence: Knowledge and Policy in Government and Industry* (New York: Basic Books, 1967); Walter Laqueur, *A World of Secrets: The Uses and Limits of Intelligence* (New York: Basic Books, 1985); Jacques Bergier, *L'espionnage scientifique* (Paris: Hachette, 1971); Albrecht Charisius and Julius Mader, *Nich Länger Geheim* (Berlin: Deutscher Militärverlag, 1969); Alexander Orlov, *Handbook of Intelligence and Guerrilla Warfare* (Ann Arbor: University of Michigan Press, 1963); and Arthur Macy Cox, *The Myths of National Security: The Peril of Secret Government* (Boston: Beacon Press, 1975), which is more hostile. For a predictably negative view of R&A, ONE, and the connection between intelligence and academe in the United States see Nikolai Yakovlev, *CIA Target—the USSR* (Moscow: Progress Publishers, 1982), pp. 112–39.

21. Kendall, "The Function of Intelligence," *World Politics,* I (July, 1949), 540–52.

22. Kent Papers, box 18: CIA, Citation file, Feb. 2, 1967.

23. RG 226, OSS, entry 37, box 5: Kent, draft, to ———, n.d. [1945].

24. Stewart Alsop, *The Center: People and Power in Political Washington* (New York: Harper & Row, 1968), pp. 237–39, 243–44.

25. Kent, *Strategic Intelligence,* p. 199.

26. Kent, *Writing History* (New York: Appleton-Century-Crofts, 1941), p. 7.

27. Lyman B. Kirkpatrick, Jr., *The U. S. Intelligence Community: Foreign Policy and Domestic Activities* (New York: Hill and Wang, 1973), p. 110.

28. *The Washington Post,* Mar., 14, and *The New York Times,* Mar. 15, 1986.

29. Kent, *Buffalo Blocks: For the Puzzled High Powered Executive* (Kentfield, Calif.: privately printed, 1970).

30. See Heinz Höhne and Hermann Zolling, *Network: The Truth about General Gehlen and His Spy Ring* (London: Secker & Warburg, 1972), pp. 58–66, 133; Reinhard Gehlen, *Der Dienst: Erinnerungen, 1942–1971* (Mainz: Hase & Koehler, 1971); Gehlen, *The Service: The Memoirs of General Reinhard Gehlen* (New York: World, 1972), a translation of *Der Dienst* with an introduction by George Bailey added; E. H. Cookridge (Edward Spiro), *Gehlen: Spy of the Century* (London: Hodder and Stoughton, 1971), pp. 126–28; and Louis Hagen, *The Secret War for Europe: A Dossier of Espionage* (London: Macdonald, 1968), pp. 35–39.

31. On Arnhem and the Battle of the Bulge, see Lyman B. Kirkpatrick, *Captains without Eyes: Intelligence Failures in World War II* (London: Macmillan, 1960). On the Cuban missile estimate see Kent's essay, "A Crucial Estimate Relived," *Studies in Intelligence* (Sept., 1969), pp. 1–18.

32. Kent Papers, box 18: aide memoire of Mar. 2, 1963, with the Cuban map and briefing notes; Vernon A. Walters, *Silent Missions* (Garden City, N.Y.: Doubleday, 1978), p. 503; David Detzer, *The Brink: Cuban Missile Crisis, 1962* (New York: Crowell, 1979), pp. 174–76. In *The Last of the Giants* (New York: Macmillan, 1970), p. 930, C. L. Sulzberger says Acheson saw de Gaulle alone, but the records show otherwise.

33. Kent Papers, box 18: notes on summit meeting of May 4–16, 1960.

34. *Ibid.*: Kent to Colonel C. B. Hansen, Oct. 15, 1951.

35. See Kent's manuscript autobiography, in the Kent Papers. Consult also *The New York Times,* Sept. 23, 26, 28, Oct. 1, 5, 1951; New Haven *Register,* Oct. 5, 1951; *Yale Daily News,* Oct. 5, 6, 1951; and Robert H. Ferrell, ed., *Off the Record: The Private Papers of Harry S Truman* (New York: Harper & Row, 1980), pp. 218–19: Truman to Krock, not sent. I wish to thank the late Sherman Kent, Basil Duke Henning, and Thomas C. Mendenhall for discussing the Yale Report with me. No copy appears to have survived, certainly not in the Kent, Dunham, Foord, or Bellinger papers. On the context of Executive Order 10290 see Donald R. McCoy, *The Presidency of Harry S. Truman* (Lawrence, Kans.: University Press of Kansas, 1984), p. 276.

36. See Robert Welch, *The New Americanism: And Other Speeches and Essays* (Boston: Western Islands, 1966), pp. 23, 203.

37. *Strategic Intelligence* was reissued by Archon Books, Hamden, Conn., and bears the date 1965, but copies were not in fact available until January 1966.

38. Kent to Kip, Feb. 18, 1966, and Mar. 17, 1967. I wish to thank Mrs. Throop M. Wilder, Jr., for supplying me with Kent's letters to Kip. These will be placed in the Kent Papers in the Yale University Library.

39. Orlov (Ann Arbor), pp. 8–9; Kent, pp. vii n., xi–xix.

BIBLIOGRAPHY

MANUSCRIPT COLLECTIONS

By far the most important manuscripts for this book were at the National Archives and in the Yale University libraries. The massive collection of official papers of the Office of Strategic Services, a veritable mudslide that moves forward steadily each year as additional volumes are declassified, is one of the most extensive and valuable bodies of documentation to become available to the historian in the last decade and by far the largest collection in the world on wartime intelligence work. John E. Taylor, who presides over the controlled avalanche of materials, is an indispensable guide to them. Of particular value for this study were the War Diaries, and a range of volumes in entries 1, 37, 99, 106, 110, 134, 147, and 176. All are in Record Group (RG) 226. Also useful were files of the

Adjutant General's Office (R.G. 94) and of the Director of Intelligence Services, Army Air Forces (R.G. 332), on G-2, held at the National Archives Records Center, Suitland, Maryland, and declassified more recently.

At Yale, the most valuable papers are the extensive collections of Norman Holmes Pearson (in the Beinecke Library) and of Sherman Kent (in the Sterling Memorial Library). The extent and organization of these collections are described in the notes to chapters 5 and 7. Other primary sources at Yale include:

Yale University Archives, Sterling Memorial Library; the papers of:

Bemis, Samuel Flagg

Berkeley College Alumni Notes

Berkeley College Scrapbooks

Buck, Polly

Calhoun College, 1939–45

Crosby, Sumner McKnight

Curtis, Lewis Perry, Family

DeVane, William C.

Dunham, William Huse

Foord, Archibald

French, Robert Dudley

Gabriel, Ralph Henry

Griswold, A. Whitney

Hemingway, Samuel B.

Henning, Basil Duke

Hovland, Carl

Institute of International Studies

Kennedy, Raymond

Kent, Tyler Gatewood

Kerrick, David B.

Kitchelt, Florence L. C.

Knollenberg, Bernard

Kone, Eugene

Lane, Arthur Bliss

Mendell, Clarence

Notestein, Wallace

Parsons, Charles

Pierson, George Wilson

Registered Students, Lists of

Secretary, Office of the, World War II Records

Seymour, Charles

Seymour, Charles, Presidential Papers

Sinai, Nathan

Sizer, Theodore

Spykman, Nicholas J.

Sussman, Harvey

University Librarian

University Publications: '41, Freshman Weekly, Furioso, Yale Literary Magazine, Vif

Watkins, Samuel C. G.

Witherspoon, Alexander

World War II Collection

Yale-China Association

Yale Daily News, 1937–1961

Yale in World War II

Elsewhere at Yale:

In the Beinecke Library, the Papers of Bryher and of James Osborn

In the Sterling Memorial Library stacks, the Human Relations Area Files and the personal files of Charles R. Walker

In storage in Davenport, Pierson, Saybrook, and Silliman colleges, the 1939–1945 records of those colleges

In the Berkeley College Master's Office, college memorabilia files

Yale Club, New York City, memorabilia

Other collections consulted include:

Carlisle Barracks, Carlisle, Penn., U.S. Army Military History Institute
    Donovan, William J., Papers

Case Western Reserve University, Cleveland, Ohio
    Shera, Jesse, Papers

College Football Hall of Fame, King's Island, Ohio
    Huntington, Ellery, Exhibit
Colorado Historical Society, Denver
    Rogers, James Grafton, Papers
Colorado, University of, Boulder
    Ninth Writers' Conference, Records
    Reynolds, George Fullmer, Collection
Columbia University, Butler Library, New York City
    Hays, Carlton J. H., Papers
    Matson, Harold, Papers
    Oral History Archive: Bancroft, Mary, typescript
Churchill College, Cambridge
    Hyde, Harford Montgomery, Papers
Dartmouth College Library, Hanover, N.H.
    Ford, Corey, Papers
Duke University Library, Durham, N.C.
    Hoover, Calvin, Papers
Harvard University, Cambridge, Mass.
    Brinton, Crane, Papers
    Langer, William L., Papers
Illinois, University of, Urbana
    American Library Association, Records
    Joint Committee on Foreign Importation, Records
Institute of Paper Chemistry, Appleton, Wis.
    Institute of Paper Chemistry, OSS Records
King's College, London, Liddell Hart Centre for Military Archives
    Myers, Edmund Charles Wolf, Papers
    Woodhouse, C. M., Papers
Lawrence University, Appleton, Wis.
    Institute of Paper Chemistry, Records
Library of Congress, Washington, D.C.
    Alsop, Joseph and Stewart, Papers
National Park System Advisory Board, Washington, D.C.
    Tangier Legation National Historic Landmark nomination records
Near East Foundation, New York City
    Dockets and Minutes of the Board of Directors' Meetings
    General Files
New Haven Colony Historical Society, New Haven, Conn.
    Seymour, George Dudley, Collection
Old Fort Museum, Fort Smith, Ark.
    Darby's Rangers, Scrapbook and memorabilia
Princeton University Library, Princeton, N.J.
    Dulles, Allen W., Papers
Roosevelt, Franklin D., Library, Hyde Park, N.Y.
    Shepardson, Whitney Hart, Papers
Virginia Historical Society, Richmond
    Bruce, David, Papers
Walpole Library, Farmington, Conn.
    Lewis, Wilmarth, Papers

Materials in private hands:

Carroll, Richard. File on the Class of 1941, in the possession of the late Mr. Carroll.

Childs, J. Rives. Copies of Childs MS., in the possession of Professor William A. Hoisington

Clark, Sidney. Letters to and from Donald Downes, in the possession of Mrs. Clark.

Downes, Donald. In the possession of the author; being transferred to the Yale University Library.

———. Letters to Gordon Browne, in the possession of Mr. Browne.

Fahs, Charles Burton. Letters in the possession of Mrs. Fahs.

Francis, Richard Lee. Tape of recollections concerning Norman Holmes Pearson; shortly to be added to the Pearson Papers in the Bienecke Library.

Holt, W. Stull. Manuscripts, in the possession of Mrs. Jocelyn Marchisio.

Kingman, Eugene. Paintings, in the possession of Mrs. Kingman.

Kip, William. Letters to Sherman Kent, in the possession of Mrs. Throop M. Wilder, Jr; soon to become part of the Kent Papers at Yale.

Pearson, Norman Holmes. Letters to his wife, Susan, held by Cooper, Tyler, and Alcorn, New Haven, Conn.

———. Letters to Felix Cowgill, in his possession.

Tompkins, Peter. Journal, in his possession.

Winn, Dilys. Tape of interview with Donald Downes, in the possession of the author; soon to become part of the Downes Papers at Yale.

INTERVIEWS AND CORRESPONDENCE

The following individuals met with me, spoke with me on the telephone, or corresponded with me to provide information, sometimes quite extensive and sometimes quite modest, that ultimately found its way into this book. Most are thanked in the notes where the information they provided was drawn upon most heavily. Some few individuals asked not to be named. I do not include here those persons who are not sources: librarians, archivists, fellow historians who examined collections I could not visit or who commented on draft chapters or paragraphs, etc., and they are thanked in the acknowledgments or the notes.

Aaron, Daniel
Addiss, Susan
Alsop, John
Angleton, James J.
Annan, Nöel
Applewhite, Edgar J., Jr.
Arndt, Richard T.
Arnstein, Robert L.
Babb, James T.
Barnes, Janet
Batchelor, Malcolm C.
Berding, Andrew
Berkeley, Roy

Bernhard, George K., Jr.
Bickel, Alexander
Bissell, Richard
Bland, Carolyn
Blee, David
Bliss, Helen D.
Bone, Robert
Brazil, John R.
Brecker, Richard L.
Brewster, Kingman, Jr.
Brooks, Robert O.
Bross, John
Brotman, Stanley S.

Browne, Gordon H.
Bryant, Douglas W.
Buckley, William F., Jr.
Bullitt, Thomas W.
Bundy, William P.
Buresch, Joan
Burke, Carl
Burling, Edward J.
Calvocoressi, Peter
Campbell, Robert F.
Cannon, Beekman
Cannon, Brevoort
Carroll, Richard
Carver, George and Ruth
Chavchavadze, David
Cheek, Leslie, Jr.
Clark, Eleanor
Clive, John
Colby, William E.
Cole, Taylor
Collingwood, Charles
Collins, J. Foster
Colwell, James L.
Corvo, Max
Costello, John F.
Cowgill, Felix
Crockett, David C.
Crosby, Sumner McKnight
Cuneo, Ernest
Curtiss, Joseph Toy
Dahl, Curtis
Danielson, J. Deering
Davis, Curtis Carroll
Day, Osborne
Dempster, Fergus
Denniston, Robin
Derrick, Robert O.
DeVane, Milton
Dill, Marshall
Dillon, Frank
Dixon, Ben F.
Dollard, Mrs. Joan
Donovan, Alan B.
Doob, Leonard
Dougherty, William
Downes, Polly W.
Dunham, William Huse
Elliott, Nicholas

Ellmann, Richard
Engley, Donald
Fahs, Mrs. Charles Burton
Farrell, John T.
Fawcett, Jane Hughes
Finch, Roy
Fodor, Eugene
Forrer, Anita
Forsythe, Carl S.
Francis, Richard Lee
Frye, Richard
Gabriel, Ralph Henry
Gage, Charles
Gallup, Donald
Galpin, Stephen K.
Gardner, Robert A.
Gay, Ruth
Giamatti, A. Bartlett
Gilbert, Reginald G. M.
Goetzmann, William H.
Goldberg, Arthur
Gordon, Ambrose
Gores, Landis
Greene, Robert S.
Guvenc, Bozkurt
Hammer, Christopher
Hanke, Lewis
Hansen, Edwin A.
Harrison, Mary Maxwell Ellett
Heckscher, August
Hilles, Susan
Hoades, Stanley
Hoisington, William A., Jr.
Holborn, Hajo
Holcombe, Harold G.
Hollander, John
Holmes, George
Hood, Cordelia
Hood, William
Hostler, Charles W.
Houston, Lawrence
Howard, Jean Alington
Howe, William E. W.
Hughes, Cherry
Hughes, Thomas
Hurt, Henry
Hyde, H. Montgomery
Jeffreys-Jones, Rhodri

Johnson, Loch K.
Johnson, William R.
Kahrl, William
Kalnay, Francis
Katz, Barry
Kaul, A. N.
Kennedy, Ruby Jo Reeves
Kent, Sherman
Kerr, Chester
Kingman, Mrs. Eugene
Kiphuth, Delaney
Kitchen, Beverly
Knox, Bernard
LaClair Cameron
Lange, H. William
Lanier, Albert G.
Leach, Joseph
Lee, Bruce
Lee, Duncan C.
Legendre, Gertrude
Liebert, Herman W.
Leslie, Nancy
Levitt, Grace Dolowitz
Lewis, Wilmarth
Lock, Owen A.
Lutkens, LaRue R.
McCargar, James
McCarthy, Mary
McConnell, Mrs. John W.
McCulloch, Mrs. John I. B.
McGrath, John J.
Mack, Maynard
McKay, Ruth C.
Maclehose, Christopher
Madden, John B.
Maddock, James
Martin, Guy
Martz, Louis
Mauldin, William
May, Georges
Mellon, Paul
Mero, Peter G.
Merriman, Daniel
Metlitzki, Dorothee
Meyer, Cord, Jr.
Meyer, Milton W.
Miler, Newton C.
Miner, Robert G.
Mohrenschildt, Dimitri von

Molden, Fritz
Morris, Donald R.
Mosle, Ted
Murphy, James R.
Naftali, Timothy J.
Nichols, Frank B.
North, Henry Ringling
Oakes, John B.
Osborn, James
Øverland, Orm
Padover, Saul K.
Page, Walter H.
Papich, Samuel J.
Parrish, Thomas
Pauker, John
Pearson, Norman Holmes
Pepper, John
Peyre, Henri
Pforzheimer, Walter L.
Phelps, Reginald H.
Pickett, Lawrence K.
Pierson, George Wilson
Porter, William Parsons
Potter, David M.
Potter, John F.
Prince, William S.
Purdy, Richard
Quinn, William W.
Raymond, Edward A.
Razis, Panos
Reid, Alastair
Roberts, Colin H.
Robbins, Mrs. Marcus
Rocca, Raymond
Rockett, Alice
Roman, Howard
Root, Leslie L.
Rosenthal, Steven T.
Roth, Lois
Rudich, Vasily
Rudin, Harry
Sawyer, John E.
Schaffner, Perdita McPherson
Schorske, Carl F.
Seccombe, Matthew
Seiferheld, David F.
Shaw, Franklin P., Jr.
Shepard, Gordon
Sherman, Margaret Elliott

Sizer, Theodore
Slyck, Deforest van
Smith, Datus
Smith, Gaddis
Smith, Mary E.
Smith, Turner Taliaferro
Smith, Warren Hunting
Smith, Wendall
Starr, Roger
Stephenson, Sir William
Stevens, Martin
Stone, Albert E.
Strange, John
Sussman, Harvey
Taft, Mary Jane
Taylor, Telford
Thompson, Karl Frederick
Thompson, Robert E. S.
Troy, Thomas F.
Twining, Kinsley
Vaill, George D.
Valentine, Mrs. Alan
Wainwright, Stuyvesant
Waith, Eugene

Waldron, John
Walker, John
Waller, John
Walz, Allen W.
Wanning, Andrews
Ward, Hugh C., Jr.
Weismiller, Edward
Welch, G. Harold
Weld, William E.
Weller, George
Welles, Benjamin
Welles, Edward O.
Wharton-Tiger, E. C.
Whiteman, Harold B.
Whittemore, Reed
Wilder, Katrinka
Will, Hubert
Williamson, Robert G.
Wilson, Junius P., Jr.
Winn, Dilys
Wolfe, Tom
Wolfers, Mrs. Arnold
Woodward, C. Vann
Wuorinen, John H.

SECONDARY ACCOUNTS

Aaron, Daniel, ed. *America in Crisis*. New York: Knopf, 1952.
Accoce, Pierre, and Pierre Quet. *A Man Called Lucy, 1939–1945*. New York: Coward-McCann, 1967.
Ackerman, E. C. *Street Man: The CIA Career of Mike Ackerman*. Miami: Ackerman & Palumbo, 1976.
Adereth, Maxwell. *The French Communist Party: A Critical History (1920–84) from Comintern to the "Colours" of France*. Manchester: Manchester University Press, 1985.
Adler, Renata. *Reckless Disregard: Westmoreland v. CBS et al., Sharon v. Time*. New York: Knopf, 1986.
Agee, James, and Walker Evans. *Let Us Now Praise Famous Men: Three Tenant Families*. Boston: Houghton Mifflin, 1960.
Agee, Philip, and Louis Wolf. *Dirty Work: The CIA in Western Europe*. Seacaucus, N.J.: Lyle Stuart, 1978.
Agrell, Wilhelm, and Bo Huldt, eds. *Clio Goes Spying: Eight Essays on the History of Intelligence*. Malmö: Lund Studies in International History #17, 1983.
Alcorn, Robert Hayden. *No Banners, No Bands: More Tales of the OSS*. New York: David McKay, 1965.
———. *No Bugles for Spies: Tales of the OSS*. New York: David McKay, 1962.
Allason, Rupert. *See* West, Nigel.

Allport, Gordon, and Leo Postman. *The Psychology of Rumor*. New York: Henry Holt, 1947.

Alsop, Stewart. *The Center: People and Power in Washington*. New York: Harper & Row, 1968.

——, and Thomas Barden. *Sub Rosa: The OSS and American Espionage*. Reprint ed. New York: Harvest, 1964.

Altieri, James J. *Darby's Rangers: An Illustrated Portrayal of the Original Rangers*. Arnold, Mo.: Ranger Book Committee, 1977.

Alumni Directory of Yale University, 1968. New Haven: Yale University, 1968.

Ambrose, Stephen E., and Richard H. Immerman. *Ike's Spies: Eisenhower and the Espionage Establishment*. Garden City, N.Y.: Doubleday, 1981.

Amery, Julian. *Sons of the Eagle: A Study in Guerilla War*. London: Macmillan, 1948.

——. *Approach March: A Venture in Autobiography*. London: Hutchinson, 1973.

Andrew, Christopher. *Secret Service: The Making of the British Intelligence Community*. London: Heinemann, 1985.

——. "Whitehall, Washington and the Intelligence Services." *International Affairs*, LII (1977).

——, and David Dilks, eds. *The Missing Dimension: Governments and Intelligence Communities in the Twentieth Century*. London: Macmillan, 1984.

Andrews, Peter. "Intelligent Intelligence." *The New York Times Book Review*, Feb. 8, 1981, p. 9.

"Aperture Card System." *United States Naval Institute Proceedings*, XC (July 1964), pp. 137–138.

Archer, Jules. *Superspies: The Secret Side of Government*. New York: Delacorte Press, 1977.

Ashman, Charles. *The CIA-Mafia Link*. New York: Manor Books, 1975.

Association of Former Intelligence Officers. *Periscope*. Washington, D.C., 1976–.

Association pour le Droit à l'information. *Intelligence: Parapolitics*. Paris: 1979–.

Austin, James D. "The Psychological Dimension of Intelligence Activities." In Alfred C. Mauer, Marion D. Tunstall, and James M. Keagle, eds., *Intelligence: Policy and Process*. Boulder, Colo.: Westview, 1985.

Auty, Phyllis, and Richard Clogg. *British Policy Towards Wartime Resistance in Yugoslavia and Greece*. London: Macmillan, 1975.

Babington-Smith, Constance. *Air Spy: The Story of Photo Intelligence in World War II*. New York: Harper & Brothers, 1957.

Bailey, Anthony. *America, Lost & Found: An English Boy's Adventure in the New World*. New York: Random House, 1980.

Bailey, F. G. "The Ordered World of the University Administrator." In George E. Marcus, ed., *Elites: Ethnographic Issues*, pp. 93–112. Albuquerque: University of New Mexico Press, 1983.

Bakeless, John. *Turncoats, Traitors and Heroes*. Philadelphia: J. B. Lippincott, 1959.

Balchin, Bernt. "Our Secret War in Scandinavia." *Colliers*, March 9, 16, 1946.

Balling, L. Christian. *Mallory's Gambit*. Boston: Atlantic Monthly Press, 1986.

Bamford, James. *The Puzzle Palace: A Report on America's Most Secret Agency.* Boston: Houghton Mifflin, 1982.

Bancroft, Mary. *Autobiography of a Spy.* New York: William Morrow, 1983.

Barker, Elizabeth. *British Policy in Southeast Europe.* London: Macmillan, 1975.

Barnes, Trevor. "The Secret Cold War: The C.I.A. and American Foreign Policy in Europe, 1946–1956." *The Historical Journal,* XXIV (1981), pp. 399–415; and XXV (1982), pp. 649–670.

Barron, John. *The KGB: The Secret Work of the Soviet Secret Agents.* New York: Reader's Digest Press, 1974.

Battaglia, Roberto. *Storia della Resistenza Italiana (8 settembre 1943–25 aprile 1945).* Turin: Einaudi, 1953.

———. *Un uomo, un partigiano.* Turin: Einaudi, 1965.

———, and Raffaello Ramat. *Un Popolo in Lotta: Testimonianze di vita italiana dall unita al 1946.* Florence: La Nova Italia, 1961.

Bazna, Elyesa, with Hans Nogly. *I Was Cicero.* London: Andre Deutsch, 1962.

Beck, Melvin. *Secret Contenders: The Myth of Cold War Counterintelligence.* New York: Sheridan Square, 1984.

Becket, Henry S. A. *The Dictionary of Espionage: Spookspeak into English.* New York: Stein and Day, 1986.

Beesly, Patrick. *Very Special Intelligence: The Story of the Admiralty's Operational Intelligence Center, 1939–1945.* London: Hamish Hamilton, 1977.

Beevor, J. G. *SOE: Recollections and Reflections, 1940–1945.* London: Bodley Head, 1981.

Behrendt, Hans-Otto. *Rommels Kenntnis von Feind im Afrikafeldzug: Ein Bericht Ober die Fiendnachrichtenarbeit, ins besondere die Funkauflärung.* Freiburg: Rombach, 1980. Translated as *Rommel's Intelligence in the Desert Campaign.* London: William Kimber, 1985.

Bellinger, Alfred. *Day's End.* New Haven: Yale University Press, 1924.

Benét, William Rose, and Norman Holmes Pearson, eds. *The Oxford Anthology of American Literature.* New York: Oxford University Press, 1938.

Bennett, Ralph F. *Ultra in the West: The Normandy Campaign of 1944–1945.* London: Hutchinson, 1979.

Benser, Günter. *Die KPD im Jahre der Befreiung: Vorbereitung und Aufbau der Legalen Kommunistischen Massenpartei.* Berlin: Dietz Verlag, 1985.

Benson, Raymond. *The James Bond Bedside Companion.* New York: Dodd, Mead, 1984.

———. "On the Trail of Ian Fleming." *The Dossier: The Official Journal of the International Spy Society,* no. 6 (Nov. 1983), pp. 22–23.

Bergier, Jacques. *L'espionage scientifique.* Paris: Hachette, 1971.

Bergin, Thomas G. *The Game: The Harvard-Yale Football Rivalry, 1876–1983.* New Haven: Yale University Press, 1984.

———. *Yale's Residential Colleges: The First Fifty Years.* New Haven: The University, 1983.

Bergonzini, Luciano. *Bologna, 1943–1945: Lettere ed osservazioni di Giorgi Amendola.* Bologna: Editrice Clueb, 1980.

———. *La Resistenza a Bologna: Testimonianze e Documenti.* 2 vols. Bologna: Instituto per la storia di Bologna, 1967–1969.

Berlin, Isaiah. *Personal Impressions.* London: Hogarth, 1980.

Bernard, Stéphane. *Le Conflit franco-marocain, 1943–56*. 3 vols. Bruxelles: Editions de l'Institute de Sociologe de l'Université Libre de Bruxelles, 1963. The first two volumes appeared as *The Franco-Moroccan Conflict, 1943–1956*. New Haven: Yale University Press, 1968.

Berton, Pierre. *My Country: The Remarkable Past*. Toronto: McClelland & Stewart, 1976.

Bertrand, Gustave. *Enigma ou la plus grande énigme de la guerre, 1939–1945*. Paris: Librarie Plon, 1973.

Beschloss, Michael R. *Mayday: Eisenhower, Khrushchev and the U-2 Affair*. New York: Harper & Row, 1986.

Bethell, Lord Nicholas. "After 'the Last Secret.' " *Encounter*, XLV (Nov. 1975), pp. 82–88.

———. *The Great Betrayal: The Untold Story of Kim Philby's Biggest Coup*. London: Hodder and Stoughton, 1984.

Bey, Umar. *Apakah CIA Itu?* Surabaja: Grip, n.d.

Blake, Lord Robert. *The Decline of Power, 1915–1969*. London: Oxford University Press, 1985.

Blitzer, Wolfe. *Between Washington and Jerusalem: A Reporter's Notebook*. New York: Oxford University Press, 1985.

Bloch, Jonathan, and Patrick Fitzgerald. *British Intelligence and Covert Action: Africa, Middle East and Europe since 1945*. Dingle, Ireland: Brandon, 1983.

Bloch, Michael. *Operation Willi: The Plot to Kidnap the Duke of Windsor*. London: Weidenfeld and Nicholson, 1984.

Blow, Rich. "The Secret Link." *The New Journal*, XVI (April 20, 1984).

Blum, William. *The CIA: A Forgotten History*. London: Zen Publishers, 1986.

Blumenson, Martin. "Intelligence and World War II: Will 'Ultra' Rewrite History?" *Army*, XXVII (Aug. 1978), pp. 442–48.

———. *Mark Clark*. New York: Congdon & Weed, 1984.

Blumenthal, Ralph. "Books of the Times." *The New York Times*. Dec. 28, 1982.

Blunt, Anthony. *Poussin*. New Haven: Yale University Press, 1980.

Bly, Herman O. *America at the Crossroads*. North Fort Myers, Fla.: Lee Constitution, 1986.

Bocca, Geoffrey. *The Moscow Scene*. New York: Stein and Day, 1976.

Bocca, Giorgio. *Storia dell'Italia Partigiana: Settembre 1943–Maggio 1945*. Bari: Editori Laterza, 1966.

de Borchgrave, Arnaude, and Robert Moss. *The Spike*. New York: Crown, 1980.

Booth, Waller B. *Mission Marcel Proust: The Story of an Unusual OSS Undertaking*. Philadelphia: Dorrance & Co., 1972.

Boyle, Andrew. *The Fourth Man: The Definitive Account of Kim Philby, Guy Burgess and Donald Maclean and Who Recruited Them to Spy for Russia*. New York: Dial, 1980. Published in Great Britain as *The Climate of Treason: Five Who Spied for Russia*. London: Hutchinson, 1979.

Braden, Tom. "The Birth of the CIA." *American Heritage*, XXVII (Feb. 1977), pp. 4–13.

———. *Eight Is Enough*. New York: Random House, 1975.

Breckinridge, Scott D. *The CIA and the U.S. Intelligence System*. Boulder, Colo.: Westview Press, 1986.

Brinton, Crane. "Letter from Liberated France." *French Historical Studies*, II (Spring 1961), pp. 1–27, and (Fall 1961), pp. 133–156.

Brissenden, R. F. "A Perfect Spy: 'Like Huckleberry Finn.' " *Quadrant,* XXX (Dec. 1986), pp. 45–49.

Brouillard, André Lèon. *See* Nord, Pierre.

Brower, Brock. "One for the Books: Private Libraries." *Town & Country,* CXL (Dec. 1986).

Bryce, Ivar. *You Only Live Once: Memoirs of Ian Fleming.* London: Weidenfeld and Nicholson, 1975.

Bryher, Winifred Ellerman. *The Days of Mars: A Memoir, 1940–1946.* New York: Harcourt, Brace Jovanovich, 1972.

Buchheit, Gert. *Spionage in zwei Veltkriegen: Schachspiel mit Menschen.* Augsburg: VPD, 1975.

Buck, Polly Stone. *We Minded the Store: Yale Life & Letters During World War II.* New Haven: privately printed, 1975.

Buckley, William F., Jr. "On the Right: Another Appeal from the States." *National Review,* XXVIII (Feb. 6, 1976), pp. 110–111. [CIA payments to Italian political parties.]

Bulletin of Yale University, Alumni Directory Number: Living Graduates and Non-Graduates of Yale University. New Haven: The Alumni Association, 1948.

Bullock, John. *Akin to Treason.* London: Arthur Barker, 1966.

Buncher, Judith F., ed. *The CIA & the Security Debate: 1971–1975.* New York: Facts on File, 1977.

Bundy, McGeorge. "The Battlefields of Power and the Searchlights of the Academy." In Edgar A. G. Johnson, ed., *Dimensions of Diplomacy.* Baltimore: Johns Hopkins University Press, 1964.

Burke, Michael. *Outrageous Good Fortune.* Boston: Little, Brown, 1984.

Burn, Michael. *The Debatable Land: A Study of the Motives of Spies in Two Ages.* London: Hamish Hamilton, 1970.

Callwood, June. *Emma: A True Story of Treason.* New York: Beaufort, 1984.

Calvocoressi, Peter. *Top Secret Ultra.* New York: Pantheon, 1980.

Campbell, Kenneth. "Bedell Smith's Imprint on the CIA." *The International Journal of Intelligence and Counterintelligence.* (ii/1986), pp. 45–62.

Campbell, Rodney. *The Luciana Project: The Secret Wartime Collaboration of the Mafia and the U.S. Navy.* New York: McGraw-Hill, 1977.

Carlson, Peter. "Secret Agents." *People* (June 7, 1982), p. 32.

Carr, Edward Hallett. *What Is History?* New York: Knopf, 1962.

Carrington, Charles E. *The Life of Rudyard Kipling.* Garden City, N.Y.: Doubleday, 1956.

Carroll, Walace. *Persuade or Perish.* Boston: Houghton Mifflin, 1948.

Carver, George. *Aesthetics and the Problem of Meaning: The Application to Aesthetics of the Logical Positivists' Verifiability Criterion of Cognitive Meaning.* New Haven: Yale University Press, 1952.

Cassidy, William L., ed. *History of the Schools and Training Branch Office of Strategic Services.* San Francisco: Kingfisher, 1983.

Cave Brown, Anthony. *Bodyguard of Lies.* New York: Harper & Row, 1975.

———. *The Last Hero: Wild Bill Donovan.* New York: Random House, 1982. Citations are to the Vintage edition, 1984.

———, ed. *The Secret War Report of the OSS.* New York: Berkley, 1976.

The Century Association. *The Century Yearbook 1984.* New York: The Association, 1984.

Cecil, Robert. "The Cambridge Comintern." In Christopher Andrew and David Dilks, eds., *The Missing Dimension: Governments and Intelligence Communities in the Twentieth Century*. London: Macmillan, 1984.

The Centennial Yale Banner: The Yearbook of the Colleges of Yale University. New Haven: The Class of 1941, 1941s, [1941].

Central Intelligence Agency. *The Rote Kapelle: The CIA's History of Soviet Intelligence and Espionage Networks in Western Europe, 1936–1945*. Washington, D.C.: University Publications of America, 1979.

Charisius, Albrecht, and Julius Mader. *Nich Länger Geheim*. Berlin: Deutscher Militärverlag, 1969.

Chatel, Nicole, and Alain Guérin. *Comrade Sorge*. Paris: Juillard, 1965.

Childs, J. Rives. *Diplomatic and Literary Quests*. Richmond: Whittet & Shepperdson, 1963.

———. *Foreign Service Farewell*. Charlottesville: Univeristy of Virginia Press, 1969.

Christie, Stuart. *Stefano delle Chiaie: Portrait of a Black Terrorist*. London: Anarchy Magazine, 1984.

Christy, Jim. *The Price of Power: A Biography of Charles Eugène Bedaux*. Toronto: Doubleday, 1984.

Clark, Mark W. *Calculated Risk*. New York: Harper, 1950.

Clayton, Aileen. *The Enemy Is Listening: The Story of the Y Service*. London: Hutchinson, 1980.

Cline, Marjorie W., Carla E. Christiansen, and Judith M. Fontaine. *Scholar's Guide to Intelligence Literature: Bibliography of the Russell J. Bowen Collection*. Frederick, Md.: University Publications of America, 1983.

Cline, Ray C. *The CIA Under Reagan, Casey & Bush*. Washington, D.C.: Acropolis Books, 1981.

———. *Secrets, Spies and Scholars: Blueprint of the Essential CIA*. Washington, D.C.: Acropolis Books, 1976. [An earlier form of the above.]

Clive, Nigel. *A Greek Experience, 1943–1948*. Wilton, England: Michael Russell, 1985.

Clogg, Richard. "The Special Operations Executive in Greece." In John O. Iatrides, ed., *Greece in the 1940s: A Nation in Crisis*. Hanover, N.H.: University Press of New England, 1981.

Coffey, Thomas M. *Iron Eagle*. New York: W. W. Norton, 1986.

Cohen, William S., and Gary Hart. *The Double Man*. New York: William Morrow, 1985.

Colapietra, Raffaele. *Benedetto Croce a la politica italiano*. Bari: Edizioni del Centro Librario, 1970.

Colby, William and Peter Forbath. *Honorable Men: My Life in the CIA*. New York: Simon & Schuster, 1978.

Coleman, Frederick. "Snapdragon: Story of a Spy." *Metro Magazine: The Magazine of Southeastern Virginia* (May 1977), pp. 24–31, 64–69.

Collier, Basil. *Hidden Weapons: Allied Secret or Undercover Services in World War II*. London: Hamish Hamilton, 1982.

Collier, Richard. *Ten Thousand Eyes*. New York: E. P. Dutton, 1958.

Collins, Larry. *Fall from Grace*. New York: Simon & Schuster, 1985.

Collins, Robert. "Master of Intrigue, Champion of Liberty." *Reader's Digest* (Canadian), December 1981.

Colville, Sir John. *The Churchillians*. London: Weidenfeld and Nicholson, 1981.

Colvin, Ian, ed. *Colonel Henri's Story: The War Memoirs of Hugo Bleicher*. London: William Kimber, 1954.

Constantinides, George C. *Intelligence and Espionage: An Analytical Bibliography*. Boulder, Colo.: Westview Press, 1983.

Cook, Blanche Wiessen. *The Declassified Eisenhower: A Divided Legacy*. Garden City, N.Y.: Doubleday, 1981.

Cook, Don. "On Revealing 'The Last Secret.' " *Encounter*, XLV (July 1975), pp. 80–86.

Cooke, Ronald C., and Roy Conyers Nesbit. *Target Hitler's Oil: Allied Attacks on German Oil Supplies, 1939–1945*. London: William Kimber, 1985.

Cookridge, E. H. *Gehlen: Spy of the Century*. London: Hodder and Stoughton, 1971.

———. *Inside SOE*. London: Arthur Barker, 1966.

———. *The Third Man: The Truth About "Kim" Philby, Double Agent*. London: Arthur Barker, 1968.

Coon, Carleton S. *A North Africa Story: The Anthropologist as OSS Agent, 1941–1943*. Ipswich, Mass.: Gambit, 1980.

Coppel, Alfred. *Thirtyfour East*. New York: Harcourt, Brace, Jovanovich, 1974.

Corson, William R. *The Armies of Ignorance: The Rise of the American Intelligence Empire*. New York: Dial Press, 1977.

———, and Robert T. Crowley. *The New KGB: Engine of Soviet Power*. New York: William Morrow, 1985.

Cot, Pierre. *Triumph of Treason*. Chicago: Ziff Davis, 1944.

Cox, Arthur Macy. *The Myths of National Security: The Peril of Secret Government*. Boston: Beacon Press, 1975.

Cox, John Hadley. *An Exhibition of Chinese Antiquities from Ch'ang-sha, Lent by John Hadley Cox*. Meriden, Conn.: Meriden Gravure, 1939.

Crane, Stephen. *The Collected Poems of Stephen Crane*. New York: Knopf, 1930.

Craveri, Raimondo. *La Compagna d'Italia e i servizi sergreti: La storia dell'ORI (1943–45)*. Milan: Viale Fulvio Testi, 1980.

Croce, Benedetto. *Quando l'Italia era Tagliata in due*. Bari: Laterza, 1948.

Cruickshank, Charles. *Deception in World War II*. Oxford: Oxford University Press, 1979.

———. *SOE in Scandinavia*. New York: Oxford University Press, 1984.

———. *SOE in the Far East*. Oxford: Oxford University Press, 1983.

Cuneo, Ernest. *Science and History*. New York: Duell, Sloan & Pearce, 1963.

Dallin, David J. *Soviet Espionage*. New Haven: Yale University Press, 1955.

Dalton, Hugh. *The Fatefull Years, 1931–45*. London: Frederick Mueller, 1957.

Daniel, Robert L. *American Philanthropy in the Near East, 1820–1960*. Athens, Ohio: Ohio University Press, 1970.

Daniels, Gordon, ed. *A Guide to the Reports of the United States Strategic Bombing Survey*. Royal Historical Society *Guides and Handbooks*, Supplementary Series no. 2. London: Royal Historical Society, 1981.

Darling, Donald. *Secret Sunday*. London: William Kimber, 1975.

———. *Sunday at Large*. London: William Kimber, 1977.

Davis, Forrest. "The Secret History of Surrender." *Saturday Evening Post*, Sept. 29, 1945.

Davis, Nathaniel. *The Last Two Years of Salvadore Allende*. Ithaca, N.Y.: Cornell University Press, 1985.

Davis, Vernon E. *History of the Joint Chiefs of Staff in WW II*. 2 vols. Washington, D.C.: Joint Chiefs of Staff Historical Section, 1953.

Deacon, Richard. *The British Connection: Russia's Manipulation of British Individuals and Institutions*. London: Hamish Hamilton, 1979.

———. *"C": A Biography of Sir Maurice Oldfield*. London: Macdonald, 1985.

———. *The Cambridge Apostles: A History of Cambridge University's Elite Intellectual Secret Society*. London: Robert Royce, 1985.

———. *A History of the British Secret Service*. London: Frederick Muller, 1969.

———. *The Israeli Secret Service*. London: Hamish Hamilton, 1977.

———. *The Silent War: A History of Western Naval Intelligence*. Newton Abbott, England: David & Charles, 1978.

———. *Within My Little Eye: The Memoirs of a Spy-Hunter*. London: Frederick Muller, 1982.

Deakin, Frederick W. *The Brutal Friendship: Mussolini, Hitler and the Fall of Italian Fascism*. New York: Harper & Row, 1962.

Deavours, Cipher A., and Louis Kruh. *Machine Cryptography & Modern Cryptanalysis*. Dedham, Mass.: Adtech Books, 1985.

Dehn, Paul, Donald Downes, and Anthony Asquith. *Orders to Kill*. Film: Arthur Rank Productions, 1959.

Delmer, Sefton. *The Counterfeit Spy*. New York: Harper & Row, 1971.

Delzell, Charles F. *Mussolini's Enemies: The Italian Anti-Fascist Resistance*. Princeton: Princeton University Press, 1961.

de Mauny, Erik. *Russian Prospect: Notes of a Moscow Correspondence*. New York: Atheneum, 1970.

Dembo, L. S. "Norman Holmes Pearson on H.D.: An Interview." *Contemporary Literature*, X (Autumn 1969), pp. 435–446.

Denniston, A. G. "The Government Code and Cypher School Between the Wars." *Intelligence and National Security*, I (Jan. 1986), pp. 48–70.

de Risio, Carlo. *Generali, Servizi Segreti e Fascismo: La guerre nella guerra, 1940–1943*. Milan: Arnoldo Mondadori, 1978.

Derogy, Jacques, and Hesi Carmel. *The Untold History of Israel*. New York: Grove Press, 1979.

de Roussy de Sales, Raoul J.J.F. *The Making of Yesterday*. New York: Reynal and Hitchcock, 1947.

Detzer, David. *The Brink: Cuban Missile Crisis, 1962*. New York: Crowell, 1979.

Deutsch, Harold C. *The Conspiracy Against Hitler in the Twilight War*. Minneapolis: University of Minnesota Press, 1968.

———. "The Historical Impact of Revealing the Ultra Secret." *Parameters, Journal of the U.S. Army War College*, VII (December 1978), pp. 2–15.

DeVane, Mable. *William Clyde DeVane, 1898–1965*. New Haven: Yale University, 1965.

DeVane, William Clyde. "The Scholar Cornered: The Dilemma of National Greatness." *The American Scholar*, XXXIII (Autumn 1964), pp. 502–511.

Dewey, A. Peter. *As They Were*. New York: Beechhurst Press, 1946.

Diamond, Sigmund. "God and the F.B.I. at Yale." *The Nation*, CCXXX (April 12, 1980), pp. 423–428.

———. "Surveillance in the Academy: Harry B. Fisher and Yale University, 1927–1952." *American Quarterly,* XXVI (Spring 1984), pp. 7–43.

Dmitri, Ivan. *Flight to Everywhere.* New York: McGraw-Hill, 1944.

Dodds-Parker, Douglas. *Setting Europe Ablaze: Some Account of Ungentlemanly Warfare.* Windlesham, Surrey: Springwood Books, 1983.

Donnelly, F. K. "A Possible Source for Nathan Hale's Dying Words." *The William and Mary Quarterly,* 3rd ser., XLII (July 1985), pp. 394–395.

Donner, Frank J. *The Age of Surveillance: The Aims and Methods of America's Political Intelligence System.* New York: Vintage Books, 1981.

Donovan, William J. *Fifth Column Lessons for America.* Washington, D.C.: n.p., 1940.

Doob, Leonard. "The Utilization of Social Scientists in the Overseas Branch of the Office of War Information." *American Political Science Review,* XLI (August 1947), pp. 649–667.

Doolittle, Hilda. *Bid Me to Live.* With afterword by Perdita Schaffner. London: Virago, 1984.

———. *End to Torment.* New York: New Directions, 1979.

———. *The Flowering of the Rod.* London: Oxford University Press, 1946.

———. *Hermetic Definition.* New York: New Directions, 1972.

———. *Notes on Thought and Vision & The Wise Sappho.* San Francisco: City Lights Books, 1982.

———. *The Walls Do Not Fall.* New York: Oxford University Press, 1944.

Dorwart, Jeffery M. *Conflict of Duty: The U.S. Navy's Intelligence Dilemma, 1919–1945.* Annapolis: Naval Institute Press, 1983.

———. "The Roosevelt-Astor Espionage Ring." *New York History,* LXII (July 1981), pp. 307–322.

Downes, Donald. *The Easter Dinner.* New York: Rinehart, 1960.

———. *Orders to Kill.* New York: Rinehart, 1958.

———. *A Red Rose for Maria.* New York: Rinehart, 1959.

———. *The Scarlet Thread: Adventures in Wartime Espionage.* New York: The British Book Centre, 1953.

Drabeck, Bernard A., and Helen E. Ellis. *Archibald MacLeish: Reflections.* Amherst, Mass.: University of Massachusetts Press, 1986.

Duffy, Francis P. *Father Duffy's Story.* New York: Doran, 1919.

Dulles, Allen. *The Craft of Intelligence.* New York: Harper & Row, 1963.

———, ed. *Great True Spy Stories.* New York: Harper & Row, 1968.

———. *The Secret Surrender.* New York: Harper & Row, 1966.

Dunlop, Richard. *Donovan, America's Master Spy.* Chicago: Rand McNally, 1982.

Dunn, Walter S., Jr. "The 'Ultra' Papers." *Military Affairs,* XLII (October 1978), pp. 134–136.

Edgar, Harold, and Benno C. Schmidt, Jr. "The Espionage Statutes and Publication of Defense Information." *Columbia Law Review,* LXXIII (May 1973), pp. 929–1087.

Edmonds, John B., ed. *St. Paul's School in the Second World War.* Concord, N.H. The Alumni Association, 1950.

Edwards, Robert, and Kenneth Dunne. *A Study of a Master Spy.* London: Houseman, 1961.

Ege, Konrad. "Buying Oman." *Counter Spy*, V (April 1981), pp. 22–27.

———. "Introducing George Bush." *Counter Spy*, V (April 1981), pp. 3–7.

Eisenberg, Dennis, Uri Dan, and Eli Landau. *The Mossad: Israel's Secret Intelligence Service—Inside Stories*. New York: Paddington Press, 1978.

Elliot, S. R. *Scarlet to Green: Canadian Army Intelligence, 1903–1963*. Toronto: Canadian Intelligence Security Association, 1981.

Elliot-Bateman, Michael, ed. *The Fourth Dimension of Warfare*. 2 vols. Manchester University Press, 1970–1974.

Ellwood, David W. *Italy, 1943–1945*. Leicester: Leicester University Press, 1985.

Ennes, James M., Jr. *Assault on* Liberty: *The True Story of the Israeli Attack on the American Intelligence Ship*. New York: Random House, 1979.

Eppler, John W. *Geheimagent in Zweiten Weltkrieg: Zwischen Berlin, Kabel und Kairo*. Preussisch Oltendorf: K. W. Schütz, 1974.

Epstein, Edward Jay. *Legend: The Secret World of Lee Harvey Oswald*. New York: McGraw-Hill, 1978.

———. "The Spy War." *The New York Times Magazine*, Nov. 28, 1980.

———. "The Spy Who Came In to Be Sold." *The New Republic*, CVIIC (July 15 and 22 [single issue], 1985, pp. 35–42, and correspondence, August 26, 30, and September 27.

———. "When the CIA Was Almost Wrecked." *Parade Magazine*, Oct. 14, 1984, pp. 8, 11.

———. "Who Killed the CIA? The Confessions of Stansfield Turner." *Commentary*, LXXX (October 1985), pp. 53–57.

———. *Inquest: The Warren Commission and the Establishment of Truth*. New York: Viking, 1966.

Faenza, Roberto, and Marco Fini. *Gli americani in Italia*. Milan: Feltrinelli, 1976.

Fain, Tyrus G., Katharine C. Plant, and Ross Milloy. eds. *The Intelligence Community: History, Organization, and Issues: Public Documents Series*. New York: R. R. Bowker, 1977.

Fairbank, John K. *Chinabound: A Fifty-Year Memoir*. New York: Harper & Row, 1982.

Faligot, Roger. *Markus: Espion allemand*. Paris: Temps Actuels, 1986.

———, and Remi Kauffer. *Au coeur de l'état, l'espionage*. Paris: Autremont, 1983.

———, and Pascal Krop. *La Piscine: Les services secrets francais, 1944–1984*. Paris: Éditions du Seuil, 1985.

Farago, Ladislav. *Burn After Reading: The Espionage History of World War II*. New York: Walker, 1961.

———. *The Game of the Foxes: The Untold Story of German Espionage in the U.S. and Great Britain During World War II*. 6th ed. New York: Bantam Books, 1978.

La Farge, Henry, ed. *Lost Treasures of Europe*. New York: Pantheon Books, 1946.

Farnham, Thomas J. *"A Child I Set Much By": A Life of Nathan Hale*. New Haven: New Haven Colony Historical Society, 1978.

Feldt, Eric A. *The Coastwatchers*. New York: Oxford University Press, 1946.

Felix, Christopher. *The Spy and His Masters: A Short Course in the Secret War*.

London: Secker & Warburg, 1963. Published in the United States as *A Short Course in the Secret War*. New York: Dutton, 1963.

———, with George Marton. *Three-Cornered Cover*. New York: Holt, Rinehart and Winston, 1972.

Ferguson, Thomas G. *British Military Intelligence, 1870–1914*. Frederick, Md. University Publications of America, Inc., 1984.

Ferrell, Robert H., ed. *Off the Record: The Private Papers of Harry S Truman*. New York: Harper & Row, 1980.

Field, John W. *Rendezvous with Destiny: A History of the Yale Class of 1937 and Its Times*. Canaan, N.H.: Phoenix, 1984.

Fielding, Xan. *Hide and Seek: The Story of a Wartime Agent*. London: Secker and Warburg, 1954.

Fisher, John. *Burgess and Maclean: A New Look at the Foreign Office Spies*. London: Robert Hale, 1977.

Fitzgerald, Penelope. *The Knox Brothers*. New York: Coward, McCann & Geoghegan, 1977.

FitzGibbon, Constance. *Secret Intelligence in the Twentieth Century*. New York: Stein and Day, 1977.

———. " 'The Ultra-Secret': Enigma in the War." *Encounter*, XlIV (Mar. 1975), pp. 81–85.

Flanner, Janet. "The Annals of Collaboration: Equivalism." *The New Yorker*, XXI (Sept. 22, Oct. 6, 13, 1945).

Foot, M.R.D. *SOE: An Outline History of the Special Operations Executive, 1940–46*. London: BBC, 1984.

———. *SOE in France: An Account of the Work of the British Special Operations Executive in France, 1940–1944*. London: H.M.S.O., 1966.

———, and J. M. Langley. *MI9: Escape and Evasion, 1939–1945*. Boston: Little, Brown, 1980.

Foote, Alexander. *Handbook for Spies*. 2nd ed. London: Museum Press, Ltd., 1953.

Ford, Corey. *Donovan of OSS*. Boston: Little, Brown, 1970.

———, and MacBain Ford. "Cloak and Dagger." *Colliers*, Oct. 6, 13, 20, 1945.

Forrer, Anita. *Rainer Maria Rilke: Briefwechsel*. Frankfurt am Maine: Insel, 1982.

Forster, E. M. *Two Cheers for Democracy*. New York: Harcourt, Brace, 1951.

Foster, Jane. *An Unamerican Lady*. London: Sidgwick & Jackson, 1980.

Fournier, Nicolas, and Edmond Legrand. *Dossier E: comme espionage*. Paris: Moreau, 1978.

Franklin, Charles. *The Great Spies*. New York: Hart, 1967.

Fraser-Smith, Charles, with Kevin Logan. *Secret Warriors: Hidden Heroes of MI6, OSS, MI9, SOE and SAS*. Exeter: The Paternoster Press, 1984.

Frazer, Philip. "Dirty Tricks Down Under." *Mother Jones*, IX (Mar. 1984).

Freed, Donald. *The Spymaster*. New York: Arbor House, 1980.

Freemantle, Brian. *CIA*. New York: Stein and Day, 1983.

Freney, Denis. *The CIA's Australian Connection*. Sydney South: Freney, 1977.

Friedman, Susan Stanford. *Psyche Reborn: The Emergence of H.D.* Bloomington, Ind.: Indiana University Press, 1981.

Friendly, Alfred. "Confessions of a Code Breaker." *The Washington Post*, Oct. 27, 1974.

Frillman, Paul, and Graham Peck. *China: The Remembered Life*. Boston: Houghton Mifflin, 1968.

Fuller, Jean Overton. *Double Webs*. London: Putnam, 1958.

———. *The Starr Affair*. London: Gollancz, 1954.

Funk, Arthur L. "American Contacts with the Resistance in France." *Military Affairs*, XXXIV (Feb. 1970), pp. 15–21.

Gage, Nicholas. *Eleni*. London: Fontana/Collins, 1983.

Galileo High School. *The Telescope*. San Francisco: The School, 1936–45.

Gallegos, Adrian. *From Capri into Oblivion*. London: Hodder and Stoughton, 1960.

Gallin, Mary Alice. *German Resistance to Hitler*. Washington, D.C.: Catholic University of America Press, 1961.

Ganier-Raymond, Philippe. *The Tangled Web*. London: Arthur Barker, 1968.

Gardiner, Muriel. *Code Name "Mary": Memoirs of an American Woman in the Austrian Underground*. New Haven: Yale University Press, 1983.

Gardner, John W., Henry A. Murray, et al. *Assessment of Men: Selection of Personnel for the Office of Strategic Services*. New York: Rinehart, 1948.

Gárlinski, Jósef. *The Enigma War*. New York: Scribner's, 1980.

Garrow, David J. *The FBI and Martin Luther King, Jr.: From Solo to Memphis*. New York: Norton, 1981.

Garwood, Darrell. *Under Cover: Thirty-five Years of CIA Deception*. New York: Grove Press, 1985.

de Gaulle, Charles. *Mémoires de guerre: L'Unité, 1943–1944*. Paris: Plon, 1956.

———. *Memoirs of Hope: Renewal and Endeavor*. New York: Simon & Schuster, 1971.

Gehlen, Reinhard. *Der Dienst: Erinnerungen, 1942–1971*. Mainz: Hase & Koehler, 1971. Translated in the United States as *The Service: The Memoirs of General Reinhard Gehlen*. New York: World Publishing, 1972.

Gelb, Norman. *Enemy in the Shadows: The World of Spies and Spying*. London: William Luscombe, 1976.

Gheysens, Roger, and Jacques de Launay. *Histoire de la guerre psychologique et sociéte*. Lausanne: Rencontre, 1970.

Gish, Lillian. *Dorothy and Lillian Gish*. New York: Scribner's, 1973.

Gleeson, James. *They Feared No Evil: The Woman Agents of Britain's Secret Armies, 1939–45*. London: Robert Hale, 1976.

Godson, Roy, ed. *Intelligence Requirements for the 1980s: Clandestine Collection*. New Brunswick, N.J.: Transaction Books, 1982.

———, ed. *Intelligence Requirements for the 1980s: Counterintelligence*. Washington, D.C.: National Strategy Information Center, 1980.

Goldston, Robert. *Sinister Touches: The Secret War Against Hitler*. New York: Dial, 1982.

Golitsin, Anatoliy. *New Lies for Old: The Communist Strategy of Deception and Disinformation*. New York: Dodd, Mead, 1984.

Gömöri, Endre. *Rejtett Szolgalat: Fejezetek a CIA történetéböl*. Budapest: n.p., 1979.

Gores, Landis. "Ultra-American: Memories of Service at the Most Secret Source." Unpublished manuscript, held by the author, New Canaan, Conn., 1984.

Graham, Robert A. "Has the Vatican Lost Confidence in the Press?" *Columbia,* Aug. 1973.

———. *Il Vaticano e il nazismo.* Rome: Cinque Lune, 1975.

———. *Vatican Diplomacy: A Study of Church and State on the International Plane.* Princeton: Princeton University Press, 1959.

Granatstein, J. L. "Spies." *Queen's Quarterly,* LXXXI (Autumn 1982), pp. 529–537.

Green, Martin. *Children of the Sun: A Narrative of "Decadence" in England After 1918.* New York: Basic Books, 1976.

Green, Stephen. *Taking Sides: America's Secret Relations with a Militant Israel.* New York: William Morrow, 1984.

Greene, Graham, and Malcolm Muggeridge. "Reflections on the Character of Kim Philby." *Esquire,* LXX (Sept. 1960), pp. 3–10.

Greene, Harris. *Inference of Guilt.* Garden City, N.Y.: Doubleday, 1982.

Gubbins, Sir Colin. "Resistance Movements in the War." *Journal of the Royal Service Institute,* XCII (May 1948), pp. 210–223.

Guérin, Alain. *Qu'est-ce que la C.I.A.?* Paris: Editions Sociales, 1968.

Guest, Barbara. *Herself Defined: The Poet H.D. and Her World.* Garden City, N.Y.: Doubleday, 1984.

Guzenhauser, Max. *Geschichte des geheimen Nachrichtendienstes: Spionage, Sabotage, und Abwehr.* Frankfurt: Bernadr und Graefe, 1968.

H.D. *See* Doolittle, Hilda.

Haestrup, Jørgen. *European Resistance Movements, 1939–1945: A Complete History.* Westport, Conn.: Meckler, 1981.

Hagen, Louis. *The Secret War for Europe: A Dossier of Espionage.* London: Macdonald, 1968.

Haines, William Wister. *Ultra and the History of the United States Strategic Air Force in Europe vs. the German Air Force.* Frederick, Md.: University Publications of America, 1980.

Haldane, R. A. *The Hidden World.* New York: St. Martin's Press, 1970.

Hall, Luella J. *The United States and Morocco, 1776–1956.* Metuchen, N.J.: Scarecrow Press, 1971.

Hamilton-Hill, Donald. *SOE Assignment.* London: William Kimber, 1973.

Hammond, Nicholas. *Venture into Greece: With the Guerrillas, 1943–1944.* London: William Kimber, 1983.

Hamson, Denys. *We Fell Among Greeks.* London: Jonathan Cape, 1946.

Haswell, Jock. *British Military Intelligence.* London: Weidenfield and Nicolson, 1973.

———. *Intelligence and Deception of the D-Day Landings.* London: Batsford, 1979.

———. *Spies and Spymakers: A Concise History of Intelligence.* London: Thames and Hudson, 1977.

———. *The Tangled Web: The Art of Tactical and Strategic Deception.* Westover, England: John Goodchild, 1985.

Havemeyer, Loomis. *Undergraduate Yale in the Second World War.* New Haven: The University, 1960.

Heald, Tim. *Old Boy Networks: Who We Know and How We Use Them.* New York: Ticknor & Fields, 1984.

Hearn, C. V. *Foreign Assignment.* London: Robert Hale, 1961.

Heckscher, August. *A Pattern of Politics*. New York: Reynard, 1947.

———. *St. Paul's: The Life of a New England School*. New York: Scribner's, 1980.

Heller, Michael. "Stalin and the Detectives." *Survey,* CCXI (1975), pp. 160–175.

Hellman, Geoffrey T. *How to Disappear for an Hour*. New York: Dodd, Mead, 1947.

———. "Profiles: The Steward of Strawberry Hill." *The New Yorker,* XXV (Aug. 6, 1949), pp. 26–37, and (Aug. 13, 1949), pp. 31–41.

———, et al. *Yale 28 War Record*. New York: A Giraldi, 1946.

Hendel, Charles W. *In Remembrance of William Clyde DeVane as Dean of Yale College*. New Haven: Pierson College, 1968.

Hersh, Burton. "Dragons Have to Be Killed." *The Washingtonian,* Sept. 1985, pp. 158–161.

Hersh, Seymour M. "The Angleton Story." *New York Times Biographical Service,* IX (June 1978), pp. 688–694.

Hervet, Francoise. "Knights of Darkness: The Sovereign Military Order of Malta." *Covert Action,* no. 25 (Winter 1986), p. 31.

Heymann, C. David. *Ezra Pound: The Last Rower—A Political Profile*. New York: Viking, 1976.

Hilsman, Roger. *Strategic Intelligence and National Decisions*. Glencoe, Ill.: The Free Press, 1956.

Hilton, Stanley E. *Hitler's Secret War in South America, 1939–1945: German Military Espionage and Allied Counterespionage in Brazil*. Baton Rouge: Louisiana State University Press, 1981.

Hinchley, Vernon. *Spy Mysteries Unveiled*. New York: Dodd, Mead, 1963.

Hinckle, Warren, and William W. Turner. *The Fish Is Red: The Story of the Secret War Against Castro*. New York: Harper & Row, 1981.

Hinsley, F. H., E. E. Thomas, C.F.G. Ransom, and R. C. Knight. *British Intelligence in the Second World War: Its Influence on Strategy and Operations*. 3 vols. London: H.M.S.O., 1979–1984.

History of the Class of 1926 Yale College. New Haven: Yale University, 1926.

A History of the German Secret Services and British Counter-Measures. Ogden, Utah: Cloak & Dagger Publications, 1986.

Hoare, Sir Samuel, Viscount Templewood. *Ambassador on Special Mission*. London: Collins, 1946.

Hodges, Andrew. *Alan Turing: The Enigma*. New York: Simon & Schuster, 1983.

Hodgson, Godfrey. *America in Our Time*. New York: Doubleday, 1976.

Hoffman, Peter. *The History of the German Resistance*. Cambridge, Mass.: Massachusetts Institute of Technology Press, 1977.

Höhne, Heinz. *Canaris: Hitler's Master Spy*. New York: Doubleday, 1979.

———. *Der Krieg im Dunkeln: Macht und Einfluss des deutschen und russischen Geheimdienstes*. Munich: Bertelsmann, 1985.

———, and Hermann Zolling. *Network: The Truth About General Gehlen and His Spy Ring*. London: Secker & Warburg, 1972.

Hoisington, William A., Jr. *The Casablanca Connection: French Colonial Policy, 1936–1943*. Chapel Hill: University of North Carolina Press, 1984.

Holden, Reuben. *Yale-in-China: The Mainland, 1901–1951*. New Haven: Yale-in-China Association, 1964.

Hollander, John. *Reflections on Espionage*. New York: Atheneum, 1976.

Holmes, W. J. *Double-Edged Secrets: U.S. Naval Intelligence Operations in the Pacific During World War II*. Annapolis: Naval Institute Press.

Holmes, Richard. "Anthony Blunt, Gentleman Traitor." *Harper's,* CCLX (Apr. 1980), pp. 102–109.

Holt, W. Stull. *Treaties Defeated by the Senate*. Baltimore: The Johns Hopkins Press, 1933.

Hondros, John. *Greece in the 1940s*. Hanover, N.H.: University Press of New England, 1981.

Hood, Stuart. *Pebbles from My Skull*. London: Hutchinson, 1963.

Hood, William. *Mole*. New York: W. W. Norton, 1982.

———. *Spy Wednesday*. New York: W. W. Norton, 1986.

Hoover, Calvin. *Memoirs of Capitalism, Communism and Nazism*. Durham: Duke University Press, 1965.

Hougan, Jim. *Secret Agenda: Watergate, Deep Throat and the CIA*. New York: Random House, 1984.

———. *Spooks: The Haunting of America—The Private Use of Secret Agents*. New York: William Morrow, 1978.

Howard, James M. "The Whiffenpoofs: Gentlemen Songsters Off on a Spree." *Yale Alumni Magazine,* XXII (Mar. 1959), pp. 9–11.

Howard, Michael. "Rigours of Recovery." *Times Literary Supplement*. Sept. 6, 1985, p. 984.

Howarth, Patrick. *Intelligence Chief Extraordinary: The Life of the Ninth Duke of Portland*. London: The Bodley Head, 1986.

———, ed. *Special Operations*. London: Routledge and Kegan Paul, 1955.

"How Did You Choose Your Academic Field?" *Yale Alumni Magazine,* XXVII (Oct. 1973), pp. 12–13.

Howe, Ellis. *The Black Game: British Subversive Operations Against the Germans During the Second World War*. London: Michael Joseph, 1982.

Howe, Thomas Carr, Jr. *Salt Mines and Castles: The Discovery and Restitution of Looted European Art*. Indianapolis: Bobbs-Merrill, 1946.

"How the British Founded Khalistan." *Sunday* (New Delhi), XIII (Feb. 22, 1986), pp. 25–27.

Hoxha, Enver. *The Anglo-American Threat to Albania*. Tiranë, Albania: n.p.: 1982.

Hughes, H. Stuart. *An Essay for Our Times*. New York: Knopf, 1950.

———. *The United States and Italy*. Cambridge, Mass.: Harvard University Press, 1953.

Hunt, David. "A Tepid Intrepid." *The Times Literary Supplement*. Sept. 3, 1982.

Hunt, E. Howard. *Bimini Run*. New York: Farrar, Straus, 1949.

———. *The Gaza Intercept*. New York: Stein and Day, 1981.

———. *The Hargrave Deception*. New York: Stein and Day, 1980.

———. *Limit of Darkness*. New York: Random House, 1944.

———. *Undercover: Memoirs of an American Secret Agent*. New York: Berkley, 1974.

Hurstfield, Julian G. *America and the French Nation, 1939–1945.* Chapel Hill: University of North Carolina Press, 1986.

Hurt, Henry. *Reasonable Doubt: An Investigation into the Assassination of John F. Kennedy.* New York: Holt, Rinehart and Winston, 1986.

———. *Shadrin: The Spy Who Never Came Back.* New York: McGraw-Hill, 1981.

Hyde, H. Montgomery. *Cynthia.* Farrar, Straus and Giroux, 1965.

———. *The Quiet Canadian: The Secret Service Story of Sir William Stephenson.* London: Hamish Hamilton, 1962. Published in the United States as *Room 3603: The Story of the British Intelligence Center in New York During World War II.* New York: Farrar, Straus and Giroux, 1963.

———. *Secret Intelligence Agent.* London: Constable, 1982.

Hymoff, Edward. *The OSS in World War II.* New York: Ballantine Books, 1972.

Iatrides, John O., ed. *Greece in the 1940s: A Nation in Crisis.* Hanover, N.H.: University Press of New England, 1981.

———. *Revolt in Athens: The Greek Communist "Second Round," 1944–1945.* Princeton: Princeton University Press, 1972.

Icardi, Aldo. *Aldo Icardi: American Master Spy.* New York: University Books, 1954.

Ind, Allison. *A Short History of Espionage.* New York: David McKay, 1963.

The Institute of Paper Chemistry. *Proceedings of the Twenty-seventh Executives' Conference, May 9–10, 1963: Thirty-Fourth Anniversary Year.* Appleton, Wis.: The Institute, 1963.

IQ/Intelligence Quarterly. Weston, Vt., 1985–.

Irving, David. *The Mare's Nest.* Boston: Little, Brown, 1965.

Isaacson, Walter, and Evan Thomas. *The Wise Men: Six Friends and the World They Made.* New York: Simon & Schuster, 1986.

Jaffary, James Freeman, ed. *A History of the Class of 1941.* New Haven: Yale University, 1941.

Jaquillard, Robert. *La Chasse aux espions en Suisse: Choses vécues—1939–1945.* Lausanne: Payot, 1947.

Jeffery, Keith. "The Government Code and Cypher School: A Memorandum by Lord Curzon." *Intelligence and National Security,* I (Sept. 1986), pp. 454–458.

Jeffreys-Jones, Rhodri. *American Espionage: From Secret Service to CIA.* New York: Free Press, 1977.

———. "The Historiography of the CIA." *The Historical Journal,* XXIII (ii/ 1980), pp. 489–496.

———. "The Socio-Educational Composition of the CIA Elite: A Statistical Note." *Journal of American Studies,* XIX (iii/1985), pp. 421–424.

Jervis, Robert. *The Logic of Perception and Misperception in International Politics.* Princeton: Princeton University Press, 1976.

John, Otto. *Twice Through the Lines.* New York: Harper, 1972.

Johns, Phil. *Within Two Cloaks: Missions with SIS and SOE.* London: William Kimber, 1979.

Johnson, Brian. *The Secret War.* New York: Methuen, 1978.

Johnson, David. *V-1, V-2: Hitler's Vengeance on London.* Briarcliff Manor, N.Y.: Stein and Day, 1982.

Johnson, Loch K. "Decision Costs in the Intelligence Cycle." In Alfred C. Maurer,

Marion D. Tunstall, and James M. Keagle, eds., *Intelligence: Policy and Process*. Boulder, Colo.: Westview Press, 1985.

———. *A Season of Inquiry: The Senate Intelligence Investigation*. Lexington, Ky.: University Press of Kentucky, 1985.

Johnson, Thomas. "Our Silent Partner in the Secret War Against Communism." *American Mercury*, XCI (Sept. 1960), pp. 3–10.

Jones, R. V. *The Wizard War: British Scientific Intelligence, 1939–1945*. New York: Coward, McCann & Geoghegan, 1978. Published in Great Britain as *Most Secret War*. London: Hamish Hamilton, 1978.

Jowitt, The Earl. *Some Were Spies*. London: Hodder and Stoughton, 1954.

Kahn, David. *The Codebreakers: The Story of Secret Writing*. New York: Macmillan, 1967.

———. "The International Conference on Ultra." *Military Affairs*, XLIII (Apr. 1979), pp. 97–98.

Kahrl, William L. "Yet Time and change shall naught prevail/To break the friendships formed at Yale." *The New Journal*, II (Feb. 9, 1969).

Karalekas, Anne. *History of the Central Intelligence Agency*. Laguna Hills, Calif.: Aegean Park Press, 1977.

Katz, Barry. *Herbert Marcuse and the Art of Liberation: An Intellectual Biography*. London: NLB, 1982.

Katz, Robert. *Death in Rome*. New York: Macmillan, 1967.

Kaufman, Louis, Barbara Fitzgerald, and Tom Sewell. *Moe Berg: Athlete, Scholar, Spy*. Boston: Little, Brown, 1974.

Kelley, Brooks Mather. *Yale: A History*. New Haven: Yale University Press, 1974.

Kelly, Richard M. "He Never Stopped Trying." *Blue Book Magazine*, Sept. 1946, pp. 42–51.

Kemp, Peter. *No Colours or Crest*. London: Cooper, 1958.

Kendall, Willmoore. "The Function of Intelligence." *World Politics*, I (July 1949), 540–552.

Kent, Sherman. *A Boy and a Pig, but Mostly Horses*. New York: Dodd, Mead, 1974.

———. *Buffalo Blocks: For the Puzzled High-Powered Executive*. Kentfield, Calif.: privately printed, 1970.

———. "A Crucial Estimate Relived." *Studies in Intelligence*, Sept. 1969, pp. 1–18.

———. *The Election of 1827 in France*. Cambridge, Mass.: Harvard University Press, 1975.

———. "Elector Lists of France's July Monarchy, 1830–1848." *French Historical Studies*, VII (Spring 1971), pp. 117–127.

———. *Strategic Intelligence for American World Policy*. Princeton: Princeton University Press, 1949. Reissued with new preface, Hamden, Conn.: Anchor, 1965.

———. "War Collection." *Yale Alumni Magazine*, March 22, 1940.

———. *Writing History*. New York: Appleton-Century Crofts, 1941.

Keogh, Andrew. *Dedication of the Sterling Memorial Library, 11 April 1931*. New Haven: The University, 1931.

Kimball, Warren F., and Bruce Bartlett. "Roosevelt and Prewar Commitments to Churchill: The Tyler Kent Affair." *Diplomatic History,* V (Fall 1981), pp. 219–312.

Kimche, Jon. *Spying for Peace: General Guisan and Swiss Neutrality.* 2nd ed. London: Weidenfeld and Nicholson, 1962.

Kipling, Rudyard. *Something of Myself.* New York: Doubleday, Doran, 1937.

Kirkpatrick, Lyman B. *Captains Without Eyes: Intelligence Failures in World War II.* London: Macmillan, 1960.

———. *The U.S. Intelligence Community: Foreign Policy and Domestic Activities.* New York: Hill and Wang, 1973.

Kirstein, Lincoln. "The Quest of the Golden Lamb." *Town & Country,* C (Sept. 1945).

Kissinger, Henry. *White House Years.* Boston: Little, Brown, 1979.

Klass, Philip J. *Secret Sentries in Space.* New York: Random House, 1971.

Knightly, Phillip. *The Second Oldest Profession.* New York: W. W. Norton, 1987.

Kogan, Norman. *Italy and the Allies.* Cambridge, Mass.: Harvard University Press, 1956.

Kone, Eugene. *Yale Men Who Died in the Second World War.* New Haven: Yale University Press, 1951.

Korbonski, Stefan. "The True Story of 'Enigma': The German Code Machine in World War II." *East European Quarterly,* XI (Summer 1977), pp. 227–234.

Kouvaras, Kōstas. *OSS—Me tēn kentrikē tou EAM [OSS—with the Central Committee EAM].* Athens: Eksantas, 1976.

Kozaczuk, Wladyslaw. *Enigma: How the German Cipher Machine Was Broken, and How It Was Read by the Allies in World War II.* Frederick, Md.: University Publications of America, 1984.

Kramish, Arnold. *The Griffin.* Boston: Houghton Mifflin, 1986.

Krasnov, Vladislav. *Soviet Defectors: The KGB Wanted List.* Stanford: Hoover Institution Press, 1985.

Kurz, Hans Rudolf. *Nachrichten zentrum Schweig.* Frauenfeld: Verlag Huber, 1972.

Lada-Mocarski, Valla. "The Last Three Days of Mussolini." *Atlantic Monthly,* CLXXVI (Dec. 1945), pp. 46–52.

Ladd, J. D. *SBS, The Invisible Raiders.* London Arms and Armour Press, 1983.

Lamphere, Robert J., and Tom Schachtman. *The FBI-KGB War: A Special Agent's Story.* New York: Random House, 1986.

Landau, Henry. *The Enemy Within: The Inside Story of German Sabotage in America.* New York: G. P. Putnam's, 1937.

Langer, Walter C. *The Mind of Adolf Hitler: The Secret Wartime Report.* New York: Basic Books, 1972.

———. "A Psychological Analysis of Adolph Hitler: His Life and Legend." 4 vols. Typescript, declassified 1968, Cross Campus Library, Yale University. Differs in some particulars from the published version.

Langer, William L., et al. *Conyers Read, 1881–1959: Scholar, Teacher, Public Servant.* Fairfax, Calif.: n.p., 1963.

———. *In and Out of the Ivory Tower: The Autobiography of William L. Langer.* New York: Neale Watson Academic Publications, 1977.

———. *Our Vichy Gamble.* New York: Knopf, 1947.

———. "Scholarship and the Intelligence Problem." *American Philosophical Society Proceedings,* XCII (Mar., 1948). pp. 43–45.

———. *Wartime Mission in Spain, 1942–1945*. New York: Macmillan, 1945.

Langhorne, Richard T. B., ed. *Diplomacy and Intelligence During the Second World War*. New York: Cambridge University Press, 1985.

Laqueur, Walter, ed. *The Second World War: Essays in Military and Political History*. London: Sage, 1982.

———. *A World of Secrets: The Uses and Limits of Intelligence*. New York: Basic Books, 1985.

Lass, Abraham H., and Norma L. Tasman, eds. *"The Secret Sharer" and Other Great Stories*. New York: New American Library, 1969.

Latham, Aaron. *Orchids for Mother*. Boston: Little, Brown, 1977.

———. "Orchids for Mother: Behind the C.I.A. Cover Story." *New York,* VIII (Apr. 7, 1975), pp. 27–40.

Latham, Earl. *The Communist Controversy in Washington*. Cambridge, Mass.: Harvard University Press, 1966.

Laurent, Frederic. *L'Orchestre Noir*. Paris: Stock, 1978.

Layne, Marion. *The Balloon Affair*. New York: Dodd, Mead, 1981.

Layton, Edwin T., with Roger Pineau, and John Costello. *"And I Was There," Pearl Harbor and Midway—Breaking the Secrets*. New York: William Morrow, 1985.

Leary, William M. *The Central Intelligence Agency: History and Documents*. Tuscaloosa, Ala.: University of Alabama Press, 1984.

Lefever, Ernest W., and Roy Godson. *The CIA and the American Ethic: An Unfinished Debate*. Washington, D.C.: Ethics and Public Policy Center of Georgetown University, 1979.

Legendre, Gertrude. *The Sands Ceased to Run*. New York: William Frederick Press, 1947.

LeMay, Curtis E., and Mackinlay Kantor. *Mission with LeMay*. Garden City, N.Y.: Doubleday, 1965.

Lett, Gordon. *Rossano: An Adventure of the Italian Resistance*. London: Hodder and Stoughton, 1955.

Leverkuehn, Paul. *German Military Intelligence*. New York: Praeger, 1945. Published in Great Britian as *German Military Intelligence*. London: Weidenfeld and Nicolson, 1954.

Lewin, Ronald. *Ultra Goes to War: The First Account of World War II's Greatest Secret Based on Official Documents*. New York: McGraw-Hill, 1978.

Lewis, Laurence. *Echoes of Resistance: British Involvement with the Italian Partisans*. Tunbridge Wells, England: Costello, 1985.

Lewis, Norman. *Naples '44*. New York: Pantheon, 1978.

Lewis, Wilmarth Sheldon. *One Man's Education*. New York: Knopf, 1967.

———. *Read As You Please*. Cleveland: The Rowfat Club, 1975.

"Life Explores World's Finest Walpole Library." *Life,* XVII (Oct. 23, 1944), pp. 116–118.

Light, Robert E., and Carl Marzani. *Cuba Versus CIA*. N.p.: n.p., 1961.

Lippincott, David. *Salt Mine*. New York: Viking, 1979.

Logoreci, Anton. *The Albanians: Europe's Forgotten Survivors*. London: Gollancz, 1977.

Long, Helen. *Safe Houses Are Dangerous*. London: William Kimber, 1985.

Lottman, Herbert R. "Dusko Popov: An Interview." *Publishers Weekly,* CCV (Apr. 22, 1974), pp. 12–13.

Louis, William Roger. *Imperialism at Bay: The United States and the Decolonisation of the British Empire, 1941–1945*. Oxford: Oxford University Press, 1977.

Loveday, Arthur F. *Spain, 1923–1948: Civil War and World War*. North Bridgewater, Somerset: Boswell, n.d.

Lovell, Stanley P. *Of Spies & Strategems*. Englewood Cliffs, N.J.: Prentice-Hall, 1963.

Luard, Nicholas. *The Orion Line*. New York: Harcourt, Brace Jovanovich, 1977.

Ludlum, Robert. *The Aquitaine Progression*. New York: Random House, 1984.

McCargar, James. *See* Felix, Christopher.

McCormick, Donald. *See* Deacon, Richard.

McCormick, William. *Special Boat Squadron*. London: William Kimber, 1984.

McCoy, Donald R. *The Presidency of Harry S. Truman*. Lawrence, Kans.: University Press of Kansas, 1984.

MacDonald, Elizabeth P. *Undercover Girl*. New York: Macmillan, 1947.

McGarvey, Robert, and Elise Caitlin. *The Complete Spy*. New York: Pedigree, 1983.

McGehee, Ralph W. *Deadly Deceits*. New York: Sheridan Square, 1983.

Macintosh, Charles. *From Cloak to Dagger: An SOE Agent in Italy. 1943–1945*. London: William Kimber, 1982.

McLachlan, Donald. *Room 39: A Study in Naval Intelligence*. New York: Atheneum, 1968.

Mackenzie, Compton. *Greek Memories*. London: Chatto and Windus, 1939.

Macksey, Kenneth. *The Partisans of Europe in the Second World War*. New York: Stein and Day, 1975.

Maclaren, Roy. *Canadians Behind Enemy Lines, 1939–1945*. Vancouver: University of British Columbia Press, 1981.

Maclean, Fitzroy. *Take Nine Spies*. New York: Atheneum, 1978.

Maclean, Kenneth. *Pierson's Masters and Fellows, 1933–1938*. Stamford, Conn.: Overbook Press, 1938.

McNamara, Francis J. *U.S. Counterintelligence Today*. Washington, D.C.: The Nathan Hale Institute, 1985.

McNeill, W. H. *The Greek Dilemma: War and Aftermath*. Philadelphia: J. B. Lippincott, 1977.

Mader, Julius, ed. *Who's Who in CIA*. Berlin: Mader, 1968.

——, Gerhard Stuchlik, and Horst Pehnert. *Dr. Sorge funkt aus Tokyo*. Berlin: Deutscher Militarverlag, 1968.

Makhali-Phal. *The Young Concubine*. New York: Random House, 1942.

Mammarella, Giuseppe. *Italy After Fascism: A Political History, 1943–1965*. Revised and enlarged edition. Notre Dame: University of Notre Dame Press, 1966.

Manderstam, L. H., with Roy Heron. *From the Red Army to SOE*. London: William Kimber, 1985.

Mann, Wilfrid. *Was There a Fifth Man?* London: Pergamon, 1982.

Marchetti, Victor. "The CIA in Italy: An Interview with Victor Marchetti." in Philip Agee and Louis Wolf, eds., *Dirty Work: The CIA in Western Europe*. Secaucus, N.J.: Lyle Stuart, 1978.

——. *The Rope-Dancer*. New York: Grossett & Dunlap, 1971.

——, and John D. Marks. *The CIA and the Cult of Intelligence*. New York: Knopf, 1974.

Marcus, George E., ed, *Elites: Ethnographic Issues*. Albuquerque: University of New Mexico Press, 1983.

Marin, German. *Una Historia Fantastica y Calculada: La CIA en el Pais de los Chilenos*. Mexico: Siglo vientiuno editores, 1976.

Marshall-Cornwall, James. *Wars and Rumours of Wars: A Memoir*. London: Secker & Warburg, 1984.

Martin, David C. *Wilderness of Mirrors*. New York: Harper & Row, 1980.

Martz, Louis L., ed. *H.D.: Collected Poems, 1912–1944*. New York: New Directions, 1983.

Mashbir, Sidney Forster. *I Was an American Spy*. New York: Vantage, 1953.

Masterman, Sir John. *The Case of the Four Friends*. London: Hodder and Stoughton, 1957.

———. *The Double-Cross System in the War of 1939–1945*. New Haven: Yale University Press, 1972.

———. *On the Chariot Wheel: An Autobiography*. London: Oxford University Press, 1975.

———. "The XX Papers." *Yale Alumni Magazine*, XXXV (Feb. 1972), pp. 7–11.

Masters, Anthony. *The Man Who Was M: The Life of Maxwell Knight*. Oxford: Blackwell, 1984.

Matt, Alphons. *Zwischen allen Fronten: Die Zweite Weltkrieg aus der Sicht des Büros Ha*. Frauenfeld: Huber, 1969.

Mauldin, William. *The Brass Ring*. New York: W. W. Norton, 1971.

May, Ernest R., ed. *Knowing One's Enemies: Intelligence Assessment Before the Two World Wars*. Princeton: Princeton University Press, 1984.

Mendall, Clarence. *Mr. Dooley Redivivus: On Acceleration*. New Haven: Branford College Press, 1942.

Menen, Aubrey. *Four Days of Naples*. New York: Seaview, 1979.

Mengungkap Kegiatan Subversip: CIA. Djilid I. Djakarta: Team Camera Press, 1965.

Metcalf, Keyes D., and Edwin E. Williams. "Notes on the Farmington Plan. *Libri*, I (i/1950), pp. 13–19.

Meyer, Cord, Jr. *Facing Reality: From World Federalism to the CIA*. New York: Harper & Row, 1980.

Michel, Henri. *The Shadow War: Resistance in Europe, 1939–1945*. London: André Deutsch, 1972.

Mihan, George. *Looted Treasure: Germany's Raid on Art*. London: Alliance Press, 1944[?]

Miler, Newton S. "Counter-Intelligence." In Roy Godson, ed., *Intelligence Requirements for the 1980's: Counterintelligence*. Washington, D.C.: Consortium for the Study of Intelligence, 1980.

Miller, James Edward. "Taking Off the Gloves: The United States and the Italian Elections of 1948." *Diplomatic History*, VII (Winter 1983), 35–55.

———. *The United States and Italy, 1940–1950*. Chapel Hill: University of North Carolina Press, 1986.

Minney, R. J. *The Films of Anthony Asquith*. South Brunswick, N.J.: A. S. Barnes, 1976.

Molden, Fritz. *Exploding Star: A Young Austrian Against Hitler*. London: Weidenfeld and Nicholson, 1978.

Montagu, Ewen. *Beyond Top Secret Ultra*. New York: Coward, McCann & Geoghegan, 1978.

———. *The Man Who Never Was*. London: Evans, 1953.

Moon, Thomas M., and Carl F. Eifler. *The Deadliest Colonel*. New York: Vantage Press, 1975.

Moore, Barrington. *Privacy: Studies in Social and Cultural History*. Armonk, N.Y.: Sharpe, 1984.

Moravec, Frantisek. *Master of Spies: The Memoirs of General Frantisek Moravec*. London: Bodley Head, 1975.

Morgan, Richard E. *Domestic Intelligence: Monitoring Dissent in America*. Austin: University of Texas Press, 1980.

Morris, Christopher. "Ultra's Poor Relations." *Intelligence and National Security,* I (Jan. 1986), pp. 111–122.

Morris, Donald R. "The Spy Who Went Out into the Cold and Never Returned." Houston *Post* (Dec. 27, 1981).

Mosley, Leonard. *The Cat and the Mice*. London: Arthur Barker, 1958.

———. *The Druid*. New York: Atheneum, 1981.

———. *Dulles: A Biography of Eleanor, Allen, and John Foster Dulles and Their Family Network*. New York: Dial Press, 1978.

Moss, Robert. *Death Beam*. New York: Crown, 1981.

Moyzisch, L. C. *Operation Cicero*. New York: Coward-McCann, 1950.

Muggeridge, Malcolm. *Chronicles of Wasted Time,* II, *The Infernal Grove*. London: Collins, 1973.

Munthe, Malcolm, *How Sweet Is War*. London: Duckworth, 1954.

Murdock, George P., et al. *Behavior Science Outlines, I*. New Haven: HRAF, 1967.

Mure, David. *Master of Deception: Tangled Webs in London and the Middle East*. London: William Kimber, 1980.

———. *Practice to Deceive*. London: William Kimber, 1977.

Murphy, Robert. *Diplomat Among Warriors*. New York: Doubleday, 1964.

Myers, E.C.W. *Greek Entanglement*. London: Hart-Davis, 1955.

Naftali, Timothy. "Yale Ph.D., O.S.S., C.I.A." Unpublished senior essay, Yale University, 1983.

Nason, Leonard H. *Contact Mercury*. Garden City, N.Y.: Doubleday, 1946.

"The Nathan Hale Statue." *The Art Interchange,* XXXII (Jan. 1894), pp. 16–17.

Navarre, Henri. *Le Service de renseignements, 1877–1944*. Paris: Plon, 1978.

Naylor, John F. *A Man and an Institution: Sir Maurice Hankey, the Cabinet Secretariat and the Custody of Cabinet Secrecy*. Cambridge: Cambridge University Press, 1984.

Nesbit, Roy C., and Ronald Cooke. *Target: Hitler's Oil*. London: William Kimber, 1985.

Neuberger, Güenter, and Michael Opperskalski. *CIA im Westeurope*. Bornheim: Lamuv, 1982.

Neustadt, Richard E., and Ernest R. May. *Thinking in Time: The Uses of History for Decision Makers*. New York: Free Press, 1986.

Newman, Bernard. *Epics of Espionage*. London: Werner Laurie, 1950.

———. *Speaking from Memory*. London: H. Jenkins, 1960.

Nicholas, Elizabeth. *Death Be Not Proud*. London: Cresset, 1958.

Nord, Pierre. *L'Intoxication: Arme absolue de la guerre subversive*. Paris: Fayard, 1971.

———. *Mes camarades sont morts*. 3 vols. Paris: Librairie des Champs-Elysées, 1947.

Northrop, Filmore S. C. *The Meeting of East and West: An Inquiry Concerning World Understanding*. New York: Macmillan, 1946.

O'Ballance, Edgar. *The Greek Civil War, 1944–1949*. New York: Praeger, 1966.

Ogilvy, David. *Blood, Brains & Beer: An Autobiography*. New York: Atheneum, 1978.

Omodeo, Adolfo. *Per la riconquista della libertá*. Naples: Macciaroli, 1944.

Omrcanin, Ivo. *Enigma Tito*. Washington, D.C.: Samizdat, 1984.

Oren, Dan A. *Joining the Club: A History of Jews at Yale*. New Haven: Yale University Press, 1986.

Origo, Iris. *War in Val D'Orcia: An Italian War Diary, 1943–1944*. Boston: Godine, 1984.

Orlov, Alexander. *Handbook of Intelligence and Guerrilla Warfare*. Ann Arbor: University of Michigan Press, 1963.

Owen, Frank. *The Eddie Chapman Story*. New York: Messner, 1954.

Padover, Saul. *Experiment in Germany: The Story of an American Intelligence Officer*. New York: Duell, Sloan, and Pearce, 1946.

Page, Bruce, David Leitch, and Phillip Knightley. *The Philby Conspiracy*. Updated edition. New York: Ballantine Books, 1981.

Paillole, Paul. *Notre espion chez Hitler*. Paris: Laffont, 1985.

———. *Services Spéciaux, 1935–1945*. Paris: Laffont, 1975.

Paine, Lauran. *Britain's Intelligence Service*. London: Robert Hale, 1979.

———. *Double Jeopardy*. London: Robert Hale, 1978.

———. *German Military Intelligence in World War II: The Abwehr*. New York: Stein and Day, 1984.

Palmer, Raymond. *The Making of a Spy*. London: Aldus Books, 1977.

Pano, Nicholas C. *The People's Republic of Albania*. Baltimore: The Johns Hopkins University Press, 1968.

Parish, James Robert, and Michael R. Pitts. *The Great Spy Pictures*. Metuchen, N.J.: Scarecrow Press, 1974.

Passy, Colonel. *Souvenirs*, II, *10, Duke Street Londres*. Monte Carlo: Raoul Solar, 1947.

The Paul C. Blum Collection: A Catalogue of Books. 2 vols. Yokohama: Archives of History, 1983.

Pearson, Anthony. *Conspiracy of Silence*. London: Quartet, 1978.

Pearson, Norman Holmes. "The Nazi-Soviet Pact and the End of the Dream." In Daniel Aaron, ed., *America in Crisis*, pp. 326–348. New York: Knopf, 1952.

Peis, Gunther. *The Mirror of Deception: How Britain Turned the Nazi Spy Machine Against Itself*. London: Weidenfeld and Nicolson, 1977.

Pendar, Kenneth, *Adventure in Diplomacy: Our French Dilemma*. New York: Dodd, Mead, 1945.

Pennypacker, Morton. *The Two Spies*. Boston: Houghton Mifflin, 1930.

Penrose, Barrie, and Simon Freeman. *Conspiracy of Silence: The Secret Life of Anthony Blunt*. London: Grafton, 1986.

Perrault, Gilles. *The Red Orchestra*. New York: Simon & Schuster, 1969.

———. *The Secrets of D-Day*. London: Arthur Barker, 1965.

Perry, George. *The Great British Picture Show*. London: Hart-Davis, Mac-Gibbon, 1974.

Persico, Joseph E. *Piercing the Reich*. New York: Viking, 1979.

Peyroles, Jacques: *See* Perrault, Gilles.

Pezeu-Massabuau, Jacques. *The Japanese Islands: A Physical and Social Geography*. Rutland, Vt.: Charles Tuttle, 1978.

Pforzheimer, Walter L. "Amassing Intelligence: In Search of Truth in Fine Condition." In Dilys Winn, ed., *Murder Ink*. 2nd ed., pp. 36–40. New York: Workman, 1984.

———. "Code Breaking—The Ultra Story." *Marine Corps Gazette*, LIV (July 1980), pp. 76–80.

Philby, Eleanor. *Kim Philby, the Spy I Married*. New York: Simon & Schuster, 1967.

Philby, H.A.R. *My Silent War*. New York: Grove Press, 1968.

Phillips, Cabell. "The Shadow Army That Fought in Silence." *The New York Times Magazine*, Oct. 7, 1945.

Phillips, David Atlee. *The Night Watch*. New York: Atheneum, 1977.

Piekalkiewicz, Janusz. *The Air War: 1939–1945*. Poole, Dorset: Blandford Press, 1985.

———. *Secret Agent, Spies and Saboteurs: Famous Undercover Missions of World War II*. New York: William Morrow, 1973.

———. *Spione, Agenten, Soldaten: Geheime kommandos im Zweitzen Weltkrieg*. Munich: Südwest, 1969. Contains minor information not in the English edition.

Pierson, George Wilson. *A Yale Book of Numbers: Historical Statistics of the College and University, 1701–1976*. New Haven: Yale University Press, 1983.

Pincher, Chapman. *Dirty Tricks*. London: Sidgwick & Jackson, 1980.

———. *The Secret Offensive*. London: Sidgwick & Jackson, 1985.

———. *Their Trade Is Treachery*. London: Sidgwick & Jackson, 1981.

———. *Too Secret Too Long*. New York: St. Martin's Press, 1984.

Pinto, Oresto. *Spy-Catcher*. New York: Harper and Brothers, 1952.

Piscitelli, Enzo, et al. *Italia, 1945–48: Le origini della Repubblica*. Turin: G. Giappichelli, 1974.

Pitt, Barrie. *Special Boat Squadron*. London: Century, 1983.

Plaut, James S. "Loot for the Master Race." *Atlantic Monthly*, CLXXVII (Sept. 1946), pp. 57–63.

Plumb, J. H. "Horace Walpole at Yale." *New York Review of Books*, V (Sept. 30, 1965), pp. 9–10.

Pollo, Stefanaq, and Arben Puto. *The History of Albania from Its Origins to the Present Day*. London: Routledge and Kegan Paul, 1981.

Pond, Hugh. *Salerno*. 2nd ed. London: William Kimber, 1961.

Popov, Dusko. *Spy/Counterspy: The Autobiography of Dusko Popov*. New York: Grosset & Dunlap, 1974.

Powers, Thomas. *The Man Who Kept the Secrets: Richard Helms and the CIA*. New York: Knopf, 1979.

Powys-Lybbe, Ursula. *The Eye of Intelligence*. London: William Kimber, 1983.

Prados, John. *The Soviet Estimate: U.S. Intelligence Analysis & Russian Strength*. New York: Dial, 1982.

Press, Sylvia. *The Care of Devils*. Boston: Beacon, 1948.

Pruden, Russell, and Thomas C. Mendenhall. "The Yale Collection of War Literature." *The Yale University Library Gazette,* XVII (July 1942), pp. 14–20.

Pujol (Garcia), Juan, and Nigel West. *Garbo*. London: Weidenfeld and Nicolson, 1985. Published in the United States as *Operation Garbo: The Personal Story of the Most Successful Double Agent of World War II*. New York: Random House, 1986.

Purdy, Anthony, and Douglas Sutherland. *Burgess and Maclean*. Garden City, N.Y.: Doubleday, 1963.

du Puy-Montbrun, Deodat. *Les armes des espions*. Paris: Ballard, 1972.

Quinn, Vincent. *Hilda Doolittle (H.D.)*. New York: Twayne, 1967.

Quirk, Akeley P. *Recollections of World War II: O.S.S. S.C.I. Unit 6th Army Group*. Fullerton, Calif.: Sultana Press, 1981.

Quirk, John Patrick, with David Atlee Phillips, Ray Cline, and Walter L. Pforzheimer. *The Central Intelligence Agency: A Photographic History*. Guilford, Conn.: Foreign Intelligence Press, 1986.

Radó, Sándor. *Codename Dora*. London: Abelost, 1977.

Ranelagh, John. *The Agency: The Rise and Decline of the CIA*. New York: Simon & Schuster, 1986.

Ransom, Harry Howe. *Central Intelligence and National Security*. Cambridge, Mass.: Harvard University Press, 1958.

———. *The Intelligence Establishment*. Cambridge, Mass.: Harvard University Press, 1970.

Read, Anthony, and David Fisher. *Colonel Z: The Secret Life of a Master of Spies*. New York: Viking, 1985.

———. *Operation Lucy: Most Secret Spy Ring of the Second World War*. New York: Coward, McCann, and Geoghegan, 1981.

Record of the Fellows of Davenport College, II. New Haven: The College, 1948.

Rees, Goronwy. *A Chapter of Accidents*. London: Chatto & Windus, 1972.

Rémy, Colonel. *Memoires d'un agent secret de la France*. Paris: Libre.

Renault-Roulier, Gilbert. *See* Rémy, Colonel.

Ribalow, Harold, and Meir Ribalow. *The Jew in American Sports*. New York: Hippocrene, 1984.

Richard Brown Baker Collects/A Selection of Contemporary Art from the Richard Brown Baker Collection. New Haven: Yale University Art Gallery, 1975.

Richelson, Jeffrey T. *The U.S. Intelligence Community*. Cambridge, Mass.: Ballinger, 1985.

———, and Desmond Ball. *The Ties That Bind*. Boston: Allen & Unwin, 1985.

Richter, Heinz. *British Intervention in Greece: From Varkiza to Civil War, February 1945 to August 1946*. London: Merlin, 1985.

Rifkind, Bernard David. *OSS and Franco-American Relations: 1942–1945*. Ann Arbor, Mich.: University Microfilms International, 1985.

Rivers, Gayle, and James Hudson. *The Five Fingers*. Garden City, N.Y.: Doubleday, 1978.

Robinson, Janice S. *H.D.: The Life and Work of an American Poet*. Boston: Houghton Mifflin, 1982.

Rohwer, Jürgen, and Eberhard Jäckel, eds. *Die Funkauklärung und ihre Rolle im Zweiten Weltkrieg*. Stuttgart: Motorbuch, 1979.

Roman, Howard. *Frog*. London: Heineman, 1978.

von Roon, Ger. *German Resistance to Hitler: Count von Moltke and the Kreisau Circle*. London: Van Nostrand Reinhold, 1971.

Roosevelt, Kermit. *The Overseas Targets: War Report of the OSS*. New York: Walker, 1976.

———. *War Report of the OSS*. New York: Walker, 1976.

Root, Waverley. *Casablanca to Katyn: The Secret History of the War*. New York: Scribner's, 1946.

Rorimer, James J. *Survival: The Salvage and Protection of Art in War*. New York: Abelard Press, 1950.

Rosenbaum, Ron. "The Shadow of the Mole." *Harper's,* CCLXVII (Oct. 1983), pp. 45–60.

Rosengarten, Frank. *The Italian Anti-Fascist Press (1919–1945)*. Cleveland: Press of Case Western Reserve University, 1968.

Roskill, Stephen W. *Hankey: Man of Secrets*. 2 vols. London: Collins, 1970–74.

Ross, Frank. *The Shining Day*. New York: Atheneum, 1981.

Rossotti, Renzo. *Top-Secret: Le Spie*. Turin: Società Editrice Internazionale, 1969.

Rothfels, Hans. *The German Opposition to Hitler: An Appraisal*. Revised edition. Chicago: Henry Regnery, 1962.

Rout, Leslie B., and John N. Bratzel. *The Shadow War*. Hanover, N.H.: University Press of New England, 1986.

Rowan, Fred. *Technospies: The Secret Network That Spies on You—and You*. New York: G. P. Putnam's, 1978.

Rowan, Richard Wilmer. *The Story of Secret Service*. New York: Literary Guild, 1938.

Ruland, Bernd. *Die Augen Moskaus: Fernschreib Zentrale der Wehrmacht in Berlin*. Zurich: Schweizer Verlagshaus, 1973.

Sage, Jerry. *Sage*. Wayne, Penn.: Miles Standish Press, 1985.

St. Paul's School. *Chapel Services and Prayers*. 4th ed. Concord, N.H.: The School, 1977.

Salvadori, Max. *Brava storia della Resistenza italiana*. Florence: Vallecchi, 1974.

Saraphes, Stephanos G. *ELAS: Greek Resistance Army*. London: Merlin Press, 1980.

Sawatsky, John. *For Services Rendered: Leslie James Bennett and the RCMP Security Services*. Toronto: Doubleday, 1982.

———. *Men in the Shadows: The RCMP Security Service*. Garden City, N.Y.: Doubleday, 1980.

Scattolini, Virgilio. *Il Vaticano contro la pace mondial*. Lugano: Societa Cooperation Operaia Editrice, 1948.

———. *Il Vaticano e la democrazia italiana*. Lugano: Societa Cooperation Operaia Editrice, 1948.

Schlesinger, Stephen, and Stephen Kinzer. *Bitter Fruit: The Untold Story of the American Coup in Guatemala*. Garden City, N.Y.: Doubleday, 1983.

Schorske, Carl E., and Elizabeth Schorske, eds. *Explorations in Crisis: Papers in International History, William L. Langer*. Cambridge, Mass.: Harvard University Press, 1969.

Schoyer, Preston. *The Indefinite River*. New York: Dodd, Mead, 1947.

Schramm, Wilhelm von. *Verrat im Zweiten Weltkrieg: Vom Kampf der Geheimdienste in Europe*. Dusseldorf: Econ, 1967.

Schrecker, Ellen. *No Ivory Tower: McCarthy and the Universities*. New York: Oxford University Press, 1986.

Scobey, Katherine. "The Making of a Poet." *The New Journal*, XVI (Feb. 3, 1984), pp. 26–34.

Scott, Dale. "The United States and the Overthrow of Sukarno, 1965–1967." *Pacific Affairs*, LVII (Summer 1985), pp. 239–264.

Scrivener, Jane. *Inside Rome with the Germans*. New York: Macmillan, 1945.

Seagrave, Gordon. *Burma Surgeon*. New York: W. W. Norton, 1943.

Seale, Patrick, and Maureen McConville. *Philby: The Long Road to Moscow*. London: Hamish Hamilton, 1973.

Secchia, Pietro. *La resistenza accusa, 1945–1973*. Milan: Mazzotta, 1973.

Segueiev, Lily. *Seule face à l'Abwehr*. Paris: Fayard, 1966.

———. *Secret Service Rendered*. London: William Kimber, 1968.

Semyonov, V. "Seventeen Moments of Spring." *Literary Gazette* (Moscow), October 19, 1983.

Serrano Suñer, Ramon. *Entre les Pyrénées et Gibralte: Notes et réflexions sur la politique espagnole depuis 1936*. Geneva: Editions du Cheval ailé, 1947.

Seth, Ronald. *Encyclopedia of Espionage*. Garden City, N.Y.: Doubleday, 1972.

Seton Watson, Hugh, "Resistance in Eastern Europe." In Patrick Howarth, ed., *Special Operations*. London: Routledge and Kegan Paul, 1955.

Seymour, George Dudley. *Documentary Life of Nathan Hale*. New Haven: privately printed, 1941.

Seymour, William. *British Special Forces*. London: Sidgwick & Jackson, 1985.

Shevchenko, Arkady N. *Breaking with Moscow*. New York: Knopf, 1985.

Shipman, David. *The Story of Cinema: An Illustrated History*. New York: Oxford University Press, 1978.

Sinclair, Andrew. *The Red and the Blue: Intelligence, Treason and the Universities*. London: Weidenfeld & Nicolson, 1986.

Sizer, Theodore. "John Marshall Phillips, 1905–1953." Publications of The Walpole Society, *The Forty-third Annual Meeting* (May 22, 1953), pp. 26–41.

———. "A Walpolean at War." Publications of The Walpole Society, *Thirty-fifth Annual Meeting* (Oct. 27, 1945), pp. 3–27.

Smiley, David. *Albanian Assignment*. London: Chatto & Windus, 1984.

Smith, Bradley F. *The Shadow Warriors: O.S.S. and the Origins of the C.I.A.* New York: Basic Books, 1983.

———, and Elena Agarossi. *Operation Sunrise: The Secret Surrender*. New York: Basic Books, 1979.

Smith, Joseph Burkholder. *Portrait of a Cold Warrior*. Reprint edition. New York: Ballantine Books, 1981.

Smith, Myron J., ed. *Cloak-and-Dagger: Biblio's Annotated Guide to Spy Fiction, 1937–1975*. Metuchen, N.J.: Scarecrow Press, 1976.

———, ed. *Secret Wars: A Guide to Sources in English*, I, Intelligence, Propaganda and Psychological Warfare, Resistance Movements, and Secret Operations, 1939–1945. Santa Barbara, Calif.: ABC-Clio, 1980.

Smith, R. Harris. *OSS: The Secret History of America's First Central Intelligence Agency*. Berkeley, Calif.: University of California Press, 1972. Citations are to the Delta edition, Dell Publishing, New York, 1973.

Smith, Warren Hunting. "Horace Walpole's Correspondence." *The Yale University Library Gazette,* LVIII (Oct. 1983), pp. 17–28.

Smyth, Denis. *Diplomacy and Strategy of Survival: British Policy and Franco's Spain, 1940–41.* Cambridge: Cambridge University Press, 1986.

Smythe, Howard McGaw. *Secrets of the Fascist Era: How Uncle Sam Obtained Some of the Top-Level Documents of Mussolini's Period.* Carbondale: Southern Illinois University Press, 1975.

Snepp, Frank. *Decent Interval.* New York: Random House, 1977.

Snow, John Howland. *The Case of Tyler Kent.* New Canaan, Conn.: Long House, 1962.

Sogno, Edgardo. *Guerra senza bandiera: Cronache della "Franchi" nella Resistenza.* Milano: Mursia, 1970.

Solomon, Flora, and Barry Litvinoff. *A Woman's Way.* New York: Simon & Schuster, 1984.

Spector, Ronald H. *Eagle Against the Sun: The American War with Japan.* New York: Free Press, 1985.

Speers, Michael F., and Nigel West. "Conspiracy Buffs Unite: Epstein vs. Shevchenko." *IQ: The Intelligence Quarterly,* I (Oct. 1985), pp. 1–2.

Sperling, Jerome. "Explorations in Elis." *American Journal of Archaeology,* XLVI (!/1942), pp. 77–89.

Spiller, Roger J. "Some Implications of Ultra." *Military Affairs,* XL (Apr. 1976), pp. 49–54.

——, and Joseph G. Dawson, III, eds. *Dictionary of American Military Biography.* 3 vols. Westport, Conn.: Greenwood, 1984.

Spiro, Edward. *See* Cookridge, E. H.

Stafford, David A. T. *Britain and European Resistance, 1940–45: A Survey of the Special Operations Executive, with Documents.* London: Macmillan, 1980.

——. "The Detonator Concept: British Strategy, SOE and European Resistance After the Fall of France." *Journal of Contemporary History,* X (1975), pp. 185–217.

——. " 'Ultra' and the British Official Histories, a Documentary Note." *Military Affairs,* XLII (Feb. 1978), pp. 29–31.

Stavrianos, Lefton S. "The Greek National Liberation Front (EAM): A Study in Resistance Organisation and Administration." *Journal of Modern History,* XXIV (i/1952), pp. 42–55.

Steiner, George. "The Cleric of Treason." *The New Yorker* (Dec. 8, 1980), pp. 158–195.

Stengers, Jean. "Enigma, the French, the Poles and the British, 1931–1940." In Christopher Andrew and David Dilks, eds., *The Missing Dimension: Governments and Intelligence Communities in the Twentieth Century.* London: Macmillan, 1984.

Steven, Stewart. *The Spymasters of Israel.* New York: Macmillan, 1980.

Stevenson, William. *Intrepid's Last Case.* New York: Villard Books, 1983.

——. *A Man Called Intrepid: The Secret War.* New York: Harcourt, Brace Jovanovich, 1976.

Strange, John G. *Fifty Years of Aspiration: An Abridged History of The Institute of Paper Chemistry.* Appleton, Wis.: The Institute of Paper Chemistry, 1980.

Strawson, John. *A History of the SAS Regiment*. London: Secker and Warburg, 1985.

Sulzberger, C. L. *The Last of the Giants*. New York: Macmillan, 1973.

Summers, Anthony. *Conspiracy*. New York: McGraw-Hill, 1980.

Suripto. *Kegagalan Agresis CIA di kuba*. Surabaja: Grip, 1965.

Sutherland, Douglas. *The Fourth Man: The Definitive Story of Blunt, Philby, Burgess and Maclean*. London: Secker & Warburg, 1980.

Suvorov, Viktor. *Aquarium: The Career and Defection of a Soviet Military Spy*. London: Hamish Hamilton, 1985.

Sweet-Escott, Bickham. *Baker Street Irregular*. London: Methuen, 1965.

Syrett, David. "The Secret War and the Historians." *Armed Forces and Society*, IX (Winter 1983), pp. 292–328.

Szulc, Tad. *Compulsive Spy: The Strange Career of E. Howard Hunt*. New York: Viking, 1974.

Tadmor, Joshua. *The Silent Warriors*. New York: Macmillan, 1969.

Taylor, A.J.P. *A Personal History*. New York: Atheneum, 1983.

Taylor, Edmond. *Awakening from History*. Boston: Gambit, 1969.

———. *Richer by Asia*. Boston: Houghton Mifflin, 1947.

———. *The Strategy of Terror: Europe's Inner Front*. Boston: Houghton Mifflin, 1940.

Taylor, John W. R., and David Mondey. *Spies in the Sky*. New York: Scribner's, 1972.

Theoharis, Athan G., ed. *The Truman Presidency: The Origins of the Imperial Presidency and the National Security State*. Stanfordville, N.Y.: Coleman, 1979.

Thompson, E. R. "Sleuthing the Trail of Nathan Hale." *IQ/Intelligence Quarterly*, II (Oct. 1986), pp. 1–4.

Tinin, David B., and Dag Christensen. *The Hit Team*. Boston: Little, Brown, 1976.

Toledano, Ralph de. *Edgar Hoover: The Man in His Times*. New Rochelle, N.Y.: Arlington House, 1973.

Tolstoy, Nikolai. *The Minister and the Massacres*. London: Century, 1986.

Tompkins, Peter. *Italy Betrayed*. New York: Simon & Schuster, 1966.

———. *The Murder of Admiral Darlan: A Study in Conspiracy*. New York: Simon & Schuster, 1965.

———. *A Spy in Rome*. New York: Simon & Schuster, 1962.

Trevor-Roper, Hugh R. "The Philby Affair: Espionage, Treason and Secret Services." *Encounter*, XXX (Apr. 1968), pp. 3–26.

———. *The Philby Affair: Espionage, Treason and Secret Services*. London: William Kimber, 1968.

Troy, Thomas F. *Donovan and the CIA: A History of the Establishment of the Central Intelligence Agency*. Frederick, Md.: University Publications of America, 1981.

———., ed. *Foreign Intelligence Literary Scene*. Washington, D.C.: February 1982–.

———. *Wartime Washington: The Secret OSS Journal of James Grafton Rogers, 1942–1943*. Frederick, Md.: University Publications of America, 1987.

Turner, Arlin. "Norman Holmes Pearson." *The Nathaniel Hawthorne Society Newsletter*, II (Spring 1976), pp. 1–2.

Turner, Stansfield. *Secrecy and Democracy: The CIA in Transition*. Boston: Houghton Mifflin, 1985.

von Uexküll, Rönn V. *Unser Mann in Berlin: Die Tätigkeit der deutschen und Schweignerischen Geheimdienste, 1933–1945*. Lucerne: Kirchberg & Steinbach, 1976.

U.S. Department of State, Historical Division. "A Survey of United States Relations with Morocco." Research Project No. 404, November, 1957.

Urban, Joan Barth. *Moscow and the Italian Communist Party: From Togliatti to Berlinguer*. Ithaca, N.Y.: Cornell University Press, 1986.

Uris, Leon. *Topaz*. New York: McGraw-Hill, 1967.

Usher, Frank Hugh. *See* Franklin, Charles.

Vachnadze, Georgii Nikolaevich. *Za kulisami odnoi diversii: kto napravlial ruku terrorista na ploshchadi Sviatogo Petra*. Moscow: Izd-vo Polit. lit-ry, 1985.

Vaill, George D. "Only One Life, But Three Hangings," *American Heritage*, XXIV (Aug. 1973), pp. 100–101.

———. *Yale: A Contesseration of Human Beings*. Bethany, Conn.: Bethany Press, 1979.

Vallee, Rudy, and Gil McKean. *My Time Is Your Time: The Story of Rudy Vallee*. New York: Ivan Obolensky, 1962.

Verne, Newton. "The Spy Who Came to Dinner." *The Washingtonian*, XX (Oct. 1984), 95–96.

Verrier, Anthony. *Through the Looking Glass: British Foreign Policy in an Age of Illusions*. London: Jonathan Cape, 1983.

Veterans of OSS, Newsletter. Washington, D.C., 1985–.

Villard, Harry. "Our Spies in North Africa." *Foreign Service Journal*, LVI (June 1979).

Volkman, Ernest. "The Search for Sasha." *Family Weekly*, October 9, 1983, pp. 1–5.

———. *Warriors of the Night: Spies, Soldiers, and American Intelligence*. New York: William Morrow, 1985.

Vosjoli, Phillipe Thyraud de. *Lamia*. Boston: Little, Brown, 1970.

Wager, Wally. "Slippery Giant of the OSS." *Men* (July 1961). 32.

Walker, David E. *Lunch with a Stranger*. London: Wingate, 1957.

Walters, Vernon A. *Silent Missions*. Garden City, N.Y.: Doubleday, 1978.

Warner, Philip. *Phantom*. London: William Kimber, 1982.

———. *The Secret Forces of World War II*. London: Granada, 1984.

———. *The Special Boat Squadron*. London: Sphere Books, 1983.

Watts, Stephen. *Moonlight on a Lake in Bond Street*. London: Bodley Head, 1961.

Wavrin, André de. *See* Passy, Colonel.

Weidersheim, William A., ed. *Uncle Sid of Yale*. New Haven: Yale Alumni Fund, 1981.

Weil, Martin. *A Pretty Good Club: The Founding Fathers of the U.S. Foreign Service*. New York: W. W. Norton, 1978.

Weismiller, Edward. *The Deer Come Down*. New Haven: Yale University Press, 1936.

———. *Serpent's Progress: The Writing of a Novel. Monday Evening Papers*. No. 15. Middletown, Conn.: Center for Advanced Studies, Wesleyan University, 1968.

——. *The Serpent Sleeping*. New York: G. P. Putnam's, 1962.

Welch, Robert. *The New Americanism: And Other Speeches and Essays*. Boston: Western Islands, 1966.

Welchman, Gordon. "From Polish Bomba to British Bombe: The Birth of Ultra." *Intelligence and National Security*, I (Jan. 1986), pp. 71–110.

——. *The Hut Six Story: Breaking the Enigma Codes*. New York: McGraw-Hill, 1982.

Weller, George. *The Crack in the Column*. New York: Random House, 1949.

West, Nigel. *The Circus: MI5 Operations, 1945–1972*. New York: Stein and Day, 1983.

——. *GCHQ: The Secret Wireless War, 1900–86*. London: Weidenfeld and Nicolson, 1986.

——. *MI6: British Secret Intelligence Service Operations, 1909–45*. New York: Random House, 1983.

——. *Unreliable Witness: Espionage Myths of the Second World War*. London: Weidenfeld and Nicolson, 1984. Published in the United States as *A Thread of Deceit: Espionage Myths of World War II*. New York: Random House, 1985.

Wheeler, M. C. *Britain and the War for Yugoslavia, 1940–1943*. Boulder, Colo.: Eastern European Monographs, 1980.

Whiting, Charles. *The Spymasters: The True Story of Anglo-American Intelligence Operations Within Nazi Germany, 1939–1945*. New York: Saturday Review Press, 1976.

Whittemore, Reed. *The Poet as Journalist: Life at the New Republic*. Washington, D.C.: The New Republic Book Co., 1976.

Whitwell, John. *British Agent*. London: William Kimber, 1966.

Widder, Arthur. *Adventure in Black*. New York: Harper & Row, 1962.

Wiens, Harold. *Atoll Environment and Ecology*. New Haven: Yale University Press, 1962.

——. *China's March into the Tropics*. Washington, D.C.: Office of Naval Research, 1952.

Wighton, Charles, and Gunther Peis. *They Spied on England: Based on the German Secret Service War Diary of General Von Lahousen*. London: Botham Press, 1958.

Wilden, Theodore. *Exchange of Clowns*. Boston: Little, Brown, 1977.

Wilensky, Harold L. *Organization of Intelligence: Knowledge and Policy in Government and Industry*. New York: Basic Books, 1967.

Wilhelm, Marian. *The Man Who Watched the Rising Sun: The Story of Admiral Ellis M. Zacharias*. New York: Franklin Watts, 1967.

Wilkinson, Burke, ed. *Cry Spy! True Stories of 20th Century Spies and Spy Catchers*. Englewood Cliffs, N.J.: Bradbury Press, 1969.

Williams, David. *Not in the Public Interest: The Problem of Security in Democracy*. London: Hutchinson, 1965.

Winkler, Alan M. *The Politics of Propaganda: The Office of War Information, 1942–1945*. New Haven: Yale University Press, 1978.

Winks, Robin W., ed. *The Historian as Detective*. New York: Harper & Row, 1969.

——. *Modus Operandi*. Boston: Godine, 1982.

Winstone, H.V.F. *The Illicit Adventure*. London: Jonathan Cape, 1982.

Winterbotham, F. W. *The Nazi Connection*. London: Weidenfeld and Nicolson, 1978.

———. *Secret and Personal*. London: William Kimber, 1969.

———. *The Ultra Secret*. London: Weidenfeld and Nicolson, 1974.

Wise, David. *The American Police State: The Government Against the People*. New York: Random House, 1976.

———, and Thomas B. Ross. *The U-2 Affair*. New York: Random House, 1962.

Witkin, Merle. "The Overseas Evacuation of British Children During World War II." Unpublished senior essay, Yale University, 1981.

Wittner, Lawrence S. "American Policy Towards Greece, 1944–1949." In John O. Iatrides, *Greece in the 1940s: A Nation in Crisis*. Hanover, N.H.: University Press of New England, 1981.

Wolff, Robert Lee. *The Balkans in Our Time*. Cambridge, Mass.: Harvard University Press, 1956.

Woodhouse, C. M. *Modern Greece: A Short History*. London: Oxford University Press, 1977.

———. *The Struggle for Greece, 1941–1949*. London: Hart-Davis, MacGibbon, 1976.

Woodward, Bob, and Carl Bernstein. *All the President's Men*. New York: Simon & Schuster, 1974.

Woolley, Sir Leonard. *A Record of the Work Done by the Military Authorities for the Protection of the Treasures of Art & History in War Areas*. London: H.M.S.O., 1947.

Worthington, Peter. *Looking for Trouble: A Journalists' Life, and Then Some*. Toronto: Key Porter, 1984.

Woytak, Richard A. *On the Border of War and Peace: Polish Intelligence Diplomacy in 1938–1939 and the Origins of the Ultra Secret*. Boulder, Colo.: East European Quarterly, 1979.

Wright, Charles Alan. "The Fictional Lawyer." *The Practical Lawyer*, XXXI (Jan. 1985).

Wyden, Peter. *Bay of Pigs: The Untold Story*. New York: Simon & Schuster, 1979.

Wynne, Greville. *Contact on Gorky Street*. New York: Atheneum, 1968.

Yakovlev, Nikolai. *CIA Target—the USSR*. Moscow: Progress Publishers, 1982.

Yale 1926–1926s Class Directory. New Haven: Yale University, 1980.

Yost, Charles W. *History and Memory*. New York: W. W. Norton, 1980.

Zacharias, Ellis M. *Secret Missions: The Story of an Intelligence Officer*. New York: G. P. Putnam's, 1946.

Zaturenska, Marya. *Selected Poems*. New York: Grove Press, 1954.

Zotiades, George B. *The Macedonian Controversy*. Thessaloniki: Institute for Balkan Studies, 1954.

Note: News reports, cited in the Notes, are omitted from the Bibliography.

Index

Acción Democrática (AD), 185
Acheson, Dean, 40, 41, 454–455
Ackerman, Edward, 90
Adamic, Louis, 106
Adams, George Burton, 26–27
Addison, Joseph, 18
Aguirre, Don José Antonio de, 176
Albania, 393–401
Alcorn, Robert Hayden, 77–78
Aldington, Richard, 311
Aldrich, Harry S., 213
Alexander, Sidney S., 88
Allende, Salvador, 446
Allport, Gordon, 44
Alsop, Stewart, 452
Alvarez del Vayo, Julio, 165
American Commission for the
    Protection and Salvage of
    Artistic and Historic
    Monuments in War Areas,
    48–49, 303
American Heritage, 19
American Library Association
    (ALA), 126, 132, 144
Amory, Robert, Jr., 412
Anderson, Eugene, 85
Angleton, Carmen Moreno, 329
Angleton, Cicely d'Autremont, 348,
    350
Angleton, Hugh Rolla, 329, 331, 332
Angleton, James Hugh, 328–330
Angleton, James Jesus, 219, 227,
    263–264, 280, 299, 300, 305,
    306, 316, 322–438
Anthology of World Poetry, 252–253
Applebaum, William, 84, 106
Applewhite, Edgar J., Jr., 405
Aranda, José, 186, 188–189, 201
Art Looting Investigation Unit,
    303–305
Asencio, José, 185

Asquith, Anthony, 224
Associated Libraries Group, 126
Atherton, Ray, 110
Atlantic, 443
Attlee, Clement, 290
Auden, W. H., 249, 253
Australia, 407n–408n
Ayer, A. J., 169

B1(A), 280, 284
Babb, James, 118, 125, 146, 147
Babbitt, Theodore, 135
Bagley, Peter, 420
Bailey, S. W. (Bill), 163
Baker, Howard H., 428
Banana, Operation, 152, 177,
    198–203
Bancroft, Hubert Howe, 99
Barghoorn, Frederick, 417
Barmine, Alexander, 176
Barnes, C. Tracy, 220, 440–441
Barnes, Harry Elmer, 79
"Barrack Room Ballads" (Kipling),
    15, 20–21
Barry, Phillip, 377–378
Barzini, Luigi, 222
Basil, 403, 407
Basque Ship's Observers project, 176
Batchelor, C. Malcolm, 255
Baxter, James Phinney, III, 44,
    70–72, 90
Bay of Pigs, 440–441, 446
Becker, Loftus E., 454–455
Becu, Omar, 174
Bedeaux, Charles, 225
Beebe, Lucius, 157
Bellinger, Alfred, 460–461
Bemis, Samuel Flagg, 42, 383
Benét, William Rose, 253, 310
Berding, Andrew, 279, 346
Berle, Adolf, 186, 202